The Social and Applied Psychology of Music

The Social and Applied Psychology of Music

Adrian C. North
Professor of Psychology,
School of Life Sciences,
Heriot Watt University,
Edinburgh, UK

and

David J. Hargreaves
Professor of Education,
Roehampton University,
London, UK

OXFORD
UNIVERSITY PRESS

OXFORD
UNIVERSITY PRESS

Great Clarendon Street, Oxford OX2 6DP
United Kingdom

Oxford University Press is a department of the University of Oxford.
It furthers the University's objective of excellence in research, scholarship,
and education by publishing worldwide. Oxford is a registered trade mark of
Oxford University Press in the UK and in certain other countries

First published 2008
Reprinted 2013

British Library Cataloguing in Publication Data
Data available

Library of Congress Cataloging in Publication Data
Data available

ISBN 978-0-19-856742-4

Whilst every effort has been made to ensure that the contents of this work,
are as complete, accurate and up-to-date as possible at the date of writing,
Oxford University Press is not able to give any guarantee or assurance that
such is the case. Readers are urged to take appropriately qualified medical
advise in all cases. The information in this work is intended to be useful to the
general reader, but should not be used as a means of self-diagnosis or for the
prescription of medication

Preface

People love music. The UK spends more annually on music than on water supply. Worldwide, people buy billions of CDs a year; listen to billions of songs on thousands of radio stations; read billions of words about music and musicians in thousands of magazines and newspapers; and travel billions of miles to thousands of concerts and nightclubs. Every year, the Eurovision Song Contest succeeds where Hitler failed by bringing millions of Europeans to their knees begging for mercy. But even though people love music, it is threatened by modern culture. For example, mainstream pop stars must follow a prevailing neo-conservative moral code or lose sales, sponsorship, and ultimately their contract with the record company. Prevailing economic policies mean that orchestras have for years complained of having to survive on a hand to mouth basis, and that unsigned pop bands must 'pay to play' in their local bar. Furthermore, in 1996 we wrote breathlessly that 'the technology even exists for a system in which any piece of music may be downloaded at will from the internet onto portable lap-top computers on a "pay-per-play" basis'. Since then iTunes and other legal and illegal online music stores and computer applications have completely changed the way many people access music. We can download almost any music we want either cheaply or even for free. We can pick up and put down music throughout the day—while doing the housework, driving a car, exercising, meeting friends, or eating in a restaurant. But just about the first thing taught in any economics class is that something only has value when the supply of it is limited: the modern ubiquity of music as a consequence of the digital revolution means that often it is regarded as unimportant or 'cheap'.

These moral, financial, and technological pressures are pushing music down a path along which mainstream musicians can't question society's morals and values; a path that means your local orchestra is once again playing *The Four Seasons*, and only then through the brand-leveraging benevolence of an insurance company; a direction that characterizes music as an entertainment product or as merely a means of boosting children's IQ, rather than as a gateway to the human spirit or evidence that the human race can produce beauty as well as a carbon footprint. We believe that the best way to safeguard music is to understand the place it occupies in everyday modern life as well as those more complex factors that explain our most profound experiences of music.

In this book we argue that an approach based in social and applied psychology can explain the position of music in the modern world. It can answer some of the oldest questions humans have asked about music, such as why some pieces elicit stronger emotional reactions than others, what makes a good musician, or why some composers are forgotten whereas others have statues erected in their honour. But an interest in social and applied psychology can also answer some of the more recent questions that have arisen concerning music, such as whether it can boost retailers' profits, whether there is a link between musical subculture and suicide, and whether music can be used to help hospital patients. Using social and applied psychology to understand some of the 'older' questions about music helps to safeguard it by allowing people to make effective arguments concerning 'music as a manifestation of the human spirit': using social and applied psychology to understand some of the more recent questions that have arisen about music helps to safeguard it against modern-day pressures such as neo-conservative protesters, accountants, and the digital revolution by demonstrating its social and financial value . This book sets out to provide social psychological answers to both these old and more recent questions concerning music.

ACN / DJH
Edinburgh / London
October 2007

Acknowledgements

We could not have completed a project of this scale without help. Most of all, we would like to thank our respective wives, Lorraine Sheridan and Linda Hargreaves, who refined our thinking when things were going well; and, just as importantly, they encouraged us, provided reality checks, and put up with our complaining when things weren't. Jon and Tom Hargreaves also provided important contributions in these respects. We are also grateful to the numerous colleagues with whom we have discussed the arguments contained in this book and/or with whom we have collaborated on the research that led us to write it: although we hesitate to single out individuals, Fran Rauscher, James Kellaris, Mark Tarrant, Raymond MacDonald, and Dot Miell have all been particularly generous with their time and ideas. Our thanks go also to those who so kindly supplied us with copies of their scholarly articles, and of course to Martin Baum and his colleagues at Oxford University Press for their patience, tolerance, and good humour. We are happy to have the opportunity to acknowledge those bodies who have funded our own research over recent years, namely, the Associated Boards of the Royal Schools of Music, the British Academy, Capital Radio, the Economic and Social Research Council, the European Union, the National Froebel Foundation, the Nuffield Foundation, the Performing Right Society, Phonographic Performance Limited, and the Qualifications and Curriculum Authority. Finally we would like to thank Mulder, Pandora, Bosworth, and Saigon for their company throughout the writing of this book.

Permissions

Figures 3.1 and 3.2 were published originally in Hargreaves, D. J., North, A. C., and Tarrant, M. (2006), The development of musical preference and taste in childhood and adolescence, in G. McPherson (ed.), *The child as musician: a handbook of musical development* (pp. 135–154). Oxford: Oxford University Press. They are reproduced here by permission of Oxford University Press. Figure 3.4 was published originally in Hargreaves, D. J., MacDonald, R. A. R., and Miell, D. E. (2005), How do people communicate using music? In D. E. Miell, R. A. R. MacDonald, and D. J. Hargreaves (eds.), *Musical communication* (pp. 1–25). Oxford: Oxford University Press. It is reproduced here by permission of Oxford University Press. Figure 3.5 was published originally in North, A. C. and Hargreaves, D. J. (1997). Liking, arousal potential, and the emotions expressed by music, *Scandinavian Journal of Psychology*, **38**, 45–53. It is reproduced here by permission of Blackwell Publishing. Figures 3.6 and 3.7 were published originally in Hevner, K. (1937), The affective value of pitch and tempo in music. *American Journal of Psychology*, **49**, 621–630. The *American Journal of Psychology* is copyright 1937 by the Board of Trustees of the University of Illinois. Figures 3.6 and 3.7 are used with permission of the University of Illinois Press. A version of Table 5.1 was published originally in Standley, J. (1995), Music as a therapeutic intervention in medical and dental treatment: research and clinical applications, in T. Wigram, B. Saperstone, and R. West (eds.), *The art and science of music therapy: a handbook* (pp. 3–22) Langhorne: Harwood. It is produced here by permission of Thomson Publishing. Figures 6.3 and 6.4 were published originally in Hargreaves, D. J., Marshall, N. and North, A. C. (2003), Music education in the 21st century: a psychological perspective. *British Journal of Music Education*, **20**, 147–163. They are reproduced here by permission of Cambridge University Press.

Contents

1

The social and applied psychology of music

The occasional experiment in the psychology of music is even today being carried on under conditions so artificial that the findings bear little relation to the affairs of real life
Paul R. Farnsworth (1948)

It goes almost without saying that music exists in a social context: the many and varied ways in which people create, perform, perceive, and react to musical sounds are vitally dependent on the specific places, times and other people present in those situations, as well as the broader historical and cultural context of musical behaviour. Paul Farnsworth published the first book on the social psychology of music in 1954, a second edition of which appeared in 1969, but the field went without further overt recognition until 1997, when we edited the first book on the subject since Farnsworth's initial explorations. There have been numerous developments since 1997 in research findings, thinking about the nature of the field, and in societal attitudes concerning music. The present book aims to provide a state of the art account of the field in the light of these developments.

In addition to academic developments, the consequences of the digital revolution also suggest that the time is right to address social and applied factors in music psychology. When producing our 1997 book we commented upon the effects of the rise of the Walkman, and other advances in miniaturization and portability. Since then this trend has accelerated massively through at least three subsequent innovations. First, the launch of illegal and then legal music download services has revolutionized the way in which people obtain their music: just prior to writing this book, British weekly sales of legally down-loaded pop songs exceeded weekly sales of CD singles for the first time; and Schramm (2006) described how CD sales in many countries had decreased by

30 to 40% since 1998. This has led to a second development, namely the popularity of high capacity, portable digital music players. Apple's iPod has enjoyed huge success, and the numerous similar devices on the market mean that individuals can now carry their entire music libraries with them wherever they go (see Bull, 2000). A third interesting development is that numerous software packages now allow any individual with a basic knowledge of computers to compose their own music or to completely transform any piece of music (such that they can, and frequently do, 're-compose' their favourite pieces).

These changes have had a pronounced effect on the hierarchy of music production and consumption. The hierarchy of 100 years ago placed at the top the composer who handed down completed pieces of music to a passive audience who listened in clearly defined environments (e.g. concert halls). In the modern era, the composer is now effectively in a process of continual negotiation with an active audience who can freely choose between and alter the works in question whenever and wherever they like. In short, it is increasingly easy and prevalent for both music listening and performing to be carried out in a wide range of different circumstances. This increasing contextualization of musical behaviour has led to a corresponding interest among researchers in the social psychology of music. Furthermore, it has led to a greater interest in how musical behaviour might have implications for other thoughts and behaviours. In other words, a great deal of research within the social psychology of music has addressed applied issues in considering how music might interact with and influence those numerous circumstances in which it is heard.

The psychology of music in general is in a very healthy state. As early as the 1970s and 1980s, two clearly identifiable sub-disciplines emerged. A seminal work in the emergence of the cognitive psychology of music was Sloboda's (1985) *The Musical Mind*, which covered topics such as musical syntax, sight-reading of music, and attention and memory in music listening. Similarly, 1986 saw the publication of Hargreaves' *The Developmental Psychology of Music*, which covered topics such as musical development in the preschooler and the development of musical preferences. Both fields have subsequently flourished, with the former following developments in mainstream cognitive psychology and making ever closer links with neuroscience and computer science; and the latter demonstrating the clear potential for developmental psychology to inform educational policy and practice. It would of course be a grave mistake to assume that these different branches of music psychology are wholly independent of one another and have separated entirely from the parent discipline. Research on topics such as the development of musical skills draws equally on both for instance, and almost any musical behaviour inevitably draws on a wide range of psychological processes including learning, creativity, motor skill, perception, and emotion.

Although the social psychology of music itself received little research attention until recent years, several cognate disciplines have a longer and more detailed history. For example, the sociology of music concerns the production of musical culture and how this relates to social organizations and conventions. Arguably the most noticeable divide separates the field into macro- and micro-sociological sub-disciplines. Macro-sociological perspectives concern the wider socio-cultural context in which music is produced and experienced. Research within this macro-sociological perspective may concern, for example, gender and sexuality, technological developments, political and economic influences, and the impact of the way in which the music industry is organized. In contrast, micro-sociological perspectives focus on smaller-scale factors such as interactions between performers, between performers and their audience, or between the fans of a particular musician. DeNora (2001, p.161) for instance notes that 'fissures within sociology are legion—*macro* (concern with large-scale institutions and trends) versus *micro* (focus on interactional processes), *quantitative* versus *qualitative*, *structuralist* (focus on social forces and trends) versus *interpretive* (focus on meaning-making activity), to name a few'. Furthermore, in practical terms there is sometimes a very blurred dividing line between music research from a sociological perspective and that from economic, ethnomusicological, anthropological, or educational perspectives. However, perhaps the most blurred boundary of all is that between sociology and social psychology.

Indeed, the distinctions within sociology mirror those within social psychology, which itself is difficult to define. Most definitions involve elements of Hewstone and Manstead's (1995, p. 588), namely that social psychology is 'the scientific study of the reciprocal influence of the individual and his or her social context'. However, many authors (e.g. Hewstone and Manstead, 1995) have distinguished explicitly between psychological social psychology and sociological social psychology. Psychological social psychology concerns the impact of social factors on individuals and typically uses experimental methods, whereas sociological social psychology focuses on the reciprocity between individuals and society usually via naturalistic methods such as observation, interviews, or diaries. Researchers within the sociological approach to social psychology have argued repeatedly and vociferously that experimental approaches are flawed and/or inappropriate. Harré (1979) for instance argued that experiments decontextualize behaviour, focus on specific actions rather than longer episodes of behaviour, and tend to adopt experimenter-based explanations for outcomes to the neglect of participants' own accounts of why they behaved in the way they did. Furthermore, a second oft cited division within social psychology is between North American and European approaches. The former focuses on the individual whereas the latter is more concerned with macroscopic social influences such as intergroup relations or cultural identity.

One other approach to defining social psychology has had a considerable impact upon our own thinking. Doise (1986) proposed that there are four 'levels of analysis' in social psychology, namely intraindividual, interindividual/situational, socio-positional, and ideological. Research at the intraindividual level investigates cognitive, perceptual, and biological processes by which people organize the social environment. Within the social psychology of music, research at this level might involve, for example, the impact of personality on musical preference. The next level of analysis, the interindividual and situational level, involves the processes that occur between individuals in a given situation. Within the social psychology of music, research at this level might involve, for example, the use of body language by members of a string quartet to coordinate the timing of their performance. The socio-positional level again considers relationships between individuals, but this time with particular reference to differences in their social position such as their group membership, or with reference to larger social institutions such as the home, schools, or the community. Within the social psychology of music, research at this level might involve, for example, the role of musical preference in forming attitudes towards others with different musical tastes. Finally, the ideological level deals with broad cultural systems of beliefs, representations, and norms. Within the social psychology of music, research at this level might involve, for example, stereotypes of musical instruments that boys and girls should play, and how these might manifest themselves (implicitly or explicitly) within an educational system. Doise suggests that most research in psychological social psychology operates at the first and second of these levels, and that in sociological social psychology at the higher levels. He also proposes that European social psychology is more likely to operate at the higher levels than is the North American approach. As such Doise's approach provides a very useful framework within which we can locate individual topics within the social psychology of music.

Our approach to the social psychology of music contains several features. First, Doise's levels of analysis seem to capture accurately the kind of research that has been carried out. As a field, the social psychology of music operates on all of Doise's levels. But, crucially, individual researchers tend to focus their activities on just one level, and the field has undoubtedly developed over recent years in a 'topic-based' manner. To single out one individual researcher for no particular reason, Tony Kemp has devoted an entire career to research on personality and music that operates entirely at the intraindividual level. In short, since individual lines of research seem to operate almost exclusively on only one of Doise's levels, the two are typically conflated. Although we believe that Doise's levels remain an extremely useful way of organizing the social psychology of music, it is also possible to focus instead on specific individual topics. The latter approach yields more or less the same organization of the field as a focus on Doise's levels, but of course makes it a simpler task to describe the routes along which individual lines of research have proceeded. Furthermore, there are a few cases where researchers have investigated a particular phenomenon from a variety of different perspectives. For example, Simonton's well-known studies of musical eminence have addressed each of Doise's levels of social influence, often within a single research design. Even here, however, Simonton's different published studies have tended to use very similar methods so that again a topic-based approach leads to clearer and simpler explanations.

Second, one particular manifestation of this 'topic-based' development of the social psychology of music has been that closely related lines of research have developed with little or no cross-pollination between them. The most obvious example of this is the dearth of linkages between research on musical likes and dislikes and research on specific emotional responses to music. These two extensive fields of research are characterized by different theories with little attempt to integrate the two. Similarly, research concerning the general public's fascination with celebrities has rarely if ever informed research on whether adolescents are predisposed to copy the licentious behaviours of their favourite musicians; historiometric analyses of the factors that influenced the development of the great classical music composers has continued without reference to research on environmental influences on the development of musical skill among groups of present day musicians or sociological work on 'superstardom'; research on the uses of music in retail has continued without reference to research on the uses of music in advertising; and we could give many other examples. Consequently a second reason why we have adopted a topic-based approach to the social psychology of music in this book is in the hope that, by juxtaposing related bodies of research that are largely unin-formed by one another, researchers will be more inclined to draw on related work and increase the coherence of the field. One immediate manifestation of this is that we have drawn on a scattered and eclectic literature that includes not just psychological and sociological approaches to social psychology but also the literature concerning psychology as a whole, and related fields such as education, economics, marketing, medicine, business studies, and communication studies: if a piece of research 'looked relevant to the social psychology of music' then, irrespective of the field that it purports to represent, we have addressed it here.

Third, as a result, we have adopted a catholic, utilitarian approach to the divisions between different approaches to the social psychology of music. We believe that all of the different approaches to social psychology can potentially contribute to understanding, and would rule out none on an a priori basis. Indeed, although interest in the social psychology of music continues to accelerate, there is not such a mass of research that it is even *possible* for us to focus solely on say, music research drawing on European psychological social psychology at the socio-positional level. We are interested in all approaches to the social psychology of music be they psychological or sociological; European or North American; intraindividual, interindividual/situational, socio-positional, or ideological. We might also add, however, that the following pages will show that different perspectives have been more influential than others in the study of particular issues and topics. For example, as we will see in Chapter 2, most of the research on composition has focused on the intraindividual or ideological levels, and with the exception of a limited number of studies on collaboration there is little work concerning composition at the interindividual/situational and socio-positional levels. Indeed, as as is shown in Chapter 4, research on musical subculture is rare in that it has adopted the perspectives of both European and North American social psychology (concerning music in the maintenance of social groups and the impact of music on delinquency respectively). These examples make clear that one of the major opportunities for future research lies not just in studying previously un-researched musical behaviours, but also in studying these from *all* of the different perspectives available to researchers in the social psychology of music.

Fourth, our coverage of these different topics is structured according to another trend that has become increasingly evident over recent years, namely a strong interest in how research findings might be applied to 'real world' problems and issues. For example, research on music in adolescence has focused increasingly on the questions of censorship and deleterious consequences of listening to pop music. Accordingly, the topics covered by this book are organized to reflect increasing levels of concern with applied questions and issues. We begin with two chapters on the 'core' areas of music psychology, namely composing/performance (i.e. making music) and listening, before then progressing to consider issues related to three general applied topics, namely music censorship and subcultures, music in business and health, and music education.

In particular we agree with many of Harré's (1979) arguments that were outlined above, and whenever possible we have emphasized research carried out using 'real' music, 'real' people, and 'real' contexts. With regard to 'real' music, the great majority of research studies within the psychology of music concern classical music. This is more justifiable in the case of research on specifically composition and performance, since many practitioners in these fields still have a strong leaning towards classical music. However, it is impossible to justify the virtual *absence* of research on composition and performance of pop music and other styles; and the continuing strong emphasis on classical music is even more untenable in other areas of research, since CD sales and radio station listening figures make it difficult to characterize this as anything but a minority interest among the general population, on a par with say, folk music. Classical music is intellectually important to the development of Western music as a whole, and is hugely important for a host of emotional, cognitive, and social reasons to those people who listen to and play it. However, in the early twenty-first century in the western world, classical music makes up such a small proportion of the general public's musical experience and interest that it is difficult to justify the amount of research attention it has received. This point has been made many times before by many different authors and we will continue to repeat it until, rather than paying 'lip service' to the idea, academics actually place more emphasis in their research on the music that most people experience as part of their everyday lives. Accordingly, whenever we could, we have focused here on pop music, although in practice classical music is nonetheless very well represented. Similarly, although a lack of research and poor access to that which does exist made this very difficult, we have also done what we could to cite research carried out outside mainstream British/North American culture, or which uses non-Western musical styles: nonetheless research from Britain and North America predominates.

Similar points apply to our emphasis on covering research involving 'real' people and 'real' contexts. A brief inspection of the journals would certainly convey the impression that psychologists believe the world to be populated largely by undergraduate students who live out their whole existence in research laboratories. Ease of access to student samples and the experimental control offered by the 'womb' of the lab explain this bias in part. Nonetheless, a theory is only a theory until it has been shown to work in practice. In order to 'work in practice' a theory has to explain the behaviour of all the relevant members of the general population going about relevant tasks as part of their working life or leisure time. For example, a complete theory of musical preference has to provide a detailed explanation why the *Wedding March* moves us to tears of joy on our special day but tears of boredom under almost any other circumstances; a complete theory of musicianship has to provide a detailed explanation of the social kudos that results from being a skilled DJ; a complete theory of musical subculture has to provide a detailed explanation of the antipathy of many classical music fans towards pop (and *vice versa*), and the role of music in explaining why a teenager dresses in a particular way, 'hangs out' in some places rather than others, or takes (certain types of) drugs. Lab-based undergraduates can only tell us so much, and for this reason we have emphasized here research that deals with the kinds of people and contexts in which the theories in question are assumed to operate in practice.

This emphasis in turn reflects a fifth feature of the present book, namely research and thinking over recent years concerning what music is actually for: ethnomusicology of course has a strong history of explaining the functions of music in many and varied societies (e.g. Gregory, 1997; Merriam, 1964), and more recent years have witnessed growing interest in evolutionary perspectives on music (e.g. Cross, 2003; Sluming and Manning, 2000; Wallin, Merker, and Brown, 2000). However, many researchers interested in the social psychology of music have also addressed the purpose of music in the modern world, and this issue runs throughout the book. Because of the technological advances mentioned above, music is part of a much greater range of everyday life experiences and activities than ever before. People now actively use music for many more different purposes in many more areas of everyday life than hitherto, and so our understanding of its effects are of more widespread and general interest within psychology. Specifically, this issue of 'purpose' brings us to a possible paradigm for the social psychology of music.

The philosopher of science Thomas Kuhn is perhaps best known for his 1962 work *The Structure of Scientific Revolutions*. In this he argues that scientific research within any field takes place within a prevailing paradigm that defines the issues of interest and how they are to be investigated. As Sloboda (1986, p. 199) put it, 'there are five characteristics of a healthy paradigm: an agreed set of central problems; agreed methods for working on these problems; agreed theoretical frameworks in which to discuss them; techniques and theories which are specific to the paradigm; research which is appropriate to the whole range of phenomena in the domain being studied'. Sloboda suggested that by the mid-1980s the psychology of music had reached this stage. He proposed that the central problem for music psychology is to explain the *structure and content* of musical experience, and that Lerdahl and Jackendoff's (1983) *Generative Theory of Tonal Music* epitomizes the concerns of this paradigm, such that the psychology of music can be considered to have 'come of age'. One other aspect of Kuhn's notion of paradigms is also particularly relevant to this argument, however. Kuhn argues that scientists' faith in the prevailing paradigm within their field is so strong that any observations that are inconsistent with it or which cannot be explained by it are attributed to a mistake on the part of the researcher or dismissed as simply irrelevant and unimportant: over time the number of inconsistent or inexplicable observations builds until they reach a critical point, and a revolution is triggered. There is a period of reflection and eventually a new paradigm for research emerges in which new questions seem important and new research methods are used to investigate them.

We believe that the prevailing paradigm of the psychology of music has changed since the 1980s, which saw the founding of identifiably cognitive and developmental psychologies of music. Specifically, the paradigm of music psychology has shifted towards social factors, and in particular current research suggests that the paradigm that many researchers are working to concerns the use of *naturalistic* as well as experimental methods to investigate the structure, content, *purpose, and implications* of musical experiences. Although experimental work on the structure and content of musical experiences has continued since the time of Sloboda's (1986) arguments, an emphasis on purpose and implications and the use of contextualized research methods has become more prominent only in recent years, most famously via the well-publicized 'Mozart effect' (see Chapter 2), although this trend can also be seen clearly in the titles of books published over the past few years such as *Psychology* for *Musicians* (our emphasis; Lehmann, Sloboda, and Woody, 2007), *Psychology* for *Performing Artists* (our emphasis; Wilson, 2002), *Musical Communication* (Miell, MacDonald, and Hargreaves, 2005), *Musical Identities* (MacDonald, Hargreaves, and Miell, 2002); and *Musical Development and Learning: The International Perspective* (Hargreaves and North, 2001). In no other branch of music psychology has this shift towards the purpose and implications of musical behaviour in naturalistic contexts been more apparent than in the social psychology of music.

In particular the progress of music psychology can be interpreted via Kuhn's notion of paradigm shifts. The cognitive and developmental branches of music psychology made good progress between the 1960s and 1980s by using lab-based, experimental methods to explain many of the 'core' issues underlying musical behaviour, namely perceptual and aesthetic reactions to music and the factors underlying skilled composition and performance. For example, as shown in Chapter 3, research on aesthetic responses to music was carried out under the impression that it 'aims not only to throw light on aesthetic phenomena but, through the elucidation of aesthetic problems, to throw light on human psychology in general' (Berlyne, 1974, p. 5). In Kuhnian terms, there was a strong belief that the prevailing paradigm, focusing on experimental cognitive and biological psychology, would ultimately answer all questions relating to preference, taste, and emotional reactions; and also begin to inform the parent discipline. However, by the 1980s researchers such as Vladimir Konečni and Dean Simonton were beginning to lose faith in the ability of experimental cognitive and biological psychology to explain responses to music. Konečni was attempting to experimentally mimic social situations in the lab, whereas Simonton was using archival data sources such as record buying guides to measure the eminence of classical music composers. Konečni (1982), for example, harked back to the sentiments expressed by Farnsworth with which this chapter began when he wrote that 'the vast majority of research studies have treated aesthetic preference and choice as if they, and the process of appreciation itself, normally occur in a social, emotional, and cognitive vacuum, as if they were independent of the contexts in which people enjoy aesthetic stimuli in daily life'(p. 498). Konečni pointed out that music is something enjoyed 'in the stream of daily life' (p. 500), for example in shops, restaurants, whilst doing housework, and so on. In Kuhnian terms, failures to explain the musical world were no longer being dismissed as irrelevant or attributed to the personal failure of scientists but rather to problems with the basic framework for research. Konečni was effectively kicking against a paradigm that said social psychological factors could be safely ignored and that lab-based methodologies could accurately capture the essentials of musical preference as they were experienced by most people. Similarly, a few years later Persson and Robson (1995, p. 39) wrote that

> In recent years the maintaining of music psychology as a strictly experimental discipline has run into difficulties. Although the need for breaking new ground has been observed by several eminent researchers, few suggestions on how to proceed have actually been made. On the basis of the current debate within the social sciences, and personal experience of field research among performing musicians, this article argues the significance of investigating the 'real world' of music in the field.

Arguments such as these led to a revision of the basic paradigm, a change in what music psychology 'is'. Compared with the early 1980s, some researchers in recent years have followed the path Kuhn said they would: they have come to see different questions as more interesting and relevant, and see different research methods as more appropriate to the investigation of these. Specifically, interest in the *purpose and implications* of musical behaviour and the use of *naturalistic* research methodologies to address these have, over recent years, become a characteristic of music psychology and the social psychology of music in particular. It is probably no coincidence that recent years have seen research on the effects of music on shoppers, on intellectual abilities, on immunity, on the experience of pain, on delinquency, on driving performance, on the ability to carry out physical labour: what links all these developments is a common interest in the purpose and implications of music experienced in everyday settings. Let us be clear, experimental cognitive and psychobiological approaches to many of the core topics in music psychology have continued since the 1980s and they continue to make good progress. What we are describing here is nonetheless a highly significant shift in the fundamental paradigm of music psychology to a greater emphasis on purposes, implications, and naturalistic methodologies. This book is titled *The Social and Applied Psychology of Music* because in the present day it is impossible to consider social topics without considering applied topics, and *vice versa*.

As such the present book reflects both the older and the more modern elements of the music psychology paradigm. In Chapters 2 and 3 for instance we describe experimental research that has addressed the structure and content of composition/performance and musical taste respectively. However, the greater part of the book concerns the more recent elements of the paradigm by highlighting the purposes and implications of musical behaviour that have been addressed via naturalistic methodologies. For example, Chapter 2 on musicianship describes research on how being a musician helps to formulate identity and on the potential association between musicianship and intellectual ability. Chapter 3 on music listening describes how people use music actively in everyday situations to address immediate goals. Chapter 4 is devoted entirely to the role of music in adolescent subculture. Chapter 5 is devoted entirely to the role of music in producing profit and health. Chapter 6 is devoted entirely to the means of optimally-educating future musicians.

On a less theoretical note, the recency of much of this research has had a considerable impact on the depth of coverage we have given to different areas. Specifically we have deliberately given much more space to new material and, given that this is scattered across journals representing may different disciplines, cited as many studies as our publisher would allow. For example, Chapter 4 is the longest chapter in the book simply because, to the best of our knowledge, it represents the first comprehensive review of psychological research on music censorship, delinquency, and subculture. Similarly, Chapter 5 represents the first major overview for more than a decade of psychological research on music purchasing and the uses of music in retail and leisure; and Chapter 6 presents the first review of the research literature on musical development and education from a specifically social psychological perspective.

We should conclude by also pointing out that it is perfectly possible to read the following pages without any reference to the issues outlined in this chapter. It is important to understand the more general context that surrounds the research and theories we describe. But this was not our primary motivation in writing the book: quite simply we hope that this book will convey our enthusiasm for the subject, and in particular that it might inspire future researchers in the same way that we were inspired by books on the subject that we read as students. In short, we hope that this book is informative, but above that we hope that it is interesting and thought-provoking.

2

Composition and musicianship

I like Toronto because nobody hates me
here—unlike New York or Vienna
Igor Stravinsky, 1972

As this quote by the great Stravinsky shows, composers and musicians are certainly susceptible to the influence of the social world. In this chapter we describe how composition and musicianship are influenced by these social factors. As described in more detail in Chapter 6, social research on music-making is certainly timely, given recent attempts by several governments and education agencies around the world to increase access to music lessons. Cooke and Morris (1996, p.127) note that music-making 'is indeed a minority activity in Britain. Less than half (45%) of all children claim to be able to play a musical instrument compared with a quarter (26%) of adults. However this still represents a market of 12 million adults and 3 million children' in the UK alone. As these figures make clear, the sheer number of people who make music on a regular basis means that social issues in composition and musicianship ought to be of interest to any music researcher and arguably to any psychologist or other social scientist. Furthermore, making music is almost certainly important to people because of social psychological factors such as achievement, motivation, creativity, and identity. Making music is an intrinsically social psychological phenomenon.

We begin the chapter by describing musical creativity: what is it, and what are the main theoretical explanations of how it occurs? In the second main section of the chapter we discuss composition, and in particular how the nature of the music a person composes (and the reputation this work subsequently obtains) can be influenced by the prevailing musical *zeitgeist* and also aspects of the composer's biographical milieu. In the final section of the chapter we consider several aspects of musicianship. These include personality differences between people who play different instruments; identity as a musician; environmental influences in the development of musical skill; evaluations of musical performances; performance anxiety; and the much-discussed 'Mozart effect'.

2.1 **Creativity**

2.1.1 **The concept of creativity**

Creativity is a prized feature of the human mind: the progress and development of the human race in many ways depends on people's capacity to generate and apply new ideas. As the pace of technological change increases, world economies are increasingly driven by the generation and application of new ideas. Indeed, competitiveness in the global market depends on the capacity for innovation. The aim of education for creativity goes well beyond economic necessity, of course. Young people need to be able to cope with social and cultural change, and with the demands of the future. It is not surprising that the study of creativity is high on the agenda in many disciplines; it has been studied by philosophers, historians, psychologists, sociologists, educators and others for many years. Trying to understand and promote creativity is also of direct interest to creative artists and scientists themselves, as well as people working in other areas of real-life application such as broadcasting, marketing, medicine, and communications.

Studying creativity immediately raises a number of difficult questions. For example, what is 'creativity' exactly, how can it be defined, how can we explain it, and can it be measured? These questions raise some fundamental paradoxes, and some would even argue that any rational analysis of creativity is impossible. Plato, for example, felt that there are inherent contradictions in talking about discovery because you either know what you are looking for, in which case there is no problem, or you do not, and can thus not expect to find anything. As he argues, 'How will you set about looking for that thing, the nature of which is totally unknown to you? Which among the things you do not know is the one you propose to look for? And if by chance you should stumble upon it, how will you know that it is indeed that thing, since you are in ignorance of it?'

The study of creativity has been likened to 'blind men's views of an elephant'; each blind man has a grasp of that part of the elephant that is in front of him, but none has an overall picture of the beast. It is generally agreed that 'creativity is the ability to produce work that is both novel (i.e. original, unexpected) and appropriate (i.e. useful, adaptive concerning task constraints' (Sternberg and Lubart, 1999, p. 3). Even so, many questions concerning the very nature of creativity remain unanswered. For example, what are the differences between creativity and intelligence; how might these differences relate to artistic and scientific thinking respectively; what is the relationship between originality and creative productivity; should creativity be defined in terms of characteristics of people, or of products; does creativity involve everyday or exceptional thinking; does creativity require inspiration, perspiration, or both; and does creativity require talent and ability, learning and expertize, or all of these?

Creativity was a neglected topic in psychology in the earlier stages of the twentieth century, and a clear landmark was J. P. Guilford's Presidential Address to the American Psychological Association on 'Creativity' in 1950; this is widely cited as having kick-started the growth of psychological research over the intervening half-century, and provided the focus for an explosion of research on the topic in the 1960s and 1970s. A good deal of this largely psychometric work was devoted to the idea that children's general levels of ability or giftedness, usually measured in terms of academic success, were being defined too narrowly, in terms of *intelligence*, which at the time largely meant the ability to do IQ tests. In other words, ability was mainly being defined in terms of problem-solving or *convergent thinking* abilities, and this was leaving out a whole area of creative or *divergent* abilities that were of equal importance in pupils' eventual success. We might add that the second author's doctoral thesis, leading to his first ever publication (Hargreaves and Bolton, 1972), was a factor analytic study using tests of divergent thinking inspired by this early surge of activity!

Contemporary views of creativity, intelligence and giftedness go well beyond mental tests and conventional academic skills, and there is increasing interest in trying to explain the processes underlying creative thinking in everyday life, and the conditions under which it can be promoted. The study of creativity is an increasingly important feature of contemporary thinking in education, with three educational research journals recently publishing special issues on creativity—the *Scandinavian Journal of Education* (2003), the *Cambridge Journal of Education* (2006), and the *International Journal of Educational Research* (2008). The same increase of interest is also apparent in psychological research, as illustrated by the American Psychological Association's 2006 launch of a new journal *Psychology of Aesthetics, Creativity and the Arts*. These developments within the psychological literature are clearly documented in Robert Sternberg's (1999) *Handbook of Creativity*, which is standing the test of time as a comprehensive, definitive, and authoritative compilation of theory and research that includes chapters by many of the most influential thinkers in the field.

2.1.2 The creative process

Some research has investigated various real-life manifestations of creativity in science, the arts, and in other fields. One obvious approach has been to look in detail at the working methods of some famous creators, and Ghiselin (1952) compiled a valuable collection of the introspective writings of a variety of eminent figures from different fields of endeavour, including Einstein, Mozart, Van Gogh, Wordsworth and Jung, to pick just a few at random. It soon becomes clear that there is no common style of working. Different creators have distinct styles. Some may indeed conform to the stereotype of a tormented genius inspired to hours of frenzied work, embodying the romantic ideal encapsulated so well by Plato's description that 'There is a third form of possession or madness, of which the Muses are the source'. Others, however, regard their work as a routine, everyday activity accomplished by clocking on at nine o'clock in the morning and working regular hours.

Introspections of this kind gave rise to descriptive accounts of the creative process such as those by Helmholtz (1896) and Wallas (1926). These proposed four distinct stages in the creative process: *preparation*, in which the problem space is defined and researched; *incubation*, a mysterious process during which there is no conscious work on the problem, and yet some kind of internal connections seem to be formed; *illumination*, which represents the 'Eureka' moment at which the solution to the problem suddenly emerges; and *verification*, which is the down-to-earth job of turning the new idea into reality by, for example, writing out the score or completing the manuscript. Walters and Gardner (1986) also used biographical information to identify the 'crystallising experiences' during which such individuals suddenly discover their gift and interests, and which change their whole approach to that domain and often the whole course of their lives.

Weisberg (1993), like other psychologists, has undertaken detailed case studies of well-known scientific discoveries and scientists. He looks in depth, for example, at the Wright brothers' invention of the first flying machine or aeroplane; at Crick and Watson's celebrated discovery of the structure of DNA, which laid the foundations for modern genetics; and at Darwin's formulation of the principle of evolution through natural selection. In each case, it appears that the process of arriving at the final breakthrough did not involve some kind of extraordinary thought process, but rather the repeated and persistent use of the methods by which ordinary people solve problems, such as reformulations, new interpretations of existing facts, and drawing on inspiration and ideas from other people or situations around them. The same general considerations apply to work in the arts. Weisberg looks in depth, amongst others, at case studies of the development of Picasso's different styles or periods of his painting; at the ways in which poets like Blake and Coleridge reported re-drafting and revising their work; and at Mozart's reports on his own composition, often written in letters to his father. Once again, the same conclusion emerges: rather than providing evidence of special or extraordinary thinking, it appears that most new discoveries in the arts arise from extensions and elaborations of ordinary thinking processes.

2.1.3 Theories of creativity

Several of the chapters in Sternberg's (1999) *Handbook of Creativity* refer to the many different approaches which have been taken to the study of creativity, the research methodologies that have been used in doing so, and the main theoretical perspectives. Sternberg and Lubart (1999) refer to two approaches which are clearly outside the realm of scientific investigation, and which indeed they regard as being 'damaging' to such investigation. These are *mystical* approaches, such as might be found in early philosophical or religious writings, or in the introspective accounts by creative thinkers mentioned above; and what they call *pragmatic* approaches, whose aim is to develop techniques for promoting creative thinking in groups like business executives, schoolchildren, and in the general public, rather than increasing our understanding of it. Indeed, something like a 'creativity industry' built up in the 1960s and 1970s, based on various 'how to' manuals which aimed to help people be more creative. Edward DeBono's idea of 'lateral thinking' was one of the most prominent, as was Alex Osborn's idea of 'brainstorming'. Some of these ideas are based on sound psychological principles, whilst others make extravagant claims that are unsupported by any evidence.

Apart from these two quite distinctive approaches, it is possible to distinguish between seven broad theoretical perspectives on creativity that are scientifically based. First, Martindale (1999) has reviewed some of the main *biological* mechanisms that have been used in attempted explanations of creativity. His brief account distinguishes between three main mechanisms: cortical arousal, hemispheric asymmetry, and frontal lobe activation. There is very little evidence for or against any of these, although the explanation of aesthetic phenomena in terms of arousal-based mechanisms has a 50-year history in the field of experimental aesthetics, as we shall see in detail in Chapter 3.

As described in more detail later in this chapter, Martindale proposes a tentative link between arousal-based mechanisms and Kris's (1952) explanation of creativity in terms of the balance between 'primary process' and 'secondary process' modes of thought. The former is the undirected, diffuse, and irrational activity that goes on in states such as dreams and hallucinations while the latter is everyday, focused and rational. Kris's hypothesis, which originated in Freudian theory (see below), is that creative people are better able than less creative people to employ primary process material in their everyday, secondary process thinking. Martindale's proposal is that intermediate levels of arousal are optimal for the promotion of secondary process thinking, whereas primary process thought is more likely to occur at high and low arousal levels. As such the relationship between arousal and creativity is complex and non-linear.

The remaining six theories are clearly and distinctly psychological in origin, and might be termed the *psychoanalytic, associative, psychometric, cognitive, computational,* and *social-personality* approaches. Sternberg and Lubart's (1999) brief review also refers to 'confluence approaches', which include varying combinations of the former, such as Czikszentmihalyi's (1996) 'systems' model, which is based on critical combinations of the characteristics of the individual, the domain (i.e. the area of creative activity, such as poetry or music), and the field (i.e. the institutions and people who control and influence a domain, such as radio and TV producers, concert promoters or critics). Another confluence model is Sternberg and Lubart's own 'investment' theory of creativity, which is based on the notion that creative people are those who can 'buy low and sell high' with respect to ideas. They can spot new ideas or approaches which are unknown or unfashionable, and work so as to make them well known and fashionable before moving on to the next project.

The *psychoanalytic* approach to creativity is based on Freud's concept of the struggle that takes place in every individual between the controlling forces of socialization and powerful, unconscious instinctual drives that are self-directed and sexual in origin. The individual employs various ego defence mechanisms in order to maintain a balance between these, and one such mechanism is sublimation. By sublimation Freud was referring to a means by which people control and resolve socially unacceptable desires that arise from their internal conflicts by diverting this energy into more socially-acceptable activities. In essence, Freud conceived of artistic creativity as a demonstration of sublimation. The ego was conceived by Freud as being that part of our psyche which regulates this balance, and so Kris's hypothesis (see above) was that creative people are those whose ego is sufficiently strong to enable primary process material to be admitted into secondary process activity. Creativity is therefore characterized by 'regression in the service of the ego' (Kris, 1952).

Another prominent idea is that creativity involves making associations between cognitive elements or objects that were previously seen as unrelated; or by seeing one of those elements or objects within a completely different context. This was the essence of Koestler's (1964) idea of 'bisociation'; and it is mirrored in Mednick's (1962) *associative* theory of creativity, originating from stimulus-response principles, in which creativity is 'the forming of associative elements into new combinations which either meet specified requirements or are in some way useful' (p. 221). For example, given a starting stimulus such as 'table', the creative person is seen as someone who is able to produce relatively unstereotyped associations to it, and then to go on to continue producing remote associations. This is termed a flat 'associative hierarchy', based on a hypothetical plot of the 'associative strengths' embodied in the person's successive responses; creative people are seen to be able to produce early responses at a lower level of associative strength (i.e. which are more unusual), and to continue to generate further unusual responses. The less creative person, on the other hand, is seen as being able to produce only stereotyped associations initially (i.e. associations at a high level of associative strength) which soon run dry, such that the ('steep') hierarchy tails off quickly. Mednick went so far as to devise the 'Remote Associates Test' in order to measure this capacity, but subsequent attempts to validate it against other psychometric tests were largely unsuccessful.

Following Guilford's (1950) lead, as we saw above, a good deal of the research on creativity in the 1960s and 1970s followed a *psychometric* approach, focusing largely on tests of divergent thinking such as the Torrance Tests of Creative Thinking (Torrance, 1974). Guilford's own work was based on his theory of the 'structure of the intellect', a factor analytic model that postulated the existence of 120 separate mental abilities organized in a three-dimensional cube. The basis of this is that five types of *operation* (one of which is 'divergent production') are carried out on four different types of *content*, and that this gives rise to six different types of *product*. More generally, a good deal of time and effort was devoted by psychometricians to attempts to show that creative thinking abilities were just as important as intelligence or problem-solving in achieving success in everyday life. Intelligence was mainly measured in terms of IQ tests, creativity was measured in terms of tests of divergent thinking, and real-life accomplishment was measured in terms of children's attainments at school. Numerous studies were then published in the psychometric literature that looked at the inter-relationships between these three domains (see Hargreaves (1986) for a fuller account of this literature); and some parallel tests of musical creativity were developed by Webster, which are still in use (e.g. Webster, 1992).

Unfortunately, the psychometric tests in the end threw little light on creativity in real life, even though they made a significant and lasting contribution to the field of psychometric testing. Educators and researchers realized that one-off 'snapshots' of creativity such as those revealed in a test were much less represen-tative and ecologically valid than assessments which were made in the context of ongoing activities, such as those within the classroom (see Gardner, 1993), such that current research on the assessment of creativity is now much more likely to employ assessments based on coursework profiles. For example, Amabile's (1982) 'consensual assessment' technique is based on the agreement between independent judges about the creativity of given products within a specific domain; and Hargreaves, Galton and Robinson (1996) also employed authentic assessment of children's work in drawing, music, and creative writing in classroom activities with their teachers.

Cognitive theories of creativity try to identify the mental plans, structures, and processes that underlie creative thinking: these might include retrieval, association, synthesis, transformation, analogical transfer, and categorical reduction (Weisberg, 1999). Some cognitive psychologists have investigated the processes underlying musical composition and improvisation by drawing analogies with other areas of skilled performance. Sloboda (1985), for example, suggests that composition/improvisation have two important features that are characteristic of all skilled performance. First, it is important for composers/improvisers to start by forming superordinate plans about their work; but having established these, it is equally important that the plans should be provisional and amenable to change according to the ways in which they actually work out in practice. Sloboda details a number of different techniques for investigating composition, including the study of composers' working sketches and the use of 'protocols' in which composers are asked to 'think aloud' as they work through sections of their work.

More generally, the cognitive approach to creativity highlights that improvisation is potentially a very fruitful area for investigation because it provides more or less direct access to creative musical processes as they happen 'live' (see reviews by Kenny and Gellrich, 2002; Lehmann, Sloboda, and Woody, 2007). One particular area that has received a certain amount of theoretical speculation and some limited empirical investigation is that of improvisation in modern jazz. Johnson-Laird (1988), for example, undertook a sophisticated theoretical analysis of the ways in which jazz improvisers steer a path between predetermined musical structures (such as chord sequences) and their own semi-arbitrary inventions; and this approach, based in artificial intelligence research, has enabled him to generate computer programmes for jazz improvisation. Other models of improvisation have also been proposed (e.g. Clarke, 1988; Pressing 1988), which follow similar principles, and which confirm the importance of investigating specific ways of working within a given domain.

Johnson-Laird's analysis demonstrates how computers and music software enable researchers to analyse the large amounts of data contained in compositions and improvisations relatively quickly and easily. Moreover, one particularly interesting methodological opportunity presented by this type of work is illustrated by Folkestad's studies of computer-based compositions by Swedish

15 to 16-year-olds (see Folkestad, 1996; Folkestad, Hargreaves and Lindström, 1998). Folkestad used the 'save as' command of a music software package to save successive drafts of the compositional work of these pupils, and used these drafts to formulate a typology of compositional strategies. There were several different strategies which fell into one of two main types: in *vertical* strategies, the piece is created section by section with all the instrumental parts completed in each case, whereas in *horizontal* strategies the melodic, harmonic or other structural aspects of the piece as a whole are created first, before instrumentation and further elaboration are added.

Johnson-Laird's (1988) development of computer programmes for jazz improvisation is a good illustration of the *computational* theories of creativity that have been proposed. Computational psychology uses ideas from the field of artificial intelligence (AI): it constructs AI models which are, in effect, operationalizations of the process being studied, and tests these models by writing computer programmes derived from them that either do or do not manage to successfully produce the behaviour in question. For example, a researcher will develop an AI model of creativity, write a computer programme that operationalizes the model of creativity, and then observe whether the computer is indeed able to demonstrate outputs that appear 'creative'. Boden (1999) provides a brief review of the small number of different computer models of musical creativity that have been proposed, as well as of the much larger number that are relevant to creativity in general. She also points out that the common idea that computational psychology mainly deals with cognitive processes is mistaken, and that this misunderstanding is exacerbated by the widespread use of the misleading term 'cognitive science': in fact, she suggests, a good deal of the early work in this field dealt with social psychology, motivation, and personality.

However, most contemporary computationalists do focus largely on cognitive processes, and AI models of creativity fall mainly into two groups, namely those dealing with *combinatorial creativity* on the one hand, and *exploratory – transformational creativity* on the other. The former deal with associative processes, such as those at the heart of the associative theories outlined above (e.g. metaphor and analogy). The latter deal with the recontextualizations and developments of ideas that occur within clearly defined conceptual spaces. These models rely on heuristics, or problem-solving guidelines, which are based on the structural constraints of a particular conceptual space, and the degree of freedom that performers are allowed within that conceptual space. For example, Johnson-Laird's programmes for jazz improvisation incorporate the harmonic and melodic rules of modern jazz chord sequences, or in other words, the structural constraints within which improvising soloists have to work within a particular style. Soloists also have a good deal of freedom within these constraints, however, for example in their choices of notes, phrasing, variations of timbre and expression, and so on; and these choices depend on many other factors such as their mood and state of mind, the contributions of the other musicians in the group (which share similar constraints and freedoms), the audience's reaction, and so on. Models that allow computers to compose via different generative systems and heuristics help us to understand how much choice and freedom human creators can employ within given forms of endeavour; and computational psychology can therefore involve a level of precision that is rare in creativity research. The corresponding disadvantage of this approach, of course, is its lack of success in accounting for the non-cognitive aspects of creativity, including social, motivational and personality factors: these are the province of the final approach.

What Sternberg and Lubart (1999) refer to as the *social-personality* approach to creativity has three main foci, namely personality factors, motivational variables, and social/cultural factors. Creativity researchers such as Barron (1968) and MacKinnon (1965) attempted to identify the personality traits associated with creativity in a series of studies of creative people such as architects and writers, and provided some limited evidence for the role of factors including independence of judgement, self-confidence, non-conformity, and risk taking. Tony Kemp (1996) more or less single-handedly pioneered this approach in trying to identify the distinctive personality types of musicians, including musical creators, and we shall review this work in more detail later in this chapter.

We shall also look in more detail at motivational factors later in this chapter, as well as in Chapter 6. For the time being, however, it is worth noting here that the clear focus of interest in terms of creativity has been in intrinsic motivation. One of the most prominent advocates of the social-personality approach is Teresa Amabile, whose book *The Social Psychology of Creativity* (1983) set out the main features of the social psychological approach, which she followed up and developed further in *Creativity in Context* (1996). Amabile adopted what she called a 'componential framework' of creativity based on the three main components of domain-relevant skills, creativity-relevant skills, and task motivation. The latter focused in particular on the importance of intrinsic motivation, and Amabile's 'intrinsic motivation hypothesis' of creativity states that 'the intrinsically motivated state is conducive to creativity, whereas the extrinsically motivated state is detrimental' (p. 107). Her own research, and those of her associates, includes experimental and psychometric studies that generally confirm this idea.

More generally, we should note also that these social and environmental factors in creativity can work at different levels. Hargreaves (1974), for example, showed that children's scores on tests of divergent thinking could be influenced by changes in the immediate classroom environment (i.e. whether the tests were administered in a conventional 'test-like' atmosphere, or whether the conditions were more playful). Numerous other studies have shown that creativity can be influenced by social and environmental factors on other levels including the educational environment (e.g. teacher characteristics, peer effects); the work environment; family influences; and broader societal and political indices (see review by Amabile, 1996). By far the largest and most methodologically sophisticated programme of research in this area is that undertaken by Dean Keith Simonton, who considered numerous biographical influences on musical composition and eminence. We turn now to a review of this work.

2.2 Composition, eminence, and fashion

The previous section tells us a great deal about the general processes that any ordinary person would go through in producing a piece of music. However an interest in the social psychology of music takes us down a different path and we move on here to considering what distinguishes a 'great' composer from an 'also ran'? The first point worth making here is simply that there is considerable agreement within a given musical culture concerning who the 'great' composers actually are, which in turn implies that, whatever the definition of 'greatness' may be, we seem to share it across the whole of society. As Simonton (1997a, p.114) notes, many people will 'debate whether Bach or Beethoven or Mozart is *the* greatest composer. What these controversies ignore is that none has entered the debate with the serious suggestion that it is Gebel or Türk or Lickl who actually deserve this distinction.'

More formal confirmation of this point is provided by Farnsworth (1969; see also Mueller and Hevner, 1942; Smith, 1987). Between 1938 and 1964 he carried out four separate polls, asking musicologists simply to nominate the most eminent classical music composers of all time. The results of the four polls are shown in Table 2.1. Although there is some minor jostling for places, composers very rarely move up or down the ranking by more than one or two places; and these rankings correlated well with other measures of eminence such as space allocations in music encyclopaedias, and counts of the frequency with which the composers' works were played by orchestras. Corresponding results were obtained for pop music by North and Hargreaves (1995a; see also North and Hargreaves, 2002; Rose and Wagner, 1995), who also found a considerable degree of consensus in participants' nominations as well as reasonable correlations between these and numerous archival measures

Table 2.1 Results of Farnsworth's polls

	Year							
	1938		**1944**		**1951**		**1964**	
1	Bach	1	Bach	1	Beethoven	1	Bach	
2	Beethoven	2	Beethoven	2	Bach	2	Beethoven	
3	Wagner	3	Mozart	3	Brahms	3	Mozart	
4	Mozart	4	Wagner	4	Haydn	4	Haydn	
5	Palestrina	5	Haydn	5	Mozart	5	Brahms	
6	Haydn	6=	Brahms	6=	Schubert	6	Handel	
7	Brahms	6=	Palestrina	6=	Debussy	7	Debussy	
8	Monteverdi	8	Schubert	8	Handel	8	Schubert	
9	Debussy	9	Handel	9	Wagner	9	Wagner	
10	Schubert	10	Debussy	10	Palestrina	10	Chopin	

of eminence such as record sales and encyclopaedia space. However, other research suggests that consensus in taste is not so universal as Farnsworth's (1969) and North and Hargreaves' (1995a) research suggests. For example, North and Hargreaves (1996a) found that consensus was much greater with regard to the 10 artworks nominated most frequently as the 'greatest' by their participants than with regard to the remaining artworks nominated. There may be a 'crème de la crème' that people really do agree over, whereas this degree of consensus breaks down as we move lower down the 'greatness' ranking to works that do have some discernible limitations over which people can disagree with one another. Similarly, Simonton (1998a) studied 496 operas by 55 composers. He found that, although the aesthetic success of these works in the modern day was positively related to their initial reception, this apparent consensus between the past and present-day judgements did appear to break down for certain periods such as 1720–1739 and 1860–1879. Simonton argues that these periods saw particularly challenging music being produced, such that it is more popular now than on its first performance; and we will return to this shortly in describing Martindale's theory of 'the clockwork muse'.

Naturally, many people have speculated on whether musical eminence has a predetermined, genetic component. Research on this itself has a fine pedigree, dating back to Galton's (1869) seminal work on hereditary genius that pointed to musical ability apparently being passed down through the generations of many family trees (e.g. the Bach family) as evidence of an inherited component to great compositional skills. Of course, sharing genes with somebody often means sharing their living environment also, such that it is often difficult to be sure whether a common degree of compositional talent is a product of genes or the environment (see section 2.3.2 below). Moreover, although obviously theoretically interesting, from a practical standpoint the search for such evidence is probably a red herring. There are many great composers who come from parents with only average levels of musicality, and many rather poor composers who are the children of at least one very gifted composer. Therefore it would, for example, be a brave music educator who did or did not offer a given child very high levels of music education in composition based purely on their lineage. Far more interesting from a practical perspective is research concerning how the outputs of eminent composers are influenced by environmental and cultural factors. Over the next few pages we consider several environmental and cultural factors that may explain the nature of the music a composer produces and also the 'greatness' of their reputation. These concern biographical influences on composition and eminence, the clockwork muse, the implications of melodic originality for a composer's future eminence, and collaboration with others.

2.2.1 Biographical influences on composition and eminence

First of all it is possible to identify biographical aspects of a composer's life that determine his prospects of becoming eminent. We say 'his' because the most clearly apparent biographical predictor of musical greatness is sex. Authors from several disciplines (e.g. Cameron, 2003; Piirto, 1991; Silverman, 1995) have asked why there are so few eminent females in many walks of life, including music. In addressing the lack of acclaimed female composers, Carl Seashore (1940, p. 88) noted that there are few sex differences in musical talent, and instead argued that the absence of women from lists of the 'musical greats' is probably because 'Women's fundamental urge is to be beautiful, loved and adored as a person; man's urge is to provide and achieve a career'! Although outrageously sexist (or at best outdated), it would seem that Seashore's arguments are not perhaps entirely discordant with present-day public opinion that continues to denigrate female musicians. North and Hargreaves (1996a) found that members of the public were extremely unlikely to nominate artworks by females in any domain as among the most important, such that, for example, only one female (Annie Lennox) was found in rankings of the top 10 classical music composers or pop musicians. Similarly, although great female composers undoubtedly exist (see Broker, 1996; Fuller, 1994) little research has focused on their defining characteristics (Sicoli, 1995; Walberg, Zhang, Cummings, and Fillipelli et al., 1996). Note also that

Simonton (1998b) presents similar data showing that judgements of the eminence of musicians are also related to their ethnicity.

As we will see in Chapter 3, effects such as these could perhaps be attributable to a kind of 'prestige effect', i.e. that music by females is automatically regarded as less 'worthy' than music by males. Effects such as this may well occur in musical composition. Goldberg (1968) gave female participants booklets containing six articles, in half of which the articles were attributed to males and in the other half to females. Articles allegedly by males were given higher ratings on 44 of the 54 measures, such as competence (see review of similar studies by Top, 1991). Two studies have employed similar methodologies but replaced written stimuli with pieces of music. Colley, North, and Hargreaves (2003) found evidence of anti-female bias in evaluations of new age music when participants were told only the name of the supposed composer of the music in question. Similarly, North, Colley, and Hargreaves (2003) found evidence of pro-female bias in female participants' evaluations of jazz excerpts and anti-female bias in male participants' evaluations. Also, participants' more specific reactions to the music (e.g. perceptions of the extent to which it was 'gentle' or 'soothing') were also influenced by gender stereotypes. Could this explain why there are so few well-known female musicians and composers?

2.2.1.1 Temporal factors

In the meantime there are other biographical factors that influence composition and eminence, and these can be divided into those that are and are not temporal in nature. Much of the research on temporal factors has concerned the possible relationship between composers' eminence and their year of birth. For example, the aptly-named team of Schubert, Wagner, and Schubert (1977) studied 80 composers finding that, compared to a sample of creative writers, the composers were more likely to be their parents' first-born child or an only child. Perhaps the best known research on this however comes from Farnsworth's data. In effect, he tested the lament of many composers that they have to die in order to become famous, such that the eminence of composers should increase in proportion to the amount of time that had passed since their death. For example, Farnsworth (1945) looked at the relationship between composers' date of birth and both their eminence ranking and also whether they were cited in two music encyclopaedias. The results did not support the 'reverence for the past' hypothesis but were instead more consistent with a 'reverence for the intermediate past' effect: neither long dead nor contemporary composers were most favoured, but instead the most nominations were given for those composers of around 100–150 years ago. North and

Hargreaves (1995a) found a different pattern for pop musicians. 275 people aged between 9 and 78 years were shown a list of 200 pop musicians/singers who had enjoyed a UK number 1 single between 1955 and 1994. These nominations were compared against the number of years that had passed since the artists in question had had their first UK number 1 single, and results demonstrated a weak, yet significant 'reverence for the recent' effect such that older artists were neglected in favour of those who had achieved their fame more recently. In addition to this, there was a slight upturn in eminence for those who achieved their first UK number 1 between 1955 and 1960 and who were perhaps perceived as trailblazers of pop music.

More recent data from North, Bland, and Ellis (2005) addressed whether specifically death leads to musicians being regarded more positively. Experimental participants were asked to read a vignette describing a male pop musician. Some versions of this vignette described how the musician had died in a plane crash (or was instead alive), and described his moral conduct in either positive or negative terms (i.e. describing how he had been convicted of sexually assaulting young fans and attacking an autograph hunter *or* campaigning for the environment and using his media profile to assist in resolving conflict in the Middle East). These manipulations had no effect on participants' ratings of how much they liked a song by the musician that they had been played. However, ratings of the emotional significance of the song were influenced by both the death and moral conduct of the musician: if the musician's moral conduct was good then his death led to his music being perceived as more emotionally profound: if moral conduct was bad then death led to a greater denigration of the significance of the song. Similarly, in a recent (as yet unpublished) study, North, Sheridan, Gillett, and Maltby (2007) asked 2,894 respondents to a web-based survey to nominate their favourite celebrity and rate the strength of their interest in this person via the Celebrity Attitude Scale: dead celebrities had less appeal. Of course, it remains to be seen how such responses can be influenced by whether the person in question is culpable in their own death, the age and career-stage of the person in question, and the extent to which they were part of a well-established sub-culture. For example, the deaths of John Lennon, Jim Morrison, Elvis Presley, and Kurt Cobain (see Chapter 4) have undoubtedly led to different public reactions.

Simonton's research on biographical factors has adopted a historiometric approach that eschews collecting data from human experimental participants and instead relies on massive archival quantitative data sources (see Simonton, 1984; 1990; 1994; 2003). Simonton (1989; see also Lindauer, 2003) considered the impact of death on composition via what he termed the 'swansong phenomenon'. He studied 1,919 compositions by 172 classical music composers that together accounted for almost 100% of the music performed in the standard repertoire. These compositions were subjected to computerized content analysis to produce a melodic originality score for each. Melodic originality was operationalized as the two-note transition frequencies for the first six notes of each composition. More simply, the initial six notes of a piece contain five two-note transitions, i.e. the transition from the first note to the second note, the transition from the second note to the third note, the transition from the third note to the fourth note and so on. Next a computer calculated the frequency with which all the various two-note transitions occurred across all the pieces of music. For example, it calculated how often there was a transition from a C to a G or from a B to a D and so on. This allowed Simonton to state the statistical probability of any particular two-note transition occurring relative to all those two-note transitions that occur across the entire corpus. This in turn then allowed the statistical probability to be calculated for each piece, so that a piece that scores highly on melodic originality contains two-note transitions that are very rare, whereas a piece that scores low for melodic originality contains two-note transitions that occur regularly.

Simonton then paid particular attention to a composer's 'swan songs', namely those pieces of music composed quite close to the composer's own death. He found that, compared to their earlier music, a composer's 'swan songs' tended to score lower in melodic originality (i.e. have relatively common note transitions), be shorter, be performed more regularly by orchestras and the like, and be rated as more aesthetically significant (e.g. masterpiece vs. seriously flawed) by an expert source. On these bases, Simonton (1989, p. 45) concluded that 'Composers in their final years seem to concentrate on producing masterworks that will permanently establish their reputation, doing so by creating works of a concise directness, as revealed by the brevity and melodic simplicity of their concluding pieces. The swan song is perhaps ... an expression of resignation, even contentment ... Consistent with this interpretation is the fact that melodic originality drops the most precipitously right before death.' It would be interesting to determine whether a similar effect occurs among successful pop music composers. These people typically cease (at least commercial) composition long before dying: do they evince a 'swansong' phenomenon towards the end of their commercial career or death, and to what extent do market forces such as record sales influence compositional originality (since, for example, extremely successful pop musicians may use the financial security they have achieved to produce music that is more experimental and less accessible)?

Simonton (1991a; see also 1997b) considered other temporal biographical factors by analysing 12,312 classical music themes (or 'hits') by 120 of the most successful classical music composers: these accounted for 89% of all the music heard in the classical repertoire. He investigated the age at which a composer first and last contributed to this pool of themes; their age when they produced their most popular (or 'best') theme; the age at which they produced the greatest number of themes; and the number of themes produced across their entire lifetime. Simonton (1991a, pp. 834–835) concluded that

> ... the typical famous composer obtains his first hit at age 26, best hit at age 40, and last hit around 52, with the age of maximum output close to that for the best hit, where the peak productivity attains 20 themes per year, in contrast to a total lifetime output averaging approximately 103 themes ... [These timings] are quite in keeping with those found in the mathematical and physical sciences, a similarity that may reflect the inherently abstract and logical nature of creativity in all of these domains.

There was also evidence that getting an early start was associated with success: composers who began both music lessons and composing at an earlier age produced their first 'hit' at an earlier age. Furthermore, 'the shorter the interval between first lessons or first composition and first hit, the higher the expected maximum annual output, lifetime productivity, and posthumous reputation' (p. 836).

2.2.1.2 Non-temporal factors

Other research by Simonton has identified several non-temporal biographical factors that may also impact upon composition, and five are particularly interesting, namely stressful life events, physical illness, competition, geographic marginality, and war. With regard to the first of these, Simonton (1980a) analysed 5,046 themes by 10 eminent classical music composers, namely Bach, Handel, Haydn, Mozart, Beethoven, Schubert, Chopin, Wagner, Brahms, and Debussy. The melodic originality of the themes was compared against a measure of stressful life events endured by the composers. To calculate this, biographical sources were used to assess whether each composer had experienced factors such as the death of a spouse, divorce, moving to a new permanent address, the birth or death of a child, or financial problems. Each of these factors was weighted according to just how stressful it was; for example, taking out a large loan was given a weighting of 20, being involved in litigation and lawsuits was given a weighting of 30, detention in jail or exile to avoid arrest was given a weighting of 63, and the death of a spouse was given a weighting of 100. Simonton found that melodic originality was greater in those works composed under times of biographical stress and speculates that (Simonton, 1980a, p. 216) 'Perhaps under stress it becomes difficult for the composer to subscribe to the standard rules of composition and instead the composer actively seeks out greater melodic freedom to symbolize the disorganized emotional states being concurrently endured.'

With regard to physical illness, Simonton (1977a) studied the same 10 composers as in his research on stressful life events. The impact of physical health was assessed by again assigning greater weight to more severe problems, such that, for example, a major illness attracted one point, an operation attracted two points, etc. This was compared against productivity, with different outputs attracting different weightings as a function of how large they were (e.g. an opera was weighted higher than a song). Although productivity was not related to stressful life events, it was related negatively to illness such that illness reduced productivity. Furthermore, Simonton (1987; see also Frosch, 1987) found a positive relationship in Beethoven's music between physical illness and melodic originality, arguing that the music composed at times of illness reflected his inner emotional state (and see also Simonton's (1993) consideration of how Mozart fits in with the more general evidence on what constitutes a musical genius).

With regard to competition, Simonton (1980b) analysed 15,618 themes by 479 composers in terms of two variables. The fame of each of the themes was assessed in terms of how often it was performed, recorded, or cited in, for example, record buying guides. These measures of thematic fame were compared against the amount of competition that each piece of music faced, which was operationalized as the total number of themes produced in a particular year. We might expect that the greater the amount of competition it faced, so the lower the likelihood of a particular piece becoming famous. However, contrary to this, Simonton found that thematic fame was positively related to competition. 'In other words, the most famous melodies tend to be ... composed in those years in which a lot of themes are being composed by other composers as well ... [This] finding implies that certain years yield a great many themes that stimulate the production of truly famous melodies' (p. 979).

With regard to geographic marginality and warfare, Simonton (1986) analysed 1,935 compositions by 172 composers, dating from the Renaissance to the middle of the twentieth century. For each 20-year period, the centre of musical activity was operationalized as the location in which the most composers were born. Geographic marginality was operationalized as the distance of each individual composer's place of birth from the centre of musical activity. Simonton found that 'the most popular compositions are less likely to be the creations of composers born an immense distance from the musical centers of the day' (p. 10). One other measure employed by Simonton was derived from ratings of the compositions by an expert in terms of their degree of accessibility, showing that 'a composer who is geographically marginal tends to create more accessible pieces' (p. 12). Finally, the study also concluded that composers born nearer to centres of compositional activity produced music with higher levels of variability in melodic originality, whereas more provincial composers produced music with more homogeneous melodic content. (Note that Simonton (1977b) presents a structural equation model of the inter-relationships between geographical marginality and several other aspects of a composer's creative milieu, such as year of birth and the availability of role models.) The study looked at two other variables also, namely international warfare and intranational warfare. The former was defined as the number of European states at war at the time each individual composition was produced; whereas the latter was defined as the number of European states suffering civil disturbance at the time of composition. Intranational war had a positive effect on the fame of the composition (defined as in earlier studies), in that 'Those works conceived when European nations were gripped by civil disturbances are more prone to be aesthetically successful' (p. 10). Intranational war was also associated with lower levels of melodic originality. International war was associated with higher levels of variability in melodic originality, and also to accessibility and another variable derived from assessment of the pieces by an expert, namely the minimum age of listener for whom the music is appropriate listening fare: Simonton concluded that 'A composition is easier to hear, and can be heard at a younger age, when it is composed ... under peacetime conditions' (p. 12).

Other researchers have adopted an economics-based approach to political order and composition. Oldani (1997), for example, found a distinct 'spike' in the number of successful musical entrepreneurs born during the Second World War, which he argued was attributable to greater achievement motivation caused by maternal anxiety during pregnancy. Similarly, Baumol and Baumol (1994) argue that the profusion of talented composers in the eighteenth-century Hapsburg empire is largely attributable to the fragmentation of the larger empire into numerous, smaller, semi-independent states. Each of these had its own court that required both entertainment and the need to garner prestige by commissioning new music, which in turn increased the number of jobs available for composers, attracting people into the profession, and providing a ready audience for them. Such conclusions are consistent with North and Hargreaves (1996a) who analysed people's nominations of their 'favourite' and the 'greatest' in a variety of artistic domains. These nominations were analysed for differences between countries in the year of birth of their nominated citizens. These analyses showed that different countries seemed to make their most important contribution at different points in history; and the pattern of these differences apparently reflected the relative economic and political prosperity of the countries at any given point in time.

For example, the only Greek artworks to be nominated were plays produced in ancient times. Similarly, the Italian artworks nominated tended to be those produced at around the time that the city states dominated the Mediterranean; the French artworks nominated tended to be those produced around the Napoleonic era; the British artworks nominated tended to be those produced at around the time that the country had a world-wide empire; and the artworks nominated from the USA tended to be those produced in the twentieth century. Whilst this may be purely coincidental, it is worth noting that more prosperous countries might be better able to patronize artists, giving them greater opportunities to produce important works: also, the involvement with other nations that is characteristic of economic and political prosperity should lead to a greater international awareness of that country's cultural products.

Note that the impact of all these non-temporal biographical factors is weak, with Simonton for example finding that they typically explained only around 5% of the variance in compositional variables such as melodic originality. Nonetheless, it would be surprising if factors such as warfare were shown to be more influential, totally dictating the nature of a composer's work, and it is more interesting that they are statistically significant at all. Furthermore, the effects identified here occurred over massive (and sometimes all but complete) samples of classical music. Consequently, while it is difficult to doubt the veracity of the findings with regard to classical music, it remains to be determined however whether similar effects would be observed in the case of pop music and other genres. For example, there was considerable artistic rivalry in the mid-1960s between UK-based The Beatles and USA-based The Beach Boys (which has been cited frequently as a factor in the production of their seminal works, namely *Sgt. Pepper's Lonely Hearts Club Band* and *Pet Sounds*): it would be interesting to see how this artistic rivalry related to Simonton's findings concerning effects on composition attributable to geographic marginality, competition, and international warfare (and domestic disquiet concerning this).

2.2.2 The clockwork muse

Colin Martindale's notion of *The Clockwork Muse* has also drawn on content analyses of very large samples of artworks. Martindale (1990, pp. 21-22) argues tongue in cheek that

> At least in private, most of us would agree that contemporary classical music sounds awful. It is dissonant; there is no detectable melody. But people have been saying the same thing about contemporary music for centuries. The major thirds (for example, C to E), which used to be considered dissonant, now sound perfectly consonant. A long time ago, there were few consonant chords; now there are many. Every time

composers began using a new chord, it sounded awful. If we want to appear cultured, we can't admit that we don't like opera. Outside of Italy, few people have ever liked opera. When opera was first introduced the cultural elite thought it an abomination. The poetry ruined the music and vice versa. Few people liked Beethoven's Moonlight Sonata when it was first played: it broke too many rules. If we dislike it today, it is for an opposite reason: it doesn't break any rules at all.

Similarly, as the quotation at the head of this chapter indicates, arguably the defining moment in Stravinsky's compositional career was the very harsh public reception at the premiere in Paris on 29 May 1913 of his ballet, *The Rite of Spring*. The highly complex music and unusual choreography led to arguments breaking out between audience members about whether what they were experiencing was truly 'art', and these arguments soon escalated into full-scale fistfights. The police failed to quell the disorder, and Stravinsky reportedly left the auditorium in tears before the end. Stravinsky's *Rite* is not alone, as riots in classical music auditoria were clearly *de rigueur* at the start of the twentieth century, being seen at, for example, a 1905 performance of Richard Strauss's *Salomé*; a 1917 performance of Erik Satie's *Parade*; a 1923 performance of George Antheil's *Ballet mécanique*; a 1923 performance of Erwin Schulhoff's *Ogelala*; a 1923 performance of Edgar Varèse's *Hyperprism*; a 1926 performance of Maurice Ravel's *Chansons madécasses*; and Stravinsky himself was a victim twice over, since a 1930 performance of his *Symphony of Psalms* went down no better than did the premiere of *The Rite* in 1913.

Similarly, we saw earlier Simonton's (1998a) finding that music from particularly 1860 to 1879 has received a much more positive reception in the present day than on first performance; and that Simonton explained this in terms of the music in question being too challenging for nineteenth-century ears. For example, Simonton describes how Bizet's *Carmen* was first performed on 3 March 1875 and received such a poor reception from audience and critics alike that Bizet grew extremely despondent, dying only three months later aged just 37. Of course, *The Rite of Spring* is now widely recognized as a seminal masterpiece, and is acceptable to most modern ears; and *Carmen* enjoys similar mass popularity. Why should music that provoked riots only 100 years ago be part of the modern mainstream? More specifically, why do reactions to music change so much over time, and in particular, what does this tell us about composition? One possible answer lies in Martindale's (1990) work on what he calls *the clockwork muse*, a theory that attempts to explain the development of creativity in all art forms, including musical composition.

Martindale begins by arguing that the nature of the music a composer writes is influenced by the audience's need for novelty. This need for novelty has the effect of making the evolution of music over time *predictable*, as though it ran by clockwork. Martindale claims that we need a *small* degree of novelty in music because of habituation. Habituation is the process by which we gradually lose interest in anything that we have experienced already. Habituation is the process by which we gradually lose interest in anything that we have experienced already. Habituation is the process by which we gradually lose interest in anything that we have experienced already. Habituation is the process by which we gradually lose interest in anything that we have experienced already. As this example shows, composers must introduce some novelty into their music if they are to avoid boring their audiences. This need for novelty is *weak* however. Society needs a considerable amount of order and predictability to be able to function, and high levels of novelty would simply produce chaos: 'Never, Salvador Dali complained, had he ordered lobster in a restaurant, and been served a baked telephone' (Martindale, 1990, p. 7). Note also that producing high levels of novelty requires a great deal of effort on the part of the producer. For instance, any attempt to rephrase the last sentence in five different ways would be difficult, and this tendency again mitigates against a composer introducing *high levels* of novelty into his or her music. In short, composers have a strong incentive to introduce some novelty into their music, but only a little.

This incentive to introduce just a little novelty into each successive composition has considerable implications. The avoidance of extreme novelty mitigates against radical and immediate changes in compositional style. However, the continual pressure to introduce slight novelty has just the same dramatic effect over time as does the sea lapping gently against a beach. There are two means by which a composer introduces novelty into his or her music and avoids habituation, namely arousal potential and primordial processing. We address the notion of musical arousal potential in more detail in the next chapter. Suffice it to say for now however that music possesses more arousal potential if it is louder or faster, more discordant, or more generally complex than other music that is around at the time. Accordingly, in order to satisfy the desire for novelty, composers will produce music that becomes incrementally louder, faster, more discordant, or more generally complicated. As such, Martindale's theory argues that over time the arousal potential of compositions should increase. Note also that some aspects of musical arousal potential can increase only to a point. For instance, sounds above 140 decibels cause physical pain and so the volume of the music is an unlikely candidate for increases in arousal potential over time. Rather Martindale argues that over time composers have instead opted to increase the arousal potential of their music by focusing on factors such as the complexity of the melody (i.e. the extent to which the melody 'chops and changes') or how 'surprising' it sounds: these can of course increase *ad infinitum*.

In describing a second means by which composers introduce novelty into their music, Martindale distinguishes between two types of cognitive process. *Conceptual* processing is logical and reality-oriented, and cannot produce novel ideas. In contrast, *primordial* processing refers to free associative and irrational thoughts: the more primordial thought in which we engage, so the more likely we are to produce novel combinations of mental elements. In order to satisfy the desire for novelty, each successive composition requires that the composer engage in more primordial processing in search of musical ideas not used already. In short, over time as a composer strives to continually introduce novelty, the impact of greater amounts of primordial processing means that work within a particular style should become more dream-like, unrealistic, bizarre, and 'weird-sounding'. There comes a point however when the amount of primordial processing required to produce new combinations of notes within the existing musical style becomes so immense that there is an easier way for composers to introduce novelty—they develop a new musical style.

For instance, there comes a point in time when a pop music composer, rather than trying to dream up new melodies based on 12-bar rock 'n' roll, finds it easier to obtain novelty by devising say funk. In short, the development of a new musical style allows a composer to achieve novelty with little primordial processing and consequent musical 'weirdness'. Over time, however, work within this new style again requires increasing amounts of primordial thought in order to achieve novelty, and the whole process begins again. The music again becomes more arousing and generally 'strange-sounding', relative to what has gone before it, and this will eventually reach a point when a new style is once again required.

Martindale presents an impressive amount of evidence supporting his theory from a wide range of different art forms. With regard to specifically music, he describes how lyrics of the top 10 pop songs in the USA showed a decrease in primordial content from 1950 to 1953 as musicians began early work on developing the rock 'n' roll style. During the rock 'n' roll years (1952-1959) the lyrics showed an increase in primordial content as composers attempted to dream up novel lyrical themes within the prevailing style. Levels of primordial content then dropped from 1960 to 1965 as the predominant rock 'n' roll style of the 1950s metamorphosed into the 1960s psychedelic style, and then primordial content began to rise again in the mid- to late-1960s once the new style was established. In another study, the epoch from 1490 to 1909 was divided into 21 consecutive 20-year periods, and compositions from eminent composers of each period were analysed. Human raters' perceptions of the arousal potential of the compositions (measured via rating scales concerning e.g. 'complex', 'tense', 'active', and 'strong') showed a significant increase over the 420-year period. The same set of compositions showed decreases in primordial content that coincided with periods of stylistic change (e.g. from the late baroque into the classical period). Martindale (1990) also reports evidence from individual composers, namely Beethoven, Chopin, and Grieg, that is sometimes (although not always) consistent with his theory. For example 'There is a correspondence between decreases in primordial content and Beethoven's stylistic changes' (p. 289); and dissonance increased significantly over time in both Chopin's and Grieg's music. Note also that, as we shall see shortly in the next section, Simonton's (1980b) analysis showed that levels of melodic originality in the music by 1479 composers generally increased throughout their life, in apparent support of Martindale's contention that arousal potential should increase over time in order to avoid audience habituation.

Martindale's highly provocative theory raises several interesting hypotheses that deserve further research attention. Most obviously there has been little research to test whether the basic principles of the theory hold for large samples of music. Five more specific aspects of the theory also seem to stand out as research candidates. First, Simonton (1993) cites Knight's (1973) description of the reaction of a violinist during the first rehearsal of one of Beethoven's *Rasoumovsky Quartets*. When the violinist queried whether what he had been asked to play was truly 'musical', Beethoven responded that it was 'not for you but for a later age'! Heavy exposure to music obviously leads to more opportunity for habituation, which in turn would be expected to lead to the individual concerned experiencing faster 'musical evolution': might this explain why composers have more radical tastes than their audiences, and tend to regard the latter as 'lagging behind' them? The same process would also predict that compositional fashions in musical styles that receive heavy media coverage (e.g. pop music) should evolve more quickly than fashions in less-exposed musical styles (e.g. folk music): the audience of the latter has fewer opportunities to habituate to the music and so there is less pressure on composers to introduce novelty.

Second, Martindale argues that some people experience a chronically high level of arousal in their everyday life as a result of living in cities rather than rural areas, experiencing rapid social change, or living during periods of social mobility. Such circumstances, Martindale contends, should lead to more arousing compositions, as composers try to produce music that is nonetheless able to 'stand out' against this arousing societal backdrop. This could relate to Simonton's findings, described above, concerning links between melodic originality and both geographic marginality and stressful life events. It also suggests that the CD collections of people living in towns will be more arousing than the collections of those living in the countryside.

Third, Martindale notes that habituation time is related negatively to the extent to which a stimulus is meaningful: we tire more quickly of a meaningless, highly complex design than we do of our children. Does this in turn imply that compositional fashions in religious music, political music, or music with sexual or otherwise sensational lyrics (see Chapter 4) should evolve more slowly than they do among other, less meaningful musical styles? Fourth, the more varied is a composer's style so the less scope there is for his or her audience to habituate, which in turn suggests that stylistic changes should occur less often. For example, people writing operas have more scope for variety (i.e. via a large number of instruments at their disposal, a libretto, a plot, a stage set, etc.) than do people composing for a string quartet or a solo instrument. Do people composing music for pop groups, jazz trios, and string quartets go through more stylistic revolutions than those composing music for operas and symphony orchestras? Finally, we should note that many of the concepts outlined in Martindale's theory overlap to some extent with research on the preference-feedback hypothesis which considers audience preferences for a particular piece of music (or other artwork) in terms of their previous exposure to it and the extent to which this is under voluntary control (see e.g. Colman, Best, and Austen, 1986; Colman, Hargreaves, and Sluckin, 1981; Colman, Sluckin, and Hargreaves, 1981; North and Hargreaves, 1997a; Sluckin, Hargreaves, and Colman, 1983).

2.2.3 Melodic originality and eminence

Of course Martindale's is not the only theory concerning what constitutes 'great' composition, and here we return briefly to Simonton's historiometric analyses of melodic originality. In addition to those studies outlined above concerning relationships between melodic originality and biographical factors, the bulk of Simonton's research on music has concerned the relationship between melodic originality and the reputation of the composer. This research has used the same very large samples and defined melodic originality in the same way as those studies described above.

As Martindale's theory makes clear, habituation and the amount of novelty contained in a piece of music are important to both composers and their audience alike. Simonton's data suggests that composers may well be in some way aware of this, using variations in melodic originality to compensate for the amount of stimulation that audiences will receive from other aspects of the music. For example, Simonton (1980b; 1986) reports how the lowest levels of melodic originality tend to be found in music such as operas and ballets that are written for the theatre; that intermediate levels of melodic originality are found in concert music (e.g. symphonies); and that the greatest levels of melodic originality are found in chamber music (e.g. sonatas, quartets, etc.). Of course the latter contain the least amount of spectacle from other sources, whereas the former have the greatest amount of spectacle from non-musical sources, employing large numbers of musicians, flamboyant costumes, towering stage sets etc. It is tempting to speculate that composers of operas and ballets implicitly understand that all this extra razzmatazz means that they have to otherwise 'keep it simple' and produce relatively undemanding music: in contrast, composers of chamber music seem to understand that the simple staging means that they have got their work cut out to maintain the audience's interest, and so they deliberately give the audience music with more novelty in order to reduce the risk of habituation.

In a similar vein, Simonton's (1987) analysis of Beethoven's music showed that his slower tempo pieces featured higher levels of melodic originality than did his faster music. Beethoven seemed to understand that people listening to the fast music might get 'overloaded' and so kept it otherwise simple. Furthermore, Simonton (1986; 1987) found that composers tend to produce less original music during periods of massive productivity, such that there is a trade-off between productivity and inventiveness; and Simonton (1995) found that a composer's first symphony contains greater variation in melodic originality than do others, suggesting that 'The neophyte composer is evidently trying to pull out all the stops' (Simonton, 1997a, p. 110); as well as highlighting numerous inter-relations between other intrinsic and extrinsic aspects of symphonic music (e.g. who the composer was, whether the work has an actual name or not, major vs. minor key).

However, the most fascinating part of Simonton's research concerns the impact of melodic originality on the fame of the music in question. Simonton measured fame in a similar to way to those studies cited earlier using, for example, space allocations in music encyclopaedias, the frequency with which the music is performed, ratings in record buying guides, etc. As Simonton (1997a, p. 111) describes, 'the popularity of a composition is an inverted backwards-J function of originality' such that pieces of low originality enjoy moderate amounts of popularity, pieces of moderate originality enjoy the highest amount of popularity, and pieces of high originality enjoy the least amount of popularity. In short, the most eminent composers are those who produce music that is not too taxing, but which nonetheless challenges the audience. For example, Simonton (1980b) found this pattern following an analysis of 15,618 musical themes by 479 classical composers. The same effect is found within the works of individual composers: Simonton (1987) found evidence of the same 'inverted-backwards-J' relationship between originality and fame in his analysis of 105 compositions (containing 593 themes) by Beethoven. As we will see in the following chapter, this pattern is remarkably similar to the predictions of Berlyne's (1971) theory of musical preference.

Other work has instead adopted a slightly different criterion of aesthetic success. Rather than the undoubtedly more democratic approach of defining success in terms of fame, an alternative is to define it in terms of the judgements of expert musicologists. In this case, Simonton (1986) found that melodic originality was related negatively to expert ratings of the 'accessibility' of the music to the general public: music experts believe that 'the weirder it sounds so the less accessible it is'! Furthermore, the same study showed that expert ratings of the aesthetic significance of pieces of music are positively related to their melodic originality: music experts believe that 'the weirder it sounds so the more artistically important it must be'! Interestingly, North and Hargreaves (2001) found that non-expert experimental participants seemed to agree with this, as they produced a positive correlation between ratings of musical quality and complexity assigned to music by The Beatles.

Other studies by Simonton have followed up Farnsworth's research with which we began this section of the chapter, and have focused directly on the eminence of composers rather than the success of their music *per se*. Simonton (1991b) analysed numerous measures of the eminence of 696 composers (e.g. assessments provided by biographical dictionaries, *Encyclopaedia Britannica*, a music encyclopaedia, and a music guide, as well as Farnsworth's original rankings, and data on performance frequencies). These measures were correlated highly with one another (see similar findings in North and Hargreaves' (1995a) investigation of pop musicians), suggesting that a single general factor may well underlie composers' eminence. Simonton (1991a) went a step further, in proposing that creative productivity is this single underlying factor; he reported that eminence was positively related to lifetime output and also the age at which the composers produced their last great work. Furthermore there is a positive relationship between output and both popularity and expert ratings of the aesthetic significance of the music in question (Simonton, 1980b; 1986). We should add that this conclusion might be tautological since success could in turn drive productivity, rather than *vice versa* as Simonton implies. In pop music, for example, a musician wins the right to produce more music (i.e. have their contract extended) if their previous recordings sell well (i.e. achieve success): commercial success leads directly to further productivity, such that it would be inevitable that the most successful musicians are the most productive. Nonetheless, although it is possible to quibble with individual findings, the historiometric approach has enormous potential for explaining musical composition, and it is amazing that so few other researchers have adopted it.

2.2.4 **Collaboration**

Before concluding this section, we should note that arguably the most overtly social psychological aspect of composition is when two or more composers collaborate together. This intrinsically social feature of composition means that it is, by definition, unconstrained, non-standardized and unpredictable. As Miell and Littleton (2004) illustrate, this in turn has meant that the existing research is largely exploratory (and perhaps theoretically rather nebulous), involving qualitative, open-ended, naturalistic accounts of collaborations involving small numbers of people (typically school pupils). As is clear from this, it will be many years before we have a good understanding of how collaboration influences the process of composition. On a more positive note, however, these characteristics also mean that much of the literature within this fast-developing field of research has adopted a common theoretical paradigm that might represent the beginning of an understanding of how collaboration occurs. This paradigm might be termed loosely as socio-cultural theory, and draws particularly on the work of Vygotsky (e.g. 1978) in emphasising the collaborative construction of knowledge via joint action and discourse, with particular emphasis on the nature and quality of any interactions (see also Chapter 6).

For example, Burnard and Younker (forthcoming) report a detailed analysis of the social and language processes involved in a composition and an arranging task given to two groups of school children; Littleton and Miell (forthcoming) analysed the talking that took place during rehearsals of a pop group comprising 15 to 16-year-olds, considering how the members construct, negotiate, and re-negotiate a shared understanding of 'their sound'; MacDonald and Miell (2000) investigated the verbal and musical communication that took place during compositions created by friends and non-friends, finding that the former involved more 'transactive communication' (i.e., interpersonal dialogue and mutual decision-making); Seddon (2004) argued that the pressure of the assessment of collaborative music can undermine relationships between the collaborators; and Dillon (2004) showed how well-designed music software could facilitate creative interactions. Furthermore, Barrett's (2006) study of a teacher-student relationship indicated that interactions in music collaboration are important not just at the actual moment of composition itself, but also in shaping more general strategies in composition such as goal-setting and providing reassurance. Hargreaves (forthcoming) noted that there are some obvious areas for empirical development in this field, such as the clearer distinction between verbal and musical communication, the use of a wider range of participant groups and musical tasks, and crucially, the development of more controlled, experimental studies. Note also that Littleton and Miell (2004) argued that the very definition of what we mean by collaborative creativity is still up for grabs, as different studies investigate work carried out by varying numbers of people with varying degrees of expertize and seniority, who (sometimes don't) complement each other in varying ways, and who are not necessarily together in the same room or even the same historical period.

Nor is there much psychological research on collaboration between *expert* composers, although a limited amount of evidence exists concerning arguably the two most commercially and artistically successful musical collaborators of all time, namely John Lennon and Paul McCartney. Everett (1999; see also Dempsey, 2004) provided a very detailed and complex musicological analysis of every work produced by The Beatles from *Revolver* onwards in terms of compositional inspiration, recording practice, and salient musical features. Although there are numerous accounts of the music by The Beatles, Everett's is particularly interesting because (in addition to simply being so detailed) it is consistent with the work on collaboration between 'ordinary' people reviewed above. In particular, Everett emphasized the *social context* of compositional collaboration. For example, he discussed the songs on *Revolver* in terms of the order in which they were composed, since progressive songs reflect the progress of Lennon and McCartney as a songwriting team. In contrast, Everett considers *Sgt. Pepper's Lonely Hearts Club Band* and *Abbey Road* in terms of the order in which the songs are presented on the albums; as any reader with an interest in The Beatles will know, *Sgt. Pepper* and *Abbey Road* were considered more as 'whole' works by the band. Similarly, Everett considers the songs on the *White Album* and *Let It Be* by composer; these songs were composed at a time when day-to-day relations between the band members were characterized by conflict and isolation.

Jackson and Padgett (1982) adopted an explicitly social psychological approach to Lennon and McCartney, producing evidence that their jointly-authored songs were lower in quality than were their individually-authored songs. This finding was attributed to social loafing, the process by which people make less effort when working collaboratively than when working alone, because in the former case it is harder to evaluate each individual's unique contribution. In contrast, Cynthia Whissell has focused on computerized content analyses of the emotion conveyed by Lennon and McCartney's lyrics, and has placed this in the context of theories of emotional response to music similar to those outlined in the next chapter. For example, Whissell (1996, p. 260; see also Whissell, 1999, 2003; Whissell and Whissell, 2000) found that, compared to McCartney, Lennon used fewer pleasant words, and more nasty, soft, and sad ones ... He also used more second person pronouns, proportionally more forms of the verb 'to be', more forms of the word 'girl', and more forms of the word 'dead'. McCartney, by comparison, used more words repeatedly, used more punctuation marks, used the conjunction 'and' more frequently, used forms of the word 'love' more often, and included more whoops and nonsense in his lyrics ... Differences across stages [in The Beatles' recording career] were often described by a significant linear trend. Pleasantness, activation, and cheerfulness all fell across the years, while nastiness and softness first rose, then fell, then rose again. Across stages, certain types of words became more frequent ('the', 'a', 'an', and whoops) while others became less frequent (first and second person pronouns, negatives, 'and', 'love', and 'girl'). Repetition and punctuation both increased across stages and words became longer.

2.3 Musicianship

In addition to creativity and composition, the final aspect of making music we shall consider is actually playing a musical instrument. In this final section of the chapter we review the research on musicianship, focusing on the personality of musicians, identity as a musician, environmental and motivational factors in the development of musical skills, social psychological factors in musical performance (such as body movements, physical attractiveness, performance anxiety, and drug use), and the current debate concerning whether playing a musical instrument brings with it other psychological benefits.

2.3.1 Personality and identity

2.3.1.1 Personality

As Kemp (1997, p. 25) argued, there is a clear need for research to

> help redress the notorious neglect of personality psychology by most music psychologists ... If one scans ... the field, a fact that cannot be overlooked is its main preoccupation with music cognition and the virtual exclusion of dynamic psychology and concern with people's less cognitive musical responses. Clearly musicians engage in highly cognitive processes ... but the view developed here is that the development of these, in many respects, is dependent upon the existence or acquisition of unusual combinations of personality factors.

Although accepting that personality influences musical behaviour only via an interaction with the physical and social environment as well as musical ability, Kemp's central argument is that personality manifests itself through musicianship. As his two extensive reviews (Kemp, 1996, 1997) make clear, in addition to their greater level of sensitivity (i.e. emotional sensitivity, imagination, intuition, and a preponderance towards 'feeling' rather than logical thinking) those particular aspects of personality relevant to musicians are *introversion/extraversion, independence, trait anxiety/neuroticism*, and *gender role orientation*.

Introversion/extraversion has been addressed by many personality theorists with some, such as Eysenck, focusing more on the social aspects (e.g. extraverts are gregarious) and others, such as Jung and Cattell, adopting a more psycho-analytic approach by stressing the inner-directedness of the introvert. Kemp's reviews show that, while musicians might be better described as introverts than extraverts, this masks a great deal of subtlety. For instance, musicians do indeed demonstrate elevated levels of detachment and self-sufficiency, consistent with their need to spend extended periods of time spent practising in isolation. However, musicians do not score more highly than most on other aspects of introversion such as seriousness and shyness. Furthermore, despite their introversion musicians still have to perform in front of others, and they are able to do so because the rich internal life that comes with intro-version gives them plenty to project to the outside world when they take to the stage.

Independence refers particularly to characteristics such as dominance and suspiciousness, but also to surgency (e.g. competitiveness, self-confidence, decisiveness), adventurousness, and imagination. Kemp's reviews demonstrate that independence is characteristic of mature and skilled musicians, whereas less mature musicians are characterized by dependency. This concept should not be confused with other findings cited by Kemp concerning *field (in)dependence*. This refers to the manner in which people perceive objects. A field dependent person tends to perceive all the elements in the object in question as inextricably joined and focuses on the organisation of a perceptual whole; whereas a field independent person tends to focus on specific parts of the object being perceived and adopts a more analytical approach. Put simply, a field dependent person would see a forest whereas a field independent person would see an individual tree against the backdrop of other trees and wonder how many different species there were overall. Kemp notes that musi-cians tend to be more field independent, and this 'enables them to analyse, extract, and reorganize the elements of music' (Kemp, 1997, p .30). Note also however that this pattern should not be taken to imply causality. For instance, someone may develop field independence as a result of the high levels of analysis involved in becoming an expert musician; or it may be that a degree of general field independence is a prequisite for developing high levels of musical skill.

Kemp treats *neuroticism and trait anxiety* as largely overlapping concepts. 'Amongst these kind of factors, adult musicians display particular tendencies towards the primary factors of emotional instability and ergic tension (a tendency to be tense and frustrated), as well as some evidence of suspi-ciousness, low self-sentiment, and apprehensiveness' (Kemp, 1997, p. 33).

In addition to this evidence on anxiety as a personality trait, a substantial amount of research has considered performance anxiety (aka. 'stage fright') in musicians, and we will return this shortly.

Gender orientation is addressed by Kemp in terms of the extent to which male and female musicians demonstrate masculinity and femininity. Crucial to this is Bem's (e.g. 1974) assertion that masculinity and femininity do not lie at opposing ends of a single dimension. Rather, masculinity and femininity are two distinct constructs, and any individual can be placed at any point on either such that it is possible, for example, to be androgynous, that is simultaneously both strongly masculine and strongly feminine. Kemp cites some evidence showing that, relative to the general population, musicians have a tendency towards androgyny, and that gender differences in personality found among the general population were significantly eroded among musicians over the age of 15 years. As Kemp (1996, p.120) argues, 'Such levels of perceptible differences as these may well result in musicians appearing to be different from ordinary people, or even strange. This may, in turn, have the effect of marginalizing them socially'.

Kemp (1996) also reviews the evidence concerning personality differences between people who play different orchestral instruments. He concludes that

> The most striking aspect of string players appears to be their introversion, particularly in terms of those factors that ... relate more closely to musicianship, namely, aloofness and self-sufficiency ... However woodwind players' introversion appears to be coupled with a degree of imagination and radicalism that eludes the string players ... Research with brass players ... [demonstrates] their considerable extraverted qualities ... Furthermore, percussion players, and particularly drummers, appear to share certain extraverted qualities of brass players (pp. 164-165).

In each case, Kemp relates these personality characteristics to the demands of learning the instrument in question. For example, he explains string players' introversion 'as reflecting the slow progress that is generally forthcoming on string instruments' (p. 164) in that a considerable amount of self-sufficiency and perseverance are required; and brass players' extraversion is explained as reflecting the fact that 'Brass playing skills may be developed in more social environments, and progress can be reasonably rapid thus eliminating the need for a more introverted temperament' (p. 165). It is interesting also that many of the actual differences between orchestral musicians identified by Kemp correspond closely with the stereotypes that orchestra members hold of each other that were identified by Davies (1978) and Lipton (1987). For example, Lipton (1987) found evidence from a survey of musicians in 16 major North American orchestras that the stereotypes of brass and string players were most dissimilar.

Research concerning non-orchestral instruments is much more scarce. Nonetheless Kemp argues that the existing evidence suggests that keyboard players demonstrate higher levels than most musicians of warm-heartedness, group dependency, conscientiousness, and conservatism (and a relative lack of anxiety); singers score higher than most on extraversion, sensitivity, and independence; conductors score higher than most for extraversion (but not for imagination or sensitivity as we might have expected they should); whereas 'Neuroticism and stress appear to characterize the popular musician as much as their classical counterparts ... As might have been expected, psychoticism appears high in drummers, guitarists, and trumpeters ... and this manifestation may relate to the hard and harsh musical styles engaged in by these instrumentalists' (p. 192).

2.3.1.2 Identity

Closely related to personality is the issue of self-concept, and the notion of 'musical identity' has received increasing attention over recent years. Interest in identity itself of course goes back to the founding of modern psychology. William James (1890) for example, was one of the first to distinguish between two components of identity, which he called the 'I' and the 'me': the latter is that part of our self-identity that is consciously experienced and known by us, whilst the 'I' is that part that is able to reflect on the 'me', i.e. which does the experiencing and the knowing. The same idea of an 'I' that reflects on social encounters is also central to Cooley's (1902) notion of the 'looking glass self', in which our identities incorporate our reflections on what other people think of us.

George Herbert Mead (1934) distinguished similarly between the personal and the social aspects of self in describing the 'I' and the 'me'. He also introduced a further concept, the 'generalized other', which is extremely useful in explaining the *development* of identity. As the 'I' develops in a social world, experiencing more and more events, situations and other people, the self-reflections of the 'me' become increasingly complex; and at around the age of 7 years or so, Mead proposed that children develop a concept of the 'generalized other' which represents their global, abstracted ('generalized') view of the world around them. In some respects, this idea has parallels with Piaget's explanation of the decline of egocentrism at this age, and also perhaps with Freud's views on the formation of the superego. All three approaches converge on the idea that aspects of the social environment are built into the self-perceptions of the developing child, and our present interest is in the specifically musical aspects of that environment.

People's *self-systems* are made up of numerous specific *self-concepts*, or *self-images*, which exist in relation to particular domains or situations in which they are most closely involved; at different times during the day I might see myself as a parent, a spouse, an office worker, a supervisor, a motorist, a tennis player, a cook, or a political activist, and *self-identity* refers to the overall view that I have of myself in which these different self-concepts are integrated. Having said this, theorists differ about the extent to which this does or does not occur: social constructionists, for example, argue that people display and develop different self-identities in interactions with others, rather than necessarily having a 'core' identity (Hargreaves, Miell, and MacDonald, 2002). In contrast, *self-esteem* is the evaluative component of the self, which has both cognitive and emotional aspects; it concerns how worthy we think and feel we are. Self-esteem can be high or low, and is not necessarily correlated with actual ability. Individuals can display a high level of ability but a low level of self-esteem in a given domain, as well as *vice versa*. Indeed, a common measure of self-esteem is the discrepancy between the ideal and the actual self: lower levels of discrepancy are associated with higher levels of self-esteem, and this is used as the basis for various empirical measures of self-esteem. Finally, *self-efficacy* refers to our view of our own ability to perform effectively in specific situations and domains. Perceptions of our own self-efficacy are not generalized aspects of self-perception, but rather are grounded in *particular* domains and contexts. It is also important to stress that self-efficacy and self-esteem are not interchangeable terms: my judgement of my own capabilities in certain domains is not necessarily related to my feelings of self-worth. I may regard myself as very poor at mastering new computer skills or electronic equipment, for example, and feel no shame in telling others about this inability; I might even take a perverse pride in it, thereby showing that I place little value on technical or mechanical skills.

Of particular interest to the development of musicianship is of course the development of different components of the self-system, and three clear trends can be identified in the literature. First, generalized aspects of the self-concept seem to become increasingly differentiated with age. Whilst young children might generalize 'being good at' one activity to their abilities in various others, an understanding emerges in middle childhood that they are good at some things but not at others (Harter, 1999). Harter suggests that these domain-specific self-images typically become integrated into a generalized self-concept at around the age of 8 years, and it may well be that musical abilities start to be differentiated from others at around this age. Second, there seems to be a declining emphasis on physical characteristics and activities in early childhood, such as sporting interests, and towards more psychological judgements involving feelings and emotions towards participation in those activities (Damon and Hart, 1988). This leads in turn to the third main trend, namely that children's self-concepts become increasingly based on comparisons with others, and their peers in particular, in middle childhood and adolescence (Harter, 1999). There is relatively little work on the extent to which these three general trends can be identified in self-systems concerning specifically musicianship. However, as we will see shortly, the concepts involved in self-systems have made a clear contribution to research on the psychology of musicianship.

Perhaps the most obvious yet important point to emerge from MacDonald, Hargreaves, and Miell's (2002) collection of essays on *Musical Identities* is simply the large number of different musical identities that can exist. For example, they begin by distinguishing identity as a practising musician from the ways in which music can help to shape non-musical aspects of identity, such as youth identity and national identity. We deal with the latter in Chapter 4 (see also Tarrant, North, and Hargreaves, 2002). However MacDonald, Hargreaves, and Miell (2002) devote most space to the issue of identity as a practising musician, or what might be regarded more specifically as the reciprocal relationship between playing a musical instrument and self-concept.

As Cook (1998) argues, many of the conventional notions concerning the roles involved in being 'a musician' are becoming hopelessly outdated. The traditional view of course is that musicianship is a specialized skill reserved for a select few; that composers lie at the top of the musical hierarchy by virtue of their position as the generators of the 'core product'; beneath them are performers who act as little more than middlemen; and beneath them are the audience, passive consumers of a mystical product that they couldn't hope to understand or appreciate as fully or as easily as does the composer. This hierarchy may have been an accurate representation of music in the nineteenth century, but it certainly isn't in the twenty-first. In the Western world at least, most people can easily afford computer software that requires no formal musical training before the user is able to produce multi-track music that is either wholly original or which samples (or even just 'plays around with') previously released music; and it is a simple task to make this music available on the web so that it can be shared with a small circle of friends as well as the rest of the world. Consequently, it is very difficult to know how, if at all, we should define the boundaries between 'composer', 'performer', and 'audience', and how these revised definitions should or even could be arranged into a musical hierarchy. In short, there is a clear need for up-to-date research concerning precisely how people in the technological world define themselves through their musical activities.

Given that a strong rationale for research on identity as a musician concerns the technological revolution of the past 20 years, it is hugely disappointing that the great majority of studies in this developing field continue to focus on people playing traditional instruments, often in the classical music education tradition. We are not aware of any psychological research concerning identity among 'digital musicians', such as, for example, how a DJ uses music to affirm self-esteem, or how 'mashing up' songs allows an individual to express their opinion of the world or merely their generation's sense of place within prevailing musical culture. Nonetheless, research on traditional music education has produced some interesting initial insights that begin to map out the specifics of the relationship between performing music and identity. One of the most consistent conclusions of this research is that it is important to establish and maintain a link between self-identity and musicianship if someone is to continue playing a musical instrument as they move from childhood to adulthood. For example, Lamont (2002) described the role of school music in developing British children's musical identity, arguing that they seem to distinguish between 'being a musician' and 'having music lessons'; the latter is regarded as something that happens to everyone as part of the national curriculum, whereas the former develops not only through very high levels of engagement with school music lessons but also when school musical activities are less exclusive and more inclusive; when children simply like their music teacher(s); and as a result of engaging in musical activities outside the classroom. This is a good example of the authenticity of children's musical experiences being determined by the social and institutional contexts in which they take place (such as inside and outside school), and we will return to this in Chapter 6.

In contrast, Borthwick and Davidson (2002) focused on the home environment as a factor in developing children's identity as a musician. They adopted a family script perspective, arguing that individual family members take on roles that support the scripted plot of family expectations concerning musical behaviour. Borthwick and Davidson's qualitative study involved interviews with 12 families, showing that

> all the parents in the study had been affected by 'scripts' during childhood within their respective families of origin. It seemed that the degree of importance given to music by members of their immediate and extended family influenced their decision to accord music a particular status and role [in the household], and this had a direct influence on their current family lifestyle. Many parents saw their own parents as key players in their children's current musical identity ... For some parents, musicianship was an inevitable part of continuing the family identity across the generations (p. 63).

Other comments made during interviews showed that a shared interest in music was a 'familial glue' that bound the household together; and that the direction of influence was two-way, in that children were capable of influencing the musical identity of their parents and particularly their music listening tastes, with one mother commenting that 'it certainly keeps me young!' (p. 69).

O'Neill (2002) drew on the literature in developmental social psychology, and described how identity as a musician should evolve as people move from early childhood towards adulthood. First, she argued that identity as a musician in young children is likely to focus on concrete issues (e.g. 'I play the piano'), whereas as we grow older the focus shifts to more sophisticated, abstract psychological factors (e.g. 'I am an expressive performer'). Second, she argues that young children have a global view of themselves (e.g. 'I am talented'; whereas older children and adolescents apply different beliefs to different domains (e.g. 'My level of musical skill cannot be improved but my sporting skills can be improved through practice'), and generally have a less positive attitude towards themselves. This implies that beliefs about ourselves might well influence the goals we pursue, since we are unlikely to persist at a task on which we believe we have little chance of success. This in turn, O'Neill argued, has implications for motivation in learning to play a musical instrument. She pointed to evidence showing that, compared to children with 'mastery-oriented' motivational patterns, children with maladaptive, 'helpless' motivational patterns avoid challenges; show low persistence; focus on the avoidance of failure rather than viewing failure as part of the learning process; show deteriorating performance in the face of failure; and in the long term show less progress in learning a musical instrument. Related to these motivational patterns is whether children adopt an 'entity' approach to musical ability (i.e. it is a fixed ability that cannot be improved upon) or an 'incremental' approach (i.e. it can be improved through practice). Children who have not played a musical instrument are far more likely to adopt an entity approach to ability; and when judging musical abilities, 'entity' people are more likely to focus on 'outcome traits' (e.g. grades, number of instruments) whereas 'incremental' people are more likely to focus on 'process traits' (e.g. practising regularly). In short, children's ability-related self-perceptions are intimately associated with their motivation to pursue musical activities, and the expressed opinions of their peers and teachers can be vitally important in their formation. This feeds back into the actual levels of ability and achievement that are reached, and so the cycle continues. We return to the issue of motivation shortly, and to the educational implications in Chapter 6.

Davidson and Burland (2006) addressed what is arguably the central topic in this area, namely the process by which an adolescent musician develops and makes decisions concerning the role of music in their future life and career. Crucial in this they argue are the adolescent's more general sense of self and the social environment in which identity as a musician develops.

Specifically, Davidson and Burland contend that musical activity continues if it contributes more generally to the fulfilment of an idealized personal identity. In particular, Davidson and Burland draw on Ibarra's (1999) notion of 'provisional selves', arguing that the adolescent 'tries out' possible selves in the process of determining a vocational identity; these provisional selves may reflect the wholesale imitation of the characteristics of a specific musical role model or the selective imitation of the characteristics of numerous musical role models. The extent to which these imitated characteristics are actually adopted is itself moderated by the extent to which they are perceived as being true to self by the adolescent concerned; and also by the extent to which they elicit positive (or negative) feedback from others.

Ideas such as these obviously require much more testing and, in particular, further data collection that reflects notions of 'musicianship' outside the scope of traditional music education. However, these ideas do deserve further attention since they link clearly to more general approaches to identity within social psychology. For example, O'Neill's arguments draw heavily on mainstream research on motivation; and Davidson and Burland's arguments appear consistent with well-known general accounts of identity and vocational development (most obviously those by Holland (e.g. 1985) and Marcia (e.g. 1966)), while also forming the outlines of a social psychological theory of vocational development as specifically a musician.

Of course it is naïve to consider musical identity in the context of idealized personal identity without also acknowledging the potential influence of stereotypes. The great majority of studies on this have concentrated on sex-typing. As Dibben (2002) points out for instance, it is only recently that women have been allowed access to any but the most domesticated forms of music-making, and it would be very short-sighted to ignore prejudices such as these in the development of musical identity. For example, Green (1997) describes a classroom study showing that teachers believed girls were more successful at singing and active as instrumentalists; and perceived them as having attitudes associated with expressivity, decoration, and delicacy. Other research shows that music in school is generally perceived as a 'feminine' subject (Boldizar, 1991; Colley, Comber, and Hargreaves, 1994) and that girls are more positive than boys in their attitudes and competence beliefs towards music (Crowther and Durkin, 1982; Eccles, Wigfield, Harold, and Blumenfeld, 1993); although this gap may close as a consequence of the introduction of music technology into the curriculum (Comber, Hargreaves, and Colley, 1993).

Sex-typing extends to individual instruments (see review by O'Neill, 1997a). For example, Abeles and Porter (1978) found that the most 'masculine' instruments are the drums, trombone, and trumpet, whereas the most feminine instruments are flute, violin, and clarinet: these patterns were largely repeated when Abeles and Porter's participants were asked to select a musical instrument for their son and daughter; by Griswold and Chroback's (1981) follow-up study using a wider range of instruments and participants; and when O'Neill and Boulton (1996) asked 9 to 11-year-old boys and girls which instruments they would most like to learn to play, and which musical instruments should or should not be played by other boys and girls. As Kemp (1996, p. 142) summarizes, 'Instruments that are soft, subtle, and high-pitched appear to be classed as suitable for girls to play; those that are large, powerful, and lower-pitched have masculine connections' (see also Cramer, Million, and Perreault, 2002), and it does not take a genius to work out the origin of these specific sex types. Harrison and O'Neill (2000) went a step further and investigated the consequences of presenting 7 to 8-year-olds with people playing gender-inappropriate instruments: rather than reducing levels of prejudice, girls liked the piano and flute less after seeing a man playing them, and girls liked the guitar less after they saw a woman playing one. As such, sex types of instrument preferences cannot be overcome by exposing children to musicians who do not confirm them.

2.3.2 Environment, motivation, and musical skill

Since personality and identity are linked to musicianship it is not terribly surprising that other social psychological influences should play a role also. Research on environmental influences on musical skill follows from the debate concerning whether musical ability is innate or can instead be acquired. Sloboda, Davidson, and Howe (1994), for example, pointed to a 'folk psychology' of music which states that musical ability is largely innate and peculiar to just a select few; and Davis (1994) reported that this view is shared by many educational professionals since 75% of those approached believed that musical skills are indeed the result of an innate gift or natural talent. This folk view of musical ability is almost certainly wrong however, and the key point to emerge from the 'nature vs. nurture' debate on musical skill is that everyone is capable of skilled musical behaviour.

As described in Chapter 3, there is a considerable amount of evidence that foetuses in the womb respond to music (see e.g. Parncutt, 2006), and Trevarthen (2002; see also Papoušek, 1996; Trehub, 2006) has reviewed the evidence demonstrating musicality in neonates. As Sloboda (2005, p. 277) argued, 'developmental research has shown that the average human infant displays musical capacities as early, if not earlier, than linguistic capacities, and in a far more developed and overt form than any capacities that might be supposed to underlie other skills such as mathematical, artistic, or athletic skills'. Some degree of musicality is common to us all and exists from a very tender age, such that it is not limited to a lucky few as the folk psychology view claims. Furthermore, there is evidence that even the 'gold standard' of a supposedly innate musical talent, namely perfect pitch, is something that can be learned and requires exposure to music early in life (e.g. Brady, 1970; Cuddy, 1968; Sergeant, 1969). Nor is there strong evidence that those with higher levels of musical skill develop these abilities more quickly than their less able peers, as the 'innate talent' approach suggests they should. Howe, Davidson, Moore, and Sloboda (1995; see also Howe, Davidson, and Sloboda, 1998; Manturzewska, 1990; Sosniak, 1990), for example, compared 257 8–18-year-old English people who were divided into five groups. These five groups represented different levels of musical ability, ranging from students at a specialist music school through to pupils at an ordinary school who had begun to learn a musical instrument but given up after six months or more. Howe et al.found very little evidence that the groups differed in the age at which they first displayed a range of musical abilities. As Kemp and Mills (2002, p. 4) argued, 'The signs of musical potential that adults think they spot [in children] are manifestations of *musical achievement* ... These are the results of musical experience and learning ... that some children have had, but others lack ... [A] child cannot sing along with a parent if the parent does not sing'. In short, we all possess some degree of inborn propensity towards musicality, people who turn out to be musically-talented don't necessarily demonstrate their ability precociously, and any indications of high levels of musicality that occur early in life are just as likely to be attributable to a favourable environment that allows skills to be demonstrated as they are to an innate talent.

Nor does this mean that genetic factors can be ignored. Gembris and Davidson (2002) point out that genetic influences on musical ability certainly include maturational staged developments (e.g. the gradual development of hand–eye dexterity with age) and certain physical capacities (e.g. a wide hand span confers an advantage on pianists), and there may well also of course be some mental aspects of musical ability that are ultimately inherited from parents. Crucially, however, these genetic factors must *interact* with the environment in mediating musical skills such that *both* are important. Gembris and Davidson point out three types of interaction between genes and environment. First is 'passive covariation' where genetic material shapes the environment. As we saw earlier when discussing the role of family scripts in musical identity, if both your parents are musical then the chances are that you will grow up in a musical environment: your genetic make-up has directly shaped the environment in which you are raised. Second is 'reactive covariation'. This is where the *recognition* of genetically influenced personality traits or needs of a child leads to the environment being changed accordingly. For example, if parents spot that the child has a natural interest in music they may buy him or her a musical instrument, thus creating an environment conducive to the development of musical ability. Third is 'active covariation'. This is where the genetically influenced personality traits or needs of a child lead to him or her actively shaping the environment him- or herself, by, for example, asking for music lessons or seeking out friends with musical interests.

Indeed, it is obvious that genetic and environmental influences need each other in order to express themselves. For example, if someone with an amazing genetic gift for the harpsichord happens to be born into a non-Western society then his or her talent will almost certainly never be realized. Conversely, it is safe to assume that if either of us was given access to all the teaching and support possible we would still never be able to write music to the level of Mozart, The Beatles, or Miles Davis: a genetic predisposition cannot be expressed without an appropriate environment, and an appropriate environment needs a naturally-talented person to make the most of it. Even the *extent*s of the importance of genetic and environmental influences on musical ability are interdependent. As Gembris and Davidson (2002, p. 18) put it, 'in domains where culture exerts a relatively homogeneous influence on development innate differences would be especially visible ... Conversely, in nonhomogeneous surroundings (e.g., with greatly varying musical training) the relative importance of the environment for causing individual differences in musical abilities increases, and the relative contribution of innate predispositions declines'. In other words, the precise contribution of genetic inheritance to musical ability depends on the extent to which the environment promotes musical ability. Environmental influences on musical ability are important, but not because they are necessarily the main determinant (although they ultimately might be). Rather, we focus here on environmental issues because, unlike genetic factors, they can be manipulated to increase everyone's prospect of achieving their musical potential.

2.3.2.1 Environmental factors in the development of musical skill

Research to date has highlighted three factors in the environment that encourage the optimal development of musical skill, namely parents, teachers, and practice (see reviews by Creech and Hallam, 2003; Davidson, Howe and Sloboda, 1997; Gembris and Davidson, 2002; McPherson and Williamon, 2006; Sloboda, 2005; and Sloboda and Davidson, 1996). As numerous studies point out, parental support appears crucial in the development of skilled musical performance (see e.g. Bastian, 1989; Brand, 1985, 1986; Manturzewska, 1995; Monsaas and Engelhard, 1990; Sloane, 1985; Sosniak, 1985; Zdzinski, 1996).

Lehmann (1997) for example describes biographical data on 14 piano prodigies (including Bach, Beethoven, Chopin, Debussy, Handel, Liszt, Mendelssohn, and Mozart) showing that 13 received regular supervised practice from a family member, and that 12 lived with their teacher for a period suggesting that the latter operated as a de facto parent. Similarly, Davidson, Howe, Moore, and Sloboda's (1996) analysis of 257 young English musicians representing five levels of musical expertize found that the most successful children were distinguished by parental involvement in music lessons (e.g. receiving feedback from teachers or even sitting in and taking notes). Furthermore, Davidson et al. also found that the most successful children had parents who increased their own involvement with music once the child began learning an instrument. One final interesting aspect of these findings is that children in the highest achieving group were particularly supported by parents up to the age of 11, after which the children's intrinsic motivation to practise took precedence; in contrast, the lowest achieving children received weak initial support from parents but saw much more forceful support during their teens as the parents made a last-ditch attempt to keep their child playing.

Although there is otherwise little evidence, the same study also highlighted the characteristics of music teachers as a further environmental influence on musical ability. Davidson, Howe, Moore, and Sloboda (1998; see also Davidson, Sloboda, and Howe, 1995/1996) focused on the first and last/current teacher that their participants had had. The highest-achieving musicians described their first music teachers as entertaining, friendly, and proficient musicians, whereas the worst-achieving musicians reported the opposite about their first music teachers. This pattern changed slightly with age: among the older participants, the lowest-achieving group still had the same attitude to their music teachers, but in the highest-achieving group the professional qualities of the teachers, such as their own degree of musical proficiency, became more salient than their personalities. More simply, in early years it is important to establish a good rapport between teacher and student redolent of friendly respect, but in later years the perceived ability of the teacher becomes more important. Furthermore, the three most successful groups of musicians tended to have individual tuition whereas the less successful musicians received only group tuition. Given that there is so little data on the impact of music teachers it is interesting that two other studies mirror the findings of Davidson, Howe, Moore, and Sloboda (1998). Both Howe and Sloboda (1991) and Sosniak (1985) found that a strong personal relationship with the first music teacher is particularly important and can for example lead to interest in one particular instrument rather than another.

Research on practice supports Thomas Edison's maxim that genius is 1% inspiration and 99% perspiration. Ericsson, Krampe, and Tesch-Römer (1993), for example, studied groups of violin students of varying ability level. Diaries completed by the violinists showed that the two most proficient groups practised alone for 3.5 hours per day over 19.5 sessions per week, whereas the least proficient group practised alone for only 1.3 hours per day over only 7.1 sessions per week. The researchers also used interviews to determine the amount of practice the violinists had accumulated over their life span. By 18 years of age the 'best' violinists had acquired 7,410 hours of practice, compared to only 5,301 hours among the 'good' violinists and 3,420 hours among the least proficient of the violinists studied. Sloboda, Davidson, Howe, and Moore (1996; and also Hallam, 1998) report similar findings from their five groups of English music students when they were asked to estimate average daily formal practice for each year of life. By the age of 12, the most proficient group practised two hours per day, whereas the least proficient group practised only 15 minutes per day. Furthermore, everyone who practised for two hours per day achieved a high level of skill, such that there was a direct link between practice and musical ability. The researchers also analysed the amount of practice required in order to pass music exams: they found that passing each exam required a requisite number of hours of practice, and the high achievers accumulated this over a shorter period of time; they weren't intrinsically better musicians who were able to get by with less effort, but rather they just worked harder. In the light of the apparent importance of practice it is interesting that musicians themselves seem less prone to buying into the idea of 'music as a natural gift'. Hallam and Prince (2003) asked professional musicians, music educators, other adults, and students to complete the statement 'Musical ability is …' and found that musicians and music educators were much more likely than the others to state that it is something that is learned or developed. Less encouragingly though, the amount of practice required means that the road to musical glory is long and steep. Another of Ericsson, Krampe, and Tesch-Römer's (1993) findings may therefore be some consolation: their two most proficient groups of violinists averaged 60.0 hours of sleep a week whereas the least proficient group slept for only 54.6 hours per week; and this is partly attributable to the proficient groups also napping during the day for 2.8 hours per week whereas the less proficient group napped for only 0.9 hours per week; hard work is important, but so is plenty of rest!

2.3.2.2 Motivation

This then raises the question of what practice strategies are most effective (see e.g. Hallam, 1995), and particularly how skilled musicians are able to carry out so much more practice than others. Parental involvement undoubtedly plays a part, and Moore, Burland, and Davidson's (2003; see also Stremikis, 2002) follow-up study identified having the mother at home during the child's early years as the critical factor in distinguishing those musically-successful children who managed to continue their progress and become professional musicians in adult life. However, the adolescents in Sloboda, Davidson, Howe, and Moore's (1996) original sample demonstrated a considerable degree of self-motivation also. Austin, Renwick, and McPherson (2006), Lehmann, Sloboda, and Woody (2007), Maehr, Pitnrich, and Linnenbrink (2002), and O'Neill and McPherson (2002) all review the different theories of musical motivation that have been put forward: given the importance of practice in developing musical skill it is worth dwelling on these theories for a moment, since although few studies to date have related them to music education they nonetheless represent a clear framework for future research.

In the context of music education, *expectancy-value theory* (Fishbein and Azjen, 1975) addresses why people should believe that playing a musical instrument will be important to them in the future. Eccles, Adler, Futterman, and Goff et al.(1983) proposed that the expectations and value attached to learning a musical instrument can be broken down into four components, namely attainment value (i.e. the importance that the person attaches to becoming a skilled musician), intrinsic interest (i.e. the pleasure derived from playing), utility value (i.e. usefulness of playing an instrument to the person's future goals, such as their career aspirations), and perceived cost (i.e. the negative implications of learning a musical instrument such as daily practice or the negative reactions of friends). O'Neill and McPherson cite research by McPherson (2000) showing that these components were understood well by children as young as 7 to 9 years old who were just beginning to play music; they could differentiate between the four components, and make clear statements in relation to each concerning the value and expectations they associated with musicianship. Moreover, the specific nature of the values and expectations elicited might explain Cooke and Morris' (1996) finding that interest in playing a musical instrument drops off sharply between the ages of 5 and 11. McPherson (2000) found that many children attached no more attainment value to music than they did to other leisure time activities, and that while many children had an intrinsic interest in playing an instrument they also attached little utility value to it. It is easy to see why so many give up. More positively, those students who made the most progress in learning their instrument were those who practised most, had made a long-term commitment to it, and who had intrinsic rather than extrinsic motivations for playing. Similarly, O'Neill (1999a) found that the importance that music students placed on music accounted for significant variations in their practice time; and Austin, Renwick, and McPherson (2006) cite research by Yoon (1997) showing that children's perceptions of music as interesting and important predicted both how much time they spent practising and whether they chose to participate in music rather than other pastimes.

Self-efficacy approaches to musical motivation (e.g. Bandura, 1997; Stipek, 1998) focus on the individual's degree of belief in both their ability and their capacity to achieve certain goals. These beliefs about the likelihood of success of course influence the choices people make; the amount of effort they put into a task and the amount of perseverance they demonstrate in the face of adversity; and their reactions to the outcome. For example, Eccles, Wigfield, and Schiefele (1998) reported that simply whether or not 8 to 11-year-olds took part in musical activities was related to their perceived musical self-efficacy. Nielsen (2004) found that Norwegian higher music education students who were high in self-efficacy were more likely to be cognitively involved in trying to learn musical material than were their peers who were low in self-efficacy. McPherson and McCormick (1999) found that levels of self-efficacy in pianists aged 9 to 18 years old before they entered an exam could predict their subsequent result, consistent with the notion that self-efficacy leads to confidence and persistence; and McCormick and McPherson's (2003; see also McPherson and McCormick, 2006) analysis of exam performance in 332 instrumentalists showed that self-efficacy was the best predictor of their actual performance. Note also that there are of course issues of causality in the relationship between self-efficacy and musicianship. Perceptions of high self-efficacy may lead to persistence and therefore greater musicianship, but it is just as plausible that high standards of musicianship lead to high perceived self-efficacy.

A *flow theory* (Czikszentmihalyi, 1990) approach to motivation concerns the extent to which someone taking part in an activity experiences feelings of concentration and control, a loss of self-awareness, and a sense that the task in question is intrinsically rewarding. These 'flow experiences' come about when the challenge posed by a task corresponds well with the level of skill that a person is able to bring to bear upon it. Retaining a sense of flow over time requires that new skills are learned by taking on new and more complex tasks. Phenomena such as these have obvious relevance to the process of learning a musical instrument, and O'Neill (1999b) considered whether they could account for variations in the amount of music practice undertaken by 12 to 16-year-old musicians. High achievers at a specialist music school and musically active people at a non-specialist school did indeed report more flow experiences than did moderate achievers at the specialist music school.

Similarly, Custodero's (1999) eight-week-long observation of four- and five-year-olds in a music classroom found that flow experiences were associated with high skill, challenge, and active engagement (see also Bailey and Davidson, 2002; Bakker, 2005; Byrne, MacDonald, and Carlton, 2003; MacDonald, Byrne, and Carlton, 2006; St. John, 2006).

Attribution theory (e.g. Heider, 1958; Kelley, 1973; Weiner, 1986) concerns the causes to which people attribute their success or failure on a given task. This approach argues that these attributions are more important in determining expectations of success in future attempts than are previous successes or failures. This has clear implications for motivation: if you believe that future attempts are likely to be successful you will persevere, even in the face of failure, such that if educators are to persuade students to keep learning a musical instrument it is important to understand their attributions of success and failure. Attributions of success and failure are made along three dimensions. First is whether a particular outcome is attributed to either an internal cause (i.e. something to do with the person) or an external cause (i.e. an outside agent or force). Second is whether an outcome is attributed to a stable (i.e. permanent) or unstable (i.e. temporary) cause. Third is whether an outcome is attributed to factors that are global (i.e. pervasive) or specific (i.e. isolated to particular localized aspects of the circumstances in question). For example, outcomes attributed to musical ability are internal, stable, and global, whereas outcomes attributed to practice are internal, unstable, and local. Therefore failures attributed to a lack of musical ability should be more likely to lead to the person giving up than if the failure is attributed to a lack of practice. In the former case the failure is due to a stable and global cause, whereas in the latter case it is due to an unstable and local cause.

Theorizing concerning attributions well outstrips the amount of data available concerning how they might be applied to music education. However in support of the ideas outlined here, Vispoel and Austin (1993; see also Austin and Vispoel, 1992, 1998; McPherson and McCormick, 2000) found that failures attributed to lack of effort or a poor learning strategy rather than a lack of ability were more likely to lead to anticipations of better future performance. Note also that music students make different attributions to differing extents: Asmus (1985) found that attributions concerning ability and effort were made most frequently, whereas task difficulty and luck were mentioned infrequently; and Arnold (1997) found that when asked to rank the importance of these same four factors then sixth-, eighth-, and tenth-grade school pupils consistently ranked effort first and luck last, although older pupils placed more emphasis on ability. Similarly, Asmus' (1986; see also Austin, 1991) analysis of attributions made by pupils in grades 4–12 found that older children were inclined to make attributions based on ability rather than effort. Research on attribution theory has also led to more specific work on motivation patterns (e.g. Dweck, 1986; O'Neill, 1997b): we saw in the earlier section on musical identity how mastery-oriented and helpless motivational patterns influence whether young musicians show persistence in the face of failure and ultimately make progress with their chosen instrument.

One of us has investigated the content of musical ability self-perceptions as part of a series of studies sponsored by the Qualifications and Curriculum Authority in England. Hargreaves, Lamont, Marshall and Tarrant (2004) compared the views of pupils, parents, and teachers about 'what it is to be good at music' along with parallel questions about art and design, dance, and drama. We asked focus groups of pupils and parents, and individual teachers to discuss three questions, namely (i) what does being good at music involve? (ii) can one be good at some aspects of music and not others? and (iii) how can one get better at music, and how would others know whether or not this had occurred? Knowledge about music and performing were both seen as especially important aspects, particularly by pupils and teachers. Music was seen as comprising a range of different skills and capacities, including non-musical skills such as learning quickly, leading a group, and having confidence. Teachers tended to emphasize the requirements of the English National Curriculum, and to conceive their views of musical ability and achievement in those terms. Parents tended to focus on skills and activities that are visible, notably those involving public performance. All three groups' responses suggested that music is no longer seen as a special talent that individuals either do or do not possess, and that it is perfectly possible to be good at some parts of it and not others. Qualifications and exams assumed lesser importance than might have been expected, and pupils' views were no less detailed and insightful than those of teachers and parents.

Before concluding, we should also make a special mention of Green's (2002) account of motivation among pop musicians, which painted a very different picture as compared to research on motivation among classical musicians within traditional music education. First, whereas classical musicians frequently regard practice as a chore, Green demonstrated that pop musicians regarded their musical activities as so enjoyable that they characterized them as 'play' not 'practice'. Second, practice typically focused almost exclusively on copying 'real' music such as parts of songs, rather than, for example, the rote-learning of scales and other technical exercises. Third, music-making often took place in group settings in which learners in effect taught each other by playing together and talking about their music. In short, there was much more evidence of fun and camaraderie among informal collectives of learners, so that motivation in general may simply be less of an issue among pop musicians than it seems to be in classical music. Aside from the implications of this for research, it suggests a potential role for pop music in encouraging people to take up and continue with a musical instrument. Indeed, it is interesting that several studies of classical musicians indicate that greater levels of practice and higher levels of attainment result when intrinsic motivation (as manifested via informal practice, improvisation, and fun) is part of the learning experience (McPherson and Renwick, 2001; Moore, Burland, and Davidson, 2003; Sloboda, Davidson, Howe, and Moore, 1996). In Chapter 6 we return to the implications of the more informal processes by which people go about learning pop music.

2.3.3 Performance

There are also clear social psychological issues in performance. The most obvious of these concerns the interpersonal relationships between members of musical groups. One potentially apocryphal story for instance tells how the nioneteenth-century German conductor Hans von Bülow so disliked two members of his orchestra, named Schultz and Schmidt, that on learning of Schultz's death von Bülow's immediate response was 'und Schmidt?' However, researchers have ignored many of the apparently obvious social psychological influences on music performance such as interpersonal conflict. For example, in one of the few studies on interpersonal relationships, Murningham and Conlon (1991) approached string quartets as an example of a social group, and argued that the more successful groups were distinguished by the recognition of the need for compromise between different members, and by a democratic approach to decision-making. Similarly, Atik (1994) argued that the position of a conductor within an orchestra is legitimized specifically by testing out the mutual trust and respect of the musicians, and by the negotiation of agreed upon expectations between composer and musicians.

Psychological research has also tended to ignore the fact that any particular musical performance occurs in a broader sociocultural context that dictates the acceptability of several practices. For example, the police would be called if an audience member at a classical concert acted in the way that he or she is expected to behave at a pop concert. These sociocultural mores extend to the performers' behaviour and vary over time. For example, pop music performers frequently communicate specific instructions to the audience to clap along in time, sing a part of the song for themselves, or be quiet (see Davidson, 2001; Frith, 1996; Kurosawa and Davidson, 2005). Similarly, Cook (1990) describes how composers in the baroque period would provide only an outline of the music and expect the musicians themselves to 'fill in' the appropriate ornamental details based on their training; and Davidson (1997) describes how it was quite normal for Beethoven to re-order or completely omit movements from performances of his sonatas, such that modern day conceptions of an 'authentic' or 'original' performance are quite different from those of earlier periods (see also Williamon, Thompson, Lisboa, and Wiffen, 2006). The majority of the research on social psychological influences in performance can be organized into two topics. Research on the first topic, visual aspects of musical performance, has focused on the impact of body movements and of performer's physical attractiveness. Research on the second topic concerns performance anxiety and drug use among musicians.

2.3.3.1 Visual aspects of performance

With regard to the first of these, one of the less regularly recognized reasons for the popularity of live music may be that the opportunity to observe the performer's body movements affords the audience a better understanding of the latter's expressive intent. In probably the best-known piece of research on this, Davidson (1994; see also Davidson 1993, 1995, 2005; Price and Winter, 1991) observed differences in body movements when a pianist performed music in deadpan, normal, or exaggerated manners. The more expressive were the intentions behind the performance, so the greater was the amount of body movement made by the pianist. Furthermore, the exaggerated body movements also led to the performance being perceived by others as more expressive. In other words, body movements made a direct contribution to both the performance itself and the audience's interpretation of it. Davidson and Correia (2002) point out that the literature on locomotion may help to produce a theory of body movement during music performance: specifically they argue that the hips may represent the 'centre of moment' which serves as a point of reference around which movements in all parts of the body are organized by the perceiver. They also draw on case study work in pointing out that expressive body movements come about only when the relevant part of the body is free from actually performing the music itself (e.g. during rests); may be predominantly rotational in nature (e.g. shoulder rotations); seem to appear consistently across performances of different styles of music, such that a given performer has his or her own 'vocabulary' of gestures; and differ in their importance, such that movements occurring at some moments during performance are more obvious indicators of expressive intention than are others.

The importance of body movement may be by no means limited to the communication of expressive intention however. Davidson and Good (2002) found that performers in small ensembles used body movements to coordinate timing, dynamics, and other expressive effects; Yarbrough (1975) found that eye contact and facial expressions made valuable contributions to inter-performer communication; Durrant (1994) found that successful conductors used body movements to communicate intentions, whereas their less success-ful counterparts emphasized verbal communication; and Decker and Kirk (1988) have specified the movements that conductors should use and their likely effectiveness. Indeed, given the apparent promise of research on body movement, it is surprising that there has been so little attempt to draw directly on the wealth of research in social psychology on non-verbal communication (see Kurkul, 2007).

Similarly, it is surprising that other aspects of mainstream social psychology have not been drawn upon by researchers interested in music performance. For example, research on groups of musicians has yet to address social facilita-tion (i.e. the process by which the positive evaluation of the performance of others improves the performance of a target individual). Research on Social Identity Theory, prejudice, and interpersonal perception may help to explain relationships between musicians in the 'workplace'. Research on conformity and obedience may explain power relationships between members of given musical groups, between a conductor and his/her orchestra, or between teachers and students. Furthermore, related fields could also make a consider-able contribution to the understanding of music performance. For example, environmental psychology can almost certainly help to describe the optimal physical conditions under which musicians should practise and perform, and under which audiences should hear music. We also look forward to more specific research focusing on the effects of performers' clothing, age, and ethnicity on audiences' perceptions of the particular genre represented by the music and the extent to which it is regarded as 'art' or 'entertainment'.

One specific example of how mainstream social psychology can make a direct contribution to understanding musical performance comes from research on physical attractiveness. Zillmann and Bhatia (1989; see also May and Hamilton, 1980; Sargent and Weaver, 1996) for instance presented partic-ipants with videos of a member of the opposite sex who described him-or herself before mentioning a preference for either classical music, country, soft rock, or heavy metal. This musical preference exerted a considerable influence on participants' reactions. Women who liked classical music were regarded as more sophisticated and more attractive, whereas liking heavy metal led to females being regarded as less sophisticated and less attractive. Men were regarded as less sophisticated when they said they liked country, and both men and women were regarded as less attractive when they liked this musical style; whereas men who liked heavy metal were perceived as more attractive. Interestingly, women were also regarded as more attractive when they shared the male participant's musical preference, consistent with other research indicating that attractiveness can be based on similarity between people's attitudes (e.g. Feingold, 1991).

This study built on findings from the 1970s indicating that we respond more positively to physically attractive people. For example, Miller (1970) presented male and female participants with photographs that had been scaled previously as low, moderate or high in physical attractiveness. Participants then recorded their impression of each photograph on an adjective checklist, and on 15 of the 17 adjective scales, the low attractiveness photographs were associated with undesirable ratings (see also Dion, 1972; Dion, Berschied, and Walster, 1972; and Walster, Aronson, Abrahams, and Rottmann, 1966). As Dion, Berschied, and Walster (1972) put it in the title of their paper, we believe that *What is beautiful is good*.

Confirmation of this in a music performance context is provided by North and Hargreaves (1997b) who investigated whether the attractiveness of the supposed performer of a piece of music could influence reactions to that music. Participants were played 20 pieces of pop music while they were simultaneously shown a picture of the supposed performer of each. At the end of each, participants were asked to rate both the performer and the music. In both cases there was again clear evidence of the physical attractiveness effect. Attractive performers were perceived as more poised, sophisticated, emotionally warm, feminine, intelligent, and likely to be popular than their unattractive counterparts; and music performed by attractive performers was liked more, perceived as possessing more artistic merit, and as being more sophisticated, intelligent, and likely to be popular than music performed by their unattractive counterparts. In other words, music by attractive performers was not only more popular, but these people were also seen as 'true artists'. Note also that male participants were influenced by attractive male performers just as much as were female participants; and female participants were taken in just as much by attractive female performers as were male participants.

Four studies by Joel Wapnick and colleagues (see also Ryan and Costa-Giomi, 2004) indicate that an attractiveness bias also exists in the evaluation of classical musicians. Wapnick, Darrow, Kovacs, and Dalrymple (1997) studied evaluations of singers when either audio only or audiovisual information on their performance was provided. Performances were judged to be better when audiovisual information was provided, and this was particularly the case for attractive male singers. More surprisingly, however, attractive females were judged to perform better than unattractive females even when *only audio* information was presented to the participants: even though the participants could not have known who was attractive and who was not, they still responded more favourably to the attractive females. Wapnick, Mazza, and Darrow (1998) replicated the study, this time replacing singers with violinists. They again found that attractive performers were rated more highly than unattractive ones in the audiovisual condition, and also that the quality of performers' dress and stage behaviour further improved ratings of them. Moreover, for both males and females, attractive performers received higher ratings in the audio only condition. The attractiveness effect was again found in both the audiovisual and also the audio only conditions when Wapnick, Mazza, and Darrow (2000) asked participants to evaluate performances given by children in their third year of piano study.

Findings such as these led Wapnick and colleagues to conclude the clear existence of an attractiveness bias in performance evaluation. Furthermore, they argued that since the bias exists even when participants only had audio information on which to base their judgement, this must mean that attractive performers are in some way favoured during their training by, for example, receiving more attention and/or encouragement from teachers. If so, then unattractive aspiring musicians could well be more likely to give up their aspirations of a musical career, and this could be tested easily by comparing the attractiveness of musicians at different career levels: players in major metropolitan symphony orchestras ought to be better-looking than their amateur and provincial counterparts. Such a process undoubtedly occurs in pop music, where the world-famous stars are often noted just as much for their beauty as their music (e.g. Elvis Presley, Debbie Harry, Jennifer Lopez, Justin Timberlake, Beyonce Knowles, and Ricky Martin to name but a few). Wapnick and colleagues also concluded that the effects on audiences' judgements involving performers' dress and stage behaviour are in some ways positive since, unlike attractiveness, these can be altered by performers. Finally, it is interesting that Ryan, Wapnick, Lacaille, and Darrow (2006) found evidence to suggest that the attractiveness bias does not occur in evaluations of very high level performers: while these results could of course be accepted simply at face value (i.e. there is no attractiveness bias in evaluations of skilled performance), Ryan and colleagues speculate that they could also be a consequence of less attractive performers simply having been already 'weeded out' lower down the music performance hierarchy.

Note also that ratings of musical performances are subject to a considerable range of other social psychological biases (e.g. Landy and Farr, 1980; McPherson and Schubert, 2004; McPherson and Thompson, 1998). These include the observer's own instrumental experience (Thompson and Williamon, 2003); the order in which performers appear on stage, such that those appearing later are favoured (Flores and Ginsburgh, 1996; Ginsburgh and van Ours, 2003; Glejser and Heyndels, 2001); the decision to play recently composed pieces and avoid popular pieces (Glejser and Heyndels, 2001); and also gender and ethnicity (Davidson and Edgar, 2003; Glejser and Heyndels, 2001; Goldin and Rouse, 2000). Similarly Thompson (2007) considered factors that might influence enjoyment of a performance. Although he emphasized how 'pre-performance' and 'during performance' factors might cluster together, what is more interesting about his data in the present context is the illustration of how so many factors outside the music itself might well relate to the enjoyment of a live concert. The specific groupings of these factors are also of interest in outlining the beginning of a theory of the enjoyment of live music. Thompson grouped 'pre-performance' factors into three clusters, namely anticipation of the music, the listener's emotional state, and familiarity and comfort with the performance environment. The 'during performance' factors were also grouped into three clusters, namely engagement of the listener with the performance; dynamic factors that interfere with attempts to pay attention emanating from both the musician (e.g. wrong notes) and elsewhere (e.g. audience noise); and stable factors that affect enjoyment (e.g. the performers appearing nervous, the performers being dressed inappropriately, the programme not fitting together well). Finally, note that the potential impact of all the biases discussed here is anything but trivial: they have the obvious potential to impact upon the prestige that results from winning a music performance competition, but the latter also predicts the degree of economic success that a musician will subsequently enjoy in later life (Ginsburgh, 2003; Ginsburgh and van Ours, 2003).

2.3.3.2 Performance anxiety and drug use

Other researchers have focused more on the performers themselves than on audience responses to them, and a particularly notable line of research has addressed performance anxiety. It is long established that musical activity can lead to physical disorders such as musculoskeletal pain, hearing impairment, and difficulties with respiration and voice production, but it is becoming increasingly clear that psychological problems are often the most serious health issue experienced by musicians. For example, Brandfonbrener (1986; see also Brandfonbrener and Kjelland, 2002) noted that musicians often experience stress as a result of the isolation and self-discipline required in order to achieve musical expertize (although we should also add here Preti, DeBiasi, and Miotto's (2001) finding that musicians had a low suicide rate relative to people working in literary and visual arts, which suggests that they do relatively well on the most acutely important measure of psychological distress.)

Arguably the most common psychological problem experienced by musicians, however, is performance anxiety (see reviews by Lehmann, Sloboda, and

Woody, 2007; Steptoe, 2001; Wilson, 1997, 2002; Wills and Cooper, 1988; and Wilson and Roland, 2002). 'Stage fright', as it is more commonly known, is experienced by the musical greats (such as Lennon or Rachmaninov) as well as novices. Wesner, Noyes, and Davis's (1990) study of 302 musicians found that 61% reported either 'marked' or 'moderate' distress at performance, and 47% reported 'marked' or 'moderate' impairment of their performance skills as a result of anxiety. Similarly, van Kemenade, van Son, and van Heesch (1995) found that 91 of their sample of 155 symphony orchestra musicians reported experiences of performance anxiety serious enough to affect their professional or personal lives. Similar results are reported by Liden and Gottfries (1974), Marchant-Haycox and Wilson (1992), Middlestadt (1990), Shoup (1995), and Steptoe and Fidler (1987).

The symptoms of performance anxiety are similar to those associated with any other phobia or fear response, namely major activation of the sympathetic branch of the autonomic nervous system which deals with the 'fight or flight' response to danger. The physiological symptoms reflect this readiness for emergency action, including for example the diversion of bodily fluids such as saliva into the bloodstream (causing a dry mouth and difficulties swallowing); a more energetic heart rate (causing palpitations); sweating to cool the skin (leading to sweaty palms); the shutting down of digestion so that energy is diverted to the muscles (causing 'butterflies' and nausea); release of stored energy from the liver (causing edginess); and the lungs working harder and airways widening (leading to breathlessness).

Unsurprisingly, performance anxiety is linked to personality traits indicative of anxiety. For example, Mor, Day, and Flett (1995) identified a link between performance anxiety and traits such as the need for excessive personal control and perfectionism (i.e. self-criticism and unrealistically high expectations of self, leading to low self-esteem and over-concern with small mistakes). Other studies show a correlation between trait anxiety (i.e. experiencing anxiety in all aspects of life) and a predisposition towards performance anxiety (Cox and Kenardy, 1992; Craske and Craig, 1984; Hamann, 1982). Similarly, Steptoe and Fidler (1987) found some evidence that greater levels of performance anxiety are experienced among younger and less experienced musicians.

Furthermore, the link to anxiety in general and symptoms such as those outlined above suggest that musicians' level of physiological arousal might well be a crucial concept in explaining the effect of stage fright on performance. The basic principle here is similar to that we will see in Chapter 3 regarding arousal and musical preference. At the risk of over-generalizing, there is an inverted-U relationship between arousal and performance on a range of tasks (Yerkes and Dodson, 1908), such that people perform at their worst under conditions of either very low or very high arousal. Wilson (2002) integrates much of the available evidence in arguing that three factors should be taken into account when applying this inverted-U model to a given individual performance: (1) the trait anxiety of the performer; some people have higher baseline arousal than others; (2) the degree of task mastery attained as arousal/anxiety will be lower when the performer knows the music well; and (3) the degree of situational stress prevailing: people experience more arousal / anxiety when their performance is to be evaluated (e.g. Abel and Larkin, 1990; Brotons, 1994) or when they perform for larger numbers of people (LeBlanc, Jin, Obert, and Siivola, 1997). We might add a fourth factor to these, namely career stress factors that professional musicians bring with them to any performance, such as work overload or underload, lack of job satisfaction, or negative work relationships (e.g. Wills and Cooper, 1988; Cooper and Wills, 1989; Steptoe, 1989).

These factors interact in determining the performer's level of arousal, such that, for example, performers prone to anxiety or who will be examined should practise more to increase their task mastery. Furthermore, the inverted-U nature of the arousal-performance relationship means that very low levels of anxiety may also lead to poorer performance: some anxiety can sometimes be a good thing. These considerations may be more important than at first seems. Hardy and Parfitt's (1991) catastrophe theory states that, under high anxiety conditions, once performers' arousal becomes super-optimal then the decline in their performance is rapid rather than the gradual decline implied by the inverted-U: in effect, performers may simply panic, such that *any* degree of super-optimal arousal may prove very detrimental.

Treatments for stage fright unsurprisingly operate by reducing anxiety. *Psychoanalytic approaches* (e.g. Gabbard, 1979; Nagel, 1993) attribute perform-ance anxiety to rather abstract processes relating to childhood experiences concerning genital exhibition and fear of parental punishment for masturba-tion. As Wilson and Roland (2002, p.52) note, 'While early childhood experi-ences may well contribute to performance anxiety, it is not clear that these need to be revisited as part of the treatment procedure'. *Behavioural therapies* (see e.g. Appel, 1976) treat performance anxiety as a phobia, and are based on the notion that the phobia is maintained because of the relief that the sufferer feels as a consequence of successfully avoiding the anxiety-inducing situation. Consequently, behavioural approaches employ techniques such as systematic desensitization in which the musician imagines increasingly sensitive perform-ance scenarios and learns to relax simultaneously. *Cognitive-behavioural thera-pies* aim to reduce the incidence of self-destructive thoughts produced by the musician (e.g. Kendrick, Craig, Lawson, and Davidson, 1982). This process may for example involve training in how to re-focus attention during perform-ance from negative and task-irrelevant thoughts onto optimistic, task-oriented thoughts. Other cognitive behavioural therapists have employed stress inoculation techniques (e.g. Salmon, 1991) in which performers are taught to anticipate the symptoms of performance anxiety and regard them positively as normal emotional reactions that can provide energy. Clark and Agras (1991) found that such techniques might be more effective than drug-based approaches. *Hypnotherapy* (e.g. Stanton, 1994) may similarly be an effective way of changing the thought processes of musicians experiencing performance anxiety. There is also some evidence that performance anxiety might be alleviated through the *Alexander Technique* (Valentine, Fitzgerald, Gorton, Hudson, and Symonds, 1995). This uses a mixture of verbal instruc-tion and actual demonstration to overcome habitual limitations in posture and movement, and is very popular among orchestral musicians (Watson and Valentine, 1987). Finally, the most commonly-used legal *drugs* in attempts to address performance anxiety are beta-blockers, which inhibit the physical manifestations of anxiety. Fishbein, Middlestadt, Ottati, Strauss, and Ellis (1988) found that they were used by 27% of professional musicians, even though there is little evidence that they actually improve performance (e.g. Brantigan, Brantigan, and Joseph, 1979; Clark, 1989; James, Griffith, Pearson, and Newbury, 1977; and James and Savage, 1984).

In addition to beta-blockers, other drugs that have been popularly associ-ated with musicians, such as alcohol and cannabis, also have anxiety-reducing properties and also induce mild euphoria. The latter effect is both a blessing and a curse, since the musician feels better about his or her performance, but also as a result of this has a disposition to take the drug again before the next performance, and this may lead to dependence. However, although there is relatively little data on the usage of drugs among musicians, what little there is suggests that usage is much less common than the stereotype suggests. Wills and Cooper (1988), for example, found that only 30% of pop musicians reported that they 'sometimes' used cannabis, and the corresponding figures for cocaine and amphetamines were 11% and 4% respectively. Similarly, Wills' (2003) study of 40 eminent jazz musicians found that although levels of psychopathology were similar to those observed among other creative groups, substance-related problems were not. Hipple, Chesky, and Young (2000) stud-ied 132 university music students, and found that reported drinking levels were generally lower than the national student average, and that perceived levels of drug use were quite low also (although Gronnerod (2002) reports that drinking was perceived as a relatively 'normal' part of musical life among people in rock bands).

A small number of other studies have taken a slightly different approach by considering the role of drugs in creativity. Although only a small proportion of these studies address *musical* creativity *per se*, the more general evidence provides an equivocal conclusion concerning the frequently made claim that illegal drugs enhance creativity. For example, in perhaps the first experimental test of such a relationship, Aldrich (1944) found that ingestion of a pyra-hexyl compound (which users reported having a similar effect to that of marijuana) led to poorer scores on the Seashore test of musical ability for nine of the 12 participants. Similarly, Kerr, Shaffer, Chambers, and Hallowell (1991) found a lack of significant differences in the use of most illegal drugs when comparing composers, writers, artists, and control participants, and argued that 'Many creative individuals described the experience of initially perceiving substances as useful to creativity, only to find them destructive in the long run' (p. 145). Hundleby (1985) surveyed 2,048 school children, finding that high achievers in a range of domains (including the arts) had below-average usage of a variety of substances including marijuana and psychedelic drugs. Plucker and Dana (1998) found only negligible negative correlations between under-graduates' creative achievement and the age at which they first used certain drugs. Edwards (1993) compared 15 substance-abusing adolescents with age-matched controls, finding that the former group gave rise to significantly lower creativity scores. Finally, Janiger and De Rios (1989) investigated 20 artists' work before and after administration of LSD, finding that 'it was not clear that the individual artist was able to produce aesthetically superior work during the period when the drug was operable' (p. 129).

In contrast, several other studies support the contention that drug use may enhance users' creative abilities. Lowe (1995) found significant (although low) positive relationships between the creativity of 619 people and their degree of substance use. Steffenhagen, McCann, and McAree (1976) found that drug users scored higher than non-users on two tests of creativity. Grossman, Goldstein, and Eisenman (1974) found positive correlations between college students' frequency of marijuana usage and scores for creativity and 'adven-turesomeness'. Gordon (1999) argued that musical hallucinations (which may be induced by illegal drug use) could be a source of artistic creativity to composers. These findings are supported by several studies focusing on drug users' motivations for their substance use. For example, Newcomb, Chou, Bentler, and Huba (1988) found that the desire to 'enhance positive affect and creativity' was one of four factors underlying adolescents' motivations for drug use. Similarly, both Lehmkuhl and Lehmkuhl (1982) and Kamali and Steer (1976) found that long-term use of drugs was related to the desire on the part of users to achieve increased creativity. Several other authors have provided less data-driven discussions of the relationship between illegal drug usage and artistic creativity (see e.g. Groce, 1991; Jenny, 1998; Lenson, 1998; Markert, 2001; and Sherrer, 1971).

This absence of a clear conclusion concerning the effect of drugs on creativity is almost certainly attributable (at least in part) to different drugs having different effects on different types of people using them in different contexts (see e.g. Krippner, 1985). Furthermore, although the use of a variety of illegal drugs may or may not *enhance* creativity, the existing literature provides no information concerning a subtly different issue, namely *how* drug usage might affect the products of creative activity. Similarly, very few quantitative studies have considered creative products that were generated outside the laboratory, such that the existing research on drugs and creativity is lacking in ecological validity. This dearth of information persists (see Greeson, 1986) despite the public's obvious fascination with the effects of drugs on several well-known pop musicians such as Brian Jones (from The Rolling Stones), Jimi Hendrix, John Lennon, Janis Joplin, Jim Morrison (from The Doors), Sid Vicious (from The Sex Pistols), John Bonham (from Led Zeppelin), and Hillel Slovak (from The Red Hot Chilli Peppers). In an initial attempt to address this, an unpublished study by North and Beauvois obtained complete sets of lyrics and dates of drug usage for five well-known pop groups/artists (namely Aerosmith, The Rolling Stones, The Incredible String Band, The Beatles, and Todd Rundgren). Computer analysis of the lyrics indicated that measures of lyrical aggression increased after periods of drug usage, whereas levels of ambivalence, cognitive terms, and cooperation decreased after such periods. Clearly more data is needed to identify whether these findings would be replicated among a much larger sample of lyrics.

2.3.4 The 'Mozart effect'

In recent years, some researchers have begun to argue that both playing and listening to music bring with them additional benefits in terms of intelligence. The story begins in 1993 with the publication of Rauscher, Shaw, and Ky's 'Music and spatial task performance' in the journal *Nature*. This reported findings from a study in which undergraduates spent 10 minutes listening to Mozart's sonata K.448, relaxation instructions, or nothing at all before then completing paper folding and cutting tasks taken from the Stanford-Binet Intelligence Scale. The latter involve drawings of a piece of paper being folded several times before having various shapes cut into it. Respondents are then asked to say what the folded and cut paper would look like when unfolded. They do this by selecting one of several pictures presented in a 'multiple choice' format. Rauscher and colleagues found that participants did better on the paper folding and cutting task after they heard Mozart than after they heard the relaxation instructions or nothing at all, such that their IQ scores were 8 to 9 points higher. The 'Mozart effect' was born. Other related studies have focused on playing rather than listening to music, showing a positive impact of music lessons on spatial reasoning skills in pre-schoolers (e.g. Rauscher, Shaw, Levine, Wright, Dennis, and Newcomb, 1997), and even that rats exposed to Mozart's music demonstrated better maze navigation skills, supporting the notion that 'musical experience may improve skills in … spatial domains' (Rauscher, Robinson, and Jens, 1998, p. 427).

Rauscher (1999, p. 827) herself has stated quite explicitly that the most common misconception of her work is that exposure to 'Mozart enhances intelligence [in general]. We made no such claim. The effect is limited to spatial-temporal tasks involving mental imagery and temporal ordering'. Nonetheless, recent years have witnessed the development of a fervent belief among the general public that exposing young children to any form of classical music will boost intelligence and other cognitive abilities. For example, the BBC News website reported on 19th May 2005 that 'many US hospitals give classical CDs to new mums. In the UK, many parents have also embraced the theory, with Classic FM's *Music for Babies* CD enjoying several weeks at the top of the classical charts earlier this year. And this week *Sound Beginnings*, a series of concerts aimed at the very young, begins in Hampshire.'

Similarly, Bangerter and Heath (2004, pp. 609–610) describe how, in 1998, the state of Georgia in the USA passed a bill to distribute free classical music CDs to new mothers: 'In an interview, the governor of Georgia and initiator of the bill said: "As you know, the brain has two lobes. The studies show that music engages both hemispheres of the brain—its creativity and emotion engage the right lobe, while rhythm and pitch engage the left. So people who receive musical exposure at a young age develop a bundle of nerves that connects those two halves"' (*Baltimore Sun*, July 6, 1998). Several other US states have acted similarly. The state of Florida passed a bill requiring state-funded day-care centers to play classical music every day (State of Florida Senate Bill 660, May 21, 1998). Books (Campbell, 1997, 2000), toys and CD collections have been marketed claiming beneficial effects of classical music. And in surveys we have conducted in California and Arizona (total $N = 496$), over 80% of respondents report some familiarity with the ME [Mozart effect]. The ME has diffused abroad, and appears in dozens of countries around the world. In 1996, the BBC's [Tomorrow's World] Megalab series tested over 8,000 students for an improvement in spatial intelligence after listening to either Mozart or rock music. In its spread, the ME has adapted to local frames of reference: an Indian newspaper describes the ME as 'music curry for the soul' (*Times of India*, March 2, 2001). Other manifestations seem comical: playing Mozart to prison inmates (*Houston Chronicle*, May 2, 1999) or even to roses during their germination (*Korea Herald*, May 22, 1999).'

Nor have academics or educational practitioners been immune to the excitement. The potential Mozart effect has been used by many to justify the inclusion of music in the school curriculum. The argument here is something like, 'Music should be taught at school because it aids maths skills'. Whether the best way to boost school maths performance is to run more music classes or more maths classes is a separate issue, but this again raises the question of whether involvement in music in general and Mozart's in particular does bring with it other benefits. Indeed, we have highlighted the lay interest in the Mozart effect simply because this stands in stark contrast to the highly controversial nature of its scientific status. While it is entirely understandable that parents, educators, and politicians want to do everything possible to help young people get a good start in life, it is almost certainly safe to say that the amount of money currently being spent far outweighs the amount of unequivocal supporting evidence.

The original research by Rauscher and colleagues led to numerous follow-up studies shortly afterwards, and Chabris (1999) carried out a meta-analysis of 16 of these to determine whether the Mozart effect really does exist. Meta-analysis provides a statistical measure of the effect size (i.e. the magnitude of the impact) of the music in question, such that the larger the effect size so the more effective was the music. Chabris concluded that the results showed an average cognitive enhancement attributable to the Mozart effect of just 0.09 standard deviations, or only 1.4 IQ points. Different studies used different measures of the effects of music, but even when considering only studies of specifically spatial-temporal skills (such as the paper folding and cutting task) the Mozart effect was worth an improvement of only .14 standard deviations or 2.1 IQ points. 'Accordingly, exposure to ten minutes of Mozart's music does not seem to enhance general intelligence or reasoning, although it may exert a small improving effect on the ability to transform visual images. However, this enhancement is essentially restricted to a single task, is one-quarter as large as that originally reported for a broader class of cognitive abilities, is not statistically significant ... and is smaller than the average variation of a single person's IQ-test performance' (Chabris, 1999, p. 826). To borrow from the title of his paper, Chabris' findings were interpreted by many as sounding a requiem for the Mozart effect, and Schellenberg's (2006) review of the evidence shows that a similar degree of scepticism persisted in the years immediately following Chabris' meta-analysis.

Rauscher (1999) contested whether Chabris should have included all the studies that he did in the meta-analysis, on the grounds that they did not test the benefits of Mozart's music claimed by her original work (concerning mental imagery and temporal ordering rather than intelligence *per se*). Whether you agree with Rauscher's criticism depends of course on whether you accept Rauscher's or Chabris' definition of which studies really do concern 'the Mozart effect': in other words, a crucial factor may be the definition of what constitutes the kind of benefits that might be expected as a result of exposure to music. For example, Hetland (2000a) published another, less well-known meta-analysis on music listening, included over 30 studies that she adjudged to concern the Mozart effect (including more emphasis than Chabris on studies concerning playing rather than listening to music), and reached much more positive conclusions concerning spatial-temporal abilities. Furthermore, we suspect that Rauscher would not be troubled too greatly by Chabris' findings that any Mozart effects that might exist are only small in magnitude: although Rauscher would expect to find *statistically significant* Mozart effects under the precise conditions she describes in her research, to the best of our knowledge she has never argued that these effects should be *massive*. Rauscher (1999) herself makes a second objection to Chabris' conclusions, noting that 'Because some people cannot get bread to rise does not negate the existence of a "yeast effect"' (p. 828). In other words, a small number of failures to replicate her findings do not mean necessarily that the Mozart effect does not exist. But to elaborate further on Rauscher's metaphor, a failure to get bread to rise usually implies that the cook doesn't understand how yeast works. We suspect that another explanation for the inconsistency in findings concerning the Mozart effect arises simply from confusion over the precise cause. If researchers do not know which aspects of the music should be effective or which variables they should impact upon then it would be expected that they would sometimes fail to obtain a Mozart effect.

There is no clear consensus yet concerning how any effect may actually come about. Rauscher and colleagues, for example, argued that passive listening to complex music such as Mozart should enhance abstract reasoning in general, including performance on spatio-temporal tasks such as the paper folding and cutting task. Other studies have suggested that the effect may occur when people enjoy the music they hear. For example, Nantais and Schellenberg (1999) found that listening to Mozart or a passage from a Stephen King story enhanced performance on paper folding and cutting providing people enjoyed what they heard; and Schellenberg and Hallam (2005) found that school pupils performed better in response to music by pop group Blur than to Mozart's. Note also, however, that this 'enjoyment explanation' finds it difficult to explain why Rauscher, Robinson, and Jens (1998) should have found that Mozart could improve the ability of rats to learn a maze, an experience they presumably could not have found enjoyable no matter what music was played. Alternatively, Thompson, Schellenberg, and Husain (2001) and Husain, Thompson, and Schellenberg (2002) argue that any effect is caused by music (or any other stimulus for that matter) increasing arousal and improving mood.

Furthermore, as Schellenberg (2001, 2003, 2006) and Rauscher and Hinton (2006) argued, it seems reasonable to suspect that the processes by which music *listening* purportedly improves cognitive performance may be different to those by which *playing* a musical instrument purportedly improves cognitive performance. For example, Chan, Ho, and Cheung (1998) and Ho, Cheung, and Chan (2003) have proposed that music lessons may have linguistic benefits, perhaps because they improve auditory temporal processing. Other studies have identified correlations between taking music lessons and mathematical abilities (Vaughn, 2000), reading abilities (e.g. Butzlaff, 2000), and spatial-temporal abilities (e.g. Hetland, 2000b). Experimental evidence from recent years suggests that the music lessons may have been *causing* the improvements in other abilities, since experimental assignment of children to the former led to gains in other domains (see e.g. Costa-Giomi, 1999; Gardiner, Fox, Knowles, and Jeffrey, 1996; Gromko and Poorman, 1988; Rauscher and Zupan, 2000; Schellenberg, 2004). Schellenberg (2006) proposes four possible explanations of the positive effects of music lessons on other intellectual abilities. First is that the effect could be 'an extension of the well-known fact that schooling raises IQ' (p. 130). Second, the 'other' benefits of music lessons may arise from one or more of the range of generic skills that these lessons would be expected to improve (e.g. fine motor skills, memory, reading). A third possible explanation is that the abstract nature of music primes abstract reasoning skills in general. Finally, learning to play music may be similar to learning a second language, and the latter 'is known to confer some non-linguistic cognitive advantages' (p. 130). For the time being, the simple truth is that we just don't know for sure how any 'Mozart effect' operates, whether any effects are stronger as a result of listening to or playing music, and what specific nature the effect might take. However, as understanding grows we might expect to find more positive evidence, such that future meta-analyses may reach more positive conclusions than that of Chabris (1999).

3

Musical preference and taste

Wagner's music is better than it sounds
Mark Twain

It goes without saying that musical preferences vary massively. If you and your friends were each to nominate your favourite piece of music it is virtually certain that you would nominate very different pieces. If you were then asked to say why you liked each piece so much then the reasons would probably be even more diverse in both their nature and their degree of sophistication. Some people, for instance, would state that their favourite music evokes certain emotions, others would attribute their preference to memories they have associated with the music, and others would say that they 'simply like it'. All this diversity, of course, poses a considerable challenge to music psychology. How could such a varied set of responses be explained? In Chapter 2 we saw the different means by which researchers have explained composers' eminence and 'greatness', but in contrast this chapter describes some of the ways in which psychologists have attempted to explain people's more mundane, everyday musical likes and dislikes. The chapter organizes the influences on musical taste into factors relating to the music, the listening situation, and the listener. After describing these influences, we provide a reciprocal response model of musical preference, discuss emotional responses to music, and finally consider research that has directly investigated people's musical likes and dislikes as they go about their daily lives.

3.1 The music

Research on how aspects of the music itself influences preference has been dominated by experimental aesthetics. We begin by describing the basic approach adopted by experimental aesthetics before then considering two of the main theories. The first was proposed by Daniel Berlyne, and concerns the effect of music (and other artistic objects) on physiological arousal. The second theory, the preference for prototypes model, focuses instead on cognitive factors.

3.1.1 **Experimental aesthetics**

The field of experimental aesthetics attempts to produce laws governing responses to all art forms. The classic methodology within this approach is influenced heavily by the late behaviourist *zeitgeist* in which the field developed. The musical 'stimulus' to which participants are asked to respond is typically monophonic, short (i.e. about 5–15 seconds long), and composed specially for the research in question, usually according to some statistical rule. This stimulus is played under laboratory conditions to undergraduate students, whose responses are then measured either by asking them to state how much they liked the music, or instead through various physiological indices such as heart rate, galvanic skin response, or other indicators of autonomic nervous system arousal. This approach has obvious advantages. The use of specially-composed music allows precise control of the experimental stimuli, and ensures that research participants have no prior experiences of the music that could influence their responses. Furthermore, playing these musical stimuli in a laboratory ensures that participants' responses cannot be influenced by outside factors, such as the nature of any tasks being carried out concurrently with the music listening. The use of undergraduate participants means that the research is carried out on a relatively homogeneous group of people well-used to taking part in psychological research. Finally, taking physiological measures of these people's responses to the music means that there is minimal distortion of the data due to participants' own ideas about how they should respond or their own biases regarding the music. In short, this classic methodology allows for the precise control of musical stimuli and the circumstances in which they are heard, and for externally observable measures of response that are unlikely to be distorted.

This powerful and well-controlled methodology has led to some correspondingly powerful findings. With its publication in 1876, Gustav Fechner's *Vorschule der Äesthetik* established experimental aesthetics as arguably the second oldest topic in experimental psychology. Fechner's approach emphasized the basic building blocks of aesthetic preferences in a variety of artistic domains, such as responses to simple shapes and geometrical forms, and with this he tested the notion of the 'aesthetic mean', namely the idea that beauty is associated with the absence of extremes. This idea can itself be traced back to ancient philosophy. Plato wrote in the *Statesman* that the arts are 'on the watch against excess and deficit … (in that) the excellence and beauty of every work of art is due to this observance and … a standard removed from the extremes'. Similarly, Aristotle wrote in the *Nichomachean Ethics* that 'a master of any art avoids excess and deficit but seeks the intermediate and chooses this'.

These ideas perhaps came to maturity in the work of Daniel Berlyne, who adopted a psychobiological approach in founding 'the new experimental aesthetics' (e.g. Berlyne, 1971; 1972; 1974). He charactered research within this approach as possessing one or more of the following features:

1. It concentrates on collative properties of stimulus patterns. Collative properties (of which more will be said later) are 'structural' or 'formal' properties, such as variations along familiar–novel, simple–complex, expected–surprizing, ambiguous–clear, and stable–variable dimensions.

2. It concentrates on motivational questions (see Berlyne, 1960, 1970, 1971).

3. It studies nonverbal behavior as well as verbally expressed judgements.

4. It strives to establish links between aesthetic phenomena and other psychological phenomena. This means that it aims not only to throw light on aesthetic phenomena but, through the elucidation of aesthetic problems, to throw light on human psychology in general. (Berlyne, 1974, p. 5)

Berlyne (1971) proposed a theory based on this approach that dominated research efforts from the 1970s until the 1990s. His theory states that preference for artistic stimuli such as music is related to their 'arousal potential', which in practical terms refers to the amount of activity they produce in the ascending reticular activating system. Music with an intermediate degree of arousal potential is liked most, and this degree of liking gradually decreases towards the extremes of arousal potential. This means that there is an 'inverted-U' relationship between preference and stimulus arousal potential (see Figure 3.1), and this relates to the well-known Wundt curve (Wundt, 1874) as well as to the arguments of Fechner, Plato, and Aristotle.

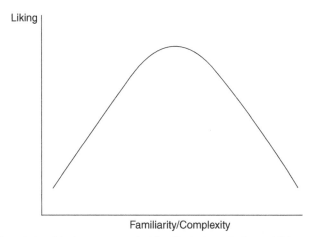

Fig. 3.1 The relationship between musical familiarity/complexity and liking

Berlyne stated that the variables that mediate arousal potential fall into three categories. First are what he called the 'psychophysical' variables, which are the intrinsic physical properties of the stimulus such as musical tempo or volume: music is said to possess more arousal potential as it gets faster or louder. Second are 'ecological' variables, which refer to the signal value or 'meaningfulness' of a particular piece of music. The final class of variables are what Berlyne called 'collative' variables. He claimed that these are the 'most significant of all for aesthetics' (Berlyne, 1971, p. 69), and they have dominated research. Collative variables concern the informational properties of the music such as its level of complexity, which can be defined as the extent to which the music seems erratic, varied, or unpredictable to the listener. As music seems to become more complex so it is said to possess more arousal potential. In addition to complexity, the other collative variable that has received a lot of research attention is familiarity: unfamiliar pieces of music are more arousing than are familiar pieces.

Berlyne took a psychobiological approach to explaining why people should prefer moderately arousing music. On its way to the cortex, the higher brain responsible for conscious thought, the auditory nerve passes through the ascending reticular activating system (ARAS), which is responsible for the degree of physiological arousal we experience. Pieces of music that are more arousing lead to more activity in the auditory nerve, which in turn means that the listener experiences a greater degree of arousal. Berlyne claimed that music of moderate arousal potential is liked most because, on their way to the higher brain, the fibres of the ARAS pass through pleasure and displeasure centres in the midbrain. The former has a lower threshold level and a lower asymptotic level than the latter. In practical terms, this means that music with low degrees of arousal potential causes activity in pleasure centres but no activity in displeasure centres. Music of moderate degrees of arousal potential causes maximal activity in pleasure centres but also begins to activate displeasure centres. Music of high degrees of arousal potential cannot cause any more activity in pleasure centres but also causes high degrees of activity in displeasure centres. The net effect of the activity in these pleasure and displeasure centres is to cause the inverted-U relationship between the arousal potential of music and liking for it.

Although this second part of the theory concerning the ARAS and pleasure centres and displeasure centres is more contentious from a physiological standpoint, four further points are worth making. First, this contentious part of Berlyne's theory represents a valuable attempt to locate the neurological bases of aesthetic judgements within a more general theoretical framework. Second, this aspect of the theory indicates how musical preferences may be based on adaptive grounds. At the risk of over-generalizing, the brain works most effectively when moderately aroused: for example, it would be hard to write an essay while feeling sleepy or very anxious. It therefore makes good sense that we should have evolved to prefer moderately arousing music. Third, as we noted earlier, the theory corresponds with several earlier ideas expressed by Wundt, Fechner, Plato, and Aristotle. Finally, under the right conditions, Berlyne's notion of an inverted-U relationship between arousal potential and liking for particular pieces of music does seem to hold.

Indeed numerous laboratory studies carried out between the 1960s and early 1980s provided evidence of an inverted-U relationship between liking for pieces of music and their complexity. Although evidence for an inverted-U relationship between liking and familiarity is less clear-cut (see e.g. Hargreaves, 1986; Zajonc, 1968), findings that are inconsistent with the theory have often been explained away by, for example, their failure to include a full-range of familiarity. We will not repeat details of these findings and arguments here, since they are reviewed extensively elsewhere (Finnäs, 1989; Hargreaves, 1986; and see notable individual studies by Crozier, 1974; McMullen, 1974; McMullen and Arnold, 1976; Simon and Wohlwill, 1968; Vitz, 1966). Of greater interest is whether an inverted-U relationship between liking for music and its arousal potential holds under everyday music listening circumstances.

There have unfortunately been few attempts to carry out this kind of work. However, what little research there is has reached encouraging conclusions. With regard to the *psychophysical* variables, Kellaris (1992) investigated the tempo of the music played by a band at various American-Greek social events. He measured musical preferences through an equally naturalistic means by timing the subsequent applause of the audience. Music of moderate tempo was applauded for longest. With regard to *complexity*, North and Hargreaves (1996b) visited several aerobic exercise and yoga classes, and found an inverted-U relationship between people's ratings of liking and complexity assigned to the music used in the classes. Furthermore, as we saw in section 2.3 of Chapter 2, one of the key conclusions of Simonton's work on melodic originality in composition is that pieces with moderate levels of originality are most popular. For example, Simonton (1980b) found this pattern following an analysis of 15,618 musical themes by 479 classical composers. If we accept Simonton's measure of originality as a proxy for complexity then this constitutes powerful evidence in support of Berlyne's theory. Three naturalistic studies concerning *familiarity* and musical preference have produced equally encouraging findings. Erdelyi (1940) considered the relationship between the plugging of 20 records on the radio and sales of the sheet music. There was an inverted-U relationship between these, implying that as plugging increased listeners' familiarity with the records, so the popularity of the latter rose and then fell. It could be argued of course that this does not necessarily support Berlyne's theory: perhaps the radio stations were simply playing the records to *reflect* their current popularity with the general public such that liking was *causing* radio airplay rather than the opposite way around as Berlyne's theory would claim. However, this was not so. Erdelyi also found that, for 18 of the 20 songs, variations in 'plugging systematically precedes sales' (p.500) by approximately 13 days. In other words, increasing plugging and therefore familiarity seemed to *cause* changes in the popularity of the music, just as Berlyne's theory would predict. Jacobovits (1966) went a step further, and reasoned that if familiarity causes liking then the quicker that familiarity increases so the quicker that liking should rise and then fall: analysis of radio airplay was consistent with this, since the more heavily that songs were plugged on the radio so the more quickly their sales rose and then tailed off. It is also worth noting that a third study by Wiebe (1940) found that although radio plugging of songs did not affect liking ratings assigned to initially well-liked music, it did affect liking for songs that were initially less popular.

Interestingly however, in contrast to this general pattern of support for Berlyne's theory, Russell (1987) found that the appearance of a song in music sales charts was associated with greater familiarity with the music; but that this change in familiarity was not associated with changes in liking for the song in question, contrary to Berlyne's theory. Russell argued that this could be due to some form of self-regulating mechanism on the part of listeners by which they limit their exposure to a song once familiarity with it has become super-optimal. In short, although Russell shows that familiarity is linked to sales, the process by which this might occur goes well beyond the scope of Berlyne's theory.

In the meantime however, research such as this, although in limited quantity, serves as a powerful demonstration of the potential of factors such as complexity and familiarity to explain instances of musical preference in naturalistic settings. Furthermore, whereas laboratory research on musical preference can be criticized for addressing likes and dislikes over only the short-term period of the testing session, the kind of methodologies described here reflect the ability of Berlyne's theory to shed light on longer-term variations in preference that occur over a period of weeks. Clearly, however, much more work of this nature is required before we can be confident in the conclusions reached, and it is surprising that data from sales charts for instance has been so neglected in research on musical preference: they represent a weekly dataset of preferences of the magnitude that most researchers could only dream of.

3.1.2 **Subjective complexity and repetition**

It is worth going a step further and addressing one other aspect of musical preference that Berlyne's theory may be able to explain. Although there is very little research on this, particularly outside the laboratory, it is very tempting to consider the putative interaction between the familiarity of a piece of music and its subjective complexity. In broad terms, there are two ways of conceptualizing the complexity of a piece of music. One means is to use a measure of *objective* complexity. As we saw in Chapter 2, it is possible to characterize a piece of music in terms of the statistical probability of one note following another, relative to the entirety of Western music. For example in the key of C major, it is quite probable that an E will follow a C, whereas an F sharp would be less probable. It is then possible to add up all such probabilities across a piece of music and then produce a final objective 'complexity' figure for the piece as a whole.

Objective measures of complexity have the obvious advantage of being very precise and of allowing large quantities of music to be considered (by, for example, computerized analysis). However, there is an alternative approach to defining complexity that perhaps sits more comfortably with the social psychology of music. *Subjective* measures of complexity make little reference to the music itself, and instead concentrate on the degree of complexity that a listener *perceives* the music to possess. In short, the researcher just asks his or her participants how complex they think a piece of music is. Such an approach is inevitably less precise, but also avoids the potentially unfounded assumption that the objective complexity inherent to a piece of music gives rise to a corresponding subjective experience on the part of the listener. The importance of this becomes apparent when we consider the interaction between the familiarity of a piece of music and its degree of subjective complexity.

As Heyduk (1975) argued, when a piece of music is new to a listener it, of course, possesses a lot of new information: every successive note tells the listener something new. However, with repeated exposure to the music, the listener knows that piece of music better. In other words, that piece of music becomes less unpredictable, it seems less erratic, and in layman's terms, the listener has a much better idea about what the music is going to do next. More formally, as familiarity increases so the objective complexity of the music remains unchanged but the subjective complexity of the music decreases. This approach to music allows for some detailed predictions concerning how repetition should affect liking for different pieces of music. If increasing familiarity leads to decreasing subjective complexity, so repeated listening to any piece of music should cause it to travel from right to left along the inverted-U between

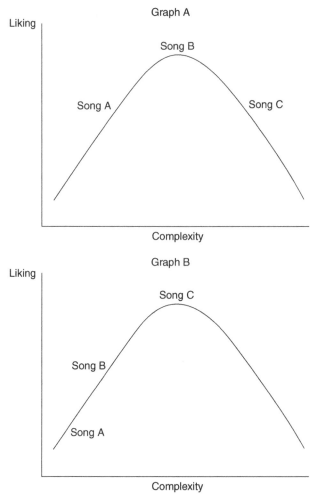

Fig. 3.2 The effects of repetition on liking for songs with different levels of complexity

liking and complexity. Figure 3.2 illustrates this point. Graph A shows the location of three songs on the inverted-U at the time when they are first heard. Song A contains *too little* complexity and is disliked. Song B contains a moderate level of complexity and so is positioned at the very peak of the inverted-U. Song C is disliked because it is *too complex*. Graph B shows what happens to the same three songs after they have been heard a few times. Increasing familiarity means that all three songs now possess less subjective complexity, and so they have travelled from right to left along the inverted-U. However, this journey has had a different effect on liking for the three songs. Song A is now even less popular now than it was at first. Song B is no longer at the peak of the inverted-U, and has instead slipped leftwards into dislike. In contrast, Song C has climbed up the inverted-U to the peak. Repeated exposure has reduced its level of subjective complexity to a degree that is liked.

Two naturalistic sources of evidence suggest that such a process may occur with regard to 'real' musical preferences over time. First, Simonton (1987) analysed 105 melodies by Beethoven in terms of their melodic originality, or the statistical probability of one note following another: as we noted above, this gives an impression of how unusual a particular melody is, and is effectively a measure of objective complexity. As Berlyne's theory would lead us to expect, Simonton found that Beethoven's moderately original works have proved to be most popular. However, crucially for the present argument, Simonton also found that those 15-20% of melodies that were just above Beethoven's average level of originality have tended to become regarded as his most significant work. In other words, Beethoven's slightly more complex pieces have been the most enduring. In short, the rather unusual Beethoven melodies that have come to be regarded as so important could well be regarded as his Song Cs: their slightly higher level of complexity has allowed them to withstand centuries of exposure.

Given this, it is also interesting to note corresponding evidence concerning arguably the greatest pop musicians of all time, The Beatles. In an unpublished study, Tuomas Eerola of the University of Jyväskylä took each of the songs from The Beatles' 12 UK albums, and used a computer to score each for complexity. He then calculated the overall complexity score for each album and compared that with the number of weeks it spent on the chart when it was first released. Figure 3.3 shows that, as with Simonton's evidence concerning Beethoven, Eerola's evidence on The Beatles again seems consistent with the relationship between liking, complexity, and familiarity. In short, the less complex an album was, so the more it enjoyed immediate popularity through a strong chart performance, but also failed to withstand the test of time: simple albums (e.g. *Please Please Me*) spent a great deal of time on the chart when first released but have arguably received comparatively little critical acclaim in the decades since. In contrast, the Beatles' more complex albums (e.g. *Abbey Road*) are the ones that, although they performed relatively badly on the charts when first released, have enjoyed the greatest degree of enduring popularity and critical acclaim since the 1960s. To express this in terms of Figure 3.2, albums like *Please Please Me* have behaved like Song Bs whereas albums like *Abbey Road* have behaved like Song Cs. Eerola produced the same effect when he looked at the performance of The Beatles' singles on both the UK and USA charts.

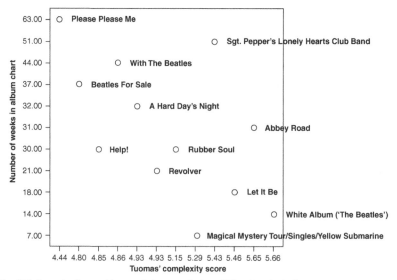

Fig. 3.3 Complexity and immediate popularity of The Beatles' albums

One other interesting aspect of Eerola's findings deserves further comment. Figure 3.3 shows that complex, challenging music is likely to lead to poor record sales in the short term. If such a phenomenon is borne out across pop music as a whole (and indeed perhaps all music) then this means that the financial pressures of the music industry are directly at odds with the notion of composers as innovators. Put simply, by the time that the public has realized that a particular piece of unusual music is good, the composer in question may have lost his / her recording contract because nobody bought the music in the few months following its initial release. Indeed, The Beatles released their most complex music, *The White Album*, on the back of the huge commercial and critical success of *Sgt Pepper's Lonely Hearts Club Band*. The album has ever since been arguably their most criticized. If The Beatles could not get away with their most challenging work immediately after the huge success of *Sgt. Pepper* then this begs the question of whether there is any hope for less acclaimed musicians who also wish to record unusual music. Clearly the sophistication of theorizing in this area far exceeds the quantity of naturalistic data available, and tests of Berlyne's theory utilizing variables such as CD sales are obviously warranted.

3.1.3 Preference for prototypes

In the 1980s and early 1990s Berlyne's theory began to be challenged by a new approach to musical preference based within cognitive psychology.

The preference for prototypes theory gained a great deal of attention since, as with Berlyne's theory, it also has an evolutionary basis. Imagine yourself as a primitive caveman returning home after a hard day's hunting through the gloom of an early evening blizzard. In the distance you hear a piercing shriek, and through the snowflakes you begin to discern something with matted orange hair running directly towards you at speed. Should you pick up your spear and attack? On the one hand, this object could be a woolly mammoth that intends to eat you for dinner: on the other hand, this object could be your wife who is angry because she made you your dinner three hours ago. If the object is a mammoth then attack would be a good idea since you could remove a threat to your genetic line and have plentiful food for your children: if the object is your wife then attack would clearly be a bad idea since it would end your prospects of further extending your genetic line. As is clear from this silly example, there are adaptive advantages of being able to classify objects in a speedy way. The preference for prototypes model is based on the notion that we should consequently prefer things that are classified easily.

Many studies in cognitive psychology have indicated that people classify stimuli by successfully matching them with an abstract schema, or 'prototype', representing the appropriate category (Posner and Keele, 1968; Reed, 1972). In other words, our everyday experiences are classified more easily if they correspond with a prototype for that kind of experience. These prototypes come about through experience of the world, so that through repeated exposures to exemplars of a category we learn what the prototype should be. To give an extreme example for the sake of clarity, light brown four-legged dogs are more typical of the category 'dog' than are bright pink three-legged dogs: the former possess the characteristics of dogs that are most typically experienced.

Although the preference for prototypes approach was first published by T.W.A. Whitfield from what was then Leicester Polytechnic (see Whitfield and Slatter, 1979; Whitfield, 1983), the theory is nowadays most closely associated with Colin Martindale (see e.g. Martindale and Moore, 1988). Martindale's version takes a neural network approach to the theory. He argues that the mind is composed of inter-connected cognitive units: each unit holds the representation of a different object. Units coding more prototypical stimuli are activated more frequently because it is these stimuli that are experienced most frequently. Therefore, units coding prototypical stimuli activate more strongly than do those coding atypical stimuli. Martindale and Moore (1988) then go on to claim that 'aesthetic preference is hypothetically a positive function of the degree to which the mental representation of a stimulus is activated. Because more typical stimuli are coded by mental representations capable of greater activation, preference should be positively related to prototypicality' (p. 661). More simply, although it has sometimes been argued that very low levels of prototypicality can also be enjoyed (e.g. Martindale, 1996), perhaps most of the occasions on which the preference for prototypes model has been operationalized have investigated simply whether preference increases with prototypicality: typical instances of any category should be preferred because they give rise to a stronger activation of the relevant cognitive representations.

Perhaps the most important aspect of research on preference for prototypes is the demonstration that the prototypicality of real-life artistic objects may be a stronger determinant of preference than their arousal-evoking qualities: this contrasts directly with Berlyne's (1971) claim that the collative variables (e.g. complexity, familiarity) are the 'most significant of all for aesthetics' (p. 69). Although the majority of research to date has concerned visual stimuli, the relevance of this to music is clear. If you listened to three songs on the radio you would probably like them to greatly differing degrees. Crucially however, these three songs will probably all be of a reasonably similar level of arousal potential. For example if you tuned in to a rock music station then all the songs will be loud and possess a fairly similar degree of melodic complexity as a result of a fairly simple verse and chorus, supplemented by a reasonably complex guitar solo. Instead what is likely to best distinguish which song you liked best is simply the extent to which each one sounded like the kind of music you usually listen to.

For example, in an early study, Moore and Martindale (1983) reported that colour typicality accounted for 79% of the variance in people's preference for random polygons, whereas complexity accounted for a meagre 1%. Similarly, Martindale, Moore, and Borkum (1990) reported seven experiments that investigated preference for polygons, line drawings, and paintings. Measures of the typicality of these consistently explained more of the variance in people's liking for them than did complexity. Martindale and Moore (1989) reported that complexity accounted for 4% of the variance in people's liking for classical music themes, whereas 51% was accounted for by typicality measures. Similar results are reported by e.g. Hekkert and van Wieringen (1990); Whitfield (1983); and Whitfield and Slatter (1979). Martindale, Moore, and West (1988, p. 94) argue that these results 'suggest that collative variables are probably a good deal less important in determining preference than Berlyne thought them to be. Furthermore, they probably determine preference via mechanisms different than those proposed by Berlyne.' Research on preference for prototypes continues in the present day (see some interesting examples by Farkas, 2002; Piters and Stokmans, 2000; Reber, Schwarz, and Winkielman, 2004; Whitfield, 2000).

We have argued however (North and Hargreaves, 2000a) that Berlyne's theory and the preference for prototypes model are by no means as incompatible as the existing research might imply. First, any attempt to assess the relative contribution of prototypicality and arousal-mediating variables will inevitably reflect the extent to which the art works vary in terms of those variables. In a set of works that vary considerably in terms of their complexity then there is plenty of scope for variations in complexity to account for differing preferences. In contrast, if the works in question vary very little in terms of complexity then it would be surprizing if complexity was able to explain differing preferences. Second, it is certainly arguable that the notion of prototypicality actually incorporates the Berlynian variables. For example, a fan of modern jazz is typically exposed to music with a high level of complexity. A fan of new age music is typically exposed to music with a low level of complexity. A fan of rock music or modern day dance music is typically exposed to fast tempi. In other words, a particular person's prototype of 'music' is imbued with factors that are crucial to Berlyne's theory also: Berlynian factors contribute to prototypicality, such that the two are not so different as they first appear. A third point follows from this. When considering the collative variables, Berlyne and other researchers have considered the extent to which music is unpredictable or erratic. Although the researchers at the time considered these factors in a 'cultural vacuum', it seems obvious that a piece of music can only seem unpredictable or erratic relative to a set of cultural expectations for how a piece of music should progress. For example a piece of Indian classical music might seem totally unpredictable or erratic to western ears but be really quite 'tame' to a listener familiar with the genre. In other words, the collative variables can only really be defined relative to a musical culture, or as we might put it instead, relative to the music to which a listener is typically exposed and for which he / she already has existing cognitive representations. In short, complexity has to be defined relative to a prototype. Finally, although he paid little attention to them relative to the collative variables, Berlyne's notion of ecological variables is also able to tap into the meaningfulness of a piece of music in just the same way as prototypicality can: although Berlyne favoured a psychobiological rather than a cognitive explanation for the effects, and believed the collative variables to be more important, both theories can accommodate any effects on liking caused by the meaningfulness of a piece of music.

Furthermore, it should be noted that the prototypicality model is itself problematic. In particular, the model starts to seem rather vague when it is used to make predictions regarding which of a set of songs should be liked most by a listener. In its raw form, the model would state simply that a listener should prefer the song that sounds most like the music he or she is usually exposed to. This of course seems all rather circular, since the model is effectively saying that we like music that sounds similar to music we like! Furthermore, the preference for prototypes model does not specify precisely which aspects of the music we respond to: in contrast, Berlyne's theory does at least say exactly what the most important aspects of music actually are. Our perspective is that Berlyne's theory and the preference for prototypes model *both* have something to offer.

More generally, the emphasis on strict experimental methods within experimental aesthetics has had three significant consequences that mean the field is unlikely to provide a complete explanation of musical preference in everyday life. First, research on experimental aesthetics has almost completely ignored the role of lyrics. It seems absurd to ignore the probability that the libretto of an opera or the lyrics of a pop song will impact upon listeners' preferences, but the existing research (including our own) does just this. Second, because it is confined to the lab, experimental aesthetics has inevitably had to focus on short-term preferences between particular pieces of music. The field has little to say, at least in a way that can be supported by data, about longer-term preferences. We saw in Chapter 2 that Simonton's work on originality could explain the eminence of composers in a manner consistent with Berlyne's theory; and Martindale's work on the clockwork muse could explain the evolution of music over time in terms of the need for novelty and arousal: it is unfortunate that so little work has taken a similar approach. Furthermore, as we will see in the remainder of this chapter and in Chapter 4, other approaches have had to be used to explain preferences held over the longer term and which reflect liking not for individual pieces of music but instead for entire musical styles and subcultures (which some authors have referred to instead as instances of musical *taste* rather than *preference*). Finally, and most importantly for us here, the reductionist approach adopted by experimental aesthetics means that it is blind to some of the more obvious sociocultural factors that shape musical preferences in the modern day. For example if you were to consider this week's music sales chart it would be very surprizing if the number 1 single and the number 111 single really differed that much in terms of either their arousal potential or their typicality of the music that the target audience usually listens to: so why should sales of the number 1 so heavily outweigh the sales of the number 111? A far more likely explanation for the differing sales performance would focus on radio airplay and a host of other social psychological factors. We discuss the role of the music industry itself in shaping the record buying behaviour of the general public in Chapter 5. In the meantime, although the ability to produce well-defined theories via experimental data is a considerable attraction of experimental aesthetics, other more social psychological factors need to be considered if we are to understand people's everyday musical likes and dislikes.

3.2 The listening situation

In Chapter 1, we noted that recent years have given rise to an increasing trend towards the recognition of social context in musical behaviour. Nowhere has this been demonstrated more literally than in research on musical preference, since a number of studies have investigated the impact of the immediate physical listening environment on musical likes and dislikes. Some of this work has been carried out in the context of experimental aesthetics, and has adopted both arousal- and typicality-based approaches to explaining why musical preferences vary from one place to another. Other work has focused on the people who are present in the immediate environment in addressing how musical preferences can be influenced by the opinions of others.

3.2.1 Konečni's arousal-based approach

There are several obvious problems with the 'classic' methodology of experimental aesthetics, outlined above, in which students are played specially-composed music under lab conditions. The most obvious is that the 'music' used in the research simply does not sound like music as most people know it. It is certainly debatable whether responses to monophonic melodic lines played (and sometimes composed) by a computer really do reflect responses to actual pop songs or other types of 'real' music. Similarly, whether undergraduates' responses to music reflect those of the population as a whole is by no means certain. Finally, and most significantly, we listen to music in a range of listening situations and not just the laboratory. In the modern world we hear music in cars, restaurants, while doing housework, and in just about any other setting in which it is possible to either be within range of a loudspeaker or wear a pair of earphones. In short, the 'classic' method may provide a great deal of reliable information about how undergraduates react to computer-generated music in a lab, but still tell us very little about how 'real' people react to 'real' music in 'real' situations.

Some psychologists interested in musical preference have faced up to criticisms such as these, and attempted to address the immediate context in which music listening occurs. We saw in Chapter 1 for example that Konečni (1982) has argued very persuasively that 'the vast majority of research studies … have treated aesthetic preference and choice as if they, and the process of appreciation itself, normally occur in a social, emotional, and cognitive vacuum, as if they were independent of the contexts in which people enjoy aesthetic stimuli in daily life' (p. 498). Konečni points out that music is something enjoyed 'in the stream of daily life ... while working, talking, eating, engaging in sexual intercourse ... What music does to people at different times, why they choose to listen to it so much, why they choose a particular type of music while engaged in a particular activity—all of these are important and unanswered questions' (p. 500).

Konečni fully embraced Berlyne's notion of the importance of moderate levels of arousal potential, but addressed also an additional source of this. Whereas Berlyne focused exclusively on arousal evoked by music, Konečni addressed arousal evoked by music *and* arousal evoked by the immediate context in which it is experienced. He argued that the listener sums arousal from both sources and selects music that will bring about, *overall*, a moderate level of arousal. For instance, a listener in a highly arousing context should choose to listen to simple music: the low complexity of the music would counteract the arousing qualities of the listening context. Similarly, if a listener is in a boring situation then he/she should choose to listen to complex music: the high complexity of the music would counteract the lack of arousal from the listening context. Konečni argued that a full feedback loop exists such that changes in the listener's mood as a result of listening to music are reflected in their behaviour. These changes in behaviour influence the listening context, and in turn the listener may change the music he or she listens to. More simply, Konečni conceives the musical and non-musical worlds as in a state of continuous interaction. As such, his research considers music listening as an episode that evolves over time rather than an isolated event that exists at one particular point in time.

Research by Konečni, Crozier, and Doob (1976) provides a good illustration of the kind of method employed and findings produced. At the beginning of the experiment, some of the participants were insulted by a confederate of the experimenter, placing them in a state of high arousal. In the main part of the research, each participant took part in 50 separate trials in each of which they could choose to listen to one of two types of computer-generated melody. One of the melodies was of high complexity whereas the other was of low complexity. Before this, however, the participants were divided into three groups. Participants in the 'annoy-wait' group were insulted, but before listening to the music they were asked to wait alone in a room. When then asked to choose between the two types of melody, they preferred the simple ones, choosing to listen to them on approximately 70% of the trials. They used the simpler melodies to counteract the high arousal caused by being insulted. The 'no annoy-wait' group had not been insulted, were not therefore in a state of high arousal, and when asked to choose between the two types of melody they showed no preference between them. Finally, the researchers employed an 'annoy-shock' group. Before choosing between the melodies, this group of participants were given the opportunity to issue what they believed were electric shocks to the confederate who had insulted them initially. Although these people were subject to an increased level of arousal as a consequence of the insult, the opportunity to retaliate would have reduced this arousal again by allowing them to 'let off steam'. Accordingly it was unsurprizing that when subsequently asked to choose between the two types of melodies the 'annoy-shock' group had no discernable preference. Overall, 'The findings ... show that a socially induced change in a listener's emotional state may strongly affect that person's aesthetic choice' (Konečni, 1982, p. 503).

Konečni and Sargent-Pollock (1976) reached similar conclusions. Since humans have a limited information processing capacity, Konečni and Sargent-Pollock therefore predicted that arousing music should reduce the amount of processing capacity that can be allocated to a concurrent task. The process is directly analogous to the functioning of a modern PC. If you play an mp3 file of a song then this reduces the amount of memory that the CPU can devote to running any other package, and the latter will run more slowly. In a similar vein, Konečni and Sargent-Pollock found that when participants carried out complex mental tasks while simultaneously listening to music, they tended to choose to listen to simple rather than complex melodies. It seems as though the participants were deliberately selecting simple, undemanding music to allow them to compensate for the demands of the cognitive task. It is interesting that, in a similar vein, North and Hargreaves (1999a) asked participants to complete five laps of a motor racing computer game. While doing this, they were forced to listen to either a loud, fast (i.e. arousing) or slow, quiet (i.e. less arousing) version of the same piece of music. Also, in some conditions participants were asked to count backwards in intervals of three, and this of course made the task even more demanding. Consistent with Konečni's arguments, lap times were slowest when participants heard the arousing version of the music and counted backwards; whereas the lap times were quickest when participants heard the less arousing music and did not have to count backwards: music and the concurrent task competed for information processing resources. Note also that the additional cognitive demand of counting backwards led to participants liking the music less: it became an irritating distraction rather than a pleasing diversion.

Konečni (1975) however perhaps provides the best demonstration of the continuing interaction between music and the listening environment over the course of an entire listening episode. As in the study by Konečni, Crozier, and

Doob (1976), some participants were insulted at the beginning of the experiment in order to increase their level of arousal. However, each participant's level of arousal was then manipulated further by playing participants melodies that varied in terms of their loudness and complexity. After both manipulations, participants were then given the opportunity to supposedly give electric shocks to the confederate who had earlier insulted some of them. Non-insulted participants administered the smallest number of electric shocks and, generally speaking, this occurred irrespective of the music they had heard. However, the number of 'shocks' given by participants who had been insulted was directly in line with the theory. The greatest number were given by participants who also heard loud, complex music, and the fewest were given by participants who had heard the quiet, simple music. Indeed, this latter group of participants in some cases were less aggressive than the participants who had not been insulted at all: the calming nature of the music was able to completely override the arousal caused by the insults and have a positive influence on subsequent behaviour.

Findings such as this appear to confirm Konečni's claim that we are 'engaged in a constant exchange with the social and nonsocial environment, of which the acoustic stimuli are a part' (Konečni, 1982, p. 501), and can explain a variety of everyday musical experiences. For example, Konečni's model can explain why we turn down the car radio when we come into heavy traffic: in psychological terms we are reducing the cognitive/arousal load from the music in an attempt to compensate for the additional load imposed by the traffic conditions. Similarly we turn up the car radio on long journeys in an attempt to boost our arousal to counteract the boredom of the drive. Konečni's findings also mirror the conclusions of some of the research on music and task performance that we shall consider in Chapter 5: for example, it might be a bad idea to listen to music while reading a textbook as the music reduces the cognitive capacity that can be devoted to the latter. Finally, it is worth noting that Konečni's discussion of arousal induced by the environment is by no means unique. Mehrabian and Russell's (1974) model of environmental psychology deals explicitly with how responses to a particular place can be shaped via an interaction between the pleasantness and arousal-evoking qualities of that place (which may of course include pleasure and arousal from whatever music is played there). As we shall see in Chapter 5, some early research of this nature has been promising.

There are also two notable criticisms of Konečni's research. First, while recognizing the limitations of lab-based studies, the research was nevertheless carried out under laboratory conditions. Although these conditions were clearly intended to model naturalistic music listening, many would still no doubt have qualms about their ecological validity (although a counterargument would be that the methods used represented a necessary compromise between the scientific rigour of experimental psychology and the kind of arguments that Konečni himself proposed). Second and more importantly, intuition suggests that Konečni's model may not be a perfect explanation of how the listening situation itself mediates musical preferences. The most obvious manifestation of this is in a modern nightclub. If you are dancing vigorously with a large group of friends then it would be surprizing if you were in anything but a state of high arousal. Konečni's model therefore predicts that the nightclubs that should be most successful would be the ones playing slow, quiet music that would reduce patrons' arousal to a moderate level. This clearly is not the case as nightclubs play loud, fast music that would further polarize their customers' level of arousal. Similarly if it is late and you are about to go to bed you would be in a state of low arousal. Konečni's model therefore predicts that there should be little you would like more than a blast of heavy rock to raise your arousal back up to a moderate level. Again, this almost certainly would not be the case in actuality. In other words it is certainly debatable whether people *always* choose to use music as a means of *moderating* their level of arousal. Furthermore, Konečni's model cannot explain why most brides in the UK come down the aisle to Mendelssohn's *Wedding March*. It would be amazing if there were any unique arousal-evoking qualities of the music that could explain its popularity. Indeed, most of the well-known requiems possess a fairly similar degree of arousal potential to the *Wedding March* but are never used at weddings. In short, the idea of arousal moderation has a great deal to offer but it simply cannot explain everything.

3.2.2 Appropriateness, typicality, and arousal-based goals

Konečni noted himself that 'I am not denying the importance of other factors that may affect aesthetic choice, including ... the appropriateness of listening to a particular piece of music in a given situation' (1982, p. 501). This is particularly interesting given more recent research that has considered the appropriateness of a piece of music for a particular listening situation within the preference for prototypes framework. One possibility is that appropriateness might be characterized as the extent to which a particular piece of music is *typical* of that usually played in the situation in question. For example, maybe the reason why the *Wedding March* is so popular is because it fits perfectly with the prototype of the music played at weddings. This massive clue as to how the situation should be classified should in turn give rise to maximal pleasure among guests. This hypothetical relationship between liking for music and its appropriateness for the listening context was confirmed in North and Hargreaves' (1996b) study in aerobics and yoga classes. As well as rating the music for liking and complexity, participants in the classes were also asked to rate how appropriate each piece was and this was defined as the extent to which it was typical of the music usually played in the class. In both the aerobics and yoga classes, ratings of liking and appropriateness were correlated positively in support of the theory; and the relationship between liking and appropriateness was just as strong as that between liking and complexity.

The possibility remains however that people will always prefer arousal-mediating music. In short, perhaps nightclubs foist arousal-polarizing music on people when really they would prefer to listen to arousal-moderating music, consistent with Konečni's model. Two further studies were carried out to test this. North and Hargreaves (1996c) presented 393 undergraduates with a brief verbal description of one of 17 different music listening situations (e.g. 'Washing the dishes', 'Early on Sunday morning', 'Your parents have come to visit'). They were then asked to rate the extent to which the music they would like to hear in those situations should possess each of 27 different characteristics. These ratings were very consistent within situations (indicating consensus in participants' judgements), but they varied considerably between different situations: musical preferences varied according to the listening environment. However, the pattern of preferences did not correspond with Konečni's model. For example, situations that seemed to be arousing (e.g. 'Jogging with your Walkman on', 'At an end-of-term party with friends') were associated with a preference for musical descriptors that would increase arousal further (e.g. 'invigorating', 'exciting/ festive', 'loud'). In contrast, ratings assigned to situations that represented a low degree of arousal (e.g. 'late at night before going to bed') were linked to a preference for musical descriptors that would reduce arousal further (e.g. 'relaxing / peaceful', 'lilting', 'quiet'). In short, it seems that the participants, far from following an arousal-moderation strategy, instead preferred music that would further polarize the degree of arousal endemic to several listening situations. But even though participants were not following an arousal-moderating strategy, a factor analysis showed that an 'arousal' factor was the most important in explaining participants' ratings. It seemed that arousal was important in everyday listening situations, but not in the way that Konečni predicted.

North and Hargreaves (2000b) carried out two experiments to investigate this further. The first was intended to mirror Konečni's research. Participants were asked to either ride an exercise bike or to lie down on some bedding and try to relax. The former of course induced a high level of arousal whereas the latter induced a low level. After doing this, participants could choose between listening to a loud, fast (i.e. arousing) or slow, quiet (i.e. much less arousing) version of the same piece of music. Consistent with Konečni's research, people preferred the music that would moderate the level of arousal resulting from their earlier activity. People who had ridden the exercise bike preferred the slow, quiet version of the music, whereas people who had relaxed preferred the loud, fast version: they were arousal-moderating. The second experiment differed from the first in only one respect. This time participants were asked to choose between the two types of music *while* they either rode the exercise bike or relaxed. This time people's preferences were almost the exact opposite of those in the first experiment. This time people who were exercising preferred the loud, fast music whereas people who were relaxing preferred the slow, quiet music. The most obvious explanation for these two sets of results centres around participants' goals. In the second experiment, participants were trying to achieve a particular arousal-based goal: people on the exercise bike had the goal of achieving a high level of arousal, whereas people who were relaxing had the goal of achieving a low level of arousal. They chose music that would further polarize their arousal because it would help them to achieve these goals. In contrast, participants in the first experiment had already finished exercising/relaxing by the time they came to listen to music. As such they had no incentive to remain in a state of polarized arousal: consequently they chose arousal-moderating music to help them 'get back to normal'.

This notion of arousal-based goals may well be able to explain much of the anecdotal evidence we have reviewed so far. For example, arousal-based goals can explain why we like loud, fast music in nightclubs: it further increases our level of arousal and generally adds to the 'party atmosphere' that we are trying to create. In contrast, before going to bed we prefer quieter, gentle music because we want to be in a state of low arousal that will help us to sleep. When driving a car in heavy traffic we have no particular arousal-based goal and so we switch to a default strategy of using music to moderate situational arousal. Indeed, it is tempting to speculate that a piece of music becomes typical for a particular situation since, to some extent at least, it helps us to achieve a particular level of arousal. (See also Apter (1984) on how cognitive factors mediate preferred arousal levels; and Martindale, Moore, and Anderson (2005) on the precise mechanism by which variables such as the listening situation might influence preference.)

As with the more theoretical debate between Berlyne's theory and the preference for prototypes model that we reviewed earlier, research on the listening situation indicates that in practical terms it is difficult to favour explanations based on arousal rather than typicality or vice versa. Furthermore, the precise means by which these variables have their influence in everyday listening situations is certainly at variance with how the original authors described them.

For example, people do not always use music to bring about a *moderate* level of arousal, but arousal nevertheless seems to be a key factor in determining the use of music to achieve particular goals. Similarly, people do like music that is prototypical of that usually heard in a particular listening context; but arousal is probably a major (although not the only) factor in determining whether music comes to be perceived as prototypical in the first place.

It is surprizing and a real shame that there is so little research on the application of experimental aesthetics to everyday musical preference. As the research here shows, the existing theories have the potential to explain a great deal of how 'real' people react to 'real' music heard in 'real' listening situations. It is worth noting a few other points also. First, it seems likely that the appropriateness of music for a particular place *causes* it to be liked, rather than *vice versa*. If liking caused music to be perceived as appropriate then an upbeat song such as *She Loves You* by The Beatles would be considered appropriate for even a solemn situation such as a funeral! Second, although we are confident that arousal plays a part in determining the appropriateness of a piece of music for a particular place, other factors must be important also. The hymns played in Christian places of worship are often musically uplifting, and promote an upbeat, happy atmosphere: if the arousal-evoking qualities of the music were all that mattered then precisely the same effect could be achieved by playing congregations disco music! Clearly we need to look at other factors also such as lyrics, the perception of appropriate instrumentation, and prejudices regarding musical styles. Third, people can only listen to appropriate music if it is actually possible to access it: but portable mp3 players with massive storage capacities allow people to access pieces from an enormous library of music wherever they may be, with obvious implications for future research. Fourth, it seems likely that, although people like music that is appropriate for the place in which it is played, this will not be the case if the music is so appropriate as to be hackneyed or 'cheesy'. For example, one of us recently visited Istanbul's beautiful Roman cistern, Yerebatan Saray Sarniçi, which played Handel's *Water Music* quietly in the background. Fifth, research is needed to determine specifically the extent to which situational factors can override personal preferences: would jazz fans prefer Chet Baker to be played at weddings for example, or would a rock fan dare to play Metallica while attempting to woo someone over a candlelit dinner? Finally, people often refer to 'background' music, meaning unimportant melodies that play while some other activity is being carried out. Although this music might not be the focus of attention, the research described here shows it clearly is anything but unimportant; and can influence our behaviour and our ability to get what we want from the listening situation.

3.2.3 **Compliance and prestige**

It would be foolish of course to believe that theories concerning arousal and prototypicality can explain everything about the effects of the listening situation on responses to music. In particular, research carried out predominantly in the 1970s highlighted the importance of compliance and prestige effects. Although operating outside the context of the theories outlined earlier in this chapter, both sets of studies undoubtedly demonstrate another aspect of the immediate listening situation that may influence responses to music.

Experimental research on conformity characterizes this as taking two distinct forms (see e.g. Levine and Russo, 1987). On the one hand are compliance effects. These arise because individuals value their membership of a particular social group. If our own opinions correspond with those of other group members then we expect to be rewarded (for example, by increased status within the group), whereas if our opinions do not correspond with those of other group members then we expect some form of social punishment (such as decreased status). In practical terms, an example of this might be a teenager saying that he or she likes a particular song just because a friend does. The other type of conformity might be termed 'informational influence'. In practical terms, this occurs when we have little or no knowledge of the music in question, and so instead we base our judgements on whatever information is available. An example of this is Mark Twain's joke with which this chapter began: if someone is told that a piece of music they don't know is by Mozart then they will probably like it more than if they are told it is by an undistinguished composer.

There are only four studies of compliance in musical judgements, and although these do not provide universal support for the notion, there is some indication that listeners will indeed 'go along' with the musical judgements of the majority, even when these judgements would seem to be clearly incorrect. Radocy (1975) played each participant a so-called 'standard' tone before then playing three comparison tones, of which one was the same pitch or loudness as the standard. Participants simply had to say which of the three options was the same as the standard tone. This basic task was repeated over 18 trials. However, before giving his or her answer, the participant first heard the answer of four other people. These four other people were, unknown to the participant, confederates of Radocy who had been instructed to all give the same, *incorrect* answer on certain critical trials. The participants complied with the incorrect judgement of the confederates on 30% of the trials involving judgements of pitch and 49% of those trials involving judgements of volume. These high compliance rates are all the more remarkable for the fact that Radocy's participants were all music students who would of course have regularly made judgements of pitch and volume.

The three remaining studies provide more direct evidence concerning specifically musical preferences. Furman and Duke (1988) used a very similar methodology to Radocy (1975). They found no evidence of compliance in the preferences of music and non-music major students concerning pop music. However when orchestral music was used then the preferences of non-music majors were subject to compliance effects. Of course, students who were not specializing in music might well be expected to be less confident when making judgements of orchestral music since they would be comparatively unfamiliar with it. Interestingly a similar finding is reported by Inglefield (1968). In this study, compliance was greatest for preferences for jazz, which again is a musical style that the ninth-grade participants would be expected to be unfamiliar with. Furthermore, in support of the notion that compliance arises out of a need for approval from a group, Inglefield also found that compliance was greater among participants who scored highly on measures of 'other-directedness', need for social approval, and dependency. In addition to musical preference, findings such as these have implications for the assessment of musical performance: when more than one person is judging an exam or an audition then their assessments must be made confidentially.

Finally, Crowther's (1985) research employed an interesting methodological development that could be easily applied by present-day researchers using computers. Crowther asked each participant to listen to one of four types of music, two of which would be liked by the participants (namely disco and rock 'n' roll) and two of which would be disliked (namely heavy metal and reggae). While they listened to the music, the participants could see a panel of lights that supposedly showed what other participants were listening to. Crowther then manipulated the read out on this panel so that it showed that the majority of participants were supposedly listening to the disliked music. The consequence of this was that the participants actually did start listening to the disliked music. Crowther considered these findings in terms of what he called minority influences on musical preference. The supposed listening preferences of the other participants were a minority influence that was able to overcome the majority influence of the individual participant's normative musical tastes.

Indeed, the phenomenon of minority influence on musical preference was investigated directly by Aebischer, Hewstone, and Henderson (1984). They drew on research in experimental social psychology showing that if a minority consistently argues an alternative position then it can win round the opinion of a majority; and that this is because the majority group will shift its judgement in order to try to avoid social conflict. Pupils at a French high school were asked to state their preference for either hard rock or new wave music and then to state their preference for either hard rock or 'contemporary music'. In both cases, hard rock was the pupils' clear favourite. The participants were then shown the supposed results of a survey regarding these musical styles. In one condition, the survey showed that pupils at their *own* school preferred new wave over hard rock. As we would expect from the research on compliance reviewed above, this majority influence led to greater liking for new wave. However in the other condition the survey showed that pupils at a *different*, lower status school preferred new wave over hard rock. This also led to an increased preference for new wave and the authors argued that this was an example of minority influence. Pupils at another school were effectively members of a different social group: the participants could not hope to be rewarded by these people for sharing similar preferences, yet still they still shifted their opinion.

Moscovici and Lage (1976) have argued that changes in opinions due to minority influence are stronger and more enduring than changes due to majority influence: this is because minority influence causes people to completely re-think the very bases of their judgements, such that they change their beliefs rather than just their behaviour. In the light of this it is interesting that Aebischer et al. also found an indirect effect of the results of the fake 'survey' on participants' responses. This survey described a general preference for new wave over hard rock, but said nothing about liking for contemporary music. Nevertheless, after seeing the survey, participants' preferences for contemporary music over hard rock also shifted in favour of the former. It is as though the participants understood the more indirect implication that hard rock was *generally* disliked, and shifted their preferences away from it. The effect of this indirect evidence on liking for contemporary music was of course weaker than the effect of the direct evidence on liking for new wave music. Nevertheless, the indirect effect on liking for contemporary music did occur and, crucially, it was *greater* when it resulted from the survey supposedly emanating from another school (i.e. a minority influence) rather than from the participants' own school (i.e. a majority influence). A finding like this is consistent with Moscovici and Lage's (1976) notion that changes in opinions resulting from minority influence should be stronger than those resulting from majority influence: when participants were exposed to the *minority* influence concerning liking for new wave over hard rock, this was more likely to generalize into a reduction in liking for hard rock compared to other musical styles. It is worth noting that similar effects were found by Mugny, Gachoud, Doms, and Perez's (1988) research on preferences for visual figures (see also Doise, Gachoud, and Mugny, 1988).

The second type of conformity is informational influence. As we noted earlier, these so-called 'prestige effects' occur when people have little or no knowledge of the music in question and so instead base their opinion on whatever information they are able to glean from other sources. Although there was earlier research concerning paintings and prose (see Farnsworth and Beaumont (1929) and Sherif (1935) respectively), the first study involving music is still perhaps the best known and a good example of the typical findings and methodology. Rigg's (1948) research was carried out just prior to the outbreak of the Second World War. Participants were played six pieces of music, which included three by Wagner, and asked to rate how much they enjoyed each. The music was then played again, but this time one group was told that Wagner was one of Hitler's favourite composers, a second group was told nothing, and a third group received a description of the music in romantic terms. After this second listening, participants' enjoyment ratings increased in all three groups, but this increase was smallest in the 'Hitler' group and greatest in the 'romantic' group. In other words, judgements were coloured by the information that people were given concerning the music. Similarly Alpert (1982) found that approval of classical music by a music teacher and a disc jockey 'increased classical music preferences and listening.' (p. 173) among fifth-grade school pupils; and Fiese (1990) found that misattributions of four musical pieces to Beethoven and Strauss could influence conducting students' judgements of which pieces were of better quality. Similar findings are reported by Chapman and Williams (1976; but see also Brittin, 1991), Castell and Hill (1985), Duerksen (1972), Radocy (1976), and Weick, Gilfillan and Keith (1973); and Geiger (1950) provides some evidence that such effects may occur in the 'real world': he describes how a radio programme of 'popular gramophone music' received only half the original audience when it was repeated a week later as a programme of 'classical music'.

The now rather dated literature concerning prestige effects on responses to music and the arts in general has been reviewed extensively by Hargreaves (1986) and Crozier and Chapman (1981) respectively; and the general pattern of findings supports the existence of prestige effects in responses to music. However, Crozier and Chapman argue that prestige effects across the arts as a whole are sometimes small, unstable, and difficult to replicate, and that there are several limitations to their scope. For instance, there seems to be less scope for them to occur in relation to familiar (rather than unfamiliar) works. Furthermore, the way in which the art works are labelled seems crucial, as is the extent to which participants pay attention to them (or try to deliberately ignore them) when making their judgements. There are also methodological problems with the existing research. In particular, individual differences have been ignored almost completely, even though factors such as suggestibility (Gudjonsson, 1984) or field independence (see below) could clearly mediate the extent to which a given person is susceptible to prestige effects. Perhaps most importantly of all, there is scant research concerning *how* prestige effects occur. Crozier and Chapman (1981) suggested that manipulating the information provided about a piece of music changes not just participants' enjoyment of that music but also more fundamental aspects of the way it is perceived. Future research may also investigate whether attribution theory can explain prestige effects (e.g. Heider, 1958; Kelley, 1973; Weiner, 1986): favourable information concerning a piece of music ought to increase the perception that the composer's ability is caused by internal factors, and is stable and global. Before moving on we should also note that prestige and conformity effects may well explain the arguments made in Chapter 2 concerning the lack of females in lists of the recognized 'great' composers; and they may also explain the evidence reviewed there concerning the impact of attractiveness on the evaluation of the performer.

3.3 **The listener**

We move on now to consider aspects of the listener that mediate musical preferences and tastes. In particular, we address socio-economic status, age, sex, personality, and the effects of musical training. Perhaps most conspicuous by virtue of its absence from this list is research on ethnicity. As Christenson and Roberts (1998, p. 87) argue, effects relating to this have not been researched a great deal because they 'are too obvious to question'. This may or may not be true in the USA (see section 2.2.2 in Chapter 4 which deals with whether racism is identifiable in music videos and section 3.4.3 of Chapter 4 which deals with whether exposure to pop music can cause racism). However, our experiences in the UK mean that we are less confident than Christenson and Roberts that the link between ethnicity and musical preference is quite so clear in Europe, for example. Nor is the link between ethnicity and musical preference necessarily as clear-cut as a 'musical apartheid' argument might suggest. For example, McCrary's (1993, p. 200; see also Bryson, 1996) research found that 'the Black listeners showed statistically significant differences in their music preferences for White and Black performers. These listeners gave stronger preference ratings when they identified the performer's race as Black. White listeners' preference ratings, however, were virtually equal for the Black and White performers.' Whether this finding would be replicated in the modern-day, in Europe, using different musical styles, or using different methodologies is impossible to tell, but the clearest message to emerge from research such as McCrary's is that existing knowledge of ethnic identity and prejudice might well contribute to our understanding of musical preference. We should also make a second general point concerning research on the listener. Whereas research on experimental aesthetics and the listening situation tends to focus on *short*-term preferences between different specific *pieces* of music, research on the listener tends to focus more on *long*-term likes and dislikes for musical *styles and genres* (i.e. what some researchers have termed musical 'taste' rather than 'preference').

3.3.1 Social class, taste publics, and massification

During the 1960s and 1970s, sociologists working on the 'mass culture hypothesis' carried out a considerable amount of research concerning the role of social class in differentiating musical preferences. Researchers interested in 'massification' argued that the music industry can minimize financial risks by ensuring maximal homogeneity in popular culture. In the name of increasing profits, the music industry avoids taking risks with new forms of music and musicians, and instead tries to sell the same type of music to the greatest number of people possible for the longest amount of time possible. Such a process leads to stagnation, a downturn in artistic standards, and a massification of musical taste. Other researchers, however, reacted to this and argued that western musical culture is instead characterized by diversification rather than massification. Perhaps the best known advocate of such an approach is Bourdieu (1971, 1984; see also DiMaggio and Useem, 1978; Francès, 1967). He contended that a proper sociology of art must address the relationship between a piece of art, its producer, and the various institutions in the 'field of production' in which cultural goods are created (e.g. conservatories, learned societies etc.). These institutions 'legitimize', or endorse, certain works and do not legitimize others, and this creates a two-tier artworld comprising 'high brow' and 'low brow' art respectively. The former obtains status through endorsement by supposedly discerning connoisseurs with access to the field of cultural production. In contrast, the existence of the latter is targeted towards consumption by a large proportion of the population and subsequent financial profit.

Bourdieu argued that individual listeners' own tastes depend on the extent to which they are members of those bodies that legitimize art and form the field of cultural production. For example, the professional, ruling classes endorse opera and so attend performances, whereas working classes are excluded from the endorsement process and must instead be content with 'low brow' music designed and marketed for the masses. In short, Bourdieu argues that our social background determines our tastes, and so sociological research has investigated how musical preferences reflect people's socio-economic status and their position within the social hierarchy. Indeed, Bourdieu's arguments are mirrored by Frith's (1990; see also 1978, 1981) work concerning specifically music. The latter distinguished between a bourgeois taste public and a commercial music world. For the former, music represents the opportunity for transcendent experience, but this opportunity exists only for those with the right sort of knowledge and interpretative skills. In contrast, the commercial music world stresses the financial profitability of music.

Quantitative research has used sociodemographic variables to categorize fans of certain musical styles into so-called 'taste publics'. These taste publics 'express values and standards of taste and aesthetics' (Fox and Wince, 1975, p. 199), such that they comprize groups of people who subscribe to a particular 'taste culture'. The research has been reviewed in some detail by Hargreaves (1986) and discussed by Shepherd (2003) and we will not repeat this here. However, it is worth describing just a few studies to illustrate the typical methods and pattern of findings.

Gans (1974), for example, identified five major American taste cultures, which could be arranged along a social class continuum, namely 'high culture', 'upper-middle culture', 'lower-middle culture', 'low culture', and 'quasi-folk low culture'. Consistent with Bourdieu's arguments, taste cultures were therefore rooted in social structure, and Gans stressed the importance of the educational attitudes and values of different socio-economic groups in this respect. Similarly, Fox and Wince (1975) identified five taste cultures among their sample of sociology undergraduates, namely 'jazz-blues', 'popular hits', 'folk music', 'rock-protest', and 'country and western'. The first, 'jazz-blues', taste public, for instance, was strongly related to hometown size (with membership related positively to size of town), religious preference (with members being predominantly atheists, agnostics and Jews, but not Catholics), and father's education and occupation (with membership being especially high amongst students whose fathers had a professional position). More generally, the two background variables that seemed to exert the strongest effects were religious preference and social class (see similar findings by Dixon, 1981; Gans, 1974; and Skipper, 1975).

Similar findings were reported following DiMaggio and Useem's (1978) survey of concert attendance in the USA. This showed that only 4% of blue-collar workers had attended a symphony orchestra concert during the past 12 months compared with 14% of managerial workers and 18% of professionals. Furthermore, attendance at classical music concerts was far more prevalent among people earning over US$15,000 per year and those with a university education than it was among those who earned less than US$5,000 or who had failed to complete high school. Pegg's (1984) survey of British concert attendance revealed a similar pattern of findings. People from upper-middle and middle classes were far more likely to attend classical music concerts than were others, whereas the audience of folk music concerts comprized predominantly middle- and working-class people.

The notion of taste publics and taste cultures has not gone without criticism, however. Zillmann and Gan (1997, p.172) argue that 'taste cultures are poorly defined. They are, for the most part, hypothetical constructs ... Surely, nobody is able to stake out the actual taste publics of heavy metal, reggae, or folk music.' Instead, Zillmann and Gan argue that taste publics are most important in that they are *thought* to exist, such that people who presume to belong to one will use clothing and behaviour to differentiate themselves from others. We will return to this point in Chapter 4. Second, 'patterns of legitimation' are constantly changing, such that what was perceived as 'low culture' can come to be perceived as legitimized 'high culture'. For example, Adorno's (e.g. 1941) work in the 1940s lumped together jazz and popular music: today, of course, jazz has been legitimized, and only the most conservative of commentators would regard it under the same heading as pop music. Third, although we would not deny Bourdieu's contention that it is important to understand the relationship between a piece of art, its producer, and the various institutions in the 'field of production' in which cultural goods are created, we would also add that any fuller understanding of music must also account for the mundane, everyday relationships between the music itself and the consumers of that music. In other words, research should address not only the means by which art is produced and legitimized, but also the means by which it is used by different people in different sociocultural contexts. For example, a school-boy may not publicly express his membership of a classical music taste public because he fears he will be bullied subsequently. Similarly, a woman may affect liking for classical music because she wishes to associate herself with the upper social class stereotype of this musical style. Fourth, it is important to remember that any given artistic product could be analysed as either 'high culture' or 'low culture', such that these labels cannot be applied uniquely to particular artistic products or domains. For example, classical music can be evaluated according to a lowbrow aesthetic (e.g. CD sales) as well as its art symbolic value, and the existence of magazines such as *NME* in the UK and *Rolling Stone* in the USA indicates that pop music can certainly be evaluated according to its art symbolic value as well as any commercial indicators of success. In short, the distinction between 'high culture' and 'low culture' resides, at least in part, within the evaluator and not within the artwork itself.

The common thread running through much of this criticism is that it is important to understand not just the production of art but also the users. Indeed, as Shepherd (2003, p. 74) argued, the research on taste publics 'operated only at the level of social groups. Little attention was paid to the social and cultural identities of individuals.' Evidence that the nature of these identities is complex would signal 'the distinct possibility that musical life has always been characterized by complex patterns of cross-fertilization and cultural hybridity' (Shepherd, 2003, p. 75). In short, an individual may represent elements of several taste publics. Indeed Shepherd goes on to cite Cohen's (1991, p. 6) argument that 'what is particularly lacking in the literature … is ethnographic data and micro-sociological detail' that would indicate this. Although a number of studies have investigated the detailed cultural and lifestyle backgrounds of individual musical movements (e.g. Crafts, Cavicchi, and Keil, 1993; Finnegan, 1989; Weinstein, 1991), it is unfortunate that research concerning micro-social differences between the fans of several musical styles is at best scarce.

In an attempt to investigate these issues, North and Hargreaves (2007a,b,c; see also Katz-Gerro, 1999; van Eijck, 2001) investigated differences in the socioeconomic status of 2,062 fans of 19 different musical styles. In addition to considering 'large scale' socio-economic factors such as employment, the research also considered micro-social indicators of socio-economic status. The results supported earlier research on taste publics in that fans of 'high art' music such as opera and classical music had higher incomes and were better educated, but this was manifested in numerous micro-social ways also such that they had greater access to financial resources (such as credit cards), paid off the greatest proportion of their credit card bill every month, spent the most money per month on food, were most likely to drink wine, and smoked and drank alcohol least. In turn this pattern of findings was consistent with other data (North and Hargreaves 2007a, 2007b) which showed that fans of classical music and opera also had other 'high art' media preferences and more conservative lifestyles and beliefs. However, a second group of fans also emerged from the analysis and the nature of their responses seems to support Shepherd's arguments concerning cross-fertilization between different taste publics. Specifically, there was a clustering of responses from fans of hip hop/rap, R&B, dance/house, and DJ-based music; and while many aspects of their lifestyle were indicative of the low socio-economic status background that might be predicted on the basis of Bourdieu's arguments, these fans also had some remarkably right-wing political attitudes. For example, these people had the least access to financial resources, paid off the smallest portion of their credit card bill every month, spent least on food every week, and had the lowest income, consistent with the notion of them being of low socio-economic status. However, these same fans were also least in favour of increasing taxes to pay for improved public services, and least in favour of retaining state-funded health care.

Given the apparent promise of research concerning lifestyle differences between fans of different musical styles, it is surprizing that so little was carried out subsequent to the initial studies on taste publics (see Hutchison and Wotring, 1993). Much of the existing research is outdated, and it is possible that taste publics no longer exist in many western societies. In particular, increasing globalisation in recent years may mean that tastes have indeed become massified (see e.g. Klein, 2001), and research concerning the inter-relationships between cultural/ethnic identity, social class, and musical preferences would be timely.

3.3.2 **Age**

Chapter 6 reviews the research concerning social psychological aspects of musical development, and for the time being we limit ourselves here to a consideration of age-related factors in specifically preference and taste. One way of considering links between age and musical preference is in terms of Berlyne's theory. This is naturally very appealing since it allows findings to be linked explicitly to one of the major theories in the literature, and it is consequently unfortunate that so little work has followed the lead of Hargreaves and Castell (1987). They argued that, because of enculturation, older people are more familiar with a range of musical pieces and styles. They then reasoned that the relationship between familiarity and subjective complexity set out in Figure 3.2 should therefore apply. That is, as people age, musical pieces and styles should move from right to left along an inverted-U. This means that pieces and styles that are too complex for children should be optimally complex for older people; and that pieces and styles that are optimally complex for children should be too simple for older people. Groups of participants in six age groups (4–5 years, 6–7 years, 7–8 years, 10–11 years, 13–14 years and 18+ years) rated their liking for four types of melody, which were selected so as to vary widely in their likely familiarity (nursery rhymes and carols, and little-known English folk song melodies respectively). The ratings of the familiar melodies showed an inverted-U relationship with increasing age, and the unfamiliar melodies showed a similar relationship to age, but crucially, with a later age-peak in liking. It is tempting to speculate that this explains why liking for classical music and jazz is so low among young people: perhaps they are not yet able to deal with the characteristically higher levels of complexity endemic to these musical styles.

3.3.2.1 Adolescence

LeBlanc (1991) has also attempted to explain the general pattern of development of musical preference across the life span. His approach was based on the concept of *open-earedness*, first proposed by Hargreaves (1982), which LeBlanc defined as 'listener tolerance' (p. 4) for a range of musical styles, and which was operationalized in terms of preference (see also Bryson, 1996). After a detailed review of the literature on the effects of maturation on changes in musical preference, LeBlanc proposed a model of the course of these which takes the form of four hypotheses, namely '(a) younger children are more open-eared, (b) open-earedness declines as the child enters adolescence, (c) there is a partial rebound of open-earedness as the listener matures from adolescence to young adulthood, and (d) open-earedness declines as the listener matures to old age' (p. 2). LeBlanc, Sims, Siivola, and Obert (1993) tested this model by obtaining preference judgements from 2,262 listeners aged between 6 and 91 years for 30-second recordings of 'art music', trad jazz, and rock. The general pattern of results conformed with the model for overall responses, as well as for responses within each of the three generic styles: there was an 'adolescent dip' in preference, followed by an increase towards adulthood, and a final decrease in preference in old age.

However, the study by LeBlanc et al. is limited in two important ways. First, musical styles were operationalized in terms of specific pieces: it is quite possible that participants in their study may have been responding to artefactual features of the pieces themselves as well as to the style from which they were drawn. Second, more importantly, participants were asked to respond to styles determined by the researchers: the adolescent 'dip' in liking that they found may be because adolescents *did* like music as much as the participants from other age groups, but simply not those styles presented by the researchers. Support for this notion is provided by Hargreaves and North (1999a) in which five age groups from across the life span were asked to nominate as many types of rock and pop, classical music, and jazz as they could. In addition to this, we also asked people to rate how much they liked each of the types they nominated using a 0-10 scale. Liking ratings assigned within each of the three styles showed the pattern we might expect, with younger people liking pop music more than older people, whereas the reverse pattern was shown for classical music and jazz. However, the average of ratings assigned to the three styles was essentially the same across all the age groups. In other words, liking for particular styles may differ between different age groups, but when people are free to respond to whichever types of music they choose to, it transpires that liking for music does not dip during adolescence, nor in any other age group.

What seems more probable is simply that different age groups may have their own musical preferences.

This conclusion is supported by research carried out since the early 1990s on people's judgements of musical eminence. For example, North and Hargreaves (1995a) recruited participants from five different age groups, namely 9–10 years, 14–15 years, 18–24 years, 25–49 years, and 50+ years. These people were all shown the same list of 200 pop groups and singers who had all enjoyed a number 1 single in the United Kingdom charts. Crucially, of these 200, 50 had had their first number 1 between 1955 and 1964, 50 had had their first number 1 between 1965 and 1974, 50 had had their first number 1 between 1975 and 1984, and 50 had had their first number 1 between 1985 and 1994. Participants were asked to choose up to 30 from the list 'who in your own personal opinion have performed music that deserves to be called to the attention of others'. The top nominations within each age group are shown in Table 3.1, in which two clear patterns are evident. First of all, a small number of 'golden greats' always do well. For example, whatever their age, everyone seemed to believe that The Beatles and Elvis Presley were eminent. However, the differences between the lists indicates a second pattern in people's nominations. In short, there was a tendency to select as eminent those artists who had their first UK number 1 single when the participants were themselves late adolescents/young adults. Late adolescence/early adulthood seems to be a sort of 'critical period' in which musical preferences become fixed.

Furthermore, North and Hargreaves (2002) investigated 12,502 nominations of the greatest pop musicians of all time gathered in response to a survey run by *The Guardian* newspaper, Channel 4 Television, and a major music retailer (HMV). Sales charts were used to determine the mean year in which people's nominated musicians achieved their first UK top 10 album. Again there was evidence for the late adolescence/early adulthood critical period. The musicians nominated by under 19-year-olds had their first UK top 10 album, on average, in 1990, whereas for 19–34-year-olds the corresponding date was 1983, for 35–54-year-olds the corresponding date was 1975, and for 55+ age group the corresponding date was 1971.

It is also interesting that the results of North and Hargreaves' two studies are consistent with earlier research by Holbrook and Schindler (1989, p. 119) who argued that 'the development of tastes for popular music follows an inverted U-shaped pattern that reaches a peak in about the 24th year' such that 'Preferences toward popular music appear to reflect tastes acquired during late adolescence or early adulthood'. Other research by the same authors concerning different stimuli has reached similar conclusions considering, for example,

Table 3.1 Top nominations for different age groups

	9–10-year-olds		14–15-year-olds		18–24-year-olds		25–49-year-olds		50+-year-olds
1	2 Unlimited	1=	The Beatles	1	The Beatles	1	The Beatles	1	The Beatles
2	Wet Wet Wet	1=	Madonna	2	U2	2	David Bowie	2	Simon & Garfunkel
3=	The Beatles	1=	Wet Wet Wet	3	Madness	3	Simon & Garfunkel	3=	Perry Como
3=	Elvis Presley	4	Elvis Presley	4	Elvis Presley	4	Elvis Presley	3=	Shirley Bassey
5	Pet Shop Boys	5	Bryan Adams	5	Eurythmics	5=	Eurythmics	3=	Cliff Richard
6=	Madonna	6	Whitney Houston	6	Madonna	5=	The Rolling Stones	3=	Harry Belafonte
6=	Michael Jackson	7	Haddaway	7	Jimi Hendrix	7	The Police	3=	Andy Williams
8	Ace of Base	8=	U2	8	The Police	8	Jimi Hendrix	8	The Shadows
9	Jazzy Jeff and The Fresh Prince	8=	Take That	9	George Michael	9	The Beach Boys	9	The Bachelors
10=	Take That / Janet Jackson	10	Ace of Base	10	The Rolling Stones	10	U2	10	Petula Clarke

preferences for movies (Holbrook and Schindler, 1996); the appearances of male and female movie stars (Holbrook and Schindler, 1994); males' preferences for automobile styles (Schindler and Holbrook, 2003); and men's tastes in female fashion models' personal appearance (Schindler and Holbrook, 1993). Holbrook (1995) found that a variety of preferences within 21 other categories such as novels, talk-show hosts, soft drinks, cereals, and toothpastes also tended to be formed during adolescence/early adulthood. Similarly, it is also worth noting Haack's (1988) data showing that nominations of the top 10 songs from between 1945 and 1982 showed a preference for music that was popular while participants were in their mid-20s (see also Rubin, Rahhal, and Poon, 1998; Schulkind, Hennis, and Rubin, 1999).

In their various papers, Holbrook and Schindler have proposed several possible explanations for this effect. The first is that the process is analogous to that which occurs during imprinting (a phenomenon in which young animals at a critical stage in their development form a strong and irreversible attachment to a parent), in that the late adolescence/early adulthood period represents a time of maximal sensitivity toward and liking for any music that we might hear. A second possible explanation they propose concerns the associations that form between particular songs and the many 'rites of passage' that occur at this stage of life. A third possible explanation concerns nostalgia, in that the music concerned was arguably more common or accessible, via for example radio airplay, when the participants were younger (although whether this argument still applies in the digital era is less clear). A fourth factor addressed by research to date concerns measures of what Holbrook and Schindler call 'nostalgia proneness' (e.g. agreement that 'Things used to be better in the old days' or disagreement with the notion that 'Things are getting better all the time'): preferences for movie stars and movies both showed an earlier age-related peak among nostalgia-prone participants than among those scoring lower on this variable. Finally, it is also worth repeating North and Hargreaves' (2002) argument that the peak in liking may occur not strictly for objects that first came to cultural prominence during late adolescence/early adulthood, but rather for objects that the participant him- or herself first became *aware of* during late adolescence/early adulthood: for example, it may still be possible to identify late adolescentearly adulthood peaks in liking for the music of the great classical music composers of the eighteenth and nineteenth centuries. Such a process may explain also why, irrespective of their age, people continue to regard The Beatles and Elvis Presley so highly: their music is present in the late adolescence/early adulthood of many people growing up in the Western world, irrespective of when this period of life actually occurred. Indeed it may be possible to link such a process to another of the main theories of musical preference, in that musical prototypes might become finalized during late adolescence/early adulthood, such that the late adolescence/early adulthood critical period is, in actuality, another manifestation of the preference for prototypes phenomenon (see Trehub and Unyk, 1991).

Direct evidence concerning these possible explanations is scant, however: we just don't know exactly why late adolescence/early adulthood might be so important, and this is an obvious candidate for research. In the meantime, however, we cannot resist pointing out that findings concerning the crystallization of musical taste during late adolescence/early adulthood might explain the common observation that 'today's pop music is rubbish compared with that of [insert year of your choice]'. It seems more accurate to argue that each generation simply has its own pop music that is not necessarily any better or worse than the pop music of any other generation. More generally, perhaps we will only really understand the development of musical taste across the lifespan through longitudinal studies that follow variations in taste in a single sample over the course of several decades. The cross-sectional studies that characterize the existing literature are assumed to provide *developmental* information: what they really provide is information on differences between age groups. As is clear from the above, the nature of these age differences is culture-dependent, and longitudinal research would minimize the effects of this. Longitudinal research would also be able to address one particular implication of research on the late adolescent / early adulthood critical period, namely that musical taste may not develop significantly in middle adulthood and old age.

3.3.2.2 Responses to music in early life

Musical preference in adulthood is not the only period of life that has been neglected. Although there is a reasonable literature concerning the musical behaviour of very young children (see reviews by Trehub, 2006; Trevarthen, 2002; and Chapter 6), recent research indicates that the origins of musical behaviour can be identified even earlier in life (see review by Parncutt, 2006). For instance, a series of studies by Peter Hepper and Sara Shahidullah has investigated the possibility that responses to music begin to develop in the mother's womb before birth (see also non-English language reports by Chen, Huang, Zhang, and Qi, 1994; Li, 1994; Salmaggi, la Torre, and Nicchia et al., 1989). Two experiments reported by Hepper (1991) illustrate the type of finding produced. Experiment 1 showed that newborns who had been exposed to the theme of a popular TV programme (*Neighbours*) during gestation exhibited changes in heart rate, number of movements, and behavioural state when they were played the same music two to four days after birth (although these effects disappeared by 21 days of age). In other words, the newborn babies recognized the music as something they 'remembered' having heard earlier. Experiment 2 found that foetuses between 29 and 37 weeks of gestational age exhibited changes in their movements when they were played a tune they had already heard earlier during pregnancy. In other words, the unborn children were able to demonstrate that they were 'remembering' music that they had heard even earlier. It is worth noting that the effects in both experiments were specific to the music heard previously rather than to any music: in other words, it seems that the foetus is not simply responding to an external stimulant, but has instead learnt on the basis of previous musical exposure.

Indeed, Shahidullah and Hepper (1993a) report that the foetus will first respond to acoustic stimulation at 20 weeks of gestational age, such that musical development may begin during mid-pregnancy (see also Hepper and Shahidullah, 1992; Shahidullah and Hepper, 1993b; Shahidullah and Hepper, 1994). Lecanuet, Graniere-Deferre, Jacquet, and DeCasper (2000) found that foetuses at 36-39 weeks could distinguish different piano notes and Shahidullah and Hepper (1994) found that foetuses at 35 weeks could better distinguish pure tone frequencies than could foetuses at 27 weeks, which again implies the *development* of music listening abilities within the womb. Similarly, Kisilevsky, Hains, Jacquet, Granier-Deferre, and Lecanuet (2004) showed how foetuses at 28-32 weeks showed an increase in heart rate to Brahms' *Lullaby* played at 105 or 110 decibels; but over time the foetuses reacted to quieter music such that Kisilevsky et al. argued that older foetuses are able to pay attention to music. There is also evidence that pre-natal music can have a positive impact on a child's post-natal development. Lafuente, Grifol, Segarra, Soriano, Gorba, and Montesinos (1998) built on the apparent ability of the foetus to respond to music by formulating their Firstart prenatal stimulation method. Their reasoning was that stimulation via music ought to enhance the intellectual and physical development of the foetus (see Chapter 2). Women in the last third of their pregnancy wore a waistband containing loudspeakers connected to a tape recorder. After birth the mothers then noted the age at which their babies developed a range of behaviours (e.g. gross and fine motor activities, linguistic development), and those who had been exposed to the music developed earlier (see also Li, 1994).

The apparent fact that foetuses can respond to music undoubtedly stems from the gestational development of the auditory system (that, of course, has to be functional once the child is born), and also from the evolutionary advantage that comes about if a newborn child is able to recognize the sound (and ideally the emotional state) of its own mother: musical development in the foetus may well be simply a 'by-product' of the development of hearing and maternal bonding. Although the foetuses in these studies are making responses that are psychologically dissimilar to the aesthetic responses shown conventionally by children and adults, the research has a number of highly provocative implications. First, from the perspective of music psychology, it highlights the argument from Chapter 1 and section 2 of this chapter that researchers must adopt a much broader definition of the terms 'music listening' and 'musical preference': foetuses' responses to music are dissimilar to those aesthetic responses made by children and adults, but nor are they *that* dissimilar. It is clear that responses to music do not develop solely during the elementary and high school years that are so often investigated. Second, research on responses to music in the foetus has implications for our understanding of the development of hearing and the early detection of deafness; and Hepper and Shahidullah (1992) have also demonstrated that a foetus' rate of habituation to auditory stimulation may discriminate children who will from those who will not be born with Down's syndrome (see also Standley, 1991a). Finally, some of the studies described here indicate that musical learning can occur during mid-pregnancy, and this may ultimately even prove to have implications for the debate on abortion.

3.3.3 Sex

Although many studies of music consider the interaction between gender and another subject of enquiry, surprisingly few have addressed the role of this factor as the primary source of variation in musical preference. Those studies that have been carried out can be classified loosely into two groups concerning attitudes towards music and uses of music respectively. With regard to the former, the consistent finding is that girls generally have more positive attitudes towards music than do boys. Crowther and Durkin's (1982) study of 12 to 18-year-olds found that this was particularly the case in their younger age groups; and that girls were also more likely to participate in musical activities. Similarly, Eccles, Wigfield, Harold, and Blumenfeld (1993) found that girls reported more positive competence beliefs and values for music than did boys. Finally, Colley, Comber, and Hargreaves (1994) studied 93 11–13-year-olds, and found that liking for school music lessons was associated with higher Femininity scores on Boldizar's Children's Sex Role Inventory.

However, an earlier study by the same authors (Comber, Hargreaves, and Colley, 1993) found that this pattern may be changing, since boys are more positive than girls in their attitudes towards music technology: the more the latter comes to the fore, the more that boys' attitudes towards music might improve. Furthermore, as we saw in more detail in Chapter 2, another area where the generally more positive attitudes of girls towards music does not hold is in the sex-stereotyping of musical instruments: although some instruments are perceived as being clearly for girls (e.g. flute, violin, clarinet) others are perceived as clearly masculine (e.g. drums, trombone, trumpet), and this seems to feed through into children's instrument preferences (see review by O'Neill, 1997a).

The data on music listening is similarly inconclusive. Sopchack (1955) reported that men and women were equally responsive to music, whereas Winold (1963) reported that females tended to be more responsive. With regard to short-term preferences between individual pieces, Abeles and Chung (1996, p. 316) conclude that 'the weight of the evidence seems to be heavily on the "no difference due to gender" end of the scale' (see e.g. Bradley, 1972; Breger, 1970; Long, 1971). However, when summarizing the effects of gender on longer-term liking for musical styles they conclude that 'Most of these studies show significant differences in the musical tastes of male and female subjects for a variety of types of music' (p. 328). The general pattern of results here suggests that women prefer 'softer' musical styles such as mainstream pop whereas males tend to prefer 'harder' styles such as rock (see e.g. Appleton, 1970; Baumann, 1960; Birch, 1962; Christenson and Peterson, 1988; Skipper, 1975). More recent evidence suggests that this trend is continuing with regard to more modern forms of pop music such as the often aggressive styles of rap and heavy rock which tend to be preferred by males (see e.g. Robinson, Weaver, and Zillmann, 1996; Took and Weiss, 1994; and Chapter 4).

One possible reason why boys tend to prefer more aggressive musical styles over the long term might be shown by research on gender differences in adolescents' uses of music. North, Hargreaves, and O'Neill (1998) asked 2465 13–14-year-olds to rate the extent to which 12 statements were reasons why they listened to music. Males were more likely than females to say that they listened to music because of the impression it could make on other people. For example, they were more likely to listen to music 'To be cool' or 'To please or impress my friends'. Females, on the other hand, were more likely than males to listen to music as a means of fulfilling their emotional needs. For example, they listened to music 'To get through difficult times' or 'To express feelings/emotions'. Put simply, girls seemed to use music listening for mood-optimization whereas boys use it more for impression management (see also Wells, 1990). In support of this, Kamptner (1995) investigated the most treasured possessions of 249 14 to 18-year-olds. She found that males tended to treasure sports equipment, music, and other objects which embodied enjoyment and *instrumental* meanings, whereas females in contrast tended to treasure jewellery, stuffed animals, and other objects embodying *interpersonal* meanings. That two unrelated studies should produce such similar findings may be more than mere coincidence.

3.3.4 **Personality**

Pearsall, Schwartz, and Russek (2002) interviewed the recipients of heart and lung transplants. The authors argued that factors such as cellular memory could explain those instances where the recipients moved towards their donors in terms of musical preference, as well as numerous other lifestyle preferences and sensory experiences. Kemp (1996) has reviewed the arguably more mundane research on both the personality correlates of musical preferences and the different listening styles people adopt. Surprizingly little research has been carried out in relation to the former, and this has on occasion yielded a confusing pattern of findings. One particular reason for this may be that there has been little attempt to address the *role* of musical preference in relation to personality. In particular, John may like a piece of music in the morning because it allows him to *project* and *reflect* a particular aspect of his personality: in contrast, later that afternoon John may dislike that same piece of music because now he wants to listen to something that allows him to *compensate* for the same aspect of his personality. Musical preference is related to personality in both cases, but the specifics of this vary as a function of the *role* of musical preference in relation to personality.

Such an argument is highlighted by the literature relating musical preferences to Eysenck's (e.g. Eysenck and Eysenck, 1975) theory of personality. Eysenck claimed that introverts experience a super-optimal baseline level of cortical arousal: in short, they need to lower their level of arousal, and so they tend to avoid stimulation (e.g. parties, conversation etc.). In contrast, extraverts experience sub-optimal baseline levels of cortical arousal: in short, they need to increase their level of arousal, and so they tend to seek out stimulation (e.g. parties, conversation etc.). This is extremely interesting of course when considered in the context of Berlyne's theory. Extraverts behave they way they do because they experience too little arousal: this means that they ought also to prefer music that has high arousal potential—music that is, for example, complex, unfamiliar, loud, or fast. In contrast, if introverts behave they way they do because they experience too much arousal then this, means that they ought to prefer music that is of low arousal potential—music that is, for example, simple, familiar, slow, and quiet. There are indeed a few findings consistent with this. For instance, Payne (1967) found that introverts prefer music with a formal structure whereas extraverts preferred music with human emotional overtones (see also Daoussis and McKelvie, 1986). As such, the music is *compensating* for aspects of personality. However, Kemp (1996, p. 126) also notes that 'it appears true that the extravert chooses music that generally makes fewer demands', or in other words, music that would do little to increase arousal and that would instead *reflect* their lower baseline level of cortical arousal.

Fortunately, other relationships between personality and musical preference appear to be more clear-cut. Furthermore, they suggest that musical preferences *reflect* rather than *compensate for* particular aspects of an individual's personality. Zuckerman's (1979) sensation seeking scale has been used in various studies investigating the relationships between preferences/attitudes and behaviours. At the risk of over-generalizing, sensation seeking is a trait defined by the need for varied, novel, and complex experiences, and the willingness to take physical and social risks for the sake of obtaining these experiences. With regard to music, several studies have found a direct association between sensation seeking and a preference for arousing music in general or heavy rock in particular (which of course tends to be loud and fast, to deal with risqué themes in its lyrics, and to be the subject of visually dynamic live performances) (e.g. Arnett, 1991, 1992; Hall, 2005; Kim, Kwak, and Chang, 1998; McNamara and Ballard, 1999; Nater, Krebs, and Ehlert, 2005; Stratton and Zalanowski, 1997; Weisskirch and Murphy, 2004; see also Chapter 4). Litle and Zuckerman (1986) found that high sensation seekers were also more likely to get emotionally involved with music, rather than merely use it as a background to other activities: in particular, the researchers found that the Experience Seeking subscale of the sensation seeking measure was correlated highly with the intensity of participants' involvement in listening to music (see also Rawlings, Barrantes and Furnham, 2000; and Rawlings, Twomey, Burns and Morris, 1998). It is tempting to speculate that this explains the finding, described in Chapter 4, that heavy rock fans tend to be immersed particularly deeply in this musical subculture.

A smaller number of studies have indicated specifically that fans of classical music score more highly on measures of conservatism whereas fans of so-called 'problem music' styles (such as rap and heavy rock) are more liberal. We deal with this research in much more detail in Chapter 4, but for the time being it is nevertheless worth mentioning a few of the findings. Lynxwiler and Gay (2000) found that participants who held conservative attitudes toward sexuality and those who attended religious services disliked heavy rock and rap. Glasgow and Cartier (1985) argued that conservatives prefer simple, familiar, and 'safe' artistic objects. McLeod, Detenber, and Eveland (2001) found that participants who listened to 'problem' music lyrics did not support their censorship, whereas participants with conservative attitudes were most likely to support censorship. McCown, Keiser, Mulhearn, and

Williamson (1997) found that psychoticism was related to a preference for music with 'exaggerated bass'.

More specifically, numerous studies have supported the more narrowly defined contention that fans of certain 'problem music' styles such as dance music, rap, and heavy rock are more involved than other fans in lifestyles containing acts of rebelliousness and anti-authoritarian behaviour. Hansen and Hansen (1991) found that heavy metal fans were higher on questionnaire measures of 'Machiavellianism' and 'machismo', and were lower on measures of need for cognition than were non-fans: similarly, punk fans were less accepting of authority than were non-fans. Robinson, Weaver, and Zillmann (1996) found that undergraduates who scored highly on measures of psychoticism and reactive rebelliousness enjoyed rebellious music videos more than did participants who scored low on these factors. Bleich, Zillmann, and Weaver (1991) assessed 16 to 19-year-old participants' trait rebelliousness and enjoyment of three 'defiant' and three 'non-defiant' rock music videos. Highly rebellious participants did not enjoy the defiant videos more than did their less rebellious peers; but highly rebellious participants enjoyed the non-defiant videos less than did non-rebellious participants, and the former group also consumed less non-defiant rock music. Dillmann-Carpentier, Knobloch, and Zillmann (2003) found that liking for defiant music was related to forms of rebelliousness. Hansen and Hansen (1990) found that experimental exposure to antisocial music videos increased participants' tolerance of antisocial behaviour (i.e. an obscene hand gesture) as compared with exposure to non-antisocial videos. Finally, Rentfrow and Gosling (2003) identified associations between several musical meta-styles and various personality factors. In particular, they found that liking for 'intense and rebellious' music was associated with openness to new experiences, athleticism, self-perceived intelligence, and verbal ability. Several protest groups have claimed that young fans of 'problem music' possess these personality attributes as a consequence of exposure to music that promotes an anti-authoritarian attitude towards society, and we will return to the issue of the direction of cause and effect in much more detail in Chapter 4.

3.3.4.1 Listening strategies

Another group of studies has investigated the different strategies people employ when listening to music. Hargreaves and Colman (1981), for instance, distinguished between 'objective-analytic' and 'affective' approaches to music listening; and Hedden (1973) found that adults employed two major listening strategies that have obvious parallels with Hargreaves and Colman's, namely 'cognitive' and 'associative' respectively. This in turn corresponds with

Smith's (1987) argument that the major distinction between expert and non-expert music listeners is that the latter adopt an emotional and referential approach, whereas the former follow a 'syntactic' strategy in which analytical, musicological processes take precedence. Two other studies (Ellis, 1995; Ellis and McCoy, 1990) suggest that listeners can analyse music more effectively if they are 'field independent' types, i.e. people who can concentrate on specific parts of whatever they perceive (see Witkin, 1965; Chapter 2). Similarly, Lewis and Schmidt (1991) report that 'intuitive' people respond to music more deeply and sensitively than do more 'sensing' people.

Two other studies have taken a very different approach to listening strategies, focusing on the music concerned rather than aspects of the listener. Hagerty (1983) reported that liking for a song decreased if it was similar to one just heard, indicating that responses to music can be optimized if similar pieces are not juxtaposed. Breckler, Allen, and Konečni (1985) conducted two experiments in which participants had to experience music and pictures respectively. These stimuli ranged from being quite pleasant to very unpleasant (e.g. four types of music and an 'aversive tone' in the music experiment, and pictures ranging from nude models to victims of assault in Experiment 2). Although participants had to expose themselves to all of these stimuli for two minutes, the *ordering* of this exposure was up to them. In both experiments, participants chose to expose themselves to the unpleasant music and pictures first, and they saved the pleasing music and pictures for the end. Furthermore, participants chose to break up runs of the most aversive music and pictures with moderately pleasing ones.

Kemp (1996), however, adds a note of caution when considering such an apparently neat set of findings. Specifically, he reminds us that the listening strategies that people choose to employ in one context (e.g. listening at home) may be quite different from those they employ in another (e.g. during psychological research or in a car). For example, the apparent differences between experts' and novices' listening strategies may really just reflect the attempts of the former to 'do their best' in a formal experimental setting, rather than any actual differences in everyday listening practices. Time limitations must play a role also: for example, someone on a five-minute car journey might be expected to jump straight to their favourite track on a CD. 'What may be emerging in some of this research [are strategies] based on people's attitudes about what the function of music is in their lives' (Kemp, 1996, p. 131). As such, there is a clear need for naturalistic, participant-centred research, and we describe some of the initial attempts at this in the final section of the chapter.

3.3.4.2 Responses to music in non-humans

Although it is certainly unusual to address species as a source of individual difference, there is some evidence that humans may not be the only creatures capable of responding to music. Ethological research on the functions, learning, and consequences of birdsong is well known (e.g. Beebee, 2004; Cooper and Goller, 2004; Garamszegi and Moller, 2004; Hall, 2004; Leboucher and Pallot, 2004; Mennill and Ratcliff, 2004; Nelson and Soha, 2004; Price and Lanyon, 2004; Slater, 2000; Ward, Lampe, and Slater, 2004); and there is also research that aims to understand human perception of music that has considered how non-humans do so (see reviews by Hauser and McDermott, 2003; Panksepp and Bernatzky, 2002; Wallin, Merker, and Brown, 2000). However, there is also a growing body of evidence concerning specifically how non-human animals do not just perceive but also react to music. The research can be divided into two loose groups, concerning respectively the impact of music on animal welfare, and the existence and modification of musical 'preferences' in non-human animals.

Several studies of animal welfare provide findings that are consistent with Konečni's research. If you recall, the latter showed how people use music to alleviate arousal from a stressful listening situation. Similarly, some of the research concerning music and animal welfare at least hints at the possibility that playing calming music to animals in captivity may be able to counteract the stress of this situation. Wells, Graham, and Hepper (2002) played human conversation, classical music, heavy metal music, pop music, and a control to 50 dogs housed in an animal rescue shelter. Classical music was therefore arguably the most soothing type of music played and it is interesting that it led to the dogs spending more time resting, more time quiet, and less time standing. In contrast, arguably the least soothing music that was played, heavy metal, led to the dogs spending more time barking. Indeed it is interesting that Wells et al. (p. 385) argue that classical music led to behaviours 'suggestive of relaxation'. In a similar vein, in an unpublished study, North, MacKenzie, and Hargreaves played fast and slow tempo music to dairy cows in their winter enclosures. Milk yield, which might be taken as an indicator of the cows' well-being, was higher in the slow than the fast music condition, which suggests that the slower music led to lower levels of stress. McCarthy, Ouimet, and Daun (1992) found that exposing rats to stress-inducing rock music could reduce their ability to heal wounds. Finally, Peretto and Kippschull (1991, p. 51) played music to mice over two weeks and found that '(1) classical music produced more interaction, including aggression; (2) country/bluegrass increased social interaction and aggression; (3) jazz and blues decreased aggression and competition; (4) easy listening increased huddling; and (5) rock tended to increase aggression but decrease sexual activity' (see similar findings by Peretto and Kippschull, 1990). There is obviously a need for more research, but the initial indications suggest that non-humans also have the potential to experience relaxation or stress in response to music.

Two other studies, although more difficult to explain in terms of Konečni's and Berlyne's research, also indicate that music may affect animal welfare. Uetakea, Hurnika, and Johnson (1997) studied 19 cows over a 69-day period in order to assess the effect of music versus no music on the cows' readiness to approach an automatic milking system (or AMS). They found 'a stimulatory effect of music, influencing [the] behavioural readiness of [the] cows to access the milking compartments of the AMS' (p. 177), with the number of cows behaving accordingly increasing from 22.3% in the absence of music up to 45.0% when music was played. Line, Markowitz, Morgan, and Strong (1991) argued that increasing the cage size of macaques had relatively little effect on their welfare compared to the provision of a 'music feeder box' under their direct control. Given findings such as these it is unsurprizing that Henley (1992) has considered the positive impact that the introduction of artistic activities can have on captive apes, elephants, and dolphins. However, two studies have also been carried out indicating that non-human species do not respond to music, such that it may not be able to promote their welfare. Cloutier, Weary, and Fraser (2000, p. 107) concluded that 'playing music or other sounds provides no improvement in conditions for piglets during handling and weaning.' Similarly Hodgetts, Waas, and Matthews' (1998, p. 337) study of red deer indicated that 'unusual disturbances (such as … loud music) do not cause long lasting changes in behavior.'

Other research on animals is interesting as it indicates that humans may not be the only species to have more overtly *aesthetic* responses to music; and shows that musical behaviour in non-humans might exist and be malleable. McDermott and Hauser (2004) found that tamarins have sound preferences (which were different to those of humans exposed to the same materials). King, West, and White (2003) found that adult and juvenile female cowbirds' preferences for different types of birdsong could be modified. Payne's (2000) long-term study of the songs of humpback whales showed how such songs arise through improvisation rather than by accident or as conveyors of information; and that these songs have a clear thematic structure. Similarly, Geissmann (2000) argued that singing behaviour has evolved independently several times in the order of primates, and that the vocalizations of non-human primates are therefore the most likely candidates for models of a precursor of human singing.

As noted earlier, other research indicates that non-humans are at least capable of making quite subtle and sophisticated discriminations between different types of music. For example, Okaichi and Okaichi (2001) showed that rats could discriminate between a version of *Yesterday* performed by The Beatles and a version performed by one of the experimenters; and that they could also distinguish Mozart's music, and the difference between music and white noise. Izumu (2000) has shown that macaques can discriminate consonant to dissonant chord changes. Chase and Hill (1999) found that koi could distinguish music from silence. McAdie, Foster, Temple, and Matthews (1993) found that hens could distinguish between music and the sounds of a water-hose, other poultry, and a train. Porter, Reed, and Neuringer (1984) found that pigeons could discriminate between Bach flute music and Hindemith viola music; and between Stravinsky's *Rite of Spring* and a Bach organ piece amongst others. College students responded similarly and the authors concluded that 'the pigeon's response to complex auditory events may be more like the human's than is often assumed' (p. 138).

Indeed, all manner of implications follow from the possibility that non-humans have responses to music, and that these are not too dissimilar from those of humans. For instance, findings such as these have been used by many as the basis of a discussion on the adaptive function of music for humans (see e.g. Wallin, Merker, and Brown, 2000). Furthermore, as with research on responses to music among human foetuses, this work with non-humans again brings into question conventional definitions of what we mean by 'listening to music' and 'musical preference'. For example, a cynic may argue that the apparent musical preferences of non-humans that we have described here are in fact just *functional* behaviours that we have anthropomorphized as 'aesthetic'. That may well be true of course, although in response to such a claim we would point out that the majority of this chapter (see also Chapters 4 and 5) has been spent describing how human 'aesthetic' responses to music are also often very *functional*. Just because non-humans' responses to music are functional does not mean that they are unlike humans' responses to music. For example we saw earlier in this section of the chapter that Wells, Graham, and Hepper (2002) found that dogs under stress in a rescue shelter reacted well to music that calmed them; whereas we saw earlier in section 2.1 of this chapter that Konečni, Crozier, and Doob (1976) found that human undergraduates under stress as a consequence of being insulted reacted well to music that calmed them: neither of these reactions to music seems any more functional or aesthetic than the other.

The findings concerning the possible impact of music on animal welfare also have at least six interesting implications for future work. First, more research is needed to identify the mechanisms by which music is responded to by non-humans. What are these precisely, and how might they interact with other environmental factors? Second, does music improve animal welfare because it masks background noise (or has other second-order effects) or, as the research on apparently more aesthetic responses to music suggests, does it work simply because the animals concerned simply enjoy it? Third, to what extent can the effects of music on animal welfare be attributed to music only: would other (non-copyrighted and therefore cheaper) sounds provide a source of relaxation or stimulation that also improves welfare? Fourth, research might also investigate the details of music presentation. For example, how much music has to be played for it to have a beneficial effect, how loud must this music be, how often does the music have to be changed, and so on? (Indeed, playing the 'wrong' types of music may well explain why Cloutier, Weary, and Fraser (2000) and Hodgetts, Waas, and Matthews (1998) found no welfare benefits of playing music to piglets and deer respectively.) Fifth, to what extent would research on specifically music support Newberry's (1995) claim that any attempt at environmental enrichment for captive animals must have functional relevance? Research addressing whether music does have functional relevance for captive non-humans may well shed light on whether their responses are truly 'aesthetic', and also on the origins and function of human musicality. Sixth, although the results of research concerning animal welfare appear broadly consistent with the ideas concerning human preferences propounded by Konečni, it may be a grave mistake to automatically assume that all species should necessarily react similarly to the same music. For example, the simple, repetitive melodies of new age music may relax a relatively unintelligent animal such as a camel, but bore the pants off a relatively intelligent one such as a chimpanzee!

Finally, there are also two ethical implications of this work. First, readers who eat meat might be unsettled to learn that their dinner tonight could be capable of enjoying Mozart, and feel motivated to change their diet accordingly. Second, it is pleasing that much of this fascinating research has featured animals in natural habitats. There are obvious ethical (as well as methodological) issues that can be overcome by continuing this practice; and in particular it would be a sad irony if the potential for long-term improvements in welfare was used by curious researchers as an excuse for inflicting short-term suffering.

3.3.5 Musical training and ability

The effects of musical training and ability on musical preference seem to be similar. At the risk of over-generalizing, the rather scanty literature indicates that people with high levels of training/ability seem to prefer more complex music than do people with low levels of training/ability. Perhaps the most transparent demonstration of this was provided by North and Hargreaves (1995b; see also a similar study by Burke and Gridley, 1990) who found that musically trained participants preferred music with a higher level of complexity than did those with no musical training. We argued that these findings were consistent with Berlyne's theory. Musical training of course involves exposure to a great deal of music. Berlyne's theory would therefore argue that the minds of musically trained people are more habituated to musically-evoked arousal than are the minds of others. Accordingly, musically trained people should need to be exposed to a greater degree of musically-evoked arousal than would others in order to achieve a moderate level of arousal. The effect is analogous to that of a drug addict who needs increasingly larger doses in order to get the same level of 'hit'.

Three other studies also support the conclusion that training/ability leads to liking for more complex music. Rubin-Rabson (1940) found that people's degree of musical training was correlated positively with the extent to which they liked 'modern' music. Fay and Middleton (1941) found that people who preferred swing music had lower levels of musical ability than those who preferred classical music. Hargreaves, Messerschmidt, and Rubert (1980) found that participants with musical training gave higher overall liking ratings to the music used in the research than did 'untrained' participants, although, crucially for our argument here, there was a significant interaction with musical style in that the effect was more pronounced for pieces of classical music than for pop.

3.4 **The reciprocal response model**

Hargreaves, Miell, and MacDonald (2005; see also Hargreaves, North, and Tarrant, 2006) have attempted to pull together these diverse influences into a single reciprocal feedback model of responses to music. Although this is by no means the first time that such a model has been attempted (see e.g. LeBlanc, 1982), that of Hargreaves et al. has the advantage of addressing specifically those three main influences described so far in this chapter, namely the music, the listener, and the listening situation. The model is described as 'reciprocal feedback' because any one of the three main influences can simultaneously influence the other two, and these influences are bi-directional. A summary of this model is shown in Figure 3.4.

The 'Music' box, for instance, incorporates all the literature on experimental aesthetics we considered at the beginning of this chapter, such as complexity,

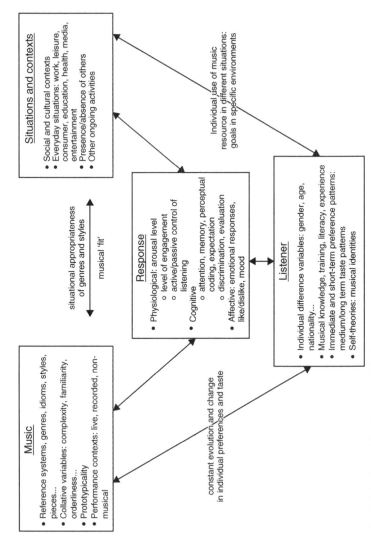

Fig. 3.4 Reciprocal feedback model of musical response

familiarity, and prototypicality (and also includes musical style—see e.g. North and Hargreaves, 1997a). The 'Situations and contexts' box incorporates situational influences on musical preferences such as contextually-determined arousal, and compliance and prestige effects. The 'Listener' box contains those individual difference variables discussed in the previous section of this chapter. In other words, it refers to influences on taste attributable to social class, age, sex, personality, and musical training.

However, the more interesting feature of the model concerns the reciprocal relations between these three 'boxes'. The relationship between the 'Music' and the 'Situations and contexts' boxes refers to the notion that some types of music are considered more appropriate for certain places. For example, we have already discussed North and Hargreaves' (1996c) finding that people agreed about the music they would expect to hear in 17 different listening situations and, as we shall see in Chapter 5, research concerning the 'fit' between music and a particular context has interesting commercial implications also. The relationship between the 'Situations and contexts' and the 'Listener' boxes refers to the findings reported above showing that individuals in particular contexts use music to achieve particular goals, be these for example optimal levels of arousal or a means of creating a public 'image' for oneself. Finally, the reciprocal relationship between the 'Listener' and 'Music' boxes illustrates how any particular response to music is related to longer-term musical tastes, through for example the relationship between a listener's familiarity with a piece of music and perceptions of the degree of complexity it contains (see Figure 3.2 and accompanying discussion); the relationship between age and musical preference; or the establishment of musical prototypes.

The model is certainly limited in focusing on only 'like-dislike' reactions to music rather than more specific emotional reactions, and (probably) only immediate responses to music rather than longer-term aspects of musical taste. However, it also embodies neatly two of the themes that have run throughout this chapter so far. Firstly, as we have seen several times, it is clear that aspects of the music, listener, and listening situation interact with one another continually in any particular instance of musical preference. Therefore, it would seem impossible to understand musical preference without fully addressing this continual interaction, and the major task facing research on musical preference over the next few years is to flesh out the details of how such an interaction occurs. More generally still, this continual interaction between the music, listener, and listening situation implies that all musical preference judgements that occur in the 'real world' (i.e. outside the lab) must necessarily have a social psychological component: there is a real *need* for social psychological input into research on musical preference.

Second, arousal- and typicality-related factors seem to underlie many aspects of musical preferences: evidence of the importance of arousal and typicality can be found in research concerning the music, the listener, and the listening situation. With regard to the music, research on experimental aesthetics has shown that arousal and typicality are crucial aspects of laboratory-based participants' musical preferences. With regard to the listener, we have seen how familiarity and subjective complexity may interact to explain age-based changes in musical taste, or how musically-evoked arousal may help to at least partly explain the relationship between personality and musical prefer-ence and also musical training and preference. We have also seen how late adolescence/early adulthood may represent a 'critical period' in which life-long musical prototypes are formed. With regard to the listening situation, we have seen how musical preferences can be shaped by levels of arousal imposed by the context in which music is heard, or by expectations about the music typically heard in a particular place. Since aspects of musical preference located within the music, listener, and listening situation share common bases in arousal- and typicality-based effects, we would *expect* aspects of the music, listener, and listening situation to interact continually. Consequently, any future effort to determine the nature of the interaction between the music, listener, and listening situation might start by trying to reach a much more detailed understanding of the nature and extent of the roles played by arousal and typicality. Specifically, to what extent can the specific models set out by Berlyne and Martindale explain preferences? Alternatively, is it impossible to use these specific models such that all we can really say is that basic aspects of physiology and cognition are involved in musical preference, as they are involved in so many other complex psychological processes?

3.5 **Emotional responses to music**

So far we have considered how liking for music can be influenced by a variety of factors, but responses to music of course also involve specific emotions. It is surprizing and very unfortunate that there is very little cross-pollination between research on musical preference and research on emotional responses to music. Part of the reason for this may be that studying emotional responses to music is especially difficult. Sloboda and Juslin (2001) identify three specific factors underlying this difficulty. First, mainstream psychology has tended to consider emotionality in terms of its adaptive value (see e.g. Lazarus, 1991; Zajonc, 1994). Since it is obviously difficult to consider emotional responses to specifically music in Darwinian terms it is correspondingly difficult to place the former in the context of many mainstream theories of emotion. Second, emotional reactions to music vary considerably from person to person and over time. Third, there are problems of ecological validity in that by closely observing an individual's emotional responses to music, researchers may fundamentally alter the nature of the process. To these problems, we would also add two more. Holbrook and Gardner (2000) raise a fourth problem, pointing out that mood is a dynamic variable. It is very difficult to consider how one particular emotional response to music is influenced by those previous emotional responses elicited by the same music. To give a simple example, a 'sad' section of a piece may seem all the more sad because the section that came before it evoked a happy mood; but in order to test this idea properly a researcher would have to be able to use music to reliably invoke a range of different moods and also address all the different possible combinations of emotions. Frijda (1989) highlights a fifth problem when discussing whether emotional responses to music (and other artistic stimuli) have the same status as emotional responses to 'real life' events. Emotional responses to artworks 'are unlike the emotions elicited by comparable events appraised as real ones. No one jumps up to warn ... Hamlet that Polonius is eavesdropping during his conversation with Ophelia' (p. 1546), so that mainstream theories of emotion simply may not generalize well to art works such as music. Indeed, Konečni, Brown, and Wanic (forthcoming) have gone so far as to question whether there even *is* a direct causal link between music and emotion.

Nevertheless Sloboda and Juslin (2001) argue convincingly that the typical characteristics of emotions can be applied to music. For example, just as the experience of certain emotions increases or decreases the probability of people acting in certain ways (e.g. people experiencing fear will close their eyes to avoid the cause of this fear), so emotions experienced in reaction to music also prime or inhibit certain behaviours (the most obvious example of which is the raucous behaviour of audiences at rock concerts). This in turn implies that the study of emotional reactions to music might still be usefully informed by mainstream theories of emotion. Sloboda and Juslin (2001) outline three major psychological approaches to conceptualizing emotion. The *categorical* approach states that people experience emotions as categories that are distinct from one another. More complex emotions are constructed through the combination of 'basic emotions' such as happiness, sadness, anger, fear, and disgust, which have adaptive value. The *prototype* approach argues that emotions are arranged hierarchically such that any particular emotion is less or more closely related to the superordinate category. For example, the top of Shaver, Schwartz, Kirson, and O'Connor's (1987) hierarchy, the superordinate level, states simply whether the emotion is positive or negative. At the middle level are basic categories of emotion, or prototypes: these represent the central concept for all the emotions within the category in question (e.g. love). At the next, subordinate, level down are all the emotions within that category (e.g. adoration, caring, compassion etc.). Finally, rather than organizing emotions according to hierarchies, *dimensional* approaches organize emotions according to their relative position along a small number of dimensions.

3.5.1 The circumplex model

Perhaps the best known dimensional theory is the circumplex model. This states that any emotion can be characterized according to its location along two dimensions, namely 'active-sleepy' and 'pleasant-unpleasant'. For example, 'tension' can be characterized as a combination of active and unpleasant; 'serenity' can be characterized as a combination of sleepy and pleasant; 'gloomy' can be characterized as a combination of sleepy and unpleasant; and 'delighted' can be characterized as a combination of active and pleasant. Furthermore, more 'extreme' emotions are located at more extreme points of the pleasantness and activity dimensions, such that, for example, 'aggressiveness' represents a greater amount of activity than does 'strength'; 'elation' represents a greater degree of pleasantness than does 'thankful'; and 'excitement' represents a greater amount of both pleasure and activity than does 'responsibility'.

North and Hargreaves (1997c) tested the theory by playing 32 pieces of pop music to participants and asking them to rate each for two factors, how much they liked it and how arousing they thought it was. A second group of participants rated each piece of music according to eight different emotions. The results are shown in Figure 3.5. In short, the results were remarkably consistent with the circumplex model. Pieces of music that were liked and arousing were also regarded as exciting, pieces that were disliked and arousing were also regarded as boring, pieces that were liked and not arousing were regarded as relaxing, and pieces that were disliked and arousing were regarded as aggressive.

In addition to being consistent with the circumplex, these findings are particularly interesting since they explain emotional responses to music in terms that are compatible with Berlyne's arousal-based theory of musical preference. As such they provide a means of integrating research on musical preference with emotional response to music, and so it is worth devoting a little time to them. In particular, North and Hargreaves' (1997c) findings are by no means uncommon. Ritossa and Rickard (2004, see also Madsen, 1998) produced similar (although weaker) findings, showing that the emotions expressed by pieces of music could be predicted by a combination of arousal,

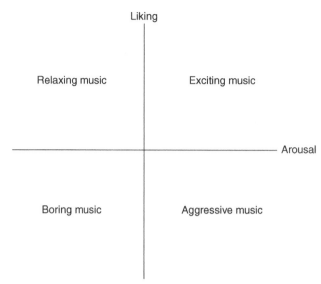

Fig. 3.5 Emotions expressed in music as a function of liking and arousal

pleasantness, and familiarity. Schubert (2004) identified a link between arousal evoked by music (particularly via loudness and tempo) and emotional responses. Similarly, two other studies show specifically that more extreme levels of arousal are associated with more extreme emotional responses to music, just as the circumplex predicts. Rickard (2004, see also McFarland, 1985) found that emotionally powerful music gave rise to greater increases in skin conductance (a measure of activity in the autonomic nervous system) than did less emotionally powerful music; and Dibben (2004) found that participants who had just exercised reported more intense emotional experiences of music than participants who had relaxed.

More generally, although it is by no means entirely consistent (e.g. Panksepp and Bekkedal, 1997), there is evidence that specific musical events do indeed lead to physiological reactions in listeners consistent with Berlyne's general approach (see reviews by Bartlett, 1996; Scherer and Zentner, 2001). For example, Khalfa, Isabelle, Jean-Pierre, and Manon (2002) found that skin conductivity response (SCR), a measure of physiological arousal, was greater when music elicited more arousing emotions (fear and happiness) than when music elicited less arousing emotions (sadness and peacefulness). Nyklicek, Thayer, and van Doornen (1997) were able to identify reliable cardiorespiratory responses to different musically-induced emotions that were 'related to the arousal dimension of self-reported emotions' (p. 304). Panksepp (1995) was able to associate particular emotional reactions to music with particular physiological responses; and Schmidt and Taylor (2001) were able to associate activity in the frontal cortex with the valence and intensity of musically-evoked emotions. Findings such as these point to the possibility that emotional responses to music may well draw on just the same mechanisms that Berlyne used to explain liking for music.

Note also that research on the circumplex is consistent with two of the best-known pieces of research concerning emotion and responses to music respectively. First, Schachter and Singer's (1962) cognitive theory of emotion states that arousal determines the *strength* of an emotion, whereas context determines the *type* of emotion experienced: it may be that musically-evoked arousal provides the basis for the strength of an emotional response to music, whereas the pleasantness of the music in question provides the contextual information in labelling the specific type of emotion experienced. Second, as the result of several studies, Hevner (1935a, 1935b, 1936, 1937; see also Farnsworth, 1954) was also able to arrange 67 emotional responses to music into an 'adjective circle', which is shown in Figure 3.6. This adjective circle comprizes eight groups of feelings, and the greater the distance between two groups of adjectives in the circle so the more dissimilar those groups are purported to be. Specifically, the arrangement of groups within the circle implies the existence of four bipolar scales: compare for example Group 1 with Group 5, Group 2 with Group 6, Group 3 with Group 7, and Group 4 with Group 8. More interestingly still, these dimensions have clear similarities with those specified by the circumplex model: in particular groups 7/8 and groups 3/4 seem to be analogous to the active-sleepy dimension of the circumplex, and groups 2 and 6 seem analogous to the pleasant-unpleasant dimension of the circumplex. Such a degree of similarity is all the more remarkable for the fact that the two sets of work were carried out independently around 50 years apart.

Hevner (1937) summarized her findings concerning the musical characteristics that give rise to the emotions in each of the eight groups within the 'adjective circle'. These are shown in Figure 3.7, in which the number in parentheses after each musical characteristic indicates Hevner's weighting of its importance. For example, Group 1 emotions are most readily evoked by a firm rhythm (with a weighting of 18), which is more important than slow tempo (with a weighting of 14): a simple harmony can also help to elicit Group 1 emotions, but is much less important with a weighting of only 3. Perhaps the most interesting aspect of Figure 3.7 however is that emotions that the circumplex would classify as more arousing seem to be evoked by musical properties that Berlyne would argue possess greater arousal potential. For example, Hevner argues that Group 7 emotions such as 'exciting' are produced

Group 6
Bright
Cheerful
Gay
Happy
Joyous
Merry

Group 7
Agitated
Dramatic
Exciting
Exhilarated
Impetuous
Passionate
Restless
Sensational
Soaring
Triumphant

Group 5
Delicate
Fanciful
Graceful
Humorous
Light
Playful
Quaint
Sprightly
Whimsical

Group 8
Emphatic
Exalting
Majestic
Martial
Ponderous
Robust
Vigorous

Group 4
Calm
Leisurely
Lyrical
Quiet
Satisfying
Serene
Soothing
Tranquil

Group 1
Awe-inspiring
Dignified
Lofty
Sacred
Serious
Sober
Solemn
Spiritual

Group 3
Dreamy
Longing
Plaintive
Pleading
Sentimental
Tender
Yearning
Yielding

Group 2
Dark
Depressing
Doleful
Frustrated
Gloomy
Heavy
Melancholy
Mournful
Pathetic
Sad
Tragic

Fig. 3.6 The Hevner adjective circle (adapted from Hevner, 1937)

Emotion Group							
1	2	3	4	5	6	7	8
Firm rhythm (18)	Minor mode (20)	Slow tempo (16)	Slow tempo (12)	Major mode (21)	Major mode (24)	Fast tempo (21)	Low pitch (13)
Slow tempo (14)	Low pitch (19)	Minor mode (12)	Simple harmony (10)	High pitch (16)	High pitch (20)	Complex harmony (14)	Firm rhythm (10)
Low pitch (10)	Slow tempo (12)	Flowing rhythm (9)	High pitch (8)	Simple harmony (12)	Simple harmony (16)	Low pitch (9)	Descending melody (8)
Ascending melody (4)	Complex harmony (7)	High pitch (6)	Major mode (3)	Flowing rhythm (8)	Flowing rhythm (10)	Descending melody (7)	Complex harmony (8)
Major mode (4)	Firm rhythm (3)	Simple harmony (4)	Ascending melody (3)	Fast tempo (6)	Fast tempo (6)	Firm rhythm (2)	Fast tempo (6)
Simple harmony (3)				Flowing rhythm (2)	Descending melody (3)		

Fig. 3.7 Weights of musical characteristics for each of Hevner's groups of emotions (adapted from Hevner, 1937)

particularly by music that is fast and has complex harmonies; whereas Group 4 emotions such as 'calm' are produced particularly by music that is slow and has simple harmonies. In short, research concerning emotional responses to music in the context of the circumplex may ultimately be reconciled with Berlyne's theory of musical preference. Emotional and like-dislike responses to music may not be nearly so dissimilar as the existing literature implies.

3.5.2 Intrinsic and extrinsic meaning

The most overt recognition of social psychological factors in emotional responses to music can be seen in much of the early thinking on the subject. This took place at the interface of philosophy, psychology, and musicology, and addressed specifically whether emotional responses to music are the result of factors *intrinsic* to the music itself or other *extrinsic* factors (see, for example, Coker's (1972) distinction between congeneric and extrageneric meanings; and Schwadron's (1967) description of isolationist and contextualist viewpoints).

3.5.2.1 Intrinsic musical meaning

Meyer (1956) proposed what is easily the best known of the intrinsic (or 'absolutist') theories (see also Hanslick, 1891; Schoen, 1940). The key concept in Meyer's theory is that of expectations. Through exposure to a particular musical culture, listeners learn what musical events should follow other musical events. In other words, the listener has an expectation as to how a given piece of music will develop, and Meyer argued that the job of the composer is to create and relieve tension in the listener as a result of deliberately violating these expectations. This act of violating expectations, Meyer argued, is what gives rise to emotional reactions in listeners. 'Affect or emotion felt is aroused when an expectation—a tendency to respond—activated by the musical stimulus situation, is temporarily inhibited or permanently blocked' (1956, p. 31). Meyer (1967, see also 1994, 2001) went on to consider the role of expectancies in terms of information theory, or more simply the statistical probability of one musical event following another. It is interesting also that Narmour's (1990, 1991) more recent account of emotion in music built on Meyer's work and provided a detailed discussion of expectations in melodic perception. Similarly, Sloboda (1991a) asked participants about their physical reactions to music, and to identify specific musical passages that would reliably produce these effects. Collating these two sources of evidence indicated that tears were evoked by melodic appoggiaturas, shivers were evoked by sudden changes in harmony, and a racing heart was evoked by syncopation. As Sloboda and Juslin (2001, p. 91) note, these musical structures 'have in common their intimate relationship to the creation, maintenance, confirmation, or disruption of musical expectations.'

There are two reasons why it is surprizing and unfortunate that this information-based aspect of Meyer's theory has not been researched more by modern-day psychologists. First, as we saw in Chapter 2, Dean Simonton's research has shown that it is possible to construct computerized databases of the expectancies inherent to several thousand melodies. These in turn may allow researchers to make very specific links between particular musical events and specific emotional responses over a very large corpus of music. Second, once we begin to discuss the probability of one musical event following another, it becomes very difficult to avoid using terms such as complexity, surprizingness, and several other factors implicated by Berlyne's arousal-based theory of liking for music: Meyer's theory may provide yet another opportunity to link liking for music with emotional responses to music.

Sloboda (e.g. 1999a) has also, however, highlighted three major problems with intrinsic theories of emotional reactions to music. First, virtually every note of a melody confirms or violates one expectancy or another, such that existing models are undoubtedly under-specified and complete models are many years away. Second, if expectations are the key to emotional reactions to music then how is it possible to have emotional reactions to music that we already know well, since in many ways almost everything that happens in the music can be said to be 'expected'? Although intrinsic theories can circumvent such arguments (by, for example, arguing that the listener learns to enjoy the means by which the composer develops and confirms/violates expectations) the means by which they do so are rather unparsimonious, and, to some extent at least, unconvincing. Third, intrinsic approaches find it difficult to explain why two people may have different emotional reactions to the same music, or why one individual might have two different reactions to the same piece over several listenings: if the music is the same then so should be people's reactions to it. It is partly because of arguments such as these that a second line of research has developed to investigate how emotional reactions might result from factors extrinsic to the music.

3.5.2.2 Extrinsic musical meaning

Extrinsic approaches to music and emotion, or so-called referentialist approaches, argue that musical meaning is derived from the extra-musical and contextual associations of the sounds. As we have already seen in our discussion of musical taste publics, some sociologists (such as Bourdieu) have proposed an extreme version of this position, arguing that music is meaningful precisely *because* of the position it occupies in structuring the world. Research on extrinsic approaches has distinguished between associative and iconic cues that result in emotional responses. Iconic cues refer to the resemblance between particular aspects of the music and the particular tone of certain emotions. For example, slow music may sound 'sleepy' because it shares the same notions of calmness and serenity. As such, the extra-musical meaning is in some ways still rooted in musical structure, such that the same music should have similar iconic meaning to different people. Cooke's (1959; see also Kaminska and Woolf, 2000) theory is arguably consistent with this approach, claiming that certain notes and melodic patterns are analogous to certain emotions; such that, for example, descending passages to the tonic are analogous to peace or rest, whereas passages moving away from the tonic are analogous to outgoing emotions.

Indeed, Bruner (1990; see also Gabrielsson and Lindström, 2001; Juslin, 2005) reviewed numerous studies from the fields of psychology and marketing, and summarized the various possible iconic meanings that different musical structures might have in terms of time-, pitch-, and texture-related factors. With regard to time-related factors, he argued that music in $^2/_4$ time is expressive of rigidity and control whereas music in $^3/_4$ time is more relaxed and abandoned; fast tempo is expressive of animation and happiness; jerky, uneven rhythms indicate complex emotions whereas even rhythms express simpler, unimpeded feelings; firm rhythms suggest a serious mood whereas smooth-flowing rhythms are more playful; and staccato notes give more emphasis to a passage than legato notes. With regard to pitch-related factors, Bruner argued that 'upward' and 'downward' movements in pitch correspond with movements up and down in the physical world as well as movements 'out-and-in' and 'away-and-back' respectively; rising and falling pitch convey a respectively growing or diminishing intensity; music in higher keys is generally considered to be happier than music in lower keys; music in the major mode expresses more animated and positive feelings than music in the minor mode; and complex harmonies are more agitated and sad than simple harmonies, which are more serene and happy. Finally, with regard to texture-related factors, Bruner argued that loudness can suggest animation or proximity whereas low volume implies tranquillity or distance; a crescendo in volume expresses an increase in force whereas diminuendo suggests a decrease in power; and that the timbre of brass instruments conveys a feeling of cold, hard force whereas reed instruments produce a lonely, melancholy expression. Although these rules undoubtedly do not apply universally, as we will see later in Chapter 5, consumer psychologists interested in the idea of musical 'fit' have utilized iconic musical meaning in an attempt to reliably influence customer's perceptions of various goods and services.

Associative cues, in contrast, refer simply to learned associations between a piece of music and non-musical factors that have emotional meaning. By its very nature, this aspect of emotional responses to music is most susceptible to social psychological influence. For example, perhaps the best-known manifestation of associative cues is the 'our song' phenomenon in which a piece of music has special meaning for lovers because they associate it with, say, their first date or their wedding day. As such, it is arguable that the emotional response to the music has just as much to do with the object it is associated with as it has to do with the music itself. Furthermore, it is clear that associative cues are almost by definition idiosyncratic, in that we would expect them to vary enormously from person to person. Nevertheless there are some associative cues held by large groups of people. For example, the majority of the population of a country will have similar reactions to their national anthem, and other pieces of music can also acquire associative meaning for large groups of people through their use in advertising and TV programmes/films.

In practical terms, although intrinsic and extrinsic arguments are often presented as irreconcilable explanations of emotional responses, there is no reason why music cannot have *both* intrinsic *and* extrinsic meanings. For example, a piece may be chosen for a funeral because it has structural properties that make it intrinsically 'sad', and this same piece may then subsequently become associated with funerals and be also perceived as 'sad' for extrinsic reasons too. Indeed, several theories argue that it is impossible to truly separate the meanings endemic to music and the meanings imposed on it by listeners. Cooke (1959) and Langer (1953), for example, both regarded emotion as an essential part of the meaning of music, rather than as a detached 'response' to a 'stimulus'. In particular, research on strong experiences of music highlights the interaction of intrinsic and extrinsic musical meanings in creating particularly powerful emotional reactions in listeners.

3.5.3 Strong experiences of music

Much of the research on strong experiences of music has drawn on Maslow's (e.g. 1968) humanistic psychology in discussing the notion of peak experiences. Maslow placed peak experiences at the top of his well-known hierarchy of human needs, referring to wonderful experiences, in response to, for example, art works, life events, or the natural world, that involve a sense of awe, complete absorption and focus, and a feeling of transcending time and space. Laksi (1961) found that of all the arts, classical music was the most frequently mentioned trigger for experiences of 'transcendent ecstasy' (see similar findings and arguments in Bakker, 2005; Konečni, 2005; Lewis, 1998, 2002, 2003; Paffard, 1970; and Panzarella, 1980).

However Alf Gabrielsson and Siv Lindström Wik's 'Strong Experiences of Music' project (see review by Gabrielsson, 2001) is by some margin the most detailed attempt to investigate massive emotional reactions to music (see Gabrielsson, 1989; Gabrielsson and Lindström, 1993, 1995; Gabrielsson and Lindström Wik, 2000, 2003). The project aimed to find out precisely how people have strong experiences of music, and to determine how these experiences are influenced by the music itself, characteristics of the listener, and the situation in which the experiences occurred. As might be expected, participants' verbal reports of their strong experiences of music varied considerably, ranging from a few lines to eight pages (including poetry). Nevertheless, it has been able to pull out several underlying themes and classify strong experiences of music into four sub-groupings, namely *intense* emotions, *positive* emotions, *negative* emotions, and *mixed/conflicting* emotions; and Gabrielsson (2001) provides some interesting supportive quotations that give a real flavour of the strength of the experiences involved.

Specifically, Gabrielsson (2001) concludes that *intense* emotions could be linked to high or low arousal states (e.g. 'This song arouses so strong feelings in me that I cannot listen to it more than once a year'; 'An internal peace that words cannot describe', p. 436). The most commonly cited *positive* emotions involved happiness, joy, elation, and bliss, and less commonly even stronger feelings such as euphoria, and feelings of intoxication (e.g. a rehearsing musician reported that 'it made me ecstatic, inconceivably exhilarated, everything concentrated to a single now', p. 437). The participants also reported highly aroused states such as enjoyment, delight, loveliness, beauty, and feelings of perfection; as well as low arousal experiences such as calm, peace, repose, safety, warmth, and love (e.g. 'A stillness that was not like anything else', p. 438). Furthermore, some of these positive emotions also contained a cognitive component, such as expectation, tension, surprise, and amazement. Instances of strong experiences of music involving *negative* emotions were relatively rare (e.g. 'A dissonance that pierced my very marrow' p. 439). Although these negative emotions were usually caused by the music itself, there were also instances of their association with factors concerning the listener and listening situation, such as painful childhood memories or death. Finally, Gabrielsson notes that examples of *mixed/conflicting* emotions were common in participants' descriptions of strong experiences of music. In particular there were reports of emotional responses to music evolving as that music progressed, and of musicians 'feeling their way' through their performance nerves. While we have focused on specifically emotional aspects of strong experiences of music, however, other types of response were common. For example, Gabrielsson reports instances of physiological and behavioural responses (e.g. tears, laughter, goosebumps, racing heart), quasi-physical feelings (e.g. 'I was filled by an enormous warmth and heat', p. 442), intensified perception, altered perception of time, loss of self-consciousness, feelings of merging with the music, feelings of freedom, and gaining new insights, to name but a few.

These examples provide a detailed account of what strong experiences of music might specifically entail, and show that these are by no means dissimilar from the non-musical peak experiences described by humanistic psychologists. However, where the 'Strong Experiences of Music' project has really come into its own is in the explicit attempt to identify *musical*, *personal*, and *situational* factors that influence strong reactions to music. With regard to the *music* itself, 'high art' styles were involved in only around half the strong experiences reported, and more generally, it was extremely difficult to associate any particular musical style with any particular strong experience of music. However, Gabrielsson has been able to identify the importance of particular chords, as well as other particular musical factors such as unusual timbres, crescendos and diminuendos, transitions from minor to major modes, and thick textures among others. Several aspects of the *listener* were also related to strong experiences of music, such as particular physical states (e.g. relaxation or illness), cognitive factors (e.g. expectations; addressing a need to listen to or play music; level of (un)familiarity with the musical style, piece or performer; and memories of the music), emotional state, and personality-related factors (e.g. maturity). *Situational* factors related to strong experiences of music could be broken down into physical factors (e.g. live versus recorded music; the physical location (e.g. at home, in a restaurant); time of day and year), social factors (e.g. the presence/absence of others, behaviour of the audience), special occasions/circumstances (e.g. during a holiday, in another country, in an unusual environment), and music performance conditions (e.g. being unrehearsed). More research is obviously needed to provide a detailed understanding of those music-, listener-, and situation-based factors linked to strong experiences of music; to determine whether and how these factors constitute rules that inevitably *lead* to strong experiences of music or only rules of thumb that are *conducive* to strong experiences; and to consider how they might interact with one another. For the time being, however, this fascinating work implies that even the most magical of our reactions to music can be studied scientifically and may be rule-based.

3.6 **Music in everyday life**

Given the implication of the reciprocal feedback model that responses to music always have a situational component, it follows that it is important to study music in those everyday contexts in which it is experienced. Sloboda and O'Neill (2001, p. 415; see also Juslin and Laukka, 2004; Stratton and Zalanowski, 2003) reflected the arguments made earlier by Konečni (see above), stating that

> music is always heard in a social context, in a particular place and time, with or without other individuals being present, and with other activities taking place which have their own complex sources of meaning and emotion. ... [Responses to music represent] actual moments of emotional feelings and displays in particular situations within particular cultures ... The prevailing contexts in which we encounter music ... include those contexts in which the most routine activities of life take place: waking up, washing and dressing, eating, cleaning, shopping, travelling.

However, research directly within such settings is scarce and only in very recent years have psychologists and sociologists begun to investigate the mundane, everyday realities of music listening.

Of course, it is extremely difficult to study mundane, everyday reactions to music since these occur over protracted periods of time outside the laboratory, and participants may not be easily able to recall the details of what occurred in any particular music listening episode. To overcome these difficulties, two British studies (Sloboda, O'Neill, and Ivaldi, 2001; North, Hargreaves, and Hargreaves, 2004) have employed the experience sampling method (see also Pincott and Anderson's (1999) market research study, which adopted a less psychological approach). Sloboda et al. provided their eight participants with a pager which they carried with them whenever awake over seven days. They were then paged once in every two-hour period between 8 a.m. and 10 p.m., and asked to complete a questionnaire concerning the most recent time they had heard music. The methodology of North et al. was essentially similar, but featured two noteworthy differences. In this case participants received a message only once per day over 14 days and were contacted via a text message sent to their mobile telephone from a free internet site. Such a technique represented a considerable cost saving relative to the use of pagers, allowing a much larger sample of 346 participants.

One of the aims of our study was simply to collect some basic normative data on whom participants listened to music with, what they listened to, and when. For instance, we found that only 26.3% of listening episodes occurred while participants were on their own; that pop was the most regularly experienced musical style (accounting for 67.1% of all listening episodes), whereas classical music accounted for only 3%; and that music was more commonly experienced during the evening, particularly between 10 p.m. and 10.59 p.m., and during weekends rather than weekdays.

However, we also tested three specific hypotheses, each of which was based on one of the three major implications of the digital revolution. The first of these is the growth of the internet as a means of obtaining music. Large internet CD retailers stock countless thousands of recordings, and these are supplemented by numerous sites allowing legal and illegal downloads of individual songs. The second major change is represented by the rise of high capacity portable digital music players, which allow an individual to carry hundreds of hours of music with them at any time. The third major change concerns the switch from analogue to digital broadcasting, which has vastly increased the number and sound quality of channels playing music around the clock. The net result of these changes is that it has never been easier to hear whatever music we want to, when we want to, whether at home or elsewhere. It would be surprising if people therefore did not use specific pieces of music to achieve very specific ends in very specific circumstances.

Accordingly, the first hypothesis we tested was that technological changes should be associated with music being common in everyday life. In support of this, we found that music could be heard on 38.6% of those occasions on which participants received their text (compared with a figure of 44% in the Sloboda et al. study), and this of course reflects a very high rate of exposure to music. Further evidence of the role of technology in modern music listening is that 49.9% of listening episodes occurred outside the home, 17.9% occurred in a public place, and a further 11.8% occurred while driving. (Note also, however, that Mehl and Pennebaker (2003) used a different method of assessing exposure to music and found that music was present in the environment of their American student sample for only 13.5% of the time).

Second, we reasoned that the high prevalence of music could have led to it being perceived as worth little: as we noted in Chapter 1, one of the central tenets of economics is that something only has value if it is in finite supply. In support of this, we found that in only 26.4% of experiences of music did participants say that listening to music was the *main* thing they were doing (with Sloboda et al. reporting a corresponding figure of only 2%). In other words, the great majority of those occasions where participants could hear music occurred while the participants were doing something else. In contrast only 11.9% of episodes occurred while participants were deliberately listening to music either at home or in a concert. Further evidence for the 'music is cheap' argument was that people had a disinterested and passive attitude toward the music that they could hear. When participants were asked to describe the function of the music, they agreed with statements such as 'It helped to create the right atmosphere.' Third, we reasoned that if people have greater access to whatever music they want when they want it, then they could well be taking this opportunity to use specific pieces of music in specific settings to serve specific functions. In support of this, there was evidence that participants thought that music served different functions depending on who they were with, what music they could hear, when they listened to it, and where they were listening. As such, this emphasizes the need to contextualize research on responses to music to reflect how its function may change depending on the listening situation.

One initial attempt to address the issue of context was made by Rana and North (forthcoming) who employed virtually the same methodology as North et al., but this time in the Pakistani city of Lahore. Pakistan is of course an Islamic country, and at the time of the research was experiencing social tensions concerning the perceived possibility of 'Westernization' and the implications of this for national sovereignty and public morality. Arguably in potential conflict with this was Pakistan's simultaneous technological development, particularly with regard to the internet and cable/satellite broadcasting, which was expected to increase people's access to music from all cultures. There were many striking similarities between the Pakistani data and that obtained from the earlier British sample. Once again, the majority of listening episodes occurred in the presence of other people; participants had the highest degree of liking for the music they could hear when they were on their own; evenings and weekends were the most common times for music listening; participants were most likely to be able to control their exposure to music in private environments, and least likely to be able to control their exposure to music while in commercial environments; and participants had different reasons for listening to music in different social settings. As such, this correspondence with the British data suggests that the utilitarian function of music in everyday life may just be a cultural universal.

However, the specific nature of this utility may well vary from culture to culture, as there were several differences between the Pakistani and British data. It was no surprise that the music that people were actually listening to differed between the British and Pakistani samples (although not as much as it might have). Furthermore, Pakistani participants tended to listen to music for apparently active reasons (rather than, for example, out of habit). Even when they had no choice but to be able to hear music (e.g. when in a shop), the Pakistani participants enjoyed the music, and it still served important positive functions for them. This contrasted with the British data showing that when participants chose to be able to hear music they did so in a more disinterested and unengaged manner, and that when they were not able to choose to hear music very few episodes resulted in enjoyment. In short, the Pakistani sample seemed less inclined to take their access to music for granted, and we speculated that this might have been because of the relatively poor state of technology (and the implications of this for access to music) that prevailed in Pakistan until recent years.

The Sloboda et al. (2001) British study adopted a much finer focus than our own work, and addressed instead the specifics of how a participant's mood changed as a consequence of hearing music. On the great majority of occasions, the everyday experience of music led to increases in participants' degree of pleasure and arousal (and this again has obvious parallels with mainstream research concerning these factors). The study also found that 35% of everyday experiences of music involved a shift away from the present situation towards for instance reminiscence, daydreams, and nostalgia; and Sloboda's (1999b) content-analysis of written descriptions of why people listened to music in everyday life also found that nostalgia was thought to be the primary function of music. In other words, the music did not just make people feel better but also seemed to transport them away from everyday concerns. However, Sloboda et al. also report instances where changes in mood again seemed to imply that music was being used by participants to achieve a particular purpose. For example, a female tidying her bedroom seemed to listen to music to allow her 'to focus attention ... away from the uninteresting domestic chore, and this focused attention was used to increase energy levels' (Sloboda and O'Neill, 2001, p. 419).

Recent sociological and ethnomusicological work has complemented the more quantitative approaches adopted by North et al. and Sloboda et al. with interview-based work that aims to capture fully the richness and complexity of responses to music in everyday life. Perhaps the best known of this is a series of interviews reported by DeNora (2000). These examined how 52 British and American women aged 18 to 77 years used music in contexts such as shopping malls, exercises classes, and during karaoke. DeNora's arguments can be seen as complementing those of North et al. and Sloboda et al. by regarding music in everyday life as a way of organizing one's internal and social world. DeNora claims that music is more than just the background to numerous activities, but rather helps to continually reconstruct the aims of these activities: 'music' is regarded more as a process than an object. In particular, the participants displayed clear awareness and understanding of the music they 'needed' to hear in particular contexts in order to achieve particular goals, and DeNora (2001, p. 170) argues that they in effect functioned as 'disc jockeys to themselves', using music to achieve specific ends that reflected not just their requirements of the current situation but also their uses of music in the past. Similarly, Crafts, Cavicchi, and Keil et al. (1993) adopted a cultural studies approach, focusing on interviews with North American music lovers aged 4 to 83 years offering in-depth and detailed insights into the complex, idiosyncratic, and eclectic roles that music played in the everyday life of the participants; and assessed these with regard to the constrictions upon musical taste imposed by the music industry (see also Kleinen, 1991; 1997). Note also that Schramm (2006) describes how music use changes when people begin downloading music and using mp3 players. Specifically, users report more positive effects, such as greater knowledge of the music, more time listening to music, and more conscientious music listening and purchasing.

The evidence covered in this chapter shows that reactions to music have value to specific individuals in specific contexts, serving particular practical goals. Despite this, however, the tremendous access we have to music in the modern world means that it is unsurprizing yet still nonetheless upsetting that on a cultural level we do not value music as highly as we should. What may prove to be the greatest contribution of all the research outlined in this chapter is that it has *quantified* the *value* of music to people in their everyday lives. Of course, this 'value' has nothing to do with pounds sterling, profit margins, or stock values. Yet there are many things in society that do not make a financial profit, but which we are nevertheless happy to support because they add value to society as a whole on a measurable day-to-day level. For example, when did streetlights ever make a profit? The evidence presented in this chapter shows that a similar principle should apply to music. It makes a measurable and valuable contribution to our daily lives, and has to be supported accordingly.

4

'Problem music' and subcultures

The market is flooded with songs today ... not even
sufficiently bad to be called immoral, but which point
with certainty to the time when their influence will
produce the positively objectionable
*Carl Laemmle, president of the Chicago-based Music
House of Laemmle (and founder of Universal Studios),
quoted in Billboard, 12 November 1910*

On 23 December 1985, Ray Belknap and James Vance from Reno, Nevada
spent the afternoon drinking beer, smoking cannabis, and listening to the
Stained Class album by heavy rock band, Judas Priest. Ray had just lost his job
and James had just quit his, leading to an angry confrontation with his
mother. Late in the afternoon they jumped out of a first floor window and
took a sawn off shotgun to a nearby churchyard with the intention of fulfilling
a suicide pact. When they arrived, 18-year-old Ray shouted 'life sucks', put the
gun under his chin and pulled the trigger, causing fatal injuries. A few
moments later, 20-year-old James did the same and, although he didn't die,
shot off the lower portion of his face. The parents sued Judas Priest and their
record company, claiming that the album their sons had been listening to all
afternoon drove them to suicide. One song on the album, *Beyond the Realms of
Death*, featured the lyrics 'He had enough/He couldn't take anymore ... This is
my life/I'll decide not you'. Another song, *Heroes End*, featured the lyric, 'Why
do you have to die if you're a hero?' The parents later claimed that the suicide
attempts also resulted from the words 'Do it' having been recorded backwards
into another song on the album, *Better By You, Better Than Me*.

The court did not rule in favour of the parents, but this case, as described by
Litman and Farberow (1994), is just one example of how protesters have
claimed that heavy rock, rap, and other forms of what has become termed
'problem music' are capable of inducing deleterious behaviours in adolescents
and young adults. In this chapter we ask whether the protesters are right to be

concerned, what action is justified, and why young people should be so interested in musical subcultures. We begin by considering the history of the problem music debate, and in particular by asking what exactly it is that parents and legislators have objected to over the years. After considering more formal content analyses of pop music songs and videos, we then describe the research that has asked directly whether an interest in problem music is associated with delinquency, drug use, permissive sexual attitudes, sexual discrimination, and self-harm/suicide. After then considering young people's ability to interpret music lyrics, we look directly at theoretical accounts of censorship and whether the available evidence suggests that young people's access to pop music should be limited. In the final section of the chapter we address the role of music in youth sub-cultures by describing the extent to which musical taste functions as a 'badge' of identity; the uses and gratifications that music provides young people; and the role of musicians as celebrities.

4.1 **Campaigns and protests: the filth and the fury**

Criticisms that pop music can *cause* negative effects among listeners are nothing new, and have led to censorship since the beginning of pop music as we know it (see McDonald, 1988; Nuzum, 2001). Indeed, in the days of Ancient Greece, Plato apparently advised of the potential threat of the media to adolescents, writing 'Then shall we allow our children to listen to any story anyone happens to make up, and so receive into their minds ideas often the very opposite of those we shall think they ought to have when they are grown up?' Aristotle added that 'Any musical innovation is full of danger to the whole state, and ought to be prohibited ... [since] when modes of music change, the fundamental laws of the state always change with them'. Similarly, in the early twentieth century, ragtime and jazz were criticized for their immoral effects on listeners. In 1951, many radio stations banned Dean Martin's *Wham Bam, Thank You Ma'am* for its apparently sexual content. In 1953, jukeboxes were outlawed within hearing distance of churches in six counties of South Carolina, and in 1954 Ruth Thompson introduced legislation to the USA Congress to ban the mailing of 'pornographic' records. Christenson and Roberts (1998) describe how during the 1950s Houston's Juvenile Delinquency and Crime Commission banned 50 records in a week simply because they were examples of rock and roll. Similarly, Ward, Stokes, and Tucker (1986) describe how Iran banned rock and roll in the 1950s because of reports of injuries caused by the wild dancing that was carried out to the music. However, certain cases have hit the headlines worldwide, and it is worth dwelling on just two of these for a moment to get a flavour of what exactly has caused the uproar and how this has changed between the 1950s and the present day.

The second half of 1956 was a turbulent time for Elvis Presley. On 5 June he made his second appearance on NBC Television's *Milton Berle Show*. In addition to performing the provocatively titled *I Want You, I Need You, I Love You*, his sexually-charged ending to *Hound Dog* caused consternation among the 40 million viewers, and earned the nickname that he apparently deplored, 'Elvis the Pelvis'. The King, however, denied using his body to sell records. 'I'm not trying to be sexy. It's just my way of expressing how I feel when I move around. My movements are all leg movements. I don't do nothing with my body ... I don't believe I'd sing the way I do if God hadn't wanted me to ... I don't think I'm bad for people. If I did ... I would go back to driving a truck'.

The bandwagon continued to rock 'n' roll however, and Elvis was soon being blamed for teenage delinquency across the country, particularly the chaotic scenes witnessed at his concerts. Elvis denied any culpability. 'If someone saw me singing and dancing, I don't see how they can think it would contribute to juvenile delinquency. If there's anything I've tried to do, I've tried to live a straight, clean life and not set any kind of a bad example.' The criticism clearly stung though since on 1 July he appeared on NBC's *Steve Allen Show* wearing a dinner jacket and singing *Hound Dog* to a basset hound, something he regarded as 'the most ridiculous performance of my entire career.' The uproar continued, however. While touring Florida in August, a judge ordered Elvis to stop moving his body while performing, with some shows being filmed by the police to check for any activity below the waistline.

By now, Elvis's line was hardening. 'If [teenagers] want to pay their money to come out and jump around and scream and yell, it's their business. They'll grow up someday and grow out of that. While they're young, let them have their fun.' Also, despite his earlier claim that God would have no objections to his stage act, the continuing furore meant that Elvis now had no choice but to distance his faith from his music. 'My religion has nothing to do with what I do now. Because the type of stuff I do now is not religious music.'

The storm eventually abated in early 1957 when Elvis finally appeared on CBS' *Ed Sullivan Show* on 6 January, following Sullivan's earlier vow never to have him on the programme. Although Elvis was filmed only from the waist up, Sullivan extended an olive branch, saying on air that he 'is a real decent, fine boy, and wherever you go, Elvis... we want to say that we've never had a pleasanter experience on our show with a big name than we've had with you. So now let's have a tremendous hand for a very nice person'. Elvis's gentle southern manners and modesty had finally won over conservative middle America, although it is arguable that the public's reaction to him in 1956 set

Elvis on a path that eschewed raucous rock 'n' roll in favour of Las Vegas lounges and Hollywood movies. That said, although apparently unintentional, the notoriety and publicity he experienced during 1956 certainly did little to harm Elvis's record sales: he spent 26 weeks at number 1 in the American charts.

The ensuing years saw continuing condemnation of pop stars for what, by present day standards, would seem like innocuous behaviour. For example, John Lennon's 1966 comment that The Beatles were 'more popular now than Jesus' led to bonfires of vinyl before the public realized that Lennon was actually describing the decline in spiritual belief among young people, rather than any delusions of his own band's omnipotence. Similarly, the 1970s saw the uprising of punk, and in particular the release of The Sex Pistols' highly unpatriotic *God Save The Queen* at the height of celebrations to mark the 25th anniversary of Queen Elizabeth II's ascension to the British throne. Featuring couplets such as 'God save the Queen/The fascist regime' and 'God save the Queen/She ain't no human being', it prompted threats of industrial action from packers at record pressing plants. The 1980s saw the rise of hyper-sexual heavy metal, and also condemnation of overt sexuality in the music of mainstream stars such as Madonna; and the 1990s gave rise to condemnation of the violent subject matter of gangsta rap tracks such as NWA's *Fuck Tha Police* and Ice-T's *Cop Killer*.

However, the contrast between the claims made against pop stars in the 1950s and the present day is perhaps illustrated best by the reaction during the late 1990s and early twenty-first century to Marilyn Manson. Manson was known as Brian Warner before changing his name partly to that of Marilyn Monroe and partly to that of 1960s serial killer, Charles Manson. Famed for his heavy make-up and 'undead Versace' appearance, he has caused controversy by vociferously opposing religious and political conservatism and particularly the mass media and gun culture. 'I'm engaged in a revolution', he once declared, 'against conservatism and ignorance, whether in American politics or American Christianity ... The thing that bugs me most about Christians [on the American religious right] is their assumption that they have a monopoly on morality [and a] right to impose their belief systems on everyone else ... I kind of see myself, among other things, as a fighter for freedom of speech'. Journalist Barbara Ellen summarized the response of Manson's targets, who believe that he 'represents everything that is decadent, evil, and anti-American. A drug-spiked apple pie smashing straight into Uncle Sam's beloved face.' His stage shows have been reviled by UK newspaper the *Daily Star* as 'pro-pervert' and 'blasphemous', and the UK's *Daily Mail* ranted that Manson is 'a rock star who promotes violent death in almost every song he sings.'

The 2000 Democratic American Vice-Presidential contender, Joe Lieberman, described Manson as 'perhaps the sickest act ever promoted by a mainstream record company'. In addition to this more 'official' censure, grass roots activists have also attacked Manson. For example, his concerts have been picketed by the religious right who in 1999 in Orlando, Florida even distributed a protest prayer against those 'foul and evil spirits who have brought/The music group Marilyn Manson into Orlando', calling on Jesus to help, 'So that they cannot sow lies/And spread discontent among our youth'.

Manson's notoriety has been achieved through a variety of acts. In one concert, for example, he opened a canister of 500 crickets with which he intended to cover his body. 'When I opened the can they had all died ... I threw up instantly and half a dozen people in the audience did the same.' After recreating elements of a fascist rally at another concert (with e.g. Nazi salutes) he said, 'I felt if I did it well enough, people would understand what I was getting at ... Some thought it was great satire, others thought I was a fascist ... Others just blindly pumped their fists and didn't notice the irony.' Numerous other, unproven, allegations abound on the internet, and they probably tell us more about Manson's reputation among the conservatives he criticizes than they do about his actual on-stage behaviour. Indeed Manson himself has said that 'The media has unfairly scapegoated the music industry and so-called Goth kids, and has speculated—with no basis in truth—that artists like myself are in some way to blame.' Instead he argues that acts of violence carried out by young people are 'a product of ignorance, hatred, and an access to guns' rather than his music.

Of course, anti-authoritarian behaviour is not something unique to pop musicians or even musicians as a whole. Picasso's *La Guernica* is perhaps the best known 'protest painting', and countless writers have been imprisoned for their views. In the musical domain, Shostakovich was reprimanded by the Russian government for his unpatriotic music; and Charlie Parker's use of drugs was widely known, as was Miles Davis's advocacy of the black civil rights movement. The reason for dwelling so long on the publicity surrounding performers such as Elvis Presley and Marilyn Manson is that it paints a clear picture of the major trend in licentious pop star behaviour. In short, this has become much more salacious over time in that behaviours, performances, and songs deemed intolerable fifty years ago are now commonplace. Videos by mainstream modern-day artists like Britney Spears and Jennifer Lopez contain just as much pelvic activity as Elvis's early performances but they have received nothing like the same level of criticism. Even the anti-authoritarian sentiments of The Sex Pistols' *God Save The Queen* seem tame when compared with Ice-T's more direct *Cop Killer* and Marilyn Manson's baiting of conservative Americans. As we saw in Chapter 2 when considering Martindale's work on 'the clockwork muse', this escalation in salaciousness is in line with the idea that all musicians have to be ever more attention-grabbing in order to maintain the public's interest. It does seem that cause for concern might be increasing, and this has led to numerous actions on the part of protesters and politicians.

The starting point of a truly organized campaign regarding music censorship can be traced to the mid-1980s when Tipper Gore, wife of the future American Vice-President Al Gore, founded the Parents' Music Resource Center (PMRC) along with several other 'Washington wives'. Not only was the PMRC concerned with explicit lyrics, but the group also argued that virgin minds were being poisoned by hidden messages and backward masking (see also Gore, 1987). The PMRC appeared before the US Senate Committee on Commerce, Science and Transportation on 19 September 1985 stressing that the group would not be satisfied until:

a) Questionable lyrics were printed and provided with their respective recordings;

b) Objectionable album covers were sold in plain brown wrappers (or sold in areas segregated from other albums);

c) Rock concerts were rated in terms of their suitability for younger age groups;

d) MTV segregated questionable videos into specific late night viewing slots.

The degree of antagonism this caused towards the PMRC is illustrated by rock musician Frank Zappa's own presentation to the Committee. In pointing out many of the practical problems and logical flaws in aiming for such goals, he argued that any ratings system 'opens the door to an endless parade of moral quality-control programs based on "Things Certain Christians Don't Like". What if the next bunch of Washington Wives demands a large yellow "J" on material written or performed by Jews, in order to save helpless children from exposure to "concealed Zionist doctrine"?' Zappa's reaction mirrored that of several other musicians. For example, rock band Megadeth sang in their 1988 song *Hook in Mouth* 'This spells out freedom, it means nothing to me/As long as there's PMRC'. Nevertheless as a result of the hearings, the industry body, the Recording Industry Association of America, asked its members to choose between two voluntary courses of action, either printing lyrics on the sleeve of records or attaching a label warning of explicit content to the front of potentially offensive albums. The latter came to be adopted and in 1990 was standardized as the well-known 'Parental Advisory – Explicit Lyrics' sticker, which is attached to around $1/3$ of the top-selling CDs in the

USA (Federal Trade Commission, 2000). It is worth noting the claim of some music industry conspiracy theorists that the real reason that record companies went along with the so-called 'Tipper sticker' was to smooth the passage of a bill to impose a tax on blank audio tapes (and other media) used in the illegal copying of music.

Nevertheless, numerous other direct measures have been taken by legislatures and law enforcement agencies against problem music. Lynxwiler and Gay (2000) reported that, up to the time of writing, 19 states of the USA had considered (but not enacted, usually on constitutional grounds) legislation to regulate the distribution of stickered CDs. Christenson and Roberts (1998, p. 229) describe some of the laws that have been considered. These would

> make it a crime to sell to minors albums with the industry's parental advisory label (Missouri, Pennsylvania, Louisiana); punish minors who buy labelled albums (a Pennsylvania bill, for instance, would sentence offending minors to 25 hours of community service at a rape crisis center); allow each township in a state to replace the state's general obscenity or 'harmful to minors' definitions with its own local standards (Ohio); ban completely the sale of all labelled albums (Leominster, MA); allow local prosecutors and judges to ban the sale of 'erotic' music to minors (Washington); and make mandatory a system of labelling sexually explicit or offensive lyrics (Missouri and other states).

Furthermore, such activities are not restricted merely to the USA. For example, in 2002 the Australian Record Industry Association and the Australian Music Retailers Association considered a revised stickering scheme that would ban the sale of certain CDs to under 18-year-olds.

In addition, interest in problem music at national level within the USA did not end with the 1985 hearings. In 1993 there were demonstrations and boycotts concerning perceived lawlessness and obscenity in rap music organized by various African American organizations (e.g. the National Association for the Advancement of Colored People), no doubt inspired in part by the 1990 ruling by a USA federal court judge that 2 Live Crew's album *As Nasty As They Wanna Be* was legally obscene (although this was later overturned in the appeal court), and the subsequent prosecution of a record store owner who sold it and (failed) attempt to prosecute the group following a Florida performance. In 1994 there were hearings of the Senate Judiciary Subcommittee on Juvenile Violence concerning purportedly anti-female lyrics by male rappers and self-degrading lyrics by female rappers. Both Bob Dole's 1996 Presidential campaign and Bill Clinton's 1996 State of the Union speech addressed the potentially negative impact of entertainment media on young people (see Grier, 2001).

In addition to these nationwide activities there are numerous instances of more localized and often bizarre actions having taken place over the past few years. Some of these are detailed on the website of the American Civil Liberties Union, and include a protest to the Kansas Attorney General over his decision to ban over 30 CDs from Kansas libraries; the arrest by a Louisiana sheriff of a skating rink owner and the confiscation (and later the court-ordered return) of 60 CDs by artists such as Britney Spears and Snoop Doggy Dog (and a Disney film soundtrack) from the rink following claims that they were involved in starting a fight in the car park; the ban by many radio stations on music by the Dixie Chicks (even after a public apology) because one group member voiced embarrassment at coming from the same state as President George W. Bush (see Rossman, 2004); the actions of police in Ohio who made a 13-year-old hand over an allegedly obscene t-shirt promoting a tour of rap group Insane Clown Posse; the suspension of a Michigan high school pupil for wearing a t-shirt promoting Korn that featured no lyrics or words apart from the band's name; and the suspension of four Texas private school students for attending a Backstreet Boys concert which violated a school policy forbidding involvement in inappropriate music.

Although the pattern of legislation has shifted constantly up until the present day, what remains clear is the direction in which the political wind is blowing, and that is very much towards censorship and the restriction of sale. There are at least three reasons why there has been so much legal and political confusion over attempts to limit young people's access to problem music. First, this is an issue that cuts right across traditional Western moral and political lines. For every conservative who is against the government meddling with business and every-day life there is a concerned parents group lobbying against a perceived affront to law and order: for every anti-censorship liberal there is a suicidal young rock fan.

A second source of legal confusion stems from young people's relationship with music. In short, although protesters have focused their attentions on the music itself, it is a mistake to assume that this music exists in a media vacuum. In reality the CDs themselves are of course just part of a multimedia market-ing extravaganza which presents adolescents with messages not just from the music and lyrics themselves but also from sophisticated promotional videos, magazine articles, CD cover art and liner notes, web sites, concerts, and t-shirts. Furthermore, the meaning conveyed by these to the adolescent audi-ence is very much a function of the circumstances in which they are presented: anxious parents and an elitist legislature sometimes forget that pop music can contain cheeky humour and irony, and are otherwise not always ideally posi-tioned to interpret the messages that musicians are trying to present to their young audience. This means that they are prone to identifying both false posi-tives (i.e. labelling music as salacious when it is not) and false negatives (i.e. failing to spot something that should concern them).

Third, following from this, it is all too easy for legislators to fall back on the 'sex and drugs' stereotype of pop music as evidence for its censorship, and to fail to recognize that young people are capable of adopting a mature, critical approach to the music they hear. One of us recently appeared on a radio programme concerning the impact of one particular artist on young people, and a pro-censorship campaigner who was also on the panel conceded that he had never even heard music by the artist in question, and more interestingly 'didn't need to'. The problem of stereotypes cuts both ways, however. It is similarly easy to portray pro-censorship campaigners as thin-skinned prigs, when in reality, as Christenson and Roberts (1998, p. 8) point out, 'For every bright, critical, actively two-parented 16-year-old watching MTV there is a gullible, enthralled 8-year-old latch-key kid watching the same stuff' and who potentially needs protection from it. This confusion means that there is a clear need for guidance based on dispassionate research, which can act as a foil to vociferous opinion based on supposition and stereotyping. As we shall see, the research on the subject suggests strongly that the truth lies somewhere in between the two extreme viewpoints adopted by pro- and anti-censorship campaigners.

4.1.1 Media effects and adolescent stereotyping

Before considering the research directly concerning music, it is worth holding back a moment longer and considering the relation between problem music and two more general areas of research, namely that concerning media effects and the stereotypes of adolescence. Research concerning media effects has over the past 15 years or so focused on whether the media do actually influence people's thoughts and behaviours. Christenson and Roberts (1998; see also Strasburger and Wilson, 2002) cite several reviews of mass media effects that describe how these are identified rarely across entire populations. For example, McGuire's (1986) review of the impact of several kinds of media content including product advertising, political campaigns, violent and stereotyped television portrayals, and television news was titled 'The myth of massive media effects', arguing that media exposure gave rise to few if any instances of wide-scale behavioural change among large numbers of listeners, readers, or viewers.

However, as McGuire and others have also acknowledged, more limited effects certainly do seem to exist, such that small groups of people can be influenced in very specific ways by specific mass media. For example, in July 2000 a joint statement issued by several academic societies in the USA (namely the American Psychological Association, the American Academy of Pediatrics, the American Academy of Child and Adolescent Psychiatry, the

American Medical Association, the American Academy of Family Physicians, and the American Psychiatric Association) stated that 'the data point overwhelmingly to a causal connection between media violence and aggressive behavior in some children'. Villani (2001, p. 392) reviewed research since 1990 on the effects of TV, films, pop music, advertising, video games, and computers/internet usage, concluding that 'The primary effects of media exposure are increased violent and aggressive behavior, increased high-risk behaviors, including alcohol and tobacco use, and accelerated onset of sexual activity'. Anderson and Bushman's (2002) meta-analysis of research on media violence and aggressive behaviour indicated that 'A positive link between media violence and aggression regardless of research method is clearly shown' (p. 2377). Indeed, although the correlations between media exposure and the various measures of aggression were typically between only 0.10 and 0.30, the authors caution that 'These effects are not trivial in magnitude. For example they are larger than the effects of calcium intake on bone mass or of lead exposure on IQ in children' (p. 2377). Similarly, Anderson and Bushman's (2001) meta-analysis showed a similar strength of relationship between exposure to violent video games and violence among players. It would be facile to dismiss more limited effects such as these as unimportant or irrelevant to music. First, as Anderson and Bushman (2002) explain, even small effects of the media on behaviour are much more alarming when placed in their true statistical context. Second, the fact that limited effects do occur in the case of non-music media suggests that they could also occur in the context of music. Although not all music may affect all people in many different ways, if just one or two very popular music CDs nevertheless increase the incidence of only one negative behaviour among a reasonable percentage of listeners then society is still faced with a strong malevolent force. More simply, problem music really could be a problem.

Given this, it is also worth considering two stereotypes of adolescence, since research on these suggests the opposite hypothesis, namely that there might not be a relationship between problem music and problem behaviour. The first of these stereotypes of adolescence is that it represents a time of 'storm and stress'. The argument here is that adolescents are helplessly attracted to problem music as it reflects their own alienation from society and conflict with parents. Research, however, paints a different picture of adolescent development. Far from being a time of storm and stress, evidence indicates that adolescents largely share the moral outlook of society in general and of their parents in particular. For example, Offer, Ostrov, Howard, and Atkinson (1988) studied a sample of 5,938 adolescents from Japan, Israel, Hungary, West Germany, Italy, Australia, Turkey, Bangladesh, Taiwan, and the

United States. Over 90% of participants in each location denied holding a grudge against their parents, and similar numbers rejected the idea that their parents were ashamed of them or would be disappointed with them in the future. Similarly, DuBois-Reymond (1989) found that 96% of Dutch adolescents were satisfied with their home life. Furthermore, although parent-adolescent conflicts undoubtedly arise from time to time, the nature of these is not terribly dramatic. As long ago as 1966, Douvan and Adelson reported that adolescents reported minor conflict with parents over minor issues (e.g. use of make-up) but little disagreement over major issues such as morality and politics. Similarly, Fogelman's (1976) study of 11,531 parents found that while 11% disagreed 'often' with their adolescent children over clothing and hairstyle, the corresponding figures for drinking, places gone to in their own time, and choice of opposite-sex friends were only 1%, 2%, 2% respectively. In short, as Coleman's (1978; 1993) focal theory points out, adolescents tend to resolve the problems they face one at a time, as and when they come into focus, such that the difficulties they face are rarely concentrated all at one time. More simply, if there is no 'storm and stress' then why should adolescents be attracted to music that deals with this?

A second stereotype of adolescence is that it represents a time of identity crisis. The idea here is that adolescents uncritically adopt the pro-drug, pro-everything-else identity of their favourite musician as they struggle immaturely to determine who they really are. Again, however, the evidence paints a different picture: while adolescence is clearly a time of identity formation, research indicates that this process is thoughtful, careful, and deliberate (e.g. Montemayor and Eisen, 1977; van der Werff, 1985); and only a small proportion of adolescents experience a period of intense, unresolved identity crisis (Hill, 1993; Meilman, 1979). More simply, if there is no identity crisis then why should adolescents adopt entirely and unquestioningly the licentious behaviours of their musical idols? Contrary to the evidence on media effects, the evidence concerning these two stereotypes of adolescence instead indicates that problem music may not link to problem behaviour. There is a clear need for research specifically on the subject, and that is what we consider next.

4.2 Prevalence and content of pop music media

Research on the problem music debate can be loosely divided into two groups, concerning respectively the prevalence and content of pop music media; and the relationship between this and actual changes in adolescents' thoughts and behaviours (see reviews by Hansen and Hansen, 2000; Knobloch and Mundorf, 2003). In this section we consider the first of these two groups of evidence. How much music media do adolescents consume and what exactly does it contain?

4.2.1 Prevalence of pop music

The first point to be made with regard to the amount of music media consumed is that adolescents have massive economic clout. Dortch (1994) found that as long ago as 1993 16 to 19-year-old boys in the USA had US$75 per week to spend and girls had US$82; and Sellers (1989) found that spending by American 12 to 19-year-olds in 1988 totalled US$55 billion, with this figure rising to US$248 billion when including also purchases made by 12 to 19-year-olds on behalf of their families (e.g. grocery shopping). Furthermore, adolescents spend a considerable amount of their money on music media: Christenson and Roberts (1998), for example, cite 1995 data from the Recording Industry Association of America showing that under 24-year-olds accounted for 40–50% of all sales of pop music in the USA. And it goes without saying that this is a very big market indeed. Frith (1987) noted that sales of mainstream pop music exceeded the US$1 billion mark as early as 1967, the US$2 billion mark by 1973, and the US$4 billion mark by 1978; Geter and Streisand (1995) estimated the pop music market in 1994 at over US$12 billion; and Rothenbuhler and McCourt (2004) described how, in 2001, people in the USA alone spent US$114 billion on 733 million CDs, records, and cassettes. The BBC News web site reports data from the British Phonographic Industry stating that in 2004 a record-breaking 174.6 million CD albums alone (excluding sales on other formats such as downloads and cassettes) were bought that year in the UK alone. Indeed the UK music industry contributes more to the national economy than does steel production or water supply; and a large proportion of this comes from adolescents buying pop music.

Given this massive financial outlay, it is unsurprising then that several studies of North American adolescents show that they spend extended periods of time with music media. Davis (1985) estimated that between grades 7 and 12 the average child has amassed 10,500 hours of deliberate exposure to music. Lyle and Hoffmann (1972) estimated that a quarter of 10-year-olds listened to music for four or more hours per day. Roberts, Foehr, and Rideout (2005) found that time spent listening to the radio plus time spent listening to CDs, tapes, and mp3 files rose from an hour a day among 8 to 10-year-olds up to two and a quarter hours a day among 15 to 18-year-olds. Christenson and Roberts (1998) argue that when all forms of exposure to music are considered (e.g. radio, deliberate music listening, and music listening in the background to another activity) then the time spent on this almost certainly outweighs time spent watching television. For example, they describe research by Roberts and Henriksen (1990) which showed that, when asked to include all incidences of exposure to music, 9th and 11th grade USA pupils estimated listening time at three to four hours per day whereas the corresponding figure for television viewing was two to two and a half hours per day.

With regard to music television, there is again evidence of high levels of exposure among North American children and adolescents. Brown, Campbell, and Fischer (1986) found that 12 to 14-year-olds watch music television for four hours per day; and 80% of their participants reported at least some exposure. Sun and Lull (1986) found that their high school pupils watched music television for two hours a day. However, exposure to music television is less frequent than exposure to other forms of music. Brown, Campbell, and Fisher (1986) and Sun and Lull (1986) indicated that less than half of adolescents watched music television on a daily basis. Similarly, Christenson (1992a) found that 98% of his 10 to 13-year-olds listened to music, whereas only 75% ever watched music videos; and that 62% had listened to music during the previous night whereas only 15% had watched music videos during the previous night. Also, more recent studies indicate much lower amounts of time spent watching music television than those figures indicated by Brown et al. (1986) and Sun and Lull (1986), with figures below an hour per day being the norm (e.g. Christenson, 1992b; Kubey and Larson, 1989; Leming, 1987; Wartella, Heintz, Aidman, and Mazarella, 1990). It is difficult to say whether these lower figures result from changes in viewing habits over time or simply from differences between the samples employed (for example, in their age or access to music television). The most important point for the time being, however, is that adolescents are certainly not strangers to the world of music video.

Also of note are several studies highlighting just how important North American adolescents believe that pop music is to them. Leming (1987) found that 46% of his 11 to 15-year-old participants regarded music as 'very important' and only 7% said that it was 'not important at all'. Steele and Brown (1995) provide numerous quotations from adolescents testifying to the role of music as one of their prized possessions. The Horatio Alger Foundation (1996) found that music was the number one non-school activity of their 13 to 17-year-olds. Christenson and Roberts (1998) describe Roberts and Henriksen's (1990) study which asked 7th to 11th grade USA school pupils what they would take with them to a desert island, and found that music media were the most preferred items. This North American data is complemented by data concerning Irish teenagers from Fitzgerald, Joseph, Hayes, and O'Regan (1995): 76% of boys and 81% of girls were interested in music as a leisure pursuit, meaning that it was the leisure activity they were most interested in. Furthermore a measure of actual leisure time activities indicated that listening to music/radio was the pursuit that girls actually participated in most frequently and the equal top pursuit for boys (together with watching television/videos).

4.2.2 Content of pop music

There are very few recent content analyses of music media, even though this content might well be expected to change with time as a consequence of both prevailing fashions and also potentially of pop music attempting to 'clean up its act'. Nonetheless, the existing research has highlighted four issues, namely the portrayal of women and sexuality, racial issues, the portrayal of destruction and violence, and why sex and violence in particular should feature so prominently in pop music media.

4.2.2.1 Women and sexuality

A few minutes spent listening to the radio will confirm that sexuality is the major theme within pop music. Cole (1971) analysed the lyrics of the top 10 songs for each year of the 1960s and found that 'love-sex was the predominant theme' (p. 389): in other words, even when 'protest pop' was arguably at its height, sexual relationships remained pop music's core subject matter. Christenson and Roberts' (1998) review indicates a gradual reduction over the past 50 years in the number of songs with a 'boy meets girl' theme from about 90% in 1941–2, 70% in 1966, 50% in the early 1980s, before recovering back up to around 70% by the late 1980s (see also Cooper, 1985). The way in which these relationships have been described also changed between the 1950s and 1980s, with growing emphasis on sexual and physical aspects of love and less on emotional aspects (e.g. Fedler, Hall, and Tanzi, 1982).

Indeed, with regard to specifically the portrayal of men and women, several protesters have criticized the *increasingly* overt sexuality of pop music and a tendency towards sexist portrayals of males and females. The best way to test this is to consider content analyses of the issue in chronological order. Wilkinson (1976) found that pop songs from 1954 to 1968 portrayed men and women similarly in terms of, for example, whether they were most likely to be primary actors or initiators in relationships (but see also Freudiger and Almquist, 1978). Hyden and McCandless (1983) found much the same with pop songs from 1972 to 1982, but they also provided early warning that changes within society since the 1960s towards sexual equality have not necessarily been reflected in pop music. They reported that males were more often portrayed as demonstrating initiative and competence, whereas females were more seductive and more powerful than men. Similarly, Baxter, de Riemer, Landini, and Leslie et al. (1985) analysed 62 music videos and found that sexual content was characterized by innuendo and suggestiveness. Sherman and Dominick (1986) found that more than 75% of the videos they sampled contained sexual suggestion (e.g. kissing, fondling), and that females were dressed provocatively about half the time they appeared.

More recent analyses have indicated much the same, in contrast with the relative egalitarian approach to sexuality in other musical styles (see e.g. Armstrong's (1986) account of sexuality in country music). Vincent, Davis, and Boruszkowski (1987) and Vincent (1989) analysed videos from 1985 to 1987, and found that over 50% of videos featured a male artist treating women in a condescending way. Seidman (1992) showed strong sex-typing of occupational roles acted out in music videos from 1987, and that women were more likely to wear sexually provocative clothing. Sommers-Flanagan, Sommers-Flanagan, and Davis (1993) found that men engaged in more aggressive and dominant behaviour in music videos than did women; that women engaged in more implicitly sexual and subservient behaviour; and that women were more frequently the object of explicit, implicit, and aggressive sexual advances. Signorielli, McLeod, and Healy (1994) analysed the commercials shown on music television, finding that females appeared less often, but that when they did they tended to have more beautiful bodies, wore skimpier clothing, and were looked at more often than others. Similarly, Gow (1996) analysed music videos from the early 1990s, finding that these under-represented women and portrayed them in a manner that emphasized physical appearance rather than musical ability. More generally, Andsager (2005; see also Andsager and Roe, 2003) has argued that sexuality performs three functions in videos, namely as a metamorphosis for a musician undergoing some form of transition; fantasy fulfilment; and as a form of power, each of which has the goal of attracting a new/greater audience.

Three studies published within the past few years show that although dubious portrayals of sexuality persist, there are also, however, some glimmers of hope. Seidman (1999) analysed music videos from 1993, comparing these with his sample of earlier videos. On the negative side, he identified that in the 1993 videos males and females were still portrayed overwhelmingly in sex-typed jobs; that males were still over-represented (63% of characters vs. 37% female characters), more adventuresome and violent; that women were still more affectionate, nurturing, and sexually pursued; and that more women wore revealing clothing (33.4% of characters vs. 7.0% of male characters). More positively, however, males were no longer more aggressive, domineering, and victimized than women; and females were no longer more dependent, fearful, and in pursuit of others sexually. Lynxwiler and Gay (2000) found that those who held conservative views toward sexuality were most likely to significantly dislike problem music, suggesting that the 'problem' may lie with the consumers of the music rather than necessarily with the music itself. Finally, Dukes, Bisel, Borega, Lobato, and Owens (2003) analysed the 100 most popular songs in the USA between 1958 and 1998. In confirmation of earlier findings they reported that 81 of the songs had lyrics about love, and that the percentage of songs concerning this did not change over time. They also found that, over time, references to love in lyrics performed by female artists decreased although women still made more references to love than men; that male artists steadily increased their use of 'sex words', while this peaked for females during 1976 to 1984; that more recent songs and songs performed by white, female artists expressed greater romantic selfishness (i.e. 'love on my terms' rather than 'love on ours or your terms'); and that the number of songs by women had increased over time towards a position of equality (from 15% of songs between 1958 and 1972, 43% between 1976 and 1984, up to 53% between 1991 and 1998). As such these findings provide some limited grounds for optimism concerning the current state of pop music. However, more generally they also indicate clear differences in music *by* and in the portrayal *of* men and women, such that sexual equality in pop music is a long way off. To give a blunt example, for every Christina Aguilera telling young girls that 'You are beautiful, no matter what they say' there is a 2 Live Crew commanding a woman to 'Nibble on my dick, like a rat does cheese'. Similarly, the furore over the 2004 MOBO awards in Britain highlighted ongoing concerns about homophobia in much modern music.

4.2.2.2 Racial issues

The racial content of pop music has received perhaps less attention, although five studies deserve brief mention. First, Dukes et al. (2003) reported that black musicians were more successful between 1991 and 1998 than at any previous point, accounting for 40% of those all-time top 100 songs that were released between 1958 and 1972, 27% of those 100 songs released between 1976 and 1984, and 63% of those 100 songs released between 1991 and 1998. Second, Hakanen (1995) surveyed the emotions that African-American teenagers had in response to rap and R&B/soul (and jazz), and notes that the predominant emotions were positive rather than negative. Rap in particular was associated with feelings of happiness and excitement. Third, in further contrast to the negative stereotype that surrounds much rap music, Cummings and Roy (2002) used rap lyrics by black artists to discuss how the ultimate goal for many is to encourage their audience to transcend the problems they face by, for example, empowering women, establishing equal race relations, assuming responsibility for their own destiny, shunning superficialities in seeking a meaningful life, avoiding violence, and working together as a community. Fourth, however, Brown and Campbell (1986) found evidence of musical 'apartheid' in that blacks were more likely to be portrayed in videos shown on Black Entertainment Television, whereas whites were more likely to be portrayed in videos shown on MTV. More direct evidence of racism was identified by Rich, Woods, Goodman, Emans, and DuRant (1998, p. 669) whose analysis of 518 music videos concluded that 'Compared with United States demographics, blacks were overrepresented as aggressors and victims [of violence], whereas whites were underrepresented. White females were most frequently victims. Music videos may be reinforcing false stereotypes of aggressive black males and victimized white females'. In summary, a lack of data makes it difficult to draw firm conclusions concerning racial issues in pop music content, although it seems that black artists are becoming accepted more into the mainstream, that rap and similar styles can convey positive emotions to teenage African-Americans, that black rap artists do not necessarily have negative intentions (contrary to the negative stereotype); but that blacks are portrayed unfairly and to differing extents on different television networks.

4.2.2.3 Violence

Other studies have focused on the prevalence of death, violence, and destructive behaviour in music media. Three studies by Wass demonstrate the popularity of music with themes concerning homicide, Satanism, and suicide (HSS) among a particular sub-group of adolescents in the USA. Wass, Raup, Cerullo, and Martel, et al.. (1988-1989) studied 694 12 to 19-year-olds, finding that 17% of the rural participants and 24% of the urban participants were fans of 'HSS rock'. Also, three-quarters of the fans were male and nearly all were white. Wass, Miller, and Stevenson (1989) studied 894 pupils in grades 9 to 12, showing that 17.5% were fans of 'HSS rock', and that relative to non-fans, 'HSS rock' fans were more likely to have parents who were never married or who had remarried, to be male, white, and enrolled in urban (rather than parochial) schools. Wass, Miller, and Redditt (1991) studied 120 13 to 18-year-old offenders. Of these, 91 were fans of rock, of whom 54% were fans of 'HSS rock'. The latter group was more likely to be white and to have dropped out of school. In short, liking for music promoting homicide, Satanism, and suicide was common, and could be traced to a subgroup of the population with distinct demographic characteristics. It would be interesting to see if fans of rap were disproportionately black but otherwise of a similar background.

Plopper and Ness (1993) illustrated the popularity of songs concerning violent death. They analysed the USA's music sales charts from 1955 to 1991 and found that only 90 of the 9,311 songs that reached the charts during this period concerned an earlier or an impending death. However, these 90 'death songs' were disproportionately popular: 25.5% of them reached number 1 compared to only 8.6% of the other songs, and while 57.8% of the 'death songs' reached the top 10 only 36.2% of the other songs did. Of those songs concerning the death of common people, murder and other forms of violence (e.g. executions, shootings of criminals) accounted for 48% of the deaths identified. Furthermore, the attitudes towards death least expressed in these songs were that life is dear and death is undeserved: references to the tangible realities of death were limited, and there was little sustained attention to grief and grieving. On a more positive point though, we should note that the popularity of death songs peaked in the 1960s, only eight of the 90 death songs were released in the 1980s and early 1990s (i.e. the end of the time period sampled by Plopper and Ness), and that the last 'novelty' death song to reach the charts was released back in 1967 (namely The Fifth Estate's *Ding Dong! The Witch is Dead*).

Other studies have studied the prevalence of violence and destruction in pop music videos. Greeson and Williams (1986) found that only 15% of the videos in their sample featured violence. Other studies from the period, however, found much higher percentages. Baxter et al. (1985) found that 53% of their sample of videos contained depictions of violence or crime, about a quarter showed physical violence against people, and 10% displayed weapons. Sherman and Dominick (1986) found that 56% of their videos included overt violence, and that only 12% of violent acts led to an actual injury. Kalis and Neuendorf (1989) found that 61% of the videos they considered contained objects or events that represented or threatened physical harm. Similarly, although Christenson and Roberts (1998) describe data from Roberts, Kinsey, and Gosh (1993) showing that 8% of the songs from 1980 to 1990 that they considered contained references to violence, they concluded that this probably represents a 'low-end estimate' (p. 135) given the subsequent rise of gangsta rap into the mainstream. In apparent confirmation of this, Tapper, Thorson, and Black (1994) found that violence was present in 29% of the rap videos they sampled, compared to only 6% of soul videos.

More recent research, however, suggests that levels of violence might be falling compared to the 1980s and early 1990s. For example, DuRant, Rich, Emans, Rome, Allred, and Woods (1997) found that 'only' 22.4% of the videos they sampled from MTV contained openly violent videos, with corresponding figures for Country Music Television and Black Entertainment Television of

11.8% and 11.5% respectively. Weapon carrying was higher among music videos on MTV (25.0%) than on Black Entertainment Television (11.5%), Video Hits One (8.4%), and Country Music Television (6.9%). Similarly, Smith and Boyson (2002) found that 'only' 15% of the videos they studied contained violence. However, the fact that more recent prevalence rates for violence are still far from ideal is illustrated by Martin and Collins' (2002, p. 855) analysis of music videos from New Zealand television, which concluded that 'violence is evident in a significant proportion of music videos'. Furthermore, although the level of violence may perhaps be falling compared to that demonstrated by earlier research, Smith and Boyson also illustrated that, as Plopper and Ness' (1993) analysis suggests, the portrayal of violence and destruction is rather casual and makes little reference to the consequences. For example, Smith and Boyson also found that 56% of the violent interactions depicted showed no injury to the victim; that 72% of all violent interactions did not feature the victim experiencing pain; that 17% of all violent scenes showed the violence being rewarded or positively reinforced; that 79% of violent scenes featured no punishments; that 88% of violent videos were presented in authentic or realistic contexts; and that only 3% of all music videos featured an anti-violence theme. In short, violence in music videos was sanitized and rarely chastized.

4.2.2.4 The popularity of sex and violence

The prevalence of sex and violence in pop music media has led a few researchers to ask whether they actually increase people's enjoyment. In particular, two studies indicate that the portrayal of sex has a positive effect on people's responses, that the effect of violence is less clear, but that sex and violence together do not enhance the appeal of videos. Hansen and Hansen (1990a) showed participants music videos with varying levels of sex and violence, and found that high violence led to negative reactions to the song and video; and also to students feeling less happy, more fearful, more anxious, and aggressive. Sexual imagery, however, did however lead to the videos having greater musical and visual appeal, although the combination of sex and violence did not. A similar study by Zillmann and Mundorf (1987, p. 316) found that 'the involvement of sexual stimuli intensified ... appreciation of the music and that violent stimuli tended to have a similar effect. However, the combination of sexual and violent images failed to enhance appreciation.' The apparent unpopularity of combinations of sex and violence may explain the DuRant, Rich, and Emans et al. (1997) finding that videos with the highest level of sexuality or eroticism are less likely to contain violence.

It is also worth noting here that other North American research by Dolf Zillmann has focused on enjoyment of love-lamenting and love-celebrating music as a function of the participants' own degree of loneliness (Gibson, Aust, and Zillmann, 2000; Knobloch, Weisbach, and Zillmann, 2004; Knobloch and Zillmann, 2003): all three studies showed some tendency towards greater preference for love-lamenting music among participants dissatisfied with their love life, and greater preference for love-celebrating music among participants who were romantically satisfied (although there were also numerous interactions involving gender). In other words, rather than talking about enjoyment of 'sex' in music, it might be more appropriate to consider the portrayal of different types of romantic relationship and the extent to which these are enjoyed by different types of person.

Indeed, the importance of considering the reactions of 'different types of person' is underscored by other studies that have directly addressed the role of individual differences in explaining reactions to sex and violence in music media. With regard to age, Christenson (1992b) found that younger adolescents aged 10 to 12 years did not feel that sexual images and lyrics were appropriate for them; and Greeson (1991) found that liking for sex in music videos was lower among college- than high school-aged participants, which implies overall that liking for sex in music may peak in the mid-teens. The latter study also reported that sex in music videos was more popular among working class participants, those who went to church less often, and males. Also with regard to participant sex, Zillmann and Mundorf (1987) found that sexual images made music seem more sensual and romantic for males, whereas females found music devoid of these visual embellishments most romantic. Bleich, Zillmann, and Weaver (1991) found that although adolescents who scored high for rebelliousness did not enjoy 'defiant' videos more than other people, they did like 'non-defiant' videos less. Clearly there is a need for more research on this topic, but what seems clear from the limited evidence available is that the relationship between sexual content, violent content, and enjoyment of music media is by no means as simple and straightforward as many pro-censorship campaigners would suggest.

4.2.2.5 Caveats

There are four caveats, however, to the general patterns identified above. First, as the research on enjoyment of sexual and violent content illustrates, factors such as age, sex, social class, religiosity, and rebelliousness all mediate the popularity of sexual and violent content in music media. Second, the great majority of the existing research originates from North America, and we still have very little data concerning the content of pop music in other regions of the world. Nonetheless, it is beyond doubt that North American music media have a global presence. Lloyd and Mendez (2001), for example, assessed the impact of music videos from the USA on 191 Botswanan 14 to 20-year-olds, reporting that more than $^2/_3$ had weekly exposure to these, and that musicians from the USA were replacing the influence of Africans on their sample. Nevertheless, all regions of the world have music of their own that may or may not have similar content to North America, and cultural differences may affect people's interpretation of the messages contained in music media from other countries. For example, Lloyd and Mendez found that the majority of their participants did not accurately perceive culture-specific language and images in the music videos from the USA. Similarly, Martin and McCracken (2001) compared marketing imagery in music videos broadcast in the UK and New Zealand, finding that UK videos had more brand references, fashion imagery, 'darkside products', and role model behaviour outcomes than in New Zealand.

Third, in addition to the need for research from cultures other than North America, the continually changing nature of pop music means that there is a need for ongoing programmes of research to detail changes in the content of modern day pop music. As society changes we might expect that the music it listens to changes as well. Nor, however, should studies from the 1980s and early 1990s be dismissed on the grounds that they are outdated. In Britain and many other countries, the most popular radio and music television stations in the present day are those that play precisely these 'golden oldies' that researchers were studying in the 1980s and 1990s. Dubious messages concerning sexuality and violence that are contained in the music of the past have survived into present day music media. Indeed it is arguable that if we want to know about the content of the majority of the music played on the radio then we should be referring directly to research from the 1980s and 1990s.

The most significant caveat, however, in terms of the problem music debate is that several studies illustrate how the content of music media varies significantly by genre: in particular, media representing styles such as heavy rock and rap have a tendency to feature the most morally dubious content, which justifies them being singled out so much by protesters. Jones (1997) assessed the prevalence of sex and violence in videos drawn from five genres, rap, hip-hop, R&B/soul, country and western, and rock. There were no differences between genres in the occurrence of more physical aspects of sex and violence, but rap videos consistently featured higher levels of socially questionable behaviours such as 'guntalk', 'drugtalk', presence of alcohol, 'bleeping' of verbal profanities, profanity, and gambling. As we have already seen, Tapper, Thorson, and Black (1994) found that violence was present in 29% of the rap videos they sampled and 17% of heavy metal videos compared to only 6% of soul videos; and that sexual innuendo, symbolism, or explicit sexual references were in 46% of rap videos and 23% of alternative rock videos compared to only 14% of classic rock videos. Christenson and Roberts (1998) cite unpublished research by Utterback, Ljungdahl, Storm, Williams, and Kreutter (1995) that compared 20 rap videos with 20 'alternative' videos, and found that of the rap videos 60% (versus 35% of alternative videos) objectified women's bodies and that 55% of the rap videos (versus 25% of alternative videos) contained 'macho' images. Smith and Boyson (2002) showed that rap (27%) and rock (20%) videos were more likely than adult contemporary videos (4%) to feature justifiable violence; and that violent scenes in rap (86%) and rock (85%) videos were more likely than those in R&B (68%) and adult contemporary (60%) to feature no punishment for the perpetrator. DuRant, Rich, and Emans et al. (1997) found that 20.4% of rap videos and 19.8% of rock videos featured violence compared to 5.9% of R&B videos and 10.8% of country videos; and that weapon carrying was also higher in rock (19.8%) and rap (19.5%) videos than in rhythm and blues (6.9%) and country (6.3%) videos. Similarly, DuRant, Rome, Rich, Alldred, Emans, and Woods (1997) found that smoking was shown in 30.1% of rap videos and 21.6% of rock videos compared to 10.9% of R&B videos and 11.7% of country videos; and that alcohol use was shown in 27.4% of rap videos and 24.7% of rock videos compared to 16.8% of R&B videos and 20.7% of country videos. They also found that 'videos with measurable levels of sexuality or eroticism were significantly more likely to contain alcohol use than videos with no referral to sexuality' (p. 1134). This glamorized depiction of alcohol contrasts with the depiction of alcohol use in 58 country songs highlighted by Connors and Alpher (1989; see also Chalfant and Beckley, 1977): in this case almost $^2/_3$ of the lyrics portrayed alcohol in terms of three negative themes, namely existential dilemmas and lessons learned, loneliness and lost love, and negative consequences; and there were few references to drinking for positive celebratory reasons.

Note, however, that dubious content is not limited exclusively to those problem music styles that have been singled out by protesters. Tapper, Thorson, and Black (1994) found that sexual imagery was present in 46% of rap videos, but also in 50% of soul videos and 45% of pop videos, and only 8% of heavy metal videos. DuRant, Rich, and Emans et al. (1997) found that 71.7% of rap videos and 76.5% of rock videos made no reference to sexuality or eroticism compared with only 45.5% of R&B videos and 54.8% of adult contemporary videos. Smith and Boyson (2002) found that there were no differences between rap, rock, R&B, and adult contemporary videos in the number of violent attacks that did not lead to consequences for the victim, the depiction of blood/gore following violence, and the humorous depiction of violence. Armstrong (1993) showed similarities in lyrics of rap and country music in terms of the portrayal of three violent crimes (i.e. murder, manslaughter, and assault) and the portrayal of toughness (i.e. physical prowess and masculinity).

In short, several studies indicate differences between the content of different musical genres, and any figures that summate data across genres must be treated with caution. Secondly however, although different studies indicate differences between the content of musical genres, the pattern of these is not completely clear-cut. Rap and rock music do tend to feature more deleterious content than other genres, and as such these genre labels do constitute a useful rule of thumb for concerned parents who would like an 'early warning' that the music their children are listening to may be problematic. However, the especially contentious nature of rap and rock relative to other musical styles is not always so apparent as the stereotypes of these might suggest.

4.3 **Effects of problem music on thoughts and behaviours**

However, just because music features content of dubious moral standing may not be sufficient to justify its censorship (although it may be sufficient evidence for some). Instead some might argue that censorship requires the case against problem music to establish not just that the music has salacious content, but also *proof* that exposure to problem music media actually *causes* deleterious effects among listeners and viewers. In the next few sections we consider the evidence concerning the effects of problem music on several attitudes and behaviours, namely delinquency and criminality, drug usage, permissive sexual attitudes, sexual and racial discrimination, and self-harm and suicide.

In each section we have very deliberately divided our presentation of the evidence into correlational and experimental studies. The reasoning behind this distinction is perhaps best described by analogy to the relationship between divorce and prior attendance at marriage counselling. A considerable proportion of married couples who divorce first go through some form of marriage counselling either formally through trained counsellors and religious leaders, or informally through close friends. Accordingly there would be a very high correlation between marriage counselling and divorce. However, nobody would attempt to claim that marriage counselling causes divorce. Rather, attendance at marriage counselling and divorce are both indicative of a deeper-rooted problem that causes both (e.g. an extra-marital affair or disagreements over children, etc.). Similarly, correlational evidence of a relationship between exposure to problem music media and problem behaviour/attitudes does not prove that the former causes the latter. Rather it indicates that, although there is a relationship between the two, there may be a deeper-rooted problem that is the real cause of both listening to problem music and also problem attitudes/behaviours. In many areas of psychology, a correlation is taken as *de facto* evidence of causality. It would be difficult to argue, for instance, that having large numbers of children with poor levels of physical and mental development *causes* towns to be polluted: the reverse causal link seems the only possible conclusion to draw from a correlation between pollution and development. However, as we shall see, although there is abundant correlational evidence of a link between exposure to problem music media and problem attitudes / behaviours, the former also tends to be associated with poor home environments and a variety of other factors that could also conceivably cause the latter. On the plus side, however, correlational research is nonetheless interesting as it tends to result from survey-based research that allows data to be collected from large groups of people concerning their everyday exposure to problem music media.

In contrast, experimental research allows researchers to directly investigate whether exposure to problem music *causes* problem attitudes/behaviours. However, this experimental evidence also suffers from a major disadvantage in the context of the problem music debate. Any research methods textbook will note that experiments are prone to demand characteristics: the experimental participant may be able to guess the hypothesis under investigation and this guides him or her to respond to any stimuli in a particular way. However, we suspect that experiments on problem music media are particularly prone to effects of this nature. Specifically, there can be very few people in the western world who are not aware of the rebellious, anti-authoritarian stereotypes of rap, heavy metal and the like. Accordingly, if they are shown a rap video and a video from a non-problem music style and asked to say which made them feel more violent, they will know what they are 'supposed' to say. Furthermore the situation is exacerbated when we remember that the great majority of the participants in experimental research are psychology and communication studies undergraduates aged between 18 and 21 years. It is hard to think of a group of people more likely to be sensitized to the hypothetical effects of pop music on behaviour.

4.3.1 Delinquency and criminality

4.3.1.1 Correlational studies

Several correlational studies have indicated that fans of problem music styles score higher on personality measures indicative of a tendency toward delinquency and criminality. For example, as we saw briefly in Chapter 3, several studies have found a direct association between sensation seeking and a preference for heavy metal music (e.g. Arnett, 1991a, 1992; Kim, Kwak, and Chang, 1998; McNamara and Ballard, 1999). Similarly, Dillman-Carpentier, Knobloch and Zillmann (2003) found that time spent listening in the laboratory to music with defiant messages was related to measures of disinhibition. Robinson, Weaver, and Zillmann (1996) found that undergraduates who scored highly on measures of psychoticism and reactive rebelliousness enjoyed rebellious videos more than did participants who scored low on these factors. Bleich, Zillmann, and Weaver (1991) assessed 16 to 19-year-old participants' trait rebelliousness and enjoyment of three 'defiant' and three 'non-defiant' rock music videos. Highly rebellious participants did not enjoy the defiant videos more than did their less rebellious peers. However, highly rebellious participants enjoyed the non-defiant videos less than did non-rebellious participants, and the former group also consumed less non-defiant rock music. North, Desborough and Skarstein (2005) found a positive relationship between psychoticism and British participants' liking for each of rap, nu metal, hip hop, and rock, but not R&B, indie music, or chart pop.

Away from the more widely recognized psychometric scales, Rubin, West, and Mitchell (2001) controlled for variations in anger and self-esteem, but still found that, as compared to most groups of fans, heavy metal fans exhibited more aggression (and a lower regard for women), and rap fans exhibited more aggression and distrust. Schwartz and Fouts (2003) compared adolescents who liked 'heavy music' (i.e. heavy metal and hard rock) and 'light music' (i.e. pop), and found that the former were more tough-minded, overly assertive in their relationships with others, less concerned with/indifferent to the feelings and reactions of others, more moody, more pessimistic, overly sensitive, discontented, more impulsive, more disrespectful of society's rules, and lower in academic confidence. Hansen and Hansen (1991a) found that heavy metal fans were higher than non-fans on 'Machiavellianism' (i.e. manipulative, cynical, and amoral) and 'machismo' (i.e. sexism and hypermasculinity); lower on 'need for cognition'; that time spent listening to heavy metal correlated positively with a belief that Satanism is widespread; and that punk fans were less accepting of authority than non-fans. Trostle (1986) found that fans of heavy metal were more likely to believe in witchcraft and the occult.

Given these personality dispositions, it is therefore unsurprising that so many correlational studies should show that fans of problem music should also score higher on actual measures of delinquency and criminality. In a recent as yet unpublished study, North and Sheridan found direct evidence that fans of problem music scored higher than non-fans on the Eysenck criminality scale. Wingood, DiClemente, Bernhardt, Harrington, Davies, Robillard, and Hook (2003) found that, compared with those who had had less exposure, participants who had had higher exposure to rap videos experienced greater unemployment and less parental monitoring. However, even when these were controlled, those with heavy exposure to rap were three times more likely to hit a teacher and more than 2.5 times as likely to be arrested during the 12-month follow-up period. Atkin, Smith, Roberto, Fediuk, and Wagner (2002) controlled for their 2,300 13 to 15-year-olds' degree of exposure to other violent media, but found that listening to problem music was still related to the commission of verbal aggression (defined as swearing, insulting or passing nasty comments). Singer, Levine, and Jou (1993) found that liking for heavy metal was related to delinquency among high school pupils with low parental control. North and Hargreaves (2006) found that British fans of problem music had carried out 20 delinquent/anti-social acts more frequently within the past two years than had non-fans; and Martin, Clarke, and Pearce (1993) found that their Australian adolescents scored higher on a delinquency scale if they liked rock/metal rather than pop. Wass, Miller, and Reditt (1991) found that people in juvenile detention were three times more likely than high school students to have heavy metal as their favourite musical style; and Epstein, Pratto, and Skipper (1990) found that 96% of their sample of adolescents with behavioural problems listed heavy metal as their favourite music.

Other correlational research has linked an interest in problem music to poor school performance. As long ago as 1966, Burke and Grinder found an inverse relationship between 13 to 17-year-olds' school marks and time spent listening to 'youth culture music'; Tanner (1981) found that Canadian teenage heavy metal fans were more likely than others to have a low commitment to school and to be delinquent (i.e. engage in fighting, damaging school property, and stealing), and that this was particularly the case among working class participants. Sun and Lull (1986) found that time spent watching music videos was negatively related to happiness at school; Larson and Kubey (1983) found that frequency of music listening was associated with lower levels of academic performance; and Christenson and Roberts (1998) report Roe's (1984) finding that low commitment to school and low academic achievement predicted liking for 'oppositional' music. Took and Weiss (1994) found that adolescent fans of heavy metal and rap were more likely than fans of other styles to have below average school grades and a history of counselling in elementary school for school problems (see also Hakanen and Wells, 1993).

Yet more correlational studies indicate that fans of problem music are more likely to engage specifically in risk-taking behaviour. For example, Arnett (1991a) compared fans and non-fans of heavy metal, finding that males fans were more likely than non-fans to engage in risky driving, risky sexual behaviour, and drug use; and that female fans were more likely than non-fans to engage in shoplifting, vandalism, risky sexual behaviour, and drug use. Similarly, Arnett (1992) found that adolescents who liked hard rock or heavy metal reported higher rates than non-fans of reckless behaviour such as drink-driving, driving over 80 mph, having sex without contraception, having sex with someone known only casually, drug use, shoplifting, and vandalism. Finally, Martin, Clarke, and Pearce's (1993) Australian study found that fans of rock/metal scored higher on a measure of risk-taking than did pop fans.

Furthermore, in addition to those British studies by North and co-workers and Martin, Clarke, and Pearce's Australian research, two other pieces of research indicate that relationships such as those described above may exist outside mainstream North American culture. Kim, Kwak, and Chang's study of 1,158 Korean adolescents found that fans of rock/heavy metal had the highest scores on an anti-social behaviour checklist; that participants who liked rock bands had high scores on measures of serious delinquency; and that fans of rock/heavy metal showed more 'light delinquency', experience seeking, and disinhibition than others. Similarly, Miranda and Claes' (2004) study of 348 French-Canadian adolescents found that liking for French rap music was linked to street gang involvement and mild drug use, even when controlling for peers' deviancy, exposure to other violent media, and the perceived importance of lyrics.

Although the bulk of the correlational evidence clearly indicates a relationship between problem music and delinquency/crime, there are several caveats to some of the studies cited above, and other correlational studies provide no evidence of a link between problem music and delinquency/crime. First, let's deal with the caveats to the studies cited above as supporting a relationship. In short, studies which investigate a third factor in addition to musical preference and a measure of delinquency/crime tend to show that the former has a strong effect in mediating the relationship between the latter two. For example, although North, Desborough, and Skarstein (2005) found that problem music fans scored higher than non-fans on psychoticism, they also reported than the frequency of carrying out delinquent acts did not differ between fans and non-fans when controlling for psychoticism. This suggests that psychoticism rather than the music itself may underlie the higher frequency of delinquency among fans of problem music. Similarly, Epstein, Pratto, and Skipper (1990) found that people with behavioural problems overwhelmingly liked heavy metal; but that musical preference could predict only participants' ethnicity and could not predict problem behaviour: ethnicity may underlie the link between problem music and problem behaviour. Singer, Levine, and Jou's (1993) finding that liking for heavy metal was related to delinquency among high school pupils with low but not high parental control implies that parental control is important in predicting delinquency/crime relative to the role of problem music. Arnett (1991a; 1992) indicated a relationship between liking heavy metal and engaging in risky behaviour, but the former was also related to higher levels of sensation seeking, negative family relationships, and, among girls, low self-esteem (Arnett, 1992), such that these are arguably more convincing explanations of engaging in risky behaviour than is musical preference. Finally, Took and Weiss (1994) indicated that gender also plays a mediating role in the relationship. Although below average school grades and a history of counselling remained significantly different between fans and non-fans of problem music when gender was taken into account, other differences between these groups of fans disappeared (namely in terms of their sexual activity, drug and alcohol use, and arrests).

Furthermore, there are numerous instances of failed attempts to establish a correlational relationship between liking problem music and crime/delinquency. With regard to personality predispositions, Schwartz and Fouts (2003) found numerous instances where fans of 'heavy music' (i.e. heavy metal and rock) had more deleterious personalities than did fans of 'light music' (i.e. pop), but this was by no means one-way traffic. They also found that fans of 'light music' scored significantly worse than fans of 'heavy music' on some measures. For example, they were overly responsible, rule-conscious, conforming in their relationships with others, struggling more with their developing sexuality, more uncomfortable toward sexual relationships, and were more concerned about being accepted by and/or fitting in with their peers. While some of these factors would steer them away from delinquency / crime (e.g. being more rule-conscious), others would not (e.g. their greater conformity to peers): indeed, Schwartz and Fouts concluded that the healthiest personalities were demonstrated by participants with eclectic musical tastes. Similarly, Gardstrom (1999) found that although rap was the preferred music of adolescent male felony offenders, only 4% of the sample perceived a connection between music listening and their deviant behaviour, and believed instead that the music was a mirror rather than a cause of their lifestyles. Adolescents are also quite cynical about the role of Satanism/the occult in their music, arguing that it is employed more as a 'publicity stunt', 'just hype', and that 'I laugh at it … it's all fake' (Arnett, 1991b, p. 91).

With regard to actual delinquent/criminal behaviour, Miranda and Claes (2004) found a link between liking French rap and street gang membership, but also that liking for American rap was linked significantly to a *lower* propensity towards theft, and that hip hop/soul were significantly linked to lower theft and lower hard drug use. North and Hargreaves (2007a) found that, although fans of hip hop/rap were among those more likely to have been arrested, the relevant percentage was no greater than for fans of blues and not a great deal higher than for fans of country and western; and also that fans of rock music were among those fans least likely to have been arrested. Furthermore, Gold (1987) found no difference in the self-image of a delin- quent group of adolescent punk fans and that of a delinquent group of adoles- cent non-fans, 'although analysis suggested group differences relative to family dynamics' (p. 535).

In summary, this correlational evidence indicates that there clearly is a rela- tionship between liking problem music and delinquency/crime. It would also be a mistake though to assume that the pattern of evidence is entirely consis- tent as there are numerous examples of either failed attempts to link problem music with delinquency/crime or cases where other forms of music have also been linked to delinquent personalities and actions. Rather, it seems that the nature of any relationship is strengthened by high psychoticism, membership of an undervalued ethnic/social group, high sensation-seeking, negative family relationships, low parental controls, and whether or not participants are male: the link between problem music and delinquency/crime is much stronger among those from these type of vulnerable backgrounds than among those from more adaptive backgrounds. It is more than a little tempting to speculate that it is these background conditions that may *cause* both liking for music which deals with victimization and also delinquency/crime.

4.3.1.2 Experimental studies

Experimental evidence paints a similarly complex picture. First let's deal with those studies that support a relationship between experimental exposure to music media portraying delinquency/crime and subsequent acts of delinquent behaviour. Harris, Bradley, and Titus (1992) observed the frequency of 'inap- propriate behaviour' in an open courtyard at a mental hospital. Hard rock and rap were played for 21 days followed by 21 days of easy listening and country, and then another 18 days of hard rock and rap. The former led to more inap- propriate behaviour being observed. Similarly, Waite, Hillbrand, and Foster (1992) found that the removal of music television from 222 hospital forensic patients led to a decrease in the frequency of overt aggressive behaviour over a 55-week period (from 44 to 27 incidents per week).

Hansen and Hansen (1990b) noted that there are at least two theoretical explanations of why exposure to music media portraying delinquency/ violence should lead to subsequent acts of delinquency. Social learning theory (Bandura, 1973; 1977; 1994) states that new behaviours can be learned through observation and direct imitation, but finds it difficult to explain effects that do not represent direct imitation of the behaviours portrayed. 'The kinds of behavioral effects measured by researchers often bear little physical resemblance to observed media behaviors, although they do fall into the same general behavioral or meaning category (e.g. aggressive acts)' (p. 359). In contrast, cognitive priming theory (Berkowitz and Rogers, 1986) argues that media violence primes additional information in memory that is related to the behaviour portrayed. This makes the entire category of information more salient, and more likely to be employed in determining social judgements and behaviour. As such, exposure to violent music media should prime related delinquent tendencies, which in turn guide assessment of the media in question and the future attitudes and behaviour of viewers/listeners.

Accordingly Hansen and Hansen (1990b) showed participants rock music videos that did or did not portray anti-social behaviours such as trashing a parent's house during a party, joyriding, or defying parents and police. Participants then saw a confederate in another room perform or not perform an anti-social hand gesture targeted at the experimenter. Participants then evaluated the confederate, and the Hansens used cognitive priming theory to predict that the anti-social videos should lead to more favourable assessments of the confederate's hand gesture than should the non-anti-social videos. The results supported this, since after exposure to the non-anti-social videos the hand gesture led to the confederate being liked less compared to when he did not make the hand gesture. However, after exposure to the anti-social videos, the hand gesture did not lead to the confederate being liked less than when he did not make the hand gesture. More simply, exposure to anti-social music media made participants more tolerant of anti-social behaviour. Similar findings occurred for participants' ratings of the extent to which the confederate was 'warm' and 'wonderful', his 'sex appeal', his 'social power', and the extent to which his behaviour was both 'irrational' and 'threatening'.

Similarly, in the first part of Johnson, Jackson, and Gatto's (1995) experiment, the inner-city African-American adolescent male participants took part in a supposed memory test in which they were shown either eight rap videos containing violent images and/or lyrics, eight non-violent rap videos, or no videos. In a 'second experiment', supposedly on decision-making skills, the participants were then asked to read a passage describing a dating couple. When an old male friend of the woman comes up to her and gives her a 'big hug and small kiss on the lips', her partner reacts violently towards the woman and the old friend. Participants had to say if the violence was acceptable and whether they would have reacted similarly. Participants then read a second passage that described two male friends. One went to college but the other chose not to. When the latter picked up the former in'his new BMW ... nice clothes and nice jewellery' the former said that he too would have these when he graduated as a lawyer, and asked the latter how he could afford these without a job. Participants were asked to state which of the men they wanted to be like, and how likely it was that the college student would become a lawyer. The results showed that participants shown the violent videos were more accepting of violence towards both the man and woman described in the first passage, and regarded themselves as more likely to react similarly if confronted with the same situation. Also, participants shown the violent videos wanted to be more like the man who acquired material wealth without a college education, and were less certain that the other young man would finish his education. Interestingly, consistent with Hansen and Hansen's (1990b) cognitive priming approach, Johnson et al. argued that 'It is possible that exposure to the violent rap videos increased the accessibility of constructs associated with violence ... [The] accessibility of such violent constructs may have led to greater acceptance of the use of violence and greater reported likelihood of engaging in violent acts' (p. 37).

Adopting a similar theoretical approach, Anderson, Carnagey, and Eubanks' (2003) five experiments indicated that exposure to violent versus non-violent music could lead to greater feelings of hostility and more aggressive thoughts. Furthermore, these findings applied whether the violence was presented in a humorous or non-humorous context. Crucially, in direct support of the cognitive priming approach, Experiments 3–5 found that violent music led to greater accessibility of violent cognitions as measured by reaction times to aggressive versus non-aggressive words or by proposing aggressive words in solution to a word completion task.

Finally, Wann and Wilson (1996) took a different approach, predicting that aggressive music videos were particularly likely to influence participants with an external locus of control (i.e. a feeling that events in their life were beyond their own personal volition). The 56 participants watched either three aggressive or non-aggressive videos and then completed a hostility scale. Although the researchers failed to find an effect of locus of control, Benjamin's (1996) re-analysis argued that the effect would have been significant had a larger sample been tested.

Before concluding this section we should also note two experimental studies that failed to support the proposed effects of exposure to violent music on delinquent thoughts and actions. Wanamaker and Reznikoff (1989) asked participants to write stories about five ambiguous pictures. While they wrote these stories they heard a rock song with either nonaggressive music and nonaggressive lyrics, aggressive music and nonaggressive lyrics, or aggressive music and aggressive lyrics. These failed to influence the degree of aggressiveness in participants' stories, or their scores on a measure of hostility. Rather than supporting the priming hypothesis, the 'Results support the hypothesis that many teenagers do not attend to rock music lyrics and that lyrics do not affect aggression' (p. 561). Similarly Gowensmith and Bloom (1997) found that exposure to heavy metal increased arousal in all participants, but did not increase levels of anger in participants who were already heavy metal fans. It is difficult to know whether to regard these two studies as mere aberrations or instead as evidence that the problem music–delinquency link is not as clear as other experimental studies suggest. Note also, however, that Verden, Dunleavy, and Powers (1989) found that music preference might follow rather than precede antisocial behaviour. In combination, however, the correlational and experimental evidence indicates that there is some form of relationship between problem music and delinquent / criminal thoughts and behaviours; that the former has the ability to prime the latter; that the relationship is probably not exclusive to mainstream North American culture; that the relationship is stronger in, but not limited to, fans of rap and heavy rock; and that the relationship may be stronger among certain vulnerable groups of adolescents than others.

4.3.2 **Illegal drugs**

In Chapter 2 we reviewed the research on drug use in musicians. Several other qualitative studies have taken a more discursive approach to the long suspected position of illegal drugs in musical subcultures. With regard to hallucinogens, Baumeister (1984) discussed the link between acid rock and LSD, arguing that the structure of the music (namely high levels of complexity within a simple chord structure) is indicative of a performer with a weak short-term memory but abundant inspiration. Similarly, Millman and Beeder (1994) discussed the re-emergence of psychedelic drug culture in the music of the early 1990s; Lyttle and Montagne (1992) considered the relationship between psychedelic drugs and the British acid house movement of the late 1980s, arguing that the music (particularly its rhythms), the settings, and the drugs were all geared towards providing altered states of consciousness; and Dotson, Ackerman, and West (1995) described the recreational use of ketamine in the acid house movement. With regard to other drugs, Klee (1998) argued that amphetamine sulphate has been popular among British youth for so long because of its links to music subcultures, such as the rave scene of the late 1980s and early 1990s; French and Power (1998) argue that alkyl nitrites (aka. poppers) were most commonly taken in nightclubs with the goal of either enhancing the music or effects of other drugs; and Peters, Kelder, Markham, Peters, and Ellis (2003) describe how abuse of codeine and promethazine hydrochloride cough syrup may be reinforced by 'an innovative form of hip-hop music called "screw"' (p. 415) (see also Gregoris and Poldrugo, 2002).

4.3.2.1 Correlational studies

There are no experimental studies concerning exposure to music and the use of illegal drugs. However, given the more discursive evidence discussed above it is perhaps unsurprising that several correlational studies have indicated a relationship between a preference for problem musical styles and the use of illegal drugs. In perhaps the first study on the issue, Robinson, Pilskaln, and Hirsch (1976) found that young men's use of marijuana, amphetamines, barbiturates, and hallucinogens (and alcohol, but not heroin) was positively related to their liking for 'protest music'. 'Usage of marijuana, for example, increased from about 25% for those having only one or no protest favorites to almost 50% among those having 2 or 3 protest favourites' (p. 125). King (1988) found that 59% of those hospitalized for substance abuse named heavy metal as their favourite style of music compared to 17% of those hospitalized for other psychiatric disorders. Martin, Clarke, and Pearce (1993) found that rock/heavy metal fans were 50% more likely to admit use of marijuana, tobacco, and alcohol than were pop fans; and Arnett (1991a; 1992) found that adolescent heavy metal fans were more likely to use drugs than adolescents with other musical preferences. Wingood, DiClemente, Bernhardt, Harrington, Davies, Robillard, and Hook (2003) found that adolescents with greater exposure to rap videos were 1.5 times more likely to use drugs over a 12 month follow-up than those with less exposure, even when controlling for factors such as employment status, parental monitoring of their whereabouts, and religiosity. Roberts, Dimsdale, East, and Friedman (1998) found that adolescents who had strong (and particularly negative) emotional responses to music were at increased risk of participating in health-risk behaviours including drug use, and that this was particularly the case among fans of rock or heavy metal. In apparent confirmation of this, Lacourse, Claes, and Villeneuve (2001) found that French-Canadian adolescents' frequency of drug use was related only weakly to measures of liking for heavy metal, but more strongly to a measure of deeper immersion in heavy metal culture, namely 'worshipping' (which included hanging posters, acquiring information about the musicians etc.). Hansen and Hansen (1991a) found that these usage patterns also appeared to permeate perceptions of social reality: heavy metal fans estimated that a greater proportion of the population had tried cocaine and marijuana than did non-fans, and that the latter perception was positively related to the amount of exposure the participants had to heavy metal music media.

Interestingly, however, although pro-censorship campaigners usually focus on heavy rock and rap music, there is also evidence of very high levels of (poly)drug use among fans of dance music. Note that these studies involved participants who were usually self-selecting and immersed heavily in the dance music 'scene', such that the figures on drug usage probably represent the 'worst case scenario'. Nevertheless, on face value the figures are extremely disturbing. Forsyth (1996) interviewed 135 participants in the Glasgow dance music scene finding that 97.8% had used cannabis, 93.3% amphetamine, 91.9% LSD, 91.1% ecstasy, 85.2% nitrites, 81.5% psilocybin, and 70.4% cocaine; that participants had tried a mean of 10.7 drugs; and that out of 17 drugs, at least half of the respondents had used 15 of them within the past year. In other words, high levels of use of several drugs seems to be the norm. Similarly, North and Hargreaves (2007a) found that of all the British music fans considered, fans of dance/house, hip hop/rap, and DJ-based music had tried the widest range of drugs, and they also had particular 'drugs of choice' that they were particularly likely to have tried, namely amphetamine, LSD, and ecstasy, partly confirming Forsyth's (1996) finding that hallucinogens were the most popular within the dance scene. Winstock, Griffiths, and Stewart (2001) found that over 70% of their 1151 respondents to a questionnaire printed in a British dance music magazine had tried each of ecstasy (96%), amphetamines (92%), cannabis (91%), amyl nitrite (77%), and LSD (71%); and that in the past month alone 86% had used ecstasy, 73% cannabis, 46% cocaine, 40% amphetamines, 22% amyl nitrite, and 10% LSD. Of those who had used the drug in the past year, participants had used cannabis on a mean of 17.9 days in the last month, benzodiazepines on 6.2 days, amphetamines on 4.7 days, ecstasy on 4.5 days, amyl nitrite on 3.8 days, and cocaine on 3.2 days. Furthermore, while 'on' ecstasy, 83% of respondents had also taken amphetamines, 82% cannabis, 58% cocaine, 51% amyl nitrite, and 30% LSD (see also Measham, Parker, and Aldridge, 1998). Lenton, Boys, and Norcross (1997) report similar results from 83 participants recruited from the rave scene in Perth, Australia. For example, 96.4% of participants had used cannabis, 90.4% LSD, 83.1% inhalants, 75.9% ecstasy, and 68.7% amphetamines; and Boys, Lenton, and Norcross (1997) showed that 80% of those who had used a drug at their last rave also used a second, and that the 'dance music drugs' (ecstasy, amphetamines, and LSD) were most commonly combined with cannabis and inhalants. Given data such as these, it is unsurprising that Winstock, Wolff, and Ramsey (2002) indicated that usage associated with dance music can act as an early warning of the arrival of a new drug.

There is also some indication that a link between dance music and illegal drugs may extend beyond those who are heavily immersed in dance music culture. Forsyth, Barnard, and McKeganey (1997) surveyed 1,523 *school pupils* in both Dundee and Perth and Kinross, and found that liking 'rave music' was positively related to use of 'rave drugs', 'hard drugs', solvents, and cannabis. For example, among the Dundee sample, 46.2% of fans of rave music had used an illegal drug at some point compared with only 8.8% of pop music fans and four of the 9 indie fans. Furthermore, the relationship survived changes in musical fashion such that the figures do not merely represent drug users affiliating themselves with the latest musical fad. Whereas the Dundee sample were tested in 1994 when rave music was still fashionable, the Perth and Kinross sample were tested in 1996 when indie music had supplanted it in British young culture. Nevertheless 38.8% of the fans of rave music had used an illegal drug at some point compared with 12.0% of pop fans and 31.4% of indie fans. In other words, the high rate of drug use among fans of dance music remained even when musical fashions changed.

Six other studies have taken a similar approach in cultures outside mainstream North American, Australian, and British society. In perhaps the most detailed of these, van de Wijngaart, Braam, de Bruin, Fris, Maalsté, and Verbraeck (1999) investigated drug usage among participants at numerous large-scale dance events in The Netherlands. Of these, 81% had tried ecstasy and 63% amphetamines; and the corresponding figures for usage during the event at which they were interviewed were 64% and 34% respectively. Furthermore, among ecstasy users, only 6% used the drug more than once per week, but 42% used it more than once a month. Similarly, in confirmation of the pattern from British research, Pederson and Skrondal (1999) found that ecstasy use among 10,812 Norwegian adolescent school pupils was higher among those interested in dance music and those who attended dance music events; and that the relationship between dance music and drug use (particularly ecstasy) persisted when controlling for gender, age, family discord, conduct problems, and depression/anxiety. Miranda and Claes' (2004) study of French-Canadian adolescents found that liking for rap music predicted use of hard drugs even when controlling for peer deviancy, consumption of violent media, and the importance participants' attached to song lyrics. Eide and Acuda (1997) found a relationship between use of both inhalants and cannabis by Zimbabwean school pupils and their orientation toward Western culture (including music) rather than local, Zimbabwean culture. Felix (2004) considered techno music culture in Spanish-speaking countries and reported that there may be two different groups, one being active and risk-taking and a second group who are more introverted and less inclined to use drugs. Finally, Baptista, Noto, Nappo, and de Araújo Carlini (2002) found that the main context for ecstasy use in São Paulo was clubs and raves playing dance music.

In other words, the link between dance music and illegal drug use has crossed many national borders.

4.3.2.2 Caveats

However, as with evidence on delinquency and criminality, there are several caveats to the conclusion that problem music is associated with use of illegal drugs. First, no fewer than eight studies show that the drugs-music link is stronger in some groups of fans, in some settings, and for some types of drugs than others, such that it would be a mistake to infer from the above that liking *all* pop music links to a predilection for *all* types of illegal drugs. Forsyth (1996) found that, among participants in the Glaswegian dance music scene, different drugs were used in different settings, such that clamping down on drug usage in nightclubs specifically would not necessarily eradicate *all* drug usage among dance music fans. For example, 59.0% of ecstasy users last did so in a nightclub, whereas only 9.0% last did so at home and only 0.8% last did so in a pub: clamping down on drug use in nightclubs might reduce specifically ecstasy use among dance music fans. In contrast, only 3.8% of heroin users last did so in a nightclub whereas 23.1% last did so at home and 65.4% last did so in another house: clamping down on drug use in nightclubs would probably have little impact on specifically heroin use among dance music fans. Similarly, van de Wijngaart, Braam, de Bruin, Fris, Maalsté, and Verbraeck (1999) found that dance music fans usually use ecstasy at dance music events rather than at home or in bars (but see also Boeri, Sterk, and Elifson (2004) who suggest that ecstasy usage practices may extend beyond nightclubs). Martin, Clarke, and Pearce (1993) found that, although rock/heavy metal fans were 50% more likely to admit use of marijuana, tobacco, and alcohol than were pop fans, fans of 'both rock/metal and pop as groups were shown to take equal amounts of sedatives and analgesics': in other words, the only difference in the two groups' drug use concerned legalized drugs and marijuana, which has semi-legal status in some countries and is often regarded as in a different class to 'hard drugs'. Hansen and Hansen (1991a) found that heavy metal fans estimated that a greater proportion of the population had tried cocaine and marijuana than did non-fans: however, these differences were not found when fans of punk were compared to non-fans, implying that the music–drugs link may be stronger among some fans of problem music than among others. Dent, Galaif, Sussman, Stacy, Burton, and Flay (1992, p. 124) found that musical preference was a 'diagnostically weak' indicator of drug, alcohol, and tobacco use among 758 Los Angeles adolescents, and although there were some highly specific exceptions, 'the popularity of particular music styles was quite similar among non-drug-exposed and drug-exposed adolescents' (p. 124).

Similarly, Miranda and Claes (2004) found that, although overall exposure to four types of rap was positively related to use of hard drugs, it explained only a small proportion of the variance in this. They also found a significant *negative* relationship between drug use and interest in hip hop/soul; and that only liking for French rap music (rather than other types of rap) was significantly and positively related to use of soft drugs (namely cannabis, tobacco, and alcohol). North and Hargreaves (2007a) found that although fans of dance/house, hip hop/rap, and DJ-based music had tried the widest range of drugs, only fans of DJ-based music had tried significantly more than had fans of indie, soul, R&B, jazz, opera, and blues; and furthermore that rock fans had, if anything, taken fewer drugs than most. Similarly, Doak (2003) found no relationship between music preferences and drug preferences among a sample of teenage substance abusers. In other words, although drug use is very common among fans of problem music, it is wrong to believe that all illegal drugs are linked equally to all problem musical styles, that drug use in some music-related contexts (e.g. dance music events) necessarily extends to several other contexts and several other drugs, and that fans of problem music always use more illegal drugs than other people.

A second caveat to the music-drugs link comes from six studies which suggest that any association between music and illegal drug use may not necessarily be *caused* by music media and music culture. For example, four studies indicate that usage is particularly high among fans of problem music with backgrounds indicative of vulnerability to drug use. For example, van de Wijngaart, Braam, de Bruin, Fris, Maalsté, and Verbraeck (1999) found that regular use of ecstasy among attendees at dance music events was more common among 16 to 21-year-olds, those with low levels of education, those working part-time or unemployed, and those with friends who also use ecstasy. Similarly, Arnett (1992) found that fans of hard rock and heavy metal were more likely to use drugs, but they were also more sensation-seeking, had negative family relationships, and (for females) had lower self-esteem. Lacourse, Claes, and Villeneuve (2001) found that frequency of drug use was related weakly to liking for heavy metal among adolescent boys and not at all among adolescent girls. Similarly, Took and Weiss (1994) found that adolescents who liked heavy metal and rap were more likely to use drugs, but that this effect disappeared when gender was controlled: in other words the effect could be explained by fans of heavy metal and rap being made up predominantly of males. Factors such as gender, low education, under-employment, drug-using friends, a sensation-seeking personality, negative family relationships, and low self-esteem might well be expected to contribute to drug usage, so that it is difficult to be certain that the music itself is the cause of drug usage. Furthermore, as we saw earlier, Roberts, Dimsdale, East, and Friedman's (1998) results suggest that it is the nature and strength of a person's emotional reaction to music, rather than the music *per se*, that may underlie the relationship between music and health-risk behaviour. It is also worth noting that Mayton, Nagel, and Parker (1990) found that lyrics and music videos were 'considered to encourage drug and alcohol use by less than 10 percent of the adolescents' they interviewed (p. 316), such that efforts to eradicate drug use through music censorship 'do not appear to be worth the energy required' (p. 317).

Third, other work suggests that pop music lyrics *per se* are unlikely to be the cause of drug usage. Markert (2001) considered 751 songs from the 1960s to the time of writing that dealt with specific drugs. Interestingly, he found that half the songs about heroin were released in the 1990s, but critically the descriptions of the drug were uniformly *negative*. Lyrics concerning cocaine were generally negative in the 1980s and 1990s, although there was more equivocation among musicians who first came to prominence in the 1960s and early 1970s. Despite its frequent association with the 1960s hippy movement, over 80% of the lyrics about LSD were released after 1980 and provide a negative assessment of the drug. Marijuana was the most frequently addressed drug, and has generally been perceived as innocuous over time. Put simply, the relationship between music media and usage of illegal drugs cannot really be linked to any overt advocacy of drugs in pop music lyrics (with the exception of marijuana). Rather any relationship between musical preference and drug use instead implies that, at worst, the drugs must be advocated by other music media (such as music journalism) rather than the music itself, even though the latter of course tends to be the target of protesters' concerns.

Indeed, three other studies also suggest that music may not be the *cause* of the music-drugs relationship. Lenton, Boys, and Norcross (1997) found high levels of drug use among participants recruited from the rave scene in Perth, Australia. Although the sample was small (N = 83), three other aspects of their data are particularly interesting. First, of those who had ever used ecstasy, 65.1% *first* did so in a 'rave related' context, which implies that this drug might well be linked strongly to dance music culture. However the corresponding percentages for other drugs were much lower (i.e. 33.3% for amphetamines, 31.2% for cocaine, 27.5% for inhalants, 22.7% for LSD, 22.6% for tranquillizers, 1.2% for cannabis, and 0.0% for heroin and other opiates). In other words, it is far from clear that dance music culture is responsible for the *onset* of the majority of drug use. Second, the respondents had a pretty good idea of the risks involved in drug use, such that drug use cannot be simply attributed to naïve individuals getting 'carried away' with excitement and taking drugs as a result: over 70% of respondents got the correct answer on seven or more questions out of 10 concerning drug-related harm; and on eight of the 10 questions, less than 10% of respondents gave the wrong answer (with fewer than 5% giving the incorrect answer for six of the questions). Although drug use is linked to musical sub-cultures, it may be more accurate to state that people who take drugs in such contexts are well informed and tend to use nightclubs and the like merely as an *opportunity* to do so.

Similarly, Lenton, Boys, and Norcross also found evidence that, with the exception again of ecstasy, any given drug was more likely to be used in settings outside 'rave culture' than in nightclubs and the like. For example, 60% had used LSD in a rave-related context in the past 12 months, but 80% had used it in other settings. Similarly, Bellis, Hughes, Bennett, and Thomson (2003) also indicated that drug use among dance music fans has a recreational rather than a specifically musical basis. They gave a questionnaire to British people as they waited to check in on their return flight to the UK from the holiday resorts of Ibiza (which has a well-established dance music scene). Participants' level of drug use was higher while on holiday in Ibiza than at home: for example 6.7% of ecstasy users took the drug five or more times per week in the UK but 36.9% did so while in Ibiza, and furthermore 'they do not appear to appear to maintain higher frequencies of use when returning to the UK' (p.1717). Similarly, significant numbers of people first tried illegal drugs while in Ibiza: for example, 16.3% of GHB users first took it in Ibiza. These findings again suggest that the dance music scene provides an opportunity for drug use, but that this is more closely linked to notions of 'having a good time' than it is to actually going to nightclubs *per se*.

A final caveat to the idea of a music-drugs link is suggested by research demonstrating the positive role of music in anti-drug initiatives. Newcomb, Mercurio, and Wollard's (2000) experimental study showed that anti-drug use TV commercials featuring pop stars (Jon Bon Jovi, Aimee Mann, Gene Simmons, and Belinda Carlisle) were more successful than otherwise equivalent commercials featuring unknown actors of similar age, ethnicity, and gender. Also, both Epstein and Sardiello (1990) and Mark (1986) provide positive reports of the role of music in anti-drug programmes (see also Wakefield, Flay, Nichter, and Giovino, 2003).

It is unfortunate that there is so little data on issues such as these, but for the time being we can conclude that there is a clear link between musical subcultures and use of illegal drugs, particularly within heavy metal and dance music subcultures. However, we can also conclude more tentatively that there are several caveats to this. First, membership of a particular musical subculture indicates a predilection for only some (and not all) types of drugs in some (and not all) settings. Second, the music–drugs relationship has not always been identified among fans of problem music, and fans of other supposedly innocuous musical styles are certainly not strangers to illegal drug use. Third, the music–drugs relationship appears to be stronger among vulnerable people, and the nature of these vulnerabilities may well indicate a predisposition toward drug use. Fourth, there is little evidence that pop music lyrics portray illegal drugs (apart from marijuana) positively, such that the lyrics themselves cannot be blamed for drug use, and that traditional methods of censorship (e.g. banning CDs, stickering albums) would be ineffective at reducing drug use. Fifth, people who use drugs in musical contexts also use them outside musical contexts, so it is hard to see why only the former should be blamed for the usage and why this should be regarded as the causal factor. As such, the music–drugs relationship is certainly troubling, but these caveats question the extent to which it can be generalized to a range of drugs and a range of musical subcultures, and also whether musical subcultures are a causal factor rather than merely a banner around which drug users (like other young people) will rally.

4.3.2.3 Alcohol and tobacco

Before concluding this section on illegal drugs we should also mention research linking musical preference to two legal yet undoubtedly harmful drugs, namely tobacco and alcohol, since many of the same arguments apply. Again there are no experimental studies but numerous correlational studies show a relationship. DuRant, Rome, Rich, Alldred, Emans, and Woods (1997) found that tobacco was portrayed in 12% of country music videos and 26% of those broadcast on MTV. As we have already seen, Martin, Clarke, and Pearce (1993) found that rock/heavy metal fans were 50% more likely to admit use of marijuana, tobacco, and alcohol than were pop fans. Miranda and Claes (2004) found that use of alcohol, tobacco, and cannabis was related to liking for French rap. Posluszna, Burtowy, and Palusinski (2004) found that smoking among high school and college students was linked to a higher preference for music associated with anxiety and a depressed mood. Wingood, DiClemente, Bernhardt, Harrington, Davies, Robillard, and Hook (2003) found that those adolescents exposed to higher levels of rap music videos were 1.5 times more likely than others to have used alcohol over a 12-month follow-up.

With regard to dance music, Forsyth (1996) found that 95.6% of participants from the Glasgow dance music scene had drunk alcohol in the past year, and that 86.2% had smoked. Forsyth, Barnard, and McKeganey (1997) found among their Dundee school-age sample that 70.7% of rave music fans had tried smoking (versus 41.4% of other fans) and that 62.7% had been drunk (versus 30.6% of others). North and Hargreaves (2007c) found numerous differences between the fans of several musical styles in terms of the amount that they drank and smoked. Fans of DJ-based music, hip hop/rap, and dance/house drank more per week than others. However, a less clear picture emerged regarding smoking. Fans of DJ-based music smoked the most, with a mean of 5.79 cigarettes per day, although fans of the innocuous musical styles of blues and 1960s pop were not far behind them.

However, many of the caveats that applied to the relationship between music and illegal drugs apply also to this general relationship between music, drinking, and smoking. First, it is not clear that fans of heavy metal, rap, and dance music always drink and smoke more than others. For example, as we have just seen, North and Hargreaves (2007c) found that fans of blues and 1960s pop smoked very nearly as many cigarettes per day as fans of DJ-based music, and that fans of other problem music styles smoked no more cigarettes per day than other non-fans. Miranda and Claes' (2004) study of 348 French-Canadian adolescents found that liking for French rap music was linked to mild drug use (i.e. cannabis, alcohol, tobacco), even when controlling for peers' deviancy, exposure to other violent media, and the perceived importance of lyrics. However, liking for other styles of rap music was unrelated to use of these drugs. Furthermore, as we saw earlier, Dent, Galaif, Sussman, Stacy, Burton, and Flay (1992, p. 124) found that musical preference was a 'diagnostically weak' indicator of drug, alcohol, and tobacco use among 758 Los Angeles adolescents.

4.3.3 **Permissive sexual attitudes**

4.3.3.1 Correlational studies

Research concerning music and permissive sexual attitudes supports the conclusion of Ward's (2003) review of the media in general (including music videos) which argued that frequent and involved exposure is associated with greater acceptance of casual attitudes about sex, higher expectations of the prevalence of sexual activity, and greater levels of sexual experience (see also Andsager and Roe, 2003; Arnett, 2002). In particular, numerous correlational studies support the notion that exposure to music media is associated with libertarian sexual attitudes, particularly among females. Hansen and Hansen (1991a) found that heavy metal fans scored higher than non-fans on a measure of hypersexuality; and this perhaps explains why the fans estimated a smaller percentage of 15 to 21-year-olds to be virgins than did non-fans. Furthermore, both these measures were positively related to the amount of exposure that participants had had to heavy metal music media. Christenson and Roberts (1998) describe Yee,

Britton, and Thompson's (1988) finding of a correlation between listening to heavy metal and approval of pre-marital sex. Schierman and Rowland (1985) found that females who scored high on a measure of sensation-seeking reported preferences for activities centred around rock music and sexually explicit material.

These attitudes are mirrored in actual sexual behaviour. Wingood, DiClemente, Bernhardt, Harrington, Davies, Robillard, and Hook's (2003) study of 522 14 to 18-year-old African-American females found that those with greater exposure to rap videos were twice as likely as those who had been less exposed to have had multiple sexual partners and 1.5 times as likely to have acquired a new sexually transmitted disease at a follow-up 12 months later (see also Strouse and Buerkel-Rothfuss, 1987). Arnett (1991a) showed that 54% of heavy metal fans versus 23% of non-fans had had sex with a casual acquaintance. Martino, Collins, Elliott, Strachman, Kanouse, and Berry (2006) conducted a longitudinal investigation of 12 to 17-year-olds. Using follow-ups one year and three years later, the 1,242 adolescents reported on their sexual behaviour and how frequently they listened to differing musical styles. People who listened to more 'sexually-degrading' lyrics at the one-year follow-up were more likely to lose their virginity; whereas exposure to 'non-degrading' content was unrelated to changes in sexual behaviour.

Again there is evidence that these relationships are not unique to North America. North and Hargreaves (2007a) found that 37.5% of British hip hop/rap fans claimed to have had five or more sexual partners during the past five years, with similar percentages for fans of DJ-based music (29.1%) and dance/house (28.7%), compared to only 14.2% of chart pop fans. Similarly, Holder-Nevins and Bain (2001) studied sexually active and virginal Jamaican teenage girls, and found that the former were particularly likely to believe that North American pop music was linked to sexually promiscuous emotional responses (e.g. 'sexy', 'loving', and 'wanting to get close to someone of the opposite sex') and feelings of loneliness. However, despite its often sexual overtones, participants believed that Jamaican dance hall music was linked more to excitement and fun than to sexuality.

As we have seen several times already, however, with regard to other attitudes and behaviours, there is also evidence that the strength of the relationship between consumption of sexually permissive music and sexual permissiveness varies from style to style. For example, Hansen and Hansen (1991a) found that levels of hypersexuality were no worse among fans of punk than non-fans, and nor did these two group differ in their estimate of the proportion of 15 to 21-year-olds who were virgins. Similarly, North and Hargreaves (2007a) found that rock fans had had no more sexual partners over the past five years than fans of jazz or blues.

The extent of the music–permissiveness relationship also may depend on several other factors. Wingood, DiClemente, Bernhardt, Harrington, Davies, Robillard, and Hook's (2003) study of 522 14 to 18-year-old African-American females found that those with greater exposure to rap videos were no less likely to use condoms than those who had been less exposed: in other words, the strength of the music–permissiveness link may depend on the measure of promiscuity in question. Furthermore, as we have already seen, Schierman and Rowland (1985) found that liking for rock music and sexually explicit material may depend on participants' level of sensation-seeking, such that the latter may well underlie the other two. Took and Weiss (1994) showed that gender plays an important role also. Their fans of heavy metal and rap were more sexually active than non-fans, but this difference disappeared when Took and Weiss accounted for the fact that a greater proportion of the former were male. Family background may also matter. Strouse, Buerkel-Rothfuss, and Long (1995) found that permissive attitudes to pre-marital sex were linked to more time spent watching music videos, particularly among females, those with a poor family life, and those who considered running away from home: there was no relationship between sexual permissiveness and watching music videos among participants who had a positive relationship with their family. The apparent relationship between promiscuous attitudes and poor family environment is easy to understand; and Strouse, Buerkel-Rothfuss, and Long argue that females are also more vulnerable to a music-promiscuity link: they are encouraged to be more sexually conservative than are boys and so have more latitude to change their permissiveness in a liberal direction; and the authors also cite evidence that females' sexuality is more influenced by exter-nal sources than is males' so that the former should be influenced more by music media (see also Chapin, 2000). One final note in defence of pop music is that two papers have described the use of rock and hip hop in AIDS inter-vention and prevention programmes (Kotarba, Williams, and Johnson, 1991; Stephens, Braithwaite, and Taylor, 1998).

4.3.3.2 Experimental studies

In short, the correlational evidence suggests a link between music and sexual permissiveness, although there are several caveats to this, which again suggest that the relationship is stronger among those from a vulnerable background. This rather equivocal conclusion is supported by two experimental studies. Both Greeson and Williams (1986) and Calfin, Carroll, and Schmidt (1993) found that experimental exposure to music videos led to participants showing greater approval of premarital sex. Wallach and Greenberg (1960), however, suggest that the effect may not be unique to pop music, finding that experimental exposure to jazz could lead to greater sexual arousal. Also, Mitchell, DiBartolo, Brown, and Barlow (1998) suggest that the effect may have less to do with any particular musical style than with the listener's emotional response to the music in question. Specifically, they found that males had more sexual arousal (as measured by penile circumference) in response to emotionally positive rather than negative music, and that emotionally negative music led to less sexual arousal than that found among a control group. In other words, any music that has a positive emotional impact on listeners/viewers leads to greater sexual arousal. Again, it seems that a relationship exists between music and permissive sexual attitudes, but this is not exclusive to *all* consumers of *solely* problem music.

4.3.4 Sexual and racial discrimination

4.3.4.1 Correlational studies

Other studies have investigated a subtly different topic, namely the relationship between exposure to music videos and anti-female beliefs and behaviours. Three correlational studies support the music-sexism relationship, although as before they suggest that the relationship may not occur for all problem music styles and may be mediated by other factors. Strouse, Goodwin, and Roscoe (1994) found that involvement with pop music (including rock music videos) was associated with attitudes indicating acceptance of sexual harassment, especially for females, but also that this was exacerbated among those from unsatisfactory or 'non-intact' families. In other words, gender and family background mediate the strength of the music–sexism link. Hansen and Hansen (1991a) found that heavy metal fans scored higher than non-fans of a measure of lack of respect for women; and that they estimated a smaller percentage of 15 to 21-year-olds to have been involved in date rape than did non-fans. Furthermore, both these measures were related positively to the amount of exposure that participants had had to heavy metal music media. Note, however, that lack of respect for women was no worse among fans of punk than non-fans, and nor did these two groups differ in their estimate of the proportion of 15 to 21-year-olds who had been involved in date rape. Rubin, West, and Mitchell (2001) found that heavy metal music listeners showed less regard for women.

4.3.4.2 Experimental studies

Three studies by Christine Hansen have attempted to test the music-sexism relationship experimentally, using cognitive priming theory (see also Ward, 2003). Hansen (1989) showed participants music videos in which there was no sex-role stereotypic material; or in which a woman was approached by a man and reciprocated his sexual interest, leading to the man treating her well (a 'boy meets girl' script); or in which the woman did not reciprocate his sexual interest leading to the man derogating her (a 'boy dumps girl' script). Afterwards, the participants watched one of two realistic male-female interactions in which a young man and woman supposedly auditioned to work as a music TV presenter. In both interactions, the male made a sexual advance toward the female. However, in one interaction the subsequent behaviour of the man and woman was consistent with the 'boy meets girl' schema; and in the other interaction their behaviour was consistent with the 'boy dumps girl' schema. Hansen's first experiment tested participants' recall of the interaction, and the second experiment tested participants' impressions of the man and woman in the interaction. The results confirmed her prediction that recall would be better when the interaction was inconsistent with the video: schema-inconsistent information ought to be unexpected by the participants and would require more processing in order to resolve the inconsistency, such that this greater processing aids recall. Experiment 2 confirmed the prediction that participants' impressions of the man and woman in the interaction ought to be more favourable when their behaviour was consistent with the video. This was because schema-consistent information is more easily processed. The results of this complex study can be summarized easily: pop videos can prime sex-role stereotypic beliefs, and these can influence the recall and evaluation of males' and females' behaviours.

Hansen and Hansen's (1988) study was very similar. Participants were first shown music videos in which men and women either were or were not depicted in sexually stereotypical ways, before then observing and appraising a man and woman interacting during an audition in a manner that again followed the 'boy meets girl' or 'boy dumps girl' script. The results again conformed to the predictions of a schema-based approach, since the man and woman were evaluated more positively along sex-typed dimensions when participants had seen the sex-typed videos. For example, when the woman reciprocated the man's sexual advances then, after viewing sex-typed videos, participants perceived her as more non-threatening, submissive, sexual, sensitive, and sympathetic than when she did not reciprocate his advances. When the man subsequently praised the woman, participants perceived him as more sexual, assertive, and dominant. Conversely, after viewing the sex-typed videos, violations of the 'boy meets girl' script (i.e. her rejecting his advances, and him derogating her subsequent to this) led to more negative evaluations of the man and woman. Furthermore, these effects were not present when participants were instead shown the neutral videos. Again the results show that pop music videos can prime sex-role stereotypic beliefs, and that these can influence subsequent evaluation of males' and females' behaviours.

Hansen and Krygowski (1994) used previous research on schemas to predict that higher levels of emotion and physiological arousal can lead to participants employing more extreme information contained within the schemas activated. 'For example, people possess different schemas for thievery that vary in their extremity: an armed robber schema would be more extreme that a shoplifter schema' (p. 26). They also argued that at least two mechanisms could underlie the effects of increased arousal on the activation of more extreme schematic knowledge. First, schema become more accessible if they are congruent with the individual's current state of arousal. Second, since arousal reduces cognitive processing capacity, people who are highly aroused are more likely to fall back on schematic processing. Consequently, Hansen and Krygowski reasoned that the priming effects of music videos ought to be stronger if individuals are in a highly aroused state, because the increased arousal would be particularly likely to trigger intense schematic information and processing. Participants watched one of four music videos before then watching an ambiguous TV commercial featuring either a man or a woman. Consistent with previous research, those who had seen a music video featuring a sexy woman rated the commercial as sexier, more humorous, less disgusting, and less aggressive than participants who had seen a music video featuring female prostitution. Similarly, participants who had seen a music video featuring a sexy male rated the TV commercial as more pleasant, amusing, sexy, and less aggressive than participants who had seen a music video featuring an 'unsexy' man. However, these effects were greater when participants also completed vigorous rather than light physical exercise, such that the high level of arousal resulting from this seemed to prime the use of more extreme schema activated by the music videos. Of course very few people watch music videos while exercising, but the salacious content of music videos might well elicit high levels of arousal from viewers that subsequently lead to more extreme evaluations of males and females.

Ward, Hansbrough, and Walker (2005) considered the effects of sex-typed music videos on the development of sex-typed gender schemas among African-American high school pupils. We have already seen that music videos portray men and women in sex-typed ways, and Ward Hansbrough, and Walker argued that with each priming of these sex-typed depictions, so sex-typed schema should become more salient in the mind of the viewer and exert a stronger influence on future judgements. In support of this, they found that the frequency with which participants watched music videos was correlated both with them holding traditional gender role attitudes and with participants' perception that it was important for women and men to be 'flash' (i.e. athletic, rich, attractive, and cool). Furthermore, experimental exposure to sex-typed rather than gender-neutral videos led to participants being more supportive of stereotypes concerning gender and sexual roles, and believing it was important for men and women to be 'flash'. Put simply, laboratory and real world exposure to sex-typed music videos both led to participants adopting stereotypical notions of gender. Crucially moreover, the effects of experimental exposure to sex-typed videos on ratings of the importance of men being 'flash' were stronger among those participants who watched music videos more frequently in real life and also among those who identified with the characters in the videos. In other words, frequent exposure to music videos outside the lab (which frequently involve sex-typed gender depictions) and heavier involvement with sex-typed videos shown in the lab increased the extent to which the experimental videos activated sex-typed schemas in gender evaluations: as such, this provides strong support for the schema-based view of the effects of videos on sexism.

Other experimental studies, although not conducted explicitly within the schematic priming approach, also provide data that are certainly consistent with it, in that participants behaved in a way that appeared to be primed by sexist music. Kalof (1999) found that exposure to a gender-stereotyped music video (for *The Way You Make Me Feel* by Michael Jackson) versus a non-sexual video (for *Stand* by REM) led to higher adversarial sexual beliefs among males and females (i.e. agreement with statements such as 'Women are usually sweet until they have caught a man, but then they let their true selves show'): at least there were no effects of the videos on measures of 'acceptance of rape myths' (e.g. agreement that 'In the majority of rapes, the victim is promiscuous or has a bad reputation'). Barongan and Hall (1995) asked participants to listen to misogynous or neutral rap music and then chose a film to show to a confederate (which was either neutral, depicted a rape, or depicted a man attacking and abusing a semi-nude woman). When participants heard misogynous rap then 30% showed the assaultive film and 70% showed the neutral film: when participants heard the neutral rap only 7% showed the sexual-violent or assaultive films and 93% showed the neutral film. Similarly, Peterson and Pfost (1989) showed male undergraduates rock videos that were erotic-violent (i.e. semi-naked women with weapons), erotic-nonviolent (i.e. semi-naked women dancing), nonerotic-violent (i.e. singer being violent), or nonerotic-nonviolent. The nonerotic-violent videos led to higher scores on a measure of adversarial sexual beliefs and more negative emotional responses (e.g. feelings of frustration and anger).

Two experimental studies, however, suggest that the music-sexism relationship is more serious for some groups of people. Ward, Hansborough, and Walker (2005) found that participants were more likely to identify with characters portrayed in non-sex-typed music videos than in sex-typed videos: this suggests encouragingly that the former are perhaps more likely to prime subsequent behaviours than are the latter. Furthermore, the effects of sex-typed videos were more extreme among vulnerable participants, specifically those who were young and male. Similarly, Maxwell (2001) found that a song was more likely to be interpreted as a literal representation of rape, battering, and sexual assault if the listener had experienced abusive behaviour. Put simply, those who have been victims of violence may be more likely to access anti-female schema when interpreting a song.

Furthermore, we have already seen how the effects of experimental exposure to music on sexism are not limited solely to exposure to 'problem music', and two studies illustrate this well. St. Lawrence and Joyner (1991) found that both sexually-violent heavy metal and relatively non-inflammatory Christian metal led to more negative attitudes to women one month later. In other words, in addition to showing that styles other than problem music can cause negative effects, it seems that it is the music itself rather than the lyrics that may cause these effects. Note also that Wester, Crown, Quatman, and Heesacker (1997) selected participants for their low level of familiarity with gangsta rap: given St. Lawrence and Joyner's findings, it is interesting that Wester et al. found, among people who were unfamiliar with the musical style, that the music alone did *not* lead to worse attitudes toward women than the absence of both music and lyrics. Since the music alone was unable to influence participants who did not know the musical style, this seems to complement St. Lawrence and Joyner's finding among participants who *did* know heavy metal that the music alone could cause negative effects. If participants knew that the music was meant to have a bad effect then it did, whereas if they did not know that the music was meant to have a bad effect then it did not. In short, although the evidence indicates a clear relationship between problem music and anti-female attitudes, it could be argued that the effect is stronger among vulnerable groups and that the broader cultural perception of a particular musical style can cause it to have an influence just as much as the specifics of the song or video in question: if so then *any* piece of music could potentially lead to anti-female attitudes. Nonetheless, of all the possible effects of music considered in this chapter, the link between problem music and sexism appears to be the one supported most by the available evidence.

4.3.4.3 Eating disorders and racial discrimination

Before concluding this section, we should also note research that has investigated two other related issues, namely eating disorders and racial discrimination. With regard to the first, we have already seen how women in music videos tend to be scantily-clad (see also Englis, Solomon, and Ashmore, 1994), and four studies have investigated whether these thin, 'ideal' body images can promote body dissatisfaction among young female viewers. Tiggemann and Pickering (1996) assessed female teenagers' exposure to music videos by presenting a list of the programmes shown on TV in the past week and asking participants to circle those they watched. Scores on this were not related to body mass index, perceived weight, or body dissatisfaction, but were correlated with scores on the 'drive for thinness' sub-scale of the Eating Disorders Inventory, even when controlling for participants' amount of exposure to other types of TV programming. Similarly, Tiggemann and Slater (2004) showed females aged 18 to 30 years music videos that either did or did not emphasize the thin appearance of women, and found that the former led to viewers feeling fatter, less confident, less physically attractive, and less satisfied with their bodies. The same videos also led to participants being more likely to compare themselves with the women shown in the videos. Note also that the effects of the 'thin women' videos on body dissatisfaction disappeared when controlling for the extent to which participants compared themselves with the women in the videos. In short, rather than the videos having a direct effect, it seems that the link between viewing 'thin women' videos and body dissatisfaction was caused by the videos prompting comparisons between the participants' own bodies and those portrayed. In apparent confirmation of this interaction of variables, Borzekowski, Robinson, and Killen (2000) found that time spent watching music videos by Californian boys and girls was related to their perception of the importance of appearance and their weight concerns, but these effects disappeared when body mass index and ethnicity were controlled. Similarly, an unpublished study by North, Sheridan, and Wilson studied females aged 16 to 30 years and found that, although self-esteem and body mass index scores were related to various measures of eating disorders, the amount of time spent watching music television was not. In short, it is not clear yet whether there is an association between exposure to music videos and eating disorders, although it would be interesting to see data that deliberately employed more vulnerable groups of participants, and specific types of videos and music.

Given this, it is interesting that three studies have investigated how negative moods induced by music can promote greater body dissatisfaction, particularly among women with a propensity towards eating disorders. In other words, it seems that any link between music and eating disorders may vary according to the nature of the music in question. For example, Kulbartz-Klatt, Florin, and Pook (1999) used classical music to induce both positive and negative moods among women with bulimia nervosa, panic disorder, or no psychological disorder. Among patients with bulimia nervosa, negative mood led to increased body width estimates and positive mood led to decreased estimates. The effects were not shown in the two other groups of women, such that they were unique to those with an eating disorder. Carter, Bulik, Lawson, Sullivan, and Wilson (1996) used music to induce a negative mood and found that this led to women with bulimia nervosa rating their own body and a picture of a woman of healthy weight as larger than did a control group. Interestingly, Carter, Wilson, Lawson, and Bulik (1995) employed classical and pop music, and showed that the type of music than can induce low moods varies considerably from person to person: it may be wrong to focus on the effects of particular problem musical *styles* rather than specific *pieces*.

Very little research has addressed the role of music in promoting/reducing racism. However, what little research there is corresponds theoretically with that on sexism; and suggests that violent and/or misogynistic rap music can have a negative priming effect on the subsequent evaluation of African-Americans. Johnson, Trawalter, and Dovidio (2000) exposed participants to violent rap before showing them either a black or white man harassing his girlfriend. Participants attributed the black man's aggression to his disposition whereas the white man's aggression was attributed much less to internal factors. Furthermore, priming this racist stereotype of blacks also led to other aspects of the stereotype being activated, and this occurred for black and white participants: irrespective of their own ethnicity, participants exposed to violent rap were less likely to hire a black than a white man for a job involving intelligence.

Similarly, Rudman and Lee (2002) presented participants with either violent and misogynistic rap or mainstream pop before asking them to take part in a seemingly unrelated person perception test. This involved participants reading a story in which a narrator describes meeting an old friend called either Donald (i.e. a typically white name) or Kareem (i.e. a typically black name). The narrator describes how Donald/Kareem refused to speak to a saleswoman, refused to pay his rent until his landlady repainted his apartment, refused to tip a waitress, got annoyed with a woman in a shop packing his bags too slowly, ignored a female co-worker, and refused a female nurse's request to donate blood. Those who had been exposed to the violent and misogynistic rap judged the friend's behaviour as more hostile, sexist, and less intelligent when the latter was called Kareem than when he was called Donald. Participants exposed to pop music judged the behaviour of Donald and Kareem similarly. Furthermore, as with Johnson, Trawalter, and Dovidio (2000), Rudman and Lee's findings were not mediated by participants' own level of racial prejudice; and the type of music employed did not influence ratings of the extent to which Donald and Kareem were perceived as popular or possessing mechanical ability, such that the violent and misogynous rap only influenced judgements of Kareem on dimensions specifically relevant to the racist stereotype. Similarly, Gan, Zillmann, and Mitrook (1997) showed white participants rap videos in which black female artists performed either 'songs of devoted love' or 'rap designed to be sexually titillating'. Participants were then asked to evaluate black and white women, and they gave more negative assessments of the black (but not the white) women after they had seen the sexual rap videos.

However, one study also demonstrates that rap music can have positive inter-racial consequences. Zillmann, Aust, Hoffman, Love, Ordman, Pope, Seigler, and Gibson (1995) investigated the effects of what they termed radical rap, by which they meant rap music with lyrics concerning cultural and political alienation, civil protest, and struggle against political and economic oppression. African-American and white school pupils were shown rock, non-political rap, and radical rap videos before taking part in a mock student-government election. The music had no effect on the candidates supported by black participants; but the radical rap videos led to white participants giving more support to a liberal African-American candidate, and less support to a candidate advocating white supremacy. Put simply, radical rap led to whites being more supportive of attempts toward racial harmony, such that the *content* of rap music is crucial in determining whether it will have a pro- or anti-social effect. Rather than focusing on the genre as a whole, it would seem more appropriate to operate on a song-by-song basis. The studies by Johnson, Trawalter, and Dovidio (2000), Rudman and Lee (2002), and Gan, Zillmann, and Mitrook (1997) show that when rap lyrics are violent or misogynistic they can prime negative stereotypes of blacks, but when they represent more of a 'cry for help' (as in the Zillmann, Aust, and Hoffman et al. (1995) study) they seem capable of activating sympathy towards the civil rights movement. Hansen (1995) argues that effects of different types of rap on inter-racial attitudes such as these can be explained easily by the notion of schema priming.

4.3.5 Self-harm and suicide

4.3.5.1 Correlational studies

The potential relationship between music media and self-harm and suicide is of course the most alarming of all those raised by protesters. It is no coincidence that the great majority of the research on this has concerned heavy metal, since this most clearly addresses alienation from mainstream society and hopelessness, and might therefore predispose listeners towards suicide. Indeed, several correlational studies support the proposed relationship between problem music, particularly heavy metal, and measures of psychological disturbance, self-harm, and suicidality. North and Hargreaves (2006) found that British fans of problem music had considered and had actually self-harmed more often during the past two years than had non-fans, and were also more likely to have wished that they were dead and to have considered suicide. Furthermore, liking for problem music/musicians could predict all these measures of self-injurious attitudes/behaviours even when controlling for self-esteem, delinquency, and a measure of participants' conservatism. When participants were asked directly about the effects of their favourite music, fans of problem music were less likely than non-fans to believe that the music told them to feel good about themselves; more likely than non-fans to believe that their favourite musician(s) would encourage them to think about both self-harming and suicide; and more likely to agree that the music they listened to could make them do things that they knew to be wrong. Also, when asked about which value was identified by their favourite musician as being most important to their future well-being, fans of problem music were disproportionately unlikely to cite factors such as being 'cheerful' and 'loving'.

Similarly, Martin, Clarke, and Pearce (1993) found significant associations between Australian adolescents' preference for rock/heavy metal and suicidal thoughts, self-harming acts, and depression, particularly among females. For example, more than 20% of male heavy metal fans and 62% of female heavy metal fans had self-harmed or attempted suicide in the past six months (compared to 8% and 14% respectively for pop fans); and heavy metal/rock fans were twice as likely as pop fans to have had suicidal thoughts during the same period. Also, Scheel and Westefeld (1999) found that heavy metal fans had lower scores than other fans on a measure of reasons for living (especially among males) and had more suicidal thoughts (especially among females).

Stack, Gundlach, and Reeves (1994) took a more unusual approach, using the number of subscriptions to *Metal Edge* magazine in the USA to measure societal interest in heavy metal subculture, and compared this to the suicide rate among the target audience for the music, namely 15 to 24-year-olds. These two variables were positively related even when controlling for various measures of social disorganization (such as divorce rates, immigration, and poverty), as well as ethnicity and levels of Catholicism. Indeed, of the variables considered, only ethnicity and divorce rates appeared to be more important than interest in heavy metal in explaining the suicide rate. Furthermore, subscriptions to *Metal Edge* were not related to the suicide rate among an older age group of 25 to 34-year-olds, which further mitigates against the spuriousness of the findings for 15 to 24-year-olds.

Away from specifically suicide and suicidal ideation, Doak (2003) found a link between musical preference and mental health diagnoses, since clinically depressed adolescents tended to prefer, rap, heavy metal, and techno; and those with mood disorder tended to prefer rap, classic rock, hard rock, heavy metal, and alternative music. As we have already seen, Schwartz and Fouts (2003) compared adolescents who liked 'heavy music' (i.e. heavy metal and hard rock) and 'light music' (i.e. pop), and found that the former were more moody, more pessimistic, overly sensitive, discontented, and more impulsive; and had more problems in their relationships with their families. Factors such as these of course might well predispose someone towards suicide, and it is interesting that about half of the adolescent school pupils interviewed by Wass, Raup, Cerullo, Martel, Mingione, and Sperring (1988–1989) thought that teenagers who were depressed or troubled could be influenced by rock music concerning homicide, Satanism, or suicide.

4.3.5.2 Experimental studies

However, there is only one piece of experimental evidence that suggests problem music could have implications for suicide/self-harm, and even this suggests that the music itself is not the cause of this. North and Hargreaves (2005) suggest that the negative effects of music on listeners may be, at least in part, due to labelling effects. Undergraduates were played one of four lyrically ambiguous pop songs before saying what they thought the song was about and how it made them feel. However, before hearing the song, participants were primed with one of two types of background information. One group was told that the song had been criticized by protesters after it was implicated in the suicide of a young fan of the group in question, while a second group was told that the song had been praised by health professionals for helping vulnerable young people work through emotional problems. These primes had a corresponding influence on ratings of the extent to which the song was 'life-destroying versus life-enhancing', whether it made the participant feel happy about themselves, and whether it would make the participant want to commit suicide if they heard it during difficult emotional times; whether participants wrote a prose description of the song that was 'life-destroying versus life-enhancing'; and several measures of how the participant felt that someone else of their own age and sex would be affected by the song. In short, labelling the song as 'life-destroying' caused it to be perceived negatively, but labelling it positively caused it to be perceived positively. In some cases of course pop songs have very unambiguous lyrics, but these findings suggest that where there is some ambiguity then the background information concerning the song can be as important as the song itself in determining its emotional effect. The pro-censorship activities of protesters against heavy metal, rap, and the like provide just this kind of background information, so that they may be exacerbating the very problem they are trying to resolve.

Other experimental evidence comes out even more strongly against the idea that problem music itself can cause suicide/self-harm. Ballard and Coates (1995) played participants either a heavy metal or rap song which featured one of three types of lyrics namely non-violent, homicidal, or suicidal. The non-violent rap songs led to higher depression scores than the more violent rap songs, and there were no effects of either musical style or type of lyric on participants' level of suicidal ideation, anxiety, or self-esteem. Rustad, Small, Jobes, Safer, and Peterson (2003) conducted two experiments in which participants were respectively shown a rock video with or without suicidal content or listened to rock music with or without suicidal content. In both cases, a subsequent story-writing task (in which participants were asked to describe what was happening in a picture) showed that watching/hearing the suicidal music raised the salience of suicide for participants. However, there were very few differences between those who had or had not been exposed to suicidal content in terms of negative mood, estimates of the probability that they would experience negative life events, hopelessness, or suicide acceptability. In other words, the suicidal content in music media primed cognitions related to suicide, but did not affect participants in a way that would increase their actual risk of suicide. Finally, although North and Hargreaves' (2006) correlational study did find higher rates of suicidal thoughts among fans of problem music, they also found crucially that listening to problem music did not pre-date suicidal thoughts and self-harming, and so cannot have caused them.

4.3.5.3 Other caveats

Indeed, several correlational studies indicate that when other intervening factors are considered then the apparent link between music and suicide indicated by correlational research disappears. It is instead more accurate to state that liking for problem music is an indicator of vulnerability, but that it is this vulnerability that appears to be the real cause of any link between music and self-harm / suicide. For example, North and Hargreaves (2006) found that low self-esteem was consistently far better at predicting suicidal and self-harming thoughts than was liking for problem music; and we also failed to identify higher rates of actual suicide attempts among fans of problem music. Stack (1998) used data from 833 respondents concerning whether they liked heavy metal and the extent to which they believed that suicide could be acceptable (e.g. in cases of having an incurable disease, being tired of living, bankruptcy, and having dishonoured one's family). Stack also used several control variables, namely age, sex, race, liberalism (i.e. education and political conservatism), religiosity, marriage, and parenthood, all of which might be expected to mediate suicidality. Liking for heavy metal was related to suicide acceptability when controlling for all the variables except religiosity. However, when the latter was also considered then the metal-suicide link disappeared, due to heavy metal fans' much lower frequency of church attendance. In other words, 'Being a heavy metal fan apparently has only an indirect effect on suicide attitudes, through metal being associated with low church attendance' (p. 393). In other words, the music-suicide link may well have its roots in factors such as self-esteem, religiosity, and a range of other factors.

Three other studies have focused on specifically family dysfunction as a cause of the heavy metal-suicide link that they identified. Schwartz and Fouts (2003) found that 'heavy music' fans experienced greater family disturbance, and speculated that this may cause their liking for the music since the latter reflects their feelings of isolation. Stack, Gundlach, and Reeves (1994) found that interest in heavy metal was linked to suicide even when controlling for divorce rates, but also found a positive relationship between divorce rates and interest in heavy metal. In other words, the divorce of parents may prime a propensity towards both heavy metal and suicide. Scheel and Westefeld (1999) found a heavy metal-suicide link, but also that their heavy metal fans scored worse on a measure of responsibility to family (i.e. family commitment and love) as a reason for not committing suicide: this again points to the family as a more prominent source of concern than any role that music might play. In perhaps the most detailed investigation of this, Martin, Clarke, and Pearce (1993) found significant associations between Australian adolescents' preference for rock/heavy metal and suicidal thoughts, but they argued that this was caused primarily by family dysfunction. A smaller percentage of the parents of rock/heavy metal fans were still married compared to pop fans, and a smaller number had access to their biological father; and twice as many rock/heavy metal fans than pop fans reported that their family relationship was 'not close'. Furthermore, gender mediated the heavy metal–suicide relationship, as many of the effects they found were much stronger among females. Also, the effects were much stronger among those who felt sad after listening to music, which suggests that any music that has such an emotional effect could be indicative of suicide risk. Given this, it is interesting that 58% of rock/heavy metal fans felt 'often happy' after listening to this music whereas only 11.2% felt 'often sad', and these percentages were very similar to those found among pop fans. Consequently, Martin et al. argue that, rather than focusing on heavy metal as a musical style, suicide preventions techniques should instead focus on particularly vulnerable heavy metal fans (i.e. females from difficult family environments who often feel sad after listening to the music).

Burge, Goldblat, and Lester (2002) also considered gender as a mediating variable, but flagged up *males* as being more at risk. They collected data on suicidal ideation as well as several control variables (hopelessness, religiosity, mania, and depression) and found that liking for rock/metal was related to suicidal ideation only among males. The position regarding gender becomes even more confusing when we consider Lacourse, Claes, and Villeneuve's (2001) findings. They reported that liking for heavy metal could predict suicide risk among female but not male French-Canadian adolescents. Furthermore, when suicide risk factors (such as alienation, drug use, and parental negligence) were considered, this positive link among females became non-significant; and a negative relationship was found in females between suicide risk and listening to heavy metal to reduce aggression. The position of gender in the putative music-suicide relationship is consequently very unclear.

Furthermore, Burge et al. (2002) pointed out that musical preferences are inter-related, and found that the preferences of their sample could be grouped into two factors, namely heavy metal/rock and 'country vs. rap'. It seems therefore that protesters may be wrong to focus solely on heavy metal, since liking for the latter is also linked to liking other related musical styles such as classic rock or punk (see also Lester and Whipple (1996), Mulder, Ter Bogt, Raaijmakers, and Vollebergh (2006), and Scheel and Westefeld (1999) who consider the music-deviance link in the context of several related musical styles). Indeed, given the Burge et al. argument that liking for heavy metal is linked to liking for a range of other musical styles, it is interesting that there is some indication that any music-suicide link is not limited solely to problem music styles. Perhaps the best known example of this concerns *Gloomy Sunday*, written in its original form in 1933 by Hungarian by Rezsô Seress, and covered by Billie Holiday (in 1941) among others. Shortly after it was written, reports from Hungary alleged individuals had taken their lives after listening to the haunting melody, or that the lyrics had been left with their last letters, leading to attempts to introduce newer, less pessimistic lyrics and an eventual ban by the BBC and many other broadcasters. Rezsô Seress jumped to his death from his flat in 1968.

More empirical work supports the argument that death and suicide are issues not just for rock and rap music. Achté, Fagerström, Pentikäinen, and Farberow (1989-1990) describe how lullabies with death-related themes exist in Finno-Ugric, Slavic, English-speaking, Spanish/Portuguese, and some Far East cultures. Three studies by Steven Stack, however, provide more direct evidence of a potential music-suicide link in musical styles other than those usually considered by protesters. Stack (2000), for example, argues that the sad themes in blues lyrics (concerning social and emotional oppression and isolation) may attract suicidal people and reinforce their suicidal attitudes. Adults were interviewed about their attitudes to the blues and also whether suicide was acceptable if a person was tired of living. Although blues fans were no more accepting of suicide than non-fans, they had lower levels of church attendance, lower levels of political conservatism, and higher levels of education, each of which was in turn associated with greater suicide acceptability. This was much more the case for white than black participants. As such, the findings are very similar to those reported earlier concerning heavy metal, namely that there is little evidence of a direct link when other suicide-mediating variables are controlled, but that the fans tend to have scores on these other variables that are indicative of greater suicide risk: any link between problem music and suicide may be no stronger than the link between blues and suicide.

Similarly, Stack (2002) considered the relationship between suicide acceptability and interest in opera subculture. He argued that 77 of the 306 opera plots described in Harrewood's (1976) *Kobbe's complete opera book* (just over 25%) involve suicide; with well-known examples including *The Flying Dutchman*, *Trovatore*, and *Otello*. Furthermore, these suicides are often shown and described in detail, and glorified as a positive and morally 'decent' response to life events. Indeed, Stack notes that a large proportion are portrayed as resulting from dishonour to the victim or his or her family (e.g. *Madame Butterfly*). Accordingly Stack argued that 'drawn to the subculture of honor in opera, opera fans should be more approving than nonfans in the case of suicide involving dishonour' (p. 432); and found that opera fans were indeed 2.37 times more accepting of suicide in cases of family dishonour than nonfans, even when controlling for factors such as church attendance, political conservatism, social bonds, and other demographic factors: any link between problem music and suicide may be no stronger than the link between opera and suicide. Furthermore, three major predictors of 'opera fandom' were being female, better educated, and elderly, such that these people perhaps constitute a more vulnerable group of opera fans.

In the best known of these studies, Stack and Gundlach (1992) followed a similar line of argument, reasoning that the themes typically found in country music (e.g. marital discord, alcohol abuse, financial strain, hopelessness) might foster suicidal thoughts among fans. They collected data from 49 large metropolitan areas within the USA on the proportion of radio airtime devoted to country, and found that this was related to the suicide rate among whites (but not blacks), the primary market for country, even when controlling for poverty, geographic location, divorce, and prevalence of gun retailers: any link between problem music and suicide may be no stronger than the link between country and suicide. Such a startling finding has inevitably attracted a considerable amount of attention and controversy (see Maguire and Snipes, 1994; Mauk, Taylor, White, and Allen, 1994; Stack and Gundlach, 1994a; b). For example, Lester and Whipple (1996) studied 93 undergraduates and found that liking for country was *not* related to depression or suicidal preoccupation. Indeed, although they found that liking for heavy metal was associated weakly with past suicidal ideation, it was not associated with current suicidal ideation or depression; and although the researchers considered five musical preferences and nine measures of suicide / personality, only five of the 45 possible correlations between these were significant. Nevertheless, Stack's findings concerning blues, opera, and country indicate the possibility that elevated levels of suicidality may not be exclusive to the fans of problem music, and there is a notable lack of research concerning the suicidality of fans of problem music relative to fans of other musical styles. For the time being, it is by no means clear that fans of problem music are the most vulnerable of all.

4.3.6 **(Mis)Interpretation of lyrics**

Stratton and Zalanowski (1994) provided a neat demonstration of the power of lyrics: for example, when played without lyrics, Hammerstein and Kern's *Why was I born?* had a positive effect on mood, but when it was played with its depressing lyrics it had the opposite effect. This point sounds obvious, but has tremendous practical importance. If the lyrics of problem music are to have a negative effect on listeners then it is important to establish whether the salacious messages they contain are interpreted as such. For example, if a particular singer really is trying to use lyrics to persuade young fans to kill themselves, then the latter have to be able to identify and correctly understand these messages. Given this, it is potentially disturbing that several studies indicate that fans of problem music know the lyrics of their favourite songs very well (e.g. Wass, Miller, and Stevenson, 1989; Wass, Raup, Cerullo, Martell, Mingione, and Sperring, 1988-1989). Furthermore, lyrics have a significance that goes well beyond simple aesthetics. For example, Rosenbaum and Prinsky (1987) found that 17% of male 12 to 18-year-olds and nearly 25% of female 12 to 18-year-olds liked their favourite song because the words expressed their own feelings. Moreover, Rouner (1990) found that 16% of a high school sample ranked music in their top three sources of information on moral guidance, and 24% placed music in their top three sources of information on social interaction. Lyrics clearly matter, but do young people interpret them accurately?

4.3.6.1 Interpretation of 'normal' lyrics

Christenson and Roberts (1998) reviewed the evidence on people's ability to interpret lyrics, showing that research has adopted three strategies. These are (1) to compare listeners' understanding with a 'definitive' interpretation; (2) to compare interpretations of the same song offered by different groups of listeners; and (3) to consider how people process lyrics without regard to the 'actual' narrative meaning of the lyric. The first of these is the most common approach and is of the greatest interest to the problem music debate: if 'problem lyrics' are to incite problem behaviour then this means that listeners must be able to understand the intended, deleterious, messages that they contain.

Research on definitive comparisons of the intended and understood meanings of lyrics involves an 'expert' who decides on the definitive interpretation. This 'expert' can be the lyricist, a parent, a pop critic, the researcher, or a panel assembled by the researcher. Denisoff and Levine (1971) considered the chart-topping song *Eve of Destruction*, but found that only 14% understood the true meaning of the lyrics (namely the massive, imminent threat of nuclear war), 45% partly understood the lyrics, 23% had no understanding of the lyrics, and 18% did not respond (either because they had not heard the song or could not make any interpretation). Robinson and Hirsch (1972; see also Robinson and Hirsch, 1969) employed several songs and showed similarly low levels of understanding on the part of listeners: depending on the song, only around 10 to 30% of participants correctly interpreted the lyrics; around 20 to 60% gave inadequate descriptions of their meaning; and the remaining participants simply did not know or did not answer. Similarly, Rosenbaum and Prinsky (1987) asked teenagers to list their three favourite songs and say what they were about. Over a third were unable to do the latter, and the remaining answers showed little correspondence with the researchers' own judgements about the meaning of the songs.

Perhaps the most dramatic demonstration of people's poor comprehension of lyrics is provided by Konečni (1984) who used print media interviews with pop stars to determine the true meanings they intended in the lyrics of several songs. For each song, the true meaning was then presented to participants along with three other, unintended, possible interpretations of the lyrics. Participants simply had to say which of the four options was the intended meaning: if they chose their answers randomly, participants would have got the correct meaning 25% of the time; and so it is interesting that they actually picked the correct meaning only 28% of the time. In statistical terms, the participants may as well have chosen their answer by sticking a pin in the answer sheet. Greenfield, Bruzzone, Koyamatsu, Satuloff, Nixon, Brodie, and

Kingsdale (1987) found that only 40% of their participants could even attempt to answer all the questions they were asked about Bruce Springsteen's *Born in the USA*, even though they had just been played the song. Older participants did better, but still made many errors: barely 50% of undergraduates studying communications showed understanding of the lyrics. Leming (1987) found that only about $^2/_3$ of participants correctly regarded *Material Girl* by Madonna as concerning materialism (despite it containing lyrics such as 'Because the boy with the cold, hard cash is always Mister Right' and 'You know that we are living in a material world'): similarly, when participants were asked to consider *Physical* by Olivia Newton-John (containing the lyrics 'Let's get into physical/Let me hear your body talk') only 36% of them correctly regarded it as a song about sex, whereas a further 36% saw it as an encouragement to take part in physical exercise. Participants were similarly confused in their assessments of *I Want a New Drug* by Huey Lewis and The News.

In short, there are undoubtedly cases where the meaning of a given set of lyrics could not be misinterpreted by even the most naïve of listeners, but we would also make four further points. First, as the research cited here illustrates, even those songs that might seem quite unambiguous are prone to misinterpretation. Second, the great majority of songs are more complex lyrically, and would therefore be expected to have different meanings to different listeners. Third, misinterpretation seems particularly likely to occur among young listeners (see also Christenson, 1992a), who are of course the target audience for pop music.

Finally, Hansen and Hansen (1991b) argue that although specific details of lyrics may be misinterpreted, this does not mean that teenagers would be expected to completely miss the point of a lyricist's true intentions. The Hansens adopted a schema approach and argued that the details of heavy metal lyrics may be misinterpreted because the music itself is physiologically arousing and often experienced at high volume, and that this imposes a heavy cognitive load that impedes processing of lyrics. However, they also argued (and demonstrated) that heavy metal lyrics can at least be understood in general thematic terms, providing they resemble existing schema. 'And if listeners are able to extract [general] themes (such as sexual seduction, suicide, violence, and Satanism) from heavy metal songs, then a great deal of equivocation must be added to the hypothesis that song lyrics do not have an effect on listeners' (p. 377). Hansen and Hansen make four further points based on the notion that lyrics may be processed schematically. First, increasing familiarity with the lyrics in question reduces the processing load associated with encoding them. As we have already seen, fans of problem music tend to be very familiar with the lyrics: this greater familiarity would facilitate detailed encoding. Second, Hansen and Hansen argued (and found) that a written copy of the lyrics reduces the amount of processing capacity required to consider them, and therefore aids comprehension. This might well mimic what happens when a teenager listens to music and reads the lyrics printed in the liner notes of a CD. (Indeed it is interesting to note that protesters in the mid-1980s argued that lyrics should be provided with recorded music: Hansen and Hansen's research suggests that this would be a bad idea as it facilitates processing of any dubious messages.) Third, schematic processing might colour the interpretation placed on ambiguous lyrics. Non-musical research on schemas shows that ambiguous information tends to be encoded as schema consistent, such that words or phrases with double meanings might be interpreted as sexual or violent etc. when presented in the context of problem music. Fourth, in cultures where English is not spoken as a first language, listeners exposed to English-language problem music will experience an even greater cognitive load as they try to translate the lyrics into their own language. This greater cognitive load should further increase the probability of schematic processing occurring, such that there is more chance of the lyrics being understood to depict the stereotypically violent and sexist themes of problem music. More simply, we have to be extremely cautious in extrapolating from the experimental research described in this section (which indicates that lyrics are misunderstood) to what actually happens on an everyday basis in adolescents' bedrooms.

4.3.6.2 Interpretation of 'masked' lyrics

Other research has taken a different approach, questioning whether 'backwards masking' of lyrics or some form of subliminal perception plays a role in affecting listeners' behaviour. Backwards masking of lyrics certainly does occur in pop music. For example, Pink Floyd's *Empty Spaces* when played backwards contains the message, 'Congratulations, you've discovered the secret message'. Protesters have seized on pranks such as this to claim that numerous recordings contain deleterious messages that are disguised by technical trickery in an attempt to indoctrinate teenagers into a life of sleaze and wrong-doing. Indeed, despite the fact that it was written 'very quickly' according to lyricist Robert Plant, Led Zeppelin's *Stairway to Heaven* is claimed to contain no fewer than six backwards messages concerning Satan in under a minute. Whether a human mind is capable of such a mental feat is open to debate. Nonetheless the state of Arkansas in the USA considered legislation in the early 1980s requiring records and tapes to carry the message 'Warning: this record contains backward masking which may be perceptible at a subliminal level when the record is played forward', and measures of this nature are by no means unique (see Vokey and Read, 1985; Walker, 1985). However, the limited research suggests that backwards masking and subliminal perception play no role in the interpretation of lyrics.

Thorne and Himelstein (1984) used three songs that had been frequently claimed to contain backwards messages. A control group of participants were played the songs backwards and asked to record their reactions, but were not told anything else. A second group were played the same music, told that masked messages could be distinguished in the songs, and were asked to write these down. A third group were again played the same and told that satanic messages had been inserted into the songs and that their job was to detect and write these down. The second, 'messages' group reported hearing more 'backwards' messages than either of the other two, and the third 'satanic' group heard more messages than the control group. Also, the third 'satanic' group reported hearing more messages about Satan than either of the other two. In other words, the suggestion that 'backwards masked' messages exist seems to prime their perception: when it is not suggested that backwards messages are present then listeners are unable to perceive them, indicating that protesters may be creating the problem by highlighting these issues. Similarly Walls, Taylor, and Falzone (1992) inserted messages into music concerning whether it was fast or slow tempo, and found that this did not influence participants' judgements of tempo.

Perhaps the real nail in the coffin for the backwards-masking argument, however, is provided by Vokey and Read (1985). They conducted several experiments in which spoken words were recorded and played backwards to participants. They showed that participants found it difficult to parse the sounds into words that they were consciously aware of, and that there was little evidence for subconscious processing of the words. For example, participants were unable to determine whether the sounds they heard were a question or a declarative statement. In another experiment, participants were presented with pairs of sentences, and performed badly when asked to indicate whether they believed the two sentences of the pair, if heard in the forward direction, would have the same meaning. In a related task, the participants were asked to judge whether each of a set of sentences, divided equally into meaningful and nonsensical sentences, would make sense if heard in the forward direction. Again performance was worse than chance levels. In yet another experiment participants were presented with backwards statements such as 'Jesus loves me, this I know' and were unable to sort them accurately into five categories, namely nursery rhymes, Christian, satanic, pornographic, and advertising. More simply, participants were unable to determine even the general gist of backwards-masked messages, even when there was no accompanying music (that could have made the task even more difficult).

Vokey and Read then presented participants with backwards messages that used homophones (i.e. words which sound alike but which have different meanings and spellings such as 'read' and 'reed'). One interesting aspect of previous research on homophones is that, when asked to spell them, people's responses can be biased by earlier priming of one of the versions. For example, if people are given the sentence 'Climbing a mountain is a remarkable feat', and then asked verbally to spell 'feat', they tend to give the spelling of the homophone that has been primed (e.g. 'feat') even though other spellings are encountered more frequently in everyday life (e.g. 'feet'). Vokey and Read presented participants with backwards messages featuring the uncommon version of a homophone (e.g. 'Climbing a mountain is a remarkable feat', 'A saxophone is a reed instrument'), and then asked participants to spell the homophone in question. Vokey and Read argued that if participants could comprehend the backwards messages then their attempts to spell the homophones would also reflect this priming of the relatively uncommon version. They didn't, and Vokey and Read concluded that since they do not seem to even be comprehended (either consciously or unconsciously), it is therefore difficult to see how backwards messages concerning Satan, suicide, or anything else could affect listeners.

4.4 **Is there a case for censorship?**

This returns us to the issue with which we began this chapter, namely whether there are grounds for censoring music. From a theoretical standpoint it is easy to understand why problem music has been subject to such an outcry. Specifically, the opinions of legislators concerning this music may be subject to biases such as 'moral panic' and the 'third-person effect'. Other researchers have suggested that the implications of legislation targeted at problem music may not correspond with those intended. These factors are evaluated here, before we summarize the evidence on the relationship between problem music and problem behaviour, and discuss the implications of this for censorship.

4.4.1 **Biases in the evaluation of problem music**

4.4.1.1 Moral panic

First, it is worth noting parallels between the problem music debate and the growing sociological literature on moral panic (e.g. Thompson, 1998), which concerns those widespread emotional outcries that occur within societies over particular social and moral issues. Indeed, the public reaction to problem music shares many similarities with that concerning issues such as the ordination of female Christian priests, paedophilia, or gay marriage. In particular, sociologists argue that public debates on issues such as these are usually triggered by one or two specific cases that are widely publicized by the media or politicians (see Greer, 2002); are characterized by extreme and deeply entrenched opinions on both sides of the debate; and are fuelled by an urgent sense that 'something must be done' by legislators (see e.g. Silverman and Wilson, 2002; Soothill and Francis, 2002; Kleinhaus, 2002). There are obvious similarities between these characteristics of moral panic and the campaigns and protests concerning problem music that we outlined earlier. Furthermore, as Ungar (2001) points out, nearly all the moral panics that have affected contemporary British society are related to youth-oriented issues (e.g. gang culture, teenage sexuality, or paedophilia), which suggests that they may in fact be interrelated.

The term 'moral panic' was first coined by Cohen (e.g. 2003) in referring to 'folk devils' that are perceived as a potential threat to society as we know it; and in particular to conflict between mods and rockers, two social groups which centred around particular musical preferences. Cohen argued that moral panics originate in the discovery of a particular problem group/factor in society, which is perceived as being more pervasive than is actually the case. This perception is reinforced by the media whenever similar instances come to light, so that the general public are sensitized to label future events as also resulting from the problem group/factor. This in turn leads to the perception of a major threat and of the urgent emotional need for a solution with severe repercussions for the 'folk devils' in question (see e.g. Silverman and Wilson, 2002; Soothill and Francis, 2002; Kleinhaus, 2002). These solutions are championed by moral entrepreneurs (e.g. Becker, 1963) who highlight what they perceive as moral failings and means of helping society as a way of furthering their own objectives.

As such, the function of moral panics is to maintain social order through the ostracizing and eventual elimination of particular problem groups/factors from mainstream society (Hier, 2003). It is therefore easy to conceive the problem music debate as involving two opposing sides in a moral panic. On the one hand, we have the desire among young consumers for music that is perceived as offering great benefits (i.e. enjoyment and excitement). On the other hand, members of mainstream society berate problem music as they feel a need to identify a 'folk devil' which is perceived as the cause of (what they perceive to be) an increasingly violent and sexually promiscuous society that threatens social order; and an urgent need to act against the musicians who produce this music as a means of ostracising it from mainstream society. Viewing pro-censorship campaigns as an instance of moral panic does not invalidate their legitimacy, of course, but certainly does explain their vehemence and tendency towards litigation.

Two studies that were not carried out in the explicit context of moral panic theory nonetheless support the notion that censorship of problem music is advocated primarily by non-fans assuming a degree of moral guardianship or responsibility. As we have already seen, Lynxwiler and Gay (2000) reported that liking for heavy metal and rap was lower among females, but also among married participants, those who held conservative attitudes toward gender roles, and those who attended religious services. We might assume that married, conservative church-goers have a keen interest in maintaining what they perceive as 'correct' moral standards. Similarly, Dixon and Linz (1997) investigated the extent to which rap was perceived as patently offensive, having prurient content, and lacking artistic merit (which are components of obscenity law in the USA). Ratings of the extent to which the music was regarded as patently offensive were related negatively to participants having uninhibited sexual values; ratings of the extent to which rap possessed pruri-ent appeal were positively related to disaffection toward society and the belief that rap contributes to societal degradation; and ratings of rap as having artis-tic merit were positively associated with disaffection toward society and appreciation of the linguistic skills involved in rap, and negatively associated with the belief that rap causes trouble. In short, both studies show unsurpris-ingly that support for censorship is higher among non-fans with conservative moral outlooks.

4.4.1.2 The third person effect

Research on the third person effect also indicates that the beliefs of protesters and problem music fans alike may not be driven solely by cold logic. McLeod, Eveland, and Nathanson (1997) argue that people should perceive media content to have a greater impact on others than on themselves, the so-called perceptual component of the third-person effect, and that this occurs particu-larly if the media in question are evaluated negatively: this perceptual bias comes about because people need to compare themselves favourably to others and thus gain self-esteem. Put simply, the perception is that 'I am not influenced by this stuff because I am intelligent and in good psychological health; but you are less intelligent/healthy than me, and so will be influenced'. Furthermore, this perception leads people to take actions to prevent this impact occurring in others, the so-called behavioural component of the third-person effect. These 'actions' in this context include attempts by protesters/legislators to 'protect our children' from problem music.

There is also a 'social distance corollary' of the third person effect. This states that the magnitude of the perceived effect of media on others should increase with the social distance between the person making the rating and the group they are making the rating about. For example, students ought to believe that the effects of media on 'others' increases as these 'others' are defined as 'other students at your university', then 'other young people in your town', and then 'the average person': there is more social distance between a student research participant and 'the average person' than there is between the student and 'other students at your university', such that the student research participant ought to believe that 'the average person' is influenced more. There is also a 'knowledge corollary' to the third-person effect. This states that people who believe themselves to be knowledgeable about the area in question should also believe themselves to be particularly unsusceptible to media influence, relative to other people who are comparative novices.

To test this, McLeod, Eveland, and Nathanson (1997) gave a questionnaire to participants that featured either violent or misogynistic rap lyrics. They were asked to estimate the effects of lyrics such as these on themselves, other students at their own university, people their age in cities like New York or Los Angeles, and the average person; and also to rate their support for music censorship, and knowledge of rap. Results supported the perceptual component of the third-person effect, since participants felt that they would be less affected by lyrics than would the other groups. There was some support for the social distance corollary since participants believed themselves to be least influenced, followed by other students at the their own university, and then other young people (although ratings assigned for 'the average person' did not indicate the perception of even greater influence). Although the results did not support the knowledge corollary, there was support for the behavioural component of the third-person effect in that support for censorship was related positively to perceptions of the extent of the effects of lyrics on others.

In a series of studies, the same team of researchers has replicated and extended these findings. For example, Eveland and McLeod (1999) provided some support for the notion that people engage in the third person effect as a means of boosting their self-esteem, finding that the size of the third-person effect was greater when people were asked to estimate the consequences of anti-social rather than pro-social rap lyrics. Eveland, Nathanson, Detenber, and McLeod (1999) employed rap and heavy metal lyrics to further support the social distance corollary when this was operationalized in terms of education and age. They also found that social distance effects were mediated by perceptions of the likelihood of the 'other' group being exposed to the music in question: they claim that this explains why their earlier study did not find that 'the average person' would be seriously affected by rap lyrics, as 'the average person' might be less likely to experience rap than would young people in New York or Los Angeles. McLeod, Detenber, and Eveland (2001) found that when estimating the effects of lyrics on others, people employ relatively naïve schemata in assuming that exposure automatically leads to influence; but that when assessing the effects on themselves people employ a much more complex model (including, for example, the role of common sense in mitigating any effects). They also found that support for censorship was strongest among females and those with conservative and paternalistic attitudes: given this it is interesting that problem music protesters have frequently been described as 'Washington wives'.

Indeed it is a fairly simple task to explain the beliefs of both protesters and problem music fans in terms of the third person effect. The perceptual component of the third-person effect means that protesters believe themselves to be relatively immune to the effects of problem music; and means that problem music fans will not believe that the music they listen to could have a bad effect on them personally. Since they tend not themselves to be young fans of problem music from vulnerable backgrounds, the protesters are at some social distance from the people who listen to problem music; and so the social distance corollary explains why they believe that the effects of this music on young fans are so serious. Furthermore, because the fans are very knowledgeable about the music, and because protesters have also 'done their homework', the 'knowledge corollary' explains why both groups of people believe that they are particularly unsusceptible to the impact of problem music, despite the irony that both groups actually listen to it more than most. Finally, the behavioural component explains why they are motivated to act, and attempt to censor (or in the case of the fans, fight against censorship of) problem music.

4.4.1.3 Consequences of censorship

Other research has considered the direct consequences of censorship, and particularly the effects of labelling certain forms of music as problematic. Of this research, only two studies have investigated the effects of attaching 'parental advisory' stickers to CDs on people's actual propensity to listen to them. Christenson (1992b) researched two competing hypotheses concerning the effects of parental advisory stickers. His 'forbidden fruit' hypothesis stated that stickers should make CDs more attractive to young people, since the threat to withdraw free choice from people should motivate them to attempt to restore it by gaining access to prohibited material. In contrast, his 'tainted fruit' hypothesis draws on research we have already seen concerning the harmonious nature of parent-child relationships during adolescence, such that stickers should be interpreted by young people as a sign that their parents would not want them to listen to the music, and thus discourage them from listening. To test this, 11 to 14-year-olds were shown albums with and without the parental advisory sticker: the albums were less popular when they bore the sticker, in support of the 'tainted fruit' hypothesis. Note, however, that the difference between evaluations of the 'stickered' and 'unstickered' albums was small (about 0.3 of a point on a five point rating scale). Consequently it is not too surprising that, in contrast to Christenson (1992b), Simmons' (1992) study of undergraduates found that when university students were told that an album was the only one to have been declared legally obscene in the UK, liking for it actually increased. In sum, together these two studies suggest that, *at best*, stickering CDs may only have a small positive effect for only children and younger adolescents. It is clearly an area that requires further research.

Studies of other consequences of censorship show that labelling music as problematic could have unintended negative effects, and this has obvious parallels with mainstream social psychological research on self-fulfilling prophecies (e.g. Snyder, 1984). For example, as we have already seen, North and Hargreaves (2005) showed that telling people that a song had been criticized by protest groups led to it being perceived as negative; and Thorne and Himelstein (1984) showed that 'backward masked' messages could be perceived in music only when participants had been told to expect them. These studies are by no means unique, however. Fried (1996) argued that rap lyrics have received a considerable amount of criticism by protesters and the media, and found that when a lyrical passage was presented as a rap (rather than a country) song participants found it more offensive, perceived it as a greater threat to civil order, and gave more support for government regulation. The same effects were found if the lyrics were associated with a black rather than a white singer, and Fried argues persuasively that the negative effect of labelling music as 'rap' is, at least in part, due to outright racism. Fried (1999) successfully replicated her earlier finding concerning the effects of labelling lyrics as 'rap', and found that the effect was stronger among older people, parents, and those who bought three or fewer CDs/tapes per year. Similarly, Dixon and Linz (1997) found that highly sexually explicit rap was rated as more patently offensive than highly sexually explicit non-rap; and Ballard, Dodson, and Bazzini (1999) asked people to rate the potential impact of a set of lyrics on behaviour: labelling the lyrics as exemplars of heavy metal or rap had no effect on ratings of whether they were likely to inspire antisocial behaviour, but did decrease the perception that they could inspire prosocial behaviour compared to those occasions when the lyrics were attributed to country or pop. In short, labelling music as problematic clearly causes it to be perceived as such: protests about music label it as a malevolent force, and may create the very problem they aim to eradicate.

These labelling effects are particular problematic given evidence on parents' use of parental advisory stickers. Bushman and Cantor's (2003) review concluded that around half of parents in the USA report using the parental advisory sticker for guidance concerning music (and that around three-quarters of parents who used the sticker found it either somewhat or very useful). However, this could be a case of the glass being half-empty rather than half-full: as we have just seen, stickers may be counter-productive if parents do not actually use them to *stop* their children listening to the music, and if around half of all parents use the sticker to these ends it also means that half do not. Furthermore, Bushman and Cantor's meta-analysis of national polls concerning all media, including music, showed that parents had an overwhelming preference for ratings that specify actual content rather than providing merely age-related recommendations: if the current parental advisory sticker was revised to include this more detailed information then again, unless it was used by parents to *prevent* access, it might be expected to have a deleterious schema-priming effect on music listeners. A second meta-analysis of all media showed that ratings schemes were a deterrent among children aged under 8 years, but that once children were 11 these ratings had a small enticement effect (particularly for boys): this is clearly consistent with the research we described earlier on the effects of specifically parental advisory stickers on the appeal of music CDs to older teenagers. In short, there is strong support among parents for a system that is used by only around half of them, and which has the clear potential to prime deleterious schema unless it is used to actually *prevent* access to problem music: furthermore, if parental pressure led to a change in the parental advisory sticker to include detailed information on content then this measure could well exacerbate the problem.

4.4.2 **Summary and implications for censorship**

It is obviously difficult to summarize the large and complex body of literature we have reviewed so far in this chapter. Nevertheless, a few clear patterns do seem to stand out. The evidence generally indicates a relationship between exposure to music media and each of delinquency, criminality, drug use, permissive sexual attitudes, sexism, racism, and self-harm. However, the correlational evidence is not as clear-cut as the stereotype and protesters suggest, and indicates that the relationships observed are much stronger among people from vulnerable backgrounds. Although the nature of these 'vulnerable backgrounds' seems to vary depending on the specific attitude/behaviour in question and from study to study, it is possible to identify several factors that have emerged on more than one occasion, namely poor school performance, membership of an undervalued social group, a sensation-seeking personality, poor family relationships and poor parenting, low self-esteem, and sex. It is entirely understandable how factors such as these could lead to both deleterious attitudes/behaviour as well as a strong interest in music that addresses these themes. These 'vulnerability' factors may well be the real cause of the link identified in several correlational studies between music and deleterious attitudes/behaviours. Furthermore, correlational research has not always identified relationships between problem music styles and problem attitudes / behaviours, and has sometimes shown correlations between the latter and non-problem music styles.

Similarly, experimental evidence *sometimes* supports the notion that problem music can cause *some* problem attitudes/behaviours. However, there is a limited amount of experimental evidence available, and the effects identified are not clear-cut in singling out problem music as a source of concern. In particular, experimental work has identified deleterious effects of supposedly non-problematic musical styles, or that the key factor may be the listener's/viewer's emotional response rather than the music *per se*, such that deleterious effects may potentially arise from any number of pieces or styles in addition to those usually targeted by protesters. Other studies show that the effects identified are greater among vulnerable groups of participants and that specific types of problem music content have the ability to promote positive effects (e.g. greater racial tolerance or the effectiveness of treatment and prevention programmes). Furthermore, although in the minority, there are several instances of experimental studies that fail to demonstrate deleterious consequences of exposure to problem music. Also, experimental tests of the interpretation of lyrics indicate that the majority of listeners will misinterpret al.l but the most unambiguous lyrics. Finally, experimental research on censorship and labelling music as problematic suggests that attempts at censorship are motivated by psychological processes of dubious logic; that such activities actually *create* the impression that the music is problematic such that people may have become erroneously prejudiced against entire musical styles, and perhaps in the case of rap have even begun to adopt racist stereotypes in evaluating individual songs; and that only around half of parents (in the USA at least) use the 'parental advisory' sticker as a source of guidance, such that the children of the remaining half are subject to unrestricted access to music with the potential to activate deleterious schema.

We noted earlier our suspicion that experimental work in this field is particularly prone to demand characteristics. However, a detailed consideration of the experimental literature raises three other concerns. First, can we be sure that effects of problem music found inside the lab also occur outside the lab? A lab-based experimental participant might be more 'accepting of violence' following exposure to a violent video, but the participant is well aware that this 'acceptance of violence' will have no further consequences. It is not clear that the same person would be more likely to act violently in the street after watching music videos at home: there would be 'real' consequences of that violence for the participant such as feeling guilty, getting into trouble with the police, or being hit back; and these consequences would surely reduce someone's propensity to act out behaviours primed by music. Rather, even if the psychological research did provide unequivocal support for a music-violence link, all that this would really show is that exposure to problem music has the potential to increase a person's *propensity* to act violently, but that this propensity is then subject to a 'reality check' before it leads to actual conduct.

Second, lab-based measures of violence, sexism, etc. in response to music videos tend to be diluted versions of the 'real thing'. For example, participants exposed to a violent music video may be more tolerant of an anti-social hand gesture made by a stranger in the safe confines of a university psychology department. But would they feel so positively about anti-social behaviour if instead they witnessed the physical assault of a friend on the street? We are quite sure that they would not, so that again the experimental evidence probably presents the worst-case scenario.

Third, one interesting correlate of sexual imagery in music media appears to be religious imagery. Pardun and McKee (1995) showed that religious imagery was present in more than $1/3$ of the 160 videos they coded, but also was twice as likely to be found in videos that also used sexual imagery than in those that did not. Furthermore, the combination of sexual and religious imagery was present in more than one quarter of the videos. Similarly, McKee and Pardun (1996) found religious imagery in around 30% of the videos they coded, and that the combination of sexual and religious imagery in combination occurred more frequently than would be expected by chance (see also McKee and Pardun, 1999). From a purely logical standpoint we could suggest therefore that any effects of sexual content in music media could really be attributable in part to increased exposure to religious material! This is obviously absurd, but does highlight the difficulty of relating any particular effect of music media to one specific aspect of the content. Even if music media do cause deleterious behaviour it is no simple act to identify those aspects of the media that cause the effect. In short, the available experimental evidence is currently a very long way from proving that problem music causes problem attitudes and behaviours.

There are also three other issues that question whether the case against problem music is as sound as protesters would have us believe. First, it is notoriously difficult to publish null results in scientific journals: there may well exist several sets of unpublished data showing no effect of problem music, again suggesting that the published research reflects the worst-case scenario. Second, if problem music was sufficient to cause problem attitudes/behaviours then we would expect to see ill-effects of this among *all* heavy rock and rap fans: the undoubted fact that the great majority of problem music fans are 'normal' shows that individual differences, and particularly factors indicative of psychological vulnerability and a predisposition toward certain problem attitudes/behaviours, must play a major role. Finally, rap and heavy metal have undoubtedly been treated harshly by protesters relative to other musical styles. Can you imagine the public outrage that would greet a new Marilyn Manson video in which a beautiful young woman committed suicide after learning that her partner loved another woman? However, this is precisely the denouement of Puccini's *Madame Butterfly*, played out nightly in opera houses around the world. If you were to respond that 'It's different, because an opera audience would be older and more sophisticated' then we might be equally patronizing and invite you to re-read the earlier section on the third-person effect. You might instead respond that 'It's different, because rock fans are more likely to come from backgrounds indicative of suicide risk'. We would agree, but also point out first that, by quite some way, not all rock fans are suicidal; that Stack (2002) found that elderly, well-educated, female opera fans were also vulnerable to suicide; and that Stack (2000) found that white blues fans might be more vulnerable than their black counterparts. It is hard to imagine any attempt by legislators to limit elderly, well-educated women's access to opera or white people's access to blues. Furthermore, given the heavy coverage that they give to suicide and related issues of hardship and despair, should blues, opera, and country music be subject to protest, and should the composers and their record companies be taken to court when the fans commit suicide?

The evidence reviewed in this chapter does not support the notion that exposure to problem music is always sufficient to cause problem attitudes/behaviours. But it is also a long way from suggesting that there are no grounds for concern, and there is evidence that exposure to problem music may be related to negative outcomes, particularly among vulnerable people to whom of course society has an especially strong duty of care. Therefore, although it is very difficult to justify attempts at wholesale prohibition, some measures regarding problem music do seem justifiable. The evidence reviewed above indicates that parental advisory stickers may have a small impact in reducing the desirability of albums to young children, but (a) parents do not seem to use them as a means of filtering material; (b) they may sometimes increase the appeal of 'stickered' material to older adolescents; and (c) the very act of labelling the music may contribute to that music having deleterious consequences. Given that the sticker is used by only around half of parents in the USA (and perhaps even fewer elsewhere), the negative effects of labelling on those adolescents who still have access to the music might outweigh the benefits to be gained by those adolescents whose parents use the sticker: our argument towards the 'parental advisory' sticker could be summarized as 'use it or lose it'.

A second strategy would be for musicians and the music industry to apply sensible self-regulation to the music media they release. By 'sensible' self-regulation we are not referring to the bowdlerising of music media. Rather, we mean a process by which musicians and the music industry ask themselves whether salacious content is something that could be jettisoned without consequence for the ability of the music to make a mature artistic comment on sensitive issues that concern young people (such as their place in the world, sexual relationships, or death). This elective approach has one particular advantage over any legislation that empowered a third party to make these evaluations: the evidence indicates that the relationships between problem music and deleterious behaviours identified in North America are also found in many other countries, and therefore it is obviously far more efficient to address any problem at source, rather than requiring each individual country to develop its own solutions.

Third, we have seen consistently that problem behaviours and salacious content can be found in a wide range of musical styles. Rap and rock music and the fans of these musical styles certainly are worse than others on some measures: but we have also seen instances where other musical styles and the fans of these score poorly on measures of salacious content and undesirable behaviour. Therefore, rather than attempting to single out particular musical styles and musicians for censure, it makes far more sense to focus concerns on individual pieces of music or individual videos. In short, a song-by-song approach is far more appropriate than a style-by-style or a musician-by-musician approach. Similarly, we have seen that some people are more vulnerable to music than others (be they fans of problem music or of opera): although it is difficult to see how this could be implemented, it implies that any censorship of music need not apply equally to all people.

Finally, perhaps the most important change that can be made certainly does involve parents and legislators working together. We have noted several times that an interest in problem music probably reflects rather than causes vulnerability on the part of listeners. Given this, it is the job of parents and governments to provide the kind of home and societal background that minimizes the number of vulnerable children and adolescents.

With regard to specifically pro-censorship legislation, we should note that Christenson and Roberts (1998) provide a detailed discussion of the legal position in the USA. More generally, however, we believe that even if a vulnerable sub-set of the population was at some point in the future shown *unequivocally* to be at risk from problem music, then it is still not clear that recourse to the law would be socially acceptable as the sole solution. There are numerous instances in which legislators can identify subsets of the population who are prone to the self-injurious behaviour in question, but have nonetheless avoided legislation targeted at them. For example, in Britain it is perfectly possible for suicidal people to buy painkillers without prescription, for smokers to buy cigarettes, or for alcoholics to buy vodka. More common still are cases where society has only allowed legislation concerning self-injurious behaviour when it is enacted in tandem with other measures that attempt to help the victims by eradicating the root source of the problem. For instance, most societies legislate against drugs but also enact treatment programmes for users, or legislate against dangerous driving but allow offenders back on the road if they can prove their safety in a subsequent driving test. In other words, legislation targeted at certain groups of the population seems usually to be acceptable to the public only when it also involves targeted educational measures and attempts to manipulate risk factors. Even if the case against music was unequivocal then we would expect legislation to go no further than in those analogous instances outlined here concerning other forms of self-injurious behaviour.

It is also possible to make several suggestions for further research work that might provide more insightful guidance for those concerned with music legislation. Ward (2003) makes several recommendations for research concerning the impact of media sexuality that can be adapted for the problem music debate. First, we need more detailed content analyses concerning whether the behaviours and attitudes in question are portrayed positively or negatively, since this would be expected to influence the likelihood of the behaviours/attitudes being mirrored in young fans. Second, research needs to consider a wide range of musical genres, since as we have seen, there are numerous instances in which fans of problem music demonstrate high levels of problem attitudes / behaviours, but where fans of other (supposedly unproblematic) styles demonstrate similarly high levels. Such an approach might encourage protest groups to place less emphasis on problem music and more on the real problem, namely people with deleterious attitudes and behaviour. Third, we need to understand more about how reactions to any particular music video are coloured by participants' previous music media history. Fourth, rather than focusing on adolescents' amount of exposure to problem music we also need to know more about their degree of involvement during that exposure time. For example, does greater involvement with music mean that any negative effects of the music are exacerbated? Fifth, we need to understand more about the role of intervening variables, particularly those such as self-esteem and family environment that in their own right indicate a vulnerable adolescent. What specific functions of problem music make it attractive to vulnerable people, and how should the music change so that it still serves these positive functions without having the potential to cause any negative 'side-effects'? Sixth, we need to expand the demographics of the samples tested and in particular to learn more about problem music outside North America and the UK. Different countries have different cultural attitudes towards deleterious behaviour, the arts, youth culture, and censorship: it would be foolish to assume that British and North American research travels well. Seventh, we need to know more about how the messages conveyed by music media interact with those conveyed by other media (e.g. films and computer games). Eighth, there is little evidence concerning viewers'/listeners' interpretations of music media. Apart from research concerning comprehension of lyrics and labelling of CDs, we have little knowledge of how, for example, teenagers interpret the messages in music videos. Do they accept them uncritically or cynically (see Arnett, 1991b)? There will be a lot more research and argument before this issue is resolved.

4.5 Musical subcultures

It is important to remember that musical subcultures certainly did not originate in the mid-1980s as a consequence of the rise of rap and the breakthrough of heavy metal into the mainstream. Rather, the history of pop music in particular is difficult to separate from the subcultures that have surrounded different genres. For example, Miller (1999, p. 229) cites John Lennon's statement in the mid-1960s that 'Beatles concerts are nothing to do with music any more. They're just bloody tribal rituals'. Indeed, youth subcultures have focused on pop music from the Teddy Boys of the 1950s, the flower children of the 1960s, and the punks of the 1970s right through to the Goths, 'metalheads' and rap fans of more recent times. More generally, of course, large numbers of young people regularly wear clothing that flags up their allegiance to a particular musical style or pop group: it represents the kind of 'brand allegiance' that most other big businesses can only dream of, and it would be terrifying if just as many young people walked around in t-shirts showing the products sold by sports equipment or computer manufacturers.

However, the problem music debate highlights the need to understand adolescent musical subcultures. For example, Einerson (1998) carried out an interview study concerning the demise of 'boy band' *New Kids on the Block*, who were so wholesome that, for example, the proceeds from their Top 10 hit *This one's for the children* were donated a cerebral palsy charity, they featured in a children's TV cartoon, and they even entered into discussions about appearing in their own video game. However, Einerson showed that female fans of the group as young as 8 years were aware of the possibility that they may be influenced by pop stars into behaviour of dubious moral standing. If this is a concern to such innocent fans of such a virtuous group of musicians then why and how do young people sometimes choose to so visibly and emphatically associate themselves with other musical subcultures that quite blatantly accentuate violence, drug use, and self-harm? Possible answers to this question are provided by research on music as an identity 'badge', the uses and gratifications approach to music, and the idolization of musicians.

4.5.1 Music as a 'badge'

There is a long tradition of sociological and journalistic writing on the role of music in specific subcultures at specific points in time (see e.g. Garofalo, 1997; Smith, 1999; Ward, 1998; and Werner, 1998 for coverage of the role of pop music in the African-American civil rights movement). Perhaps the best known academic work of this nature is described in Frith's (1981) analysis of teenage musical subcultures in West Yorkshire. He contrasted the role of music for sixth-formers (who were taking university entrance exams) and fifth-formers (who were yet to make the decision whether they would attempt these exams). The former group tended to stress the deeper meaning of the music, particularly as a means of expressing their own individuality and unconventionality. Frith also noted the existence of numerous specific musical subcultures, each with its own dress code and worldview. In particular, Frith (1981, p. 217) suggests that subcultures form around pop music styles precisely because 'all adolescents use music as a badge' which communicates values, attitudes, and opinions to others. For example, this 'badge' function of music may explain why fans of problem music have a tendency toward anti-authoritarian attitudes/behaviours (see also Reddick and Beresin, 2002).

Similarly, as we saw in Chapter 3, North and Hargreaves (2007a, b, c) attempted to provide a detailed examination of the micro-social lifestyle choices that surround musical subcultures. Specifically they related liking for each of 19 musical styles to numerous attitudes and behaviours concerning interpersonal relationships, living arrangements, political and moral beliefs, crime, media preferences, leisure time preferences, travel, personal finances, education, employment, and health. Two aspects of the findings are of particular interest. First of all, we were surprised by just how specific the differences were between different groups of fans, since they differed frequently on very fine-grained variables such as their favourite alcoholic drink, the number of baths/showers they took per week, whether they preferred indoor or outdoor activities, and whether they recycled household waste. Second, these specific differences between musical subcultures mirrored well-established theories. For example, fans of rap and other problem music styles had comparatively libertarian values, and fans of opera were clearly part of a 'high culture' taste public drawn from high social classes (see Chapter 3).

Far less common, however, are data-driven attempts to describe the role of music in identity in a manner that might be expected to survive particular historical periods and musical fashions. One notable exception to this is DeNora (1999) who used ethnographic interviews with 52 women aged 18 to 78 years from the USA and UK to argue that music is a resource that allows people to organize 'their on-going work of self-construction' (p. 32). For example, respondents used music to structure and remind themselves of 'who they were' at a certain moment, season, or era; and they deliberately chose to listen to pieces of music that reaffirmed their current identity. In short, DeNora (1999) indicated that music may well serve identity-related functions that go far beyond short-term musical fads or means of expressing one's own position relative to the social hierarchy.

4.5.1.1 Social identity theory

Perhaps the most promising psychological attempt to investigate the broader role of music in identity has been carried out by Mark Tarrant and colleagues (see e.g. Tarrant, North, and Hargreaves, 2002). This research focused on social identity theory (SIT—see Tajfel, 1978; Tajfel and Turner, 1986; Turner, 1975; see also Ashmore, Deaux, and McLaughlin-Volpe, 2004), which is itself based on earlier research on inter-group relations. Categorizing oneself as a member of one group, an in-group, automatically excludes other people who are members of an out-group. This categorization provides a sense of 'self', or a social identity, which in turn can guide subsequent behaviour. Social identity contrasts with 'personal identity', which becomes salient when no obvious social categorizations are in play and focuses instead on personal, idiosyncratic attributes such as personality or intelligence.

Specifically, SIT argues that as soon as group membership becomes salient so group members act to discriminate in favour of the in-group and against the out-group. In several studies (most famously Tajfel, Flament, Billig, and Bundy, 1971; Billig and Tajfel, 1973), Tajfel and colleagues have demonstrated precisely this pattern of discrimination when asking participants to divide up money between in-group and out-group members. Rather than simply dividing the money equally or awarding the greatest amount of money possible to ingroup members, participants will instead attempt to maximize the difference between the amounts awarded to in-group and out-group members respectively. Furthermore, there is also some evidence that self-esteem mediates the strength of this discriminatory behaviour (see e.g. Abrams and Hogg, 1988; Branscombe and Wann, 1994; Hunter, Brien, and Grocott, 1999; Hunter, Platow, Howard, and Stringer, 1996). When self-esteem is low or threatened then attempts to discriminate increase, and successful discrimination increases self-esteem.

A small number of studies have supported the predictions of SIT in musical behaviour. Knobloch, Vorderer, and Zillmann (2000) found that perceiving a shared musical taste fostered positive appraisals of another person and a greater desire to befriend them. North and Hargreaves (1999b) found that participants responded more positively to an individual when he or she she was described as a fan of a prestigious (e.g. pop) rather than a non-prestigious (e.g. country) musical style. Tarrant, Hargreaves, and North (2001) found much the same: adolescents believed that pupils at their own school (an in-group) would like three prestigious musical styles more than would pupils at a different school (an out-group), whereas they thought that pupils at their own school would like non-prestigious music less than would pupils at a different school. Put simply, these two studies show discrimination in favour of an in group and against an out-group whether musical preference is used as the basis (North and Hargreaves, 1999b) or the measure (Tarrant, Hargreaves, and North, 2001) of group categorisation. Furthermore, Tarrant, Hargreaves, and North (2001) found evidence to support the self-esteem portion of SIT: participants with lower levels of self-esteem were particularly likely to believe that pupils at a different school should like non-prestigious music and that pupils at their own school should like prestigious music. In other words, they seemed motivated to use estimates of musical preferences as a means of presenting their in-group in a favourable light and thus gaining self-esteem from this (see also Tekman and Hortacsu, 2002).

In addition to this, Tarrant, North, Edridge, Kirk, Smith, and Turner (2001) demonstrated the particularly important role that music played in social identity processes, relative to other media and leisure interests. Furthermore, Tarrant and North (2004) related musical social categorization effects to attribution theory. As we saw in Chapter 2, attribution theory concerns how people explain behaviours in terms of three factors, namely internality, stability, and globality. Tarrant and North found that when an in-group member was described as going to a pop concert (i.e. behaving in a socially-positive manner) then this was attributed more to internal reasons (e.g. their decision 'was likely to have been an entirely personal one'), stable reasons (e.g. 'the person is likely to go to similar events often'), and global reasons (e.g. 'the person is likely to perform related behaviours in the future') than when an outgroup member went to the same concert; whereas this pattern was reversed when the person was described as going to a classical music concert (i.e. behaving in a socially-negative manner). Tarrant, North, and Hargreaves (2002, p. 140) drew on social identity theory in proposing a more formal statement of the relationship between music and identity as follows;

1. through the affiliation of their peer groups with certain styles of music, adolescents associate those groups with the meta-information which such affiliation generates;

2. through intergroup comparison, this affiliation can be exaggerated or diminished according to the value connotation of that meta-information, and in response to social identity needs'.

Nor is the role of music in identity unique to adolescence and pop music. For example, in Chapter 2 we discussed the development of identity as a musician. Similarly, Folkestad (2002) discussed the role of music in maintaining national identity. Specifically, he distinguished between national identity, cultural identity, and ethnic identity, arguing that nationality is the 'cement' that holds together different geographical regions despite their cultural and ethnic differences: the sense of a 'nation' is really the marriage between a legally-defined state and culture. As such, it is impossible to address national identity and music without reference to political questions concerning statehood particular to the geographical region in question: for example, we can only consider the validity of Beethoven's *Ode to Joy* as the European Union's anthem relative to a person's definition of themselves as European or alternatively as, for example, Scottish, Basque, or Estonian. Folkestad even goes so far as to note that, consistent with SIT, music seems to play a particularly important role in national identity in countries that have had their legal and cultural sovereignty seriously threatened over extended periods of time.

Of course, much more research is required concerning the role of music in maintaining identity and self-esteem before we can be confident regarding these speculative conclusions. However, if the initial positive signs described above are borne out by future work then SIT forces us to view the problem music debate in a different light. Rather than necessarily being a threat to the moral values and physical health of young people, problem music could perhaps be regarded instead as a positive phenomenon in at least two ways. First, it can be seen as a positive way for teenagers to respond to the perceived *threat* of an older, politically and economically powerful out-group that 'just doesn't understand' the developmental tasks they face. By defining themselves in terms of musical subcultures, teenagers can gain self-esteem through membership of a group that they perceive as morally superior, rather than by defining themselves otherwise as isolated, helpless individuals. Indeed, McNair and Powles (2005) provide a discursive account of the role of rap in promoting collective well-being among African-Americans. Second, membership of problem music subcultures could be particularly helpful to vulnerable teenagers. In addition to gaining self-esteem, membership of a strong problem music subculture allows these people to define themselves less in terms of personal identity with all the negative associations this involves as a consequence of their vulnerable background; and to instead define themselves in terms of a more positive collective identity (see e.g. Caldwell, Kohn-Wood, Schmeelk-Cone, Chavous, and Zimmerman, 2004). Such a process might well explain why problem music styles are associated with particularly strong 'tribal' subcultures formed of individuals from vulnerable backgrounds. Similarly, rap music's preoccupation with urban strife within the African-American community could be interpreted in the light of SIT as a self-esteem boosting assertion of in-group identity in reaction to the perceived threat to an undervalued social group from a white, conservative out-group that is believed to possess disproportionate economic and political clout. Just the same process might explain why minority ethnic groups value radio and TV stations playing 'their' music (such as the BBC *Asian Network* or BBC *Radio nan Gaidheal*).

There are also two more negative consequences of regarding musical subcultures as a manifestation of social identity processes. SIT can explain why (and indeed predicts that) fans of problem music should be antagonistic towards outgroup members such as the fans of other musical styles. For example, the Whitsun weekend of 1964 saw street riots in several coastal towns in southern England between over 1000 ska-loving 'mods' and Elvis Presley and Gene Vincent loving 'rockers' (with the whole mess dramatized famously in the 1979 film *Quadrophenia*). The more strongly that an individual identifies with a particular musical subculture, so the more that he / she should strive to preserve the perceived superiority of that subculture over another. Similarly, given Dibben's (2002) arguments concerning the role of music in the formulation of gender identity, it is easy to use SIT to understand the disproportionate appeal of problem music to young males. By identifying themselves with a musical subculture centred around often violent and sexual themes, young males can gain self-esteem by defining their identity in stereotypically masculine terms.

More generally, Ashmore, Deaux, and McLaughlin-Volpe (2004) quite rightly note that group membership is often a complex notion, arguing that different people may join the same group for different motives, and also that individuals can classify themselves at multiple levels within that group. For example, some people may become rap fans because they simply like the rhythms, others because they feel it addresses issues that worry them such as racial oppression, and others because they enjoy videos featuring scantily-clad women: it would be inappropriate to regard these people as equally committed members of a homogenous group to which they are all equally conscious of belonging, which they value equally (both in public and in private), in which they are likely to have an equal behavioural involvement (e.g. buying the same CDs and t-shirts, 'hanging out' in the same kind of social groups, having the same level of civic commitment), and which they will belong to until the same age. Similarly, a teenager may class him- or herself as a fan of the band Poison, glam metal, and heavy metal, but it is not yet clear which level of this group hierarchy would be most salient in defining group membership at a given time. Although further work is needed to address issues such as these, it is clear that musical subculture can be explained to some extent at least by SIT, as well as by other similar theories of collective identity such as social categorization theory (Turner, 1987), identity theory (Stryker, 1987), and Cross' (1991) stage theory of nigrescence (see also Dweck, 1999).

4.5.1.2 Stereotypes of musical taste

Given the role of intergroup processes in the formation and maintenance of musical subcultures, it is no surprise that numerous studies have highlighted the existence of negative stereotypes of the fans of many different musical styles. The extent to which these musical stereotypes are time-specific is at best uncertain, as is the issue of whether negative stereotypes would automatically lead to lower self-esteem among the fans (see e.g. Crocker and Major, 1989), but they clearly do constitute a source of concern. In particular, research has tended to address the stereotypes of problem music fans. Fried (2003), for instance, found that whereas fans of heavy metal were stereotyped as a threat to themselves (e.g. through drug abuse or suicide), fans of rap were stereotyped as a threat to others through criminal and aggressive behaviour. Similarly, Binder (1993) investigated the coverage of heavy metal and rap in North American newspapers and news magazines between 1985 and 1990. Heavy metal was discussed in terms of protecting fans from corruption whereas rap was more likely to be discussed in terms of it being a danger to society. However, rap was portrayed very differently in periodicals (e.g. *Ebony*) aimed predominantly at the African-American market. Here, there were no instances of rap music being described as harmful: instead discussion of rap focused particularly on it representing an art form concerning important messages. Fischoff (1999) also provides evidence of the particularly negative stereotype concerning rap. He was a witness in the murder trial of a young African-American, in which the prosecution cited violent, misogynistic lyrics written by the defendant as evidence of guilt. In a piece of research carried out on behalf of the defence, Fischoff showed that this fact alone meant that the defendant was seen by participants as more likely to have committed the murder than if he had not been presented as authoring such lyrics. The most startling evidence of all, however, concerning the stereotyping of problem music fans comes from Rosenbaum and Prinsky's (1991) study. In this, hospitals with adolescent psychiatric care programmes responded to a hypothetical situation in which the parents' main concern with their child was the rock music the child listened to, together with the related clothing the child wore and the related posters on the child's bedroom wall. 83% of the facilities indicated that the child needed hospitalization.

Note, however, that musical stereotypes are not limited to heavy metal and rap. North and Hargreaves (1999b) found a high level of consensus in the stereotypes that British undergraduates held concerning the fans of three styles, namely classical music, chart pop, and indie music. Classical music fans were perceived as religious, of high social class, old, highly educated, male, pro-establishment, and sophisticated. Chart pop fans were perceived as unreligious, teenagers, relatively uneducated, female, conventional, unsophisticated, and interested in physical appearances, having fun, being popular, American culture, and technology. Indie music fans were perceived as university-aged, well-educated, male, anti-establishment, non-sexist, non-racist, and unconventional. A follow-up study of 10 to 11-year-olds found that they also held similar stereotypes of the fans of chart pop and classical music. Similarly, Bryson (1996) found that education and political tolerance were linked to a reduced tendency to dislike a range of musical styles (defined as 'musical intolerance'), whereas racism was associated with intolerance of musical styles associated stereotypically with predominantly non-white audiences.

Research on self-to-prototype matching (e.g. Niedenthal, Cantor, and Kihlstrom, 1985), however, suggests a more positive side to the stereotypes of fans of different musical styles. The self-to-prototype matching hypothesis is based on the assumption that individuals are motivated to reinforce their current self-image (see e.g. Kihlstrom and Cantor, 1984; Tesser and Campbell, 1983), and argues that if this is the case then self-to-prototype matching 'is quite serviceable' as a means of predicting people's lifestyle preferences (Niedenthal, Cantor, and Kihlstrom, 1985 p. 575). Put simply, the probability of a person selecting one particular lifestyle option should increase with the degree of overlap between their self-concept and their prototype of the kind of person who usually selects that option.

Several studies have supported the self-to-prototype matching hypothesis in considering the intention to begin smoking (Chassin, Presson, Sherman, Corty, and Olshavsky, 1981), and preferences for housing (Niedenthal, Cantor, and Kihlstrom, 1985), occupations (Moss and Frieze, 1993), types of psychotherapy (Niedenthal and Mordkoff, 1991), and leisure activities (Burke and Reitzes, 1981). In a similar vein, consumer psychologists have argued that product choice is influenced by the degree to which the perceived characteristics of the goods in question correspond with the self-concept of the purchaser (see e.g. Dittmar, 1992). Given this, North and Hargreaves (1999b) tested the validity of self-to-prototype matching as a means of predicting membership of musical subcultures. Participants were presented with a list of 30 statements and asked to rate the extent to which each was true of themselves (i.e. a measure of self-image), typical rap fans (i.e. a measure of the rap stereotype), and typical chart pop fans (i.e. a measure of the chart pop stereotype), before then stating whether they themselves were more a fan of rap or of chart pop. Among rap fans, the correlation between ratings of self and rap fans on the 30 statements was higher than the correlation between ratings of self and chart pop fans. Among chart pop fans, the correlation between ratings of self and chart pop fans on the 30 statements was higher than the correlation between ratings of self and rap fans. In other words, in selecting between the two subcultures, participants seemed to be deciding which group of fans they themselves were more similar to. Furthermore, consistent with SIT, there was evidence that participants' self-esteem increased with the extent to which they identified with the fans of their preferred musical style. Given the support for the self-to-prototype matching hypothesis in research on a range of lifestyle choices, and the clear abundance of stereotypes concerning the fans of different musical styles, it would seem that self-to-prototype matching offers another possible route for research concerning the role of self-image in membership of musical subcultures.

4.5.2 **The uses and gratifications approach**

Howitt (1998) argued that the media have an effect on the public through one of three models. The first, 'cause and effect', model is highlighted by research on the problem music debate. This model states that media have a direct (positive or negative) impact on the public as a result of their content, and this has clear links with the well-known 'hypodermic needle' model of media influence (Hirsch, 1971). Howitt's second model, 'cultural ratification', states that the role of the media is to stabilize society by reinforcing core beliefs and maintaining the status quo. The model is clearly not supported by research on the problem music debate (but is supported by the research described in Chapter 3 concerning the notions of taste cultures and taste publics). Howitt's third model is termed 'uses and gratifications' (see Rosengren, Wenner, and Palmgreen, 1985). This states that the impact of the media is limited by the extent to which they help the public to achieve particular goals. Indeed, the literature reviewed in Chapter 3 concerning everyday uses of music could be seen as supporting such a model, but there is also a reasonably large body of quantitative sociological/social psychological work that directly addresses the uses and gratifications of music.

A key feature of much of the uses and gratifications research is the focus on simply asking adolescents why they listen to music (usually in response to an open-ended question or by asking participants to select from a list of options provided by the researcher). Such an approach is obviously commendable, crediting young people with the ability to understand why they are so interested in music. There are methodological problems as well though. For example, this method presents a biased view of why young people listen to music, namely their own. Furthermore, it is by no means clear that introspection of this nature is a reliable means of determining people's motivations (see e.g. Leahey, 1994; Maier, 1931; Nisbett and Wilson, 1977); and other research shows that self-knowledge develops during rather than prior to adolescence (e.g. Harter, 1986), such that adolescents may provide imperfect data about their own motivations for music listening. Put simply, it is important to recognize that uses and gratifications research tells us why adolescents *believe* they listen to music, although it may not necessarily tell us why they *actually* do this.

Uses and gratifications research is subject to a second, more practical problem. It is obviously tempting to rank order the many different uses and gratifications of music in terms of their importance, and many studies have indeed attempted to provide percentages reflecting the frequency with which different uses and gratifications are employed by people. Findings of this nature are, however, rather inconsistent. For example, research has shown that mood management can be of little (Gantz, Gartenberg, Pearson, and Schiller, 1978), intermediate (Sun and Lull, 1986), or great (Roe, 1985) importance to adolescents as a reason for listening to music. One explanation for this is provided by North and Hargreaves (1996c). They reported that the functions of music varied across 17 different hypothetical music listening situations (e.g. at a nightclub), such that the uses and functions of music seem to be context-dependent. Furthermore, we shall see shortly that other research has shown that the uses and gratifications of music interact with factors such as age, sex, social class, and ethnic origin. It is, therefore, spurious to produce overall figures concerning the relative frequency with which music is used for a given reason. The brief review that follows deliberately shies away from any such an attempt (and such a review is provided by Christenson and Roberts (1998) anyway), and focuses instead on how these uses and gratifications might be classified.

As evidence of the range of uses and gratifications of music for teenagers, Christenson and Roberts (1998, p. 42) cite 34 factors in their 'partial inventory', such as pleasure, relief of tension, identification with a subculture, or masking out of unwanted sounds. They go on to argue that there are three types of social functions of music, namely quasi-social, socializing, and cultural. Although other models of uses and gratifications of music exist (see e.g. Arnett (1995), and Steele and Brown's (1995) adolescent media practice model), Christenson and Roberts' is perhaps the most coherent given the parallel with Doise's (1986) levels of influence in social psychology that we discussed briefly in Chapter 1. Quasi-social functions can be seen as operating on the intraindividual level, socializing functions at the interindividual level, and cultural functions at the social-positional and ideological levels.

Research on quasi-social uses of music has looked at two main functions, namely the alleviation of loneliness and mood management. With regard to loneliness, in addition to a particular tendency for females more than males to listen to music just to alleviate short-term loneliness (e.g. Gantz, Gartenberg, Pearson, and Schiller, 1978; Larson, Kubey, and Colletti, 1989), research shows that adolescents also use music to prepare for future social interactions. For example, Dominick (1974) reported that keeping up with latest musical trends via the radio was important to those with a lot of friends; Clarke (1973) found that the amount of time that adolescents spent reading pop music magazines was related to the number of friends they had who shared their musical taste; and Brown and O'Leary (1971) found that adolescents' integration into pop music culture was linked to their number of friends, and that this integration was very socially prestigious.

With regard to mood management it goes almost without saying that, like everyone else, adolescents will use music to achieve or alleviate particular moods (e.g. Arnett, 1991b; Gantz, Gartenberg, Pearson, and Schiller, 1978; Wells, 1990). However, Christenson and Roberts (1998) point out that research on mood management is complicated by several factors. In particular, adolescents' reliance on music for mood control varies according to dimensions such as age and sex (e.g. Larson, Kubey, and Colletti, 1989) and social class (e.g. Frith, 1981). Furthermore, it is not precisely clear what is meant by 'mood management', since for example Arnett (1991b) describes how half of his male heavy metal fans listened to the music when angry: it is not clear whether such a process would produce catharsis or an exacerbation of the mood, although Christenson and Roberts (1998) cite arguments by Oliver (1990) which propose two possible reasons why catharsis may be the more likely explanation. First, it may be 'mood managing' to listen to negatively-valenced music while in a negative mood since it provides a downward social comparison such that the listener's own plight seems less serious. Second, it may be important to distinguish moods from 'meta moods', in that the former can be negative while the latter can be simultaneously positive: put simply, we can feel sad but feel good about that. Another approach to defining what exactly is meant by mood management is suggested by Behne's (1996) notion of 'Musikerleben': this refers to a process by which musical behaviour can be interpreted in the context of other aspects of participants' lifestyles (e.g. the emotional problems that they face). In this regard Behne identified nine distinct listening styles that could be regarded as nine different types of mood management, namely compensating, concentrated, emotional, distancing, vegetative, sentimental, associative, stimulative, and diffuse.

Socializing uses of music reflect attempts to achieve specific aims during interactions between individuals. They fall into three main categories, namely setting a mood, filling silence, and facilitating interpersonal interaction (through, for example, dancing or by providing a source of conversation). Again, these uses of music interact with several other variables. For example, females tend to use music for these ends more than do males (Carroll, Silbergleid, Beachum, Perry, Pluscht, and Pescatore, 1993; Gantz, Gartenberg, Pearson, and Schiller, 1978), and in different ways (North, Hargreaves, and O'Neill, 2000). Kuwhara (1992) and Lull (1992) both suggested that African-Americans are more involved than whites in dancing. Musical subculture seems to be important also: Kortaba and Wells' (1987) ethnographic study of a nightclub found that heavy metal fans did not socialize across genders as much as other fans, and that the latter were more likely to laugh, hug, kiss, and smile, such that the music was much less the focus of the social event.

Cultural uses of music reflect how people use music when they are operating as a member of a social group. Christenson and Roberts (1998, p. 60) stated that, 'none of the "uses and gratifications" studies reviewed ... report explicit evidence of ... subcultural or oppositional uses. It is possible of course that the methods used to elicit the information are too blunt to detect such uses'. This must be seen in the context of the experimental research on SIT reviewed earlier which suggests that adolescents may well (consciously or not) still use music to these ends. Furthermore, the frequency with which music is used for these 'tribal' ends probably depends very much on whether group membership is salient at the moment in question (e.g. Tajfel and Turner, 1986).

In conclusion, existing research on the uses and gratifications of music probably raises more questions than it answers. However, it also serves a valuable function in the problem music debate by demonstrating that music is not always received passively, and that instead young people are perfectly capable of using music actively to achieve certain emotional and everyday ends. Indeed, this notion of teenagers as active consumers of music on a mundane, everyday basis adds further credence to our earlier argument that vulnerable people ought to be more attracted to problem music. Research on uses and gratifications shows it is perfectly plausible that such people would regularly seek out music dealing with difficult themes in order to 'get a handle' on what is happening in their life. We are not alone in this view. Roe (1995) goes so far as to argue that delinquency and the use of socially disvalued media such as problem music are both self-esteem boosting reactions to poor school performance and therefore lower social status. Indeed, although there are probably as many uses and gratifications of music as there are people, the most socially significant of these during adolescence may prove to be the use of music to reconcile oneself with a vulnerable background.

4.5.3 Idolization of musicians

One particularly extreme form of musically-defined identity is of course the idolization of a favourite musician. This idolization can include membership of fan clubs and collecting memorabilia, or more disturbingly can even involve stalking of the musician and accusations concerning copycat suicides in which fans have ended their own life in a manner similar to that of the musician. In this section, we accordingly review the research on idolization of musical celebrities, stalking of musicians, and copycat suicide. Note that idolization of some form is not unique to pop music: Dolly Parton and Daniel O'Donnell are well-known examples of strongly idolized musicians from other genres. Moreover, several studies have described the idolization of Elvis Presley. Olson and Crase (1990) are among many authors (see also Doss, 1999; but also Duffett, 2003) who describe how Elvis has become a 'spiritual leader' who allows fans to express their own hopes, often during 'pilgrimages' to his former home, Gracelands. Similarly, Fraser and Brown's (2002) ethnographic study of Elvis fans and impersonators shows how many people have deliberately modelled their values and lifestyles on those of The King.

However, research on the idolization of musicians has paid most attention to problem music. Cardinal Joseph Ratzinger (later to become Pope Benedict XVI) wrote in his *The Spirit of the Liturgy* (2000) that 'Rock... is the expression of the elemental passions, and at rock festivals it assumes a sometimes cultic character, a form of worship, in fact, in opposition to Christian worship.'

In apparent confirmation of this, Arnett (1991b) asked heavy metal fans and non-fans to name three people whom they most admired, and found that 61% of the metal fans named at least one musician whereas only 13% of non-fans did so. However, perhaps the most promising line of enquiry concerning the idolization of problem musicians has employed the Celebrity Attitude Scale (CAS, McCutcheon, Lange, and Houran, 2002).

4.5.3.1 Musicians as celebrities

The CAS measures the extent to which the respondent is interested in and relates to the life of his or her favourite celebrity, who can be from the world of music or elsewhere. McCutcheon, Lange, and Houran (2002) proposed that the CAS contains three sub-scales that effectively represent three different types of celebrity worship, namely *entertainment-social, intense-personal*, and *borderline-pathological. Entertainment-social* celebrity worship refers to a 'normal' degree of interest in the life of the participant's favourite celebrity. It is manifested by, for example, a desire to discuss the celebrity with friends, and agreement that learning about the celebrity through magazines or newspapers represents 'having a good time'. *Intense-personal* celebrity worship involves the participant feeling that he or she has a strong personal 'connection' with the celebrity. It is manifested by, for example, a feeling that the celebrity is a fault-less soulmate, about whom the individual has frequent thoughts. As is clear, this form of celebrity worship is arguably less positive than the *entertainment-social* form. Finally, *borderline-pathological* celebrity worship is arguably the most deleterious form. It is manifested through a variety of bizarre beliefs such as a shared secret code through which the individual can communicate with the celebrity, a belief that the celebrity would come to help the individual in times of distress, and feelings that the celebrity would be pleased to meet the respondent in intimate settings such as the former's car or home.

Two recent studies have investigated the relationship between CAS scores, musical preferences, and other factors. On the negative side, North and Hargreaves (2006) asked participants to complete the CAS with regard to their favourite musician and found that those who named a musician from a problem music style had higher CAS scores, indicating higher levels of 'celebrity worship'. Problem music fans also had higher scores on two sub-scales that appeared in participants' responses, namely 'entertainment-social' celebrity worship and another factor concerning a propensity to mimic the licentious activities of the favourite musician. Furthermore, high CAS scores were associated with whether the participant had considered self-harming. However, North, Desborough, and Skarstein (2005) again asked participants to complete the CAS with regard to their favourite musician and found that fans of problem music did not score higher than non-fans. As such, it is unclear whether fans of problem music do indeed idolize their musical heroes more than anyone else. What is arguably more interesting in the present context is that both studies showed a considerable range in CAS scores across all participants. In other words, fans of musicians from a variety of genres gave rise to some very high and very low CAS scores: just because these CAS scores may or may not be related to particular musical preferences does not preclude the fact that some participants idolized their favourite musicians strongly.

Although little research has so far concerned specifically music and the CAS, we have dwelt on it since several studies indicate links between CAS scores and other factors. As such, these other studies provide several strong clues about the factors that are likely to be linked to the idolization of specifically musicians. For example, McCutcheon, Lange, and Houran (2002) propose that celebrity worship within an individual develops in a manner consistent with addiction. They argue that 'a compromised identity structure' (p. 412) leads to absorption with a celebrity in an attempt to establish identity and a sense of fulfilment. Because the celebrity does not reciprocate this relationship, some individuals are driven to ever greater extremes in order to maintain their satisfaction with it, and this leads to more extreme forms of celebrity worship. Given what we have already seen about the vulnerable backgrounds of problem music fans, we might well, according to this model, expect them to particularly idolize their favourite musicians. Similarly, although several authors have provided more anecdotal evidence concerning the analogy between celebrity worship and religion, Maltby (2004) was able to identify a negative relationship between a measure of religious puritanism and CAS scores: in other words, people who disagree with notions of Divine law and church authority tend to neglect religious worship in favour of celebrity worship (see also Maltby, Houran, Lange, Ashe, and McCutcheon, 2002). This might again predict that problem music fans (who tend not to be religious—Arnett, 1991; North and Hargreaves, 2007a) should be particularly likely to idolize their favourite musicians.

Other research shows a higher incidence of celebrity worship among young people (Ashe and McCutcheon, 2001; Larsen, 1995) which again suggests that pop music fans should be more prone to idolization of musicians; links between celebrity worship and a 'game playing love style' (McCutcheon, 2002), which may relate to the relationship between problem music and misogyny; and a relationship between celebrity worship and poorer mental health (Maltby, Day, McCutcheon, Gillett, Houran, and Ashe, 2004), which may relate to evidence indicating the relatively poor mental health of problem music fans (Doak, 2003; Schwartz and Fouts, 2003). Furthermore, Maltby,

Houran and McCutcheon (2003) found evidence associating different types of celebrity worship with aspects of Eysenck's (e.g. Eysenck and Eysenck, 1975) personality dimensions. Specifically, they argued that entertainment-social celebrity worship reflects some of the extraversion personality traits (sociable, lively, active, venturesome), that intense-personal celebrity worship reflects some of the neuroticism traits (tense, emotional, moody), and that borderline-pathological celebrity worship seems to reflect some of the psychoticism traits (impulsive, anti-social, egocentric). It is easy to see how these personality factors would again lead to many of the attitudes and behaviours we have already seen to be linked to problem music. These ideas based on CAS research are obviously speculative but are clear candidates for future research.

Other research on celebrities suggests clear hypotheses for research on the idolization of specifically musicians. North, Bland, and Ellis (2005) found that musicians were more likely to be nominated as participants' favourite 'celebrities' rather than as their favourite 'heroes' (i.e. people who made a long-lasting and important contribution to society); and that attitudes to heroes were characterized by greater emotional involvement and drive for affiliation and less 'disdain' than were attitudes towards celebrities. This may begin to explain the difference in public attitudes towards musical heroes (e.g. John Lennon, Jim Morrison, Jimi Hendrix) and musical celebrities (e.g. Robbie Williams, Britney Spears, Justin Timberlake), and why people collect memorabilia associated with the former (e.g. old guitars, original transcriptions of lyrics) much more than the latter. Similarly Boon and Lomore (2001; see also Raviv, Bar-Tal, Raviv, and Ben-Horin, 1996) investigated the relationships of 17 to 35-year-olds with celebrities to whom they were moderately or strongly attracted (and who were predominantly male musicians and actors). These idols did not affect participants' self-concept or self-worth, and only modest amounts of time, money and thought were devoted to them. However, about half of the participants felt that their idol had influenced their attitudes and beliefs or inspired them to pursue a particular activity, and there were numerous relationships between measures of 'investment' in the celebrity, 'attraction strength', 'perceived intimacy', 'perceived influence', and participants' attempts to change aspects of their personality, appearance, and attitudes to become more similar to their favourite celebrity. The resulting detailed model devised on the basis of these findings has direct implications for research on the influence of musicians on attitudes and behaviour.

4.5.3.2 Stalking of musicians

The borderline pathological sub-scale of the CAS implies that whereas some people may simply join a fan club or put a poster up on their bedroom wall, other fans may go to very extreme lengths to establish a link between themselves and a favourite musician. Perhaps the most extreme form of this concerns the stalking of musicians, in which 'fans' develop an unusually high degree of obsession or fixation, often as a consequence of mental disorder; and this has been suffered by the likes of John Lennon, Madonna, Agnetha Fältskog, Robbie Williams, Gloria Estefan, Billie Piper, George Harrison, Linda Ronstadt, Vanessa Mae, Whitney Houston, Sheena Easton, Britney Spears, Mel C, Olivia Newton-John, Michael Jackson, and Björk. This can manifest itself through the fan perceiving him- or herself to have a personal relationship with the musician (sometimes in response to messages within the music supposedly aimed directly at the fan), coming to the musician's house, writing several times a day to the musician, plotting to kidnap the musician or their family, physical attack, or in the case of John Lennon, murder.

Hoffmann and Sheridan's (2005) review suggests that the stalking of public figures such as media celebrities and politicians may be increasing, and that many stalkers may target multiple victims either in a serial or simultaneous manner, with each individual being targeted for around two years. Furthermore, such cases tend to go unreported either because the stalking is dealt with via private security companies, and the victim wishes to keep their victim status private, or because the victim feels that recourse to the law may exacerbate the problem. For example, when Madonna was ordered to testify in person against an individual who had allegedly targeted her, she commented that, 'we have somehow made his fantasies come true [in that] I am sitting in front of him and that is what he wants'. Hoffmann and Sheridan go on to suggest that, although violence may be a rare outcome of celebrity stalking (relative to stalking of members of the general public), in cases where violence is involved there is almost always an earlier period of planning and preparation, so that the violence is rarely the product of an impulsive individual who has temporarily lost control. Instead, acts of violence are viewed by the stalking perpetrator as a means of achieving objectives such as becoming (in)famous or incarcerated, achieving power or revenge over the celebrity, or getting killed. Given this element of planning, Hoffman and Sheridan argue that it is possible to identify fans who pose a threat to the physical well-being of public figures, and recommend adopting a case-by-case approach in using threat management strategies.

4.5.3.3 Copycat suicide

Two other studies have investigated another very negative aspect of the idolization of musicians, namely copycat suicide. Although this may sound far-fetched it is worth noting that Phillips (1974), for example, found that after the suicide of Marilyn Monroe, the USA and UK together saw 363 more suicides than would be expected statistically in the month following her death (equivalent to a 12.04% rise in the USA and a 9.83% rise in the UK). Indeed, Rustad, Small, Jobes, Safer, and Peterson (2003) note that many other (although not all) studies have shown a link between suicide rates and the prevalence of suicide-related newspaper stories, television reports and fictional depictions. We are only aware of two similar studies concerning the death of a musician, with both concerning the impact of the 1994 suicide of Seattle-based Kurt Cobain.

Seelow (1996) describes the anxiety and incomprehension in Cobain's lyrics, and Schaller (1997) linked Cobain's increasing fame to increased use of first-person singular pronouns in his lyrics, arguing that this supports the hypothesis that his growing fame led to greater self-consciousness, which was in turn self-destructive. Jobes, Berman, O'Carroll, Eastgard, and Knickmeyer (1996) describe the course of events leading to Cobain's suicide and the immediate response of health professionals in Seattle, such as attendance at a candlelit public memorial vigil for Cobain to disseminate information about a suicide crisis telephone service. They also report data on suicides in metropolitan Seattle in the seven-week period following Cobain's suicide. There was a clear rise in calls to a local suicide crisis line, and 'a virtual prototype copycat suicide' (p. 262) in which the decedent was a Cobain fan who killed himself in the same manner and made explicit references to Cobain in his suicide note (although he was also 'a heavy substance abuser, was isolated and depressed, had previous suicidal thoughts, and had a father who committed suicide' (p. 262) in a similar way). However, 'During this period, there were 24 suicides … When compared to the same period … one year earlier, there were actually fewer suicides in 1994 (1993 prevalence = 31).' They conclude from all this that the speedy and targeted reaction of Seattle's health professionals had a positive, preventative role. They also note that the absence of an increased suicide rate could also be attributable to the unromantic manner of his suicide (which necessitated the use of dental records to make a positive identification), and the (usually) responsible media portrayal of Cobain's suicide: 'the general message was, "great artist, great music … stupid act, don't do it; here's where to call for help"' (p. 263).

It is also pleasing that even less ambiguous evidence is reported by Martin and Koo (1997). They compared the Australian suicide rate in the 30 days following the announcement of Cobain's suicide with corresponding data for each year back to 1989. Among males, the 1994 suicide rate was lower than for 1992 and 1993 and was more similar to the 1989 and 1990 rates. Among females there was a small but steady decline in suicide rates over the five years that was sustained into 1994. Also there was no evidence of an increase in 1994 in suicides using the same method as Cobain. In short, the Cobain suicide did not appear to lead to copycat suicides.

It is obviously very dangerous to make generalizations based on two studies of the effects of a single suicide, and it must be remembered that both Phillips (1974) and Rustad, Small, Jobes, Safer, and Peterson (2003) did find that 'copycat' suicides may take place. However, it is clearly good news that Cobain's suicide did not apparently lead to a spate of copycats. Indeed, it is also reassuring that Lacourse, Claes, and Villeneuve (2001) failed to identify a relationship between 'worshipping' heavy metal (i.e. hanging posters, acquiring information about singers, etc.) and increased suicide risk; and that three studies indicate that fans of heavy metal do not believe that their music can encourage suicide and self-harm, and can dissipate anger (Arnett, 1991b; Wass, Miller, and Redditt, 1991; Wass, Raup, Cerullo, Martel, Mingione, and Sperring, 1988-1989; but also North and Hargreaves, 2006). Nevertheless it would be equally dangerous to assume that there is no cause for concern, and in the unfortunate event of a similar suicide occurring in the future we would urge the media to again run an assertive prevention campaign of the type that was apparently successful in 1994 in Seattle and Australia.

In conclusion, we saw in Chapter 3 that different cohorts of adolescents each have their own version of 'pop music', and so it is unsurprising that adults should be prone to misunderstanding the effects of the music that their children listen to and the musical subcultures that they join. However, it is also ironic and saddening that the baby boomers who embraced freedom of artistic expression in the 1960s should lie behind so much of the protest and legislation aimed at pop music in the present day. Just as saddening is that so much of the research treats musical subcultures and the problem music debate as North American (and to a lesser extent British) phenomena. While it is understandable that researchers wish to address pop music from their own cultural perspective, the export of North American and British pop music through radio and satellite television means that any social ills associated with the former are likely to crop up anywhere in the world. In addition to this moral argument, there is also a strong scientific case for research in other cultures: since musical subcultures are such an intrinsically social phenomenon there is presumably much to be learned by investigating the relative roles of society and music *per se* in shaping them and the deleterious behaviour they are associated with. Finally, even though so much of the research in this area is carried out by researchers interested in communication studies, it is unfortunate that so few people have investigated the interaction between different music media. For example, we still have little understanding of the interaction of music and lyrics (see e.g. Besson, Faïta, Peretz, Bonnel, and Requin, 1998), let alone one between music and video, radio, the 'image' of the band in question, and the 'image' of the typical fans, to name but a few.

This chapter has provided some tentative answers concerning the problem music debate, and we are optimistic that most and perhaps all of the theories and methodologies needed to address unanswered questions already exist. Rather, the major challenge facing researchers will be to make reliable, practical recommendations based on theory and data. These recommendations will need to be made vociferously since they will very likely call into question the stereotypical assumptions and lazy arguments which are propagated by both powerful protest groups and media-savvy musicians; and which are often accepted without sufficient scrutiny by journalists who are simply hungry for a good story. The problem music debate will ultimately be resolved in newspapers rather than academic journals, and it requires not just good research but good *communication* of that research to the general public.

5

Music, business, and health

Extraordinary how potent cheap music is
Noel Coward, *Private Lives*

It is obviously easy to view music through rose-tinted spectacles and forget that most of the 'organized' music we hear (e.g. CDs and concerts etc.) exists solely because at some point in time, somebody thought it would directly or indirectly serve their financial or political interests. To give two obvious examples, only the most ill-informed or naïve could have regarded the July 1985 *Live Aid* and July 2005 *Live 8* concerts as primarily musical events (see Westley, 1991). Similarly, Pincott and Anderson (1999, p. 109) reported that '7.3 billion musical items are broadcast and publicly performed each year' by radio stations, shops, restaurants and the like in the UK alone, and it is very hard to believe that this is motivated by philanthropy. Nor is the use of music for financial or political gain unique to pop music in the twentieth and twenty-first centuries. For example, Lanza (1994) describes how, in Greek mythology, Orpheus played his lyre to inspire Jason and the Argonauts' quest for the Golden Fleece. Plato advocated the health-promoting function of music, arguing that 'Rhythm and harmony find their way into the inward places of the soul'. The third century Roman grammarian Censorinus wrote that 'music serves to make toil as bearable as may be, as when it is used by the steersman in a moving galley', and a flute orchestra purportedly accompanied the erection of the walls of Rome's Messina. During the Middle Ages, Christian soldiers of the early Crusades hired battlefield musicians to play the same Arabic military music that the Saracens had used to defeat them in previous battles, and monks would perform Gregorian plainsong outside the monastery to uplift agricultural workers. Trainee musicians are often appalled to learn that many pieces from the standard classical repertoire were written specifically as background music. Bach's *Goldberg Variations* were written to help cure the insomnia of the man who commissioned them, Count Kaiserling; and Mozart and Telemann were also both well aware of the need to compose background music for the court.

In the previous chapter we considered how music might influence attitudes and behaviours among primarily adolescents. In this chapter we consider another line of research that has also considered the impact of music on attitudes and behaviours, but this time in the context of effects that have implications for the economic 'bottom line'. The most obvious commercial aspect of music involves buying pre-recorded CDs, and this chapter begins by considering the music industry itself. How does industry organization affect the music that is released on CD and played on the radio, and how do people choose to buy music (or make illegal 'pirate' copies)? From here we consider the effects that music might have in advertising, and then in other retail and service-based businesses such as shops, restaurants, and hotels. Finally, we consider two indirect economic benefits of music, namely its ability to influence productivity in the workplace, and its ability to promote physical health.

5.1 **The music industry**

In Chapter 4 we described evidence on the prevalence of record sales, and it is worth reiterating some of these huge figures if only to exemplify the scale of the business. A 2003 report by market research agency Mintel described how 225.7 million pre-recorded albums were sold in the UK alone in 2002, representing retail sales of £2.03 billion; and how 18 British music magazines between them had a total net circulation per issue of 1,211,382 copies. (And since classical music or jazz were unable to account for more than 5% of retail sales, it is easy to see why they are so neglected by the music industry.) Similarly, the Recording Industry Association of America report that in 2005, people in the USA alone spent US$105 billion on 705 million CDs. Although the current market is slowing (e.g. the 2005 figures were 8.0% down on 2004), the 'big picture' is nevertheless one of massive sales and earnings. Music is very big business. This section of the chapter describes research at the interface of psychology, economics, and sociology on how the music business works and how this influences musical behaviour. We consider the link between musical innovation and music industry concentration; how and why superstardom is important to the music industry; models of music purchasing and attempts to explain piracy; and finally the process of radio station programming.

5.1.1 **Tin Pan Alley and music industry innovation**

'Tin Pan Alley' was christened in 1900 by songwriter Monroe H. Rosenfeld, who was commissioned by the *New York Herald* to write a piece on the new sheet music publishing industry that had emerged on West 28th Street between Broadway and Sixth Avenue. Rosenfeld thought that the din of countless upright pianos that he heard through the open windows, muffled by the use of newspapers on the strings, was reminiscent of rattling pans. Although the location of Tin Pan Alley moved around the city (as Irving Caesar claimed, so as to remain 'close to the nearest buck'), for the following 50 years it was to dominate popular songwriting. As Scott (1999) shows, it still operates in effect today with record companies in New York and Los Angeles being disproportionately likely to release hit records (even when accounting for the number of record companies there, including the 'majors'). Over the years, Tin Pan Alley became synonymous with the profit-driven motives of the music industry as George Gershwin, Cole Porter and colleagues, while certainly not forsaking aesthetic standards, composed with *popularity* in mind. Indeed, Gershwin himself started out as a song plugger, employed by the Remick company when only 14 years old to demonstrate their latest songs to professional entertainers short of material; and Cole Porter is reported to once have said that 'My sole inspiration is a telephone call from a producer'. Highly entertaining accounts of Tin Pan Alley are provided by John Shepherd (1982) and Philip Furia (1990); and Jimmy Cauty and Bill Drummond (1988), who reached number 1 in the British charts as *The KLF*, have described the modern-day equivalent of Tin Pan Alley in their self-explanatory *The Manual: How to Have a Number One Hit the Easy Way*.

Academic interest in the music industry is by no means limited to Britain and North America (see e.g. Blewett and Farley, 1998; Capling, 1996; Ellis, 2001; Gebesmair and Smudits, 2001; Fosu-Mensah, Duran, and Stapleton, 1987; Laing, 1986; Reddi, 1985). Indeed, a brief flick through these or any British or North American sources on the business would be sufficient to cure a music purist of the notion that the industry operates for the cultural and aesthetic benefit of musicians and their audience. Rothenbuhler and McCourt (2004, p.226; see also Frith, 1992; Laing, 2003), for example, describe the situation well, noting that 'Record companies do not "create" music; instead they obtain music from contractually bound songwriters and musicians, who (in theory) benefit from the company's distribution and promotional services'. 'Session' musicians employed by the companies are not paid well for their work, and even the most successful of performers will rarely receive royalty payments on sales of their recordings at more than 15% (although see also Clemons, Bin, and Lang, 2002). Out of these royalties are deducted costs related to the recording of the music and the production of videos, to name but two, and if one particular recording fails to make a profit then the outstanding debt is typically carried over and applied to royalties due on future recordings. Songwriters at least also have the opportunity to boost their payments by royalties based on so-called mechanical rights (i.e. the physical manifestation of a song on a CD or in sheet music) and performing rights (which are paid whenever a song is recorded or played in public). However, even the means by which we hear pre-recorded music is determined by the self-interest of the music industry (see e.g. Klaes, 1997). Although CDs undoubtedly provide better sound quality, their predominance may not be unrelated to the fact that their manufacture is also more reliable and has lower labour costs than vinyl; and since they are smaller and lighter they also have lower shipping costs as well. Perhaps we are being overly cynical here but it may be an interesting parallel that, in its early days, the music industry adopted Berliner's discs which were cheaper and easier to reproduce, store, and handle, rather than Edison's cylinders which offered better sound reproduction. The music business is far more interested in profit than aesthetics.

Nor can the music industry really be criticized for such self-interested business methods: in addition to the fact that the *raison d'être* of record companies is profit rather than charity, Vogel (1998) estimated that only one in 10 records manages to so much as break even, such that when one does make a profit it has to cover the losses made by nine others. Added to this of course are the huge entry barriers to the pre-recorded music mass market (see Alexander, 1994a; Wilson and Stokes, 2004). While it costs little to record music on your home PC and sell it on the internet, the costs of producing, marketing, and distributing a CD through retailers worldwide are staggering. As a consequence of factors such as these, the music industry has long employed mergers, conglomeration and vertical integration (see Gander and Rieple, 2002), with many major record companies at some time owning or having been owned by instrument manufacturers, audio equipment manufacturers, film studios, or music retailers. Two obvious consequences of this are that it introduces economies of scale (see Fairchild, 1996) both in administration and by allowing cross-promotion between different parts of the business (e.g. music by artist X appearing on the soundtrack of a film produced by a studio with links to their record company), and that it limits the prospects for competition from other companies (see e.g. Alexander, 1994b).

Unsurprisingly this has led to the music industry being controlled largely through an oligopoly of very large multinational companies. For example, a report by Mintel (2003) notes that six companies together had over three-quarters of the British album market in 2001, with Universal alone accounting for 26% (but see also Hesmondhalgh, 1998; 1999); and suggests that further mergers are likely. This concentration led to investigation of the music industry in the 1990s by the UK's Monopolies and Mergers Commission (Towse, 1997). Rothenbuhler and McCourt (2004) report similar data for the USA. This industry 'concentration' has interesting implications of its own. For instance, the costs of producing, marketing, and distributing a CD are fairly constant whether it sells 5000 or 500,000 copies. It therefore makes sense for record companies to aim to sell as many copies as they can of a relatively small number of CDs. Such a strategy maximizes returns on a small initial outlay (and financial risk).

It should therefore come as no surprise that several studies show there is a negative correlation between the concentration of the music industry and both the amount of innovation and diversity represented by the music on the charts (Peterson and Berger, 1975; Rothenbuhler and Dimmick, 1982; see also Anderson, Hesbacher, Etzkorn, and Denisoff, 1980). Put simply, the more that a small number of companies control the charts (i.e. greater concentration) so the *slower the turnover* of songs on the charts (i.e. lack of diversity) and the *smaller number of new artists* there are that reach the charts (i.e. lack of innovation). In effect, the small number of companies exploit their market dominance by taking the opportunity to spend money on only a small number of recordings and therefore minimize their financial exposure. For example, with regard to diversity, Rothenbuhler and Dimmick (1982) reported that in 1980 only nine firms had hit records in the USA, and there were only 82 top 10 records and 17 number one records. In contrast, 1975 saw much less concentration with 21 firms having hit records, and there was a larger number of top 10 records (111) and number one records (37). In other words, the structure of the music industry directly influences music buying behaviour. Furthermore, both Peterson and Berger (1975) and Rothenbuhler and Dimmick (1982) provided some indication that a lack of diversity leads to falling sales, since some potential customers are unable to identify music that matches their taste. Years with greater diversity tended to feature higher overall sales as there are more songs 'out there' that listeners have the opportunity to like and subsequently buy. In other words, if we accept diversity and innovation as measures of musical creativity, and sales as a measure of the overall popularity of 'music' at a given point in time, then oligopolistic control of the music industry, although understandable from an economic perspective, is bad news for music lovers.

Such provocative conclusions have not gone unchallenged. Lopes (1992), for example, argued that Peterson and Berger's and Rothenbuhler and Dimmick's model is simply outdated. He points to the more recent strategy among major companies of establishing semi-autonomous labels (see Gander and Rieple, 2004), and provides evidence that this allows high levels of innovation and diversity to exist within a still highly-concentrated market. Alexander (1996; see also 1997) criticized the use of the number of top 10 songs as a measure of diversity, arguing that a large number of songs that all actually sound very similar to one another does not truly indicate musical variation. Instead, he defined diversity in terms of how unusual the music was (by, for example, considering whether it was in 4/4 time, and whether the melody was confined to a single octave). Such an approach has obvious parallels with experimental aesthetics (see Chapter 3). Alexander argued that using this method, diversity is maximized by moderate levels of industry concentration whereas both high and low levels of concentration lead to decreased diversity (although Peterson and Berger (1996) in turn disagreed).

5.1.2 **Superstardom**

We have already seen how the industry favours making money through huge sales of a small number of albums, and two strategies have been adopted for achieving this. The first is the use of vast promotional campaigns, such that once a particular title begins to sell it attracts a marketing budget that is hugely disproportionate to that enjoyed by others. A second strategy is the use of a star system, a limited roster of acts whose recordings are virtually guaranteed to sell in huge quantities. Economic research on this subject has investigated the so-called 'superstar phenomenon' (e.g. Rosen, 1981; 1983). This states that as incomes rise so the demand for 'quality' goods and services will increase: this in turn should lead to supply-side economies of scale such that the price of 'quality' goods falls. Since inferior goods are regarded by consumers as imperfect substitutes for slightly superior ones (e.g. slightly better music), 'small differences in talent become magnified in larger earnings differences' and therefore commercial success (Rosen, 1981, p.846). Indeed, a very small number of musicians do seem to enjoy hugely disproportionate degrees of success even though they are only a little better than many of their peers. For example, Fox and Kochanowski (2004) noted that, by 2001, Elvis Presley had 27 USA platinum singles whereas Mariah Carey in second place had only 8, and the three artists tied for third place (Boyz II Men, Whitney Houston, and Michael Jackson) had only 7 each. Most people would probably agree that although Elvis is better, he is probably not *three times* more talented than Michael Jackson, such that he has a disproportionately high number of platinum singles. Similarly, Chung (1994) noted that of the 1,377 performers who received a gold record in the USA between 1958 and 1989, only 10.8% of them (i.e. 149 performers) accounted for 43.1% of all gold records awarded. Consistent with this, Hamlen (1991) showed that there was a relationship between total record earnings and the voice quality of singers, but that at higher levels the relative increase in earnings exceeded the relative increase in singing ability; again, small increments in talent were rewarded disproportionately.

A variation of this model is proposed by MacDonald (1988) who argued that the music industry is a multi-layered market. At first musicians compete with each other in an entry-level market (e.g. playing in bars). This market consists of lower income consumers who have more spare time and who can therefore afford to 'risk' listening to a greater range of musicians, some of whom of course won't be very good. Some musicians in this market will be of higher ability, however, and will therefore succeed more. These better musicians are then allowed to compete in more select markets (e.g. performing in higher quality venues charging higher admission fees). These markets comprise consumers with higher incomes but also less spare time: these consumers are less able to afford the 'risk' of listening to poor musicians during the more limited time that they have available. In short, low quality musicians are filtered out of the market such that only the best are presented to higher-paying consumers with less spare time, and consequently small differences in musical talent lead to disproportionate financial reward. Adler (1985) pointed out, however, that this filter of musical talent may not work perfectly, as some better musicians will be excluded and some poor musicians allowed up to the next layer of the market as a result of social psychological factors such as sexual and racial discrimination and physical attractiveness. In support of this argument, Hamlen (1994) used data from the USA music charts from 1955 to 1987 to show that the average 'cost' of being a black musician was equivalent to approximately one hit album. More simply, musical talent alone is not able to completely explain musicians' relative success.

Others have gone a step further. Adler (1985) proposed that musical talent may not necessarily be related to superstardom *at all*. This argument is based on an economic consideration of aesthetic judgements which states that the more an individual knows about music so the more that he or she will enjoy listening to it: as such, individuals should be motivated to acquire 'consumption capital' by gaining knowledge of music by either listening to it or talking to others about it. 'The accumulation of knowledge through discussion with others is relatively easy if all participants share common prior knowledge. If some artist is lucky and emerges as a star, the consumer would be better off patronizing this star even if he or she is no more talented than other non-star artists. The stardom factor operates independently of the existence of a hierarchy of talent' (Crain and Tollison, 2002, p. 1). In short, we are motivated to be interested in *well-known* musicians, irrespective of their level of talent, since this minimizes the difficulties we have in finding other people with whom we can talk about the musician, gain consumption capital, and therefore greater future enjoyment. As such the disproportionate popularity of a small number of musicians is self-perpetuating. The corollary of this is that 'Consumer choice will not always promote the survival of the most talented if [obtaining] consumption capital [regarding them] is costly' (Crain and Tollison, 2002, p. 8). If it is difficult to find out information about a musician (even if he or she is talented) then the effort involved in obtaining this consumption capital may not justify the greater resulting enjoyment.

It seems very unlikely that musical talent (albeit defined loosely) should be totally unrelated to commercial success. Nevertheless, this is a field in which theory far outstrips research. In particular, issues relating to the reliable measurement of 'talent' and 'success' seem to have held back researchers testing why precisely the superstardom effect should occur, although several attempts have been made to apply statistical models to explain the precise nature it takes (e.g. Chung and Cox, 1994, 1998; Cox, Felton, and Chung, 1995; Fox and Kochanowski, 2004; Strobl and Tucker, 2000). Similarly, at present we just don't know how these theories of commercial success relate to lab-based theories of musical preference outlined in Chapter 3 or to research on the idolization of musicians outlined in Chapter 4. However, the provocative implications of research on superstardom mean that it represents a clear candidate for future research.

5.1.3 **Music purchasing**

Surprisingly little research has investigated the more specific question of why people buy particular songs or CDs. This limited research can be divided into five loose headings: namely, research on music consumption and sales charts; effects due to individual differences; pricing strategies; on-line music purchasing; and live music. The lack of coherence between these studies reflects their dispersal across psychology, economics, marketing, and computing journals, and there is a clear need for a programme of research that allows theoretical ideas to develop. In the meantime, however, there are nonetheless several apparently isolated findings with obvious and immediate commercial relevance.

5.1.3.1 **Music consumption and sales charts**

With regard to research on music consumption and sales charts, Lacher (1989) noted that music differs from other products in several ways. For example, we have many opportunities to sample music before buying (e.g. through the radio), rarely buy the same music twice, and consume the music repeatedly although it has little obvious utilitarian value; and this suggests that the purchasing of recorded music may require specialized theoretical explanations. In light of this, Lacher and Mizerski (1994; see also Lacher, 1994) proposed a model of music consumption in which 'sensorial', 'imaginal', 'emotional', and 'analytical' responses to music all contributed towards three constructs that may hypothetically influence the recorded music purchase decision, namely overall affective response, experiential response (e.g. being 'swept up' into the experience of the music), and the need to re-experience the music. Their research suggested that these three constructs were all related to music purchase intentions, although the need to re-experience the music was the strongest predictor of such intentions.

Similarly, Meenaghan and Turnbull (1981) employed a variety of archival measures (e.g. radio airplay, record sales) to present data illustrating the typical 'product life cycle' of successful pop singles. The central feature of this was that successful records moved through five stages in a typically 16 week-long period between their release and final abandonment by the music industry. In stage 1 ('pre-release'), songs and artists were selected for their likely market performance. Stage 2 ('buzz-creation') was short, occurring just before and during release, and was characterized by promotion by the record company in an attempt to persuade TV and radio stations that the song was not a risk. Stage 3 ('pre-threshold') occurred between release and entry into the charts, and was characterized by the media deciding whether to feature the song: such exposure was a crucial determinant of record sales, and typically preceded them. Stage 4 ('commercial life', or the time spent on the chart) was approximately 11 weeks long. During the early weeks of this stage, radio airplay was the most important determinant of sales, and was used as a guide to which songs should receive TV exposure. If a song reached the Top 20 it tended to receive television coverage, and this then became more closely associated with sales than was radio airplay. Stage 5 ('final decline') corresponded with falling sales, and was very short. Sales were often negligible within only three weeks of a song leaving the chart, although the speed of this decline tended to correspond with that of the earlier sales increase.

Three other studies have focused more on the use of data from music sales charts to predict future popularity and record sales. Dixon's (1982) analysis of the chart performance of singles and albums in the USA between September and December 1979 indicated that numerous patterns within these charts did exist. For example, the position at which a recording entered the chart was the most powerful predictor of the highest position it reached and how long its popularity was sustained. Similar findings are reported by Strobl and Tucker (2000) who analysed the complete UK album charts for 1991 and 1992. They found that initial popularity as well as seasonal demand (i.e. entering the chart at Christmas) and type of album (e.g. greatest hits compilations) appeared to influence the longevity of an album's chart tenure. They also supported the 'superstar' theory, finding that during the period between 1980 and 1993 'a few albums have spent a long time period, while many have spent a very short time period in the charts' (p. 121). In a similar vein, North and Hargreaves (1995a) found that there were low to moderate, although nonetheless significant, positive correlations between the performance of 200 artists on the UK and USA sales charts; and also that the number of years that had passed since a performer enjoyed their first number 1 single and the duration of their chart career (i.e. the amount of time that passed between their first and last recording reaching the charts) were both positively related to the amount of space they were allocated in music encyclopaedias.

Two other models focus less on the music itself and more on economic factors associated with the performance of a given single/album on the sales charts. Crain and Tollison (1997) studied all 912 songs that reached number 1 in the USA between 1940 and 1988 in terms of tempo, duration, and the number of weeks they spent at number 1. These measures were compared against data on the economy (e.g. interest rates, personal income) and related variables (e.g. availability of substitutes for music, such as television), and the relationships between these indicated that changes in the internal structure of successful songs were tied to market forces. For example, the music charts were dominated less by a small number of performers as there were more FM radio stations (and therefore presumably a greater range of music that was presented to listeners) and a faster growing teenage population (i.e. a greater number of consumers). 'One way to interpret these results is that the monopoly positions of top performers ... were broken down by demand (a burgeoning teenage population) and new technological forces (the growth of FM stations)' (p. 196). Similarly, the tempo of the songs bought by consumers was related positively to the number of military deaths and the 'misery index' (i.e. unemployment rate plus inflation rate). The length of songs was negatively related to military deaths, prime interest rate, and advertising expenditure, and positively related to earnings and the dominance of a small number of artists in occupying the number 1 position.

Similarly, Burke (1996a) quantified the link between the singles and albums charts, finding that 40% of songs which appeared in the annual British top 100 singles chart also appeared on albums in the top 100 albums in the same year (and typically in the same quarter). This percentage dropped considerably the year after and was close to 0 afterwards, such that 'a particular tune has ... a commercial life of about two years in the albums market' (p. 147). Burke also noted that, singles are usually produced at a loss to the record company. He argues that, since success in the singles and albums charts tends to occur simultaneously, it seems that record companies are willing to sell singles at a loss because of an 'advertising effect' on album sales rather than because they were using singles as a means of testing the likely market for an album.

Other studies that we described in Chapter 3 have attempted to identify how music sales charts can be influenced by radio airplay. For example, Erdelyi (1940) found that for 18 of the 20 songs considered, the extent of their plugging on the radio preceded variations in sales by approximately 13 days, implying that the radio airplay was driving sales. Similarly, Jacobovits' (1966) data found that the frequency with which songs were played on the radio was related positively to the speed with which their chart performance waxed and waned; and Wiebe (1940) found that radio plugging of songs that were initially less popular led to their popularity increasing (see also Brentar, Neuendorf, and Armstrong, 1994; Geiger, 1950; Russell, 1987). Baldwin and Mizerski (1985) studied the relative impact of radio and music television in promoting sales. They found that MTV was more effective than the radio in promoting recall and recognition of the song, arguing that this was because the addition of visuals provided more memory cues, but that affect and purchase intention were uninfluenced.

The amount of data entry and manipulation involved means that studies using sales chart data such as these are often very time-consuming. Furthermore, they inevitably lack the explanatory power of experimental research, and the explanations for the findings obtained are often by necessity rather speculative. However, the use of music sales data in research allows total sampling, such that any firm conclusions that can be reached are extremely powerful. Indeed, given this it should not be surprising that several authors have produced more overtly statistical economic forecasting models that attempt definitive quantification of the movement of songs on the sales charts (Bradlow and Fader, 2001), the diffusion of compact discs (Bewley and Griffiths, 2001; 2003; Ishii, 1984), online music sales (Fader and Hardie, 2001), and the relation between sales and radio airplay (Moe and Fader, 2001), advance orders (Moe and Fader, 2002), and sales of previous albums (Lee, Boatwright, and Kamakura, 2003).

5.1.3.2 Individual differences

The limited research concerning individual differences has implicated opinion leadership in music purchasing. Opinion leadership refers to the tendency of some consumers to influence others directly by giving advice and directions for seeking out, buying, and using the music in question. Perhaps the best-known marketing application of this concerns 'stealth marketing' techniques in which key opinion formers are recruited by businesses to promote their products directly to others in their peer group (see e.g. Kaikati and Kaikati, 2004; Klein, 2001). Flynn, Goldsmith, and Eastman (1996; see also Flynn, Goldsmith, and Eastman, 1994; Goldsmith and De Witt, 2003) found that students' degree of opinion leadership in music (i.e. agreement with items such as 'My opinions influence what types of recordings other people buy') was associated positively with the extent to which they read music magazines, listened to music, shopped at record stores, and spent money on music recordings. In contrast, scores on a scale of opinion seeking (i.e. the opposite of opinion leadership) were mostly unrelated to the four measures of interest in music. In a similar vein, Flynn, Eastman, and Newell (1995) used a neural network approach and found that the frequency that students shopped for music could be predicted by (in order of importance) opinion leadership, involvement with music, age, perceived knowledge of music, social class, marital status, race, gender, and actual knowledge of music. Although the demographic range of a student sample is obviously limited, this finding might imply that personality-related variables are more important than sociodemographic variables. In apparent confirmation of another aspect of Flynn, Eastman, and Newell's (1995) findings, Pucely, Mizerski, and Perrewe (1988) also found a link between music purchasing and involvement with music. Similarly, Swoboda (1998) found that the probability of a customer using in-store information systems to learn more about CDs was positively related to frequency of purchase, interest in the products, and media involvement.

5.1.3.3 Pricing strategies

Other research on music purchasing has focused on pricing strategies and customers' in-store behaviour. Some of this work is more economic in nature (Harchaoui and Hamdad, 2000; Mixon and Ressler, 2000), and many studies focus on consumer behaviour in general rather than music *per se*. Nonetheless, two studies have produced particularly relevant findings. Mixon, Trevino, and Bales (2004) investigated 'just-below' pricing strategies (i.e. prices ending in '.99' or '.95'), showing that these are used more' in rap than classical music and more in-store than on-line. They argue that this supports the idea that retailers are more likely to employ just-below pricing when selling to customers such as rap fans who are younger and less educated. Coley and Burgess (2003) found that men were more likely than women to impulse buy music CDs and DVDs, consistent with their generally greater propensity toward impulse buying of technology and entertainment items.

5.1.3.4 On-line music purchasing

Numerous other studies have considered specifically on-line music purchasing in reflection of the considerable market share gained by on-line CD retailers such as Amazon, CDNow, and others (see Fox, 2004; Rabinovich, Bailey, and Carter, 2003). Although the findings are difficult to integrate, several particular studies stand out. Merrilees and Fry (2002; see also Almeida, Meira, Ribeiro, and Ziviani, 1999; Hoffman and Novak, 2000) found that attitudes towards online CD retailers were determined principally by interactivity and trust (rather than e.g. navigability or fun). Johnson, Moe, Fader, Bellman, and Lohse (2004; see also Bellman, Lohse, and Johnson, 1999) also found evidence that on-line music purchasers are rather impatient, indicating that households visit only 1.3 CD sites during a typical active month of CD purchasing, with 70% of the households visiting only one site.

Other research has considered what happens once a customer has selected a particular on-line music retailer. Again a key aspect of customer behaviour seems to be impatience. Rajala and Hantula (2000) found that a delay of around four seconds in providing information about the availability of a CD in a particular on-line shop was sufficient to reduce participants' inclination to shop on the same site in future or recommend it to a friend, and delays of over only half a second led to reduced perceptions of service quality. One area in which internet music shoppers are potentially more patient concerns postal delivery fees: Hantula and Bryant (2005) modelled the trade-off between delivery fees and delivery periods for CDs, showing that 'delivery fees are regarded as a swap of money for time' (p. 153). Cooke, Sujan, Sujan, and Weitz (2002; see also Drèze and Zufryden, 1997) considered the personalized recommendations of particular CDs made by internet music retail sites, and particularly how best to recommend CDs that would be unfamiliar to the customer. When the latter were presented in the context of CDs that were liked and familiar to the participant then they were regarded more positively (presumably because the unfamiliar CDs came to be regarded as similar to the CDs that the participant liked and was familiar with). But when people were also provided with a short musical excerpt taken from the unfamiliar CDs then this led to participants contrasting them with familiar CDs, and the former were evaluated less positively (see also Nowak, Shamp, Hollander, and Cameron, 1999). Finally, Adelaar, Chang, Lancendorfer, Byoungkwan-Lee, and Morimoto (2003) devised three types of web pages concerning CDs: these each contained the music itself together with either the text of the lyrics, still images from the song's music video, or the music video itself. Displaying the text of the lyrics had a greater effect on the impulse buying intent than showing still images of the music video. Furthermore, although participant sex did not predict intent to impulse buy, high arousal did. As a consequence of findings such as these, Molteni and Ordanini (2003), Ozer (2001), Sivadas, Grewal, and Kellaris (1998), and Vijaysarathy and Jones (2000) point out that internet music shoppers may fall into different market segments, all of which require different marketing strategies.

5.1.3.5 Live music

Finally, as Victor Borge once put it so well when playing to a half-empty house in a Michigan city, 'Flint must be an extremely wealthy place: I see that each of you bought two or three seats'. The ongoing battle 'to put bums on seats' has been the subject of several studies that have adopted an economic or business studies perspective on audience attendance at live music events. For example, Reddy, Swaminathan, and Motley (1998) analysed the predictors of success of Broadway shows, finding that New York newspaper theatre critics have a significant impact on the success of shows, with the *New York Times*' critic wielding twice as much influence as the critics from the *Daily News* or the *New York Post*. There are numerous other instances of similarly fascinating findings (e.g. Borgonovi, 2004; Connolly and Krueger, 2005; Earl, 2001; Forbes, 1984; Frey, 1994, 1996; Gazel and Schwer, 1997; Goldfarb, 1994; Hodgson, 1992; Kolb, 2002; Krueger, 2005; Kushner and Brooks, 2000; Laing and York, 2000; Lewis and Brooks, 2005; Lewis and Seaman, 2004; Martorella, 1977; Minor, Wagner, Brewerton, and Hausman, 2004; Prieto-Rodriguez and Fernandez-Blanco, 2000; Royne-Stafford and Tripp, 2000; Royne-Stafford, Tripp, and Bienstock, 2004).

5.1.4 **Music piracy**

5.1.4.1 Incidence

The 'dark side' of music purchasing is of course the field of music piracy. Rothenbuhler and McCourt (2004; see also Asvanund, Clay, Krishnan, and Smith, 2004; McFedries, 2005) summarized the history of music piracy, and in particular the sudden rise in popularity in the late 1990s of peer-to-peer filesharing software that allowed vast quantities of mp3s and other digital files to be shared between internet users. The scale of the problem is revealed by Jones and Lenhart (2004), who studied USA telephone polling data on music downloading obtained from several thousand participants between April 2000 and March 2001. Over these dates, between 21% and 29% of respondents had downloaded music over the internet. A 2003 report by market research agency Mintel noted that 14% of British internet users also regularly downloaded music. Similarly, Teston (2002) found that 72% of his sample of 264 seventh-grade school pupils had actually engaged in digital music piracy; and 37% of Walsh, Mitchell, Frenzel, and Wiedmann's (2003) sample of 4000 German internet users contacted during 2001 regularly downloaded music from the internet. These percentages of course represent the potential for a massive loss of sales. In counter to this, services such as Napster (before it became a fully legal music download tool) argued that use of their software actually increased music sales by allowing people the opportunity to 'try' the music before buying it. The financial markets apparently agreed: Navissi, Naiker, and Upson (2005) found that legal events that harmed the prospects of Napster also harmed the market value (by an average of 18%) of a sample of 41 music companies in the USA, whereas positive legal news for Napster led to on average an 8.97% increase in the market value of the 41 music companies.

However, the money market's opinion was not shared by the downloaders. Jones and Lenhart (2004) found that only 13% of music downloaders regarded it as stealing (see also Taylor, 2004), and that only 21% subsequently bought the music 'most of the time' such that illegal downloading was leading rarely to sales. Indeed, Jones and Lenhart used their data to estimate that in the summer of 2000 there were 11 million users of Napster in the USA, sharing approximately 1.5 billion songs. Similarly, Teston (2002) found that 52% of his sample of seventh-grade school pupils advocated piracy (compared to only 10% for bike theft). Moreover, Hui and Png (2003; see also Rob and Waldfogel, 2004) analysed international music CD sales from 1994 to 1998 and found that decreasing demand for CDs coincided with increased piracy; and estimated that piracy led to a 6.6% reduction in sales in 1998 (although the effect was only 42% of that claimed by the music industry). In addition to the ease with which computers can burn copies of CDs (see Bishop, 2004) and the longer established practice of 'bootlegging' concerts (e.g. Marshall, 2001; Naghavi and Schulze, 2001; Neumann and Simpson, 1997), it is understandable that figures such as these meant that a great deal of ink was spilled by those interested in the law (e.g. Channel, 2004; Ince, 2004; Landes and Lichtman, 2003; Langenderfer and Cook, 2001; Schleimer and Freundlich, 2001; Zepeda, 2002), business studies (e.g. Bach, 2004; McCourt and Burkart, 2003), and sociology/cultural studies (e.g. Cooper and Harrison, 2001; Taylor, Demont-Heinrich, Broadfoot, Dodge, and Jian, 2002), with work addressing the implications for many countries/regions such as Australia (Papadopoulos, 2000), the Caribbean (Nurse, 2000), Italy (Evansburg, Fiore, Welch, Chua, and Eremitaggio, 2004), Taiwan (Chiou, Huang, and Lee, 2005); and Vietnam (Vietnam studios face the music, 2002).

5.1.4.2 Correlates of piracy

Psychological research concerning *why* people should engage in music piracy lags behind data. Certainly demographic factors seem to be related to piracy. Jones and Lenhart (2004) found that downloaders were disproportionately male, and tended to be more experienced internet users from lower income and educational groups. Odell, Korgen, Schumacher, and Delucchi (2000) found that 49.6% of North American university-aged males used the internet to obtain music compared to only 26.9% of females. Similarly, Papadopoulos (2003; 2004; see also Burke, 1996b) used economic data to show that levels of music piracy were related to low income (i.e. the legitimate price of a CD as a function of wages) as well as the size and efficiency of black market distribution channels: if legitimate CDs are perceived as expensive relative to income then people will substitute them more readily with pirate copies depending on how available these are. Ang, Cheng, Lim, and Tambyah's (2001) sample of 3,621 Singaporean participants showed that males and those from low income groups were more favourable about music piracy. As such, these studies describe the low income, male archetypal music downloader.

However, Molteni and Ordanini (2003) caution against the dangers of treating music pirates as a homogenous group, and three studies support this by indicating that individuals' value systems also play a significant role in mediating piracy. Gopal, Sanders, Bhattacharjee, Agrawal, and Wagner's (2004) model showed a significant relationship between music piracy and participants' ethical/moral concerns, the value they placed on justice, their perception of the amount of money saved through piracy, and the size of the piracy network in which the individual was a member (e.g. a friendship group that copies CDs for one another). For example, the model showed that ethical concerns were related negatively to the size of the piracy network to which an individual belonged, which was in turn related positively to perceptions of the amount of money saved through music piracy. Chiou, Huang, and Lee (2005) found that attitudes and behavioural intentions concerning music piracy were influenced negatively by participants' satisfaction with the copyrighted CDs they currently owned, the extent to which favourite musicians were idolized, perceived prosecution risk, perceptions of the magnitude of the consequence of piracy for the musicians/record companies in question, and perceived social consensus concerning the immorality of piracy. Ang, Cheng, Lim, and Tambyah's (2001) study found that, compared with those who did not purchase counterfeits, those who did purchase had more trust in the shops that sold them and regarded the purchase as less risky. Attitudes toward piracy were related positively to value consciousness (i.e. a desire to pay low prices), and negatively to a measure of ethical concern and 'normative susceptibility' (a desire to impress others and 'keep up with the Joneses'). Furthermore, purchasers of counterfeit CDs had few moral qualms regarding the practice. Although these studies make little or no reference to one another, it is interesting that they highlight, in addition to other factors, the importance of ethical and moral concerns, the role of friends, and the desire to save money: such a degree of overlap is surely not mere coincidence.

Two further studies have attempted to cluster the many different reasons that individuals may have for purchasing/pirating music, and consider how these differ between individuals. North and Oishi (2006) investigated why British and Japanese participants chose to buy rather than obtain pirate copies of music CDs. Two separate studies indicated that participants' main reasons for buying could be grouped into four factors concerning the consequences of friendship, need to control and be involved with the music, music industry promotion, and need to re-experience the music. British participants scored higher than their Japanese counterparts on the first and last of these, and participants' scores on these factors were also related to several other individual differences. For example, scores on the 're-experience the music' factor were related negatively to a measure of experience seeking: participants who buy (rather than pirate) CDs in order to re-experience the music tend more generally to avoid new experiences and to instead favour the familiar. Similarly, Walsh, Mitchell, Frenzel, and Wiedmann's (2003) study of 4,000 German internet users found four motive clusters relating to willingness to pay for music downloads, namely assortment and time advantage (e.g. easy access to unreleased or otherwise unavailable songs), independence (i.e. freedom from the constraints of the music industry such as store opening hours), trend consciousness (i.e. belief that the internet is fashionable and that existing music suppliers are not), and topicality (i.e. access to up to date music). They also identified three distinct groups of downloaders prepared to pay for online music. 'Demanding downloaders' scored high on all four motive clusters, particularly 'trend consciousness' and 'topicality'. In contrast, 'general download approvers' had the lowest scores on the motive clusters, particularly 'independence'. Finally, 'procurement autonomous' downloaders also had low scores on all the motive clusters except independence: it is specifically the prospect for autonomy that appeals to these people.

The specific findings of these studies may or may not be replicated by future research, but even so they highlight two important points. First, complex motives underlie the decision to purchase/pirate music, and these go well beyond the price advantage enjoyed by pirated music. Any successful attempt to prevent piracy will ultimately have to account for more overtly psychological factors and not rely simply on reducing the cost of legitimate music: music piracy is an economic process, but it is a psychological process also, and other factors such as a desire to be involved with the music can only be addressed by non-price-related measures such as liner notes etc. Second, following from this, anti-piracy measures and legal music download sites will have to allow for differences between different groups of consumers in terms of, for example, their need to control and be involved with music, their procurement autonomy, or their desire to impress friends; one size will not fit all in the battle against piracy.

5.1.5 **Radio programming**

The dispiritingly financial focus of the music industry is perhaps most apparent in radio programming, the process by which music is selected for radio airplay. Rothenbuhler and McCourt (1992) note that radio programming is the final stage in the music industry's pre-selection of music on behalf of the public.

> Songwriters, for example, may strive to write a hit, but must first write something that a producer and performer will select to record. Record producers may want to produce hits, but the recording session first must produce material acceptable to the executives in charge of recording budgets, artists' contracts, and release schedules. Songs that aren't recorded, recordings that aren't released, releases that aren't promoted aggressively, and records that don't get airplay cannot become hits ... [Consequently] those who occupy decision-making positions in the radio industry are indeed very powerful (pp. 103–104).

Nevertheless the radio industry does not love music. Rather, the radio industry loves to carry advertising, which allows it to make a profit, and music is nothing more than a means of attracting a particular segment of the population at large that can be presented to advertisers who want to sell to them (Hennion and Meadel, 1986; Rothenbuhler, 1985, 1987; Rothenbuhler and McCourt, 1992). Indeed, Albarran (2004) notes that one of the reasons that radio stations even play music at all (rather than featuring rolling news, for example) is that this represents the cheapest type of programming, and that further economies are achieved through conglomeration of radio stations which allows practices such as the use of 'voice tracking' in programme production (in which a DJ records the links between songs in a single short sitting before these links are then sent to 'sister' stations who use them to assemble their own programmes).

Radio uses music to attract a particular segment of the population through the use of a *format* that governs the specific type of music played. Different stations in the same area will adopt different formats to attract different parts of the total available audience, and this in turn minimizes competition. Alternatively, a new station may copy a format already run successfully by an existing station in the area, providing the audience is sufficiently large/potentially profitable (see Greve and Taylor, 2000). The use of music solely to attract advertising revenue leads to tremendous conservatism in music policy, and this manifests itself in numerous specific ways. First, rather than striving to play music that listeners like, the real goal of radio stations is to avoid playing songs that listeners might not like: familiar and unobjectionable songs help to avoid 'audience tuneout'. Second, record companies will try to ensure airplay for their songs by producing material that fits neatly into radio station formats (see Negus, 1993). Third, the process by which a song arrives on a radio station playlist emphasizes tried and trusted methods, such as the experience of station employees and record company promoters, an emphasis on musical superstars with broad appeal, and occasionally direct imitation of the output of competing stations (since the prospect of hearing the same music will deter listeners from switching stations). The conservatism of music policy on commercial radio is illustrated well by Hendy (2000; see also Berry and Waldfogel, 1999; Machill, 1996). He studied the British radio station BBC Radio 1, which is not funded through advertising, and which therefore has relatively little incentive to specifically try to avoid audience tuneout. During 1996 one in four songs played on Radio 1 was 'pre-release' whereas the corresponding figures for two national commercial stations, Atlantic 252 and Virgin, were one in 67 and one in 19 respectively, such that Radio 1 was much more likely to play music of unproven broad public appeal.

Ahlkvist and Faulkner (2002; see also Ahlkvist, 2001) interviewed staff at 28 stations in the USA and concluded that, within the broader set of constraints described above, there are four methods by which a radio programmer selects songs for airplay. The 'subjective repertoire' refers to decisions based on the programmer's own aesthetic evaluation of the songs and artists. Common features of this approach are passion for music on the part of the programmer, and a desire to 'break' new songs. The 'objective repertoire' refers to programming decisions based on market research, a conservative approach toward 'breaking' new songs, and attempts to operate autonomously of record company marketing. The 'populist repertoire' involves trying to evaluate potential songs 'like a listener', and selecting particular songs for airplay according to the criteria the programmer believes are used by the station's listeners. Finally, the 'synergistic repertoire' refers to programming decisions that are influenced by collaboration with record companies. For example, the radio station will play the particular song from a new album that the record company wants them to, but will in return receive promotional benefits such as an exclusive interview with the band in question. Furthermore, Ahlkvist and Fisher (2000) note that practices common to the subjective approach and a focus on local audiences (part of the populist approach) protect against standardization of musical output between different stations, whereas the research-based objective approach reflects practices that lead towards standardization.

More generally, what is very clear from the above is the complete divorce between research on the music industry and music psychology. At present it could be argued that much of the research concerning the former in some way supersedes research on the latter: the opinions of a small number of individuals within the music industry dictate what music people will actually listen to, irrespective of the predictions of psychological theory. Paradoxically, the longer-term prospects for psychological research in this area seem good, however. The interactivity of the internet and digital broadcasting effectively short-circuit the pre-selection processes of the music industry, since anybody with access to the technology can obtain whatever music they want on demand. As a consequence, psychology's greater focus on the individual means it is ideally placed to address the increasing complexity in people's musical behaviour that will be the inevitable consequence of technological innovation. The less that the music industry controls what people hear, so the more importance will accrue to psychological explanations at an individual level concerning who is listening to what and why. Furthermore, with regard to conventional music industry practice, a considerable psychological literature addresses specifically who should like what music, and how music is used by listeners in the course of their everyday lives (see Chapters 3 and 4). This could surely inform radio programming decisions, and also help to explain music purchasing and why some musicians should be candidates for superstardom.

5.2 **Music and advertising**

We shift now from a focus on the music as a product itself to situations where music is used as a means of selling something else, and specifically to considering the roles of music in advertising and in physical commercial environments. With regard to the former, recent research has queried the role of music and advertising in young people's tobacco and alcohol usage (e.g. Knight and Chapman, 2004; Robinson, Chen, and Killen, 1998; Wakefield, Flay, Nichter, and Giovino, 2003), and more generally the impact that watching music television may have on consumption habits (e.g. Englis, 1991). Of course music may have numerous uses in advertising. Hecker (1984), for instance, stressed that music might attract attention, implicitly or explicitly carry the message, create emotional states, or act as a mnemonic cue; Taylor and Johnson (2002) discussed international differences in the roles that music plays in marketing; and Scott (2002; see also Blair and Hatala, 1992) described the potential to use different types of music in order to appeal to different age groups.

This potential utility seems to be reflected by the frequency with which advertisers actually use music. For example, Stewart and Furse (1986) found music in 42% of the 1,000 television commercials they considered, and Stewart and Koslow (1989) reported a similar frequency in a different large sample of adverts. Furthermore, Appelbaum and Halliburton (1993) reported that this figure increased to 89.3% when considering advertisements screened internationally, and indicated that music is typically the predominant element in these advertisements. Similarly, Furnham, Abramsky, and Gunter (1997) found that music was present in over 80% of adverts aimed at children. Furthermore, Balasubramanian (1990) was able to show that TV adverts were liked more as their musical component was perceived as less complex or less active, whereas liking for the adverts was positively related to the perceived 'beauty' of the music they contained. Whilst this clearly suggests the importance of music in television commercials, research has rarely addressed what impact it may have (Borgerson and Schroeder, 2002). The main explanations proposed so far are based on three key concepts, namely classical conditioning, elaboration likelihood, and the more recent notions of sonic branding and sponsorship.

5.2.1 **Classical conditioning**

The traditional approach to advertising might be summarized as the 'attitude towards the brand' approach, in which advertisers aim to influence consumers' beliefs concerning the likely consequences of consuming the product in question (e.g. that a detergent will leave your hands soft). However, in the 1980s this began to give way to the 'attitude toward the ad' approach, which instead focused on attempting to ensure that customers liked the advertising for the product. This approach was based on evidence showing that the emotional consequences of being exposed to a television advert were themselves important mediators of consumer behaviour (see review by Brown and Stayman, 1992). In particular, this evidence came from researchers employing a conditioning-based approach in which pairing a product (conditioned stimulus) with a liked piece of music (unconditioned stimulus) should produce an association between the two, and therefore liking for the product (a conditioned response) (see review by DiClemente and Hantula, 2003). Gorn's (1982) well-known research illustrated the phenomenon well. Participants were shown a slide of either a light blue or beige coloured pen and at the same time they heard music that was either liked (taken from the film *Grease*) or disliked (Indian classical music). Participants were then told that they could take one of the two types of pen home with them as a reward for their efforts: 79% chose the pen associated with liked music. Several other marketing studies have reported findings generally consistent with the classical conditioning approach (Bierley, McSweeney, and Vannieuwkerk, 1985; Blair and Shimp, 1992; Gorn, Goldberg, and Basu, 1993; Gorn, Pham, and Sin, 2001; Groenland and Schoormans, 1994; Miniard, Bhatla, and Sirdeshmukh, 1992; Simpkins and Smith, 1974; and Tom, 1995), and Brader (2005) found that responses even to political adverts could be conditioned, such that enthusiasm-eliciting background music led to greater interest in the campaign in question and willingness to vote.

Although the conditioning hypothesis is described in several sources as though it was well researched and proven beyond doubt, it is worth pointing out also, however, that there have been failed attempts to demonstrate it. Pitt and Abratt (1988) were unable to use music to condition preferences for red and blue condoms, and Alpert and Alpert (1989, 1990) found that the mood associated with different greeting cards could not be conditioned by pairing them with happy and sad music (although purchase intentions could be). Others have raised methodological objections to the existing research. Olsen and Pracejus (2004) point out that the majority of studies fail to address the interaction of emotional and other responses to different aspects of a given advert. Dunbar (1990) argued that the importance of the attitude toward the ad approach may be over-emphasized by the use of still rather than moving pictures in research. Murray and Murray (1996) found differences in the musical content of TV adverts from the USA and Dominican Republic; and concluded that their findings 'lend support to a theory of music that incorporates culture as a key element. They do not fit well with present conceptualisations of music based on classical conditioning or affect response theories that posit global and invariant effects of music across all populations' (p. 60). Kellaris and Cox (1989) argued that apparent conditioning effects may result from demand artefacts: their participants' pen selections were influenced by merely *imagining* that they heard liked or disliked music associated with the pens, such that conditioning effects may arise from participants' expectations rather than any effect of the music *per se* (although non-musical attempts to replicate this finding have themselves failed, e.g. Kim, Allen, and Kardes, 1996). Perhaps most significantly, Middlestadt, Fishbein, and Chan (1994) found that music raised or lowered the salience of various aspects of the apple juice advertised in their research: 23% of participants who saw the commercial with music noted 'drinking a natural drink' as one of the benefits of the juice, whereas this figure fell to 4% in a no music condition. In other words, music influenced *beliefs* about the advertised product, and this impact on beliefs as well as emotions is a fundamental part of research on music and the elaboration likelihood model.

5.2.2 Elaboration likelihood, involvement, and musical fit

Whilst the classical conditioning approach may have its faults as a complete model of musical effects in advertising, it has made a clear contribution to the more detailed Elaboration Likelihood Model. Gorn (1982) conducted a second experiment to test the generality of conditioning effects, and the main difference between this and his first experiment described above was that half of the participants were not told they would receive a pen until they were asked to actually choose between the two pen colours: the remaining partici-pants were told at the beginning of the study that they would receive a pen for having taken part. The participants who did not know that they would be choosing a pen tended to choose the pen advertised with liked music, whereas the participants who did know that they would be choosing a pen tended to choose the pen that was advertised with information emphasising that it did not smudge. In other words, musical conditioning seemed to occur when participants had no reason to evaluate the advertised product, whereas product information was more important when participants were motivated to process product-relevant information.

Findings such as these can be explained in terms of the Elaboration Likelihood Model (or ELM—Petty and Cacioppo, 1981; Petty, Cacioppo, and Schumann, 1983). The ELM states that there are two routes to persuasion, central and peripheral. In the central route, attitudes are formed through consideration of information relevant to the object in question (for example, whether the pen in question smudges). In the peripheral route, someone forms their attitudes without thinking actively about the object and its attributes, but instead by *associating* the object with positive or negative cues, such as liked or disliked music: in other words, by some form of conditioning mechanism. The central route is used when elaboration likelihood is high: in other words, the person has the *motivation, opportunity*, and *ability* to process (or elaborate on) information about the product. This has been termed 'high involvement' with the advertisement. Persuasion occurs via the peripheral route when people are in a state of 'low involvement' with the advertisement, and do not have the motivation, opportunity, or ability to elaborate on the information they have regarding the attitude object: conditioning may be influential under these circumstances because people invoke simpler cues and heuristics when forming their attitudes. Consequently, advertising cues such as liked music should be more important in persuasion when the viewer is unwilling or unable to evaluate overt commercial messages concerning the advertised brand.

Park and Young (1986; see also Bozman and Muehling, 1994; Muehling and Bozman, 1990) supported the predictions of the ELM in hair shampoo adverts employing music. One group of participants was asked to try to learn about the effectiveness of the shampoo. This gave them the motivation to process the information in the advert, and meant that they would be highly involved with it. Participants in another group were asked to imagine that they had no need to buy shampoo. This meant that they had no motivation to process the information in the advert, and this would be expected to bring about a low level of involvement. Consistent with the ELM, music had a positive effect for low-involvement participants, leading to, for example, better brand attitudes than for those participants in a no music condition. However, music had a distracting effect for participants in the high-involvement group, leading to lower brand attitudes than for those in a no music condition. In other words, it seems that some sort of conditioning effect operated for low involvement participants, but that the music hampered the attempts of high involvement participants to learn about the shampoo. (See also Thorson, Christ, and Caywood (1991) on involvement and music in political commercials).

Similar conclusions have been reached by a small number of other recent studies that have instead adopted a resource matching approach to music in advertising. Olsen (1997) provided data to support his argument that when the available cognitive resources for processing an advert are insufficient, the processing will be incomplete and so retention will be hindered. As the cognitive resources available increase to a point where they match those required, information will be processed completely and retention improved. Music may therefore reduce recall as it distracts the listener and therefore reduces the resources available to process the advertising messages. For example, Olsen (2002; see also Olsen 1994, 1995) found that advertising information highlighted by a short period of silence was recalled better than information highlighted by music (which requires more processing resource); and Hahn and Hwang (1999) found that advert recall was lower when those adverts featured music at 120 bpm (which would require more processing resources) rather than 90 bpm. There are two caveats however to this 'music hampers recall' conclusion of the resource matching approach. First, the effect would *not* be expected to occur when listeners are actively focused on the content of the advert itself: under these circumstances they might well just ignore the music and devote no processing resources to it whatsoever. Second, over longer periods of time, background music may facilitate retention by maintaining attention and decreasing the number of thoughts that consumers have concerning topics other than the advert and product. When the resources available for processing an advert outstrip those required then people may simply 'drift off': the use of music increases the resources required to process the advert up to a point where they match those available and this helps to maintain consumers' attention.

5.2.2.1 Musical 'fit'

Indeed, other research goes a step further and argues that certain types of music can be helpful for highly-involved consumers who are actively focused on processing the messages contained in advertising. MacInnis and Park (1991; see also Lord, Lee, and Sauer, 1995; Zhu and Myers-Levy, 2005) argued that music might still have a positive influence on high-involvement consumers if it 'fits' the advertisement, or corresponds with 'consumers' subjective perceptions of the music's relevance or appropriateness to the central ad message' (p. 162). In essence, music that fits the advertisement should be effective for high-involvement consumers because the music primes relevant beliefs about the product while consumers are actively considering it. For example, while a consumer is actively considering the messages in a perfume advert, the gentle classical music in the background might be priming perceptions concerning 'sophistication' or 'femininity'. As such, the music works by conveying and activating relevant, related *information*: this of course contrasts with the classical conditioning approach which focuses on using music to elicit positive *emotional* responses to the advert, and the resource matching approach which regards *all* music as somehow the same, irrespective of the messages that different pieces may convey.

MacInnis and Park (1991) provided some initial support for the impact of musical fit in a study of shampoo commercials using the song *You Make Me Feel Like a Natural Woman* as appropriate music: musical fit positively influenced the responses of high-involvement consumers, and therefore seemed to be priming relevant knowledge. Several other studies have demonstrated the potentially positive impact of musical fit in advertising contexts. For example, Kellaris, Cox, and Cox (1993) obtained similar results in radio advertisements when instrumental rather than lyrical properties were used to promote music-message congruency. Similarly, Alpert, Alpert, and Maltz (2005) played happy and sad music while participants were shown greetings cards. Participants were asked to say how likely they were to purchase the card for a happy (i.e. for a friend's birthday) or sad (i.e. for a hospitalized friend) occasion. Participants said they were more likely to purchase the card for a sad occasion when sad rather than happy music was played; and that they were more likely to purchase the card for a happy occasion when happy rather than sad music was played.

North, Hargreaves, MacKenzie, and Law (2004) reasoned that if musical fit operates by conveying information concerning the product then this ought to facilitate recall of the claims made during advertising. Specifically, they argued that if musical fit increases the activation of related cognitive concepts, then proof of this process requires that research demonstrate a change in the activation of those concepts in the minds' of participants. Five adverts were prepared (for a fictional internet bank, people carrier, nappies, a chocolate bar, and a soft drink), and music that either did or did not fit with the central claims of the adverts was superimposed on these. Participants were then asked to recall the product that was advertised (e.g. a chocolate bar), the brand that was advertised (e.g. *Rhapsody*), and the product claims that were advertised (e.g. indulgent). For all three measures, recall was better in the musical fit condition. This suggested that musical fit did operate specifically by activating certain knowledge-based constructs in the minds of participants. Similarly, Oakes and North (2006) manipulated musical fit in the context of a radio advert for cosmetic surgery by varying only the timbre of the instruments involved. Congruent piano music led to higher recall for the name of the product and the advertised benefits than did incongruent church organ or steel drum renditions of the same music.

Other research has led to similar findings. Stewart and Punj (1998; see also Furnham, Burgland, and Gunter, 2002; Hitchon, Duckler, and Thorson, 1994; Stewart, Farmer, and Stannard, 1990; Tavassoli and Han, 2002; Tavassoli and Lee, 2003) approached members of the general public in order to assess their memory for an advertising campaign. They adopted a dual-coding framework in arguing that music should particularly facilitate recall of non-verbal elements of the advertising, whereas a verbal prompt should particularly facilitate recall of verbal elements of the advertising. Participants were played the musical jingle featured in the advert and asked to try to recall what they could. This musical cue did indeed prime recall of visual (i.e. non-verbal) elements of the adverts. In particular, respondents who were played the jingle seemed particularly prone to recall the setting, motion, or action when describing the advert compared to respondents who were given a verbal prompt for recall. Furthermore, Miller and Marks (1992; 1997) found some evidence that congruent sound effects led to a radio advert producing more images in the mind of listeners and more brand information being learned than when those sound effects were absent. More generally, it is worth pointing out of course that this process of musical fit has marked parallels with the research on cognitive priming and the effects of music videos that we reviewed in the previous chapter; the research on preference-for-prototypes that we reviewed in Chapter 2; and also the research on the effects of musical fit in physical commercial environments that is reviewed in section 5.3.2.3 below.

5.2.2.2 Problems for research on advertising

However, despite this apparent promise, there are four significant problems faced by research concerning music and advertising. First, it is possible to explain almost any finding in terms of the highly complex theories that have been produced concerning elaboration likelihood, involvement, and fit. For example, resource-matching explanations suggest that the presence of music in an advert may *reduce* recall because it detracts from the cognitive resources available for advert processing, whereas research on musical fit suggests that the presence of music may *enhance* recall, providing it is congruous with expectations. Furthermore, Heckler and Childers (1992; see also Houston, Childers, and Heckler, 1987) argue that *incongruity* between different elements of an advert may improve recall by encouraging deeper processing, such that incongruous music may be optimal in facilitating recall of advertising. As such, *any* finding can be presented as 'consistent with previous research'. This is so problematic here because there are indeed numerous instances of studies yielding data inconsistent with the predictions of the approaches outlined above. For example, Morris and Boone (1998) found few differences in brand attitudes and purchase intent when participants were shown adverts with either no music or music that fitted the product playing in the background; and Brooker and Wheatley (1994) found that differing musical tempi (with the different processing resources they require) had no effect on unaided recall of radio adverts. Such inconsistencies in research findings are no doubt due to the very complex stimuli and cognitive processes involved in advertising research. Future studies should investigate non-linear relationships between variables, and over the short term at least, adopt very reductionist experimental methods that sacrifice ecological validity for the sake of greater insight into the conditions under which certain theories do and do not operate.

Second, it is by no means clear that participants relate to the stimuli with which they are presented as exemplars of 'fit' and 'no fit' in the manner in which experimenters wish them to. For example, Hung (2000; see also Hung, 2001; McQuarrie and Mick, 1999) showed participants coffee commercials in which the music either supposedly did or did not fit with the visual images, and found that participants were nonetheless able to resolve the incongruity in the 'non-fit' versions and derive meanings from them. For example, avant garde music combined with visuals showing a rainforest setting led to perceptions of South America, adventure, and strong coffee; whereas music that was 'simple', 'reedy', and 'primitive' (p. 27) combined with black and white visuals of an artistic man and woman in a sparsely-decorated space led to perceptions of mystery and non-conformity. Similarly, Vitouch (2001) showed participants an excerpt from Billy Wilder's film *The Lost Weekend* that contained either the original, optimistic music or pessimistic music (Barber's *Adagio for Strings*). In both cases, participants were quite able to form expectations for future plot development (with these expectations mirroring the emotional tone of the music). Both Hung and Vitouch's studies suggest that there may be no such thing as 'no fit' in the mind of research participants who are understandably motivated to assume that researchers would present them only with coherent stimuli, and who subsequently try to determine sensible meanings in whatever stimuli are placed in front of them.

Third, when defining musical 'fit', it is often unclear whether researchers are referring to the degree of fit with a particular commercial stereotype (e.g. the notion that banks are 'trustworthy', that chocolate is an 'indulgence', or that cars are 'exciting') or are instead referring to 'fit' with the messages unique to the advert in question, such that music could enhance recall of the latter even when these contradict the former. Semiotics may make a valuable contribution in understanding exactly what messages people take from particular pieces of music (see e.g. Beasley and Danesi, 2002; Floch, 2001). Following from this, although far from impossible, we should also note that musical fit may be difficult to apply in practice: as we saw in Chapters 2 and 3, there are numerous factors that can mediate the message that any given individual will take from a given piece of music. Although some crass musical stereotypes do not leave much room for misinterpretation (e.g. the notion that accordions are in some way always 'French', or that classical music is in some way always 'sophisticated'), any attempt to move beyond these may lead to miscommunication. Researchers and practitioners must be cautious and explicit in predicting the effects that their music should have.

Finally, although obvious, it is nonetheless important to point out one other major methodological problem with almost all advertising research concerning music. Most of this research is conducted in laboratories using participants who are there as a consequence of being enrolled on a relevant undergraduate degree course. These people under these circumstances are far more disposed to pay attention to the adverts with which they are presented than are the great majority of TV viewers or radio listeners. In particular, there is a real paucity of longitudinal research concerning the longevity of any effects of music, and whether these lead to any changes in actual high street spending, which is after all the purpose of advertising. Data from the lab can help to build theories but may not necessarily tell us about how the general public respond to advertising, and thus field testing will, at some point, be unavoidable.

5.2.3 Sonic branding, jingles, and sponsorship

Over recent years, practitioners have shown growing interest in another possible mechanism by which music may be used in marketing, namely sonic branding (see e.g. Fulberg, 2003; Jackson, 2003). Sonic branding can be seen as having grown from the old-fashioned jingle (Buchanan, 2005), and can be defined loosely as the attempt to use very short periods of music and other auditory cues to convey core brand values and prime brand recognition whenever customers come into contact with a company (e.g. in advertising, on their web site, in their premises, while waiting on hold on the phone). As such, sonic brands are the auditory equivalent of a visual company logo, and recent well-known examples can be found in marketing for Intel, Duracell, McDonalds, or perhaps most famously British Airways' use of Delibes' *Flower Duet* from the opera *Lakmé*. Jill McDonald, British Airways' general manager of global marketing, effectively defined sonic branding when she stated that 'We use *Lakmé* to try and give an audio version of the BA service. We chose something calm, relaxing, and classic ... We use sound in every part of our service to present ourselves to people ... *Lakmé* is just the audio equivalent of a "red carpet" for customers where we try and capture all the values of BA' (Mortimer, 2005, pp. 28–29).

From a psychological perspective, it might be most apt to characterize sonic branding as a special case of musical fit, an instance in which the music used in advertising (and other forms of marketing) aims to raise the salience of certain brand attributes in the minds of potential customers. As such, we might regard the evidence on musical fit as directly relevant to the issue of whether sonic branding can actually achieve its aims. Specifically, research on musical fit showed that music that conveys a certain message can influence consumers into regarding the associated company in a similar way: if this process works in advertising, it seems reasonable to assume that it should also work in specifically sonic branding.

Quantitative evidence concerning specifically sonic branding is limited to say the least, however. Nonetheless, four studies on the effectiveness of jingles do provide some grounds for optimism (at least concerning sonic brands that feature lyrics), and may be analogous to the use of music for sonic branding. Tom (1990) played real TV adverts that had had all mention of the product name deleted, and asked participants to try to recall what the adverts were for. Music created specifically for the advertised product was a more effective memory cue than were hit songs or parodies of those songs, and Tom argued that this was because the former had only ever been heard in the context of advertising for the product. Sonic brands are also usually (or in some cases exclusively) heard in the context of the company in question, and may therefore have a similar effect on memory. Wallace (1991) played participants three verses of a song either sung or spoken, and asked them to write down the text they had heard as accurately as possible. After completing a distractor task, participants recalled 81% of the words when they had been sung but only 67% of words when they had been spoken: Wallace (p. 240) explained this as resulting from music acting as a frame for the text whereby, for example, 'The music defines the number of lines, chunks words and phrases, [and] identifies the number of syllables'. In the context of sonic branding this implies that music with lyrics is an effective way to promote recall of a short, simple message concerning a company. Yalch (1991) produced similar findings when participants were shown 20 advertising slogans that had been presented earlier either verbally or in the context of a musical jingle. Participants were given an 'aided recall task' in which they were presented with only the slogans and asked to state which brand each slogan was associated with. People's ability to associate slogans with brands was better when the slogans had been presented earlier in the context of a musical jingle than when the slogans had been presented verbally. This again implies that music may facilitate recall of a short message about a company or product, and points to the potential effectiveness of jingles and sonic branding. A second experiment by Yalch showed that the positive effects of jingles on aided recall occurred particularly after only one rather than two exposures to the advertising, which implies that sonic branding and jingles may be a particularly effective way of reaching people.

Finally, the findings of Tavassoli and Han (2002) hint at a possible limitation of sonic branding. They point out that around one quarter of the world's population write in logographic script (e.g. Mandarin Chinese) in which the characters represent meaning rather than units of sound (as per the alphabetic script of other languages such as English). Consequently, English words tend to be coded using phonological methods, whereas a Chinese reader can access the meaning of logographs without the mediation of phonology, and instead relies more on visual processes. Tavassoli and Han point to this difference in explaining their finding that participants could associate sonic branding more readily with brand names presented in English than with brand names presented in Mandarin: the English brand names were processed by phonological means whereas the Mandarin brand names were processed visually, and so there is more opportunity to associate other sounds such as sonic branding with the former. Put simply, sonic branding and jingles may be less effective in cultures using logographic scripts.

It is also possible to interpret the concept of 'branding' more generally to include those occasions where businesses associate themselves with particular pieces of music, musicians, or music festivals in an attempt to improve their corporate image (see Blackwell and Stephan, 2004; Doonar, 2004; Fan and Pfitzenmair, 2002; King and Foster, 2001). Indeed, a small number of studies have directly addressed the relationship between music and commercial sponsorship. For example, Pincus (2005) presented data indicating that certain musical styles are associated not just with certain products, but also with certain specific brands. For example, Smirnoff vodka was associated most with dance music, whereas Evian water was associated most with pop; and Vans' clothing was associated most with indie/rock, whereas Puma was associated most with rap, and Levi's with pop. Indeed, Pincus (2004) describes research showing that 64% of 14 to 25-year-olds cited music as their greatest influence when selecting between different brands.

Furthermore, musicians themselves are by no means innocent bystanders in the appropriation of music by business: Phillips (2001) describes how musicians themselves function as brands through for example the launch of eponymous clothing lines and websites, and by allowing themselves (rather than just their music) to be used in advertising (such as, for example, the appearance of U2 in adverts for Apple's iPod). Similarly, Englis, Solomon, and Olofsson (1993) found evidence that consumption imagery in music videos varied by genre, such that certain musicians, in effect, promote the use of certain products. 'For example, rap stands out for the prevalence of "darkside" products (drugs, weapons, and alcohol), while dance music stands out for its emphasis on fashion, heavy metal for band-related products, and new wave music for its *relative* absence of consumption imagery' (p. 29).

However, increasing links between music and brands may have negative implications in the longer term: Englis and Pennell (1994) describe several studies by themselves and others showing that fans can particularly resent 'their' music being appropriated by businesses for commercial ends, and that this can have negative consequences for attitudes towards the latter. Furthermore, Oakes (2003) presents evidence that questions the effectiveness of business sponsorship of musical events. Participants recruited from a classical music festival and a jazz festival could recall only 0.86 and 0.65 festival sponsors respectively per respondent: this was despite the fact that the two festivals had 57 and 18 sponsoring organizations or individuals respectively. Three other studies of music and branding provide evidence that is more positive for the marketing industry but also more disturbing for society at large. Both van den Bulck and Beullens (2005) and Collins, Schell, Ellickson, and McCaffrey (2003) showed a positive relationship between awareness/use of alcohol among school pupils and their degree of exposure to music videos. Similarly, Friedman (1986) noted an increase in the use of brand names in the top 10 American hit songs for each year between 1946 and 1980, arguing that this constituted evidence that American culture was becoming increasingly commercialized and that 'word of author' advertising presented to consumers in these artistic contexts may be more likely to be accepted uncritically by them.

5.3 Music in commercial environments

The use of music in retail and leisure settings such as hotels, restaurants and the like has long been the source of considerable light-hearted derision. As Lanza's (1994) fascinating *Elevator Music* describes, the playwright

J. B. Priestley once bragged of having 'had it turned off in the best of places', and comedian Lily Tomlin once expressed fears that the guy who invented piped music might be inventing something else! The situation perhaps reached its zenith (or some would say its nadir) with the invention of piped music in the 1920s by Brigadier General George Owen Squier, a graduate of the prestigious West Point military academy; and in the present day, the provision of music in retail and leisure settings is a multi-million dollar industry that employs the latest satellite and computer technology.

To complement the public derision to which piped music is subject, there is a UK-based celebrity pressure group, 'Pipedown', dedicated to its removal. Founded in the 1990s, Pipedown has managed to attract a number of celebrity endorsers from British music such as Julian Lloyd Webber, Lesley Garrett, and Simon Rattle, and now has branches worldwide. Members write letters to organizations that use piped music, and are issued with calling cards that they can leave with a particular business. These cards say, for example, 'I left your establishment without buying anything simply because of the piped music', or 'I have enjoyed my meal/drink here, but I will not return for one reason only: the piped music'.

Indeed, numerous anecdotes point to just how controversial piped music can be. For example, London's well-known musical duo Chaz and Dave promised in their manifesto for the city's mayoral election that they would ban piped music in pubs. In May 2000, golfers in Stuart, Florida were in conflict with neighbouring pig farmer, Paul Thompson: the dispute centred over the country music Thompson played to his pigs which could also be heard from the 15th hole. (Thompson played the music since he claimed that it 'reduces stress, enhances tenderness of the meat, lets the animal grow faster and fatten quicker', and as we saw in Chapter 3, he may have been right.) Similarly, while shopping malls have long used piped music, we have personal experience of hearing its use on shopping streets in Japan, France, and Florida. The US military apparently used cover versions of middle of the road pop songs to break the fighting spirit of the Viet Cong. The Glastonbury pop music festival which takes place in the south-west of England has long been well known for its primitive washing facilities and promotion of counter-culture attitudes: in recent years however it has begun to feature piped music in its toilets. Perhaps most interesting is the case of a man in the USA who sued a bus company successfully over the piped music played on board. Apparently he saw no reason why he should have to listen to music he did not order, and eventually had his argument upheld by the USA Supreme Court: his right to the freedom of assembly had been violated, contravening the first amendment to the USA's constitution.

But what does Pipedown complain about specifically? Their web pages (www.pipedown.info/) claim that:

- Piped music raises blood pressure and depresses the immune system; and also causes problems for tens of millions of people with tinnitus or other hearing problems

- Piped music was named as 'the single thing *most detested* about modern life' by 17% of people in an opinion poll

- 'Despite all the hype about differing types of piped music affecting people's shopping habits, there is no impartial evidence to show that piped music increases sales by one penny'

- 'Pipedown believes that all music is devalued by being used as acoustic wallpaper or a marketing tool'

In short, campaigners' arguments seem to have two bases. The first is that piped music does not work, and may even be harmful. The second is that this is a 'freedom of choice' issue. As Peter Donnelly, a director of the Canadian 'Right to Quiet Society' explains, 'Owners and staff justify forcing music on us by saying most people like it. But that argument ignores the right of individuals to make their own choices. Most people like coffee, but the greeter at Wal-Mart doesn't force you to drink a cup before letting you shop in the store.' Using arguments such as these, protesters against piped music won perhaps their biggest victory to date in 2000. British Conservative politician Robert Key received the backing of fellow MPs for his attempt to ban piped music in public places such as airports, doctors' surgeries, and bus stations. Only a lack of Parliamentary time meant that Key's proposals never became law.

Balanced against claims such as these are those of the companies that provide in-store music. Unsurprisingly, their opinion regarding the effectiveness of piped music is very different. Perhaps the most famous company, the Muzak Corporation, features many testimonials from businesses on its web site (www.muzak.com). For example, a manager from fast food chain McDonald's states that their piped music 'is an excellent vehicle to support ... McDonald's core equities, special offers and products ... [and is] designed to generate increased traffic within a site.' Another executive claimed that 'The audio [marketing] worked so well [that our] video tape sold out'. Another said that 'We generate ... sales daily from the Muzak on-hold messages.' Most of the other in-store music companies make similar claims. Obviously it is easy to put this kind of statement to the test. As Ng's (2003) review illustrates, there is an extensive literature on numerous aspects of commercial environments that may influence consumer behaviour, and recent years have seen considerable attention devoted to the impact of music specifically (see earlier reviews by Bruner, 1990; Herrington and Capella, 1994; Oakes, 2000). Indeed, Areni (2003a; see also Areni 2003b; Morrison and Beverland, 2003) found that hotel and pub managers certainly had strong beliefs and theories concerning the power of atmospheric music, only some of which mirrored findings from the academic literature. Specifically, 'the more managers believed atmospheric music: (a) influences customers to interact with staff, (b) must vary according to the time of day, (c) can draw customers into an establishment or drive them away, (d) makes customers stay longer than they otherwise would, and (e) eliminates unacceptable silences, the more they agreed that it influences the revenues, gross margins, and operating profits of their establishments' (p. 263). Moreover, Pincott and Anderson (1999) report that in 1997 there were over a quarter of a million commercial premises in the UK alone that were licensed to play music. Academic research on the issue can be categorized into four main areas concerning the effects of musically-induced pleasure and arousal, knowledge activation effects, research on waiting and time perception, and workplace morale and productivity respectively.

5.3.1 **Pleasure and arousal-based effects**

5.3.1.1 The speed of customer activity

A number of studies have investigated the effect of music on the speed of customer activity. It is possible to regard these studies as drawing on that part of Berlyne's (1971) theory of musical preference (see Chapter 3) which says that as music becomes louder or faster it causes more arousal in the listener: one correlate of greater arousal is faster physical activity on the part of the listener, and so it is unsurprising that several studies on customer activity predict that as music becomes more arousing (e.g. louder, faster), so customers should behave more quickly.

Smith and Curnow (1966) were perhaps the first to investigate the effects of music on the speed of customers' activity. They played 'loud' and 'soft' music to 1,100 customers in two American supermarkets over eight half-day sessions. The researchers then measured the time at which customers entered the store, the time they left, and the amount of money they spent. The results showed that people spent less time in the store when loud music was played than when soft music was played (averages of 17.64 minutes and 18.53 minutes respectively). There was no difference in the amount of money people spent when loud and soft music were played. However, because people spent less time in-store when loud music was played, this means that loud music led to a faster rate of spending than did soft music. The authors point out that these effects cannot be attributed to differential rates of crowding, and that both types of music were liked equally by customers. Smith and Curnow concluded that 'if the store manager wishes to manipulate the number of persons in his [*sic*] store at any one time, he may do so by increasing or decreasing the volume of the music being played' (p. 256).

Milliman's (1982) paper is perhaps the best known in all the literature on music and consumer behaviour. The study 'was conducted in a medium-size store operated by a large nationally known chain of supermarkets' (p. 88), and was carried out over a nine-week period between New Year and Easter. Three different types of instrumental background music were played in the supermarket, namely no music, fast music (> 93 bpm), and slow music (< 73 bpm). The time that a total of 45 customers took to move between two points of the store was timed between 7pm and 8pm on each Wednesday, and Milliman also measured daily gross sales. Slow tempo music led to shoppers on average taking 127.53 seconds to move between the two points in the supermarket; fast tempo music led to a timing of 108.93 seconds; and no music led to a timing of 119.86 seconds. Milliman argued on the basis of this that 'there is sufficient evidence to conclude that the tempo of in-store background music can significantly affect the pace of ... supermarket customers' (p. 9). However, perhaps the most interesting aspect of the study concerned gross daily sales. Average sales when no music was played are not reported, although slow music led to average daily sales of US$16,740.23 whilst fast music led to a daily average of US$12,112.85: slow music led to 38.2% higher average daily sales than did fast music. The most likely explanation of this is that because slow music led to people shopping slowly, they were also more likely to browse and so see more products: shoppers spent less time in the store when fast music was played, and so would not have dwelt on so many products.

Milliman's (1986) paper was essentially an attempt to replicate his earlier findings in a different commercial setting. The 1986 study was carried out in a medium-sized restaurant that was 'above-average priced' (p. 287). Testing was carried out on 1,392 groups of customers on Friday and Saturday evenings over eight consecutive weekends from mid-September to mid-November. Slow music was played on four Fridays and four Saturdays, and fast music was played on four Fridays and four Saturdays. There were no significant differences between the two types of music on measures of the amount of time it took for customer groups to be seated; the number of customer groups who left the restaurant before being seated; or the amount of money spent by customer groups on food. The latter result is probably because virtually all customers ate one dish from each course, and it would be socially unacceptable to eat more. However, the music did have a statistically significant effect on three other measures. First, customer groups differed in the amount of time they took to eat their meals: customers in the slow music condition required on average 56 minutes whilst customers in the fast music condition required on average 45 minutes. Second, customer groups in the slow music condition spent on average US$30.47 on drinks from the bar during their meal, whereas the corresponding figure for the fast music condition was significantly lower (US$21.62). Third, the average estimated gross margin per customer group in the slow music condition was US$55.82, whilst the corresponding figure in the fast music condition was US$48.62. Although this might seem encouraging at first, it is worth remembering that customers stayed in the restaurant for longer when slow music was played: estimated gross margins *per minute* in the fast and slow music conditions were very similar at US$1.00 and US$1.08 respectively. In other words, slow music did not lead to diners buying goods with a higher margin: rather it led to higher margins simply because diners spent longer in the establishment and as a consequence they bought more drinks. As such, these findings support those obtained in the 1982 supermarket study.

Roballey, McGreevy, Rongo, Schwantes, Steger, Wininger, and Gardner (1985) were concerned with whether Milliman's effects would generalize to other customer activities. Their study had three conditions, namely slow music (average of 56 beats per minute); fast music (average of 122 beats per minute), and no music. The music comprised 'instrumental, nonclassical selections' (p. 221) which were played at a constant volume level over the central public address system of a university staff cafeteria. The study was conducted over 16 days between noon and 1.30 p.m. A small sample of only 11 diners was observed by two experimenters posing as fellow patrons. The main measure taken was average bites per minute, which was recorded over a 10 minute period, and the researchers found that fast music led to 4.40 bites per minute; slow music led to 3.83 bites per minute; and no music led to 3.23 bites per minute. Although the authors do not state which particular conditions led to significant differences, fast music clearly led to more bites per minute than did either slow music or no music. Interestingly, in contrast to Milliman's (1986) findings, Roballey et al.. also reported that there were no differences between the different types of music in terms of the total time taken to eat meals: perhaps fast music led to more bites, but with each bite containing less food!

Sullivan's (2002) research was carried out in a medium-sized mid-range restaurant in a British city centre. He investigated the impact on the amount of time spent in the restaurant and spending on both food and drink of no music, volume of the music, tempo of the music, and the popularity of the music. Soft music once again led to longer meal durations than did loud music (72.75 vs. 59.75 minutes respectively). Perhaps because it influenced the amount of time customers spent in the restaurant, the volume of the music also influenced the amount that customers spent. When soft music was played customers spent more per head on food (UK£7.16) than when loud music was played (UK£6.66), and the same effect was found for sales of drinks (UK£3.70 versus UK£3.33 respectively).

Caldwell and Hibbert (2002; see also Caldwell and Hibbert, 1999) tested the effects of musical tempo and liking for the music on time spent in a Glaswegian restaurant and expenditure therein. Tempo again influenced the amount of time spent dining, with slow music leading to slower dining times (96.56 minutes) than fast music (80.59 minutes). The greater time spent in the restaurant led to corresponding effects on sales. Slow music also led to more money being spent on drink per head than did fast music (UK£9.12 versus UK£6.04 respectively) and the same pattern held for spending on food (UK£18.14 versus UK£16.14 respectively). Liking for the music was also related positively to time spent dining and spending, consistent with Sullivan's (2002) findings. It is also worth noting Herrington and Capella's (1996) finding that although tempo and volume did not have an effect on the shopping time of supermarket customers, liking for the music was associated significantly with longer shopping times.

Since fast music seems to lead to faster eating, McElrea and Standing (1992) tested the parallel hypothesis that fast music should lead to fast drinking. The music used was 'a recording of the same medley of songs, played either quickly or slowly on a piano (132 or 54 beats respectively on a metronome)' (p. 362) at a quiet background volume. Forty laboratory participants were asked to drink a can of soda to ostensibly rate its flavour; although the researchers were really interested in the amount of time it took people to finish the drink. As with the research on eating, the results showed that fast music led to significantly faster drinking than did slow music (with averages of 9.70 minutes versus 13.52 minutes respectively). Similarly, McCarron and Tierney (1989) played no music, quiet music, or loud music while participants were left to drink as much as they wanted from a supply of soft drinks: total consumption of the drinks was related positively to the volume of the music. Similarly, Guéguen, Le Guellec, and Jacob (2004) studied 120 patrons at a bar in a rural area of France and at a second bar situated in an urban area. Loud and quiet pop music was played on two Saturday nights, and observers counted the number of drinks per person that were ordered. Loud music led to more drinks per person being ordered than did quiet music.

With the notable exception of Herrington and Capella's (1996) research, the studies reviewed above point to a clear conclusion: arousing (e.g. loud or fast) music seems to make customers do things more quickly than does less arousing (e.g. quiet or slow) music. The business implications of these studies are obvious and extensive, and can be easily put into practice by managers. For example, if music can increase or decrease the speed of customers to do things then it may be wise to play different types of music in different parts of a store: slow music, for example, could be played to encourage people to linger in neglected areas, whereas fast music could be used to relieve congestion in crowded areas. A more general implication of some of the studies reviewed above is that there may be a trade-off between the speed of customer activity and the amount of money that customers spend: slow music may lead to slower shopping but also more spending. The optimal resolution to this conflict depends on the goals that a given business is attempting to address with its music. For example, the manager of a town centre fast food restaurant should play fast music during weekend lunchtimes when his or her establishment is very busy and there is a need for space: however, slow music should be played early on a week-day morning when the restaurant is quiet, as this may encourage customers to linger and perhaps spend more. Note also that two studies (Knibbe, van de Goor, and Drop, 1993; van de Goor, Knibbe, and Drop, 1990) show that, in everyday life, heavy drinking of alcohol tends to occur in the presence of loud music. Such an effect is precisely what might be expected in the light of these studies, but does question whether pubs and bars should not play slower, quieter music in an attempt to encourage more sensible drinking practices.

These implications are also tempered by a few factors. First, it is interesting that Herrington and Capella (1996) found no effects of tempo and volume on shopping times as this suggests that it is potentially inaccurate to state that musical tempo will *always* increase the speed of customer activity: there must be some circumstances under which the effects outlined here do not operate. Second, following from this, it seems likely that customers' other goals mediate any tempo/volume effects. For example, if a parent visited a supermarket just prior to collecting their child from school, it seems very unlikely that slow/quiet music would be sufficient to induce them to leave their child alone at the school gate. Third, the relative importance of tempo/volume and liking for the music in question remains undetermined, and until the picture is clearer it would make sense for practitioners to attempt to address both factors. Fourth, the consistency of the findings suggests it may be worthwhile attempting to carry out what would be admittedly a difficult 'proof of the concept' study in which direct measures of arousal (e.g. elevated heart rate) are taken from shoppers. It would also be interesting to investigate the extent to which complexity and those other arousal-mediating variables addressed by Berlyne's (1971) theory (see Chapter 3) could lead to similar effects to tempo and volume; and the extent to which slow, quiet in-store music could alleviate elevated feelings of arousal resulting from crowding or excessive temperature.

With regard to the latter, it is worth noting that Eroglu, Machleit, and Chebat (2005) studied the interaction between musical tempo and in-store crowding. As we saw in Chapter 3, Konečni (e.g. 1982) has argued that listeners aggregate the arousal they experience as a consequence of the music and the listening situation, and as a consequence of this they should prefer combinations of musical and situational arousal that lead to a moderate level of arousal overall. As such, it is interesting that Eroglu, Machleit, and Chebat (2005) found that evaluations of a trip to a shopping mall in both hedonic terms (e.g. the degree of agreement with statements like, 'This shopping trip was truly a joy') and utilitarian terms (e.g. the degree of agreement with statements like, 'I accomplished just what I needed to on this shopping trip') were highest when slow music was paired with high crowding and when fast music was paired with low crowding. The authors themselves explain their findings in terms of an arguably rather unparsimonious schema incongruity approach. However, as compared with slow music and low crowding or with fast tempo and high crowding, Konečni's arguments would indeed predict that combinations of slow music and high crowding or fast music and low crowding should give rise to moderate levels of arousal and be most successful.

5.3.1.2 Liking for commercial environments

Other research has focused more directly on the emotional impact of music experienced in retail environments and how this interacts with arousal-evoking characteristics. A good deal of this work has been carried out in the context of the Mehrabian and Russell (1974) model of environmental psychology. This model characterizes responses to environments in terms of approach and avoidance behaviours. These are (i) a desire to physically stay in (approach) or to leave (avoid) the environment; (ii) a desire or willingness to look around and to explore the environment (approach) versus a tendency to avoid moving through or interacting with the environment (avoidance); (iii) a desire or willingness to communicate with others in the environment (approach) versus a tendency to avoid interacting with others or to ignore communication attempts from others (avoidance); and (iv) the enhancement (approach) or hindrance (avoidance) of satisfaction with tasks performed. Whether or not individuals carry out approach or avoidance behaviours depends on their emotional response to the environment, which can in turn be conceptualized in terms of pleasure, arousal, and dominance. Research tends to focus on only pleasure and arousal. In short, responses to the environment involving pleasure increase the likelihood of approach behaviours, whereas responses involving displeasure increase the likelihood of avoidance behaviours. These basic effects of pleasure/displeasure are amplified by the degree of arousal that a person experiences.

The available research provides some support for this model, particularly concerning the notion that liked music leads to approach behaviours. Studies described earlier by Caldwell and Hibbert (2002), Herrington and Capella (1996), and Sullivan (2002) all found that liking for the music was related to the amount of time spent in commercial premises. Furthermore, both Kerr, Yore, Ham, and Dietz (2004) and Boutelle, Jeffery, Murray, and Schmitz (2001) found that installing a music system on a stairwell could promote use of those stairs, and argued that this was because the music improved the aesthetic qualities of that environment. North, Tarrant, and Hargreaves (2004) found that uplifting rather than annoying music played in a gym could influence the extent to which people were prepared to be helpful (by offering to distribute leaflets on behalf of a charity for disabled athletes). Dubé, Chebat, and Morin (1995) employed a video simulation of a bank branch featuring classical music excerpts that varied in the amount of pleasure and arousal that they elicited. High levels of musically-evoked pleasure (and arousal) led to higher desire to affiliate (e.g. friendliness towards a bank clerk). Sweeney and Wyber (2002) found that musically-evoked pleasure affected intended approach behaviours toward a video simulation of a women's clothes shop, and that arousal contributed to this when the store environment was pleasurable. Areni, Sparks, and Dunne (1996) found that the effects of different types of music on pleasure affected perceptions of clothes stores in terms of service quality, the quality of the merchandise, the pleasantness of the shopping experience, and higher prices. Dubé and Morin (2001) found evidence that pleasurable rather than relatively unpleasurable background music improved evaluations of the physical environment of a clothes shop, and that this in turn led to liking for the store in general. North and Hargreaves (1996d) found a positive correlation between liking for the music played in a student cafeteria and liking for the cafeteria itself; and that when liked music was played, diners were more likely to visit the source of the music, namely a stall offering advice on typical student-related issues (e.g. safe sex). Baker, Levy, and Grewal (1992) manipulated the ambience of a simulated card and gift shop by featuring either background classical music and soft lighting or foreground pop music and bright lighting. The researchers also manipulated a 'social' factor by having either three employees, one of whom greeted the participant, or one employee who ignored the participant. Higher levels of pleasure and arousal induced by these manipulations led to greater willingness to buy from the shop. Note also that Tai and Fung (1997) also found some evidence supporting the Mehrabian and Russell model in predicting customers' responses to a CD store.

However, evidence on the Mehrabian and Russell model concerning specifically musically-evoked arousal is at best mixed. As we have just seen, some studies have indeed shown that the effects of musically-induced pleasure are amplified by arousal. But other studies do not show that arousal amplifies the effects of pleasure. Research by Dubé, Chebat, and Morin (1995) (described earlier) failed to find any evidence that musically-evoked arousal amplified the effects of musically-evoked pleasure, as did Chebat, Vaillant, and Gélinas-Chebat (2000). Although the three pieces of music employed in the latter's video simulation of a travel agent were all 'highly pleasurable' (p. 413), low and moderately arousing music led to greater desire to affiliate with the travel agent employee than did highly-arousing music. If musically-induced arousal amplifies the effects of musically-induced pleasure (as the Mehrabian and Russell model claims), and the music played in the study was 'highly pleasurable', then low- and moderately-arousing music should have had a *worse* effect than highly-arousing music. Furthermore, musically induced arousal did not influence participants' intent to buy, and moderately arousing music led to the greatest degree of acceptance of the travel agent's arguments.

Several other studies also suggest that the Mehrabian and Russell model may not represent the ideal means of capturing the effects of musically-induced pleasure and arousal on consumer behaviour. First, although North and Hargreaves' (1996d) study found that liking for the music in a student cafeteria could enhance several approach behaviours, these effects were confounded by musically-evoked arousal. Specifically, a separate paper (North and Hargreaves, 1996e) reporting data from the same study showed that the most liked music was of a moderate level of complexity, with disliked music being of low and high complexity. As noted in the coverage of Berlyne's theory in Chapter 3, musical complexity is related to arousal, so that it is debatable whether musically-evoked pleasure and arousal really are as independent as Mehrabian and Russell's model implies. Second, Machleit and Eroglu (2000) showed that methods of conceptualizing emotion proposed by Izard (1977) and Plutchik (1980) outperformed Mehrabian and Russell's 'by offering a richer assessment of emotional responses to the shopping experience' (p. 101). Finally, as El Sayed, Farrag, and Belk (2003) discuss, results concerning pleasure and arousal from Western and non-Western shopping environments may not necessarily correspond. In short, liking for in-store music appears to elicit approach behaviours, but it is less clear how this relates to musically-evoked arousal and whether these two factors are best considered in the context of the Mehrabian and Russell model.

5.3.2 **Knowledge activation effects**

More recent years have also witnessed research on knowledge-activation effects of music in commercial settings. This research has employed music to activate the associations that people have with a particular piece of music or musical style, with the intention of influencing not only purchasing decisions but also the perceived atmosphere of in-store environments. The existing research on this can be grouped into three areas, namely perceptions of the environment, patronage, and purchasing.

5.3.2.1 Perception of the environment

Research concerning the effects of music solely on perceptions of the environment is limited and lacks an obvious theoretical focal point. Nonetheless, several specific findings and different models of the relationship have been proposed, and might be put to use readily by practitioners. North, Hargreaves, and McKendrick (2000) played different musical styles in a city centre bank and also a bar, asking customers to rate the premises along several adjectival scales. Different musical styles gave rise to different 'atmospheres' in the premises, and these 'atmospheres' could be summarized along a small number of factors, namely how upbeat, aggressive, and dignified/cerebral the premises seemed. Baker, Grewal, and Parasuraman (1994) found that classical music and soft lighting led to people inferring that merchandise and service quality would be higher, when compared to top 40 music and bright lighting; and that classical music was associated more with the image of a prestigious store than was pop music. Spangenberg, Grohmann, and Sprott's (2005) study was carried out in the USA between Halloween and Thanksgiving, and found that when Christmas-related music and scent were both employed simultaneously they led to more favourable store attitudes, greater pleasure and also a stronger intention to visit the store: when music and scent were incongruous however then the advantages of each largely disappeared. Similarly, Mattila and Wirtz (2001) adopted a gestalt approach, finding that when ambient scent and music were congruent with each other in terms of their arousing qualities, consumers rated a gift store more positively, and showed greater levels of approach and impulse buying: the combination of a low arousal scent (lavender) and slow music was successful, as was the combination of a high arousal scent (grapefruit) and fast music, such that the *coherence* of the atmosphere was crucial. We will return to the issue of congruity and musical fit shortly, but for the time being, the Spangenberg et al. study and Mattila and Wirtz's research indicates that in-store music can be effective if it helps to promote a very specific aspect of the environment. Furthermore, Yalch and Spangenberg (1993) studied the impact of music on purchasing, but perhaps the most interesting aspect of their study was the description of how different types of music can be used in-store to promote 'zoning', the practice whereby different parts of the same store are made to appear conceptually different. Note also that Lageat, Czellar, and Laurent (2003) focused on how different psychophysical attributes of the sound of a product itself could promote the notion of 'luxury', and there is every reason to assume that the methodology and findings could be applied to music *per se*.

5.3.2.2 Patronage

Four other studies have focused on how the knowledge activated by in-store music may directly affect patronage. Sirgy, Grewal, and Mangleburg (2000) describe a model concerning how the perceived congruency between in-store factors such as music and customers' self-image may influence the decision to patronise certain stores rather than others. Put simply, in-store music provides a message about the kind of person who would be expected to visit a particular store, and such a model would be easy to test. Sirgy et al. also point out that such a process ought to distinguish between actual self (e.g. a consumer with little money), ideal self (e.g. that consumer's aspiration to be wealthy), and social self (e.g. that consumer's desire to appear at least 'upwardly-mobile' in the eyes of others). Similar conclusions concerning the role of self-image were reached by DeNora and Belcher's (2000) qualitative research on the use of music in clothes retailing: these are summed up well by the title of their paper, namely 'When you're trying something on you picture yourself in a place where they are paying this kind of music'. Grewal, Baker, Levy, and Voss (2003) also drew on the potential for music to convey a particular message. They constructed a video simulation of a jewellery store, and found that when this store featured classical music this enhanced the evaluation of the store's atmosphere because it promoted the notion of a luxurious environment: this in turn promoted store patronage intentions. Similarly, Babin, Chebat, and Michon (2004) provided data from consumers in a shopping mall supporting a model concerning how the appropriateness of in-store factors such as music can positively influence perceptions of merchandise quality, in-store affect, and approach/avoidance behaviours toward the mall.

5.3.2.3 Purchasing

In the case of both Grewal, Baker, Levy, and Voss' (2003) and the Babin et al. (2004) research, patronage intentions were enhanced by the ability of music to communicate a message that corresponded with the general image of the premises in which it was played. This leads neatly into the most commercially-relevant of all the research on knowledge-activation effects. This concerns how the 'fit' between the knowledge activated by in-store music and particular products and product attributes can promote certain beliefs about a product, raise the salience of certain products or product features, and increase actual purchasing.

For example, North, Hargreaves, and McKendrick (1997; 1999a) considered the effect of music on wine sales in a supermarket. The research used an aisle-end display featuring four shelves of French and German wines, with each shelf featuring one French wine and one German wine of a similar price and degree of dryness/sweetness. On the top shelf of the display was a small music player, which on alternate days over two weeks played either stereotypically French music (e.g. the French national anthem played on an accordion) or stereotypically German music (e.g. Bierkeller songs). When German music was played then German wine outsold French by two bottles to one. However, when French music was played then French wine outsold German by five bottles to one. Customers seemed to be predisposed to buying the wine that 'fitted' with the music, and the results are consistent with the notion that customers' knowledge about the music was priming the recognition or selection of one of the two types of wine. Similarly, Areni and Kim (1993) investigated the effect of music on the amount of money that customers spent in a wine cellar. They found that classical music and Top 40 songs had no effect on the number of bottles of wine sold; but that classical music led to more expensive wine being bought, with customers spending on average US$7.43 compared with US$2.18 when top 40 music was played. The authors argued that spending more money on wine fits with the affluent, sophisticated image of classical music, such that the stereotypes surrounding classical music activated related thoughts in customers. In particular, these effects mirror those identified by Grewal, Baker, Levy, and Voss (2003) who found that classical music led to more positive patronage intentions concerning a jewellery store.

The notion that the upmarket, affluent, sophisticated stereotype of classical music can prime spending has obvious commercial implications; and these were investigated more by North and Hargreaves (1998) and North, Shilcock, and Hargreaves (2003). North and Hargreaves' (1998) study was carried out over four days in a university cafeteria, during which time pop music, classical music, easy listening music, or no music were played. Customers were asked to rate the premises on several adjectival scales, with different types of music leading to different 'atmospheres'. Specifically, pop music led to the cafeteria being perceived as 'fun' and 'upbeat'; easy listening led to the cafeteria being perceived as rather 'downmarket' and 'cheap'; no music led to a rather unclear atmosphere; but classical music led to the perception of the cafeteria as 'sophisticated' and 'upmarket', in apparent support of Areni and Kim's (1993) contention.

Furthermore these different 'atmospheres' were associated with spending intentions. Diners were also asked to state the maximum they would be prepared to spend that day on each of a list of 14 items on sale (e.g. a slice of pizza, a pot of fruit yoghurt, a can of cola). When no music was played, diners said they would spend on average a total of UK£14.30 on the 14 items. The corresponding figures for when easy listening and pop were played were UK£14.51 and UK£16.61 respectively. In contrast, the corresponding figure for classical music was UK£17.23. In other words, music influenced the amount that customers were prepared to spend on precisely the same products in precisely the same place. Furthermore, as with the earlier Areni and Kim study, customers seemed to behave in a way that 'fitted' with the music, being willing to spend most when the cafeteria seemed 'sophisticated' (i.e. when classical music was played), spend the next highest amount when the cafeteria seemed 'fun' (i.e. when pop music was played), and spend least when the cafeteria seemed 'downmarket' (i.e. when easy listening music was played) or had an unclear image (i.e. when no music was played). Similarly, North, Shilcock, and Hargreaves (2003) played classical music, pop music, and no music over 18 nights in a restaurant and found that classical music was associated with higher spending per head (UK£32.52) than was either pop music (UK£29.46) or no music (UK£29.73). Again it seems as though the upmarket impression of the premises created by classical music prompted customers to behave in a consistent manner and spend more money.

Two other studies have reported similar findings. Wilson's (2003) study in an Australian restaurant found similar results to North and Hargreaves (1998) and North, Shilcock, and Hargreaves (2003), even when diners' income, age, reason for dining out (e.g. with friends, attending a business convention), and level of familiarity with the restaurant were accounted for. Lammers (2003) found that although musical style (rock versus classical) did not matter, restaurant customers spent more when quieter rather than louder music was played, and concluded that an important factor in this may have been the congruity between the quietness of the music and the rather serene atmosphere of the restaurant itself. Note also that findings such as these are consistent with those described earlier concerning musical fit in advertising.

5.3.2.4 Unresolved issues concerning musical fit

This is an encouraging set of findings with the obvious potential to increase profits. However several issues concerning musical fit in retail and leisure settings require more attention before the research can be put to full commercial use. First, it could be argued that using music to such ends is unethical since it could help to persuade customers to spend more money than they would otherwise, or to select products that they do not necessarily want. We believe that this potential criticism is unfounded on both ethical and practical grounds. From an ethical perspective, we believe that the use of music to achieve such ends is no more unethical than other means used by businesses. For example, most people would not regard it as unethical for restaurant waiters to dress smartly in order to create an atmosphere thought to be conducive to spending; and if French music is used to boost sales of French wine is this really any more unethical than hanging French flags by the display? From a practical perspective, although it is of course a research issue, we simply find it hard to believe that music could be used to persuade people to buy products they don't want or can't afford. For example, it is extremely unlikely that a customer would choose to buy a Renault car rather than a Volkswagen simply because the showroom played French music: musical fit would only play a part when the customer was otherwise undecided between the two options. Similarly, musical fit may be more effective for some types of products than for others. Schlosser (1998) for example provided evidence supporting the notion that the impact of a given piece of in-store music would be based on the extent to which it enhanced a desired social identity on the part of a consumer (e.g. using classical music to reinforce a customer's self-perception that he is affluent and successful): given this, Schlosser argues it is understandable that she should have found that the impact of environmental music was maximized for 'social identity products' (i.e. those which communicate a particular identity on behalf of the purchaser); and relatively unimportant in the case of products that are utilitarian and therefore intrinsically rewarding.

This in turn leads to a second issue raised by the limited research that has already been carried out on musical fit, namely *why* such effects should occur. To the best of our knowledge only one study has attempted to test an explanation of this. As described above in the section on advertising, North, Hargreaves, MacKenzie, and Law (2004) argued that musical fit operates by priming the activation of mental concepts containing information related to the music, and in support of this they found that musical fit could promote recall of associated products. If correct, this approach would also predict that musical fit should lead to consumers being able to recognize products more quickly when they are presented in context of related music; or to in-store decisions being regarded by consumers as easier or less problematic when music 'fits' well with certain products. Note, however, that Hume, Dodd, and Grigg (2003) found that purchasing was not affected by playing strongly stereotyped music in a wine store. Similarly, Alpert and Alpert (1990) found that sad music led to higher purchase intentions towards a sad greetings card than did happy music, but also led to higher purchase intentions towards a happy greetings card as well. Findings such as these indeed suggest that research concerning the effects of musical fit on purchasing is still very much in its early stages, and that theoretical issues must be resolved before the potential effects can be employed reliably. Future studies may therefore benefit by drawing on research and theory concerning priming, heuristics, and schemata.

The third issue raised by research such as this concerns how exactly 'musical fit' might be defined in a degree of detail that is both commercially useful and scientifically testable. At present, the idea of musical fit is very experimenter-centred: it is defined in terms of the image of the product in the opinion of the experimenter, and researchers investigate the effect of the music they have chosen on the variables they are interested in. However, a customer may perceive the music differently to the way the experimenter intended: for example, classical music may be perceived as 'old fashioned' rather than 'upmarket'. Similarly, customers may not relate positively to those aspects of the product made more salient by music: for example, the music played in a car dealership may correspond with the 'reliable' image of the manufacturer, but this could be unappealing to customers who are instead only interested in buying cars that are 'sporty' or 'exciting'. As described in Chapter 3 and earlier in this chapter (see also Turley and Milliman's (2000) review of the effects of store atmosphere on shopping behaviour), numerous attempts have been made to define the means by which people respond to music, and also the effect of music on perceptions of the immediate environment. It seems plausible that these may ultimately provide a basis on which musical 'fit' can be defined in a theoretically-driven manner. However, a great deal more work is required if this is to come to fruition and, as Pan and Schmitt's (1996) arguments make clear, there is very likely to be a strong cross-cultural element to any truly valid process.

5.3.3 Time perception and waiting

5.3.3.1 Discrete event models

A third line of research concerning music in commercial environments has concerned its potential impact on time perception and waiting time. Many businesses play music to waiting customers on the assumption that this will make the time pass more quickly and/or pleasantly. However, research suggests that the real effects of music on time perception are much more complicated. Many researchers interested in so-called discrete events models have argued that time perception is related positively to the number of events that are processed within a given period (e.g. Levin and Zackay, 1989; Ornstein, 1969). In effect, the mind invokes a heuristic that 'it takes more time for more things to happen', such that music that requires a greater amount of processing should lead to longer time duration estimates than should music that requires less processing. For example, Kellaris and Altsech (1992) (see also Cameron, 1996; Kellaris, Mantel, and Altsech, 1996) found that, for females at least, loud music led to longer time estimates than did soft music: several authors (e.g. Konečni, 1982) have suggested that loud music seems to require more processing than does soft music. Similarly, in a study that perhaps possesses greater ecological validity, Oakes (2003) drew on the notion that fast music contains more information than slow music: he found a positive correlation between the tempo of music played while students waited to register for their courses and their perception of the amount of time for which they had been kept waiting. Similarly, Polkosky and Lewis (2002) found that a slow tempo non-musical stimulus (namely a 'ticking' sound) led to participants under-estimating the response time of a 'telephony-speech recognition' computer application. Moreover, Bailey and Areni (2006a) played participants either eight short songs or four long songs while they solved word puzzles for 20 minutes. The former led to longer time duration estimates, and Bailey and Areni (2006a) argued that each song represented a distinct trace in memory, such that the eight songs led to the perception that more had happened during the target period.

Other research within this approach has directly addressed the old maxim that 'time flies when you're having fun'. James Kellaris, however, has demonstrated the opposite, namely that disliked music can lead to people underestimating the duration of a passage of time whereas liked music leads to people overestimating the duration of a passage of time: in effect, time does *not* always fly when you're having fun. Kellaris has explained this in terms of two factors. First, the 'Pollyanna principle' (e.g. Matlin, 1989) states that pleasant information is processed and recalled more effectively. Second, we have already seen that time perception is related positively to the amount of information processed within the given period. Consequently, Kellaris and Mantel (1994) used these two lines of research to explain their finding that, for females at least, disliked music led to shorter time estimations than liked music: following the Pollyanna principle, they argued that less information was encoded and retrieved when disliked (i.e. unpleasant) music was played, and that this reduction in the amount of information processed subsequently led to shorter time estimates (see also Kellaris and Altsech, 1992). Similarly, Hui, Dubé, and Chebat (1997) found that liking for the music heard in a video simulation of a bank was linked positively to time estimates. Furthermore, Kellaris and Kent (1992) related these effects to structural musical properties. They found that perceived duration was longest when people heard music in a major mode (i.e. music that was emotionally positive), and shortest when people heard music in a minor mode (i.e. music that was emotionally negative).

5.3.3.2 Attentional models

Bailey and Areni (2006b; see also Chebat, 2004), however, argue that this work provides an incomplete picture of the role of music in time perception. They do not deny that music can influence time perception via discrete events models, but they also contend that it can have an effect by diverting attention away from the internal monitoring of time through so-called attentional models of time perception. Bailey and Areni argue that the impact of background music on time perception depends crucially on whether people are preoccupied with the passage of time. On some occasions, people are doing some other task during a waiting period, and are not focusing on the passage of time. This means that when people are asked to estimate the passage of time, these duration estimates have to be based on attempts to *reconstruct* the period that has passed such that people base their duration estimates on this reconstruction. Under these circumstances, people use discrete events models of the type investigated by Kellaris.

However, Bailey and Areni argue that sometimes people *are* disposed to monitor the passage of time, and when they do so then attentional models are more important in determining time duration estimates. This method of estimating time leads to music having very different effects to those set out by discrete events models. When people are actively monitoring the passage of time, then any stimulus (including music) that draws attention away from this monitoring will reduce the amount of temporal information available. Since there is less temporal information available, perceived duration is shortened. Bailey and Areni note that the results of four studies are consistent with this attentional model. MacNay (1996), North and Hargreaves (1999c), Roper and Manela (2000), and Guéguen and Jacob (2002) employed methodologies in which participants were simply asked to wait (in a medical exercise facility, an experimental laboratory, a psychiatric care waiting room, and an on-hold telephone setting respectively). As such, people would be monitoring the passage of time, the presence of music in these settings would distract attention from the passage of time, less temporal information would be encoded subsequently, and this in turn would lead to the amount of waiting time seeming shorter. Shorter time duration estimates were indeed found in all four studies.

Bailey and Areni argue that three other studies have yielded findings that are also probably consistent with the 'attentional models' argument. Yalch and Spangenberg (1990) found that foreground pop music led to under 25-year-old shoppers reporting shorter shopping duration estimates than did background music, whereas the reverse was true for older shoppers. Bailey and Areni argue that younger shoppers would have liked and listened to the pop music more, and that this would have reduced the amount of attention they paid to the passage of time, leading to shorter duration estimates. In contrast the older shoppers would have liked the background music more, and this explains their shorter duration estimates when this music was played. Similarly, Lopez and Malhotra (1993) and Cameron, Baker, Peterson, and Braunsberger (2003) both found a negative correlation between liking for music and time duration estimates, exactly as Bailey and Areni would predict. Indeed, the main appeal of Bailey and Areni's arguments is that they are able to reconcile apparently contradictory sets of findings: the results obtained by MacNay (1996), North and Hargreaves (1999c), Roper and Manela (2000), Guegen and Jacob (2002), Yalch and Spangenberg (1990), Lopez and Malhotra (1993), and Cameron et al. (2003) are all difficult to reconcile with discrete events models. Similarly, many of the findings obtained by people working on discrete events models (e.g. Kellaris) are themselves difficult to reconcile with attentional models and the notion that sometimes time really does fly when you're having fun.

Future research should directly compare the effects of music under circumstances in which participants either are or are not focusing on the passage of time. Furthermore, given the complexity of time perception, and the number of factors along which music varies, it is unsurprising that at least five studies suggest that the discrete events and attentional models in their current state, although extremely helpful, may still not be complete explanations of the relationship between music and time duration. First, Chebat, Gelinas-Chebat, and Filiatrault (1993) investigated the effects of musical tempo on the perceived duration of a video-simulated bank queue. Musical tempo did not directly affect perceived time spent in the queue as both the discrete events and attentional models (and Oakes' (2003) findings) predict it should have. Second, North, Hargreaves, and Heath (1998) played fast and slow music in a gym. Again, musical tempo did not influence time duration estimates in any single direction, as both discrete events and attentional models perhaps predict it should have. However slow music led to less *accurate* time duration estimates: this was explained in terms of participants rating the slow music as less appropriate for a gym such that the inappropriateness may have confused people's attempts to monitor time. The apparent role of the appropriateness of the music for the listening situation suggests that context and expectations may also be important factors.

Third, North, Hargreaves, and McKendrick (1999b) placed an advert in a local newspaper asking people to call a number and receive payment for completing a questionnaire on attitudes. In practice, we never actually answered the phone and instead put callers on hold, measuring how long they waited before hanging up. While on-hold the participants heard either music by The Beatles, pan-pipe cover versions of the same songs, or a brief spoken message that repeated regularly. Contrary to the discrete events and attentional models, this manipulation had no effect at all on callers' perception of the amount of time they had waited on-hold, even though the music by The Beatles and the pan-pipe covers were liked significantly more than the spoken message. However, callers did actually wait longer in the presence of pan-pipe music. After they had hung up, callers were phoned back, and their responses to a questionnaire suggested that the longer actual waiting times in response to the pan-pipe music could have been because it was associated with the phone service also being rated as less stressful or because the pan-pipe music was rated as corresponding more closely with callers' expectations concerning typical on-hold music: either factor may have led to longer actual waiting times, but the effects of neither can be explained simply by discrete events or attentional models.

Fourth, to some extent, Mantel and Kellaris' (2003) findings are consistent with the discrete events model: when people were played radio adverts for a restaurant, those that required a greater amount of information processing also led to longer time duration estimates. However, Mantel and Kellaris' results also show that it is important to consider not just consumers' perception of the amount of information contained in an advert (or for that matter any other commercial stimulus), but also their *ability to process* the stimuli with which they are presented. Mantel and Kellaris found that when the resources required to process the advert matched those available, people processed the advert in full: consistent with the discrete events model, they accordingly believed that more time had passed. When the resources required to process the advert did not match the resources available people were predisposed either to use heuristics to process the advert (when too little resource was available) or simply to 'drift off' (when too much resource was available) meaning that little of the advert was processed: this in turn meant that, consistent with the discrete events model, people did not think that much time had passed. In other words, the main finding was consistent with the discrete events model; but the findings also show that a consumers' *ability to process* an advert, an on-hold telephone system, or a supermarket check-out queue affects their perception of the passage of time just as much as does the amount of information that these stimuli provide in their own right. A conversation with a spouse on the sofa, irritation at waiting on-hold, or a screaming baby sitting in the supermarket trolley all affect the *ability* to process time, and are just as relevant to a consumer's time perception as are the commercial stimuli under the direct control of businesses.

Finally, as with Yalch and Spangenberg (2000), Gulas and Schewe (1994) found that familiar music led to longer time duration estimates than did unfamiliar music: Bailey and Areni (2006b) argue that both these findings are consistent with a discrete events model since familiar music is more accessible in memory, such that more events are associated with the target interval, which in turn leads to longer duration estimates. In contrast, we would argue that Yalch and Spangenberg's (2000) and Gulas and Schewe's (1994) findings are not perhaps so consistent with a discrete events model, since familiar music could also have been predicted to lead to *shorter* duration estimates: unfamiliar music contains more new information than familiar music, leading to more events being coded in memory, which in turn could lead to longer duration estimates.

5.3.3.3 Problems and opportunities for research on time perception

Indeed, this particular point illustrates one of the major problems with research in this area, namely that it is possible to explain almost any finding in terms of the complex theories that exist concerning time perception and / or responses to music. Antonides, Verhoef, and van Aalst's (2002) study demonstrates the issue further. They found that music led to greater overestimation of on-hold waiting time than did providing information about expected waiting time. It is difficult to determine which of these two stimuli would have been a greater distraction from attempts to monitor the passage of time (which is important according to attentional models), or which of the two stimuli would have conveyed the greatest degree of information (which is important according to discrete events models): it is subsequently difficult to predict which stimulus should have led to shorter time perception, and therefore whether the results support existing theories. We fear it may be some time yet before practitioners can be presented with a neat set of guidelines that can be used to reliably influence consumers' time perceptions.

There are other, simpler, limitations of the research on time perception. First, it has tended to be carried out in laboratories using student participants: the effects need to be replicated in commercial environments with 'real' customers. Second, the research tends to use short periods of time (e.g. 30-second adverts, on-hold telephone queues of five minutes). People are often presented with advertising, on-hold queues, etc. for much longer periods in real commercial environments, and again we need to determine whether music can influence time perception over these longer time periods. Third, the practical utility of approaches to time perception based on emotional responses to music (such as liking) is perhaps limited: if a given company attracts a diverse range of customers then it may be difficult to select music that all customers will react to similarly; and research focusing on structural aspects of music such as tempo or volume may be easier to put into commercial practice. Despite these problems, however, part of the appeal of the findings concerning time perception is their complex, sometimes counter-intuitive nature, and they certainly deserve further research. Once the effects obtained can be predicted more reliably they will allow retailers to use music to decrease the perception of elapsed time in queues, or make consumers believe that services have been consumed for longer than is actually the case. The commercial benefits of effects such as these are potentially very large; and so are the potential ethical implications.

Finally, we should make six more general comments before concluding our coverage of the impact of music on consumers. First, the research reviewed above has almost without exception considered only the short-term impact of music on consumers in the setting in which that music is played. This does not rule out the possibility that music may also have longer-term effects that may also transfer to other settings. For example, hearing music in one branch of a retail chain may have effects that transfer to other shops during the same shopping trip or other branches during subsequent shopping trips. Indeed, two studies suggest that music may influence consumers on an even broader, cultural level. A survey reported in 1998 ('"Cool Britannia" boosts the image of British goods abroad') found that over 50% of 1000 exporting manufacturers believed that the resurgence of British pop music in the mid to late 1990s helped to make British goods more desirable overseas. Similarly, Zullow (1991) found that levels of pessimistic rumination in the lyrics of best-selling pop songs could predict changes in consumer optimism, which could in turn predict growth in Gross National Product. The effects of music on consumer behaviour may well not be limited to specific instances of music heard in specific premises. Note also that the research outlined above by no means necessarily exhausts the potential range of effects of specific pieces of music played in specific commercial settings. The effects outlined above seem to operate via general psychological processes such as arousal, knowledge activation/priming, and the transfer of emotional responses to in-store music onto emotional responses to the premises themselves: given that so many other aspects of consumer behaviour might be influenced by these general processes, there are grounds to suspect that the research cited here taps only a limited range of all the commercial effects that music might have.

Second, we began this section of the chapter by presenting some of the claims of protest groups that campaign against piped music. The existing research directly refutes one claim made by protesters, namely that there is no evidence showing the commercial benefit of piped music. The research described here shows that music could well affect the speed with which customers shop and diners eat; the products customers choose; the amount they are prepared to spend; store atmosphere; how long people will wait; how long they think they have been kept waiting; and the places that they will go to. The literature indicates moreover that the 'right' kinds of music can lead to increases in turnover of sometimes 10% or more. As such, background music makes clear commercial sense. It is worth noting that some of the other arguments proposed by protesters against piped music can be refuted by common sense. For example, if customers dislike piped music so much then the high street should be full of businesses advertising the fact that they don't play it. If society can tolerate a death from starvation every 3.6 seconds (see www.thehungersite.com), it is hard to imagine how or why Liberace playing at the deli counter could promote universal disgust. Furthermore, protesters claim that large numbers of eminent musicians support a ban on piped music, but we suspect that their agents and managers would not since this ban would cut off a lucrative source of royalty payments. Also, if piped music devalues all music, does this also mean that turquoise paint in a supermarket devalues Picasso's blue period, or that TV adverts devalue great films such as *Citizen Kane*? Similarly, protesters have campaigned against piped music on health grounds, arguing that excessive, unwanted noise can cause increased blood pressure. Later in this chapter we will describe research showing the positive impact of music on immunity and other health-related variables; and although excessive, unwanted noise may well have a negative impact on health we would also note that living on an airport flight path is not the same thing as hearing Elgar in an elevator. As a consequence, protesters should focus on other arguments that do have more merit. For example, the available literature (and common sense) certainly cannot refute protesters' claims that loud piped music causes problems for customers with hearing difficulties. Protesters are also almost certainly right to point out that the cost of piped music will probably at some point be passed on to consumers; and focus their campaigning on particularly crass and inappropriate uses of piped music.

Third, although music has the potential to lead to commercial gain, many businesses often play the 'wrong' kinds of music, irritating customers and making the premises feel frenetic or downmarket. The research reviewed here shows that when several types of music are played then the 'wrong' types of music often perform dramatically worse than the 'right' kinds of music: piped music must not be treated as a single object, with the only decision facing managers being whether or not to play it. Rather, the research shows that different types of music will have different effects. It is the job of managers to decide what commercial goals they want music to achieve; to select the right type of music to achieve those goals; and to assess whether the music they choose is actually achieving these goals. Our experience suggests however that store managers are sometimes simply too lazy to consider the music they play: they will for example often allow staff to bring in CDs from home, even though they wouldn't dream of letting staff set their own pricing policy, wear whatever clothes they wanted to, use old paint tins from the garage to paint the shop walls, or take control of any other aspect of in-store marketing on an *ad hoc* basis. Of those businesses that do take care over their music policy, the great majority outsource this to a specialist music company and carry out very little monitoring or assessment of what they get in return: no business would simply trust another to dictate their pricing policy, pay to screen a new TV advert without previewing it first, or fail to assess the commercial impact of implementing a new type of cash register.

Fourth, much of the research in this field is ghetto-ized. For example, we saw in Chapter 3 that most of the research within music psychology concerning arousal has focused on factors such as complexity and familiarity: most of the research within consumer psychology concerning musical arousal has ignored this and focused instead on factors such as tempo and volume. Similarly, although mainstream theories of consumer psychology and marketing can be seen in the literature on music and consumer behaviour, there remain numerous attempts to re-invent the wheel in which researchers ignore studies published outside their immediate area of expertize. It is worth noting that in compiling this section of the chapter we identified relevant research in journals concerning consumer psychology, environmental psychology, music psychology, cognitive psychology, business studies, public health, marketing, management, economics, and sociology. All can make a contribution, and none can be ignored.

Fifth, one criticism levelled by managers against the academic research in this field is that the work is often too theoretical to be put into commercial practice by non-specialists. Of course researchers sometimes do not do everything possible to communicate the practical applications of their work to practitioners. However, we would also add to this the old adage that there's nothing so practical as a good theory. Theoretical accounts of the effects of piped music allow us to explain why the effects in question have occurred: if we can explain why the effects have occurred then practitioners can control them to their advantage. There is clear scope for collaboration between practitioners and academics, since both bring something to the party. Academics can bring knowledge of the existing literature and research methods: managers can bring insights into which hypotheses are of practical relevance.

Finally, and most importantly of all, despite problems such as these, the clear 'headline' conclusion from this research is unarguable: music in retail and leisure environments can, if used in a manner suggested by the research findings, have a positive commercial impact. This positive conclusion chimes with the conclusions of Garlin and Owen's (2006) meta-analysis of 32 studies in the area. As noted in Chapter 2, meta-analysis provides a statistical measure of the effect size (i.e. the magnitude of the impact) of the music in question. Garlin and Owen's analysis showed 'small-to-moderate, yet quite robust effects in terms of background music and the dependents: value returns, behaviour duration and affective response' (p. 755).

5.3.4 **Workplace morale and productivity**

The majority of the research on music in retail and leisure settings focuses on customers. However, there is a smaller literature addressing the other group of people likely to be influenced by music in such contexts, namely the staff who work there. Interest in the role of music in the workplace began in earnest during the Second World War when researchers investigated the role of music in maintaining morale and reducing fatigue among factory employees (Antrim, 1943; Beckett, 1943; Halpin, 1943; Jones, 1941; Kerr, 1942a, b; Kerr 1943a, b, c, d, e; Kerr, 1946; Kirkpatrick, 1943a; Pepinsky, 1944); and improving productivity and reducing errors among production line workers (Cardinell, 1943; Humes, 1941; Hough, 1943; Kirkpatrick, 1942; Kirkpatrick, 1943b; Reynolds, 1943; Selvin, 1943). It is interesting that many of the main topics of concern to researchers have changed little since the days of Spam, spivs, and the Siegfried line, and research has continued concerning the effects of workplace music on morale, productivity in boring or repetitive tasks, and employees' ability to carry out physical work, as well as more 'modern' topics such as the effects of office noise and related research on driving performance and cognitive task performance.

5.3.4.1 Morale

Research on using music to maintain morale has little theoretical basis. Instead it rests on a simple premise. When we hear music we like it can put us in a better mood: similarly, when we hear music we like in the workplace it can put us in a better mood in the workplace. The research on staff morale shows unsurprisingly that this is precisely what happens. Nor are the consequences of this trivial. For example, Connolly and Viswesvaran (2000) reviewed all the research that quantified the relationship between workers' moods and their job satisfaction. The main conclusion was that between 10% and 25% of variations in job satisfaction are attributable just to variations in workers' moods. Similarly, unpublished data collected by North, Hargreaves, and McKendrick in a computer assembly plant found that playing music that the employees liked led to mood ratings that were 20.1% higher than in a 'no music' condition and 14.2% higher than in a 'neutral music' condition. Similar findings are reported by Devereux (1969), Jacoby (1968), Lesiuk (2005), Uhrbrock (1961), and Webb (1995). One other interesting manifestation of the effects of music on employees' mood and morale is reported by Au, Chan, Wang, and Vertisnsky (2003). They played music to traders on financial markets, finding that music that put the traders in a good mood led to them losing money whereas music that put the traders in a neutral or negative mood led to them making profit. The authors attributed this to the 'good mood' traders being over-confident in taking unwarranted risks and making less accurate decisions.

5.3.4.2 Productivity on boring or repetitive tasks

Research on the effects of music on employees engaged in boring or repetitive tasks is similarly unencumbered by complex theoretical baggage. Numerous possible explanations for such effects have been proposed including the reduction of fatigue and tension, increases in arousal, and the masking of background noise, although there is no reason to assume that any of these explanations should be mutually exclusive. Indeed, Oldham, Cummings, Mischel, Schmidtke, and Zhou (1995) supported many of these possible explanations in carrying out perhaps the best-known piece of research in the area. Office employees either were or were not given personal music players to use over four weeks. Employees in the 'music condition' showed significant improvements in performance, had lower intentions to leave for other jobs, were more satisfied with the company they worked for, and were in a better mood. This seemed to be because the music helped the workers to relax and overcome the stress of work. Furthermore, 'employees in relatively simple jobs responded most positively' (p. 547) to the music. The only bad effects of wearing a music player were found for those employees working on very complex jobs, and this is likely because 'employees in complex jobs are more involved or absorbed in their work than those in simple jobs and, therefore, are less likely to attend to and benefit from music in the workplace' (p. 550). Consistent with these findings, Fox and Embrey (1972) addressed specifically the ability of music to increase arousal and decrease fatigue in two experiments looking at the effect of music on fault detection workers. In the first study, six participants in a psychological laboratory examined small metal parts on a conveyor belt. As the experiment progressed over a 30-minute period, the number of faulty parts missed by participants increased (i.e. they got worse at detecting faults). However, this drop-off in performance was only half as bad in the presence of lively music as it was in the absence of music. The second experiment was very similar, this time using 8 factory-based employees whose normal job was to inspect for faults in products on a production line. When no music was played, the employees identified 51% of the faulty parts: lively music led to a higher detection rate of 69% of all faulty parts (see also Aseev and Mishin, 1971; Gereb, 1966; Nafde, 1974; H. C. Smith, 1947).

5.3.4.3 Physical work and exercise

Much of the research that is relevant to the effects of music on employees' ability to carry out physical labour has been carried out in the context of various quasi-sporting activities, presumably because these are relatively easy to carry out and quantify under laboratory conditions (e.g. time taken to cycle a mile on an exercise bike). In short, the research here shows that music can help people to produce more physical labour, although the theoretical basis for this is still contentious. Three explanations have been proposed. First, some researchers argue that the positive effects of music on physical exertion are based on arousal, such that sedative music reduces heart rate, which in turn leads to greater endurance (e.g. Copeland and Franks, 1991). Second, some researchers claim that music can help physical performance simply because it distracts attention from the amount of fatigue experienced (e.g. Boutcher and Trenske, 1990): people spend their time listening to the music rather than thinking about how tired they feel. A third explanation is that music can function as a reward, such that people will exert themselves more if they hear music as a reward for this effort (e.g. Hume and Crossman, 1992): the pleasure to be gained from music outweighs the discomfort of greater exertion. Karageorghis and Terry's (1997) review of the effects of music in sport and exercise emphasizes that music may be particularly beneficial under conditions of sub-maximal physical exercise, which of course characterizes the kind of physical work typically carried out in the workplace. They also highlight the benefits of music that is in time with the rhythm of the physical work in question. This so-called *synchronous* music experienced under conditions of sub-maximal exercise has typically been shown to be most effective, and has the potential to improve performance, reduce the amount of perceived exertion, and enhance mood.

5.3.4.4 Office noise

Modern working practices have given rise to a fourth area of research concerning the impact of office noise. Although this is clearly relevant to the impact of music on staff, our coverage will be brief since the research does not concern music *per se*. In general, this research has led to four conclusions which all follow from the notion that background noise is distracting and unpleasant.

First, the great majority of the research shows that office noise has negative effects on employees' performance (e.g. Banbury and Berry, 1997, 1998; Guski, 1975; Jones and Broadbent, 1979; Knez and Hygge, 2002; Loewen and Suedfeld, 1992; A. P. Smith, 1985). Second, office noise is related to reduced job satisfaction, dislike of the office environment, and even medical symptoms (e.g. Ferguson, 1973; Hedge, 1982; Klitzman and Stellman, 1989; Krause, Lynch, Kaplan, Cohen, Goldberg, and Salonen, 1997; Mital, McGlothlin, and Faard, 1992; Nelson, Kaufman, Burt, and Karr, 1995; Rishi, Sinha, and Dubey, 2000; Rodríguez-González, Fernández, and Sabucedo-Cameselle, 1997; Sundstrom, Herbert, and Brown, 1982; Sundstrom, Town, Rice, and Osborn et al., 1994). Third, office noise increases stress among employees (e.g. Evans and Johnson, 2000; Kjellberg, Landström, Tesarz, and Söderberg et al., 1996). Finally, the negative effect of office noise is exacerbated when employees do not believe that they can control it, when it is perceived as unnecessary, or when employees have not been exposed to office noise previously (e.g. Banbury and Berry, 1997; Kjellberg, Landström, Tesarz, and Söderberg et al., 1996; Sailer and Hassenzahl, 2000; Spieth, 1956; Veitch, 1990; Willner and Neiva, 1986). It is also worth noting that at least one study (Young and Berry, 1979) has directly addressed the positive role that music can play in masking office noise.

5.3.4.5 Driving

Research on driving has adopted numerous differing perspectives that reflect the complexity of driving. First, most people are familiar with the 'boy racer' who drives a heavily customized car at reckless speed while loud music thumps out of the massive bass bin that occupies the space where the back seat used to be. Accordingly, Ramsey and Simmons (1993; see also Melka and Pelant, 1999) investigated whether exposure to music in this manner can actually harm hearing. They recruited 10 young drivers in their cars and asked them to play the music they usually listen to at a typical volume level. The mean sound level of the music was 99 dbA (equivalent to being inside a subway train, or being close to a lorry horn). However, this masked considerable variation between the 10 individuals, whose music led to them receiving between 5% and 530% of their daily permissible healthy 'noise dose'. However a mean 'dose' of 108.5% indicated that, providing no other noise was experienced, 'the *average* owner of a high-powered car stereo is probably safe from any risk of noise-induced hearing loss' (p. 109).

Other research has focused on how the tempo and rhythm of the music may harm driving performance. Brodsky (2001), for example, confirmed his prediction that fast-paced music would increase heart rate, thus leading to increased driving speed and increased traffic violations (e.g. disregarded red lights); and similar results are reported by both Konz and McDougal (1968) and Zendel, Slawinski, and Pearson (2003). Other researchers have demonstrated similar effects while instead attributing the findings to either (a) music interfering with the cognitive processes involved in driving or (b) music reducing the amount of cognitive resources available for processing driving-related information. For example, North and Hargreaves (1999a; see also Ayres and Hughes, 1986; I. D. Brown, 1965) found that both loud, fast music (versus slow, quiet music) and a backwards-counting task increased the time it took participants to complete five laps of a motor racing computer game.

Note also, however, that Consiglio, Driscoll, Witte, and Berg's (2003) simulated driving task found that listening to music did not slow the time it took participants to press the brake pedal once they had seen a red braking light up ahead. Furthermore, music led to quicker reaction times than when the participants talked to a passenger or on a phone, and to reaction times that were only 4% (and not significantly) slower than in a control condition that featured neither music nor conversation. More simply, the effects of music on driving may not be uniformly negative, and we suspect that under boring driving conditions (such as those in the Consiglio et al. study), any short-term negative effects of music on distraction may be offset by the ability of music to maintain alertness over time. For example, Beh and Hirst (1999; see also Turner, Fernandez, and Nelson, 1996) showed that loud music was associated with increased reaction times in driving-related tasks carried out under 'high demand conditions', but also that quieter music could indeed have positive effects in maintaining vigilance. Furthermore, in addition to potentially improving vigilance during undemanding driving, three other studies show a second potential benefit of in-car music, namely the possibility of counteracting 'road rage' in congested traffic or when drivers are under time pressure (Wiesenthal, Hennessy, and Lubertacci, 2003; Wiesenthal, Hennessy, and Totten, 2000, 2003). There is even evidence (Iwamiya, 1997) that relaxing in-car music makes the scenery outside the window look better!

5.3.4.6 Productivity on complex tasks

Other research has considered the effects of music on performance on demanding cognitive tasks other than driving, such as homework or other similarly intellectual activities; and the rather diffuse set of findings that exists at present no doubt reflects the tremendous number of variables involved. These variables fall into four groups concerning the *task*, the *music*, the *person*, and the *situation*. First are variables related to the *task* itself such as its difficulty (e.g. Arkes, Rettig, and Scougale, 1986; Davies, Land, and

Shackleton, 1973; Oldham et al., 1995), or whether it is verbal, mathematical, or visuo-spatial in nature (e.g. Jausovec and Habe, 2005). Second are variables concerning the *music* such as whether it features lyrics (which may interfere with performance on verbal tasks) (e.g. Crust, Clough, and Robertson, 2004; Furnham, Trew, and Sneade, 1999), the extent to which it is distracting (e.g. loud, unfamiliar, complex) or attended to (e.g. Blood and Ferriss, 1993; Davenport, 1972; Hallam, Price, and Katsarou, 2002; Kallinen, 2002; Smith and Morris, 1977), or the style of music in question and whether, as some well-known research indicates, music composed by Mozart can increase visuo-spatial task performance (see e.g. Bangerter and Heath, 2004; Rauscher, Shaw, and Ky, 1993; see also our review in Chapter 2). Third are variables concerning the *person* carrying out the task such as his or her degree of interest in, motivation towards, and experience of the task in question (e.g. Hallam and Price, 1998; Iwata, 1975; Stanton, 1973), his or her intelligence and whether he or she is used to hearing background music (e.g. Etaugh and Ptasnik, 1982; Mitchell, 1949), and his / her personality, mood, and degree of alertness (e.g. Bittman, Bruhn, Stevens, Westengard, and Umbach, 2003; Crust, Clough, and Robertson, 2004; Furnham and Bradley, 1997; Plante, Marcotte, Manuel, and Willemsen, 1996). Finally, also relevant are a range of other *situational* variables such as the simultaneous presence of stimuli other than music (e.g. TV, other people) (e.g. Pool, Koolstra, and van der Voort, 2003), and the presence of 'everyday' drugs such as caffeine, alcohol, or nicotine (e.g. Ward and Lewis, 1987). This range of variables indicates the difficulty of carrying out research in this area, and when we also consider that complex interactions may exist between all of these factors it is easy to understand why a truly definitive piece of research on the subject has yet to be carried out.

5.4 **Music and health**

Music can also lead to financial gain in one other particularly important way. At the time of writing, the state-funded National Health Service in the UK has an annual budget well in excess of UK£90 billion. This serves as just one example of how, every year, Western countries spend billions of pounds on drugs and other medical procedures that less wealthy countries can unfortunately only dream of providing for their citizens. Research, however, suggests that music can provide numerous benefits in healthcare settings at a fraction of the cost of the latest drug regimes. This research has the obvious potential to save large sums of money in Western economies and to provide hitherto unknown benefits to people living in less wealthy countries.

Some of the means by which music has been used to impact directly upon health are often surprising to the general public. For example, on 18 June 2004, *USA Today* reported how the subway system in Seoul has attempted to reduce the number of people leaping to their death in front of the trains by using optimistic, stress-reducing music (e.g. Ben E. King's *Stand By Me*; Rod Stewart's *Sailing*; and Simon and Garfunkel's *Bridge Over Troubled Water*). This is played in conjunction with specific spoken messages requesting for example 'Dear passengers, let's think again about the parents and sisters and brothers we love and the preciousness of our life'; signs on the train saying, for example, 'Giving up your life will inflict an unbearable pain on your family and society!'; and emergency buttons on platforms so that other passengers can warn authorities of anybody they suspect may be about to attempt suicide.

However, to hope that music might play such a dramatic role in public health seems less bizarre when considered in the context of the research literature. Music therapy has a long history of using music to alleviate chronic psychological disorders and problems associated with long-term physical impairment; and this section of the chapter begins with a brief overview. Although this practice dates back to ancient times (see Ansdell, 2004; Horden, 2000; Meinecke, 1948), Ansdell and Pavlicevic (2005, p.194) note that 'most contemporary music therapy has concentrated on eliciting clients' participation in direct communicative musicing … [There has been] a distinct move away from a discourse of healing (or curing) to one where, for music therapists today, communication itself is a more modest therapeutic aim … [Music therapy] increasingly presents itself as a psychosocial intervention, rather than a curative medical one'. We then move on to cover research outside this approach to music therapy. This second body of research has been carried out more overtly within a medical model of health, aims directly to use music as a means of healing or curing, and concerns music in medical settings such as hospitals, and dentists' and doctors' practices where it has been used in the treatment of acute disorders that are not primarily psychological: as such music is used as an acute adjunct to other short-term medical treatments for physical illnesses (e.g. drugs or surgery). Note that this division of the field mirrors that employed by Bruscia (1987) in distinguishing between respectively music *as* therapy and music *in* therapy.

5.4.1 Models of music therapy

The literature on conventional music therapy in the treatment of chronic psychological and physical disorders has addressed a variety of conditions. Although the conditions most frequently associated with this approach to music therapy concern learning difficulties and mental health, music has also been used in attempts to help people with other problems such as physical impairments, people with hearing and visual problems, the institutionalized elderly, and people in the criminal justice system. This research has been reviewed extensively and regularly since the end of the Second World War (e.g. Aldridge, 1996; Ansdell, 1995; Bright, 2002; Bruscia, 1987; Bunt, 1994, 1997; Bunt and Hoskyns, 2002; Bunt and Pavlicevic, 2001; Dokter, 1994; Heal and Wigram, 1993; Lathom-Radocy, 2002; Licht, 1946; Meinecke, 1948; Munro, 1993; Nordoff and Robbins, 1971, 1977; Pavlicevic, 1997, 1999; Pavlicevic and Ansdell, 2004; Payne, 1993; Peters, 1987; Podolsky, 1954; Pratt, 1993; Priestley, 1975; Ruud, 1980, 1998; Schullian and Schoen, 1948; Soibelman, 1948; Standley, 1991b; Stige, 2002; Unkefer, 1990; Unkefer and Thaut, 2002; van de Wall, 1946; Wigram, Saperston, and West, 1995). We will not attempt to repeat this extensive coverage here. However, in order to give a flavour of the discipline it is worth briefly reviewing Bunt's (1997) description of how music therapists have used four main treatment models, namely the medical model, psychoanalysis, behaviour therapy, and humanistic psychology.

As the term suggests, the medical model emphasizes the impact of music on physiological indices such as heart rate and breathing. As Bunt points out, such an approach dominated the early literature as music therapy emerged in hospitals, but is limited in two important ways. First, work within the medical model focuses on instantaneously occurring and potentially temporary effects to the detriment of longer-term effects that may not even show themselves immediately. Second, research within the medical model often neglects emotional factors, and particularly how these might interact with physiological changes among clients, with the consequence that the outcomes of a music therapy session are idiosyncratic to the individuals concerned. These potential limitations notwithstanding, we shall see in the next section how research within the medical model has nonetheless contributed a great deal to attempts to provide direct assistance to people experiencing acute disorders of a non-psychological origin.

Although Freud would undoubtedly fume at the distinction from a medical model, Bunt's second model concerns psychoanalytic approaches to music therapy. As with much of psychoanalytic theory, a precise, concise description of this model is difficult to pin down. However, therapists working within this approach emphasize the symbolic nature of a client's musical behaviour (and indeed other behaviours) during a therapy session, such that overt behaviours are interpreted as indicative of internal states that the therapist subsequently attempts to connect with. Bunt (1997, pp. 255–256) gives the example of how 'For example, a child may play a drum at a quick tempo which is taken by the therapist to indicate a feeling of excitement: the therapist then plays the drum (or responds via another modality such as the voice) at a similar tempo but also loudly. Turntaking between the child and therapist may then ensue'.

Behaviour therapy approaches draw heavily on classical learning theory as proposed by the behaviourists. As such, they emphasize processes such as the reinforcement of desired behaviour through reward, and the withholding of reward when undesired behaviours are shown. Such approaches have been used with particular effect in educational settings in which researchers have shown how using contingent music listening as a reward can reinforce the likelihood of school pupils improving their academic performance, paying greater attention in class, or misbehaving less. Nor are these effects trivial, as illustrated by Standley's (1996) meta-analysis of research on music as a reinforcement in educational and therapeutic settings: she concluded that benefits attributable to contingent music were nearly three standard deviations greater than in control or baseline conditions; that music was more effective as a contingent reward for desirable behaviour than were other possible rewards; and that the beneficial effects regularly generalized to other academic and social behaviours that w ere not reinforced directly by the music. Nevertheless, the criticisms that have been levelled at behaviourism over the years can also be adapted and subsequently applied to behavioural approaches to music therapy. In particular, behavioural music therapy in the strict sense ignores unobservable psychological states and treats physical symptoms rather than the psychological causes of disorders, no matter how relevant these might seem.

Finally, humanistic approaches to music therapy focus on self-actualization and making the most of one's potential, individual differences, freedom of choice, and self-esteem. They emphasize relationships, the treatment of the whole person, and Rogerian notions of empathy and acceptance within the therapeutic process. Furthermore, humanistic approaches are unique in that the other approaches to music therapy outlined here focus almost entirely on non-conscious processes. For example, the medical model focuses on physiological processes, the psychoanalytic model focuses on the unconscious, and the behavioural model simply denies the scientific utility of anything that is not directly observable. Instead, in common with all humanistic psychology, the humanist approach to music therapy is the only one to focus overtly on conscious processes such as hope, acceptance, volition, and all the other feelings that most people would regard as the very stuff of human life. We began this section by noting that music therapy has the potential to be very cost-effective. Nonetheless, although rather vague, the processes and outcomes linked to humanistic music therapy have a warmer hue that is especially welcome in an age in which the health benefits of any therapy are so often reduced to dehumanized, accountancy-style metrics such as the length of hospital stay or the cost of drugs. If we accept that healthcare is about people rather than illness or economics then it is hard to be anything but very sympathetic towards humanistic approaches.

5.4.2 Music and physical health

5.4.2.1 Standley's meta-analysis

Vickers (2000) discussed how growing evidence of their effectiveness means that a range of complementary medicines including music are being used more in the treatment of physical disorders. Perhaps the most convincing evidence concerning music specifically is provided by Standley (1995; see also Aldridge, 1993; Standley, 1986). She carried out a meta-analysis of 55 studies concerning the effects of music on actual patients who were undergoing treatment for a wide variety of medical and dental disorders. As noted in Chapter 2, meta-analysis provides a statistical measure of the effect size (i.e. the magnitude of the impact) of the music in question, such that the larger the effect size so the more effective was the music. For example, an effect size of 3 means that the music condition led to scores that were three standard deviations more positive than those obtained in the 'no music' control condition. Standley's analysis indicated that music had been used in attempts to treat 129 different medically-related dependent variables, and that the effect was positive on 125 of these. By means of illustration, the 10 health-related factors showing the greatest effects of music are shown in Table 5.1.

Indeed, data such as these allow us to make a simple, dramatic case for the potential role of music in medicine. As Standley (1995, p. 3) herself puts it in her opening paragraph,

> If given an option, would most pregnant women elect to reduce the length of labor by an average of two hours? Would the patient in the surgical recovery room choose to awaken from the anaesthesia sooner, with fewer side effects and less pain? Would persons with chronic pain prefer to use less analgesic medication, thereby reducing possible side effects? Would those undergoing consequential medical treatment opt for reduced anxiety during its course? Research shows that music provides the above medical benefits and more, and that most people perceive their preferred music to be relaxing and beneficial to their recovery.

Furthermore, 'The overall mean effect size for all 129 dependent variables was 0.88. Therefore the average therapeutic effect of music in medical treatment was almost one standard deviation greater than that without music' (p. 4). Arguments (and effect sizes) such as these not only help to guide the efforts of researchers towards areas where music has particularly positive effects, but will also help to convince the medical profession of the potential of music relative to other, more expensive, treatment regimes.

Table 5.1 The 10 health-related factors showing the greatest effects of music in medical and dental studies (adapted from Standley, 1995)

Effect of music		Effect size
Podiatric pain	Bob (1962)	>3.28
Paediatric respiration	Ammon (1968)	3.15
Pulse (in dental patients)	Oyama, Hatano, and Sato et al. (1983)	3.00
Use of analgesia (in dental patients)	Monsey (1960)	2.49
EMG	Martin (1987)	2.38
Use of analgesia (in dental patients)	Gardner and Licklider (1959)	2.36
Blood pressure (in dental patients)	Oyama, Hatano, and Sato et al. (1983)	2.25
Pain	Rider (1985)	2.11
Medication in paediatric surgery patients	Siegel (1983)	2.11
EMG	Martin (1987)	2.10

Standley also calculated effect sizes according to a range of independent variables. With regard to sex, music was less effective for males than it was for females. With regard to age, children responded more positively to music than did adults and infants. With regard to the means of measuring the effectiveness of music, patients' self-reports tended to produce more conservative evidence than did behavioural observations or physiological measurements. With regard to the means of presenting the music, live music from a trained music therapist had a greater effect than did recorded music. With regard to diagnosis, the effects of music were greatest for dental patients and those experiencing chronic pain, and smallest (although nonetheless still helpful) for obstetric, coma, and cancer patients. Pain relief was greatest when that pain was temporary (e.g. as in dental treatment or headaches) rather than resulting from deep tissue injury (e.g. as in childbirth, surgery, or cancer). Similarly, the effect of music varied depending on the specific variable in question, being greatest for those factors shown in Table 5.1, and smallest (although still helpful) for the length of labour during childbirth, the amount of anaesthesia required, the number of days for which a patient remains hospitalized, and measures of neonates' behaviour.

Standley concluded by describing a classification of seven different means by which music is employed in medical and dental settings; with different means being used to address different problems. First, *passive music listening* was used most frequently to reduce pain, anxiety or stress; to enhance the effects of anaesthetic/analgesic drugs (or reduce their usage); or to reduce the length of hospitalization. The typical method involves playing the patient's preferred music prior to the event that actually causes pain or anxiety, telling the patient that the music will help, and allowing the patient to control the music as much as possible. Specific instances of the effectiveness of this include the use of pre-operative music to reduce anxiety and the amount of anaesthesia required; perioperative music to reduce anxiety and mask operating room sounds; post-operative music to promote waking, reduce the use of analgesia, and to reduce the negative after-effects of anaesthesia; music during kidney dialysis to reduce discomfort and serve as a distraction; music to reduce pain and anxiety in burn victims undergoing treatment; music to reduce pain and enhance the effects of analgesics among cancer patients; music to decrease intracranial pressure in coma patients; music to reduce pain and stress and decrease the length of hospital stays among neonates; and music to reduce pain in so-called 'office treatments' such as abortions, dental procedures, and podiatric treatments.

Second, *active music participation* is used most frequently to focus attention on exercise or to structure exercise, with the aim of reducing pain from joint movement, increase a patient's ability to move, or shorten childbirth labour. The typical method involves selecting appropriate exercises, selecting music that helps to promote the specific *kind* of movement in question (for example, Standley recommends disco music for the promotion of forceful movements and waltz music for fluid movements), and then continually refining the nature of the music played as the patient's movements improve. Specific instances of the effectiveness of this include the use of music during pregnancy to structure Lamaze exercises; during childbirth to focus attention and structure breathing; to help those with respiratory deficiencies to structure their deep breathing exercises or structure coughing to relieve congestion; to structure physical therapy schemes for burn and other patients; or to help those with gait disturbances.

Third, *music and counselling techniques* are used most frequently to reduce distress among patients (and their families) who are dying, seriously ill, or permanently disfigured or disabled. This method involves simply playing music to provide opportunities for pleasure, reminiscence, closure, or to initiate discussion; to help patients (and their families) identify and develop their abilities; to help patients recognize and think about crucial decisions they need to take; and to assist in interpersonal relationships.

Fourth, *music and developmental or educational objectives* involves using music to reinforce or structure learning among children who are hospitalized for extended periods. The aim is to help them achieve educational goals and more general developmental milestones indicative of growing independence, such as feeding themselves or walking rather than being carried. The typical method involves telling the child that music is to be used as a reinforcer for achieving predetermined educational or developmental goals, determining whether those goals have been met, and if so providing music. Other variations of this approach involve creating educational musical activities that address the specific objectives facing the child; setting the child musical 'assignments' to promote independence; and inviting parents to take part in musical activities with the child, having them reinforce demonstrations of independence or other instances of developmental progression.

Fifth, *music and stimulation* approaches aim to provide auditory stimulation; to make patients more aware of and responsive toward stimuli experienced through other senses; and to reduce depression due to the lack of stimulation in conventional medical environments. When attempting to increase responsiveness, the typical method involves playing the patient's preferred music through a pillow speaker while simultaneously stimulating other senses by, for example, stroking, moving visual stimuli, and providing pleasant smells. When the patient begins to respond these stimuli are removed, and others are then presented in an attempt to broaden the range of stimuli that elicit a reaction. After a time, the therapist begins to present the stimuli that elicited a response in conjunction with a human voice, in an attempt to encourage the patient to respond to the latter. Specific instances of the effectiveness of this approach include the use of music to elicit responses from patients who are comatose or brain-damaged, patients who have experienced strokes, or premature babies. Alternatively, when this approach is used to reduce depression resulting from lack of stimulation, the patient's preferred music is played in conjunction with attempts to stimulate other senses, and evidence of pleasure or creativity is reinforced. Specific instances of the effectiveness of this include attempts to help patients such as burn victims, organ transplant patients, and patients with infectious diseases who are typically forced to endure sterile environments.

Sixth, *music and biofeedback* is used to reinforce or structure physiological responses in order to increase patients' awareness, self-control, and their monitoring of their physiological state. The typical method involves using the patient's preferred music as a reward for achieving a desired physiological state, or music may instead be used simply to help the patient relax. Over time, the therapist helps the patient to transfer these skills to non-medical settings so that they can be used in everyday life. Specific instances of the effectiveness of this include using music to help patients with epilepsy to reduce the frequency of seizures by relaxing and reacting calmly to stress; improving blood flow and lowering blood pressure, heart rate, and tension in coronary patients; and promoting relaxation among sufferers of migraines.

Finally, *music and group activity* approaches aim to promote positive interpersonal interactions which in turn reduce depression due to social isolation or long-term hospitalization, and increase feelings of happiness. The typical method involves using a variety of activities that are relevant and appropriate to the age group in question and also their physical condition. These activities (which might include live music) involve a mixture of focused listening and participation on the part of patients and medical staff alike. Instances of pleasure, creativity, and verbalizations not concerning illness are reinforced, and the session ends with relaxation to prepare patients for rest.

5.4.2.2 Explanations of the health effects of music: pain, stress, immunity, and neonates

Standley's (1995) meta-analysis provides a detailed and powerful case concerning the impact of music on a range of disorders. In some cases, the analysis also describes (albeit briefly) *why* music should have such positive benefits. For example, it is easy to see why music should be effective in those forms of music therapy Standley terms *active music participation, music and counselling techniques*, and *music and group activity*. Similarly, the behaviourist approach that explains the effectiveness of approaches concerning *music and developmental or educational objectives, music and stimulation*, and *music and biofeedback* is also well understood. However, it is arguable that the outcomes elicited by Standley's first type of therapy are the most exciting. As described above, *passive music listening* techniques have implications for finance-related variables such as the amount of drugs that patients require and also the amount of time that they spend in hospital. Given this, it is worth spending a little while longer on the mechanisms that might explain how passive music listening could have direct health benefits, since a thorough understanding promotes effective use. Research on these mechanisms has concerned the effect of music in relieving pain, relieving stress, boosting immunity, and in issues related to pregnancy, childbirth, and neonates.

Michel and Chesky's (1995) survey indicated that 41% of music therapists used music to relieve pain. Interest in the effects of music on pain began in earnest in the 1960s with the gate control theory (e.g. Melzack and Wall, 1965) which argued that the experience of pain was mediated by the mind, and was not attributable to simply the passive reception by the brain of pain messages from other parts of the body. Specifically, as Melzack, Weisz, and Sprague (1963, p. 240) argued, the intensity and quality of pain experiences can be mediated by 'expectation, suggestion, level of anxiety, the meaning of the situation in which injury occurs, attention-distraction levels, competing sensory stimuli, and other psychological variables'. This has led to two theories concerning how music can mediate pain. Researchers such as Maslar (1986; see also Brown, Chen, and Dworkin, 1989; Locsin, 1981; Whipple and Glynn, 1992) drew on the 'distraction and competing stimuli' element of the gate control theory to argue that music that patients enjoy may reduce their experience of pain by *distracting their attention* away from the pain and on to the music itself. Indeed, Mitchell, MacDonald, Knussen, and Serpell's (2007) survey of 318 chronic pain sufferers found that distraction and relaxation were the most frequently reported perceived benefits of music. A second possible explanation for the effect of music on pain concerns the 'expectation, suggestion, and meaning of the situation' part of the gate control theory. Both Brown, Chen, and Dworkin (1989) and Mitchell, MacDonald, Knussen, and Serpell (2007) amongst others argue that music can relieve pain by increasing people's *perceived control* over the pain: in short, if patients believe that they have access to a means of pain control via, for example, music then this belief itself decreases the aversiveness of pain.

A considerable amount of research over recent years has addressed music and pain relief. Much of this is atheoretical, and there are very few instances of studies that *directly* test the implications of the two possibilities set out above. For instance, if music reduces pain by distracting attention then this ought to reduce the amount of pain that patients can actually recall at a later date. However, although support is not unanimous, the great majority of the research published over recent years provides data that are at least *consistent* with the two possibilities set out above. This can be seen in studies of numerous aspects of pain relief such as;

- Chronic pain (Colwell, 1997; Jacobi and Eisenberg, 2001-2002; Kenny and Faunce, 2004; Leão and da Silva, 2004; Selm, 1991; Siedlecki, 2005)

- Pain experienced during treatment (Davis, 1992; Fauerbach, Lawrence, Haythornthwaite, and Richter, 2002; Fowler-Kerry and Lander, 1987; Hekmat and Hertel, 1993; Koch, Kain, Ayoub, and Rosenbaum, 1998; Megel, Houser, and Gleaves, 1998; Menegazzi, Paris, Kersteen, Flynn, and Trautman, 1991; Nilsson, Rawal, Unestähl, Zetterberg, and Unosson, 2001; Perlini and Viita, 1996; Tanabe, Ferket, Thomas, Paice, and Marcantonio, 2002; but see also Aitken, Wilson, Coury, and Moursi, 2002; Arts, Abu-Saad, Champion, Crawford, Fisher, Juniper, and Ziegler, 1994; Ayoub, Rizk, Yaacoub, Gaal, and Kain, 2005; Binek, Sagmeister, Borovicka, Knierim, Magdeburg, and Meyenberger, 2003; Broscious, 1999; Cepeda, Diaz, Hernandez, Daza, and Carr, 1998; Haythornthwaite,

Lawrence, and Feuerbach, 2001; Stermer, Levy, Beny, Meisels, and Tamir, 1998)

- Pain experienced post-treatment (Good, 1995; Good, Anderson, Ahn, Cong, and Stanton-Hicks, 2005; Good, Stanton-Hicks, Grass, Anderson, Choi, Schoolmeesters, and Salman, 1999; Kim and Koh, 2005; Masuda, Miyamoto, and Shimizu, 2005; Tse, Chan, and Benzie, 2005; Tusek, Church, and Fazio, 1997; Voss, Good, Yates, Baun, Thompson, and Hertzog, 2004; Zhang, Li, Xu, and Feng, 2000; Zimmerman, Nieveen, Barnason, and Schmaderer, 1996) and;

- Pain experienced specifically by cancer patients and those undergoing palliative care (e.g. Abrams, 2001; Aldridge, 2003; Magill, 2001; Magill-Levreault, 1993; Trauger-Querry and Haghighi, 1999; Zaza, Sellick, Willan, Reyno, and Browman, 1999).

The efforts of music therapists to relieve stress have either been an end in themselves or with the goal of alleviating some other condition associated with stress (such as pain). Pelletier's (2004) meta-analysis of 22 studies concerning specifically the effects of music on stress (see also Hanser, 1985) indicated that music and music-assisted relaxation techniques were successful to this end, and also that the amount of stress reduction varied according to age, the type of stress in question, the means by which the music was used, the listener's musical preference, and their prior level of musical experience. Of course the research on experimental aesthetics described in Chapter 3 describes the musical properties that give rise to low levels of arousal and relaxation. But what is most impressive about the music therapy research on stress are those instances in which calming music has been shown to lead to reductions in direct biological indicators of stress such as cortisol (e.g. Flaten and Åsli, 2006; Fukui and Yamashita, 2003; Khalfa, Bella, Roy, Peretz, and Lupien, 2003; Nilsson, Unosson, and Rawal, 2005; but see also Migneault, Girard, Albert, Chouinard, Boudreault, Provencher, Todorov, Ruel, and Girard, 2004) or blood pressure (e.g. Chafin, Roy, and Gerin, 2004; Knight and Rickard, 2001; Triller, Erzen, Duh, Petrinec-Primozic, and Kosnik, 2006). High levels of cortisol are associated with numerous specific health problems, and generally lowered immunity. The size of these effects is also impressive: Miluk-Kolasa, Obminski, Stupnicki, and Golec (1994), for example, provided patients with information about surgery to be performed the next day, and within 15 minutes this produced a 50% increase in cortisol levels. However, after one hour, patients who had not been played music still had elevated cortisol levels, whereas patients exposed to music showed a decrease in cortisol to a level that was 35% lower than their baseline and that was similar to that observed in a non-surgical control group who were merely in hospital for observation. More generally, numerous studies over recent years have indicated that music may help to alleviate various indices of stress and have similar benefits among;

- Patients awaiting imminent treatment (e.g. Cooke, Chaboyer, Schluter, and Hiratos, 2005; Haun, Mainous, and Looney, 2001; Kain and Caldwell-Andrews, 2005; Kain, Cladwell-Andrews, and Wang, 2002; Tansik and Routhieaux, 1999; Wang, Kulkarni, Dolev, and Kain, 2002; Whipple, 2003; Yung, Kam, Lau, and Chan, 2003)

- Patients undergoing treatment (e.g. Barrera, Rykov, and Doyle, 2002; Bittman, Berk, Shannon, Sharaf, Westengard, Guegler, and Ruff, 2005; Ganidagli, Cengiz, Yanik, Becerik, and Unal, 2005; Kain, Wang, Mayes, Krivutza, and Teague, 2001; Schneider, Schedlowski, Schurmeyer, and Becker, 2001; Walsh, Martin, and Schmidt, 2004; Yilmaz, Ozcan, Basar, Basar, Batislam, and Ferhat, 2003; Yang, Li, Zhang, and Zhang, 2003; Zhang, Fan, Manyande, Tian, and Yin, 2005); and

- Patients who have been treated (e.g. MacDonald, Mitchell, Dillon, Serpell, Davies, and Ashley, 2003; Magee and Davidson, 2002; Nilsson, Unosson, and Rawal, 2005)

This research on music and stress has, in more recent years, led to two particularly interesting offshoots, the first of these being the effect of music on immunity. The reasoning behind this is that if (i) music can affect the autonomic nervous system and lower stress (or conversely increase feelings of well-being), and (ii) that lowered stress (or increased well-being) is associated with improved immune functioning, then music ought to relate to immune functioning (see e.g. Brennan and Charnetski, 2000; Kreutz, Bongard, Rohrmann, Hodapp, and Grebe, 2004). A smaller number of researchers have favoured a more direct route, arguing that the emotional responses caused by the effect of music on the limbic system cause direct changes in immune system functioning (see e.g. Abrams, 2001; Murrock, 2005). In reality, the precise mechanism by which such an effect may occur remains an empirical question. In the meantime, it is noteworthy that many studies support the contention of all the theorists, namely that music can improve immune system functioning (typically measured by levels of salivary immunoglobulin A, which is an indicator of the ability of the respiratory system to fight off infection) and therefore maintain good health (e.g. Brennan and Charnetski, 2000; Charnetski, Brennan, and Harrison, 1998; Goff, Pratt, and Madrigal, 1997; Hucklebridge, Lambert, Clow, Warburton, Evans, and Sherwood, 2000; Kuhn, 2002; McCraty, Atkinson, Rein, and Watkins, 1996; Núñez, Mañá,

Liñares, Riveiro, Balboa, Suárez-Quintanilla, Maracchi, Méndez, López, and Freire-Garabal, 2002; Rider, 1990; Rider and Achterberg, 1989; Rider and Weldin, 1990; Zachariae, Hansen, Andersen, Jinquan, Petersen, Simonsen, Zachariae, and Thestrup-Pedersen, 1994).

There is a clear need for future research that determines the reliability of the effect of music on immunity using a variety of music types and patient groups; how specifically the effect occurs; whether it can be produced through group therapy or requires one-to-one administration (since the effect may be based on the music producing relaxation or positive moods, and different types of music will be needed in order to achieve this in different listeners); the extent to which cognitive processes mediate any effects of music on immunity (Koelsch and Siebel, 2005); the extent to which any effects of music exist in isolation (since many studies employ music in conjunction with guided imagery or some other means of inducing relaxation); and the length of time for which any positive effect endures (particularly since Rider, Achterberg, Lawlis, Goven, Toledo, and Butler (1990) found that music could decrease symptomology when measures of the latter were taken both three and six weeks later). In the meantime, the apparent link between music listening and the functioning of the immune system may explain why currently unpublished data collected by one of our Ph.D. students, Shabbir Rana, identified a positive correlation between the number of hours per week spent listening to music and scores on the General Health Questionnaire, indicating that people who listen to a lot of music enjoy better health. It may similarly explain findings that involvement with cultural activities is associated positively with health (Beck, Cesario, Yousefi, and Enamoto, 2000; Konlaan, Bjorby, Bygren, Weissglas, Karlsson, and Widmark, 2000; Kreutz, Bongard, Rohrmann, Hodapp, and Grebe, 2004; Kuhn, 2002; Michalos, 2005; and Montello, 1995).

A second way in which the impact of music on stress has particularly stimulated research over recent years concerns the uses of lullabies with premature babies. Standley (2002; see also Standley's (1991a) overview) carried out a meta-analysis of 10 studies that had used lullabies to help premature and low birth weight infants in neonatal intensive care units (NICUs). As noted earlier, the larger the effect size so the more effective was the music. For example, an effect size of 1 means that the music condition led to scores that were one standard deviation more positive than those obtained in a control condition. Standley's analysis of the 10 studies showed that music could affect (with the effect size in parentheses) the number of days in hospital (0.50), weight gain (0.84), and behaviour state (0.73) (Caine, 1991); oxygen saturation (1.19) (Cassidy and Standley, 1995); heart rate (0.92), oxygen saturation (0.86), behaviour state (1.95), days in hospital (0.49), and weight gain (0.49) (Coleman, Pratt, Stoddard, Gerstmann, and Abel, 1997); oxygen saturation (0.70), behaviour state (1.26), and heart rate (0.46) (Collins and Kuck, 1991); oxygen saturation (1.05) and behaviour state (0.88) (Flowers, McCain, and Hilker, 1999); oxygen saturation (1.29) (Moore, Gladstone, and Standley, 1994); days in hospital (0.55) and weight gain (0.81) (Standley, 1998); non-nutrituve sucking rate (0.73) (Standley, 2000); feeding rate (0.87) (Standley, 1999); and oxygen saturation (1.03) (Standley and Moore, 1995).

As Standley (2002, p. 111) herself concludes, these 'results demonstrate that music therapy procedures provide significant benefits to premature infants that are consistent across the following diverse variables: the ... gestational age of the infant ... ; the decibel level of the music within a range of 55 to 80 dB; the mode of delivery (free field/earphones); and the birth weight of the infant. Additionally, results are consistent [and positive] across all variables measured.' Standley also notes that there are three fundamental methodologies that can be observed in these studies. The first method concerns the use of 20–30 minute periods of pre-recorded lullabies to induce calmness, increase oxygen saturation, or to increase language stimulation. The second method concerns the use of sung lullabies to sustain homeostasis with the goal of encouraging neurological development and tolerance of greater future stimulation. The third method involves using music to reinforce sucking with the goal of enhancing the baby's feeding ability. Note also that several other studies have been published in recent years concerning the uses of music with premature babies (e.g. Blumenfeld and Eisenfeld, 2006; Lai, Chen, Chang, Hsieh, Huang, and Chang, 2006), and the role of music during pregnancy and childbirth in general (see e.g. Browning, 2000, 2001; Chang and Chen, 2005; Liebman and MacLaren, 1991; Schwartz, 1997; Shiraishi, 1997; Sidorenko, 2000; and McKinney's (1990) review).

Before concluding our coverage of music and health we should also make two final points. First of all, even as little as 20 or 30 years ago, many would have been surprised by the effects of music on health described here. There is no *a priori* reason to assume that the medical benefits of music should necessarily be limited to those outlined above. Many of the effects described here are based on using contingent music as a reward for the patient demonstrating desired behaviours, or using calming and / or enjoyable music as a means of distraction and stress-reduction. It is possible to think of many health-related processes in addition to those addressed here that might also be improved by such processes. For instance, both Lai and Good (2005) and Tan (2004) showed that music can improve sleep quality, and Kimata (2003) showed that music can alleviate allergic responses. Second, it is nonetheless important not to get over-excited regarding the effects of music on health. Although music can lead to health gains that are extremely cost-effective, healthcare administrators and the like need to determine the costs and benefits of paying music therapists' salaries relative to other treatment approaches. Similarly, much more work is needed concerning the health benefits of music relative to, firstly, more conventional medical interventions (e.g. drugs), and secondly, other forms of alternative therapy such as humour (see e.g. Lehrner, Marwinski, Lehr, Johren, and Deecke, 2005; Mitchell, MacDonald, and Brodie, 2006; Parris and Smith, 2003; Robb, 2000; Szabo, Ainsworth, and Danks, 2005). In the meantime, the apparent relationship between music and health represents an area of rich promise for societies around the world.

6

Musical development and education

Every child is an artist. The problem is how to remain
an artist once he grows up
Pablo Picasso (1881–1973)

In some countries, such as in parts of Africa and South America, the idea of
going to a school or some other educational institution to 'learn music' seems
faintly ridiculous. In these societies music is a natural part of everyday life:
people sing, play, and dance from a very early age, and music accompanies
many aspects of work and leisure. What then are the purposes of art or music
education; and can they vary from society to society? Picasso's insightful
remark captures this essential paradox, as does Igor Stravinsky's comment that
'My music is best understood by children and animals'. People's musical development occurs naturally as they grow up in society, and yet this development
is also shaped by the educational contexts and institutions in which it takes
place. Furthermore, despite the apparent differences that exist in what different
cultures mean by 'music education' it seems that, even over extended periods
of time, societies have agreed with one another that it is important. For example,
Socrates stated as long ago as the fifth century BC that 'Musical training is a
more potent instrument than any other ... making the soul of him who is
rightly educated graceful, or of him who is ill-educated ungraceful.'

In this chapter we turn to the vast and interrelated topics of musical
development and education across the life span, both of which are the
subjects of ever-growing literatures of books, journals, and research theses.
Amongst the more prominent landmarks in the psychological literature are
the books by Hargreaves (1986), Deliège and Sloboda (1996), and McPherson
(2006). We shall make no attempt to undertake a comprehensive review:
instead, our approach will be from specifically the social psychological
perspective, and we will identify the unique insights that this approach

has to offer. This is likely to be fruitful because the widespread adoption of a social agenda has become very clear and explicit in developmental psychology and education. Developmental psychologists' conceptions of the process of development have changed radically over the last two or three decades, and we have argued elsewhere that it therefore makes sense to talk about the developmental social psychology of music and music education (Hargreaves, Marshall and North, 2003).

Butterworth (1992) suggested that the study of cognitive development has gone through three clear phases over this period. The first phase was dominated by Piagetian theory, in that the main interest was in the thinking of the individual child. The second phase was characterized by a focus on the interpersonal context of that thinking, with the effects of the immediate social milieu upon it. This arose from demonstrations by Bryant (1974) and others that the immediate context of Piagetian tasks has a strong influence upon children's performance on them. The same issue was central to demonstrations by Donaldson (1978) and others that the linguistic content of these tasks—of the way in which the questions were framed, and the expectations that this generated—led children to construct 'human sense' explanations of the task situations. The attribution of motives and intentions to the participants involved was shown to influence their performance, and this finding had broad educational implications, which went well beyond the explanation of logical thinking. The third phase rests on the view that the acquisition of knowledge can *only* be explained in terms of its physical and social context— that we must think in terms of *situated cognition*—and this is the predominant view that exists today. The 'social context' exists on several different levels, of course, and we saw in Chapter 1 for instance how researchers such as Doise (1986) have differentiated between four different levels.

This chapter is in two broad sections. In the first, we approach the literature on musical development by considering how the social perspective has influenced developmental psychology and education as a whole, and then go on to look at the impact on our view of musical development from infancy through to adulthood. This includes a consideration of four theoretical issues which are currently salient in the developmental psychology of music, namely the interaction between biological predispositions and the influence of the social context; the putative existence of stages in cognitive and artistic development; the domain-specificity or modularity of different aspects of learning; and the different considerations which apply to normative and expert development in music. We go on to comment on some of the main theoretical models of musical development, and to evaluate their usefulness from a social psychological point of view.

In the second part of the chapter we look at the field of music education, and at the formal and informal learning processes that take place within it. Our own 'globe' model of the opportunities available in music education provides a means of organizing this diverse field: the distinctions between activities that take place *inside* and *outside* musical and educational institutions, and the concept of musical identities, again prove to be useful. We go on to look at international variations in music educational practices and institutions, and in particular at the aims and objectives of different national systems and at the outcomes that they might promote. Finally, we consider the processes of learning and teaching themselves: how do different forms of informal and formal learning take place in different learning environments, and what parts are played by teachers and pupils in setting the music learning agenda?

6.1 Musical development

6.1.1 The socio-cultural perspective

The socio-cultural perspective has become the dominant approach in many areas of developmental and educational psychology, as we briefly explained above, and it is important to understand some of the origins and contemporary implications of this. In the next three sections we outline the pioneering contributions of Piaget and Vygotsky, two of the founding fathers of the discipline, and then go on to look at some more recent developments, and in particular at cultural-historical activity theory (CHAT), drawing on musical examples wherever this is possible.

6.1.1.1 Piaget and Vygotsky

In developmental psychology and education as a whole, the socio-cultural perspective has become the prevailing orthodoxy. Children are no longer seen as Piagetian 'mini-scientists', whose thinking develops through a common developmental sequence regardless of the specific cultural events, situations, and groups which they experience. The main originator of the socio-cultural approach was the Russian psychologist Lev Vygotsky, who died of tuberculosis in 1934 at the age of just 38, and whose major contribution to developmental psychology has only been recognized and developed in the West in recent decades. Vygotsky rejected the idea that 'the child is an adult in miniature', proposing instead that we start out as social beings: we interact with others, observing what they say and do, and gradually internalize those actions so that they become a part of our own thinking.

In this sense, the social environment—our parents, family members, peers, teachers, and so on—forms the basis of our own individual development: Vygotsky (1966, p. 37) suggested that 'the relations between the higher mental functions were at one time real relations among people'. He considered that individuals' development within a given culture was based on the use of signs, which served the function of communicating with other people; and that these signs, which are internal mental representations, could therefore be seen to have their origin in external social relationships. It follows that speech, which is the most powerful human sign system, was considered to be the central function of social relations; and that this social function could be seen as leading on to the vital role of speech in the development of behaviour and personality. The idea that 'we become ourselves through others' was formulated as a 'general genetic law of cultural development as follows: *any function in the child's cultural development appears on the stage twice, on two planes, first on the social plane and then on the psychological*, first among people as an *intermental category* and then within the child as an *intramental category*' (p. 40).

In one sense, this is the reverse of Piaget's view, in which individuals assimilate the social world around them to their own thinking: in contrast, Vygotsky's view is that social relationships actually determine individuals' thinking. Piaget and Vygotsky also had different views of the relationships between language, thought, and action. Piaget's view was essentially that language is a medium of representation through which thinking expresses itself, and which plays no major formative role. For Piaget, thinking derives from actions, so that actions and speech serve quite different functions. Vygotsky's view, on the other hand, was that language and actions (i.e. practical activity) converge in early childhood, and that this convergence represents the origins of practical and abstract intelligence.

Vygotsky proposed that the development of thought and speech are independent in very young children, such that thinking is 'preverbal', and language is correspondingly devoid of thought, such as in early crying or babbling. At around the age of two years, however, there is an important convergence in which prelinguistic thought and preintellectual language combine to give rise to a new form of behaviour involving verbal thought and rational speech. 'This crucial instant, when speech begins to serve intellect, and thoughts begin to be spoken, is indicated by two unmistakable objective symptoms: (1) the child's sudden, active curiosity about his words, his question about every new thing, "What is this?" and (2) the resulting rapid, saccadic increases in his vocabulary' (Vygotsky, 1986, p. 82). Between the ages of two and seven or so, speech then serves the functions of both monitoring and directing internal thought, as well as the external function of communicating with others.

Vygotsky's view that social and cultural networks are incorporated into the development of thought itself meant that the interactions between teacher and learner gain far more prominence than in Piagetian theory; and these are explained in terms of the *zone of proximal development* (ZPD): this is probably Vygotsky's best known concept, and has profound educational implications. Vygotsky defined the ZPD as the discrepancy between the child's actual level of performance on a task at a given point in time and his or her potential level of performance on that task given appropriate instruction. This is quite different from the Piagetian idea of self-paced activity because it places *the capacity to learn from instruction* at the heart of the theory of development. In the UK at least, there has been a corresponding clear shift in the 1980s and 1990s away from the emphasis on 'child-centred' and self-paced learning that predominated in the 1960s and 1970s, and it seems quite likely that these changes in pedagogical policy reflect the theoretical shift towards a greater emphasis upon the process of instruction.

This shift is also associated with a growth of research studies on how children learn from their peers, either in pairs or in larger groups, and on how they learn from teachers and other instructors. One important concept which has emerged in the latter context is that of *scaffolding*: David Wood, Jerome Bruner and others have investigated the details of the processes by which the teachers and learners work together in solving problems. In one widely-cited study, for example, Wood, Bruner and Ross (1976) observed individual 3 to 5-year-olds working together with their mothers on the task of building a ziggurat—a wooden pyramid made up of small pieces. Through the detailed observations of these pairs, they found that the mothers very clearly monitored the children's level of thinking in relation to the task, and modified their own behaviour accordingly so as to give the child the optimum chance of completing the task.

The mothers seemed to work with an 'implicit theory of the learner's acts', and modified their teaching strategies according to their children's behaviour. Wood, Bruner, and Ross identified five different tutorial functions with respect to this particular task, as well as five more general strategies, namely *recruiting attention, making the task limits manageable, maintaining direction, controlling frustration*, and *modelling the solution*. Choosing the appropriate strategies for the child's level of thinking, and building upon this, was termed 'contingent teaching', and the mothers were described as 'scaffolding' the course of the child's approach to the problem. Similarly, and in a more explicitly musical context, Adachi (1994) explored three possible roles of adults in adult–child musical duets, namely as 'transmitters of musical signs', as 'practice partners', and as 'co-players'. Furthermore, Byrne (2005) has described some specific ways in which the principle of scaffolding might be applied in the music classroom. For example, Byrne explains how musical improvisational ability, or instrumental technique, might be developed by means of what he called a 'pattern and echo' technique, in which the teacher sets up a pattern for the pupil to play back, and then gradually develops the complexity of the patterns provided according to the learner's level of ability. This is a good example of what Wood, Bruner, and Ross called 'contingent instruction', which skilful teachers can use to suit pupils' different paces of learning.

There is one interesting theoretical divergence between Piaget and Vygotsky in explaining how this kind of learning might take place. Piaget's view was that, unlike adult–child interactions, peer interactions between children constitute a negotiation between partners of equal status. Since he viewed many children as being 'egocentric' below the age of seven, any discussion and learning which gives rise to learning involves *conflict*, since one partner is forced to listen to the other's point of view; and it follows from this that conflict forms the basis of collaborative learning. This is quite the opposite of Vygotsky's point of view, since the idea of the ZPD is that *co-operative* interaction is precisely what leads to learning: learning takes place because of co-operation rather than conflict. Since a great deal of music-making is carried out as a part of social group activity, these ideas have an important bearing on the explanation of musical development, and we will return to this theme later in the chapter.

Even though Piaget himself was well aware of the importance of the socio-cultural context on learning, this has become one of several well-trodden lines of criticism of his theory, and some of its basic tenets are nowadays rejected. Perhaps the clearest consensus is that very few contemporary psychologists place the same emphasis as Piaget on the role of logical operations— the notion that thinking strives towards higher levels of logic, or scientific analysis—and this is particularly true for the explanation of development in an artistic domain such as music. Nevertheless, Piaget's thinking about the course of development has been adopted and refined by various subsequent theorists, some of whom have become known as neo-Piagetians, and whose theories propose alternative mechanisms in order to explain developmental change.

6.1.1.2 Post-Piagetian and Vygotskian developments

This is not the place to elaborate upon post-Piagetian and post-Vygotskian developments, but we might briefly outline five key concepts that have been influential in the more recent socio-cultural literature. The first of these is *speed of processing*: Case (1985), for example, suggests that the speed with which people can extract information from their environment increases with age, so that children are slower than adults in this respect. In particular, children have more limited 'working memories', so that the complexity of the constructs with which they can deal is inevitably less than for older people. Similarly, we could say that the 'mental models' that children have of the world are less complex than those of adults (Halford, 1993). Both of these ideas concerning working memories and mental models constitute different explanations of some of the same age-related changes that were observed by Piaget. Whereas Piaget explained them in terms of the development of logical structures, Case, Halford and others concentrated upon ways in which the development of speed of processing and mental models in children gradually enable them to hold an increasing number of relationships simultaneously in mind. The relevance of these ideas to musical development can be seen readily in the extensive literature on the development of musical expertize (see e.g. Sloboda (1991b), and section 6.1.5 of this Chapter). For example, it is well established in this field that good sight-readers are better able than poor sight-readers to spot recognizable patterns or 'chunks' in the musical score, and that this enables them to process the information contained in the score at a much faster rate.

The second key concept that forms an important part of current thinking is that of *modularity*. Whereas Piaget's view was that developmental stages herald *global* aspects of change that encompass all aspects of knowledge and experience, a more common recent view is that different aspects of knowledge develop at different speeds, and in different ways, because of the diverse cultural environments in which this occurs. Children's developing knowledge of language, for example, may follow a different path from their developing musical knowledge, which may in turn differ from their emerging social knowledge, and so on: in other words, development is probably more 'modular', or domain-specific, than Piaget suggested, so that age-related changes in music may be unrelated to those in other domains. This issue is discussed in more depth in section 6.1.4.

One prominent neo-Piagetian theorist, Karmiloff-Smith (1992), argued that explanations of development should go 'beyond modularity'. She claimed that innate mechanisms governing development do exist, such as the natural capacity to extract regularities and patterns in language: because of this emphasis, she agreed with Piaget that language and cognition do interact in some way, and that neither are wholly independent nor completely modular. In other words, Karmiloff-Smith seemed to propose a compromise between the Piagetian 'global' view on the one hand, in which developments in one domain are seen as functionally related to those in others, and the 'domain-specific' view of Howard Gardner and others (see section 6.1.4 below), according to which they are independent. Wood (1998) summarized this complex issue by supporting the 'compromise' view that it may be possible to eventually produce a theoretical synthesis which on the one hand acknowledges the modularity of mind, thereby taking account of the importance of the social context, but which is simultaneously able to incorporate the idea that interrelationships and interactions do occur between different symbol systems.

This new interest in situated cognition has given rise to more detailed investigations of the interactions between teacher and learner, and the third of our influential theoretical ideas has emerged as a development of the idea of scaffolding, which we discussed earlier. Rogoff (1990) has suggested that *guided participation* may be a useful and general way of describing teaching and learning. Guided participation displays four main characteristics. First, that tutors act as a link, or bridge between the knowledge and understanding of the learner and the demands of the task; second, that tutors provide an overall structure or context in which the learner is encouraged to seek a solution, rather than losing sight of the goal of the activity; third, that guided problem-solving enables learners to take an active, participatory role in problem-solving; and fourth, that as learning progresses, the responsibility for it gradually transfers from the teacher to the learner. Whilst consistent with the Vygotskian approach, Rogoff's view goes beyond the notion of the ZPD by emphasizing that children take an active part in their own socialization. They do not simply learn existing rules from adults and peers, but actively seek out and structure the assistance of those around them in learning how to solve new problems. In this way, individual creativity is seen as occurring within the broader social community of thinkers: individual learning builds on the existing technology, knowledge, and experience that have been developed collectively.

This idea is the basis of our fourth key concept: Rogoff (2003) suggested that these *communities of practice* (i.e. the attitudes, skills, procedures, practices and 'ways of doing things' that have been developed by particular communities of thinkers) are essentially social and cultural in nature. This means that the arts, and particularly music, are specifically incorporated into this approach. Young (2005) demonstrated this point very clearly in her account of musical communication between adults and young children, in which she undertook a detailed analysis of the musical dialogue that took place in a play session between a community musician and a four-year-old child. Her description of the background to this session, and of the way in which it developed over time, enabled her to show how the processes of imitation, elaboration, and organization were all observable in this episode of shared musical play.

Rogoff's notion of guided participation has a lot in common with the fifth influential idea to follow from the increased interest in situated cognition, namely Lave and Wenger's (1991) notion of *legitimate peripheral participation*. This also refers to the process by which learners participate in communities of practice: individual learning is defined in terms of 'changing our ability to participate, to belong, to negotiate meaning. And this ability is configured socially with respect to practices, communities, and economies of meaning where it shapes our identities' (Wenger, 1998, p. 226). The development of expertize in a given field therefore requires learners to become full participants in the social and cultural practices of a given community. This does not mean that learning in a community of practice can only occur collectively: individual learning can also occur as part of a group undertaking. For example, Green's (2001) study of how young musicians learn to play in pop bands out of school revealed many of the processes of informal learning involved, and we shall look at some of these in more detail in section 6.2.3.1. One of the most important features of this learning is that it takes place in groups, rather than individually: this means that the individual members of the group were able to develop their own personal techniques and creativity by means of observations of and discussions with other members of the band—of their own particular community of practice.

Communities of practice are characterized in three main ways, which we will again illustrate using the example of aspiring rock stars such as those studied by Green. They share a *domain* of knowledge, which defines a set of issues (e.g. the current pop style or a band that the young musicians are trying to emulate); a *community* of people who care about this domain (e.g. the musicians' personal friends and peers, and perhaps, as their learning progresses, those who come to see them play); and the shared *practice* that they are developing to be effective in this domain (Wenger, McDermott and Snyder, 2002). A remarkably detailed account of the shared practices that were developed by one aspiring group of young pop musicians has been painstakingly compiled by Everett (2001), in his detailed analyses of the emerging compositional skills of a young group from Liverpool who were inspired by the British skiffle craze in 1956-7, and by American rock and roll. This group started life as a skiffle duo called the Black Jacks, and was formed in 1956 by John Lennon on guitar and vocals with his friend Pete Shotton on washboard played with thimbles. The band was soon to become The Quarry Men, to add further talented young musicians, and the rest is history: we shall simply add that Everett's documentary and music theoretical analyses of Lennon and McCartney's earliest compositions leave no stone unturned in documenting the shared practices which they first developed, and which were to have such a resounding influence on the history of popular music and culture.

Margaret Barrett (2005) has developed the idea of children's communities of musical practice, particularly in relation to young children's music-making. She draws in particular on studies of children's playground chants and musical games (e.g. Harwood, 1998; Marsh and Young, 2006) to show how peers can have a powerful influence as 'pedagogues' in musical learning and development. Campbell's (2002) extensive cross-cultural studies of various musical cultures also illustrate the wide variety of communities of children's musical practice, and show how these practices fulfil various different psychological, social, and cultural functions.

6.1.1.3 Cultural-historical activity theory

Three central concepts in Vygotsky's theory, as we saw at the start of section 6.1.1.1, are actions, language, and social settings, and his view of the first of these has provided the basis of another strand of socio-cultural theory which has developed rapidly over the last decade or two, and which has been applied to areas as diverse as human–computer interaction, and teacher training. At the heart of the theory was the idea that when people encounter an object in their environment, they act upon and interpret it through the mediation of 'cultural tools'. Cultural tools can be either internal (e.g. symbolic systems such as language, concepts, or scripts) or external (e.g. books or computers). For example, a preschooler might come across a rattle or a tambourine at her playgroup, and use it to beat out a regular rhythm for the other children to jump or dance to: the social activity which might ensue, and indeed its potential for the development of a symbolic system (e.g. naming different types of jumps or dances) is mediated by this 'cultural tool'. The concept of tool mediation means that we do not respond to an object directly, but with reference to the cultural norms that are involved in other people's use of those same tools: any further development of our preschooler's role as percussionist for her playgroup companions, for example, is likely to be shaped by their previous experiences and understanding of jumping or dancing games. This basic mediational model is shown in Figure 6.1.

The model shows that individual learning occurs via repeated social interactions with others, i.e. through joint activities with shared cultural tools. Vygotsky's view is thus extremely broad-ranging, and typical of Russian psychology in the sense that it seeks to explain the broad features of learning from a top-down, global perspective, rather than to deal with more specific learning issues from the 'bottom up'. Vygotsky's view of the cultural mediation of actions is considered by Engeström (2001) to be the first of three generations of research in what has become known as cultural-historical activity theory (CHAT), or more simply activity theory, which has become an important current formulation of the social-cultural approach.

The second generation of research was able to move beyond the analysis of actions of individual people to the collective analysis of groups, and this

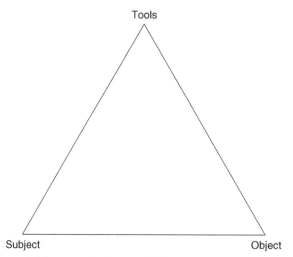

Figure 6.1 Vygotsky's basic mediational model

important distinction was developed by one of Vygotsky's two main collaborators, A.N. Leont'ev (1981). Whereas Vygotsky's original view was that individuals are active agents in their own development, and that activities are defined in terms of everyday life events and circumstances, Leont'ev's conception of individual activities as located within collective practice can be viewed as providing 'a means for relating social institutional and individual psychological phenomena' (Wertsch, 1985, p. 215). This leads to the concept of distributed cognition—the idea that individual learning is partly shaped by that of others via collective activity; and furthermore, that collective activity does not involve just those other people who are present at that moment in time, but includes also the history and the social and political relationships that exist in the whole community. To pursue our example above, the actual dancing games that are led by the emerging preschool percussionist in our fictional playgroup could easily incorporate elements of national nursery rhymes, folk songs, or songs heard on TV.

The third generation of research on activity theory involved the incorporation of conceptual tools to deal with dialogue and interactions within activity systems, i.e. with the ways in which people talk to one another and interact in social groups of any size. This approach has been developed by Yrjö Engeström and his associates (e.g. Engeström, 1987; Engeström and Miettinen, 1999), who have formulated an expanded view of activity systems, and of the ways they function and change. In activity theory, the activity system as a whole, rather than the individual, is the basic unit of analysis for understanding human learning and development: individuals' musical learning, for example, should be considered within the context of the musical activities of the groups of which they are part (e.g. their families, peer groups, school classes, community institutions). Figure 6.2 shows Engeström's view of an activity system. The top triangle is Vygotsky's original, as in Fig. 6.1. The *subject*(s) can be an individual or a group; the *object* is the 'object of study', or the domain of activity on which the subject acts. If we take the hypothetical example of a group of musicians in the Western classical tradition rehearsing a new piece for a concert performance, then the subject would be the group as a whole, and the object would be the piece of music to be performed. The object is linked to an *outcome*, in this case, a successful performance of the piece. As in Vygotsky's original model, the relationship between these two is mediated by the cultural tools involved (e.g. the score, the musical instruments).

Engeström's model adds three new components to Vygotsky's original. The *community* refers to the community of people who are also engaged in that activity: this could be a school music class or a group of professional musicians; or it could also be a much wider social or cultural group, such as an online group of music students from different universities. In the case of our example, the community could be defined as the audience present at the performance, the radio audience for a broadcast of the performance, or even the wider community of musical performers and listeners, all of whom might have an

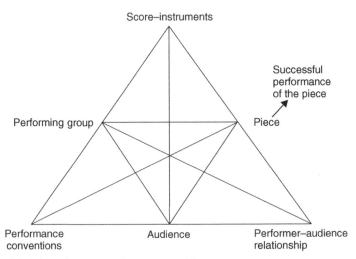

Figure 6.2 Rehearsing a new piece as an activity system

interest in or a view about that particular performance. This community is regulated by certain *rules*—the norms and values which shape the activity, and which may be explicit and formal or implicit and informal. In our example, these are the conventions regarding the performance itself, and the relationship with the audience (e.g. the piece is divided into three movements, which are divided by silent intervals; the audience, who remain silent, applaud only at the end of the whole performance). There is also a *division of labour* within that community, such that certain tasks are undertaken by some members of the community, and others by other members (e.g. the performers and the listeners in our hypothetical musical community).

It is important to reiterate that the basic unit of analysis here is the activity system, and not the individual: the individual's development and learning can only be understood in the context of the system as a whole. The causes of change and development in the individual occur as a result of the development of internal tensions and contradictions within the activity system, and Engeström introduced the notion of the 'expansive cycle' to explain how this happens. As novices begin to acquire competence and expertize with the domain of the object, so they begin to internalize some of its elements: once this has been established, innovations and changes introduced by the learner initiate expansion outwards, by a process of 'creative externalisation'.

If we adapt our example above to refer to the first rehearsal of a newly-formed school music group at the beginning of term ('the subject'), the members who have never previously played in groups could be described as novices with respect to ensemble playing, even though they may be reasonably competent on their instruments. As they begin to rehearse the piece they are playing, they begin to learn not only the piece itself (the 'object'), but also something about the abilities, attitudes, and musical personalities of their fellow group members. As they gradually get to know the piece, and adapt to each others' playing styles and idiosyncrasies, they begin to internalize some of the aspects of this 'domain' as a whole: after a while, they may begin to improve upon their ways of working together, and to introduce innovation and change ('expansion'). The expansive cycle refers to the developments and changes that occur in activity systems as a result of this opposition between internalisation and externalisation, and so the systems evolve.

Musical learning is an obvious domain in which these ideas could be applied; and although Burnard and Younker (forthcoming) have made a start on this by trying to explain children's collaborative creative music-making in terms of activity theory, virtually no empirical research has been carried out: this is an important task for further theoretical elaboration and empirical investigation.

6.1.2 **Biological predispositions and the social context**

Studies of infant socialization over the last two or three decades (e.g. Papoušek, 1996; Trehub, 2006) show that the very heart of development involves the interaction between the biological predispositions of both the infant and the caregiver, and the social environment. When mothers are observed with their newborns, they are seen to behave in ways that are biologically predetermined: they display this in their patterns of facial expression gaze, speech, and even in particular ways of holding the baby. At the same time, babies have been shown to take the lead in many early interactions—usually by means of crying or smiling—and mothers respond accordingly. Mothers construct meaning in the cries and smiles of their babies, who in turn gradually interpret the facial expressions and vocalisations of their mothers as having different meanings; and so increasingly complex patterns of interaction gradually develop which involve mutual constructions of meaning. This process, in which infants 'make sense of the world', represents the interaction between the biological and the social.

Trevarthen (1999) has proposed that these interactions are themselves inherently musical in character, and that what he calls 'communicative musicality' characterizes the behaviour of both infants and caregivers in these interactions. Investigations of talk, singing, and other rhythmic games with infants show that the general features of interactive or communicative musicality are displayed in the anticipatory movements and emotions that develop between infants and their caretakers. Furthermore, Trevarthen considers that music communicates with young babies because it connects with what he calls an 'intrinsic motive pulse', which is generated within the brain. This involves the ability to detect regularities in musical elements, sensitivity towards the acoustic elements of the qualities of the human voice, and the ability to perceive 'narrative' structures in vocal or musical performances.

Papoušek (1996) has also spoken of infant musicality in terms of the development of speech and communication, suggesting that 'speech, as a uniquely human form of communication, represents an unusually effective means of biological adaptation. It has allowed unprecedented possibilities in accumulation, integration and distribution of information, it has enabled the development of specific forms of culture, and it has provided opportunities to overcome biological constraints' (p. 38). If early musicality is an integral part of early speech and language, then these same biological considerations presumably apply.

Although newborn infants possess a fully developed innate capacity for crying, speech-related sounds are of course heard in the social and cultural environment, and so are partly learnt. The Papoušeks research has demonstrated that parents scaffold the infant's vocal behaviour so as to increase different kinds of vocal expertize, and that these vocalizations gradually start to acquire emotional meanings (Papoušek and Papoušek, 1982). Caregivers' infant-directed speech is different from their adult-directed speech in that it tends to be higher in pitch, and contains more sustained vowels, rhythmic regularities, and expanded pitch contours. Caregivers and infants can thus be seen as working together in constructing musical meanings from early vocalisations. Parents reinforce the musical aspects of these early vocalizations, and also sing songs and lullabies (Trehub, 2006). Gradually, vocal/musical play gives rise to speech and words on the one hand, and to more specific musical activities such as imitation or improvising on the other, so that singing develops a sphere of activity in its own right.

Trehub and her co-researchers (see e.g. Trehub, 2006; Trehub, Schellenberg and Hill, 1997) have been interested in the biological predispositions that infants bring to *listening*. Their extensive programme of research shows that infants are sensitive to melodic contour, to octaves, to simple frequency ratios, to rhythmic patterns, and to some aspects of harmony. Trehub suggests that these capacities, along with the richness of the musical environment and their strong interest in expressive performances qualify infants as 'musical connoisseurs'. Because these predispositions seem to occur in the absence of prolonged exposure to music, Trehub mounts a strong case for attributing these music processing skills to biological predispositions, arguing for early biologically-based perceptual preferences which are culture-general; although she also points out that there is evidence for culture-specific processing by as early as the age of 12 months or so (e.g. Hannon and Trehub, 2005).

6.1.3 Does musical and artistic development proceed in stages?

One central question about the nature of development has been whether it is *continuous*, with skills and knowledge increasing in a smooth, accumulative fashion with age, or whether it is *discontinuous*, proceeding in a series of qualitatively different steps. Piaget's stage theory, which is by far the best-known version of the latter view, is not now generally accepted in its original form, as we pointed out earlier, and there are probably three main reasons for this. In summary, these are (a) that doubts exist about the functional coherence of the stages; (b) that the acquisition of logical operations is probably not a common developmental goal, and alternative explanations might be more appropriate; and (c) that social and cultural diversity in cognitive development should be given much more weight (see section 6.1.1 above, and also Hargreaves, 1986, 1996). In this section we start with this general debate about the nature of development in general, and use that as the background to a discussion of development in the arts in general, and in music in particular.

We would like to suggest that the current consensus of opinion in the debate is that development has *multiple* endpoints: individuals build up a repertoire of behaviours whose heterogeneity precludes any idea of a general direction. Bamberger (2006) took this view further, suggesting that 'Musical development is enhanced by continuously evolving interactions among multiple organising constraints along with the disequilibrium and sensitivity to growing complexity that these entanglements entrain' (p. 71). In other words, she is suggesting that there is no common goal or 'endpoint' of musical development which is reached by all, or even by most children. Various developing skills are constantly interacting with one another as children encounter different situations and have different experiences, such that development proceeds in several different directions all at once. Both of these views reject the traditional idea that age-related developmental stages exist in artistic and musical development. The most clear-cut stage theory is that of Parsons (1987), which is explicitly modelled on Kohlberg's Piagetian-style stage theory of moral development. Parsons' theory was based on the visual arts: he proposed that all children go through five stages of increasing cognitive sophistication, from 'favouritism', in which children simply take pleasure in art works with little cognitive discrimination, to 'autonomy', in which the artist is able to adopt a mature, reflective attitude towards the cultural value of particular works.

The criticisms of this theory follow the lines of the more general critique above. One instance of these is provided by Kindler and Darras (1997), who felt that the idea of linear development towards some common end state is inappropriate in the arts. The latter of course have many possible end states or 'goals', and are characterized by their very diversity. For example, the goal of one young painter may be to express particular moods, feelings or emotional states in his work, a second may want to tell an autobiographical story, and a third may be far more concerned about producing a realistic representation of the objects that he selects as his subjects. None of these three approaches is any better or worse than either of the other two: they are all equally valid artistic aims, and represent different artistic goals. Kindler and Darras also complain that other stage theories in the visual arts tend to over-concentrate on the development of visual realism, i.e. on the 'photographic' depiction of things as they actually appear, and on developments in childhood. They consequently fail to address the non-representational aims of some young artists, as well as further artistic developments in adolescence and adulthood.

A contrasting theoretical view is that of the 'symbol system' theorists, namely Howard Gardner and his colleagues, who have worked at Harvard

University's Project Zero over the last three or four decades. Gardner's view places the child's acquisition and use of symbols at the heart of development in general, and of artistic development in particular. Symbols are organized into different systems, which can either be *denotational* in the sense that they have a precise referential meaning, such as in number systems; or they can be *expressive*, such as in music or abstract art. Symbol systems in the domains of language, drama, drawing, music or indeed mathematics can draw on both of these types of symbol; and Gardner (1973) felt that one of the main tasks of developmental psychology should be to show how adult competences in these different symbol systems emerges from their origins in early childhood. His celebrated and well-known theories of 'multiple intelligences' could be seen as an important part of his own attempt to achieve that aim (see e.g. Gardner, 1983).

The acquisition of symbols was also a central part of Piaget's account of development in preschoolers, which formed part of his equally well-known stage theory of development, but Gardner (1973) departed from the Piagetian view by suggesting that there is no need to propose developmental stages for the arts because 'the groupings, groups and operations described by Piaget do not seem essential for mastery or understanding of human language, music, or plastic arts' (p. 45). Gardner's alternative view was that young children display a surprisingly high level of artistic competence and knowledge, which seems to occur without any direct intervention on the part of teachers or parents. This early precocity seems to be followed by a decline in middle childhood before a recovery in later childhood, such that development can be described as 'U-shaped' (Gardner and Winner, 1982). It is also worth pointing out that these precocious abilities tend to be more observable in perceptual or comprehension skills than necessarily in production skills, although the 'U-shaped curve' also occurs in certain aspects of artistic production, notably in children's drawing (see e.g. Gardner, 1989).

Gardner and his colleagues nevertheless allow that certain psychological structures can be discerned across different symbol systems, and that these may follow a developmental sequence. Wolf and Gardner (1981), for example, suggest that children pass through three 'waves of symbolisation'. They propose, in brief, that children move from 'enactive representation' in infancy, in which babies' internal symbols are based on physical actions such as sucking or touching the objects and toys around them; through 'mapping' at around the age of three years, in which symbols are developed in make-believe play and early drawings; through to 'digital mapping' at around the age of four years, which shows more precise correspondence between the child's symbols and the objects and events that are symbolized in the outside world. By the age of five or six years, children have become able to use cultural symbol systems such as musical notation or written language.

There seems to be little doubt that regular age-related changes in artistic behaviour do occur: older children are generally more advanced than younger ones in the ways they engage with the arts, and in their potential range of achievements, although the developmental route is by no means linear or clear-cut. This conclusion is also borne out by cross-cultural research on artistic development: Newton and Kantner's (1997) review, for example, shows that there were some similar age-related patterns of development among children in different societies. However, to return to the question in the title of this section, this does *not* imply that Piagetian-style developmental stages exist in the arts. Although there may indeed be regular age-related changes that may occur in different societies, and even across different art forms (see also sections 6.1.4 and 6.1.6), it does not follow that these derive from the generic processes of cognitive development that Piaget proposed. The socio-cultural perspective implies that any age-related developments that derive from cognitive change are shaped by the specific social and cultural contexts within which they occur, such that we cannot conclude that artistic development progresses via cognitive stages. It is interesting to note in passing that Vygotsky, whose approach is usually seen as being in direct opposition to that of Piaget in certain respects (see section 6.1.1.1), was also interested in the notion of developmental stages. This interest was developed subsequently by El'Konin (1971) in terms of the different activities that predominate in children at different age levels. These ideas are very different in nature from Piagetian-style changes in cognitive capacity, however.

6.1.4 Is musical development domain-specific?

Parsons' Piagetian-style stage theory of artistic development implies that the stages apply across all art forms, rather than in specific domains. Although he does not deal in any detail with domains other than visual art, Parsons' theory implies that generalized age-related changes occur in artistic thinking and that the effects of these can then be observed in visual art, in music, in drama, in writing, and so on. The 'symbol system' view, on the other hand, is based on the idea that developments which occur within particular symbol systems, or artistic domains, have no implications for those in any other domains, since they demand completely different skills and techniques, which are applied to specific sets of knowledge and materials.

The question then is whether artistic developments are or are not *domain-specific*, and our focus here is upon whether or not musical development has anything in common with that in the other arts. This is equivalent to the question of modularity, which was raised in section 6.1.1.2: are the different components of our developing cognitive systems inter-related, or independent of one another? The current consensus seems to be that development is much more diverse and culture-specific than Piaget proposed, such that most theorists would argue for some degree of modularity in development: levels of sophistication and attainment in some domains of knowledge may be much more advanced than those in others. This view is developed most clearly in Gardner's theory of multiple intelligences (see e.g. Gardner, 1983, 2003).

However, as we pointed out earlier, Karmiloff-Smith (1992) has argued that we must move *beyond* modularity, and that we must also acknowledge that developing systems of knowledge and skill do at least *interact* with one another, so that developmental regularities may indeed exist at a broader level of description. In the case of artistic development, it may be possible to reconcile a modular account, in which developments within each art form proceed independently, with the view that integration across different modular systems can and does occur, as exemplified by Wolf and Gardner's (1981) notion of 'waves of symbolisation'.

This concurs with the view that 'although medium-specific aspects of musical development clearly do exist, most notably at very high levels of skill and expertize, it is nevertheless possible to delineate general features of the course of artistic development which do exist across domains, and which do display regular changes with age' (Hargreaves, 1996, p. 153). There is no reason why a modular approach, which emphasizes social and cultural differences between individuals, should be incompatible with an acknowledgement of the interactions between different art forms, and the cross-modal generalities that exist. Wood (1998) makes this point when discussing theories of the development of intelligence more generally, concluding that 'There seems to be a general movement, then, which seeks to acknowledge the fact that minds do exhibit a modular structure (as many studies of infancy show) but that later development also involves more general, cross-modular integration and exploits the cognitive practices and sign systems made available by the culture in which development takes place' (p. 281).

This important theoretical question has obvious practical implications. Some arts educators argue that different arts subjects can be regarded as an integrated whole, and therefore work in music, writing and painting, for example, might be combined in projects in drama or video. On the other hand, proponents of discipline-based arts education (see Smith, 2000) argue that specialized skills should be developed in each of the artistic domains, so that there is no need to speak in terms of generalized aesthetic understanding. Although arts-specific skills clearly need to be taught as such, this does not necessarily seem to be incompatible with their integration within particular educational activities: it may well be possible to reconcile the two views.

6.1.5 Normative and expert development in music

'Development' in its widest sense refers to overall changes in the patterning of behaviour with age, and includes two quite distinct aspects; these might be termed enculturation (or acculturation) and training. Enculturation refers to age-related changes that occur spontaneously in a given culture, without any conscious effort or direction. In contrast, training gives rise to age-related changes that arise from conscious, directed intervention. Enculturation results in *normative* development—changes that happen naturally as children grow up in a given culture; whereas training results in what might be called specialist, or *expert* development. A good deal of developmental research has been carried out on normative development in music, investigating those advances in the ability to process pitch, tonality, rhythm, harmony and so on which occur without specific training (see e.g. Hargreaves, 1986). In recent years, however, there has been a growth of research on the development of specialist or expert musical skill, and on the environmental conditions which best promote it (see e.g. Parncutt and McPherson, 2002; Williamon, 2004; and also Chapter 2).

These two aspects of development may, however, have more in common than it seems. We have already encountered Trehub's notion of infants as 'musical connoisseurs', and Gardner's proposal that young children can display precocious musical abilities. Davidson (1994) pointed out that musically untrained children can display surprisingly sophisticated abilities given the appropriate conditions, and that musically untrained adults 'can solve musical problems at least at the level of undergraduate music students who have years of performance experience in their background' (p. 102). Sloboda (1991b) took this idea further in suggesting that it may be wrong to view expertize as something special and rare; a more appropriate view may be that 'becoming expert' in socially-defined ways is the process of connecting 'intrinsic expertize to the outside world so that it becomes manifest in particular types of behaviours in particular types of situations' (p. 245). In other words, we could say that every member of a culture is a musical expert, in particular as manifested in perceptual abilities, but that this expertize needs to be translated into the ability to sing or play: it is to these latter skills that the study of musical expertize has been largely directed.

The study of expert musical development has drawn on the cognitive psychology of skill learning rather than on developmental theory. Sloboda (1994) has suggested that four general conclusions can be drawn from this literature, namely that expert musical skills are dependent on the ability of the performer to detect pattern and structure in the material; that the level of skill exhibited depends much more on the amount of relevant practice undertaken than on any other factor; that skills tend to become automatic, or unconscious, as they are practised; and that they tend to be specific to certain domains of activity, and therefore not to be susceptible to transfer to others. We might add, in the light of more recent research on emotion and music (see e.g. Cook and Dibben, 2001), that the apprehension of pattern and structure in musical material is inextricably bound up with the expression of emotion via those structures.

Most research in this area has adopted one of two main methodological approaches. The first has been to make comparisons between experts and novices so as to illuminate some of the processes underlying complex activities such as composition and performance (see e.g. Ericsson and Smith, 1991), or jazz improvisation (see e.g. Hargreaves, Cork and Setton, 1992). The second has been to carry out biographical studies of high achievers in music, and several studies have undertaken detailed analyses of the environmental determinants of excellence in expert musicians. It is worth pointing out here that one important and distinctive part of this latter approach is the study of musical savants, such as Sloboda, Hermelin and O'Connor's (1985) studies of NP, and Adam Ockelford's more recent work with the precocious blind jazz pianist Derek Paravicini (see e.g. Ockelford, 2007; Ockelford and Pring, 2005).

The distinction between normative and expert musical development has important educational implications, since it parallels the distinction between specialist and generalist methods of music education. Specialist tuition (usually of instrumental skills) is typically carried out in conservatories and at specialist music schools, whereas generalist music education is that which all pupils encounter in their regular schooling. It would be a great mistake to make the obvious link between normative development and generalist music education on the one hand, and expert development and specialist music education on the other, however. The borderlines between these areas are blurring as a result of technological developments, as well as of changes in social attitudes towards different musical styles, particularly within the institutions in which they are taught. Furthermore, the importance of *informal* alongside *formal* music learning is receiving increasing recognition, and is arguably the most important single issue in music education today (see Hargreaves, Marshall and North, 2003; and section 6.2 of this chapter).

6.1.6 Theoretical models of musical development

Having set out the main theoretical issues involved in explaining musical development, we now move on to use the socio-cultural perspective to evaluate the main theoretical models that have been proposed. The first review of these models was attempted by one of us, with Marilyn Zimmerman, in the first edition of the *Handbook of Research on Music Teaching and Learning* (Hargreaves and Zimmerman, 1992). At that time we summarized the current state of play of developmental theories in terms of four identifiable shifts of opinion: these shifts were (a) away from the notion of universal developmental stages and towards greater diversity and domain specificity; (b) towards a search for universals in cognitive function (as in information-processing and computational approaches) rather than in cognitive structure; (c) towards increasing interest in symbolic representation; and (d) away from the view of development as 'unfolding', and towards a more Vygotskian emphasis on the role of the tutor or instructor.

We carried out a detailed review of three main theories, namely Swanwick and Tillman's (1986) 'spiral' model, Serafine's (1988) developmental view of 'music as cognition', and the symbol system approach, principally associated with Howard Gardner and his group; and evaluated the evidence for each of them. We also tried to assess the success of each theory in dealing with three critical questions, namely (a) does each theory deal with musical production, perception, performance and representation; (b) does each theory deal specifically with developmental progression; and (c) does each theory deal specifically with music? In the second edition of the *Handbook*, this review was updated and extended by Runfola and Swanwick (2002), who drew extensively on our original chapter. They outline their own views on the three theories identified in the original, with an extended account of subsequent empirical work on and theoretical critiques of the Swanwick and Tillman 'spiral' model; and also cast their net more widely to include Edwin Gordon's (1976, 1997) music learning theory, and the work of other theorists associated with the Harvard Project Zero group, in particular Lyle Davidson and Larry Scripp (e.g. Davidson and Scripp, 1989), and Jeanne Bamberger (1991). They also cite Hargreaves and Galton's (1992) more general descriptive model of the normative developmental changes that occur across different art forms.

Hargreaves and Galton's (1992) model was revised in certain respects by Hargreaves (1996), who described five age-related phases in artistic development, namely the *sensorimotor* (in which artistic expression takes the form of physical action sequences such as scribbling or vocal babbling), *figural* (in which children's representations in drawing or in singing convey the overall form or shape of the subject, but not its fine detail), *schematic* (in which figural representations acquire the beginnings of adult artistic conventions), *rule systems* (which employ fully-fledged artistic conventions), and *professional* phases (in which the artist can employ a variety of styles and conventions according to task demands, and remain independent of them). This broad description of age-related changes in artistic and musical development is generally accepted as providing a rough and ready map, drawn at a very broad level of generality, of development in these areas. It is 'rough and ready' in the sense that there is huge scope for individual variation within each developmental phase. Furthermore, a good deal of the empirical research on which such an account is based implicitly adopts the view that these age changes have their origins in cognitive maturation, which is often linked with the existence of Piagetian-style developmental stages. We outlined some of the problems of this view earlier, and indeed many contemporary developmental psychologists in the UK and elsewhere would reject stage-type theories for a number of different reasons (see e.g. Goswami, 2001).

This explains why we deliberately use the term *phase* rather than *stage*, in order to avoid the Piagetian connotations, including the implication of functional coherence within each phase, and perhaps also the associations with logical-scientific thinking, which are probably quite inappropriate in the arts. Another feature of Hargreaves' model is its implication that that cross-modular generalities can be made across different art forms, which are based on a detailed analysis of the empirical literature, though no attempt was made to propose any underlying theoretical mechanism (which is why we refer to the model as being descriptive rather than explanatory). This is not to say, of course, that domain-specific or intra-modular developments are not themselves important: but as we saw earlier in the chapter, current thinking is moving *beyond* the idea of strict modularity, such that the identification of cross-modal regularities is acceptable.

A socio-cultural perspective on musical development should presumably try to build social-cultural contexts into developmental descriptions such as this. Swanwick and Tillman's (1986) spiral model does go some way towards this by incorporating the distinction between of the 'personal' and 'social' poles of development. In brief, the spiral model consists of four age-related 'levels' or 'layers' of musical thinking, which are based on *materials, expression, form,* and *value* respectively: the model proposes that there is a developmental shift from an 'assimilatory, personal response to music' to 'accommodatory social sharing' on each of these four levels. This terminology indicates that the model is based on Piagetian theory, and therefore suffers from the same limitations of general stage theories that we reviewed earlier in this chapter: that is, the 'personal' and 'social' poles of development in the model refer to the nature of the child's activity rather than to the specific social contexts in which development occurs.

A similar distinction is also central to Schubert and McPherson's (2006) much more recent account of the development of emotion perception in music, which is also based on the notion of a developmental spiral. Schubert and McPherson propose 'that throughout childhood different forces work in parallel in a spiral like manner and that decoding information from music is a dynamic combination of one-to-one (veridical) connections and general (schematic) connections' (p. 193); and go on to specify the details of these connections at four different age levels. In the first level, for example, (infancy to two years), the veridical connections arise from babies' biological predisposition to respond to the emotional content of vocal signals, such as the expression of primary emotions like happiness, excitement, sadness, or surprise in the mother's voice: this is part of the evolutionary need for social bonding. The developing perception of emotion in response to music is also mediated by the absorption of cultural norms, however: more complex, secondary emotions such as embarrassment, guilt, envy, and pride arise from the experience of social situations in which infants begin to learn the rules and standards for evaluating their own behaviour, and that of others. The latter are what Schubert and McPherson call schematic connections; and these authors suggest that 'the mechanism for emotional detection by the infant is primarily, though not exclusively, schematic' (p. 199).

Lamont (1998, 1999) attempted to build social-cultural contexts into developmental descriptions by incorporating certain aspects of Bronfenbrenner's (1979) *ecological systems theory* into her developmental model of musical pitch representation in children. Bronfenbrenner's theory postulates four levels of system nested within each other: *micro*systems are the immediate settings of the child's life (e.g. families, peer groups, schools); the links between these form *meso*systems (such as the ways in which what happens at home affects what happens at school); *exo*systems are the broader settings which exert more indirect influence (e.g. parents; employment); and *macro*systems are those which exert their influence most indirectly (e.g. economic policies, social class institutions).

Lamont suggests that musical development can be seen as 'a constant and ongoing process of mediation between the social and cultural domain—which embodies the values of a particular culture and leads to particular kinds of activities—and the personal and individual domain, within which individuals' representations are formed' (p. 5). Lamont's model of the development of pitch perception then maps five developmental phases in the personal and individual domain on to four contexts in the social and cultural domain. 'Primitive capacities' are the basic auditory systems which infants bring to their perception of musical sounds, and are limited by innate constraints such as the limits of working memory and processing capacity; these are associated with 'early musical experiences' in the social and cultural domain. The development of a 'listening grammar', in the second phase, includes a basic sensitivity to differences between sounds, and an understanding of diatonic scale membership, and is seen as part of 'school music'. 'Figural understandings', in the third phase, involve the development of increasing sensitivity to tonal differentiation and to features of the tonal hierarchy, and are seen as part of 'musical activities'; and 'formal' and 'explicit understandings', in the fourth and fifth phases, are seen as part of 'formal training', culminating in the development of a wide range of strategies that can be used in different musical situations, and a metacognitive awareness of different musical forms and styles.

Lamont's model has a good deal in common with those of Swanwick and Tillman, and Hargreaves and Galton, and is able to say very little about any specific influences within the social and cultural domain. We are forced to conclude therefore that, in spite of these efforts, attempts to build specific social and cultural contexts into developmental phase/stage models are ultimately likely to fail because stage theories are essentially individual rather than social. Phase or stage models represent generalized descriptions of the ways in which individual children's thinking develops, and this generality precludes any specification of social circumstances and cultural contexts. This is one reason why Piaget's stage theory is rejected by many advocates of the socio-cultural approach. Although it is useful to know children's approximate capabilities at different ages, and although older children are demonstrably capable of performing at a higher level than younger ones in most respects, any explanation of development based on individual capabilities can only ever tell part of the story.

One effect of the prominence of the socio-cultural perspective in studies of development and education more generally has been a growth of interest in the self-perceptions of the learner and the teacher; at their perceptions of each other, and at the relationship between these. The concept of *identity*, of long-standing interest in sociology and other fields as well as in psychology, provides us with a vehicle for doing this. In the field of music, Hargreaves, Miell, and MacDonald (2002) have explored the notion of *musical identities* from this point of view in a book with that title. The book argues that people's developing musical identities have their origins in biological predispositions towards musicality, and that they are subsequently shaped by other people, groups, situations, and social institutions that they encounter as they develop in a particular culture.

This approach puts a new perspective on the explanation of musical development: not only does it represent a way in which socio-cultural factors might be built into the explanation of individual development, but it may also start to explain how individuals' views of themselves can actually determine their motivation and subsequent performance in a domain such as music. It holds out the promise of explaining musical development 'from the inside' by trying to understand how individuals perceive and conceptualize their own musical development, which might itself be important in shaping that development. As we saw in Chapters 2 and 4, the concept of musical identity has the potential to enable us to make significant advances in the developmental social psychological study of musical development.

6.2 Music education

When discussing musical identity in Chapter 2, we saw that different children have different ideas about what constitutes 'learning music' and being 'good at music' and that these in turn may be different to the ideas held by parents and teachers concerning what 'music education' and 'musical ability' may involve. One of the main reasons why pupils, teachers, and parents have different views of what it is to be 'good at music' is that this encompasses an increasingly diverse range of skills and abilities, and music educators need to be able to take this diversity on board. Partly as a result of rapid social and technological change, music education is changing very quickly in the UK, as in many other countries. Informal music-making and listening, which usually takes place outside school, is becoming seen as just as important as the formal music-making that takes place in schools, universities and conservatories, for example. One consequence of this is that some of the traditional distinctions at the heart of curricula and systems in music education for many years are being rethought. These include the distinction between 'specialist', and 'general' or 'curriculum' music at school; that between institutional and community music-making; and even that between the teacher and the learner of music.

In England, the Government's *Music Manifesto* (DfES, 2004) follows this view by adopting a much broader and more 'joined-up' perspective on music education than has traditionally been held. It is based on the idea that music is something to be participated in by everyone, and across the lifespan. It should no longer be the specialized territory of a small number of experts or professionals with highly specialized and cultivated skills, but something accessible to all. The implication is that we need to *apply* educational thinking to those areas of life in which music occurs: in studios, in therapeutic and clinical settings, in communities, in the media, and in orchestras and commercial businesses. By doing so, music educators can capitalize on the power of music to promote the emotional, social, and cognitive development of pupils of all ages.

First, we consider the *contexts* of music education. For example, what should be taught and learnt at school; how might that relate to what is taught and learnt out of school; what is the modern-day role of institutions such as conservatories, universities, and community organizations; and how are these questions answered in different countries? This last question gives us an important global perspective on all of these issues, and so we directly address the question of international variations. We also use the international perspective in the second section, which deals with the *aims and objectives* of music education. For example, how important is instrumental tuition; what constitutes being a musician in the digital era; and do the benefits extend beyond musical learning? Finally, in the third section we consider the processes of *learning and teaching* in music: how much of music is self-taught rather than learnt from others; how do contexts influence the nature of and the ways in which we learn; and what is the role of music teachers?

6.2.1 Contexts of music education

We said in the introduction to this chapter that its central focus is on the social and cultural contexts of musical development and learning, and we concentrate next on contexts at institutional and cultural levels. These also exert their influence at the individual and interpersonal levels, however, and we deal with the latter in more depth in section 6.2.3.

6.2.1.1 A globe model of opportunities in music education

We start with one of two theoretical models that were developed by one of us as part of the work of the Music Development Task Group of the Qualifications and Curriculum Authority, the body responsible for music education policy in schools in England. One of their concerns is to ensure that school music should forge important links between the home, the school, and the wider world, and that it should develop pupils' ability to listen and appreciate a wide variety of music and to make judgements about musical quality (QCA, 2002).

This 'globe' model summarizes the wide range of *opportunities* available to pupils within music education, conceived as widely as possible. It is shown in Figure 6.3, and is organized around three bipolar dimensions. The vertical dimension distinguishes between formal, institutional contexts that lead to qualifications and careers (the 'northern hemisphere' of the model), and informal ones, which do not. The horizontal dimension distinguishes between statutory and elective provision: the 'western hemisphere' includes in-school music provision in all its forms, and the 'eastern hemisphere' includes all of those opportunities that are optional, voluntary, and self-selected by pupils. One important implication of the model is that the 'northern and southern hemispheres' should receive equal status and attention, since music education in many countries has a traditional focus on formal provision, and on the 'north-eastern' quadrant in particular. The third dimension, 'specialist-generalist', derives from an earlier model of teaching methods in music education (Hargreaves, 1996), and shows that opportunities at both of these levels exist in all four quadrants. The model shows that 'formal-informal' cannot be equated with 'specialist-generalist'; very high levels of specialist performance can be found in 'informal' musical activities.

The 'north-eastern' quadrant refers to the traditional 'specialist musician' route, usually involving instrumental grade examinations, ensembles and orchestras provided by local education and music agencies, which can lead on to the conservatory, and to careers in professional music. The 'generalist' sector of this quadrant includes opportunities in music-related fields such as in sound recording, or music technology.

Figure 6.3 shows that the 'generalist' sector of the model's 'south-eastern' quadrant incorporates what has been called the 'third environment' (see Heath, 2001); this refers to those contexts in which musical learning takes place in the absence of parents or teachers. These could include off-site locations such as playgrounds, garages, youth clubs, or the street, i.e. those places which are neither at school nor at home: but the third environment

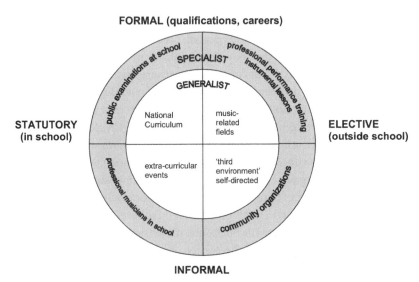

Figure 6.3 A 'globe' model of opportunities in music education (from Hargreaves, Marshall and North, 2003)

could also include one's bedroom, or even a school classroom, *given the absence of any formal activity or adult supervision*, and this latter point is the critical defining feature of the 'third environment'. The 'specialist' sector of this quadrant includes community organizations in which these skills can be developed to 'specialist' levels without formal qualifications, such as in local choirs, or the brass bands of northern England.

The model's 'north-western' quadrant includes the different kinds of provision that take place in schools: in England, for which this model was developed, this largely refers to the National Curriculum, which has determined provision up to the age of 16 since it was introduced in 1988. Music is a statutory part of this curriculum up to the age of 16, although no formal assessment is involved. The specialist sector of this quadrant refers to those pupils who go on to take public examinations in music: they enter for the Advanced level of the General Certificate of Secondary Education, usually at age 18. Different forms and levels of such examinations exist in other countries, of course. Finally the 'south-western' quadrant of the model includes the informal music education provision that is available in schools. This includes extra-curricular activities such as school concerts and plays at the 'generalist' level, and 'specialist' activities such as composer-in-residence schemes, or other contact with professional musicians.

6.2.1.2 International variations

There are striking differences between the contexts, aims and objectives, and processes of teaching and learning of different countries, so that international comparisons are valuable in our attempt to characterize music education in the new millennium. Both Campbell (2006) and Walker (2006) have addressed some important conceptual issues involved in making international comparisons within music education. Campbell explores 'global practices' of children's learning of music, pointing out the existence of similarities between the ways in which this occurs across all cultures, even though the specific cultural values and practices of local homes, families and communities form its basis. Walker stresses the importance of specific cultural traditions, citing Merriam's (1997) view that music is considered by ethnomusicologists to be one of the most stable elements of culture, and suggesting that 'music is one of the most important elements through which a child maintains a stable cultural identity, even when cultural traditions and associated life-styles have all but disappeared' (p. 439).

We undertook a large-scale comparative review of 15 different countries from around the world (Hargreaves and North, 2001) by asking eminent music educators in each country to review three main aspects of their national provision, namely 'aims and objectives', 'contents and methods', and 'student issues'. Although this provision varied widely, it was nevertheless possible to identify several issues of common concern, in particular (a) the tension between the Western classical tradition, Western pop music, and traditional local musics; (b) the role of general and specialist provision in the curriculum; (c) the aims and objectives of music education; and (d) the question of music learning in and out of school. The last two of these issues are dealt with in sections 6.2.2, 6.2.2.1 and 6.2.3.1.

The countries covered by our review varied considerably in physical and demographic characteristics such as geographical size, cultural diversity, population, and economic wealth. China incorporates 56 nationalities with numerous different languages, for example, and India includes a vast range of political, cultural, and musical traditions: both countries represent centuries of philosophical tradition concerning questions of moral and personal development and education which inevitably bear on their views of the arts and the role of arts education. Recent technological developments mean that Western (largely Anglo-American) pop music is available to an increasingly large proportion of the world's population, and this is having a powerful effect not only on people's musical experience and consumption, but also upon more general aspects of popular culture, including leisure interests, clothing styles, and social attitudes.

In China, the world's most populated country, Western pop culture appears as yet to have had relatively little impact upon music education. The tradition and predominance of Confucian philosophy emphasizes the role of music and the arts in promoting virtuous, moral living, yet this exists alongside a very strong and professional tradition of Western-style conservatory musical training, with all of the individual competitiveness that this involves. Similar tensions exist on the Indian and African continents. Farrell (2001) pointed out that a wide range of classical, popular, folk, and religious musical traditions co-exist in India, such that India is 'at the crossroads' as far as the resolution of these diverse and sometimes conflicting influences is concerned. Primos' (2001) account of music education in South Africa revealed a similar tension between the Western classical tradition, which has been a prominent influence in the past, African music, and the influx of pop culture.

The same tension also exists in more technological societies such as Japan, in which there is a long-standing tradition of promoting Japanese traditional music. Murao and Wilkins (2001) described some of the ways in which the Japanese Ministry of Education, Science, Sports and Culture is trying to deal with this issue within the education system. These include conscious attempts to 'fuse' Eastern and Western musical styles by composers writing music for children's use in the classroom, and the statutory requirement for school music teachers to teach Japanese traditional music and learn a traditional instrument.

The second issue of common international concern stems from the distinction between 'general' and 'specialist' music education. Most countries offer both of these, but vary in the ways in which each is provided in and out of school, and in the balance that is struck between them. Specialist music education is typically offered as an elective subject at the higher age levels of different school systems, and pupils intending to go on to a career in music typically seek additional tuition outside the school alongside that they receive within it. General music is typically offered at the lower age levels, and is usually taught either by specialist musicians or by general class teachers with extra training in general music; and the issue of which of these types of teacher is best qualified to do so can be a controversial issue.

In many countries, 'specialist' music education involves largely Western classical music, and this may explain some of the tensions described above. A very clear and detrimental example of this is in Poland, where Jankowski and Miklaszewski (2001) identified two distinct systems of general and specialist music education. The former involves conventional skills such as the development of ear training, performance skills, and reading notation, as well as some creative work, and the latter involves preparation for very high levels of formal achievement in the Western classical tradition. Jankowski and Miklaszewski suggested that the system as a whole fails on both counts. The aims of general music education are over-ambitious, given the resources available, and this results in a failure to equip many pupils with basic levels of musical skill. Similarly, the aims of specialist music education are so ambitious that many young aspiring musicians experience high levels of stress, and drop out of the system.

6.2.1.3 Learning music inside and outside school

The balance between musical learning in and out of school varies widely across different countries. In many parts of South America and Africa, for example, music is an integral part of everyday life: it is a natural part of work, play, rituals, ceremonies, religious and family occasions. Oliveira (2001), for example, describes the rich, multicultural musical heritage of the South American continent, and explains that a good deal of this is passed on from generation to generation informally rather than via school settings. The *bossa nova*, *tropicalia*, *marcho-rancho* and other distinctively South American styles are learnt in games and plays in families, inner city locations, bars, night clubs, and on beaches, rather than in school.

In countries where the provision of school music is relatively scarce, informal music-making assumes prominence, but in the UK there is a very clear divergence between music inside and outside school, particularly at the secondary school level. In the decade or so leading up to the millennium, official evidence such as examination entry statistics and school inspection reports, as well as large-scale independent research studies (e.g. Harland, Kinder, and Lord et al., 2000; Ryan, Boulton, O'Neill and Sloboda, 2000) suggested that a good deal of lower secondary school music was unsuccessful, unimaginatively taught, and out of touch with pupils' interests; and there was a good deal of debate about the 'problem of secondary school music'. Ross (1995), for example, argued that music was one of the least popular subjects in secondary school because attempts to modernize the music curriculum had failed, and because music teachers were unable or unwilling to adapt to the new challenges created by the rapid increase in music-making out of school.

This led to concern within the music profession, as well as to changes within the government's education policy, culminating in the launch of its *Music Manifesto* in July 2004 (DfES, 2004). This recommended much greater integration between schools and others outside school, including broadcasters, conservatories, the music business, and musicians themselves. There are encouraging signs that the 'problem of school music' may be declining as a result: pupils' music-making in and out of school, as well as their enjoyment of it, seem to be on the increase in England at least. One study that provided support for this idea was carried out by one of us as part of a team commissioned by the Music Development Task Group of the Qualifications and Curriculum Authority in England (see Lamont, Hargreaves, Marshall and Tarrant, 2003). We administered a *Pupils' Music Questionnaire* to 758 girls and 721 boys aged between 8 and 14 years, carried out interviews with head teachers and teachers responsible for music in the same schools, and conducted focus group discussions with 134 of the same pupils.

The questionnaire results revealed that 67% of pupils overall reported enjoying their class music lessons. There was a general decline with age in this figure between primary and secondary pupils, and an interesting gender effect: whereas the girls' enjoyment ratings declined steadily with age, those for boys showed a slight increase from years 6 to 9. Looking in more detail at *why* pupils report enjoying class music lessons showed that playing musical instruments and singing were the most popular activities. Approximately 25% of pupils were learning a musical instrument at school, and of those who were not, approximately 40% said that they would like to. Furthermore, consistent with other studies cited in Chapter 4, when questioned about music out of school, virtually all pupils reported listening regularly, mostly to popular styles such as dance, rock, drum 'n' bass, and R&B; 14-year-olds reported listening for approximately 13 hours per week. But this level of interest outside school was not limited solely to *listening* to music. Over half of the sample reported creating or playing music outside school regularly, and for a significant length of time; of those who did not, almost half said that they would like to. Playing music outside school occurred in various places, with parents or siblings in the home, or in choirs and bands in the community. Three-quarters of pupils reported having at least one instrument at home: piano or keyboard and recorder were the most popular instruments, with guitar and violin close behind. Overall, 30% of pupils were learning to play an instrument outside school, and of those not doing so, 45% said they would like to.

Music outside school is provided by organizations based in the community in many countries. Some of these are provided by the state, such as the municipal music schools in Scandinavia, which take pupils of all ages and levels of ability, and which form an important part of the lives of local communities. These parallel the Japanese 'culture schools' (see Murao and Wilkins, 2001) and the German 'Volkshochschule' (see Gembris, 2001). Other community organizations are less formally organized: the *bandas* in Portugal, for example, are essentially local amateur groups, but can attain high standards of musicianship. Their members are drawn from across generations: men, women, boys and girls of all ages are part of a musical tradition that is passed from grandparents, to parents, to children (see Mota, 2001). Mota points out that the *bandas* enable many people to read and write music, play instruments, and take place in public events regardless of age, gender, or ability; these opportunities are not necessarily available in the school system.

6.2.2 Aims and objectives

'What are arts and music education for?' is the central question here, and our international review revealed two main underlying issues. The first is whether the development of musical experience and expertize is an end in itself, such that music education serves mainly to promote musical and artistic skills, or whether it should have broader personal and cultural aims. There are clear differences between Eastern and Western countries in this respect. Arts and music educators in countries including Korea, Japan and China, with a foundation in Confucian philosophy, place much greater emphasis on the moral and spiritual role of the arts than their Western counterparts; their primary aim is to develop the character of pupils. In Japan, for example, the emphasis is on 'educating students through music' rather than on 'teaching music to students' (Murao and Wilkins, 2001).

In the West, on the other hand, there is much more interest in the non-musical benefits of music education; and this is epitomized by the recent interest in the so-called 'transfer' effects of participation in the arts, in which their presence in the curriculum is partly justified in terms of their benefits for other aspects of learning such as reading, spatial skills, language learning, social and emotional development, and so on (see e.g. Hetland and Winner, 2000). As we saw in more detail in Chapter 2, perhaps the best-known example of this is in the research carried out since the mid-1990s on the so-called 'Mozart effect', originally stimulated by an article by Frances Rauscher and her colleagues in *Nature* (Rauscher, Shaw and Ky, 1993), which showed that a group of undergraduates who listened to 10 minutes of Mozart's music performed better on a spatial ability test than matched groups who received either relaxation instructions or silence. The Rauscher et al. original paper gave rise to a wealth of replication attempts and further research on the theme of the social and cognitive benefits of listening to and performing music, as well as stimulating a commercial industry of CDs and tapes based on the notion that 'classical music makes you smarter'. Although the idea that listening to music somehow 'makes you smarter' or raises IQ is a massive oversimplification and overgeneralization of the original scientific findings, and although questions have been raised about the possibility that such effects may be mediated by arousal and mood (see Schellenberg, 2006), there is nevertheless some clear evidence for the positive effects of listening to and performing music for certain spatial, verbal and social abilities under certain conditions.

The second main issue concerning aims and objectives is the extent to which music education should be teacher- or pupil-centred. The Indian guru-shishya system, for example, epitomizes the teacher-centred approach (see Farrell, 2001). In this system the pupil (literally) sits at the feet of the teacher (the guru), and learns the philosophy, traditions, and techniques of the music over many months and years. This contrasts sharply with the highly pupil-centred 'creativity' movements which predominate in Australia, in the UK, and in North and South America, and in which pupils' self-expression and originality are seen as far more important in the early stages of learning than technique or tradition.

The teacher-centred approach focuses on pupils adapting to the requirements of the teacher and to the musical culture, whereas the pupil-centred approach suggests that the curriculum should be adapted to the level and specific needs of the child. These two broad approaches do seem to be associated with Eastern and Western approaches to music education respectively, although the division between the two is frequently blurred in the actual teaching methods adopted in different countries. Creative music-making is now encouraged in countries such as Poland, Korea, Japan, and China, for example, and composition and improvisation are encouraged in many different forms in many different musical cultures.

6.2.2.1 A model of the outcomes of music education

Figure 6.4 shows a conceptual model of the potential outcomes of music education, which has three main origins. It was developed along with the model of opportunities in music education (section 6.2.1.1) as part of the work of the Music Development Task Group of the Qualifications and Curriculum Authority in England and it also draws on our psychological analysis of the functions of music (Hargreaves and North, 1999b), and on our international review (Hargreaves and North, 2001). The model is based on a broad division between three main types of outcome, namely *musical-artistic*, *personal*, and *social-cultural* outcomes. All of these are 'personal' in the sense that they describe the effects of music learning on the individual, but the three-way typology affords more detail, and also enables us to specify interactions or overlaps between these three main aspects.

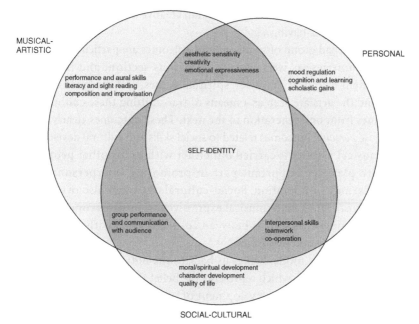

Figure 6.4 The potential outcomes of music education (from Hargreaves, Marshall and North, 2003)

Musical skills such as performance, sight-reading, singing, ear training, literacy, and composition and improvisation are the basis of specialist conservatory training, and also form part of the early stages of musical training in many countries. These are closely associated with broader *musical-artistic* skills such as emotional expression in performance, musicological understanding, aesthetic appreciation and discrimination, and creativity in improvisation and composition, and these latter skills are shown in the intersection between 'musical-artistic' and 'personal' in the model.

The *personal* outcomes of music education are of two main types in the model. The first relates to cognition, learning and scholastic gains: this is exemplified by the literature on the 'transfer effects' of music (see previous section and Chapter 2), which seeks to demonstrate that musical and artistic learning promote development in these wider domains. The second type concerns emotional development; our analysis of the functions of music for individuals suggests that the regulation of moods and emotional states is an important component. We referred earlier to the Japanese emphasis on 'educating the student through music' rather than on 'teaching music to students', and this reflects a clear emphasis on personal outcomes. The aims of the national curriculum framework for the arts in Australia have a similar emphasis on a holistic view of the 'core goals' of arts education, which include the promotion of confident self-expression, creative and innovative thinking, being involved, and 'having a go'.

The third broad group of *social-cultural* outcomes are particularly prized in Eastern countries, as we saw in the previous section, and include the development of moral character, spiritual values, and the 'quality of life': music and the arts are seen as a means of transmitting these cultural ideals and values from one generation to the next. These outcomes clearly overlap with those *personal* outcomes related to social skills and cultural development. Most musical activity is carried out either with or for other people, and therefore plays an important part in promoting interpersonal skills, teamwork, and co-operation. Social-cultural outcomes also overlap with *musical-artistic* ones, since musical expressiveness involves communication with the audience, as well as between co-performers within a group, or between composer and performer.

The centre of the model brings us back to the notion of identity that we explored in Chapter 2, which represents the belief that the ultimate outcome of music education is the development of individual self-identity. In this sense, the model represents a mapping of the different aims and objectives of music education, as well as of the ways in which these might be internalized within the individual.

6.2.3 Learning and teaching

We looked in section 6.2.1 at the contexts of music education, identifying the school, home, and the 'third environment' as the main domains likely to shape the nature of music learning. The model of opportunities presented in 6.2.1.1 is based on the interaction between the school-centredness of these contexts and with their level of formality: we define formal and informal learning situations as those that either do or do not lead to qualifications and careers. The model also incorporates the interactions between these two distinctions, and the level of specialization at which the musical activities take place. The co-existence of these three dimensions in the model means that they are conceived as being independent of one another; formal and informal music learning can take place, at generalist or specialized levels, in school-based as well as out of school contexts.

It is also worth pointing out here that Campbell (2006) makes a further distinction between one type of informal learning which is 'only partly guided, occurring outside institutionalized settings through the prompting of non-consecutive directives, frequently by expert musicians to novices', and another type of informal learning which is 'enculturative, occurring naturally, non-consciously, and without direct instructional activity of any sort' (p. 416). The power and importance of this latter form of natural informal learning, which Campbell suggests may form the beginnings of an 'ethnomusicology of children', is demonstrated vividly in some ingenious studies by Mito (2004, 2007). Given the increasing body of evidence that young people are involved deeply in music listening in everyday life, and that pop music plays a central role in their lifestyles (see section 6.2.1.3), Mito investigated the role of daily musical activities in the acquisition of musical skill.

Mito's doctoral thesis included observational and experimental studies, typified by Mito (2004). This observational study compared the performances of three groups of participants on a task involving the memorization of a contemporary Japanese pop ('J-pop') song over four repeated trials. Two of the groups had received formal musical training; and of those, one group listened regularly to pop music (the 'pop-immersed musicians'), while the other group did not (the 'non-immersed musicians'). The third group (the 'non-musicians') were undergraduates with no formal musical training, but who all listened regularly to pop music. Mito's results showed very clearly that the non-musicians performed at the highest level on all four trials, that the pop-immersed musicians had an intermediate level of performance, and that the non-immersed musicians had the lowest level of performance on the memory task. This result is completely counter-intuitive, showing as it does that non-musicians can outperform musicians on a musical task. Mito suggests that this is probably because J-pop songs have complex rhythmic structures which are not easily notated: the musicians' self-reported tendency to mentally transform the song into notation before trying to memorize it actually depressed rather than enhanced their performance. Mito's result confirms that the distinction between formal and informal modes of music learning may be as important as that between formal and informal learning situations, and we consider the former in more detail in the next section.

6.2.3.1 Formal and informal learning

We start by trying to identify the main features of the distinction between formal and informal learning, drawing on earlier attempts by Folkestad (2005, 2006), Green (2005a), and Hargreaves and Marshall (2003), and can identify four main dimensions. The first, which we have already covered, refers to the *contexts* of learning. Our own interest has been in differences between home, school, and the 'third environment', and Folkestad referred to this dimension as the 'situation'. The second dimension, which is perhaps the crucial defining feature of the distinction between formal and informal learning, is *autonomy and ownership*. School music usually involves the teacher's control of the curriculum, as well as of the direction of the activities taking place. Music out of school, on the other hand, is typically self-directed: the learners set their own agenda, adopt their own ways of working, and this often engenders high levels of motivation and commitment. Folkestad took this further by suggesting that ownership involves decisions about the 'what', 'how', 'where' and 'when' of musical activities.

The third dimension is what Folkestad (2005) called *learning style*. This is 'the nature and quality of the learning process' (p. 283), which is similar to the concept of 'working methods'. Several different aspects of learning styles/ working methods can be identified. Folkestad, for example, specified 'intentionality', which he saw as the explicit aim of the activity from the learner's point of view (e.g. learning a skill, or giving a performance). Green's (2005a) analysis specified four further features of the learning process that are helpful here. She pointed out that informal music learning typically (a) involves playing and copying recordings by ear, rather than working from notation or from spoken or written instructions; (b) takes place in groups rather than individually, such that peer learning occurs consciously and unconsciously through discussion, observation, and imitation; (c) proceeds in top-down rather than in bottom-up fashion, in the sense that learners usually work with real-world pieces of music in their own idiosyncratic ways, whereas formal music education typically involves a planned progression from simple to more complex skills and achievements; and (d) tends to involve the integration of listening, performing, improvising and composing activities, in the service of creativity, rather than their differentiation and increasing specialization, as in formal learning.

The fourth dimension, which we will term *learning content*, refers to the 'what' of music learning, and in particular, the focus on different styles and genres. As long ago as the late 1960s, Swanwick (1968) raised the issue of 'pop music in school', and attitudes towards it have changed markedly since then. As Folkestad (2005, p. 280) pointed out, 'popular music is already present in school, brought there by the students, and in many cases also by the teachers, as part of their musical experience and knowledge'. In spite of the inclusion of a wide range of musical styles in many music curricula around the world, the widespread adoption of a multicultural approach in many people's everyday music listening, and the acknowledgement of the importance of traditional local musics, school music is still nevertheless typically associated with 'serious' genres, most notably Western 'classical' music, whereas music out of school is typically associated with pop and rock. This was clearly spelt out in two of our own studies.

North, Hargreaves and O'Neill's (2000) survey of 2,465 British 13 to 14-year-olds showed that they perceived the benefits of playing and listening to pop music (including 'enjoyment', 'exercising creativity and imagination', 'relieving tension and stress') as being very different to those for classical music ('to please parents and teachers'). Similarly, Boal-Palheiros and Hargreaves' (2001) study of 9 to 10 and 13 to 14-year-old school pupils in the UK and Portugal found that they associated school music listening with motivation for learning, being active, and the content of particular lessons, but associated home music listening with enjoyment, emotional mood and social relationships. More generally, we saw in Chapter 4 that pop music plays a central role in the lifestyle of most teenagers, and indeed constitutes a 'badge of identity' for many of them, such that this constitutes another important aspect of informal learning.

The interrelationships between these four dimensions of formal and informal learning—*contexts, autonomy and ownership, learning style*, and *learning content*—determine the *authenticity* of secondary school music for pupils, and thereby its likely success. The challenge for school music teachers is somehow to be able to capitalize on the high levels of motivation and commitment that informal music learning can engender, but to do so within the school environment. Berkaak and Ruud (1994) carried out an ethnological study of the nature of informal learning within rock bands, and Green's (2001) study of how young musicians learn to play in pop bands out of school encouraged her to attempt to introduce the same informal learning methods inside school. The apparent success of her initial attempts to teach pop music in school using informal methods have even encouraged her to try to introduce classical music learning using the same methods (Green, 2005a, 2005b). The detailed results of this research are not yet available, and so it is too early to evaluate the effectiveness and wider applicability of this approach, but it may provide one very positive way forward in dealing with the 'problem of secondary school music'.

6.2.3.2 Teacher and pupil agendas of music learning

Many secondary school music teachers are the products of the Western classical tradition, which is based largely in the conservatoire, and this model still dominates a good deal of secondary school music. For example, an analysis of the qualifications of 74 postgraduate secondary music teaching students in the TIME (Teacher Identities in Music Education) project, representing approximately one-fifth of all such students in the UK at that time, showed that the overwhelming majority had advanced school examination passes in music (General Certificate of Education 'A level'), advanced classical performance qualifications (Associated Boards grade 8 instrumental or vocal qualifications), as well as an undergraduate music degree: very few came from non-classical backgrounds involving pop or jazz (Hargreaves, Welch, Purves and Marshall, 2003).

This background may be inappropriate for the demands of the contemporary secondary school classroom, however, as teachers trained in classical music may be relatively inexperienced in other genres. York's (2001) survey of 750 heads of secondary school music revealed that, although they had a good knowledge of mainstream Western classical music, of 'old' (more than 25 years) pop music, and of musicals and opera, their engagement with current pop music and modern jazz was 'patchy and in many cases inadequate' (p. 1). As part of his questionnaire, York provided 18 titles of well-known works chosen so as to represent a wide range of styles, including classical music from the baroque, classical and romantic periods, jazz, Broadway musicals, and various pop styles, and asked them to say whether they knew the work, and to name the 'composer or most associated performer' in each case. Whilst over 95% of the sample were predictably able to name the composers of *The Four Seasons*, *Eine Kleine Nachtmusik*, the *Ode to Joy* and *Mars* from *The Planets*, only 29.5% could name the composer of *Le Marteau sans Maître*, and only 15.0% could name Miles Davis as the composer of *Kind of Blue*, the best-selling and probably most widely-known jazz record of all time. Whilst over 90% said they knew *Jailhouse Rock*, *Hey Jude*, *Waterloo* and

Bohemian Rhapsody, however, only 13.1% had any familiarity with Fatboy Slim's dance music classic *The Rockafeller Skank*, and only 9.2% could name who performed it.

The primary focus of the TIME project was upon the developing identities of classroom music teachers, which is beyond our scope here; but it is important to realize that teachers' own musical preferences and identities inevitably influence their implicit views about music learning in their pupils. Teachers can obviously exert a powerful influence upon pupils' developing musical identities, and their own musical identities are formed within exactly the same social and educational contexts. In other words, the musical identities of teachers and pupils are interdependent, such that we cannot study the development of the latter in isolation.

Another of our own research projects looked directly at the issue of mutual teacher-pupil learning agendas in respect of the ownership of creative arts work in the primary classroom. In the Development of Learning and Teaching the Arts (DELTA) project, we investigated primary school teachers' assessments of their pupils' work in visual art, creative writing, and music (see e.g. Hargreaves, Galton and Robinson, 1996). As part of this, teachers and pupils answered open-ended questions about the aims of arts activities in school, and about what pupils learned from doing them (Hargreaves, Galton, Robinson and Windridge, 2002). Our analysis of the responses showed that, whereas teachers typically expressed the straightforward 'child-centred' view that the teacher's main role is to provide a supportive environment in which pupils can develop autonomously, some pupils expressed a more complex view which recognizes the implicit 'mutual agendas' which exist concerning the ownership of creative arts work in school, and which seem to be negotiated between teacher and pupil.

For example, in response to questions about what is learnt from doing arts activities, some pupils revealed the view that the teacher was the arbiter of quality (e.g. in creative writing): *'you take it to Mrs X (teacher) and she reads through it and tells you whether it is finished or not'*. However, others expressed the opposite view, indicating that they felt they had ownership themselves: *'I wouldn't want her to tell us what to do. If she wanted that she should do it herself, it wouldn't be ours'*. More generally, pupils seemed simultaneously to acknowledge that a piece of work could be their own, but that in a different sense they were also doing it for the teacher, who set the formal agenda. This perspective is expressed in some pupils' responses to questioning about their likely reactions to teachers asking them to change their work:

◆ *'I'd wish I was in her position. I'd wish she were me and I was her and I could tell her to do it again'*.

- *'She is cleverer than me, she is the teacher and I'm still a kid. She'd know better, but I thought that was good and I did change it a bit and if she still insults me I don't think it is nice, I would get quite cross'.*
- *'She has to tell us what to do. She is the teacher. But I wouldn't be very happy. It would make me feel like doing it ten times as good'.*
- *'If I had done my best, bad. If I hadn't tried, not bad'.*

These last two responses in particular reveal the subtlety and complexity of these children's views of the criteria of success in creative activities at school, of the implicit roles played out by pupils and teachers, and of their mutual perceptions of these roles: pupils' views of musical learning and achievement are no less detailed and insightful than those of teachers and parents. This is more likely to be the case in the creative arts than in any other subject area because there are no correct or incorrect solutions to most problems, and because the evaluation of different solutions is inevitably subjective. In a very real sense, the only person truly qualified to evaluate or assess a piece of work is the person who produced it; and in this respect pupils are of course more 'expert' than their teachers.

The other sense in which pupils are more expert than teachers is in their knowledge of current pop music, as we saw from York's (2001) survey. However, Green's encouraging results from her attempts to teach pop music in school using informal methods (see above) involve two paradoxes. The first was her observation that when teaching others, these young musicians tend to do so in traditional, formal ways: this first paradox probably results from the second, namely that as soon as teachers and other adults attempt to become involved in these activities, they cease to be part of the 'third environment', and may thereby lose their essential appeal. The relationship between teachers and pupils in these situations is a delicate one, and demands a good deal of mutual respect.

The musical identities of teachers and pupils are interdependent, as we pointed out earlier. Teachers and pupils are subject to largely the same social and cultural influences, and they have a mutual understanding of the school music learning agenda as a whole, but they nevertheless seem to adopt different implicit agendas and roles within it, as is shown by the DELTA project results above. Teachers seem to focus on the requirements of the curriculum, and to evaluate pupils' achievements in terms of general curriculum goals such as developing creative expression and aesthetic awareness; pupils recognize this, but simultaneously take account of other factors in the learning agenda, including what their teachers expect of them, and the expectations of parents and peers. Teachers and pupils negotiate the course of music learning within specific social contexts and implicit rule systems.

6.3 **Conclusion**

We can conclude this wide-ranging chapter by saying that the *contexts* of music-making and music listening are critical in determining the course of musical development and learning, as well as its authenticity for learners in music education. The developmental social psychology of music has already acknowledged this through the general adoption of a socio-cultural perspective, as we saw earlier; and music education is also beginning to do so in different ways. The social perspective requires us to evaluate different composers, pieces, and musical styles according to the discourses and aesthetic standards that apply in particular cultural contexts (see Frith, 1996; Walker, 1990), and the international perspective is particularly useful in this respect. Although many school music curricula have taken this multicultural perspective on board, there remains a powerful legacy of conceptual divisions: between 'classical' and 'popular', ethnic and Western, old and new, good and bad. This can still be seen in the associations that exist between music in and out of school, and classical and pop/rock respectively, in many pupils' minds. Evaluations of quality or 'seriousness' are still often linked, quite inappropriately, with particular genres or styles.

The social perspective enables us to gain a deeper understanding of the effects of the many ways in which the contexts of music learning are diversifying as the pace of globalization and technological development continues to increase. Music psychologists and educators are being forced to rethink the traditional distinctions between normative and expert development in music; between music in and out of school; between formal and informal music-making and learning; and even that between the teacher and the learner itself.

7

Concluding remarks

A conclusion is the place where you got tired of
thinking
Steven Wright

In mapping out the social and applied psychology of music, we suggest that
the 1980s paradigm for music psychology, based heavily within experimental
cognitive psychology, was able to provide answers about musical behaviour,
but also that it simply didn't always ask the right questions, often addressing
topics that bore little relationship to 'music' as it is experienced by most
people. As noted in Chapter 1, the rise of the social and applied psychology of
music can be linked to the digital revolution and the continuing dominance of
pop music in CD sales, radio station listening figures, and concert
attendances. The earlier paradigm makes sense if musical behaviour follows
the 'classical music model' in which middle-aged, well-educated people sit in
comfortable chairs while listening carefully to (or playing) compositions by
dead, white central European males: under these circumstances it becomes
acceptable, even desirable, to carry out research without reference to the
context of musical behaviour because the ways in which people are playing and
listening to the music are themselves largely de-contextualized. Indeed, the
whole point of the hallowed hush of the traditional concert hall, the detailed
obsequiousness of the announcer on a classical music radio station, or the
'armchair model' of music listening is to stress the central importance of the
music itself and remove all outside distractions and influences, such that full
attention is paid. The 1980s paradigm, driven by experimental cognitive
psychology and the notion of classical music as high art, asserted that music
exists on its own terms, and should be studied as such.

However, the 'baby boom' generation of the 1960s is now approaching
pensionable age. To most of them and to most members of subsequent
generations, 'music' is less about dead, white central Europeans, and more
about black African-Americans and other people from social housing projects
in their own country. Specifically, three of the major differences between

classical music and pop music are that the latter is aimed at a target market that is self-consciously youthful (at least in attitude if not always in chronology); that the music came to prominence at a time of rapid technological advancement that led to it being readily accessible; and that the audience places less emphasis on revering the music as high art and more on it as a 'friend' that supports them throughout their everyday life, so that pop is less like a god and more like a dog. This is not to say that pop music cannot lead to profound emotional experiences (see Chapter 3, for example), but that the youthful and less reverential nature of our relationship with it, together with increased access as a result of the digital revolution, means that the music is itself much more contextualized. The greater contextualization of music in the modern era, and particularly pop music, means that different questions become interesting and relevant to research: these contextualized questions almost inevitably *have to* address social influences on musical behaviour and the implications of musical behaviour for everyday life.

This theme of the contextualization and application of music and music psychology has emerged repeatedly throughout the course of this book. For example, how can we understand musical preference without also understanding the factors underlying radio airplay that dictate whether the great majority of the population will ever get to hear the song in question in the first place? How can we understand the role of music in subculture without studying the large numbers of young people who wear t-shirts depicting the covers of their favourite CDs? How can we say that music makes you 'feel good' without attempting to address the direct health-related implications of this? How can we understand musicianship without addressing how being able to play the guitar means that an adolescent boy can get a better-looking girlfriend? How can we understand music education without appreciating the broader musical and socio-political culture to which young people belong? The old paradigm for music psychology continues to use experimental cognitive psychology to address interesting questions concerning the details of how people process musical stimuli and demonstrate highly-skilled musical performance ability; and it can also provide the 'building blocks' on which contextualized and applied research is based. But it cannot in its own right adequately address many of the most apparent aspects of our everyday musical behaviour.

Make no mistake, this is not just a theoretical issue. Through its emphasis on experimental cognitive psychology and approach to classical music as 'high art', the old paradigm failed to point out the social, emotional, and financial value that music has to the general public going about their everyday lives. As such, when the 1980s saw the re-emergence of tight public spending controls and conservative morality, music psychology was unable to offer any counter to the arguments that music budgets should be cut, that musicians who failed to conform to conventional ideology should be censored, or that more generally music just didn't really *matter*. In contrast, the social and applied paradigm directly concerns why music *matters*.

Furthermore, although many of the topics of research that the social and applied paradigm leads to may be new to music psychology, they have been a concern to society for centuries. It is no coincidence that in each of the preceding chapters we have been able to include quotations from the ancient Greek philosophers. For example, in Chapter 2 we saw how Plato was well aware of the importance and methodological difficulties of studying creativity. In Chapter 3 we saw how Plato's and Aristotle's theories of aesthetics pre-empted Berlyne's influential work. In Chapter 4 we saw how Plato and Aristotle were concerned with the negative impact of music on social order. In Chapter 5 we saw that, although the ancient Greeks were not able to predict the rise of piped music in supermarkets, they were aware of the effects of music on physical labour and argued vociferously that music could promote psychological health and well-being. In Chapter 6, we saw how Socrates stressed the importance of music education for the good of the individual and of society. In other words, these issues have been of concern to society ever since the Roman Empire was founded, the Celts began arriving in the British Isles, and Carthage was the dominant economic power in Europe and northern Africa. It is surprising then that other topics dominated music psychology until only recently. But social psychological and applied issues are now at the heart of the discipline: we hope and believe that the social and applied psychology of music is well placed to put the case for the defence of music as a cherished object in twenty-first- century society.

References

Abel, J. L. and Larkin, K. T. (1990). Anticipation of performance among musicians: physiological arousal, confidence, and state anxiety. *Psychology of Music*, 18, 171–182.

Abeles, H. and Chung, J. W. (1996). Responses to music. In D. A. Hodges (ed.), *Handbook of music psychology* (2nd edn.) (pp. 285–342). San Antonio: IMR Press.

Abrams, A. (2001). Music, cancer, and immunity. *Clinical Journal of Oncology Nursing*, 5, 222–224.

Abrams, D. and Hogg, M. A. (1988). Comments on the motivational status of self–esteem in social identity and intergroup discrimination. *European Journal of Social Psychology*, 18, 317–334.

Achté, K., Fagerström, R., Pentikäinen, J., and Farberow, N. L. (1989–1990). Themes of death and violence in lullabies of different countries. Omega: *Journal of Death ad Dying*, 20, 193–204.

Adachi, M. (1994). The role of the adult in the child's early musical socialization: a Vygotskian perspective. *Quarterly Journal of Music Teaching and Learning*, 5, 26–35.

Adelaar, T., Chang, S., Lancendorfer, K. M., Byoungkwan-Lee, K. M., and Morimoto, M. (2003). Effects of media formats on emotions and impulse buying intent. *Journal of Information Technology*, 18, 247–266.

Adler, M. (1985). Stardom and talent. *American Economic Review*, March, 208–212.

Adorno, T. W. (1941). On popular music. *Zeitschrift für Sozialforschung*, 9, 17–49.

Aebischer, V., Hewstone, M. R., and Henderson, M. (1984). Minority influence and musical preference: innovation by conversion not coercion. *European Journal of Social Psychology*, 14, 23–33.

Ahlkvist, J. A. (2001). Programming philosophies and the rationalization of music radio. *Media, Culture and Society*, 23, 339–58.

—— and Faulkner, R. (2002). 'Will this record work for us?': managing music formats in commercial radio. *Qualitative Sociology*, 25, 189–215.

—— and Fisher, G. (2000). And the hits just keep on coming: music programming standardization in commercial radio. *Poetics*, 27, 301–325.

Aitken, J. C., Wilson, S., Coury, D., and Moursi, A. M. (2002). The effect of music distraction on pain, anxiety and behavior in pediatric dental patients. *Pediatric Dentistry*, 24, 114–118.

Albarran, A. B. (2004). The economics of the contemporary radio industry. In A. Alexander, J. Owers, R. Carveth, C. A. Hollifield, and A. N. Greco (eds.), *Media economics: theory and practice* (3ʳ edn) (pp. 207–220). Mahwah: Lawrence Erlbaum Associates.

Aldrich, C. K. (1944). The effect of a synthetic marihuana-like compound on musical talent as measured by the Seashore test. *Public Health Reports*, 59, 431–433.

Aldridge, D. (1993). Music therapy research: I. A review of the medical research literature within a general context of music therapy research. *Arts in Psychotherapy*, 20, 11–35.

Aldridge, D. (1996). *Music therapy research and practice in medicine: from out of the silence.* London: Jessica Kingsley Publishers.

Aldridge, D. (2003). Music therapy references related to cancer and palliative care. *British Journal of Music Therapy*, 17, 17–25.

Alexander, P. J. (1994a). New technology and market structure: evidence from the music recording industry. *Journal of Cultural Economics*, 18, 113–123.

Alexander, P. J. (1994b). Entry barriers, release behavior, and multiproduct firms in the music recording industry. *Review of Industrial Organization*, 9, 85–98.

Alexander, P. J. (1996). Comment on Peterson and Berger, ASR, April 1975: entropy and popular culture: product diversity in the popular music recording industry. *American Sociological Review*, 61, 171–174.

Alexander, P. J. (1997). Product variety and market structure: a new measure and a simple test. *Journal of Economic Behavior and Organization*, 323, 207–214.

Almeida, V. A. F., Meira, W., Ribeiro, V. F., and Ziviani, N. (1999). Efficiency analysis of brokers in the electronic marketplace. *Computer Networks*, 313, 1079–1090.

Alpert, J. (1982). The effect of disc–jockey, peer, and music teacher approval of music on music selection and preference. *Journal of Research in Music Education*, 30, 173–186.

Alpert, J. I. and Alpert, M. I. (1989). Background music as an influence in consumer mood and advertising responses. *Advances in Consumer Research*, 16, 485–491.

Alpert, J. I. and Alpert, M. I. (1990). Music influences on mood and purchase intentions. *Psychology and Marketing*, 7, 109–133.

Alpert, M. I., Alpert, J. I., and Maltz, E. N. (2005). Purchase occasion influence on the role of music in advertising. *Journal of Business Research*, 58, 369–376.

Amabile, T. M. (1982). Social psychology of creativity: a consensual assessment technique. *Journal of Personality and Social Psychology*, 433, 997–1013.

Amabile, T. M. (1983). *The social psychology of creativity*. New York: Springer Verlag.

Amabile, T. M. (1996). *Creativity in context*. Boulder: Westview Press.

Ammon, K. (1968). The effects of music on children in respiratory distress. *American Nurses Association Clinical Session*, 127–133.

Anderson, B., Hesbacher, P., Etzkorn, K. P., and Denisoff, R. S. (1980). Hit record trends, 1940–1977. *Journal of Communication*, 30, 31–43.

Anderson, C. A. and Bushman, B. J. (2001). Effects of violent video games on aggressive behavior, aggressive cognition, aggressive affect, physiological arousal, and pro–social behavior: a meta-analytic review of the scientific literature. *Psychological Science*, 12, 353–359.

Anderson, C. A. and Bushman, B. J. (2002). The effects of media violence on society. *Science*, 29, 2377–2378.

Anderson, C. A., Carnagey, N. L., and Eubanks, J. (2003). Exposure to violent media: the effects of songs with violent lyrics on aggressive thoughts and feelings. *Journal of Personality and Social Psychology*, 84, 960–971.

Andsager, J. (2005). Seduction, shock, and sales: research and functions of sex in music video. In T. Reichert and J. Lambaise (eds.), *Sex in Consumer Culture*. Mahwah: Erlbaum.

Andsager, J. and Roe, K. (2003). "What's your definition of dirty, baby?": sex in music video. *Sexuality and Culture: an Interdisciplinary Quarterly*, 7, 79–97.

Ang, S. H., Cheng, P. S., Lim, E. A. C, and Tambyah, S. K. (2001). Spot the difference: consumer responses towards counterfeits. *Journal of Consumer Marketing*, 18, 219–235.

Ansdell, G. (1995). *Music for life: aspects of creative music therapy with adult clients*. London: Jessica Kingsley Publishers.

Ansdell, G. (2004). Music as medicine: the history of music therapy since antiquity. *Psychology of Music*, 323, 440–444.

Ansdell, G. and Pavlicevic, M. (2005). Musical companionship, musical community: music therapy and the process and value of musical communication. In D. Miell, R. A. R. MacDonald, and D. J. Hargreaves (eds), *Musical communication* (pp. 193–213). Oxford: Oxford University Press.

Antonides, G., Verhoef, P. C., and van Aalst, M. (2002). Consumer perception and evaluation of waiting time: a field experiment. *Journal of Consumer Psychology*, 12, 193–202.

Appel, S. S. (1976). Modifying solo performance anxiety in adult pianists. *Journal of Music Therapy*, 133, 2–16.

Appelbaum, V. and Halliburton, C. (1993). How to develop international advertising campaigns that work: the example of the European food and beverage sector. *International Journal of Advertising*, 12, 223–241.

Appleton, C. R. (1970). The comparative preferential response of black and white college students to black and white folk and popular musical styles. *Ph.D. Dissertation, New York University*.

Apter, M. J. (1984). Reversal theory, cognitive synergy, and the arts. In W. R. Crozier and A. J. Chapman (eds.), *Cognitive processes in the perception of art* (p. 411–426). Amsterdam: North–Holland.

Areni, C. S. (2003a). Examining managers' theories of how atmospheric music affects perception, behaviour and financial performance. *Journal of Retailing and Consumer Services*, 10, 263–274.

Areni, C. S. (2003b). Exploring managers' implicit theories of atmospheric music: comparing academic analysis to industry insight. *Journal of Services Marketing*, 17, 161–184.

Areni, C. S. and Kim, D. (1993). The influence of background music on shopping behavior: classical versus top forty music in a wine store. *Advances in Consumer Research*, 20, 336–340.

Areni, C. S., Sparks, J. R., and Dunne, P. (1996). Assessing consumers' affective responses to retail environments: a tale of two simulation techniques. *Advances in Consumer Research*, 233, 504–509.

Arkes, H. R., Rettig, L. E., and Scoudale, J. D. (1986). The effect of concurrent task complexity and music experience on preference for simple and complex music. *Psychomusicology*, 6, 51–60.

Armstrong, E. (1993) The rhetoric of violence in rap and country music. *Sociological Inquiry*, 633, 64–83.

Armstrong, E. G. (1986). Country music sex songs: an ethnomusicological account. *Journal of Sex Research*, 22, 370–378.

Arnett, J. (1991a). Heavy metal music and reckless behavior among adolescents. *Journal of Youth and Adolescence*, 20, 573–592.

Arnett, J. (1991b). Adolescents and heavy metal music: from the mouths of metalheads. *Youth and Society*, 233, 76–98.

Arnett, J. (1992). The soundtrack of recklessness: musical preferences and reckless behaviour among adolescents. *Journal of Adolescent Research*, 7, 313–331.

Arnett, J. (2002). The sounds of sex: sex in teens' music and music videos. In J. D. Brown, J. R. Steele, and K. Walsh–Childers (eds.), *Sexual teens, sexual media: investigating media's influence on adolescent sexuality* (pp. 253–264). Mahwah: Lawrence Erlbaum Associates.

Arnett, J. J. (1995). Adolescents' uses of the media for self–socialization. *Journal of Youth and Adolescence*, 24, 519–533.

Arnold, J. A. (1997). A comparison of attributions for success and failure in instrumental teaching among sixth, eighth, and tenthgrade students. *Update: Applications of Research in Music Education*, 155, 19–23.

Arts, S. E., Abu–Saad, H. H., Champion, G. D., Crawford, M. R., Fisher, R. J., Juniper, K. H., and Ziegler, J. B. (1994). Agerelated response to lidocaineprilocaine (EMLA) emulsion and effect of music distraction on the pain of intravenous cannulation. *Pediatrics*, 933, 797–801.

Aseev, V. G. and Mishin, Y. T. (1971). Work rest schedule in performing a particularly monotonous task. *Voprosy Psychologii*, 17, 110–120.

Ashe, D. D. and McCutcheon, L. E. (2001). Shyness, loneliness, and attitude toward celebrities. *Current Research in Social Psychology*, 6, 124–133.

Ashmore, R. D., Deaux, K., and McLaughlinVolpe, T. (2004). An organizing framework for collective identity: articulation and significance of multidimensionality. *Psychological Bulletin*, 130, 80–114.

Asmus, E. P. (1985). Sixth graders' achievement motivation: their views of success and failure in music. *Bulletin of the Council for Research in Music Education*, 85, 1–13.

Asmus, E. P. (1986). Student beliefs about the causes of success and failure in music: a study of achievement motivation. *Journal of Research in Music Education*, 343, 262–278.

Asvanund, A., Clay, K., Krishnan, R., and Smith, M. D. (2004). An empirical analysis of network externalities in peer-to-peer music-sharing networks. *Information Systems Research*, 15, 155–174.

Atik, Y. (1994). The conductor and the orchestra: interactive aspects of the leadership process. *Leadership and Organization Development Journal*, 133, 22–28.

Atkin, C. K., Smith, S. W., Roberto, A. J., Fediuk, T. and Wagner, T. (2002). Correlates of verbally aggressive communication in adolescents. *Journal of Applied Communication Research*, 30, 251–268.

Au, K., Chan, F., Wang, D., and Vertinsky, I. (2003). Mood in foreign exchange trading: cognitive processes and performance. *Organizational Behavior and Human Decision Processes*, 91, 322–338.

Austin, J. R. (1991). Competitive and noncompetitive goal structures: an analysis of motivation and achievement among elementary band students. *Psychology of Music*, 19, 142–158.

Austin, J. R. and Vispoel, W. P. (1992). Motivation after failure in school music performance classes: the facilitative effects of strategy attributions. *Bulletin of the Council for Research in Music Education*, 111, 1–23.

Austin, J. R. and Vispoel, W. P. (1998). How American adolescents interpret success and failure in classroom music: relationships among attributional beliefs, selfconcept and achievement. *Psychology of Music*, 26, 26–45.

Austin, J., Renwick, J., and McPherson, G. E. (2006). Developing motivation. In G. E. McPherson (ed.), *The child as musician: a handbook of musical development* (pp. 213–238). Oxford: Oxford University Press.

Ayoub, C. M., Rizk, L. B., Yaacoub, C. I., Gaal, D., and Kain, Z. N. (2005). Music and ambient operating room noise in patients undergoing spinal anesthesia. *Anesthesia and Analgesia*, 100, 1316–1319.

Ayres, T. J. and Hughes, P. (1986). Visual acuity with noise and music at 107 dbA. *Journal of Auditory Research*, 26, 65–74.

Babin, B. J., Chebat, J. C., and Michon, R. (2004). Perceived appropriateness and its effect on quality, affect and behavior. *Journal of Retailing and Consumer Services*, 11, 287–298.

Bach, D. (2004). The double punch of law and technology: fighting music piracy or remaking copyright in a digital age? *Business and Politics*, 6, 1–33.

Bailey, B. A. and Davidson, J. W. (2002). Adaptive characteristics of group singing: perceptions from members of a choir for homeless men. *Musicae Scientiae*, 6, 221–256.

Bailey, N. and Areni, C. S. (2006a). Keeping time to the tune: background music as a quasi clock in retrospective duration judgments. *Perceptual and Motor Skills*, 102, 435–444.

Bailey, N. and Areni, C. S. (2006b). When a few minutes sound like a lifetime: does atmospheric music expand or contract perceived time? *Journal of Retailing*, 82, 189–202.

Baker, J., Grewal, D., and Parasuraman, A. (1994). The influence of store environment on quality inferences and store image. *Journal of the Academy of Marketing Science*, 22, 328–339.

Baker, J., Levy, M., and Grewal, D. (1992). An experimental approach to making retail store environmental decisions. *Journal of Retailing*, 68, 445–460.

Bakker, A. B. (2005). Flow among music teachers and their students: the crossover of peak experiences. *Journal of Vocational Behavior*, 66, 26–44.

Balasubramanian, S. K. (1990). Temporal variations in the evaluation of television advertisements: the role of key nonverbal cues. *Advances in Consumer Research*, 17, 651–657.

Baldwin, L. and Mizerski, R. (1985). An experimental investigation concerning the comparative influence of MTV and radio on consumer market responses to new music. *Advances in Consumer Research*, 12, 476–481.

Ballard, M. E. and Coates, S. (1995). The immediate effects of homicidal, suicidal, and nonviolent heavy metal and rap songs on the moods of college students. *Youth and Society*, 27, 148–168.

Ballard, M. E., Dodson, A. R. and Bazzini, D. G. (1999). Genre of music and lyrical content: expectation effects. *Journal of Genetic Psychology*, 160, 476–487.

Bamberger, J. (1991). *The mind behind the musical ear*. Cambridge: Harvard University Press.

Bamberger, J. (2006). What develops in musical development? in G. E. McPherson (ed.), *The child as musician* (pp. 69–92). Oxford: Oxford University Press.

Banbury, S. and Berry, D. C. (1997). Habituation and dishabituation to speech and office noise. *Journal of Experimental Psychology: Applied*, 33, 181–195.

Banbury, S. and Berry, D. C. (1998). Disruption of officerelated tasks by speech and office noise. *British Journal of Psychology*, 89, 499–517.

Bandura, A. (1973). *Aggression: a social learning analysis*. Englewood Cliffs: PrenticeHall.

Bandura, A. (1977). *Social learning theory*. Englewood Cliffs: PrenticeHall.

Bandura, A. (1994). Social cognitive theory of mass communication. In J. Bryant and D. Zillmann (eds.), *Media effects: advances in theory and research* (pp. 61–90). Hillsdale: Erlbaum.

Bandura, A. (1997). *Selfefficacy: the exercise of control.* New York: Freeman.

Bangerter, A. and Heath, C. (2004). The Mozart effect: tracking the evolution of a scientific legend. *British Journal of Social Psychology,* 43, 605–623.

Baptista, M. C., Noto, A. R., Nappo, S., and de Araújo Carlini, E. (2002). The use of ecstasy (MDMA) in S„o Paulo city and surroundings: an ethnographic study. *Jornal Brasileiro de Psiquiatria,* 51, 81–89.

Barongan, C. and Hall, G. C. N. (1995). The influence of misogynous rap music on sexual aggression against women. *Psychology of Women Quarterly,* 19, 195–207.

Barrera, M. E., Rykov, M. H., and Doyle, S. L. (2002). The effects of interactive music therapy on hospitalized children with cancer: a pilot study. *Psycho-Oncology,* 11, 379–388.

Barrett, M. (2005). Musical communication and children's communities of musical practice. In D.E. Miell, R. MacDonald and D.J. Hargreaves (eds.), *Musical communication* (pp. 261–280). Oxford: Oxford University Press.

Barrett, M. (2006). 'Creative collaboration': an 'eminence' study of teaching and learning in music composition. *Psychology of Music,* 34, 195–218.

Barron, F. (1968). *Creativity and personal freedom.* New York: Van Nostrand.

Bartlett, D. L. (1996). Physiological reactions to music and acoustic stimuli. In D. A. Hodges (ed.), *Handbook of music psychology (*2nd edn.*)* (pp. 343–385). San Antonio: IMR Press.

Bastian, H. G. (1989). *Leben für Musik: eine BiographieStudie über musikalische (Hoch-)Begabungen.* Mainz: Schott.

Baumann, V. H. (1960). Teenage music preferences. *Journal of Research in Music Education,* 8, 75–84.

Baumeister, R. F. (1984). Acid rock: a critical reappraisal and psychological commentary. *Journal of Psychoactive Drugs,* 16, 339–345.

Baumol, W. J. and Baumol, H. (1994). On the economics of musical composition in Mozart's Vienna. *Journal of Cultural Economics,* 18, 171–198.

Baumol, W. J. and Bowen, W. G. (1966). On the rationale of public support. In R. Towse (ed.), *Baumol's cost disease: the arts and other victims* (pp. 213–224). Cheltenham: Edward Elgar.

Baxter, R. L., de Riemer, C., Landini, A., and Leslie, L. et al. (1985). A content analysis of music videos. *Journal of Broadcasting and Electronic Media,* 29, 333–340.

Beasley, R. and Danesi, M. (2002). *Persuasive signs: the semiotics of advertising.* Berlin: de Gruyter.

Beck, R. J., Cesario, T. C., Yousefi, A., and Enamoto, H. (2000). Choral singing, performance perception, and immune system changes in salivary immunoglobulin A and cortisol. *Music Perception,* 18, 87–106.

Becker, H. S. (1963). *Outsiders: studies in the sociology of deviance.* New York: Free Press.

Beckett, W. (1943). *Music in war plants.* Oxford, England: War Production Board. Antrim, D. K. (1943). Music in industry. *Musical Quarterly,* 29, 275–290.

Beebee, M. D. (2004). The functions of multiple singing modes: experimental tests in yellow warblers, Dendroica petechia. *Animal Behaviour,* 67, 1089–1097.

Beh, H. C. and Hirst, R. (1999). Performance on driving-related tasks during music. *Ergonomics,* 42, 1087–1098.

Behne, K. E. (1996). The development of 'Musikerleben' in adolescence. In. I. Deliege and J. Sloboda (eds.). *Musical beginnings, origins, and development of musical competence* (pp. 143–159). Oxford: Oxford University Press.

Bellis, M. A., Hughes, K., Bennett, A., and Thomson, R. (2003). The role of an international nightlife resort in the proliferation of recreational drugs. *Addiction*, **98**, 1713–1721.

Bellman, S., Lohse, G. L., and Johnson, E. J. (1999). Predictors of online buying behavior. *Communications of the ACM*, **42**, 32–38.

Bem, S. L. (1974). The measurement of psychological androgyny. *Journal of Consulting and Clinical Psychology*, **42**, 155–162.

Benjamin, A. J. (1996). The influence of locus of control and aggressiveness of rock music videos on aggression: a reanalysis and methodological critique of Wann and Wilson (1996). *Journal of Social Behavior and Personality*, **14**, 491–498.

Berkaak, O. A. and Ruud, E. (1994). *Sunwheels. Fortellinger om et rockeband*. Oslo: Universitetsforlaget.

Berkowitz, L. and Rogers, K. H. (1986). A priming effect analysis of media influences. In J. Bryant and D. Zillmann (eds.), *Perspectives on media effects* (pp. 57–81). Hillsdale: Erlbaum.

Berlyne, D. E. (1960). *Conflict, arousal, and curiosity*. New York: McGraw-Hill.

Berlyne, D. E. (1970). Motivational problems. In J. Lindhart (ed.). *Proceedings of the International Conference on Psychology of Human Learning, Vol. 1*. Prague: Institute of Psychology, Czechoslovak Academy of Sciences.

Berlyne, D. E. (1971). *Aesthetics and psychobiology*. New York: Appleton-Century-Crofts.

Berlyne, D. E. (1972). Experimental aesthetics. In P. C. Dodwell (ed.). *New Horizons in Psychology 2* (pp. 9–32). Hammondsworth: Penguin.

Berlyne, D. E. (1974). The new experimental aesthetics. In D. E. Berlyne (ed.). *Studies in the new experimental aesthetics: steps toward an objective psychology of aesthetic appreciation* (pp. 1–25). New York: Halsted Press.

Berry, S. T. and Waldfogel, J. (1999). Public radio in the United States: does it correct market failure or cannibalize commercial stations? *Journal of Public Economics*, **71**, 189–211.

Besson, M., Faïta, F., Peretz, I., Bonnel, A.-M., and Requin, J. (1998). Singing in the brain: independence of lyrics and tunes. *Psychological Science*, **9**, 494–498.

Bewley, R. and Griffiths, W. E. (2001). A forecasting comparison of classical and Bayesian methods for modelling logistic diffusion. *Journal of Forecasting*, **20**, 231–247.

Bewley, R. and Griffiths, W. E. (2003). The penetration of CDs in the sound recording market: issues in specification, model selection and forecasting. *International Journal of Forecasting*, **19**, 111–121.

Bierley, C., McSweeney, F. K., and Vannieuwkerk, R. (1985). Classical conditioning of preferences for stimuli. *Journal of Consumer Research*, **12**, 316–323.

Billig, M. and Tajfel, H. (1973). Social categorization and similarity of intergroup behaviour. *European Journal of Social Psychology*, **3**, 27–52.

Binder, A. (1993). Constructing racial rhetoric: media depictions of harm in heavy metal and rap music. *American Sociological Review*, **58**, 753–767.

Binek, J., Sagmeister, M., Borovicka, J., Knierim, M., Magdeburg, B., and Meyenberger, C. (2003). Perception of gastrointestinal endoscopy by patients and examiners with and without background music. *Digestion*, **68**, 5–8.

Birch, T. E. (1962). Musical taste as indicated by records owned by college students with varying high school music experiences. *Ed.D. Dissertation, University of Missouri*.

Bishop, J. (2004). Who are the pirates? The politics of piracy, poverty, and greed in a globalized music market. *Popular Music and Society*, 27, 101–106.

Bittman, B., Berk, L., Shannon, M., Sharaf, M., Westengard, J., Guegler, K. J., and Ruff, D. W. (2005). Recreational musicmaking modulates the human stress response: a preliminary individualized gene expression strategy. *Medical Science Monitor*, 11, BR31–40.

Bittman, B., Bruhn, K. T., Stevens, C., Westengard, J., and Umbach, P. O. (2003). Recreational musicmaking: a costeffective group interdisciplinary strategy for reducing burnout and improving mood states in longterm care workers. *Advances in Mind-Body Medicine*, 19, 4–15.

Blackwell, R. and Stephan, T. (2004). *Brands that rock*. Hoboken, New Jersey: Wiley.

Blair, M. E. and Hatala, M. N. (1992). The use of rap music in children's advertising. *Advances in Consumer Research*, 19, 719–724.

Blair, M. E. and Shimp, T. A. (1992). Consequences of an unpleasant experience with music: a secondorder negative conditioning perspective. *Journal of Advertising*, 21, 35–43.

Bleich, S., Zillmann, D., and Weaver, J. B. (1991). Enjoyment and consumption of defiant rock music as a function of adolescent rebelliousness. *Journal of Electronic and Broadcasting Media*, 35, 351–366.

Blewett, R. A. and Farley, M. (1998). *Institutional constraints on entrepreneurship in Kenya's popular music industry*. Gainesville: University Press of Florida.

Blood, D. J. and Ferriss, S. J. (1993). Effects of background music on anxiety, satisfaction with communication, and productivity. *Psychological Reports*, 72, 171–177.

Blumenfeld, H. and Eisenfeld, L. (2006). Does a mother singing to her premature baby affect feeding in the neonatal intensive care unit? *Clinical Pediatrics*, 45, 65–70.

Boal–Palheiros, G. M. and Hargreaves, D. J. (2001). Listening to music at home and at school. *British Journal of Music Education*, 18, 103–118.

Bob, S. R. (1962). Audioanalgesia in paediatric practice: a preliminary study. *Journal of the American Podiatry Association*, 52, 503–504.

Boden, M. (1999). Computer models of creativity. In R. J. Sternberg (ed.), *Handbook of creativity* (pp. 351–372). Cambridge: Cambridge University Press.

Boeri, M. W., Sterk, C. E., and Elifson, K. W. (2004). Rolling beyond raves: ecstasy use outside the rave setting. *Journal of Drug Issues*, 34, 831–860.

Boldizar, J. P. (1991). Assessing sex typing and androgyny in children: the Children's Sex Role Inventory. *Developmental Psychology*, 27, 505–515.

Boon, S. D. and Lomore, C. D. (2001). Admirer-celebrity relationships among young adults: explaining perceptions of celebrity influence on identity. *Human Communication Research*, 27, 432–465.

Borgerson, J. L. and Schroeder, J. E. (2002). Ethical issues of global marketing: avoiding bad faith in visual representation. *European Journal of Marketing*, 36, 570–594.

Borgonovi, F. (2004). Performing arts attendance: an economic approach. *Applied Economics*, 36, 1871–1885.

Borthwick, S. J. and Davidson, J. W. (2002). Developing a child's identity as a musician: a family 'script' perspective. In R. A. R. MacDonald, D. J. Hargreaves, and D. E. Miell, D. E. (eds.), *Musical identities* (pp. 60–78). Oxford: Oxford University Press.

Borzekowski, D. L. G., Robinson, T. N., and Killen, J. D. (2000). Does the camera add 10 pounds? Media use, preceived importance of appearance, and weight concerns among teenage girls. *Journal of Adolescent Health*, 26, 36–41.

Bourdieu, P. (1971). Intellectual field and creative project. In M. F. D. Young (ed.), *Knowledge and control* (pp. 161–188). London: Collier-Macmillan.

Bourdieu, P. (1984). Distinction: a social critique of the judgement of taste. London: Routledge.

Boutcher, S. H. and Trenske, M. (1990). The effects of sensory deprivation on perceived exertion and affect during exercise. *Journal of Sport and Exercise Psychology*, 12, 167–176.

Boutelle, K. N., Jeffery, R. W., Murray, D. M., and Schmitz, K. H. (2001). Using signs, artwork, and music to promote stair use in a public building. *American Journal of Public Health*, 91, 2004–2006.

Boys, A., Lenton, S., and Norcross, K. (1997). Polydrug use at raves by a Western Australian sample. *Drug and Alcohol Review*, 16, 227–234.

Bozman, C. S. and Muehling, D. (1994). The directional influence of music backgrounds in television advertising. *Journal of Applied Business Research*, 10, 14–18.

Brader, T. (2005). Striking a responsive chord: how political ads motivate and persuade voters by appealing to emotions. *American Journal of Political Science*, 49, 388–405.

Bradley, I. L. (1972). effect on student musical preference of a listening program in contemporary art music. *Journal of research in Music Education*, 20, 344–353.

Bradlow, E. T. and Fader, P. S. (2001). A Bayesian lifetime model for the 'Hot 100' Billboard songs. *Journal of the American Statistical Association*, 96, 368–381.

Brady, P. T. (1970). Fixed–scale mechanism of absolute pitch. *Journal of the Acoustical Society of America*, 48, 883–887.

Brand, M. (1985). Development and validation of the Home Musical Environment Scale for use at the early elementary level. *Psychology of Music*, 13, 40–48.

Brand, M. (1986). Relationship between home musical environment and selected musical attributes of second-grade children. *Journal of Research in Music Education*, 34, 111–120.

Brandfonbrener, A. G. (1986). An overview of the medical problems of musicians. *Journal of American College Health*, 34, 165–169.

Brandfonbrener, A. G. and Kjelland J. M. (2002). Music medicine. In R. Parncutt and G. E. McPherson (eds.), *The science and psychology of music performance* (pp. 83–96). Oxford: Oxford University Press.

Branscombe, N. R. and Wann, D. L. (1994). Collective self-esteem consequences of outgroup derogation when a valued social identity is on trial. *European Journal of Social Psychology*, 24, 641–657.

Brantigan, C., Brantigan, T., and Joseph, N. (1979). The effect of betablockade on -stage fright: a controlled study. *Rocky Mountain Medical Journal*, 76, 227–233.

Breckler, S. J., Allen, R. B., and Konečni, V. J. (1985). Mood-optimizing strategies in aesthetic–choice behavior. *Music Perception*, 2, 459–470.

Breger, I. (1970). Affective response to meaningful sound stimuli. *Perceptual and Motor Skills*, 30, 842.

Brennan, F. X. and Charnetski, C. J. (2000). Stress and immune system function in a newspaper's newsroom. *Psychological Reports*, 87, 218–222.

Brentar, J. E., Neuendorf, K. A., and Armstrong, G. B. (1994). Exposure effects and affective responses to music. *Communication Monographs*, 61, 161–181.

Bright, R. (2002). *Supportive eclectic music therapy for grief and loss: a practical handbook for professionals*. St. Louis: Magna Music Baton.

Brittin, R. V. (1991). The effect of overtly categorizing music on preference for popular music styles. *Journal of Research in Music Education*, 39, 143–151.

Brodsky, W. (2001). The effects of music tempo on simulated driving performance and vehicular control. *Transportation Research Part F: Traffic Psychology and Behaviour*, 4, 219–241.

Broker, M. (1996). *The work of female composers from 1150–1995*. Devon: Arthur W. Stockwell.

Bronfenbrenner, U. (1979). *The ecology of human development*. Cambridge: Harvard University Press.

Brooker, G. and Wheatley, J. J. (1994). Music and radio advertising: effects of tempo and placement. *Advances in Consumer Research*, 21, 286–290.

Broscious, S. K. (1999). Music: an intervention for pain during chest tube removal after open heart surgery. *American Journal of Critical Care*, 8, 410–415.

Brotons, M. (1994). Effect of performing conditions on music performance, anxiety, and performance quality. *Journal of Music Therapy*, 31, 63–81.

Brown, C. J., Chen, A. C., and Dworkin, S. F. (1989). Music in the control of human pain. *Music Therapy*, 8, 47–60.

Brown, I. D. (1965). Effect of a car radio on driving in traffic. *Ergonomics*, 8, 475–479.

Brown, J. D., Campbell, K., and Fischer, L. (1986). American adolescents and music videos: why do they watch? *Gazette*, 37, 19–32.

Brown, R. and O'Leary, M. (1971). Pop music in an English secondary school system. *American Behavioral Scientist*, 14, 401–413.

Brown, S. P. and Stayman, D. M. (1992). Antecedents and consequences of attitude toward the ad: a meta–analysis. *Journal of Consumer Research*, 19, 34–51.

Browning, C. A. (2000). Using music during childbirth. *Birth*, 27, 272–276.

Browning, C. A. (2001). Music therapy in childbirth: research in practice. *Music Therapy Perspectives*, 19, 74–81.

Bruner, G. C. (1990). Music, mood, and marketing. *Journal of Marketing*, 54, 94–104.

Bruscia, K. (1987). *Improvisational models of music therapy*. Springfield: Charles C Thomas.

Bryant, P. E. (1974). *Perception and understanding in young children*. London: Methuen.

Bryson, B. (1996). 'Anything but heavy metal': symbolic exclusion and musical dislikes. *American Sociological Review*, 61, 884–899.

Buchanan, L. (2005). New laws of the jingle. *Harvard Business Review*, 83, 20.

Bull, M. (2000). *Sounding out the city: personal stereos and the management of everyday life*. New York: Berg.

Bunt, L. (1994). *Music therapy: an art beyond words*. London: Routledge.

Bunt, L. (1997). Clinical and therapeutic uses of music. In D. J. Hargreaves and A. C. North (eds.), *The social psychology of music* (pp. 249–267). Oxford: Oxford University Press.

Bunt, L. and Hoskyns, S. (eds.) (2002). *The handbook of music therapy*. London: Routledge.

Bunt, L. and Pavlicevic, M. (2001). Music and emotion: perspectives from music therapy. In P. Juslin and J. A. Sloboda (eds.), *Music and emotion* (pp. 181–201). Oxford: Oxford University Press.

Burge, M., Goldblat, C., and Lester, D. (2002). Music preferences and suicidality: a comment on Stack. *Death Studies*, 26, 501–504.

Burke, A. E. (1996a). The dynamics of product differentiation in the British record industry. *Journal of Cultural Economics*, 20, 145–164.

Burke, A. E. (1996b). How effective are international copyright conventions in the music industry? *Journal of Cultural Economics*, **20**, 51–66.

Burke, M. J. and Gridley, M. C. (1990). Musical preferences as a function of stimulus complexity and listeners' sophistication. *Perceptual and Motor Skills*, **71**, 687–690.

Burke, P. J. and Reitzes, D. C. (1981). The link between identity and role performance. *Social Psychology Quarterly*, **44**, 83–92.

Burke, R. and Grinder, R. (1966). Personality–oriented themes and listening patterns in teenage music and their relation to certain academic and peer variables. *School Review*, **74**, 196–211.

Burnard, P. and Younker, B.A. (in press). Using Engeström's activity theory (AT) as an analytical lens to investigate interaction in children's collaborative creative music making. *International Journal of Educational Research*.

Bushman, B. J. and Cantor, J. (2003). Media ratings for violence and sex: implications for policymakers and parents. *American Psychologist*, **58**, 130–141.

Butterworth, G. (1992). Context and cognition in models of cognitive growth. In P. Light and G. Butterworth (eds.), *Context and cognition: ways of learning and knowing* (pp. 1–13). Hillsdale: Lawrence Erlbaum.

Butzlaff, R. (2000). Can music be used to teach reading? *Journal of Aesthetic Education*, **34**, 167–178.

Byrne, C. (2005). Pedagogical communication in the music classroom. In D. E. Miell, R. MacDonald and D. J. Hargreaves (eds.), *Musical communication* (pp. 301–319). Oxford: Oxford University Press.

Byrne, C. MacDonald, R. A. R., and Carlton, L. (2003). Assessing creativity in musical compositions: flow as an assessment tool. *British Journal of Music Education*, **20**, 277–290.

Caine, J. (1991). The effects of music on the selected stress behaviors, weight, caloric and formula intake, and length of hospital stay of premature and low birth weight neonates in a newborn intensive care unit. *Journal of Music Therapy*, **28**, 180–192.

Caldwell, C. and Hibbert, S. (1999). Play that one again: the effect of music tempo on consumer behavior in a restaurant. *European Advances in Consumer Research*, **4**, 58–62.

Caldwell, C. and Hibbert, S. (2002). The influence of music tempo and musical preference on restaurant patrons' behavior. *Psychology and Marketing*, **19**, 895–917.

Caldwell, C. H., Kohn–Wood, L. P., Schmeelk–Cone, K. H., Chavous, T. M., and Zimmerman, M. A. (2004). Racial discrimination and racial identity as risk or protective factors for violent behaviors in African American young adults. *American Journal of Community Psychology*, **33**, 91–105.

Calfin, M. S., Carroll, J. L., and Shmidt, J. (1993). Viewing music-videotapes before taking a test of premarital sexual attitudes. *Psychological Reports*, **72**, 475–481.

Cameron, M. A. (1996). Responses to delay in services: the effects of music volume and attribution. *Dissertation Abstracts International Section A: Humanities and Social Sciences*, **57(6-A)**.

Cameron, M. A., Baker, J., Peterson, A. and Braunsberger, K. (2003). The effects of music, wait-length evaluation, and mood on a low-cost wait experience. *Journal of Business Research*, **56**, 421–430.

Cameron, S. (2003). The political economy of gender disparity in musical markets. *Cambridge Journal of Economics*, **27**, 905–917.

Campbell, D. G. (1997). *The Mozart effect*. New York: Avon Books.

Campbell, D. G. (2000). *The Mozart effect for children*. New York: William Morrow.

Campbell, P. S. (2002). The musical cultures of children. In L. Bresler and C. Marme Thompson (eds.), *The arts in children's lives: context, culture and curriculum* (pp. 57–69). Dordrecht: Kluwer Academic Publishers.

Campbell, P. S. (2006). Global practices. In G. E. McPherson (ed.), *The child as musician* (pp. 415–437). Oxford: Oxford University Press.

Capling, A. (1996). The conundrum of intellectual property rights: domestic interests, international commitments and the Australian music industry. *Australian Journal of Political Science*, 31, 301–320.

Cardinell, R. L. (1943). The statistical method in determining the effects of music in industry. *Journal of the Acoustical Society of America*, 15, 133–135.

Carroll, R., Silbergleid, M., Beachum, C., Perry, S., Pluscht, P., and Pescatore, M. (1993). Meaning of radio to teenagers in a niche-programming area. *Journal of Broadcasting and Electronic Media*, 37, 159–176.

Carter, F. A., Wilson, J. S., Lawson, R. H., and Bulik, C. M. (1995). Mood induction procedure: importance of individualising music. *Behaviour Change*, 12, 159–161.

Carter, F., Bulik, C. M., Lawson, R. H., Sullivan, P. F., Wilson, J. S. (1996). Effect of mood and food cues on body image in women with bulimia and controls. *International Journal of Eating Disorders*, 20, 65–76.

Case, R. (1985). *Intellectual development: birth to adulthood*. New York: Academic Press.

Cassidy, J. W. and Standley, J. M. (1995). The effect of music listening on physiological responses of premature infants in the NICU. *Journal of Music Therapy*, 32, 208–227.

Castell, K, C. and Hill, E. (1985). The effects of stylistic information on ratings of ambiguous music. *Bulletin of the British Psychological Society*, 38, A58.

Cauty, J. and Drummond, B. (1988). *The manual: how to have a number one the easy way*. London: Ellipsis.

Cepeda, M. S., Diaz, J. E., Hernandez, V., Daza, E., and Carr, D. B. (1998). Music does not reduce alfentanil requirement during patient–controlled analgesia (PCA) use in extracorporeal shock wave lithotripsy for renal stones. *Journal of Pain and Symptom Management*, 16, 382–387.

Chabris, C. F. (1999). Prelude or requiem for the 'Mozart effect'? *Nature*, 400, 826–827.

Chafin, S., Roy, M., and Gerin, W. (2004). Music can facilitate blood pressure recovery from stress. *British Journal of Health Psychology*, 9, 393–403.

Chalfant, H. P. and Beckley, R. E. (1977). Beguiling and betraying: the image of alcohol use in country music. *Journal of Studies on Alcohol*, 38, 1428–1433.

Chan, A. S., Ho, Y. C., and Cheung, M. C. (1998). Music training improves verbal memory. *Nature*, 396, 128.

Chang, S. and Chen, C. (2005). Effects of music therapy on women's physiologic measures, anxiety, and satisfaction during cesarean delivery. *Research in Nursing and Health*, 28, 453–461.

Channel, C. S. (2004). The twisted path of the music file–sharing litigation: the cases that have shaped the litigation and the RIAA's litigation strategy. *Intellectual Property and Technology Law Journal*, 16, 6–12.

Chapin, J. R. (2000). Adolescent sex and mass media: a developmental approach. *Adolescence*, 35, 799–811.

Chapman, A. J. and Williams, A. R. (1976). Prestige effects and aesthetic experiences: adolescents' reactions to music. *British Journal of Social and Clinical Psychology*, 15, 61–72.

Charnetski, C. J., Brennan, F. X., and Harrison, J. F. (1998). Effect of music and auditory stimuli on secretory immunoglobulin A (IgA). *Perceptual and Motor Skills*, 87, 1163–1170.

Chase, A. R. and Hill, W. (1999). Reliable operant apparatus for fish: audio stimulus generator, response button, and pellet-dispensing nipple. *Behavior Research Methods, Instruments and Computers*, 31, 470–478.

Chassin, L., Presson, C. C., Sherman, S. J., Corty, E., and Olshavsky, R. W. (1981). Self–images and cigarette smoking in adolescence. *Personality and Social Psychology Bulletin*, 7, 670–676.

Chebat, J. C. (2004). Effects of music induced arousal on the assessment of quality in two service situations. *Paper presented at the Eric-Langeard Seminars in Services, Lalonde-les-Maures, France.*

Chebat, J. C., Vaillant, D., and Gé linas-Chebat, C. (2000). Does background music in a store enhance salespersons' persuasiveness? *Perceptual and Motor Skills*, 91, 405–424.

Chebat, J. C., Gelinas-Chebat, C., and Filiatrault, P. (1993). Interactive effects of musical and visual cues on time perception: an application to waiting lines in banks. *Perceptual and Motor Skills*, 77, 995–1020.

Chen, D., Huang, Y., Zhang, J, and Qi, G. (1994). Effects of fetal music and stroking stimulus on infant development of intelligence, motor function, and behavior. *Chinese Mental Health Journal*, 8, 148–151.

Chiou, J. S., Huang, G., and Lee, H. (2005). The antecedents of music piracy attitudes and intentions. *Journal of Business Ethics*, 57, 161–174.

Christenson, P. (1992a). Preadolescent perceptions and interpretations of music videos. *Popular Music and Society*, 16, 63–73.

Christenson, P. (1992b). The effects of parental advisory labels on adolescent musical preferences. *Journal of Communication*, 42, 106–113.

Christenson, P. G. and Peterson, J. B. (1988). Genre and gender in the structure of music preferences. *Communication Research*, 15, 282–301.

Christenson, P. G. and Roberts, D. F. (1998). *It's not only rock and roll: popular music in the lives of adolescents*. Cresskill: Hampton Press.

Chung, K. H. and Cox, R. A. K. (1994). A stochastic model of superstardom: an application of the Yule distribution. *Review of Economics and Statistics*, 76, 771–775.

Chung, K. H. and Cox, R. A. K. (1998). Consumer behavior and superstardom. *Journal of Socio–Economics*, 27, 263–270.

Clark, D. B. (1989). Performance related medical and psychological disorders in instrumental musicians. *Annals of Behavioural Medicine*, 11, 28–34.

Clark, D. B. and Agras, W. S. (1991). The assessment and treatment of performance anxiety in musicians. *American Journal of Psychiatry*, 148, 598–605.

Clarke, E. (1988). Generative principles in music performance. In J. A. Sloboda (ed.), *Generative processes in music* (pp. 1–26). Oxford: Oxford University Press.

Clarke, P. (1973). Teenagers' coorientation and information-seeking about pop music. *American Behavioral Scientist*, 16, 551–556.

Clemons, E. K., Bin, G., and Lang, K. R. (2002). Newly vulnerable markets in an age of pure information products: an analysis of online music and online news. *Journal of Management Information Systems*, 19, 17–41.

Cloutier, S., Weary, D. M., and Fraser, D. (2000). Can ambient sound reduce distress in piglets during weaning and restraint? *Journal of Applied Animal Welfare Science*, 3, 107–116.

Cohen, S. (1991). *Rock culture in Liverpool: popular music in the making*. Oxford: Clarendon.

Cohen, S. (2003). *Folk devils and moral panics: the creation of mods and rockers* (3rd edn.) 3. London: Mae Gibbon and Kee.

Coker, W. (1972). *Music and meaning*. New York: Free Press.

Cole, R. R. (1971). Top songs in the sixties: a content analysis of popular lyrics. *American Behavioral Scientist*, 14, 389–400.

Coleman, J. (1978). Current contradictions in adolescent theory. *Journal of Youth and Adolescence*, 7, 1–11.

Coleman, J. (1993). Adolescence in a changing world. In S. Jackson and H. Rodriguez–Tome (eds.), *Adolescence and its social worlds* (pp. 251–268). Hove: Erlbaum.

Coleman, J. M., Pratt, R. R., Stoddard, R. A., Gerstmann, D. R., and Abel, H. H. (1997). The effects of the male and female singing and speaking voices on selected physiological and behavioral measures of premature infants in the intensive care unit. *International Journal of Arts Medicine*, 5, 4–11.

Coley, A. and Burgess, B. (2003). Gender differences in cognitive and affective impulse buying. *Journal of Fashion Marketing and Management*, 7, 282–295.

Colley, A. M., North, A. C., and Hargreaves, D. J. (2003). Gender bias in the evaluation of new age music. *Scandinavian Journal of Psychology*, 44, 137–143.

Colley, A., Comber, C., and Hargreaves, D. J. (1994). Gender effects in school subject preferences: a research note. *Educational Studies*, 20, 13–18.

Collins, R. L., Schell, T., Ellickson, P. L., and McCaffrey, D. (2003). Predictors of beer advertising awareness among eighth graders. *Addiction*, 98, 1297–1306.

Collins, S. and Kuck, K. (1991). Music therapy in the neonatal intensive care unit. *Neonatal Network*, 9, 23–26.

Colman, A. M., Best, W. M., and Austen, A. J. (1986). Familiarity and liking: direct tests of the preference–feedback hypothesis. *Psychological Reports*, 58, 931–938.

Colman, A. M., Hargreaves, D. J., and Sluckin, W. (1981). Preference for Christian names as a function of their experienced familiarity. *British Journal of Social Psychology*, 20, 3–5.

Colman, A. M., Sluckin, W., and Hargreaves, D. J. (1981). The effect of familiarity on preference for surnames. *British Journal of Psychology*, 72, 363–369.

Colwell, C. M. (1997). Music as distraction and relaxation to reduce chronic pain and narcotic ingestion: a case study. *Music Therapy Perspectives*, 15, 24–31.

Comber, C., Hargreaves, D. J., and Colley, A. (1993). Girls, boys and technology in music education. *British Journal of Music Education*, 10, 123–134.

Connell, J.P. (1990). Context, self, and action: a motivational analysis of self-system processes across the life span. In D. Cicchetti (ed.), *The self in transition: infancy to adulthood* (pp. 61–97). Chicago: University of Chicago Press.

Connolly, J. J. and Viswesvaran, C. (2000). The role of affectivity in job satisfaction: a meta–analysis. *Personality and Individual Differences*, 29, 265–281.

Connolly, M. and Krueger, A. B. (2005). *Rockonomics: the economics of popular music*. National Bureau of Economic Research.

Connors, G. J. and Alpher, V. S. (1989). Alcohol themes within country-western songs. *International Journal of the Addictions*, 24, 445–451.

Consiglio, W., Driscoll, P., Witte, M., and Berg, W. P. (2003). Effect of cellular telephone conversations and other potential interference on reaction time in a braking response. *Accident Analysis and Prevention*, 35, 494–500.

Cook, N. (1990). *Music, imagination, and culture*. Oxford: Oxford University Press.

Cook, N. (1998). *Music: a very short introduction*. Oxford: Oxford University Press.

Cook, N. and Dibben, N. (2001). Musicological approaches to emotion. In P. N. Juslin and J. A. Sloboda (eds.), *Music and emotion: theory and research* (pp. 45–70). Oxford: Oxford University Press.

Cooke, A. D. J., Sujan, H., Sujan, M., and Weitz, B. A. (2002). Marketing the unfamiliar: the role of context and item-specific information in electronic agent recommendations. *Journal of Marketing Research*, 39, 488–497.

Cooke, D. (1959). *The language of music*. Oxford: Oxford University Press.

Cooke, M. and Morris, R. (1996). Music making in Great Britain. *Journal of the Market Research Society*, 38, 123–134.

Cooke, M. Chaboyer, W., Schluter, P., and Hiratos, M. (2005). The effect of music on preoperative anxiety in day surgery. *JAN Journal of Advanced Nursing*, 52, 47–55.

'Cool Britannia' boosts the image of British goods abroad. (1998). *Management Services*, 42, 4–16.

Cooley, C. H. (1902). *Human nature and social order*. New York: Shocken.

Cooper, B. G. and Goller, F. (2004). Multimodal signals: enhancement and constraint of song motor patterns by visual display. *Science*, 303, 544–546.

Cooper, C. and Wills, G. I. (1989). Popular musicians under pressure. *Psychology of Music*, 17, 22–36.

Cooper, J. and Harrison, D. M. (2001). The social organization of audio piracy on the Internet. *Media, Culture and Society*, 23, 71–89.

Cooper, V. W. (1985). Women in popular music: a quantitative analysis of feminine images over time. *Sex Roles*, 13, 499–506.

Copeland, B. L. and Franks, B. D. (1991). Effects of types and intensities of background music on treadmill endurance. *Journal of Sports Medicine and Physical Fitness*, 15, 100–103.

Costa–Giomi, E. (1999). The effects of three years of piano instruction on children's cognitive development. *Journal of Research in Music Education*, 47, 198–212.

Cox, R. A. K., Felton, J. M., and Chung, K. H. (1995). The concentration of commercial success in popular music: an analysis of the distribution of gold records. *Journal of Cultural Economics*, 19, 333–340.

Cox, W. J. and Kenardy, J. (1993). Performance anxiety, social phobia, and setting effects in instrumental music students. *Journal of Anxiety Disorders*, 7, 49–60.

Crafts, S. D., Cavicchi, D., Keil, C., and the Music in Daily Life Project (1993). *My music*. Hanover, New Hampshire: Wesleyan University Press/University Press of New England New England.

Crain, W. M. and Tollison, R. D. (1997). Economics and the architecture of popular music. *Journal of Economic Behavior and Organization*, 32, 185–205.

Crain, W. M. and Tollison, R. D. (2002). Consumer choice and the popular music industry: a test of the superstar theory. *Empirica*, 29, 1–9.

Cramer, K. M., Million, E., and Perreault, L. A. (2002). Perceptions of musicians: gender stereotypes and social role theory. *Psychology of Music*, 30, 164–174.

Craske, M. G. and Craig, K. (1984). Musical performance anxiety: the three-systems model and self-efficacy theory. *Behavioral Research Therapy*, 22, 267–280.

Creech, A. and Hallam, S. (2003). Parent-teacher=pupil interactions in instrumental music tuition: a literature review. *British Journal of Music Education*, 20, 29–44.

Crocker, J. and Major, B. (1989). Social stigma and self-esteem: the self-protective properties of stigma. *Psychological Review*, 96, 608–630.

Cross, I. (2003). Music, cognition, culture, and evolution. In I. Peretz and R. Zatorre (eds.), *The cognitive neuroscience of music* (pp. 42–56). Oxford: Oxford University Press.

Cross, W. E. (1991). *Shades of Black: diversity in African-American identity*. Philadelphia: Temple University Press.

Crowther, R. D. (1985). A social psychological approach to adolescents' musical preferences. *Psychology of Music*, 13, 64.

Crowther, R. D. and Durkin, K. (1982). Sex- and age-related differences in the musical behaviour, interests and attitudes towards music of 232 secondary school students. *Educational Studies*, 20, 13–18.

Crowther, R. D. (1982). Sex- and age-related differences in the musical behaviour, interests and attitudes towards music of 232 secondary school students. *Educational Studies*, 8, 131–139.

Crozier, J. B. (1974). Verbal and exploratory responses to sound sequences varying in uncertainty level. In D. E. Berlyne (ed.), *Studies in the new experimental aesthetics* (pp. 27–90). New York: Wiley.

Crozier, W. R. and Chapman, A. J. (1981). Aesthetic preferences, prestige, and social class. In D. O'Hare (ed.), *Psychology and the arts* (pp. 242–278). Brighton: Harvester.

Crust, L., Clough, P. J., and Robertson, C. (2004). Influence of music and distraction on visual search performance of participants with high and low affect intensity. *Perceptual and Motor Skills*, 98, 888–896.

Cuddy, L. L. (1968). Practice effects in the absolute judgement of pitch. *Journal of the Acoustical Society of America*, 43, 1069–1076.

Cummings, M. S. and Roy, A. (2002). Manifestations of Afrocentricity in rap music. *Howard Journal of Communications*, 1, 59–76.

Custodero, L. A. (1999). Constructing musical understandings: the cognition-flow interface. *Bulletin of the Council for Research in Music Education*, 142, 79.

Czikszentmihalyi, M. (1990). *Flow*. New York: Harper and Row.

Czikszentmihalyi, M. (1996). *Creativity: flow and the psychology of discovery and invention*. New York: Harper Collins.

Damon, W. and Hart, D. (1988). *Self-understanding in childhood and adolescence*. Cambridge: Cambridge University Press.

Daoussis, L. and McKelvie, S. J. (1986). Musical preferences and effects of music on a reading comprehension test for extraverts and introverts. *Perceptual and Motor Skills*, 62, 283–289.

Davenport, W. G. (1972). Vigilance and arousal: effects of different types of background stimulation. *Journal of Psychology: Interdisciplinary and Applied*, 82, 339–346.

Davidson, J. W. (1993). Visual perception and performance manner in the movements of solo musicians. *Psychology of Music*, 21, 103–113.

Davidson, J. W. (1994). What type of information is conveyed in the body movements of solo musician performers? *Journal of Human Movement Studies*, 6, 279–301.

Davidson, J. W. (1995). What does the visual information contained in music performances offer the observer? Some preliminary thoughts. In R. Steinberg (ed.), *Music and the mind machine: psychophysiology and psychopathology of the self of music* (pp. 105–114). New York: Springer.

Davidson, J. W. (1997). The social in music performance. In D. J. Hargreaves and A.C. North (eds.), *The social psychology of music* (pp. 209–228). Oxford: Oxford University Press.

Davidson, J. W. (2001). The role of the body in the production and perception of solo vocal performance: a case study of Annie Lennox. *Musicae Scientae*, 5, 235–256.

Davidson, J. W. (2005). Bodily communication in musical performance. In In D. E. Miell, R. A. R. MacDonald, and D. J. Hargreaves (eds.), *Musical communication* (pp. 215–237). Oxford: Oxford University Press.

Davidson, J. W. and Burland, K. (2006). Musician identity formation. In MacPherson, G. E. (ed.), *The child as musician: a handbook of musical development* (pp. 475–490). Oxford: Oxford University Press.

Davidson, J. W. and Correia, J. S. (2002). Body movement. In R. Parncutt and G. E. McPherson (eds.), *The science and psychology of music performance* (pp. 237–250). Oxford: Oxford University Press.

Davidson, J. W. and Edgar, R. (2003). Gender and race bias in the judgement of Western art music performance. *Music Education Research*, 5(2), 169–181.

Davidson, J. W. and Good, J. M. M. (2002). Social and musical coordination between members of a string quartet. *Psychology of Music*, 30, 186–201.

Davidson, J. W., Howe, M. J. A., and Sloboda, J. A. (1997). Environmental factors in the development of musical performance skills over the life span. In D. J. Hargreaves and A. C. North (eds.), *The social psychology of music* (pp. 188–206). Oxford: Oxford University Press.

Davidson, J. W., Howe, M. J. A., Moore, D. G., and Sloboda, J. A. (1998). The role of teachers in the development of musical ability. *Journal of Research in Music Education*, 46, 141–160.

Davidson, J. W., Howe, M. J. A., Moore, D. G., and Sloboda, J. A. (1996). The role of parental influences in the development of musical ability. *British Journal of Developmental Psychology*, 14, 399–412.

Davidson, J. W., Sloboda, J. A., and Howe, M. J. A. (1995/1996). The role of parents and teachers in the success and failure of instrumental learners. *Bulletin of the Council for Research in Music Education*, 127, 40–44.

Davidson, L. (1994). Song singing by young and old: a developmental approach to music. In R. Aiello and J. A. Sloboda (eds.), *Musical Perceptions* (pp. 99–130). Oxford: Oxford University Press.

Davidson, L. and Scripp. L. (1989). Education and developmental in music from a cognitive perspective. In D. J. Hargreaves (ed.), *Children and the Arts* (pp. 59–86). Milton Keynes: Open University Press.

Davies, D. R., Land, L., and Shackleton, V. J. (1973). The effects of music and task difficulty on performance at a visual vigilance task. *British Journal of Psychology*, 64, 383–389.

Davies, J. B. (1978). *The psychology of music*. London: Hutchinson.

Davis, C. A. (1992). The effects of music and basic relaxation instruction on pain and anxiety of women undergoing in-office gynecological procedures. *Journal of Music Therapy*, 29, 202–216.

Davis, M. (1994). Folk music psychology. *The Psychologist*, 7, 537.

Davis, S. (1985, summer). Pop lyrics: a mirror and molder of society. *Et Cetera*, 167–169.

Decker, H. and Kirk, C. (1988). *Choral conducting: focus on communication*. New Jersey: Prentice-Hall.

DeLiège, I. and Sloboda, J.A. (eds.) (1996). *Musical beginnings: origins and development of musical competence*. Oxford: Oxford University Press.

DeLiège, I. (1997). *Perception and cognition of music*. Hove: Psychology Press.

Deliège, I. and Wiggins, G. (eds.) (2006). *Musical creativity: multidisciplinary research in theory and practice*. Hove: Psychology Press.

Dempsey, J. M. (2004). McCartney at 60: a body of work celebrating home and hearth. *Popular Music and Society*, 27, 27–40.

Denisoff, R. S. and Levine, M. H. (1971). The popular protest song: the case of 'Eve of Destruction'. *Public Opinion Quarterly*, 35, 119–124.

DeNora, T. (1999). Music as a technology of the self. *Poetics*, 27, 31–56.

DeNora, T. (2000). *Music in everyday life*. Cambridge: Cambridge University Press.

DeNora, T. (2001). Aesthetic agency and musical practice: new directions in the sociology of music and emotion. In P. N. Juslin and J. A. Sloboda (eds.), *Music and emotion: theory and research* (pp. 161–180). Oxford: Oxford University Press.

DeNora, T. and Belcher, S. (2000). 'When you're trying something on you picture yourself in a place where they are playing this kind of music': musically sponsored agency in the British clothing retail sector. *Sociological Review*, 48, 80–101.

Dent, C. W., Galaif, J., Sussman, S., Stacy, A. W., Burton, D. and Flay, B. R. (1992). Music preference as a diagnostic indicator of adolescent drug use. *American Journal of Public Health*, 82, 124.

Devereux, G. A. (1969). Commercial background music: its effect on workers' attitudes and output. *Personnel Practice Bulletin*, 25, 24–30.

DfES. (2004). *The Music Manifesto*. http://www.musicmanifesto.co.uk/

Dibben, N. (2002). Gender identity and music. In R. A. R. MacDonald, D. J. Hargreaves, and D. E. Miell, D. E. (eds.), *Musical identities* (pp. 117–133). Oxford: Oxford University Press.

Dibben, N. (2004). The role of peripheral feedback in emotional experience with music. *Music Perception*, 22, 79–115.

DiClemente, D. F. and Hantula, D. A. (2003). Applied behavioral economics and consumer choice. *Journal of Economic Psychology*, 24, 589–602.

Dillmann–Carpentier, F., Knobloch, F., and Zillmann, D. (2003). Rock, rap, and rebellion: comparisons of traits predicting selective exposure to defiant music. *Personality and Individual Differences*, 35, 1643–1655.

Dillon, T. (2004). "It's in the mix baby": exploring how meaning is created within music technology collaborations. In D. E. Miell and K. Littleton (eds.), *Collaborative creativity: contemporary perspectives* (pp. 144–157). London: Free Association Books.

DiMaggio, P. and Useem, M. (1978). Social class and arts consumption: the origins and consequences of class differences in exposure to the arts in America. *Theory and Society*, 5, 141–161.

Dion, K. K. (1972). Physical attractiveness and evaluation of children's transgressions. *Journal of Personality and Social Psychology*, 24, 207–213.

Dion, K. K. Berschied, E. and Walster, E. (1972). What is beautiful is good. *Journal of Personality and Social Psychology*, 24, 285–290.

Dittmar, H. (1992). *The social psychology of material possessions*. Hemel Hempstead: Harvester Wheatsheaf.

Dixon, R. D. (1981). Musical taste cultures and taste publics revisited: a research note of new evidence. *Popular Music and Society*, 8, 2–9.

Dixon, R. D. (1982). LP chart careers: indices and predictors of ascent and descent in popularity. *Popular Music and Society*, 8, 19–43.

Dixon, T. L. and Linz, D. G. (1997). Obscenity law and sexually explicit rap music: understanding the effects of sex, attitudes, and beliefs. *Journal of Applied Communication Research*, 25, 217–241.

Doak, B. A. (2003). Relationships between adolescent psychiatric diagnoses, music preferences, and drug preferences. *Music Therapy Perspectives*, 21, 69–76.

Doise, W. (1986). *Levels of explanation in social psychology*. Cambridge: Cambridge University Press.

Doise, W. Gacoud, J-P., and Mugny, G. (1986). Direct and indirect social influence on aesthetic choices in different intergroup contexts. *Cahiers de Psychologie Cognitive*, 6, 283–301.

Dokter, D. (1994). *Arts therapies and clients with eating disorders: fragile board*. London: Jessica Kingsley Publishers.

Dominick, J. (1974). The portable friend: peer group membership and radio usage. *Journal of Broadcasting*, 18, 164–169.

Donaldson, M. (1978). *Children's minds*. London: Fontana.

Doonar, J. (2004). Harmonious sponsorship. *Brand Strategy*, 185, 52–53.

Dortch, S. (1994, July). Why teens have less green. *American Demographics*, 9.

Doss, E. (1999). *Elvis culture: fans, faith and image*. Lawrence, KA: University of Kansas Press.

Dotson, J. W., Ackerman, D. L., and West, L. J. (1995). Ketamine abuse. *Journal of Drug Issues*, 25, 751–757.

Douvan, E. and Adelson, J. (1966). *The adolescent experience*. New York: Wiley.

Drèze, X. and Zufryden, F. (1997). Testing web site design and promotional content. *Journal of Advertising Research*, 37, 77–91.

Dubé, L. and Morin, S. (2001). Background music pleasure and store evaluation: intensity effects and psychological mechanisms. *Journal of Business Research*, 54, 107–113.

Dubé, L., Chebat, J. C., and Morin, S. (1995). The effects of background music on consumers' desire to affiliate in buyer seller interactions. *Psychology and Marketing*, 12, 305–319.

DuBois–Reymond, M. (1989). School and family in the lifeworld of youngsters. In K. Hurrelmann and U. Engel (eds.), *The social world of adolescents: international perspectives* (pp. 213–228). New York: de Gruyter.

Duerksen, G. L. (1972). Some effects of expectation on evaluation of recorded musical performance. *Journal of Research in Music Education*, 20, 268–272.

Duffett. M. (2003). False faith or false comparison? A critique of the religious interpretation of Elvis fan culture. *Popular Music and Society*, 26, 513–522.

Dukes, R. L., Bisel, T. M., Borega, K. N., Lobato, E. A., and Owens, M. D. (2003). Expressions of love, sex, and hurt in popular songs: a content analysis of all–time greatest hits. *Social Science Journal*, 40, 643–650.

Dunbar, D. S. (1990). Music, and advertising. *International Journal of Advertising*, 9, 197–203.

DuRant, R. H., Rich, M., Emans, S. J., Rome, E. S., Allred, E., and Woods, E. R. (1997). Violence and weapon carrying in music videos: a content analysis. *Archives of Pediatrics and Adolescent Medicine*, 151, 443–448.

DuRant, R. H., Rome, E. S., Rich, M., Alldred, E., Emans, S. J., and Woods, E. R. (1997). Tobacco and alcohol use behaviors portrayed in music videos: a content analysis. *American Journal of Public Health*, 87, 1131–1135.

Durrant, C. (1994). Towards an effective communication: a case for structured teaching of conducting. *British Journal of Music Education*, 11, 56–76.

Dweck, C. S. (1986). Motivational processes affecting learning. *American Psychologist*, 41, 1040–1048.

Dweck, C. S. (1999). *Self-theories: their role in motivation, personality and development.* Hove: Psychology Press.

Earl, P. E. (2001). Simon's travel theorem and the demand for live music. *Journal of Economic Psychology*, 22, 335–358.

Eccles, J., Adler, T. F., Futterman, R., Goff, S. B., Kaczala, C. M., Meece, J. L. and Midgley, C. (1983). Expectancy, values, and academic behaviours. In J. T. Spence (ed.), *Achievement and achievement motives: psychological and sociological motives* (pp. 75–146). San Francisco: Freeman.

Eccles, J., Wigfield, A., Harold, R. D., and Blumenfeld, P. (1993). Age and gender differences in children's self-and task perceptions during elementary school. *Child Development*, 64, 830–847.

Eccles, J., Wigfield, A., and Schiefele, U. (1998). Motivation to succeed. In N. Eisenberg (ed.), *Handbook of child psychology: Volume 3. Social, emotional and personality development* (5th edn.) (pp. 1017–1095). New York: Wiley.

Edwards, J. (1993). Creative thinking abilities of adolescent substance abusers. *Journal of Group Psychotherapy, Psychodrama and Sociometry*, 46, 52–60.

Eide, A. H. and Acuda, S. W. (1997). Cultural orientation and use of cannabis and inhalants among secondary school children in Zimbabwe. *Social Science and Medicine*, 45, 1241–1249.

Einerson, M. J. (1998). Fame, fortune, and failure: young girls' moral language surrounding popular culture. *Youth and Society*, 30, 241–257.

El Sayed, I. M., Farrag, D. A., and Belk, R. W. (2003). The effects of physical surroundings on Egyptian consumers' emotional states and buying intentions. *Journal of International Consumer Marketing*, 16, 5–27.

El'Konin, D. B. (1971). Toward the problem of stages in the mental development of children (trans. N. Veresov). *Voprosy Psikhologii*, 4, 6–20.

Ellis, M. C. (1995). Field dependence–independence and texture discrimination in college non–music majors. *Psychology of Music*, 23, 184–189.

Ellis, M. C. and McCoy, C. W. (1990). Field dependence/independence in college nonmusic majors and their ability to discern form in music. *Journal of Research in Music Education*, 38, 302–310.

Ellis, P. (2001). MTV vs. Channel V. *Asian Case Research Journal*, 5, 167–201.

Engeström, Y. (1987). *Learning by expanding: an activity theoretical approach to developmental research.* Helsinki: Orienta-Konsultit Oy.

Engeström, Y. (2001). Expansive learning at work: toward an activity theory reconceptualisation. *Journal of Education and Work*, 14, 133–161.

Engeström, Y. and Miettinen, R. (1999). Introduction, and activity theory and individual and social transformation. In Y. Engeström, R. Miettinen, and R. L. Punamäki (eds), *Perspectives on activity theory* (pp. 1–16 and 19–38). Cambridge: Cambridge University Press.

Englis, B. G. (1991). Music television and its influences on consumers, consumer culture, and the transmission of consumption messages. *Advances in Consumer Research*, 18, 111–114.

Englis, B. G. and Pennell, G. E. (1994). 'This note's for you': negative effects of the commercial use of popular music. *Advances in Consumer Research*, 21, 97.

Englis, B. G. Solomon, M. R., and Ashmore, R. D. (1994). Beauty before the eyes of the beholders: the cultural encoding of beauty types in magazine advertising and music television. *Journal of Advertising*, 23, 49–64.

Englis, B. G. Solomon, M. R., and Olofsson, A. (1993). Consumption imagery in music television: a bi–cultural perspective. *Journal of Advertising*, 22, 21–33.

Epstein, J., Pratto, D., and Skipper, J. (1990). Teenagers, behavioral problems and preferences for heavy metal and rap music: a case study of a Southern middle school. *Deviant Behavior*, 11, 381–394.

Epstein, J., and Sardiello, R. (1990). The Wharf Rats: a preliminary examination of Alcoholics Anonymous and the Grateful Dead Head phenomena. *Deviant Behavior*, 11, 245–257.

Erdelyi, M. (1940). The relation between 'radio plugs' and sheet sales of popular music. *Journal of Applied Psychology*, 24, 696–702.

Ericsson, K. A. and Smith, J. (eds.) (1991). *Toward a general theory of expertize: prospects and limits*. New York: Cambridge University Press.

Ericsson, K. A., Krampe, R., and Tesch–Römer, C. (1993). The role of deliberate practice in the acquisition of expert performance. *Psychological Review*, 100, 363–406.

Eroglu, S. A., Machleit, K. A., and Chebat, J. C. (2005). The interaction of retail density and music tempo: effects on shopper responses. *Psychology and Marketing*, 22, 577–589.

Etaugh, C. and Ptasnik, P. (1982). Effects of studying to music and post-study relaxation on reading comprehension. *Perceptual and Motor Skills*, 55, 141–142.

Evans, G. W. and Johnson, D. (2000). Stress and open-office noise. *Journal of Applied Psychology*, 85, 779–783.

Evansburg, A. R., Fiore, M. J., Welch, B., Chua, L., and Eremitaggio, P. (2004). Italian anti–piracy law includes prison term. *Intellectual Property and Technology Law Journal*, 16, 22–23.

Eveland, W. P. and McLeod, D. M. (1999). The effect of social desirability on perceived media impact: implications for third-person perceptions. *International Journal of Public Opinion Research*, 11, 315–333.

Eveland, W. P., Nathanson, A. I., Detenber, B. H., and McLeod, D. M. (1999). Rethinking the social distance corollary: perceived likelihood of exposure and the third–person perception. *Communication Research*, 26, 275–302.

Everett, W. (1999). *The Beatles as musicians: Revolver through the Anthology*. Oxford: Oxford University Press.

Everett, W. (2001). *The Beatles as musicians: The Quarry Men through Rubber Soul*. New York: Oxford University Press.

Eysenck H. J. and Eysenck S. B. G. (1975). *Manual of the Eysenck Personality Questionnaire*. London: Hodder and Stoughton.

Fader, P. S. and Hardie, B. G. S. (2001). Forecasting repeat sales at CDNOW: a case study. *Interfaces*, 31, S94–S107.

Fairchild, C. (1996). What you want when you want it: altering consumption and consuming alternatives. *Media, Culture and Society*, 18, 659–668.

Fan, Y. and Pfitzenmair, N. (2002). Event sponsorship in China. *Corporate Communications*, 7, 110–116.

Farkas, A. (2002). Prototypicality–effect in surrealist paintings. *Empirical Studies of the Arts*, 20, 127–136.

Farkas, A. (1945). Musical eminence and year of birth. *Journal of Aesthetics and Art Criticism*, 44, 107–109.

Farkas, A. (1948). Sacred cows in the psychology of music. *Journal of Aesthetics*, 7, 48–51.

Farkas, A. (1954). A study of the Hevner adjective list. *Journal of Aesthetics and Art Criticism*, 13, 97–103.

Farkas, A. (1969). *The social psychology of music (2nd edition)*. Ames: Iowa State University Press.

Farnsworth, P.R. (1945). Musical eminence and year of birth. *Journal of Aesthetics and Art Criticism*, 4, 107–109.

Farnsworth, P.R. (1948). Sacred cows in the psychology of music. *Journal of Aesthetics*, 7, 48–51.

Farnsworth, P.R. (1954). A study of the Hevner adjective list. *Journal of Aesthetics and Art Criticism*, 13, 97–103.

Farnsworth, P.R. (1969). *The social psychology of music* (2nd edn.). Ames: Iowa State University Press.

Farnsworth, P.R. and Beaumont, H. (1929). Suggestion in pictures. *Journal of General Psychology*, 2, 363–366.

Farrell, G. (2001). India. In D. J. Hargreaves and A. C. North (eds.), *Musical development and learning: the international perspective* (pp. 56–72). London: Continuum.

Fauerbach, J. A., Lawrence, J. W., Haythornthwaite, J. A., and Richter, L. (2002). Coping with the stress of a painful medical procedure. *Behaviour Research and Therapy*, 40, 1003–1015.

Fay, P. J. and Middleton, W. C. (1941). Relationship between musical talent and preferences for different types of music. *Journal of Educational Psychology*, 32, 573–583.

Fechner, G. T. (1876). *Vorschule der äesthetik*. Leipzig: Breitkopf and Hartel.

Federal Trade Commission. (2000). *Marketing violence to children: a review of self-regulation and industry practices in the motion picture, music recording, and electronic game industries*. Washington: Federal Trade Commission.

Fedler, F., Hall, J., and Tanzi, L. (1982). Popular songs emphasize sex, de-emphasize romance. *Mass Communication Review*, 9, 10–15.

Feingold, A. (1991). Sex differences in the effects of similarity and physical attractiveness on opposite-sex attraction. *Basic and Applied Social Psychology*, 12, 357–367.

Felix, R. (2004). Understanding youth culture: techno music consumption at live events in Spanish speaking countries. *Journal of International Consumer Marketing*, 16, 7–37.

Ferguson, D. (1973). A study of occupational stress and health. *Ergonomics*, 16, 649–664.

Fiese, R. K. (1990). The effects of non-musical cues on the rankings of music scores by undergraduate conducting students based on judgements of quality. *Journal of Band Research*, 25, 13–21.

Finnäs, L. (1989). A comparison between young people's privately and publicly expressed musical preferences. *Psychology of Music*, 17, 132–145.

Finnegan, R. (1989). *The hidden musicians: music-making in an English town.* Cambridge: Cambridge University Press.

Fischoff, S. P. (1999). Gangsta' rap and a murder in Bakersfield. *Journal of Applied Social Psychology*, 29, 795–805.

Fischoff, S. P. and Ajzen, I. (1975). *Belief, attitude, intention, and behavior: an introduction to theory and research.* Reading: Addison-Wesley.

Fishbein, M., Middlestadt, S. E., Ottati, V., Strauss, S., and Ellis, A. (1988). Medical problems among ISCOM musicians: overview of a national survey. *Medical Problems of Performing Artists*, 3, 1–8.

Fitzgerald, M., Joseph, A. P., Hayes, M., and O'Regan, M. (1995). Leisure activities of adolescent schoolchildren. *Journal of Adolescence*, 18, 349–358.

Flaten, M. A. and Åsli, O. (2006). The effect of stress on absorption of acetaminophen. *Psychopharmacology*, 185, 471–478.

Floch, J. M. (2001). *Semiotics, marketing, and communication: beneath the signs, the strategies.* London: Palgrave MacMillan.

Flîres, R. and Ginsburgh, V. (1996). The Queen Elizabeth music competition: how fair is the final ranking? *Journal of the Royal Statistical Society, Series D, The Statistician*, 45, 97–104.

Flowers, A. L., McCain, A. P., and Hilker, K. A. (1999). *The effects of music listening on premature infants.* Paper presented at the Biennial Meeting, Society for Research in Child Development, Albuquerque.

Flynn, L. R., Eastman, J. K., and Newell, S. J. (1995). An exploratory study of the application of neural networks to marketing: predicting rock music shopping behavior. *Journal of Marketing Theory and Practice*, 3, 75–85.

Flynn, L. R., Goldsmith, R. E., and Eastman, J. K. (1994). The King and Summers Opinion Leadership Scale: revision and refinement. *Journal of Business Research*, 31, 55–64.

Flynn, L. R., Goldsmith, R. E., and Eastman, J. K. (1996). Opinion leaders and opinion seekers: two new measurement scales. *Journal of the Academy of Marketing Science*, 24, 137–147.

Fogelman, K. R. (1976). *Britain's sixteen year olds.* London: National Children's Bureau

Folkestad, G. (1996). *Computer based creative music making: young people's music in the digital age.* Doctoral thesis, University of Göteborg. Göteborg, Sweden: Acta Universitatis Gothoburgiensis.

Folkestad, G. (2002). National identity and music. In R. A. R. MacDonald, D. J. Hargreaves, and D. Miell (eds.), *Musical identities* (pp. 151–162). Oxford: Oxford University Press.

Folkestad, G. (2005). Here, there and everywhere: music education research in a globalized world. *Music Education Research*, 7, 279–287.

Folkestad, G. (2006). Formal and informal learning situations or practices vs. formal and informal ways of learning. *British Journal of Music Education*, 23, 135–145.

Folkestad, G., Hargreaves, D. J. and Lindström, B. (1998). Compositional strategies in computer-based music-making. *British Journal of Music Education*, 115, 83–97.

Forbes, D. (1984). Risk management on Broadway: keeping popular show–stoppers from causing financial disasters. *Risk Management*, 31, 100–102.

Forsyth, A. J. M. (1996). Places and patterns of drug use in the Scottish dance scene. *Addiction*, 91, 511–521.

Forsyth, A. J. M., Barnard, M., and McKeganey, N. P. (1997). Musical preference as an indicator of adolescent drug use. *Addiction*, 92, 1317–1325.

Fosu-Mensah, K., Duran, L., and Stapleton, C. (1987). On music in contemporary West Africa. *African Affairs*, 86, 227–240.

Fowler-Kerry, S. and Lander, J. R. (1987). Management of injection pain in children. *Pain*, 30, 169–175.

Fox, J. G. and Embrey, E. D. (1972). Music: an aid to productivity. *Applied Ergonomics*, 3, 202–205.

Fox, M. (2004). E–commerce business models for the music industry. *Popular Music and Society*, 27, 201–220.

Fox, M. A. and Kochanowski, P. (2004). Models of superstardom: an application of the Lotka and Yule distributions. *Popular Music and Society*, 27, 507–522.

Fox, W. S. and Wince, M. H. (1975). Musical taste cultures and taste publics. *Youth and Society*, 7, 198–224.

Francès, R. (1967). Communication persuasive et communication esthétique. *Journal de Psychologie*, 4, 415–430.

Fraser, B. P. and Brown, W. J. (2002). Media, celebrities, and social influence: identification with Elvis Presley. *Mass Communication and Society*, 5, 183–206.

French, R. and Power, R. (1998). A qualitative study of the social contextual use of alkyl nitrites (poppers) among targeted groups. *Journal of Drug Issues*, 28, 57–76.

Freudiger, P. and Almquist, E. M. (1978). Male and female roles in the lyrics of three genres of contemporary music. *Sex Roles*, 4, 51–65.

Frey, B. S. (1986). The *Salzburg* festival: an economic point of view. *Cultural Economics*, 10, 27–44.

Frey, B. S. (1994). The economics of music festivals. *Journal of Cultural Economics*, 18, 29–39.

Fried, C. B. (1996). Bad rap for rap: bias in reactions to music lyrics. *Journal of Applied Social Psychology*, 26, 2135–2146.

Fried, C. B. (1999). Who's afraid of rap: differential reactions to music lyrics. *Journal of Applied Social Psychology*, 29, 705–721.

Fried, C. B. (2003). Stereotypes of music fans: are rap and heavy metal fans a danger to themselves or others. *Journal of Media Psychology*, 8, *downloaded from http://www.calstatela.edu/faculty/sfischo/Fried%20rev.pdf*

Friedman, M. (1986). Commercial influences in the lyrics of popular American music of the postwar era. *Journal of Consumer Affairs*, 20, 193–213.

Frijda, N. H. (1989). Aesthetic emotions and reality. *American Psychologist*, 44, 1546–1547.

Frith, S. (1978). *The sociology of rock*. Constable: London.

Frith, S. (1981). *Sound effects: youth, leisure and the politics of rock 'n' roll.* New York: Pantheon.

Frith, S. (1987). The industrialisation of popular music. In J. Lull (ed.), *Popular music and communication* (pp. 53–77). Newbury Park: Sage.

Frith, S. (1990). What is good music? *Canadian University Music Review*, 10, 97–8.

Frith, S. (1992). The industrialization of popular music. In J. Lull (ed.), *Popular music and communication (2nd ed.)* (pp. 49–74). Thousand Oaks: Sage.

Frith, S. (1996). *Performing rites*. Oxford: Oxford University Press.

Frosch, W. A. (1987). Moods, madness, and music: I. Major affective disease and musical creativity. *Comprehensive Psychiatry*, 28, 315–322.

Fukui, H. and Yamashita, M. (2003). The effects of music and visual stress on testosterone and cortisol in men and women. *Neuroendocrinology Letters*, 24, 173–180.

Fulberg, P. (2003). Using sonic branding in the retail environment: an easy and effective way to create consumer brand loyalty while enhancing the in–store experience. *Journal of Consumer Behaviour*, 3, 193–198.

Fuller, S. (1994). *The Pandora guide to women composers: Britain and the United States 1629–present*. London: HarperCollins.

Furia, P. (1990). *The poets of Tin Pan Alley: a history of America's great lyricists*. Oxford: Oxford University Press.

Furnham, A. and Bradley, A. (1997). Music while you work: the differential distraction of background music on the cognitive test performance of introverts and extraverts. *Applied Cognitive Psychology*, 11, 445–455.

Furman, C. E. and Duke, R. A. (1988). Effect of majority consensus on preferences for recorded orchestral and popular music. *Journal of Research in Music Education*, 36, 220–231.

Furnham, A., Abramsky, S., and Gunter, B. (1997). A cross-cultural content analysis of children's television advertisements. *Sex Roles*, 37, 91–99.

Furnham, A., Bergland J., and Gunter B. (2002). Memory for television ads as a function of advertisement-programme congruity. *Applied Cognitive Psychology*, 16, 525–545.

Furnham, A., Trew, S., and Sneade, I. (1999). The distracting effects of vocal and instrumental music on the cognitive test performance of introverts and extraverts. *Personality and Individual Differences*, 27, 381–392.

Gabbard, G. O. (1979). Stage fright. *International Journal of Psychoanalysis*, 50, 383–392.

Gabrielsson, A. (1989). Intense emotional experiences of music. In *Proceedings of the 1st International Conference on Music Perception and Cognition* (pp. 371–376). Kyoto: Japanese Society of Music Perception and Cognition.

Gabrielsson, A. (2001). Emotions in strong experiences with music. In P. N. Juslin and J. A. Sloboda (eds.), *Music and emotion: theory and research* (pp. 431–449). Oxford: Oxford University Press.

Gabrielsson, A. and Lindström, S. (1993). On strong experiences of music. *Musikpsychologie: jahrbuch der Deutschen Gesellschaft für Musikpsychologie*, 10, 118–139.

Gabrielsson, A. and Lindström, S. (1995). Can strong experiences of music have therapeutic implications? in R. Steinberg (ed.), *Music and the mind machine: the psychophysiology and psychopathology of the sense of music* (pp. 195–202). New York: Springer.

Gabrielsson, A. and Lindström, S. (2001) The influence of musical structure on emotional expression. In P. N. Juslin and J. A. Sloboda (eds.), *Music and emotion: theory and research* (pp. 223–248). Oxford: Oxford University Press.

Gabrielsson, A. and Lindström Wik, S. (2000). Strong experiences of and with music. In D. Greer (ed.), *Musicology and sister disciplines: past, present, and future* (pp. 100–108). Oxford: Oxford University Press.

Gabrielsson, A. and Lindström Wik, S. (2003). Strong experiences related to music: a descriptive system. *Musicae Scientiae*, 7, 157–217.

Galton, F. (1869). *Hereditary genius: an inquiry into its laws and consequences*. Macmillan: London.

Gan, S., Zillmann, D., and Mitrook, M. (1997). Stereotyping effect of Black women's sexual rap on White audiences. *Basic and Applied Social Psychology*, 19, 381–399.

Gander, J. and Rieple, A. (2002). Inter–organisational relationships in the worldwide popular recorded music industry. *Creativity and Innovation Management*, 11, 248–254.

Gander, J. and Rieple, A. (2004). How relevant is transaction cost economics to inter–firm relationships in the music industry? *Journal of Cultural Economics*, 28, 57–79.

Ganidagli, S., Cengiz, M., Yanik, M., Becerik, C., and Unal B. (2005). The effect of music on preoperative sedation and the bispectral index. *Anesthesia and Analgesia*, 101, 103–106.

Gans, H. J. (1974). *Popular culture and high culture: an analysis and evaluation of taste*. New York: Basic Books.

Gantz, W., Gartenberg, H. M., Pearson, M. L., and Schiller, S. O. (1978). Gratifications and expectations associated with pop music among adolescents. *Popular Music and Society*, 6, 81–89.

Garamszegi, L. Z. and Moller, A. P. (2004). Extrapair paternity and the evolution of bird song. *Behavioral Ecology*, 15, 508–519.

Gardiner, M. F., Fox, A., Knowles, F., and Jeffrey, D. (1996). Learning improved by arts training. *Nature*, 381, 284.

Gardner, H. (1973). *The arts and human development*. New York: John Wiley.

Gardner, H. (1983). *Frames of mind: the theory of multiple intelligences*. New York: Basic Books.

Gardner, H. (1989). Zero–based arts education: an introduction to Arts Propel. *Studies in Art Education*, 30, 71–83.

Gardner, H. (1993). *Multiple intelligences: the theory in practice*. New York: Basic Books.

Gardner, H. (2003). *MI after 20 years*. Paper presented at the American Educational Research Association, Chicago.

Gardner, H. and Winner, E. (1982). First intimations of artistry. In S. Strauss (ed.), *U-shaped behavioral growth* (pp. 147–168). New York: Academic Press.

Gardner, W. J. and Licklider, J. C. (1959). Auditory analgesia in dental operation. *Journal of the American Dental Association*, 59, 1144–1150.

Gardstrom, S. C. (1999). Music exposure and criminal behavior: perceptions of juvenile offenders. *Journal of Music Therapy*, 36, 207–221.

Garlin, F. V. and Owen, K. (2006). Setting the tone with the tune: a meta-analytic review of the effects of background music in retail settings. *Journal of Business Research*, 59, 755–764.

Garofalo, R. (1997). *Rockin' out: popular music in the USA*. Needham Heights: Allyn and Bacon.

Gazel, R. C. and Schwer, R. K. (1997). Beyond rock and roll: the economic impact of the Grateful Dead on a local economy. *Journal of Cultural Economics*, 21, 41–55.

Gebesmair, A. and Smudits, A. (eds.) (2004). Global repertoires: popular music within and beyond the transnational music industry. Aldershot: Ashgate.

Geiger, T. (1950). A radio test of musical taste. *Public Opinion Quarterly*, 14, 453–460.

Geissmann, T. (2000) Gibbon songs and human music from an evolutionary perspective. In N. L. Wallin, B. Merker, and S. Brown (eds.), *The origins of music* (pp. 103–123). Cambridge: MIT Press.

Gembris, H. (2001). Federal Republic of Germany. In D. J. Hargreaves and A. C. North (eds.), *Musical development and learning: the international perspective* (pp. 40–55). London: Continuum.

Gembris, H. and Davidson, J. W. (2002). Environmental influences. In R. Parncutt and G. E. McPherson (eds.), *The science and psychology of music performance* (pp. 17–30). Oxford: Oxford University Press.

Gerbner, G., Gross, L., Morgan, M., and Signorielli, N. (1994). Growing up with television: the cultivation perspective. In J. Bryant and D. Zillmann (eds.), *Media effects: advances in theory and research* (pp. 17–41). Hillsdale: Erlbaum.

Gereb, G. (1966). Some methodological implications of model experiments in the study of monotony. *Pszichologiai Tanulmanyok*, 9, 563–579.

Geter, T. and Streisand, B. (1995, 25th September). Recording sound sales: the music industry rocks and rolls to the newest financial rhythms. *U.S. News and World Report*, 67–68, 70, 72.

Ghiselin, B. (ed.) (1952). *The creative process*. Cambridge: Cambridge University Press.

Gibson, R., Aust, C. F., and Zillmann, D. (2000). Loneliness of adolescents and their choice and enjoyment of love-celebrating versus love-lamenting popular music. *Empirical Studies of the Arts*, 18, 43–48.

Ginsburgh, V. (2003). Awards, success and aesthetic quality in the arts. *Journal of Economic Perspectives*, 17, 99–111.

Ginsburgh, V. A. and van Ours, J. C. (2003). Expert opinion and compensation: evidence from a musical cometition. *American Economic Review*, 93, 289–296.

Glasgow, M. R. and Cartier, A. M. (1985). Conservatism, sensation-seeking and music preferences. *Personality and Individual Differences*, 6, 393–395.

Glejser, H. and Heyndels, B. (2001). Efficiency and inefficiency in the ranking in competitions: the case of the Queen Elisabeth music contest. *Journal of Cultural Economics*, 25, 109–129.

Goff, L. C., Pratt, R. R., and Madrigal, J. L. (1997). Music listening and S-IgA levels in patients undergoing a dental procedure. *International Journal of Arts Medicine*, 5, 22–26.

Gold, B. D. (1987). Self–image of punk rock and nonpunk rock juvenile delinquents. *Adolescence*, 22, 535–544.

Goldberg, P. (1968). Are women prejudiced against women? *Transaction*, 5, 28–30.

Goldfarb, R. S. (1994). A Davis–Bacon musicale: symphony orchestras as migrant labor. *Journal of Labor Research*, 5, 427–33.

Goldin, C. and Rouse, C. (2000). Orchestrating impartiality: the impact of 'blind' auditions on female musicians. *American Economic Review*, 90, 715–741.

Goldsmith, R. E. and De Witt, T. S. (2003). The predictive validity of an opinion leadership scale. *Journal of Marketing Theory and Practice*, 11, 28–35.

Good, M. (1995). A comparison of the effects of jaw relaxation and music on postoperative pain. *Nursing Research*, 44, 52–57.

Good, M., Anderson, G. C., Ahn, S., Cong, X., and Stanton-Hicks, M. (2005). Relaxation and music reduce pain following intestinal surgery. *Research in Nursing and Health*, 28, 240–251.

Good, M., Stanton–Hicks, M., Grass, J. A., Anderson, G. C., Choi, C., Schoolmeesters, L. J., and Salman, A. (1999). Relief of postoperative pain with jaw relaxation, music and their combination. *Pain*, 81, 163–172.

Gopal, R. D., Sanders, G. L., Bhattacharjee, S., Agrawal, M., and Wagner, S. C. (2004). A behavioral model of digital music piracy. *Journal of Organizational Computing and Electronic Commerce*, 14, 89–105.

Gordon, A. G. (1999). Creativity, hyperesthesia, and mental illness. *Canadian Journal of Psychiatry*, 344, 91.

Gordon, E. E. (1976). *Learning sequence and patterns in music.* Buffalo: Tometic Associates Ltd.

Gordon, E. E. (1997). *A music learning theory for newborn and young children.* Chicago: G. I. A. Publications, Inc.

Gore, T. (1987). *Raising PG kids in an X–rated society.* Nashville: Abingdon.

Gorn, G. J. (1982). The effect of music in advertising on choice behavior: a classical conditioning approach. *Journal of Marketing,* **46,** 94–101.

Gorn, G. J., Goldberg, M. E., and Basu, K. (1993). Mood, awareness, and product evaluation. *Journal of Consumer Psychology,* **2,** 237–256.

Gorn, G., Pham, M. T., and Sin, L. Y. (2001). When arousal influences ad evaluation and valence does not (and vice versa). *Journal of Consumer Psychology,* **11,** 43–55.

Goswami, U. (2001). Cognitive development: no stages please—we're British. *British Journal of Psychology,* **92,** 257–277.

Gow, J. (1996). Reconsidering gender roles on MTV: depictions in the most popular music videos of the early 1990s. *Communication Reports,* **9,** 151–161.

Gowensmith, W. N. and Bloom. L. J. (1997). The effects of heavy metal music on arousal and anger. *Journal of Music Therapy,* **34,** 33–45.

Green, L. (1997). *Music, gender, education.* Cambridge: Cambridge University Press.

Green, L. (2001). *How popular musicians learn: a way ahead for music education.* Aldershot: Aldgate.

Green, L. (2002). *How popular musicians learn: a way ahead for music education.* Aldershot: Ashgate.

Green, L. (2005a). *Meaning, autonomy and authenticity in the music classroom: professorial lecture.* Institute of Education, University of London.

Green, L. (2005b). The music curriculum as lived experience: children's 'natural' music learning processes. *Music Educators' Journal,* **91,** 27–32.

Greenfield, P. M., Bruzzone, L., Koyamatsu, K., Satuloff, W., Nixon, K., Brodie, M., and Kingsdale, D. (1987). What is rock music doing to the minds of our youth? A first experimental look at the effects of rock music lyrics and music videos. *Journal of Early Adolescence,* **7,** 315–329.

Greer, C. (2002). *Sex crime and the media: sex offending and the press in a divided society.* Cullompton: Willan.

Greeson, L. E. (1986). Discussion of media influences and other selected issues in adolescent psychology texts. *American Psychologist,* **41,** 1385–1386.

Greeson, L. E. (1991). Recognition and ratings of television music videos: age, gender, and sociocultural effects. *Journal of Applied Psychology,* **21,** 1908–1920.

Greeson, L. E. and Williams, R. A. (1986). Social implications of music videos for youth: an analysis of the content and effects of MTV. *Youth and Society,* **18,** 177–189.

Gregoris, L. and Poldrugo, F. (2002). Alcohol abuse as a theme in contemporary Italian song writers. *Alcoholism: Journal on Alcoholism and Related Addictions,* **38,** 27–33.

Gregory, A. H. (1997). The roles of music in society: the ethnomusicological perspective. In D. J. Hargreaves and A. C. North (eds.), *The social psychology of music* (pp. 123–140). Oxford: Oxford University Press.

Greve, H. R. and Taylor, A. (2000). Innovations as catalysts for organizational change: shifts in organizational cognition and search. *Administrative Science Quarterly,* **45,** 54–80.

Grewal, D., Baker, J., Levy, M., and Voss, G. B. (2003). The effects of wait expectations and store atmosphere evaluations on patronage intentions in service–intensive retail stores. *Journal of Retailing*, 79, 259–268.

Grier, S. A. (2001). The Federal Trade Commission's report on the marketing of violent entertainment to youths: developing policy-tuned research. *Journal of Public Policy and Marketing*, 20, 123–132.

Griswold, P. A. and Chroback, D. A. (1981). Sex-role associations of music instruments and occupations by gender and major. *Journal of Research in Music Education*, 29, 57–62.

Groce, S. B. (1991). What's the buzz? Rethinking the meanings and uses of alcohol and other drugs among small–time rock 'n' roll musicians. *Deviant Behavior*, 12, 361–384.

Groenland, E. A. G. and Schoormans, J. P. L. (1994). Comparing mood-induction and affective conditioning as mechanisms influencing product evaluation and product choice. *Psychology and Marketing*, 11, 183–197.

Gromko, J. E. and Poorman, A. S. (1988). The effect of music training on preschoolers' spatial–temporal task performance. *Journal of Research in Music Education*, 46, 173–181.

Gronnerod, J. S. (2002). The use of alcohol and cannabis in non–professional rock bands in Finland. *Contemporary Drug Problems*, 29, 417–443.

Grossman, J. C., Goldstein, R., and Eisenman, R. (1974). Undergraduate marijuana and drug use as related to openness to experience. Psychiatric Quarterly, 48, 86–92.

Gudjonsson, G. H. (1984). A new scale of interrogative suggestibility. *Personality and Individual Differences*, 5, 303–314.

Guéguen, N, Le Guellec, H., and Jacob, C. (2004). Sound level of background music and alcohol consumption: an empirical evaluation. *Perceptual and Motor Skills*, 99, 34–38.

Guéguen, N. and Jacob, C. (2002). The influence of music on temporal perceptions in an on–hold waiting situation. *Psychology of Music*, 30, 210–214.

Guilford, J. P. (1950). Creativity. *American Psychologist*, 5, 444–454.

Gulas, C. and Schewe, C. (1994). Atmospheric segmentation: managing store image with background music. In R. Acrol and A. Mitchell (eds.), *Enhancing knowledge development in marketing* (pp. 325–330). Chicago: American Marketing Association.

Guski, R. (1975). An experiment on the relationship between noise intensity, awareness of the situation, and performance. *Zeitschrift für Experimentelle und Angewandte Psychologie*, 22, 584–599.

Haack, P. A. (1988). An exploratory study of popular music preferences along the age continuum. *Paper presented at the meeting of the Music Educators National Conference, Indianapolis, Indiana, USA.*

Hagerty, M. R. (1983). Variety seeking among songs which vary in similarity. *Advances in Consumer Research*, 10, 75–79.

Hahn, M. and Hwang, I. (1999). Effects of tempo and familiarity of background music on message processing in TV advertising: a resource-matching perspective. *Psychology and Marketing*, 16, 659–675.

Hakanen, E. A. (1995). Emotional use of music by African American adolescents. *Howard Journal of Communications*, 5, 214–222.

Hakanen, E. A. and Wells, A. (1993). Music preference and taste cultures among adolescents. *Popular Music and Society*, 17, 55–69.

Halford, G. S. (1993). *Children's understanding: the development of mental models.* Hillsdale: Erlbaum.

Hall, A. (2005). Sensation seeking and the use and selection of media materials. *Psychological Reports*, 97, 236–244.

Hall, M. L. (2004). A review of hypotheses for the functions of avian duetting. *Behavioral Ecology and Sociobiology*, 55, 415–430.

Hallam, S. (1995). Professional musicians' approaches to the learning and interpretation of music. *Psychology of Music*, 23, 111–129.

Hallam, S. (1998). The predictors of achievement and dropout in instrumental tuition. *Psychology of Music*, 26, 116–132.

Hallam, S. (2002). Musical motivation: towards a model synthesising the research. *Music Education Research*, 4, 225–244.

Hallam, S. and Prince, V. (2003). Conceptions of musical ability. *Research Studies in Music Education*, 20, 2–22.

Hallam, S. and Price, J. (1998). Can the use of background music improve the behaviour and academic performance of children with emotional and behavioural difficulties? *British Journal of Special Education*, 25, 87–90.

Hallam, S. and Price, J., and Katsarou, G. (2002). The effects of background music on primary school pupils' task performance. *Educational Studies*, 28, 111–122.

Halpin, D. D. (1943). Industrial music and morale. *Journal of the Acoustical Society of America*, 15, 116–123.

Hamann, D. L. (1982). An assessment of anxiety in instrumental and vocal performers. *Journal of Research in Music Education*, 30, 77–90.

Hamlen, W. A. (1991). Superstardom in popular music: empirical evidence. *Review of Economics and Statistics*, 73, 729–733.

Hamlen, W. A. (1994). Variety and superstardom in popular music. *Economic Inquiry*, 32, 395–406.

Hannon, E. E., and Trehub, S. E. (2005). Tuning in to musical rhythms: infants learn more readily than adults. *Proceedings of the National Academy of Sciences*, 102, 12639–12643.

Hansen, C. H. (1989). Priming sex-role stereotypic event schemas with rock music videos: effects on impression favorability, trait inferences, and recall of a subsequent male-female interaction. *Basic and Applied Social Psychology*, 10, 371–391.

Hansen, C. H. (1995). Predicting cognitive and behavioural effects of gangsta rap. *Basic and Applied Social Psychology*, 16, 43–52.

Hansen, C. H. and Hansen, R. D. (1988). How rock music videos can change what is seen when boy meets girl: priming stereotypic appraisal of social interactions. *Sex Roles*, 19, 287–316.

Hansen, C. H. and Hansen, R. D. (1990a). The influence of sex and violence on the appeal of rock music videos. *Communication Research*, 17, 212–234.

Hansen, C. H. and Hansen, R. D. (1990b). Rock music videos and antisocial behavior. *Basic and Applied Social Psychology*, 11, 357–369.

Hansen, C. H. and Hansen, R. D. (1991a). Constructing personality and social reality through music: individual differences among fans of punk and heavy metal music. *Journal of Broadcasting and Electronic Media*, 35, 335–350.

Hansen, C. H. and Hansen, R. D. (1991b). Schematic information processing of heavy metal lyrics. *Communication Research*, 18, 373–411.

Hansen, C. H. and Hansen, R. D. (2000). Music and music videos. In D. Zillmann and P. Vorderer (eds). *Media entertainment: the psychology of its appeal* (pp. 175–196). Mahwah: Lawrence Erlbaum Associates.

Hansen, C. H. and Krygowski, W. (1994). Arousal–augmented priming effects: rock music videos and sex object schemas. *Communication Research*, 18, 24–47.

Hanser, S. B. (1985). Music therapy and stress reduction research. *Journal of Music Therapy*, 22, 193–206.

Hanslick, E. (1891). *The beautiful in music.* London: Novello.

Hantula, D. A. and Bryant, K. (2005). Delay discounting determines delivery fees in an e–commerce simulation: a behavioral economic perspective. *Psychology and Marketing*, 22, 153–161.

Harchaoui, T. M. and Hamdad, M. (2000). The prices of classical recorded music: a hedonic approach. *International Journal of Industrial Organization*, 18, 497–514.

Hardy, L. and Parfitt, G. (1991). A catastrophe model of anxiety and performance. *British Journal of Psychology*, 82, 163–178.

Hargreaves, D. J. (1974). Situational influences on divergent thinking. *British Journal of Educational Psychology*, 44, 84–88.

Hargreaves, D. J. (1982). The development of aesthetic reactions to music. *Psychology of Music, Special Issue*, 51–54.

Hargreaves, D. J. (1986). *The developmental psychology of music.* Cambridge: Cambridge University Press.

Hargreaves, D. J. (1996). The development of artistic and musical competence, in I. deLiège and J. A. Sloboda (eds.), *Musical beginnings: the origins and development of musical competence* (pp. 145–170). Oxford: Oxford University Press.

Hargreaves, D. J. (1999). Developing musical creativity in the social world. *Bulletin of the Council for Research in Music Education*, 142, 22–34.

Hargreaves, D. J. (forthcoming) Invited commentary on 'Music education: a site for collaborative creativity'. *International Journal of Educational Research*.

Hargreaves, D. J. and Bolton, N. (1972). Selecting creativity tests for use in research. *British Journal of Psychology*, 63, 451–462.

Hargreaves, D. J. and Castell, K. C. (1987). Development of liking for familiar and unfamiliar melodies. *Council for Research in Music Education Bulletin*, 91, 665–669.

Hargreaves, D. J. and Colman, A. M. (1981). The dimensions of aesthetic reactions to music. *Psychology of Music*, 99, 15–20.

Hargreaves, D. J., Cork, C. A. and Setton, T. (1991). Cognitive strategies in jazz improvisation: an exploratory study. *Canadian Music Educators Journal*, 33, 47–54.

Hargreaves, D. J. and Galton, M. (1992). Aesthetic learning: psychological theory and educational practice. In B. Reimer and R. A. Smith (eds.), *1992 N.S.S.E. yearbook on the arts in education* (pp. 124–150). Chicago: N.S.S.E.

Hargreaves, D. J., Galton, M., and Robinson, S. (1996). Teachers' assessments of primary children's classroom work in the creative arts. *Educational Research*, 38, 199–211.

Hargreaves, D. J., Galton, M., Robinson, S., and Windridge, K. (2002). Why do children do creative arts work at school? Teacher and pupil views. *Bulletin of the Council for Research in Music Education*, 153/4, 109–113.

Hargreaves, D. J., Lamont. A., Marshall, N., and Tarrant. M. (2004). What is 'being good at music'? *NAME (National Association of Music Educators) Magazine*, 13, 4–7.

Hargreaves, D. J. and Marshall, N. A. (2003). Developing identities in music education. *Music Education Research*, 5, 263–273.

Hargreaves, D. J. and North, A. C. (2003). Music education in the 21st century: a psychological perspective. *British Journal of Music Education*, 20, 147–163.

Hargreaves, D. J., Messerschmidt, P., and Rubert, C. (1980). Musical preference and evaluation. *Psychology of Music*, 8, 13–18.

Hargreaves, D. J., Miell, D. E., and MacDonald, R. A. R. (2002). What are musical identities, and why are they important? in R. A. R. MacDonald, D. J. Hargreaves and D. E. Miell (eds.), *Musical identities* (pp. 1–20). Oxford: Oxford University Press.

Hargreaves, D. J., Miell, D. E., MacDonald, R. A. R. (2005). How do people communicate using music? in Miell, D. E., MacDonald, R. A. R., and Hargreaves, D. J. (eds.) *Musical communication* (pp. 1–25). Oxford: Oxford University Press.

Hargreaves, D. J. and North, A. C. (eds.) (1997). *The social psychology of music*. Oxford: Oxford University Press.

Hargreaves, D. J. and North, A. C. (1999a). Developing concepts of musical style. *Musicae Scientiae*, 3, 193–216.

Hargreaves, D. J. and North, A. C. (1999b). The functions of music in everyday life: redefining the social in music psychology. *Psychology of Music*, 27, 71–83.

Hargreaves, D. J. and North, A. C., Hargreaves, D. J. and North, A. C. (eds.) (2001). *Musical development and learning: the international perspective*. London: Continuum.

Hargreaves, D. J. and North, A. C., and Tarrant, M. (2006). The development of musical preference and taste in childhood and adolescence. In G. McPherson (ed.), *The child as musician: a handbook of musical development* (pp. 135–154). Oxford: Oxford University Press.

Hargreaves, D. J., Welch, G., Purves, R. and Marshall, N. (2003). The identities of music teachers. In R. Kopiez, A. C. Lehmann, I. Wolther and C. Wolf (eds.), *Proceedings of the 5th Triennial ESCOM conference* (pp. 178–181). University of Hanover, Germany.

Hargreaves, D. J. and Zimmerman, M. (1992). Developmental theories of music learning. In R. Colwell (ed.), *Handbook for research in music teaching and learning* (pp. 377–391). New York: Schirmer/Macmillan.

Harland, J., Kinder, K., Lord, P., Stott, A., Schagen, I., Haynes, J., Cusworth, L. White, R. and Paola, R. (2000). *Arts education in secondary schools: effects and effectiveness*. Slough: NFER.

Harré, R. (1979). *Social being*. Oxford: Blackwell.

Harris, C. S., Bradley, R. J., and Titus, S. K. (1992). A comparison of the effects of hard rock and easy listening on the frequency of observed inappropriate behaviors: control of environmental antecedents in a large public area. *Journal of Music Therapy*, 29, 6–17.

Harrison, A. C. and O' Neill, S. A. (2000). Children's gender-typed preferences for musical instruments: an intervention study. *Psychology of Music*, 28, 81–97.

Harrison, A. C. and O' Neill, S. A. (2002). II. The development of children's gendered knowledge and preferences in music. *Feminism and Psychology*, 12, 145–152.

Harter, S. (1986). Cognitive–developmental processes in the integration of concepts about emotions and the self. *Social Cognition*, 4, 119–151.

Harter, S. (1999). *The construction of the self: a developmental perspective*. New York: Guilford Press.

Harwood, E. (1998). Music learning in context: a playground tale. *Research Studies in Music Education*, 11, 52–60.

Haun, M., Mainous, R. O., and Looney, S. W. (2001). Effect of music on anxiety of women awaiting breast biopsy. *Behavioral Medicine*, 27, 127–132.

Hauser, M. D. and McDermott, J. (2003). The evolution of the music faculty: a comparative perspective.*Nature Neuroscience*, 6, 663–668.

Haythornthwaite, J. A., Lawrence, J. W., and Fauerbach, J. A. (2001). Brief cognitive interventions for burn pain. *Annals of Behavioral Medicine*, 23, 42–49.

Heal, M. H. and Wigram, T. (eds.) (1993). *Music therapy in health and education*. London: Jessica Kingsley Publishers.

Heath, S. B. (2001) Three's not a crowd: plans, roles and focus in the arts. *Educational Researcher*, 30, 10–17.

Hecker, S. (1984). Music for advertising effect. *Psychology and Marketing*, 1, 3–8.

Heckler, S. E. and Childers, T. L. (1992). The role of expectancy and relevancy in memory for verbal and visual information: what is incongruency? *Journal of Consumer Research*, 18, 475–492.

Hedden, S. K. (1973). Listeners' responses to music in relation to autochthonous and experiential factors. *Journal of Research in Music Education*, 21, 225–238.

Hedge, A. (1982). The open–plan office: a systematic investigation of employee reactions to their work environment. *Environment and Behavior*, 14, 519–542.

Heider, F. (1958). *The psychology of interpersonal relationships*. New York: Wiley.

Hekkert, P. and van Wieringen, P. C. W. (1990). Complexity and prototypicality as determinants of the appraisal of cubist paintings. *British Journal of Psychology*, 81, 483–495.

Hekmat, H. M. and Hertel, J. B. (1993). Pain attenuating effects of preferred versus non–preferred music interventions. *Psychology of Music*, 21, 163–173.

Helmholtz, H. von (1896). *Vorträge und Reden*. Brunswick: Friedrich Vieweg.

Hendy, D. (2000). Pop music radio in the public service: BBC Radio 1 and new music in the 1990s. *Media, Culture and Society*, 22, 743–761.

Henley, D. R. (1992). Facilitating artistic expression in captive mammals: implications for art therapy and art empathicism. *Art Therapy*, 9, 178–192.

Hennion, A. and Meadel, C. (1986). Programming music: radio as mediator. *Media, Culture and Society*, 8, 281–303.

Hepper, P. G. (1991). An examination of fetal learning before and after birth. *Irish Journal of Psychology*, 12, 95–107.

Hepper, P. G. and Shahidullah, S. (1992). Habituation in normal and Down's syndrome fetuses. *Quarterly Journal of Experimental Psychology: Comparative and Physiological Psychology*, 44B, 305–317.

Herrington, J. D. and Capella. L. M. (1994). Practical applications of music in service settings. *Journal of Services Marketing*, 8, 50–65.

Herrington, J. D. and Capella, L. M. (1996). Effects of music in service environments: a field study. *Journal of Services Marketing*, 10, 26–41.

Hesmondhalgh, D. (1998). The British dance music industry: a case study of independent cultural production. *British Journal of Sociology*, 49, 234–251.

Hesmondhalgh, D. (1999). Indie: the institutional politics and aesthetics of a popular music genre. *Cultural Studies*, 13, 34–61.

Hetland, L. (2000a). Listening to music enhances spatial-temporal reasoning: evidence for the 'Mozart effect'. *Journal of Aesthetic Education*, 34, 105–148.

Hetland, L. (2000b). Learning to make music enhances spatial reasoning. *Journal of Aesthetic Education*, 34, 179–238.

Hetland, L. and Winner, E. (eds.) (2000). Special issue: the arts and academic achievement: what the evidence shows. Journal of Aesthetic Education, 34.

Hevner, K. (1935a). The affective character of the major and minor modes in music. *American Journal of Psychology*, 47, 103–118.

—— (1935b). Expression in music: a discussion of experimental studies and theories. *Psychological Review*, 42, 186–204.

—— (1936). Experimental studies of the elements of expression in music. *American Journal of Psychology*, 48, 246–268.

—— The affective value of pitch and tempo in music. *American Journal of Psychology*, 49, 621–630.

Hewstone, M. and Manstead, A. S. R. (1995). Social psychology. In M. Hewstone and A. S. R. Manstead (eds.), *The Blackwell encyclopaedia of social psychology* (pp. 588–595). Oxford: Blackwell.

Heyduk, R. G. (1975). Rated preference for musical composition as it relates to complexity and exposure frequency. *Perception and Psychophysics*, 17, 84–91.

Hier, S. P. (2003). Risk and panic in late modernity: implications of the converging sites of social anxiety. *British Journal of Sociology*, 54, 3–20.

Hill, P. (1993). Recent advances in selected areas of adolescent development. *Journal of Child Psychology and Psychiatry*, 34, 69–99.

Hipple, J. Chesky, K., and Young, J. (2000). Alcohol use patterns and perceptions of substance abuse among university music majors: a preliminary investigation. *TCA Journal*, 28, 102–110.

Hirsch, P. (1971). Sociological approaches to the pop music phenomenon. *American Behavioral Scientist*, 14, 371–388.

Hitchon, J., Duckler, P., and Thorson, E. (1994). Effects of ambiguity and complexity on consumer response to music video commercials. *Journal of Broadcasting and Electronic Media*, 38, 289–306.

Ho, Y. C., Cheung, M. C., and Chan, A. S. (2003). Music training improves verbal but not visual memory: cross sectional and longitudinal explorations in children. *Neuropsychology*, 17, 439–450.

Hodgetts, B. V., Waas, J. R., and Matthews, L. R. (1998). The effects of visual and auditory disturbance on the behaviour of red deer (Cervus elaphus) at pasture with and without shelter. *Applied Animal Behaviour Science*, 55, 337–351.

Hodgson, P. (1992). Is the growing popularity of opera in Britain just another nineties media myth? Market research provides the answer. *Journal of the Market Research Society*, 34, 405–418.

Hoffman, D. L. and Novak, T. P. (2000). How to acquire customers on the web. *Harvard Business Review*, 78, 179–188.

Hoffmann, J. and Sheridan, L. P. (2005). The stalking of public figures: management and intervention. *Journal of Forensic Sciences*, 66, 1459–1465.

Holbrook, M. B. (1995). An empirical approach to representing patterns of consumer tastes, nostalgia, and hierarchy in the market for cultural products. *Empirical Studies of the Arts*, 13, 55–71.

—— and Gardner, M. P. (2000). Illustrating a dynamic model of the mood–updating process in consumer behavior. *Psychology and Marketing*, 17, 165–194.

—— and Schindler, R. M. (1989). Some exploratory findings on the development of musical tastes. *Journal of Consumer Research*, 16, 119–124.

—— —— (1994). Age, sex, and attitude toward the past as predictors of consumers' aesthetic tastes for cultural products. *Journal of Marketing Research*, 31, 412–422.

—— —— (1996). Market segmentation based on age and attitude toward the past: concepts, methods, and findings concerning nostalgic influences on customer tastes. *Journal of Business Research*, 37, 27–39.

Holder–Nevins, D. and Bain, B. (2001). Popular music and sexual behavior among female adolescents in Jamaica: a case control study. *Journal of HIV/AIDS Prevention and Education for Adolescents and Children*, 4, 149–160.

Holland, J. L. (1985). *Making vocational choices: a theory of vocational personalities and work environments* (2nd ed.). Englewood Cliffs: Prentice-Hall.

Horatio Alger Foundation. (1996). *The mood of American youth*. Alexandria: Horatio Alger Foundation of Distinguished Americans.

Horden, P. (2000). *Music as medicine: the history of music therapy since antiquity*. Aldershot: Ashgate.

Hough, E. (1943). Music as a safety factor. *Journal of the Acoustical Society of America*, 15, 124.

Houston, M. J., Childers, T. L., and Heckler, S. E. (1987). Picture-word consistency and elaborative processing of advertisements. *Journal of Marketing Research*, 24, 359–369.

Howe, M. J. A., Davidson, J., and Sloboda, J. A. (1998). Innate talents: reality or myth? *Behavioural and Brain Sciences*, 31, 399–442.

—— —— Moore, D. G., and Sloboda, J. A. (1995). Are there early childhood signs of musical ability? *Psychology of Music*, 23, 162–176.

—— and Sloboda, J. A. (1991). Young musicians' accounts of significant influences in their early lives: 2. Teachers, practising, and performing. *British Journal of Music Education*, 8, 53–63.

Howitt, D. (1998). *Crime, the media and the law*. London: Wiley.

Hucklebridge, F., Lambert, S., Clow, A., Warburton, D. M., Evans, P. D., and Sherwood N. (2000). Modulation of secretory immunoglobulin A in saliva; response to manipulation of mood. *Biological Psychology*, 53, 25–35.

Hui, K. L. and Png, I. (2003). Piracy and the legitimate demand for recorded music. *Contributions to Economic Analysis and Policy*, 2, article 11, 1–22.

Hui, M, K., Dube, L., and Chebat, J. C. (1997). The impact of music on consumers' reactions to waiting for services. *Journal of Retailing*, 73, 87–104.

Hume, K. M. and Crossman, J. (1992). Musical reinforcement of practice behaviors among competitive swimmers. *Journal of Applied Behavior Analysis*, 25, 665–670.

Hume, L., Dodd, C.A., Grigg, N.P. (2003). In–store selection of wine: no evidence for the mediation of music? *Perceptual and Motor Skills*, 96, 1252–1254.

Humes, J. F. (1941). The effects of occupational music on scrappage in the manufacturing of radio tubes. *Journal of Applied Psychology*, 25, 573–587.

Hundleby, J. D. (1985) Drug usage and outstanding performance among young adolescents. *Addictive Behaviors*, 10, 419–423.

Hung, K. (2000). Narrative music in congruent and incongruent TV advertising. *Journal of Advertising*, 29, 25–34.

Hung, K. (2001). Framing meaning perceptions with music: the case of teaser ads. *Journal of Advertising*, 30, 39–49.

Hunter, J. A., O'Brien, K. S., and Grocott, A. C. (1999). Social identity, domain specific self-esteem and intergroup evaluation. *Current Research in Social Psychology*, 4, 160–177.

—— Platow, M. J., Howard, M. L., and Stringer, M. (1996). Social identity and intergroup evaluative bias: realistic categories and domain specific self-esteem in a conflict setting. *European Journal of Social Psychology*, 26, 631–647.

Husain, G., Thompson, W. F., and Schellenburg, E. G. (2002). Effects of musical tempo and mode on arousal, mood, and spatial abilities. *Music Perception*, 20, 151–171.

Hutchison, T. W. and Wotring, C. E. (1993). Musical preferences among clientele of a non–thematic night club: a study of diversification. *Popular Music and Society*, 17, 43–62.

Hyden, C. and McCandless, N. (1983). Men and women as portrayed in popular music lyrics. *Popular Music and Society*, 9, 19–26.

Ibarra, H. (1999). Provisional selves: experimenting with image and identity in professional adaptation. *Administrative Science Quarterly*, 44, 764–791.

Ince, R. (2004). Copy cats. *Police Review*, 13 Aug 2004, 18–20.

Inglefield, H. G. (1968). The relationship of selected personality variables to conformity behaviour reflected in the musical preferences of adolescents when exposed to peer group leader influences. *Unpublished doctoral dissertation, Ohio State University*.

Ishii, K. (1984). Analysis of diffusion by differential equation models. *Japanese Journal of Behaviormetrics*, 12, 11–19.

Iwamiya, S. (1997). Interaction between auditory and visual processing in car audio: simulation experiment using video reproduction. *Applied Human Science*, 16, 115–119.

Iwata, O. (1975). Concentration on performance as a determinant in the effect of acoustic environment upon performance. *Japanese Journal of Psychology*, 46, 91–99.

Izard, C. E. (1977). *Human emotions*. New York: Plenum.

Izumu, A. (2000). Japanese monkeys perceive sensory consonance of chords. *Journal of the Acoustical Society of America*, 108, 3073–3078.

Jackson, D. M. (2003). *Sonic branding: an essential guide to the art and science of sonic branding*. Basingstoke, Hampshire: Palgrave Macmillan.

Jackson, J. M. and Padgett, V. R. (1982). With a little help from my friend: social loafing and the Lennon-McCartney songs. *Personality and Social Psychology Bulletin*, 8, 672–677.

Jacobi, E. M. and Eisenberg, G. M. (2001–2002). The efficacy of Guided Imagery and Music (GIM) in the treatment of rheumatoid arthritis. *Journal of the Association for Music and Imagery*, 8, 57–74.

Jacoby, J. (1968). Work music and morale: a neglected but important relationship. *Personnel Journal*, 47, 882–886.

Jakobovits, L. A. (1966). Studies of fads: 1. The 'hit parade'. *Psychological Reports*, 18, 443–450.

James, I. M., Griffith, D. N. W., Pearson, R. M., and Newbury, P. (1977). Effect of oxprenolol on stage–fright in musicians. *Lancet*, 2, 952–954.

—— and Savage, I. (1984). Beneficial effect of nadolol on anxiety–induced disturbances of performance in musicians: a comparison with diazepam and placebo. *American Heart Journal*, 44, 1150–1155.

James, W. (1890). *The principles of psychology, Vol.1*. New York: Holt.

Janiger, O. and De Rios, M. D. (1989). LSD and creativity. *Journal of Psychoactive Drugs*, 21, 129–134.

Jankowski, W. and Miklaszewski, K. (2001). Poland. In D. J. Hargreaves and A. C. North (eds.), *Musical development and learning: the international perspective* (pp. 134–150). London: Continuum.

Jausovec, N. and Habe, K. (2005). The influence of Mozart's sonata K.448 on brain activity during the performance of spatial rotation and numerical tasks. *Brain Topography*, 17, 207–218.

Jenny, L. (1998). Recit d'experience et figuration. *Revue Francaise de Psychanalyse*, 62, 937–946.

Jo, E. and Berkowitz, L. (1994). A priming effect analysis on media influences: an update. In J. Bryant and D. Zillmann (eds.), *Media effects: advances in theory and research* (pp. 43–60). Hillsdale: Erlbaum.

Jobes, D. A., Berman, A. L., O'Carroll, P., Eastgard, S. and Knickmeyer, S. (1996). The Kurt Cobain suicide crisis: perspectives from research, public health and the news media. *Suicide and Life Threatening Behavior*, 26, 260–271.

Johnson, E. J., Moe, W. W., Fader, P. S., Bellman, S., and Lohse, G. L. (2004). On the depth and dynamics of online search behavior. *Management Science*, 50, 299–308.

Johnson, J. D., Jackson, L. A., and Gatto, L. (1995). Violent attitudes and deferred academic aspirations: deleterious effects of exposure to rap music. *Basic and Applied Social Psychology*, 16, 27–41.

—— Trawalter, S., and Dovidio, J. F. (2000). Converging interracial consequences of exposure to violent rap music on stereotypical attributions of blacks. *Journal of Experimental Social Psychology*, 36, 233–251.

Johnson-Laird, P. N. (1988). Freedom and constraint in creativity. In R. J. Sternberg (ed.), *The nature of creativity: contemporary psychological perspectives* (pp. 202–219). Cambridge: Cambridge University Press.

Jones, A. N. (1943). Music in industry. *Texas Personnel Review*, 2, No. 4, pp. 94–98.

Jones, D. and Broadbent, D. E. (1979). Side–effects of interference with speech by noise. *Ergonomics*, 22, 1073–1081.

Jones, K. (1997). Are rap videos more violent? Style differences and the prevalence of sex and violence in the age of MTV. *Howard Journal of Communications*, 8, 343–356.

Jones, S. and Lenhart, A (2004). Music downloading and listening: findings from the Pew Internet and American Life Project. *Popular Music and Society*, 27, 185–199.

Juslin, P. N. (2005). From mimesis to catharsis: expression, perception, and induction of emotion in music. In D. E. Miell, R. A. R. MacDonald, and D. J. Hargreaves (eds.), *Musical communication* (pp. 85–115). Oxford: Oxford University Press.

—— and Laukka, P. (2004). Expression, perception, and induction of musical emotions: a review and a questionnaire study of everyday listening. *Journal of New Music Research*, 33, 217–238.

—— and Sloboda, J. A. (eds.) (2001). *Music and emotion: theory and research*. Oxford: Oxford University Press.

Kaikati, A. M. and Kaikati, J. G. (2004). Stealth marketing: how to reach consumers surreptitiously. *California Management Review*, 46, 6–22.

Kain, Z. N. and Caldwell–Andrews, A. A. (2005). Preoperative psychological preparation of the child for surgery: an update. *Anesthesiology Clinics of North America*, 23, 597–614.

—— Caldwell–Andrews, A., and Wang, S. M. (2002). Psychological preparation of the parent and pediatric surgical patient. *Anesthesiology Clinics of North America*, 20, 29–44.

—— Wang, S. M., Mayes, L. C., Krivutza, D. M., and Teague B. A. (2001). Sensory stimuli and anxiety in children undergoing surgery: a randomized, controlled trial. *Anesthesia and Analgesia*, 92, 897–903.

Kalis, P. and Neuendorf, K. A. (1989). Aggressive cue prominence and gender participation in MTV. *Journalism Quarterly*, 66, 148–154, 229.

Kallinen, K. (2002). Reading news from a pocket computer in a distracting environment: effects of the tempo of background music. *Computers in Human Behavior*, 18, 537–551.

Kalof, L. (1999). The effects of gender and music video imagery on sexual attitudes. *Journal of Social Psychology*, 139, 378–385.

Kamali, K. and Steer, R. A. (1976). Polydrug use by high-school students: involvement and correlates. International Journal of the Addictions, 11, 337–343.

Kaminska, Z. and Woolf, J. (2000). Melodic line and emotion: Cooke's theory revisited. *Psychology of Music*, 28, 133–153.

Kamptner, N. L. (1995). Treasured possessions and their meaning in adolescent males and females. *Adolescence*, 30, 301–318.

Karageorghis, C. I. and Terry, P. C. (1997). The psychophysical effects of music in sport and exercise: a review. *Journal of Sport Behavior*, 20, 54–68.

Karmiloff-Smith, A. (1992). *Beyond modularity: a developmental perspective on cognitive science.* Cambridge: MIT Press.

Katz-Gerro, T. (1999). Cultural consumption and social stratification: leisure activities, musical tastes, and social location. *Sociological Perspectives*, 42, 627–646.

Kellaris, J. J. (1992). Consumer esthetics outside the lab: preliminary report on a musical field study. *Advances in Consumer Research*, 19, 730–734.

—— and Altsech, M. B. (1992). The experience of time as a function of musical loudness and gender of listener. *Advances in Consumer Research*, 19, 725–729.

—— and Cox, A. D. (1989). The effects of background music in advertising: a reassessment. *Journal of Consumer Research*, 16, 113–118.

—— —— and Cox, D. (1993). The effect of background music on ad processing: a contingency explanation. *Journal of Marketing*, 57, 114–125.

Kellaris, J. J. and Kent, R. J. (1992). The influence of music on consumers' temporal perceptions: does time fly when you're having fun ? *Journal of Consumer Psychology*, 1, 365–376.

Kellaris, J. J. and Mantel, S. P. (1994). The influence of mood and gender on consumers' time perceptions. *Advances in Consumer Research*, 21, 514–518.

—— —— and Altsech, M. B. (1996). Decibels, disposition, and duration: the impact of musical loudness and internal states on time perceptions. *Advances in Consumer Research*, 23, 498–503.

Kelley, H. H. (1973). The processes of causal attribution. *American Psychologist*, 28, 107–128.

Kemp, A. E. (1996). *The musical temperament: psychology and personality of musicians.* Oxford: Oxford University Press.

—— (1997). Individual differences in musical behaviour. In D. J. Hargreaves and A. C. North (eds.), *The social psychology of music* (pp. 25–45). Oxford: Oxford University Press.

—— and Mills, J. (2002). Musical potential. In R. Parncutt and G. E. McPherson (eds.), *The science and psychology of music performance* (pp. 3–16). Oxford: Oxford University Press.

Kendrick, M. J., Craig, K. D., Lawson, D. M., and Davidson, P. O. (1982). Cognitive and behavior therapy for musical performance anxiety. *Journal of Consulting and Clinical Psychology*, 50, 353–362.

Kenny, B. J. and Gellrich, M. (2002). Improvisation. In R. Parncutt and G. E. McPherson (eds.), *The science and psychology of music performance* (pp. 117–134). Oxford: Oxford University Press.

Kenny, D. T. and Faunce G. (2004). The impact of group singing on mood, coping, and perceived pain in chronic pain patients attending a multidisciplinary pain clinic. *Journal of Music Therapy*, 41, 241–258.

Kerr, A., N., Yore, M. M., Ham, S. A., and Dietz, W. H. (2004). Increasing stair use in a worksite through environmental changes. *American Journal of Health Promotion*, 18, 312–315.

Kerr, B., Shaffer, J, Chambers, C., and Hallowell, K. (1991). Substance use of creatively talented adults. *Journal of Creative Behavior*, 25, 145–153.

Kerr, W. A. (1942a). Psychological effects of music as reported by 162 defense trainees. *Psychological Record*, 5, 205–212.

—— (1942b). Factor analysis of 229 electrical workers' beliefs in the effects of music. *Psychological Record*, 5, 213–221.

—— (1943a). Attitudes toward types of industrial music. *Journal of the Acoustical Society of America*, 15, 125–130.

—— (1943b). Music for workers. *Personnel Journal*, 22, 32–34.

—— (1943c). The psychological background of industrial broadcasting. *Psychological Bulletin*, 40, 341–349.

—— (1943d). Where they like to work: work place preference of 228 electrical workers in terms of music. *Journal of Applied Psychology*, 27, 438–442.

—— (1943e). Three studies in plant music. *Factory Management and Maintenance*, 101, No. 11, p. 280.

—— (1946). Worker attitudes toward scheduling of industrial music. *Journal of Applied Psychology*, 30, 575–578.

Khalfa, S., Bella, S. D., Roy, M., Peretz, I., and Lupien, S. J. (2003). Effects of relaxing music on salivary cortisol level after psychological stress. *Annals of the New York Academy of Sciences*, 999, 374–376.

—— Isabelle, P., Jean–Pierre, B., and Manon, R. (2002). Event–related skin conductance responses to musical emotions in humans. *Neuroscience Letters*, 328, 145–149.

Kihlstrom, J. F. and Cantor, N. (1984). Mental representations of the self. In L. Berkowitz (ed.), *Advances in experimental social psychology (Vol. 7)* (pp. 1–47). New York: Academic Press.

Kim, I., Kwak, K., and Chang, G. (1998). Rock music and Korean adolescents' antisocial behaviour. *Korean Journal of Developmental Psychology*, 11, 27–38.

Kim, J., Allen, C. T., and Kardes, F. R. (1996). An investigation of the mediational mechanisms underlying attitudinal conditioning. *Journal of Marketing Research*, 33, 318–328.

Kim, S. J. and Koh, I. (2005). The effects of music on pain perception of stroke patients during upper extremity joint exercises. *Journal of Music Therapy*, 42, 81–92.

Kimata, H. (2003). Listening to Mozart reduces allergic skin wheal responses and in vitro allergen-specific IgE production in atopic dermatitis patients with latex allergy. *Behavioral Medicine*, 29, 15–19.

Kindler, A. M. and Darras, B. (1997). Map of artistic development. In A. M. Kindler (ed.), *Child development in art* (pp. 17–44). Reston: NAEA.

King, A. P., West, M. J., and White, D. J. (2003). Female cowbird song perception: evidence for plasticity of preference. *Ethology*, 109, 865–877.

King, P. (1988). Heavy metal music and drug abuse in adolescents. *Postgraduate Medicine*, 83, 295–304.

King, S. A. and Foster, P. R. (2001). "No problem, mon": strategies used to promote reggae music as Jamaica's cultural heritage. *Journal of Nonprofit and Public Sector Marketing*, 8, 3–16.

Kirkpatrick, F. H. (1942). Music and the factory worker. *Psychological Record*, 5, 197–204.

—— (1943a). Take the mind away. *Personnel Journal*, 22, 225–228.

—— (1943b). Music in industry. *Journal of Applied Psychology*, 27, 268–274.

Kisilevsky, B. S., Hains, S. M. J., Jacquet, A. -Y., GranierDeferre, C., and Lecanuet, J. P. (2004). Maturation of fetal responses to music. *Developmental Science*, 7, 550–559.

Kjellberg, A., Landström, U., Tesarz, M., and Söderberg, L. et al. (1996). The effects of nonphysical noise characteristics, ongoing task and noise sensitivity on annoyance and distraction due to noise at work. *Journal of Environmental Psychology*, 16, 123–136.

Klaes, M. (1997). Sociotechnical constituencies, game theory, and the diffusion of compact discs. An inter–disciplinary investigation into the market for recorded music. *Research Policy*, 25, 1221–1234.

Klee, H. (1998). The love of speed: an analysis of the enduring attraction of amphetamine sulphate for British youth. *Journal of Drug Issues*, 28, 33–56.

Klein, N. (2001). *No logo*. London: Flamingo.

Kleinen, G. (1991). Rock music: the aesthetic and sociology of a mass medium. *Jahrbuch fur Volksliedforschung*, 36, 145–147.

—— (1997). Bigger than life: rock and pop in the USA: a musical world. *Jahrbuch fur Volksliedforschung*, 42, 191–192.

Kleinhaus, M. M. (2002). Criminal justice approaches to paedophilic offenders. *Social and Legal Studies*, 11, 233–255.

Klitzman, S. and Stellman, J. M. (1989). The impact of the physical environment on the psychological well–being of office workers. *Social Science and Medicine*, 29, 733–742.

Knez, I. and Hygge, S. (2002). Irrelevant speech and indoor lighting: effects on cognitive performance and self–reported affect. *Applied Cognitive Psychology*, 16, 709–718.

Knibbe, R. A., van de Goor, I., and Drop, M. J. (1993). Contextual influences on young people's drinking rates in public drinking places: an observational study. *Addiction Research*, 1, 269–278.

Knight, F. (1973). *Beethoven and the age of revolution*. New York: International Publishers.

Knight, J. and Chapman, S. (2004). 'Asian yuppies ... are always looking for something new and different': creating a tobacco culture among young Asians. *Tobacco Control*, 13, 22–29.

Knight, W. E. J. and Rickard, N. S. (2001). Relaxing music prevents stress-induced increases in subjective anxiety, systolic blood pressure, and heart rate in healthy males and females. *Journal of Music Therapy*, 38, 254–272.

Knobloch, S. and Mundorf, N. (2003). Communication and emotion in the context of music and music television. In J. Bryant, D. Roskos-Ewoldsen, et al. (eds.), *Communication and emotion: essays in honor of Dolf Zillmann* (pp. 491–509). Mahwah: Lawrence Erlbaum Associates.

—— Vorderer, P., and Zillmann, D. (2000). Der Einfluβ des Musikgeschmacks auf die Wahrnehmung möglicher Freunde im Jugendalter / The impact of music preferences on the perception of potential friends in adolescence. *Zeitschrift für Sozialpsychologie*, 31, 18–30.

—— Weisbach, K., and Zillmann, D. (2004). Love lamentation in pop songs: music for unhappy lovers? *Zeitschrift fur Medienpsychologie*, 16, 116–124.

—— and Zillmann, D. (2003). Appeal of love themes in popular music. *Psychological Reports*, 93, 653–658.

Koch, M. E., Kain, Z. N., Ayoub, C., and Rosenbaum, S. H. (1998). The sedative and analgesic sparing effect of music. *Anesthesiology*, 89, 300–306.

Koelsch, S. and Siebel, W. A. (2005). Towards a neural basis of music perception. *Trends in Cognitive Sciences*, 9, 578–584.

Koestler, A. (1964). *The act of creation*. New York: Macmillan.

Kolb, B. M. (2002). Ethnic preference for the arts: the role of the social experience as attendance motivation. *International Journal of Nonprofit and Voluntary Sector Marketing*, 7, 172–181.

Konečni, V. J. (1975). The mediation of aggressive behavior: arousal level vs. anger and cognitive labelling. *Journal of Personality and Social Psychology*, 32, 706–712.

—— (1982). Social interaction and musical preference. In D. Deutsch (ed.). *The psychology of music* (pp. 497–516). New York: Academic Press.

—— (1984). Elusive effects of artists' 'messages'. In W. R. Crozier and A. J. Chapman (eds.) *Cognitive processes in the perception of art* (pp. 71–96). Amsterdam: Elsevier.

—— (2005). The aesthetic trinity: awe, being moved, thrills. *Bulletin of Psychology and the Arts*, 5, 27–44.

—— Brown, A., and Wanic, R. A. (in press). Comparative effects of music and recalled life events on emotional state. *Psychology of Music*.

—— Crozier, J. B., and Doob, A. N. (1976). Anger and expression of aggression: effects on aesthetic preference. *Scientific Aesthetics/Sciences de l'Art*, 1, 47–55.

—— and Sargent–Pollock, D. (1976). Choice between melodies differing in complexity under divided–attention conditions. *Journal of Experimental Psychology: Human Perception and Performance*, 2, 347–356.

Konlaan, B. B., Bjorby, N., Bygren, L. O., Weissglas, G., Karlsson, L. G., and Widmark, M. (2000). Attendance at cultural events and physical exercise and health: a randomized controlled study. *Public Health*, 114, 316–319.

Konz, S. and McDougal, D. (1968). The effect of background music on the control activity of an automobile driver. *Human Factors*, 10, 233–244.

Kortaba, J. and Wells, L. (1987). Styles of adolescent participation in an all–ages rock 'n' roll nightclub: an ethnographic analysis. *Youth and Society*, 18, 398–417.

Kotarba, J. A., Williams, M. L., and Johnson, J. (1991). Rock music as a medium for AIDS intervention. *AIDS Education and Prevention*, 3, 47–49.

Krause, N. Lynch, J., Kaplan, G. A., Cohen, R. D., Goldberg, D. E., and Salonen, J. T. (1997). Predictors of disability retirement. *Scandinavian Journal of Work, Environment and Health*, 23, 403–413.

Kreutz, G., Bongard, S., Rohrmann, S., Hodapp, V., and Grebe, D. (2004). Effects of choir singing or listening on secretory immunoglobulin A, cortisol, and emotional state. *Journal of Behavioral Medicine*, 27, 623–635.

Krippner, S. (1985). Psychedelic drugs and creativity. *Journal of Psychoactive Drugs*, 17, 235–245.

Kris, E. (1952). *Psychoanalytic exploration in art.* New York: International Universities Press.

Krueger, A. B. (2005). The economics of real superstars: the market for rock concerts in the material world. *Journal of Labor Economics*, 23, 1–30.

Kubey, R. and Larson, R. (1989). The use and experience of the new video media among children and young adolescents: television viewing compared to the use of videocassettes, video games, and music videos. *Communication Research*, 17, 107–130.

Kuhn, D. (2002). The effects of active and passive participation in musical activity on the immune system as measured by salivary immunoglobulin A (SlgA). *Journal of Music Therapy*, 39, 30–39.

Kulbartz-Klatt, Y. J., Florin, I., and Pook, M. (1999). Bulimia nervosa: mood changes do have an impact on body width estimation. *British Journal of Clinical Psychology*, 38, 279–287.

Kurkul, W. W. (2007). Nonverbal communication in one-to-one music performance instruction. *Psychology of Music*, 35, 327–362.

Kurosawa, K. and Davidson, J. W. (2005). Nonverbal interaction in popular performance: a case study of The Corrs. *Musicae Scientiae*, 9, 111–137.

Kushner, R. J. and Brooks, A. C. (2000). The one–man band by the quick lunch stand: modeling audience response to street performance. *Journal of Cultural Economics*, 24, 65–77.

Kuwhara, Y. (1992). Power to the people, y'all: rap music, resistance, and black college students. *Humanity and Society*, 16, 54–73.

Lacher, K. T. (1989). Hedonic consumption: music as a product. *Advances in Consumer Research*, 16, 367–373.

—— (1994). An investigation of the influence of gender on the hedonic responses created by listening to music. *Advances in Consumer Research*, 21, 354–358.

—— and Mizerski, R. (1994). An exploratory study of the responses and relationships involved in the evaluation of, and in the intention to purchase new rock music. *Journal of Consumer Research*, 21, 366–380.

Lacourse, E., Claes, M., and Villeneuve, M. (2001). Heavy metal music and adolescent suicidal risk. *Journal of Youth and Adolescence*, 30, 321–332.

Lafuente, M. J., Grifol, R., Segarra, J., Soriano, J., Gorba, M. A., and Montesinos, A. (1998). Effects of the Firstart method of prenatal stimulation on psychomotor development: the first six months. *Journal of Prenatal and Perinatal Psychology and Health*, 12, 197–208.

Lageat, T., Czellar, S., and Laurent, G. (2003). Engineering hedonic attributes to generate perceptions of luxury: consumer perception of an everyday sound. *Marketing Letters*, 14, 97–109.

Lai, H., Chen, C., Chang, F., Hsieh, M., Huang, H., and Chang, S. (2006). Randomized controlled trial of music during kangaroo care on maternal state anxiety and preterm infants' responses. *International Journal of Nursing Studies*, 43, 139–146.

—— and Good, M. (2005). Music improves sleep quality in older adults. *JAN Journal of Advanced Nursing*, 49, 234–244.

Laing, D. (1986). The music industry and the 'cultural imperialism' thesis. *Media, Culture and Society*, 8, 331–341.

—— (2003). Music and the market: the economics of music in the modern world. In M. Clayton, T. Herbert, and R. Middleton (eds.), *The cultural study of music: a critical introduction* (pp. 309–320). London: Routledge.

—— and York, N. (2000). The value of music in London. *Cultural Trends*, 10, 1–34.

Laksi, M. (1961). *Ecstacy: a study of some secular and religious experiences*. London: Cresset Press.

Lammers, H. B. (2003). An oceanside field experiment on background music effects on the restaurant tab. *Perceptual and Motor Skills*, 96, 1025–1026.

Lamont, A. (1998). *The development of cognitive representations of musical pitch.* Unpublished PhD thesis, University of Cambridge.

——(1999) *A contextual account of developing representations of music.* Paper presented at the International Conference on Research in Music Education, Exeter University, April 1999.

—— (2002). Musical identities and the school environment. In R. A. R. MacDonald, D. J. Hargreaves, and D. E. Miell, D. E. (eds.), *Musical identities* (pp. 41–59). Oxford: Oxford University Press.

—— Hargreaves, D. J., Marshall, N. and Tarrant, M. (2003). Young people's music in and out of school. *British Journal of Music Education*, 20, 1–13.

Landes, W. and Lichtman, D. (2003). Indirect liability for copyright infringement: Napster and beyond. *Journal of Economic Perspectives*, 17, 113–124.

Landy, F. J. and Farr, J. L. (1980). Performance rating. *Psychological Bulletin*, 87, 72–107.

Langenderfer, J. and Cook, D. L. (2001). Copyright policies and issues raised by A and M Records v. Napster: 'The Shot Heard 'Round the World' or 'Not with a Bang but a Whimper?' *Journal of Public Policy and Marketing*, 20, 280–288.

Langer, S. (1953). *Feeling and form.* New York: Scribner.

Lanza, J. (1994). *Elevator music.* London: Quartet Books.

Larson, R. W. (1995). Secrets in the bedroom: adolescents' private use of media. *Journal of Youth and Adolescence*, 24, 535–550.

Larson, R. and Kubey, R. (1983). Television and music: contrasting media in adolescent life. *Youth and Society*, 15, 13–31.

—— —— and Colletti, J. (1989). Changing channels: early adolescent media choices and shifting investments in family and friends. *Journal of Youth and Adolescence*, 18, 583–599.

Lathom-Radocy, W. (2002). *Pediatric music therapy.* Springfield: Charles C. Thomas.

Lave, J. and Wenger, E. (1991). *Situated learning: legitimate peripheral participation.* Cambridge: Cambridge University Press.

Lazarus, R. S. (1991). *Emotion and adaptation.* Oxford: Oxford University Press.

Leahey T. H. (1994). *A history of modern psychology.* London: Prentice Hall.

Leão E. R. and da Silva, M. J. P. (2004). Music and chronic muscular-skeletal pain: the evocative potential of mental images. *Revista Latino-Americana de Enfermagem*, 12, 235–241.

LeBlanc, A. (1982). An interactive theory of musical preference. *Journal of Music Therapy*, 19, 28–45.

—— (1991). Effect of maturation/aging on music listening preference: a review of the literature. *Paper presented at the Ninth National Symposium on Research in Music Behavior, Canon Beach, Oregon, U.S.A.*

—— Jin, Y. C., Obert, M., and Siivola, C. (1997). Effects of audience on music performance anxiety. *Journal of Research in Music Education*, 45, 480–486.

—— Sims, W. L. Siivola, C., and Obert, M. (1993). Music style preferences of different-age listeners. *Paper presented at the Tenth National Symposium on Research in Music Behavior, University of Alabama, Tuscaloosa, Alabama, U.S.A.*

Leboucher, G. and Pallot, K. (2004). Is he all he says he is? Intersexual eavesdropping in the domestic canary, Serinus canaria. *Animal Behaviour*, 68, 957–963.

Lecanuet, J. P., Graniere–Deferre, C., Jacquet, A.–Y., DeCasper, A. J. (2000). Fetal discrimination of low–pitched musical notes. *Developmental Psychobiology*, 36, 29–39.

Lee, J., Boatwright, P. and Kamakura, W. A. (2003). A Bayesian model for prelaunch sales forecasting of recorded music. *Management Science*, 49, 179–196.

Lehmann, A. C. (1997). The acquisition of expertize in music: efficiency of deliberate practice as a moderating variable in accounting for sub-expert performance. In I. Deliège and J. A. Sloboda (eds.), *Perception and cognition of music* (pp. 161–187). Hillsdale: Erlbaum.

—— Sloboda, J. A. and Woody, R. H. (2007). *Psychology for musicians: understanding and acquiring the skills*. Oxford University Press: New York.

Lehmkuhl, U. and Lehmkuhl, G. (1982). Psychische Wirkungen und Motivation bei laengerfristigem Haschischkonsum Jugendlicher: Welche Bedeutung besitzen 'Bewusstseinserweiterungen' und 'mystische Erfahrung'? Zeitschrift fur Kinder und Jugendpsychiatrie, 10, 322–332.

Lehrner, J., Marwinski, G., Lehr, S., Johren, P., and Deecke, L. (2005). Ambient odors of orange and lavender reduce anxiety and improve mood in a dental office. *Physiology and Behavior*, 86, 92–95.

Leming, J. (1987). Rock music and the socialization of moral values in early adolescence. *Youth and Society*, 18, 363–383.

Lenson, D. (1998). Drugs. *Literature and Psychology*, 44, 23–40.

Lenton, S., Boys, A., and Norcross, K. (1997). Raves, drugs and experience: drug use by a sample of people who attend raves in Western Australia. *Addiction*, 92, 1327–1337.

Leont'ev, A. N. (1981). *Problems of the development of mind*. Moscow: Progress Publishers.

Lerdahl, F. and Jackendoff, R. (1983). *A generative theory of tonal music*. London: MIT Press.

Lesiuk, T. (2005). The effect of music listening on work performance. *Psychology of Music*, 33, 173–191.

Lester, D. and Whipple, M. (1996). Music preference, depression, suicidal preoccupation, and personality: comment on Stack and Gundlach's papers. *Suicide and Life–Threatening Behavior*, 26, 68–70.

Levin, I. and Zackay, D. (eds.) (1989). *Time and human cognition*. Elsevier Science.

Levine, J. M. and Russo, E. M. (1987). Majority and minority influence. In C. Hendrick (ed.), *Review of personality and social psychology, vol. 8* (pp. 13–54). Newbury Park: Sage.

Lewis, B. E. and Schmidt, C. P. (1991). Listeners' response to music as a function of personality type. *Journal of Research in Music Education*, 39, 311–321.

Lewis, G. B. and Brooks, A. C. (2005) A question of morality: artists' values and public funding for the arts. *Public Administration Review*, 65, 8–17.

—— and Seaman, B. A. (2004). Sexual orientation and demand for the arts. *Social Science Quarterly*, 85, 523–538.

Li, H. (1994). Experimental study on the affection of fetal music on the fetus. *Acta Psychologica Sinica*, 26, 51–58.

Licht, S. (1946). *Music in medicine*. Oxford: New England Conservatory of Music.

Liden, S. and Gottfries, C. (1974). Beta–blocking agents in the treatment of catecholamine–induced symptoms in musicians. *Lancet*, 2, 529.

Liebman, S. S. and MacLaren, A. (1991). The effects of music and relaxation on third trimester anxiety in adolescent pregnancy. *Journal of Music Therapy*, 28, 89–100.

Lindauer, M. S. (2003). *Aging, creativity, and art: a positive perspective on late-life development*. New York: Kluwer Academic/Plenum.

Line, S. W., Markowitz, H., Morgan, K. N., and Strong, S. (1991). Effects of cage size and environmental enrichment on behavioural and physiological responses of rhesus macaques to the stress of daily events. In M. A. Novak and A. J. Petto (eds.), *Through the looking glass: issues of psychological well-being in captive nonhuman primates* (pp. 160–179). Washington: American Psychological Association.

Lipton, J. P. (1987). Stereotypes concerning musicians within symphony orchestras. *Journal of Psychology*, 12, 85–93.

Litle, P., and Zuckerman, M. (1986). Sensation seeking and music preferences. *Personality and Individual Differences*, 7, 575–577.

Litman, R. E. and Farberow, N. L. (1994). Pop–rock music as precipitating cause in youth suicide. *Journal of Forensic Sciences*, 39, 494–499.

Littleton, K. and Miell, D. E. (2004). Collaborative creativity: contemporary perspectives. In D. E. Miell and K. Littleton (eds.), *Collaborative creativity: contemporary perspectives* (pp. 1–8). London: Free Association Books.

—— —— (forthcoming). Collaborating outside school: the band as a learning community. *International Journal of Educational Research*.

Lloyd, B. T. and Mendez, J. L. (2001). Botswanan adolescents' interpretation of American music videos: so that's what that means. *Journal of Black Psychology*, 27, 464–476.

Locsin, R. G. (1981). The effect of music on the pain of selected post-operative patients. *Journal of Advanced Nursing*, 6, 19–25.

Loewen, L. J. and Suedfeld, P. (1992). Cognitive and arousal effects of masking office noise. *Environment and Behavior*, 24, 381–395.

Long, N. H. (1971). Establishment of standards for the Indiana Oregon Music Discrimination Test based on a cross-section of elementary and secondary students with an analysis of elements of environment, intelligence and musical experience and training in relation to musical discrimination. *Council of Research in Music Education Bulletin*, 25, 26–32.

Lopes, P. D. (1992). Innovation and diversity in the popular music industry, 1969 to 1990. *American Sociological Review*, 57, 56–71.

Lopez, L. and Malhotra, R. (1991). Estimation of time intervals with most preferred and least preferred music. *Psychological Studies*, 36, 203–209.

Lord, K. R., Lee, M. S., and Sauer, P. L. (1995). The combined influence hypothesis: central and peripheral antecedents of attitude toward the ad. *Journal of Advertising*, 24, 73–85.

Lowe, G. (1995). Judgments of substance use and creativity in 'ordinary' people's everyday lifestyles. *Psychological Reports*, 76, 1147–1154.

Lowis, M. J. (1998). Music and peak experiences: an empirical study. *Mankind Quarterly*, 39, 203–224.

—— (2002). Music as a trigger for peak experiences among a college staff population. *Creativity Research Journal*, 14, 351–359.

—— (2003). Peak emotional experiences and their antecedents: a survey of staff at a British university college. *Korean Journal of Thinking and Problem Solving*, 13, 41–53.

Lull, J. (1992). Popular music and communication: an introduction. In J. Lull (ed.), *Popular music and communication* (2nd edn.) (pp. 1–32). Newbury Park: Sage.

Lyle, J. and Hoffmann, H. R. (1972). Children's use of television and other media. In E. A. Rubinstein, G. A. Comstock, and J. P. Murray (eds.), *Television and social behavior. Reports and papers: Vol 4. Television in day to day life: patterns of use* (pp. 129–256). Washington: U.S. Government Printing Office.

Lynxwiler, J. and Gay, D. (2000). Moral boundaries and deviant music: public attitudes toward heavy metal and rap. *Deviant Behavior*, 21, 63–85.

Lyttle, T. and Montagne, M. (1992). Drugs, music, and ideology: a social pharmacological interpretation of the Acid House movement. *International Journal of the Addictions*, 27, 1159–1177.

MacDonald, G. (1988). The economics of rising stars. *American Economic Review*, March, 155–166.

MacDonald, R. A. R., Byrne, C., and Carlton, L. (2006). Creativity and flow in musical composition: an empirical investigation. *Psychology of Music*, 34, 292–306.

MacDonald, R. A. R., Hargreaves, D. J. and Miell, D. E. (eds.) (2002). *Musical identities*. Oxford: Oxford University Press.

—— and Miell, D. E. (2000). Creativity and music education: the impact of social variables. *International Journal of Music Education*, 36, 58–68.

—— Mitchell, L. A., Dillon, T., Serpell, M., Davies, J. B., and Ashley, E. A. (2003). An empirical investigation of the anxiolytic and pain reducing effects of music. *Psychology of Music*, 31, 187–203.

Machill, M. (1996). Musique as opposed to music: background and impact of quotas for French songs on French radio. *Journal of Media Economics*, 9, 21–36.

Machleit, K. A. and Eroglu, S. A. (2000). Describing and measuring emotional response to shopping experience. *Journal of Business Research*, 499, 101–111.

MacInnis, D. J. and Park, C. W. (1991). The differential role of characteristics of music on high– and low–involvement consumers' processing of ads. *Journal of Consumer Research*, 18, 161–173.

MacKinnon, D. W. (1965). Personality and the realisation of creative potential. *American Psychologist*, 20, 273–281.

MacNay, S. K. (1995). The influence of preferred music on the perceived exertion, mood, and time estimation scores of patients participating in a cardiac rehabilitation exercise program. *Therapy Perspectives*, 13, 91–96.

Madsen, C. K. (1998). Emotion versus tension in Haydn's Symphony no. 104 as measured by the two-dimensional continuous response digital interface. *Journal of Research in Music Education*, 46, 546–554.

Maehr, M. L., Pitnrich, P. R., and Linnenbrink, E. A. (2002). Motivation and achievement. In R. Colwell and C. Richardson (eds.), *The new handbook of research on music teaching and learning* (pp. 348–372). Oxford: Oxford University Press.

Magee, W. L. and Davidson, J. W. (2002). The effect of music therapy on mood states in neurological patients: a pilot study. *Journal of Music Therapy*, 39, 20–29.

Magill, L. (2001). The use of music therapy to address the suffering in advanced cancer pain. *Journal of Palliative Care*, 17, 167–172.

Magill-Levreault, L. (1993). Music therapy in pain and symptom management. *Journal of Palliative Care*, 9, 42–48.

Maguire, E. and Snipes, J. B. (1994). Re-assessing the link between country music and suicide: comment on Stack and Gundlach. *Social Forces*, 73, 1239–1243.

Maier, N. R. F. (1931). Reasoning in humans. II. The solution of a problem and its appearance in consciousness. *Journal of Comparative Psychology*, 12, 181–194.

Maltby, J. (2004). Celebrity and religious worship: a refinement. *Journal of Psychology*, 138, 286–288.

—— Day, L., McCutcheon, L. E., Gillett, R., Houran, J., and Ashe, D. D. (2004). Personality and coping: a context for examining celebrity worship and mental health. *British Journal of Psychology*, 95, 411–428.

—— Houran, J., Lange, R., Ashe, D., and McCutcheon, L. E. (2002). Thou shalt worship no other godsunless they are celebrities: the relationship between celebrity worship and religious orientation. *Personality and Individual Differences*, 32, 1157–1172.

—— —— and McCutcheon, L. E. (2003). Locating celebrity worship within Eysenck's personality dimensions. *Journal of Nervous and Mental Disease*, 191, 25–29.

Mantel, S. P. and Kellaris, J. J. (2003). Cognitive determinants of consumers' time perceptions: the impact of resources required and available. *Journal of Consumer Research*, 29, 531–538.

Manturzewska, M. (1990). A biographical study of the life-span development of professional musicians. *Psychology of Music*, 18, 112–139.

—— (1995). Das elterliche Umfeld herausragender Musiker. In H. Gembris, R. D. Kraemer, and G. Maas (eds.), *Musikpädagogische Forschungsberichter 1994* (pp. 11–22). Augsburg: Wissner.

Marchant–Haycox, S. E., and Wilson, G. D. (1992). Personality and stress in performing artists. *Personality and Individual Differences*, 13, 1061–1068.

Marcia, J. E. (1966). Development and validation of ego-identity status. *Journal of Personality and Social Psychology*, 3, 551–558.

Mark, A. (1986). Adolescents discuss themselves and drugs through music. *Journal of Substance Abuse Treatment*, 3, 243–249.

Markert, J. (2001). Sing a song of drug use-abuse: four decades of drug lyrics in popular music. From the sixties through the nineties. *Sociological Inquiry*, 71, 194–220.

Marsh, K. and Young, S. (2006). Musical play. In G. E. McPherson (ed.), *The child as musician* (pp. 289–310). Oxford: Oxford University Press.

Marshall, L. (2001). The social organization of audio piracy on the Internet. *Media, Culture and Society*, 26, 163–181.

Martin, B. A. S. and Collins, B. A. (2002). Violence and consumption imagery in music videos. *European Journal of Marketing*, 36, 855–873.

—— and McCracken, C. A. (2001). Music marketing: music consumption imagery in the UK and New Zealand. *Journal of Consumer Marketing*, 18, 426–436.

Martin, G. and Koo, L. (1997). Celebrity suicide: did the death of Kurt Cobain influence young suicides in Australia? *Archives of Suicide Research*, 33, 187–198.

—— Clarke, M., and Pearce, C. (1993). Adolescent suicide: music preference as an indicator of vulnerability. *Journal of the American Academy of Child and Adolescent Psychiatry*, 32, 530–535.

Martin, M. (1987). *The influence of combining preferred music with progressive relaxation and biofeedback techniques on frontalis muscle.* Unpublished MSc thesis, Southern Methodist University.

Martindale, C. (1990). *The clockwork muse: the predictability of artistic change.* New York: Basic Books.

—— (1996). A note on the relationship between prototypicality and preference. *Empirical Studies of the Arts*, 14, 109–113.

—— (1999). Biological bases of creativity. In R. J. Sternberg (ed.), *Handbook of creativity* (pp. 137–152). Cambridge: Cambridge University Press.

Martindale, C. and Moore, K, (1988). Priming, prototypicality, and preference. *Journal of Experimental Psychology: Human Perception and Performance*, 14, 661–670.

—— and Moore, K. (1989). Relationship of musical preference to collative, ecological, and psychophysical variables. *Music Perception*, 6, 431–455.

—— —— and Anderson, K. (2005). The effect of extraneous stimulation on aesthetic preference. *Empirical Studies of the Arts*, 23, 83–91.

—— —— and Borkum, J. (1990). Aesthetic preference: anomalous findings for Berlyne's psychobiological theory. *American Journal of Psychology*, 103, 53–80.

—— —— K. and West, A. (1988). Relationship of preference judgements to typicality, novelty, and mere exposure. *Empirical Studies of the Arts*, 6, 79–96.

Martino, S. C., Collins, R. L., Elliott, M. N., Strachman, A., Kanouse, D. E., and Berry, S. H. (2006). Exposure to degrading versus nondegrading music lyrics and sexual behavior among youth. *Pediatrics*, 118, 430–441.

Martorella, R. (1977). The relationship between box office and repertoire: a case study of opera. *Sociological Quarterly*, 18, 354–366.

Maslar, P. M. (1986). The effect of music on the reduction of pain: a review of the literature. *Arts in Psychotherapy*, 13, 215–219.

Maslow, A. (1968). *Toward a psychology of being (2nd edition).* New York: Van Nostrand Reinhold.

Masuda, T., Miyamoto, K., and Shimizu, K. (2005). Effects of music listening on elderly orthopaedic patients during postoperative bed rest. *Nordic Journal of Music Therapy*, 14, 4–14.

Matlin, M. W. (1989). *Cognition.* Chicago: Holt, Rinehart, and Winston.

Mattila, A. S. and Wirtz, J. (2001). Congruency of scent and music as a driver of in–store evaluations and behavior. *Journal of Retailing*, 77, 273–289.

Mauk, G., Taylor, M., White, K. R., and Allen, T. S. (1994). Response to Stack and Gundlach's 'The effect of country music on suicide': an 'Achy Breaky Heart' may not kill you. *Social Forces*, 72, 1249–1255.

Maxwell, J. P. (2001). The perception of relationship violence in the lyrics of a song. *Journal of Interpersonal Violence*, 16, 640–661.

May, J. L. and Hamilton, P. A. (1980). Effects of musically evoked affect on women's interpersonal attraction toward and perceptual judgements of physical attractiveness of men. *Motivation and Emotion*, 44, 217–238.

Mayton, D. M., Nagel, E. A., and Parker, R. (1990). The perceived effects of drug messages on use patterns in adolescents. *Journal of Drug Education*, 20, 305–318.

McAdie, T. M., Foster, T. M., Temple, W., and Matthews, L. R. (1993). A method for measuring the aversiveness of sounds to domestic hens. *Applied Animal Behaviour Science*, 37, 223–238.

McCarron, A. and Tierney, K. J. (1989). The effect of auditory stimulation on the consumption of soft drinks. *Appetite*, 13, 155–159.

McCarthy, D. O., Ouimet, M. E., and Daun, J. M. (1992). The effects of noise stress on leukocyte function in rats. *Research in Nursing and Health*, 15, 131–137.

McCloud, S. (2003). Popular culture fandoms, the boundaries of religious studies and the project of the self. *Culture and Religion*, 4, 187–206.

McCormick, J. and McPherson, G. E. (2003). The role of self–efficacy in a musical performance examination: an exploratory structural equation analysis. *Psychology of Music*, 31, 37–51.

McCourt, T. and Burkart, P. (2003). When creators, corporations, and consumers collide: Napster and the development of on–line music distribution. *Media, Culture and Society*, 25, 333–350.

McCown, W., Keiser, R., Mulhearn, S. and Williamson, D. (1997). The role of personality and gender in preference for exaggerated bass in music. *Personality and Individual Differences*, 23, 543–547.

McCrary, J. (1993). Effects of listeners' and performers' race on music preferences. *Journal of Research in Music Education*, 41, 200–211.

McCraty, R., Atkinson, M., Rein, G., and Watkins, A. D. (1996). Music enhances the effect of positive emotional states on salivary IgA. *Stress Medicine*, 12, 167–175.

McCutcheon (2002). Are parasocial relationship styles reflected in love styles? *Current Research in Social Psychology*, 7, 82–93.

McCutcheon, L. E., Lange, R., and Houran, J. (2002). Conceptualization and measurement of celebrity worship. *British Journal of Psychology*, 93, 67–87.

McDermott, J. and Hauser, M. (2004). Are consonant intervals music to their ears? Spontaneous acoustic preferences in a nonhuman primate. *Cognition*, 94, B11–B21.

McDonald, J. (1988). Censoring rock lyrics: a historical analysis of the debate. *Youth and Society*, 19, 294–313.

McElrea, H. and Standing, L. (1992). Fast music causes fast drinking. *Perceptual and Motor Skills*, 75, 362.

McFarland, R. A. (1985). Relationship of skin temperature changes to the emotions accompanying music. *Biofeedback and Self Regulation*, 10, 255–267.

McFedries, P. (2005). The iPod people. *IEEE Spectrum*, 42, 76.

McGuire, W. (1986). The myth of massive media impact: savagings and salvagings. In G. Comstock (ed.), *Public communication and behaviour* (pp. 173–257). Orlando: Academic Press.

McKee, K. B. and Pardun, C. J. (1996). Mixed messages: the relationship between sexual and religious imagery in rock, country, and Christian videos. *Communication Reports*, 9, 163–171.

—— —— (1999). Reading the video: a qualitative study of religious images in music videos. *Journal of Broadcasting and Electronic Media*, 43, 110–122.

McKinney, C. H. (1990). Music therapy in obstetrics: a review. *Music Therapy Perspectives*, 8, 57–60.

McLeod, D. M., Detenber, B. H., and Eveland, W. P. (2001). Behind the third–person effect: differentiating perceptual processes for self and other. *Journal of Communication*, 51, 678–695.

——McLeod, D. M., Eveland, W.P., and Nathanson, A. I. (1997). Support for censorship of violent and misogynic rap lyrics: an analysis of the third–person effect. *Communication Research*, 24, 153–174.

McMullen, P. T. (1974). Influence of number of different pitches and melodic redundancy on preference responses. *Journal of Research in Music Education*, 22, 198–204.

——McMullen, P. T. and Arnold, M. J. (1976). Preference and interest as a function of distributional redundancy in rhythmic sequences. *Journal of Research in Music Education*, 24, 22–31.

McNair, J. and Powles, J. (2005). Hippies versus hip–hop heads: an exploration of music's ability to communicate an alternative political agenda from the perspective of two divergent musical genres. In D. Miell, R. A. R. MacDonald, and D. J. Hargreaves (eds.), *Musical Communication* (pp. 339–360). Oxford: Oxford University Press.

McNamara, L., and Ballard, M. E. (1999). Resting arousal, sensation seeking, and music preference. *Genetic, Social, and General Psychology Monographs*, 125, 229–250.

McPherson, G. E. (ed.) (2006). *The child as musician*. Oxford: Oxford University Press.

—— and McCormick, J. (1999). Motivational and self–regulated learning components of musical practice. *Bulletin of the Council for Research in Music Education*, 141, 98–102.

—— —— (2000). The contribution of motivational factors to instrumental performance in a music examination. *Research Studies in Music Education*, 15, 31–39.

—— —— (2006). Self-efficacy and music performance. *Psychology of Music*, 34, 322–336.

—— and Renwick, J. M. (2001). A longitudinal study of self-regulation in children's musical practice.*Music Education Research*, 3, 169–186.

—— and Schubert, E. (2004). Measuring performance enhancement in music. In A. Williamon (ed.), *Musical excellence: strategies and techniques to enhance performance* (pp. 61–82). Oxford: Oxford University Press.

—— and Thompson, W. F. (1998). Assessing music performance: issues and influences. *Research Studies in Music Education*, 10, 12–24.

—— and Williamon, A. (2006). Giftedness and talent. In G. E. McPherson (ed.), The child as musician: a handbook of musical development (pp. 239–256). Oxford: Oxford University Press.

McQuarrie, E. F. and Mick, D. G. (1999). Visual rhetoric in advertising: text–interpretive, experimental, and reader–response analyses. Journal of Consumer Research, 26, 37–54.

Mead, G. H. (1934). Mind, self and society. Chicago: University of Chicago Press.

Measham, F., Parker, H., and Aldridge, J. (1998). The teenage transition: from adolescent recreational drug use to the young adult dance culture in Britain in the mid-1990s. *Journal of Drug Issues*, 28, 9–32.

Mednick, S. A. (1962). The associative basis of the creative process. *Psychological Review*, 69, 220–232.

Meenaghan, A. and Turnbull, P. W. (1981). The application of product life cycle theory to popular record marketing. *European Journal of Marketing*, 15, 1–50.

Megel, M. E., Houser, C. W., and Gleaves, L. S. (1998). Children's responses to immunizations: lullabies as a distraction. *Issues in Comprehensive Pediatric Nursing*, 21, 129–145.

Mehl, M. and Pennebaker, J. W. (2003). *The sounds of social life: a psychometric analysis of students' daily social environments and natural conversations. Journal of Personality and Social Psychology*, 84, 857–870.

Mehrabian, A. and Russell, J. A. (1974). *An approach to environmental psychology.* Cambridge: MIT Press.

Meilman, P. W. (1979). Cross–sectional age changes in ego identity status during adolescence. *Developmental Psychology*, 15, 230–231.

Meinecke, B. (1948). Music and medicine in classical antiquity. In D. M. Schullian and M. Schoen (eds.) *Music and medicine* (pp. 47–95). Oxford: Henry Schuman.

Melka, A. and Pelant, P. (1999). Psychoacoustic methods applied to SKODA passenger car development programmes: intentions and first experiences. *Acustica*, 85, 657–660.

Melzack, R. and Wall, P. D. (1965). Pain mechanisms: a new theory. *Science*, 150, 971–979.

Menegazzi, J. J., Paris, P. M., Kersteen, C. H., Flynn, B., and Trautman, D. E. (1991). A randomized, controlled trial of the use of music during laceration repair. *Annals of Emergency Medicine*, 20, 348–350.

Mennill, D. J. and Ratcliff, L. M. (2004). Overlapping and matching in the song contests of black-capped chickadees. *Animal Behaviour*, 67, 441–450.

Merriam, A. P. (1964). *The anthropology of music.* Evanston: Northwestern University Press.

—— (1997). *The anthropology of music.* Chicago: Northwestern University Press.

Merrilees, B. and Fry, M. L. (2002). Corporate branding: a framework for e-retailers. *Corporate Reputation Review*, 5, 213–225.

Meyer, L. B. (1956). *Emotion and meaning in music.* Chicago: University of Chicago Press.

—— (1967). *Music, the arts, and ideas.* Chicago: University of Chicago Press.

—— (1994). Emotion and meaning in music. In R. Aiello and J. A. Sloboda (eds.), *Musical perceptions* (pp. 3–39). Oxford: Oxford University Press.

—— (2001). Music and emotion: distinction and uncertainties. In P. N. Juslin and J. A. Sloboda (eds.), *Music and emotion: theory and research* (pp. 341–360). Oxford: Oxford University Press.

Michalos, A. (2005). Arts and the quality of life: an exploratory study. *Social Indicators Research*, 71, 11–59.

Michel, D. E. and Chesky, K. S. (1995). A survey of music therapists using music for pain relief. *Arts in Psychotherapy*, 22, 49–51.

Middlestadt, S. E. (1990). Medical problems of symphony orchestra musicians: from counting people with problems to evaluating interventions. *Revista Interamericana de Psicología*, 24, 159–172.

—— Fishbein, M., and Chan, D. K.-S. (1994). The effect of music on brand attitudes: affect- or belief-based change? in E. M. Clark, T. C. Brock, and D. W. Stewart (eds.), *Attention, attitude, and affect in response to advertising* (pp. 149–216). Hillsdale: Lawrence Erlbaum Associates.

Miell, D. E. and Littleton, K. (eds.) (2004). *Collaborative creativity: contemporary perspectives.* London: Free Association Books.

—— MacDonald, R. A. R., and Hargreaves, D. J. (eds.) *Musical Communication.* Oxford: Oxford University Press.

Migneault, B., Girard, F., Albert, C., Chouinard, P., Boudreault, D., Provencher, D., Todorov, A., Ruel, M., and Girard, D. C. (2004). The effect of music on the neurohormonal stress response to surgery under general anesthesia. *Anesthesia and Analgesia*, 98, 527–532.

Miller, A. G. (1970). Role of physical attractiveness in impression formation. *Psychonomic Science*, 19, 241–243.

Miller, D. W. and Marks, L. J. (1992). Mental imagery and sound effects in radio commercials. *Journal of Advertising*, 21, 83–93.

—— —— (1997). The effects of imagery–evoking radio advertising strategies on affective responses. *Psychology and Marketing*, 14, 337–360.

Miller, J. (1999). *Flowers in the dustbin: the rise of rock and roll*. London: Simon and Schuster.

Milliman, R. E. (1982). Using background music to affect the behavior of supermarket shoppers. *Journal of Marketing*, 46, 86–91.

—— (1986). The influence of background music on the behavior of restaurant patrons. *Journal of Consumer Research*, 133, 286–289.

Millman, R. B. and Beeder, A. B. (1994). The new psychedelic culture: LSD, ecstasy, "rave" parties and the Grateful Dead. *Psychiatric Annals*, 24, 148–150.

Miluk–Kolasa, B., Obminski, S., Stupnicki, R., and Golec, L. (1994). Effects of music treatment on salivary cortisol in patients exposed to pre-surgical stress. *Experimental and Clinical Endocrinology*, 102, 119–120.

Miniard, P. W., Bhatla, S., and Sirdeshmukh, D. (1992). Mood as a determinant of postconsumption product evaluations: mood effects and their dependency on the affective intensity of the consumption experience. *Journal of Consumer Psychology*, 1, 173–195.

Minor, M. S., Wagner, T., Brewerton, F. J., and Hausman, A. (2004). Rock on: an elementary model of customer satisfaction with musical performances. *Journal of Services Marketing*, 18, 7–18.

Mintel (2003). *Pre–recorded music, June 2003*. London: Mintel.

Miranda, D. and Claes, M. (2004). Rap music genres and deviant behaviors in French–Canadian adolescents. *Journal of Youth and Adolescence*, 33, 113–122.

Mital, A., McGlothlin, J. D. and Faard, H. F. (1992). Noise in multiple-workstation open–plan computer rooms: measurements and annoyance. *Journal of Human Ergology*, 21, 69–82.

Mitchell, A. H. (1949). The effect of radio programs on silent reading achievement of ninety–one sixth grade students. *Journal of Educational Research*, 42, 460–470.

Mitchell, L. A., MacDonald, R. A. R., and Brodie, E. E. (2006). A comparison of the effects of preferred music, arithmetic and humour on cold pressor pain. *European Journal of Pain*, 10, 343–351.

—— —— Knussen, C., and Serpell, M. A. (2007). A survey investigation of the effects of music listening on chronic pain. *Psychology of Music*, 35, 39–59.

Mitchell, W. B., DiBartolo, P. M., Brown, T. A. and Barlow, D. H. (1998). Effects of positive and negative mood on sexual arousal in sexually functional males. *Archives of Sexual Behavior*, 27, 197–207.

Mito, H. (2004). Role of daily musical activity in acquisition of musical skill: comparisons between young musicians and nonmusicians. *Bulletin of the Council for Research in Music Education*, 161/2, 1–8.

—— (2007). *Learning musical skills through everyday listening*. Unpublished PhD thesis, Roehampton University, London.

Mixon, F. G. and Ressler, R. W. (2000). A note on elasticity and price dispersions in the music recording industry. *Review of Industrial Organization*, 17, 465–470.

—— Trevino, L. J., and Bales, A. R. (2004). Justbelow pricing strategies in the music industry: empirical evidence. *International Journal of the Economics of Business*, 11, 165–174.

Moe, W. W. and Fader, P. S. (2001). Modeling hedonic portfolio products: a joint segmentation analysis of music compact disc sales. *Journal of Marketing Research*, 383, 376–385.

—— —— (2002). Fast-track article using advance purchase orders to forecast new product sales. *Marketing Science*, 21, 347–364.

Molteni, L. and Ordanini, A. (2003). Consumption patterns, digital technology and music downloading. *Long Range Planning*, 36, 389–406.

Monsaas, J. A. and Engelhard, G. (1990). Home environment and the competitiveness of highly accomplished individuals in four talent fields. *Developmental Psychology*, 26, 264–268.

Monsey, H. L. (1960). Preliminary report of the clinical efficacy of audioanalgesia. *Journal of California State Dental Association*, 36, 432–437.

Montello, L. (1995). Music therapy for musicians: reducing stress and enhancing immunity. *International Journal of Arts Medicine*, 4, 14–20.

Montemayor, R. and Eisen, M. (1977). The development of self-conceptions from childhood to adolescence. *Developmental Psychology*, 13, 314–319.

Moore, D. G., Burland, K., and Davidson, J. W. (2003). The social context of musical success: a developmental account. *British Journal of Psychology*, 94, 529–549.

Moore, K. and Martindale, C. (1983). Preference for shapes varying in color, color typicality, size, and complexity. *Paper presented at the International Conference on Psychology and the Arts, Cardiff.*

Moore, R., Gladstone, I., and Standley, J. (1994). *Effects of music, maternal voice, intrauterine sounds and white noise on the oxygen saturation levels of premature infants.* Unpublished paper presented at the National Conference, National Association for Music Therapy, Inc., Orlando, FL.

Mor, S., Day, H., and Flett, G. (1995). Perfectionism, control, and components of performance anxiety in professional artists. *Cognitive Therapy and Research*, 19, 207–225.

Morgan, L. A., Hargreaves, D. J. and Joiner, R. W. (2000). Children's collaborative music composition: communication through music. In R. Joiner, K. Littleton, D. Faulkner and D.E. Miell (eds.) *Rethinking collaborative learning* (pp. 52–64). London: Free Association Press.

Morris, J. D. and Boone, M. A. (1998). The effects of music on emotional response, brand attitude, and purchase intent in an emotional advertising context. *Advances in Consumer Research*, 25, 518–526.

Morrison, M. and Beverland, M. (2003). In search of the right instore music. *Business Horizons*, 46, 77–82.

Mortimer, R. (2005). Flying high with Lakmé . *Brand Strategy*, 189, 28–29.

Moscovici, S. and Lage, E. (1976). Studies in social influence: III. Majority versus minority influence in a group. *European Journal of Social Psychology*, 6, 149–174.

Moss, M. K. and Frieze, I. H. (1993). Job preferences in the anticipatory socialization phase: a comparison of two matching models. *Journal of Vocational Behavior*, 42, 282–297.

Mota, G. (2001). Portugal. In D. J. Hargreaves and A. C. North (eds.), *Musical development and learning: the international perspective* (pp. 151–162). London: Continuum.

Muehling, D. D. and Bozman, C. S. (1990). An examination of factors influencing effectiveness of 15–second advertisements. *International Journal of Advertising*, 9, 331–344.

Mueller, J. H. and Hevner, K. (1942). *Trends in musical taste.* Bloomington, Indiana: Indiana University Publishers.

Mugny, G., Gachoud, J–P., Doms, M., and Perez, J. A. (1988). Influences majoritaire et minoritaire directe et indirecte dans un paradigme de choix é sthetiques. *Schweizerische Zeitschrift für Psychologie / Revue Suisse de Psychologie*, 47, 13–23.

Mulder, J., Ter Bogt, T., Raaijmakers, Q., and Vollebergh, W. (2006). Music taste groups and problem behavior. *Journal of Youth and Adolescence*, 363, 313–324.

Munro, S. (1993). *Music therapy in palliative/hospice care.* St. Louis: Magna Music Baton.

Murao, T. and Wilkins, B. (2001). Japan. In D. J. Hargreaves and A. C. North (eds.), *Musical development and learning: the international perspective* (pp. 87–101). London: Continuum.

Murningham, J. K. and Conlon, D. E. (1991). The dynamics of intense work groups: a study of British string quartets. *Administrative Science Quarterly*, June, 165–186.

Murray, N. M. and Murray, S. B. (1996). Music and lyrics in commercials: a cross–cultural comparison between commercials run in the Dominican Republic and in the United States. *Journal of Advertising*, 25, 51–63.

Murrock, C. J. (2005). Music and mood. In A. V. Clark (ed.), *Psychology of moods* (pp. 141–155). Hauppauge: Nova Science Publishers.

Nafde, M. (1974). Rhythm and work. *Scientia Paedagogica Experimentalis*, 11, 95–102.

Nagel, J. J. (1993). Stage fright in musicians: a psychodynamic perspective. *Bulletin of the Menninger Clinic*, 57, 492–503.

Nantais, K. M. and Schellenberg, E. G. (1999). The Mozart effect: an artifact of preference. *Psychological Science*, 10, 370–373.

Narmour, E. (1990). *The analysis and cognition of basic melodic structures: the implication-realization model.* Chicago: University of Chicago Press.

—— (1991). The top-down and bottom-up systems of musical implication: building on Meyer's theory of emotional syntax. *Music Perception*, 9, 1–26.

Nater, U. M., Krebs, M., and Ehlert, U. (2005). Sensation seeking, music preference, and psychophysiological reactivity to music. *Musicae Scientiae*, 9, 239–254.

National Advisory Committee on Creative and Cultural Education (1999). *All our futures: creativity, culture, and education.* London: DfEE.

Navissi, F., Naiker, V., and Upson. S. (2005). Securities price effects of Napster-related events. *Journal of Accounting, Auditing and Finance*, 20, 167–183.

Negus, K. (1993). Plugging and programming: pop radio and record promotion in Britain and the United States. *Popular Music*, 12, 57–68.

Nelson, D. A. and Soha, J. A. (2004). Perception of geographical variation in song by male Puget Sound white-crowned sparrows, Zonotrichia leucophrys pugetensis. *Animal Behaviour*, 68, 395–405.

Nelson, N. A., Kaufman, J. D., Burt, J., and Karr, C. (1995). Health symptoms and the work environment in four nonproblem United States office buildings. *Scandinavian Journal of Work, Environment and Health*, 21, 51–59.

Neumann, M. and Simpson, T. A. (1997). Smuggled sound: bootleg recording and the pursuit of popular memory. *Symbolic Interaction*, 20, 319–341.

Newberry, R. C. (1995). Environmental enrichment: increasing the biological relevance of captive environments. *Applied Animal Behaviour Science*, 44, 229–243.

Newcomb, M. D., Chou, C-P., Bentler, P. M., and Huba, G. J. (1988). Cognitive motivations for drug use among adolescents: longitudinal tests of gender differences and predictors of change in drug use. Journal of Counseling Psychology, 35, 426–438.

—— Mercurio, C., and Wollard, C. A. (2000). Rock stars in anti–drug-abuse commercials: an experimental study of adolescents' reactions. *Journal of Applied Social Psychology*, 30, 1160–1185.

Newton, C. and Kantner, L. (1997). Cross-cultural research in aesthetic development: a review. In A. M. Kindler (ed.), *Child development in art* (pp. 165–182). Reston: NAEA.

Ng, C. F. (2003). Satisfying shoppers' psychological needs: from public market to cyber-mall. *Journal of Environmental Psychology*, 23, 439–455.

Niedenthal, P. M., Cantor, N., and Kihlstrom, J. F. (1985). Prototype matching: a strategy for social decision making. *Journal of Personality and Social Psychology*, 48, 575–584.

—— and Mordkoff, J. T. (1991). Prototype distancing: a strategy for choosing among threatening situations. *Personality and Social Psychology Bulletin*, 17, 483–493.

Nielsen, S. G. (2004). Strategies and self-efficacy beliefs in instrumental and vocal individual practice: a study of students in higher music education. *Psychology of Music*, 323, 418–431.

Nilsson, U., Rawal, N., Unestähl, L. E., Zetterberg, C., and Unosson, M. (2001). Improved recovery after music and therapeutic suggestions during general anaesthesia: a double–blind randomized controlled trial. *Acta Anaesthesiologica Scandinavica*, 45, 812–817.

—— Unosson, M., and Rawal N. (2005). Stress reduction and analgesia in patients exposed to calming music postoperatively: a randomized controlled trial. *European Journal of Anaesthesiology*, 22, 96–102.

Nisbett, R. E. and Wilson T. D. (1977) Telling more than we can know: verbal reports on mental processes. *Psychological Review*, 84, 231–259.

Nordoff, P. and Robbins, C. (1971). *Therapy in music for handicapped children*. London: Gollancz.

—— —— (1977). *Creative music therapy*. New York: John Day.

North, A. C., Bland, V., and Ellis, N. (2005). Distinguishing heroes from celebrities. *British Journal of Psychology*, 96, 39–52.

—— Colley, A. M. and Hargreaves, D. J. (2003). Adolescents' perceptions of the music of male and female composers. *Psychology of Music*, 313, 139–154.

—— Desborough, L. and Skarstein, L. (2005). Musical preference, deviance, and attitudes towards celebrities. *Personality and Individual Differences*, 383, 1903–1914.

—— and Hargreaves, D. J. (1995a). Eminence in pop music. *Popular Music and Society*, 19, 41–66.

—— —— (1995b). Subjective complexity, familiarity, and liking for popular music. *Psychomusicology*, 14, 77–93.

—— —— (1996a). Affective and evaluative responses to the arts. *Empirical Studies of the Arts*, 14, 207–222.

—— —— (1996b). Responses to music in aerobic exercise and yogic relaxation classes. *British Journal of Psychology*, 87, 535–547.

—— (1996c). Situational influences on reported musical preference. *Psychomusicology*, 15, 30–45.

—— —— (1996d). The effects of music on responses to a dining area. *Journal of Environmental Psychology*, 16, 55–64.

—— ——(1996e) Responses to music in a dining area. *Journal of Applied Social Psychology*, 24, 491–501.

—— —— (1997a). Liking for musical styles. *Musicae Scientiae*, 1, 109–128.

—— —— (1997b). The effect of physical attractiveness on responses to pop music performers and their music. *Empirical Studies of the Arts*, 15, 75–89.

—— —— (1997c). Liking, arousal potential, and the emotions expressed by music. *Scandinavian Journal of Psychology*, 38, 45–53.

—— (1998). The effect of music on atmosphere and purchase intentions in a cafeteria. *Journal of Applied Social Psychology*, 28, 2254–2273.

—— —— (1999a). Music and driving game performance. *Scandinavian Journal of Psychology*, 40, 285–292.

—— —— (1999b). Music and adolescent identity. *Music Education Research*, 1, 75–92.

—— —— (1999c). Can music move people? The effects of musical complexity and silence on waiting time. *Environment and Behavior*, 313, 136–149.

—— —— (2000a). Collative variables versus prototypicality. *Empirical Studies of the Arts*, 18, 13–17.

—— —— (2000b). Musical preference during and after relaxation and exercise. *American Journal of Psychology*, 113, 43–67.

—— —— (2001). Complexity, prototypicality, familiarity, and the perception of musical quality. *Psychomusicology*, 17, 77–80.

—— —— (2002). Age variations in judgements of 'great' art works. *British Journal of Psychology*, 933, 397–405.

—— —— (2005). Labelling effects on the perceived deleterious consequences of pop music listening. *Journal of Adolescence*, 28, 433–440.

—— —— (2006). Problem music and self-harming. *Suicide and Life-Threatening Behavior*, 363, 582–590.

—— —— (2007a). Lifestyle correlates of musical preference: 1. Relationships, living arrangements, beliefs, and crime. *Psychology of Music*, 35, 58–87.

—— —— (2007b). Lifestyle correlates of musical preference: 2. Media, leisure time, and music. *Psychology of Music*, 35, 179–200.

—— —— (2007c). Lifestyle correlates of musical preference: 3. Travel, money, education, employment, and health. *Psychology of Music*, 35, 473–497.

—— —— and Hargreaves, J. J. (2004). The uses of music in everyday life. *Music Perception*, 22, 63–99.

—— —— and Heath, S. (1998). Musical tempo and time perception in a gymnasium. *Psychology of Music*, 26, 78–88.

—— —— MacKenzie, L., and Law, R. (2004). The effects of musical and voice 'fit' on responses to adverts. *Journal of Applied Social Psychology*, 34, 1675–1708.

—— —— and McKendrick, J. (1997). In-store music affects product choice. *Nature*, 3903, 132.

—— —— ——(1999a). The effect of music on in–store wine selections. *Journal of Applied Psychology*, 84, 271–276.

—— —— —— (1999b). Music and on-hold waiting time. *British Journal of Psychology*, 90, 161–164.

—— —— —— (2000). The effects of music on atmosphere and purchase intentions in a bank and a bar. *Journal of Applied Social Psychology*, 30, 1504–1522.

—— —— and O'Neill, S. A. (2000). The importance of music to adolescents. *British Journal of Educational Psychology*, 70, 255–272.

——and Oishi, A. (2006). Music CD purchase decisions. *Journal of Applied Social Psychology*, 36, 3043–3084.

—— Sheridan, L., Gillett, R., and Maltby, J. (2007). Death, attractiveness, moral conduct, and celebrity worship. *Manuscript submitted for publication*.

—— —— and Maltby, J. (submitted). Attributional style, self esteem, and celebrity worship. *Journal of Media Psychology*.

—— Shilcock, A., and Hargreaves, D. J. (2003). The effect of musical style on restaurant customers' spending. *Environment and Behavior*, 35, 712–718.

—— Tarrant, M., and Hargreaves, D. J. (2004). The effects of music on helping behaviour: a field study. *Environment and Behavior*, 36, 266–275.

Nowak, G. J., Shamp, S., Hollander, B., and Cameron, G. T. (1999). Interactive media: a means for more meaningful advertising? in D. W. Schumann and E. Thorson (eds.), *Advertising and the world wide web* (pp. 99–117). Mahwah: Lawrence Erlbaum Associates.

Núñez, M. J., Mañá, P., Liñares, D., Riveiro, M. P., Balboa, J., Suárez-Quintanilla, J., Maracchi, M., Méndez, M. R., López, J. M., and Freire-Garabal, M. (2002). Music, immunity and cancer. *Life Sciences*, 71, 1047–1057.

Nurse, K. (2000). Copyright and music in the digital age: prospects and implications for the Caribbean. *Social and Economic Studies*, 49, 53–81.

Nuzum, E. (2001). Parental advisory: music censorship in America. New York: Perennial.

Nyklicek, I., Thayer, J. F., and van Doornen, L. J. P. (1997). Cardiorespiratory differentiation of musically-induced emotions. *Journal of Psychophysiology*, 11, 304–321.

O'Neill, S. A. (1997a). Gender and music. In D. J. Hargreaves and A. C. North (eds.), *The social psychology of music* (pp. 46–63). Oxford: Oxford University Press.

——(1997b). The role of practice in children's early musical performance achievement. In H. Jørgensen and A. C. Lehmann (eds.), *Does practice make perfect? Current theory and research on instrumental practice* (pp. 53–70). Oslo: Nordes Musikhøgskole.

—— (1999a). The role of motivation in the practice and achievement of young musicians. In S. W. Yi (ed.), *Music, mind, and science* (pp. 420–433). Seoul: Seoul National University Press.

—— (1999b). Flow theory and the development of musical performance skills. *Bulletin of the Council for Research in Music Education*, 141, 129–134.

—— (2002). The self-identity of young musicians. In R. A. R. MacDonald, D. J. Hargreaves, and D. E. Miell, D. E. (eds.), *Musical identities* (pp. 79–96). Oxford: Oxford University Press.

—— and Boulton, M. J. (1996). Boys' and girls' preferences for musical instruments: a function of gender? *Psychology of Music*, 24, 171–183.

—— and McPherson, G. E. (2002). Motivation. In R. Parncutt and G. E. McPherson (eds.), *The science and psychology of music performance* (pp. 31–46). Oxford: Oxford University Press.

Oakes, S. (2000). The influence of the musicscape within service environments. *Journal of Services Marketing*, 14, 539–556.

—— (2003). Demographic and sponsorship considerations for jazz and classical music festivals. *Service Industries Journal*, 23, 165–178.

—— (2003). Musical tempo and waiting perceptions. *Psychology and Marketing*, 20, 685–705.

—— and North, A. C. (2006). The impact of background musical tempo and timbre congruity upon ad content recall and affective response. *Applied Cognitive Psychology*, 20, 505–520.

Ockelford, A. (2007). *In the key of genius: the extraordinary life of Derek Paravicini*. London: Hutchinson.

—— and Pring, L. (2005). Learning and creativity in a prodigious musical savant. Proceedings of International Society for Low Vision Research and Rehabilitation Conference 2005 ('Vision'), *International Congress Series* 1282, 903–907. Amsterdam: Elsevier.

Odell, P. M., Korgen, K. O., Schumacher, P., and Delucchi, M. (2000). Internet use among female and male college students. *CyberPsychology and Behavior*, 3, 855–862.

Offer, D., Ostrov, E., Howard, K. I., and Atkinson, R. (1988). *The teenage world: adolescents' self-image in ten countries*. New York: Plenum.

Okaichi, Y. and Okaichi, H. (2001). Music discrimination by rats. *Japanese Journal of Animal Psychology*, 51, 29–34.

Oldani, R. (1997). Causes of increases in achievement motivation: is the personality influenced by prenatal environment? *Personality and Individual Differences*, 22, 403–410.

Oldham, G. R., Cummings, A., Mischel, L. J., Schmidtke, J. M. and Zhou, J. (1995). Listen while you work: quasi-experimental relations between personal stereo headset use and employee work responses. *Journal of Applied Psychology*, 80, 547–564.

Oliveira, A. (2001). South America. In D. J. Hargreaves and A. C. North (eds.), *Musical development and learning: the international perspective* (pp. 187–201). London: Continuum.

Olsen, G. D. (1994). Observations. The sounds of silence: functions and use of silence in television advertising. *Journal of Advertising Research*, 343, 89–95.

—— (1995). Creating the contrast: the influence of silence and background music on recall and attribute importance. *Journal of Advertising*, 24, 29–44.

—— (1997). The impact of interstimulus interval and background silence on recall. *Journal of Consumer Research*, 233, 295–303.

—— (2002). Salient stimuli in advertising: the effect of contrast interval length and type on recall. *Journal of Experimental Psychology: Applied*, 8, 168–179.

—— and Pracejus, J. W. (2004). Integration of positive and negative affective stimuli. *Journal of Consumer Psychology*, 14, 374–384.

—— and Crase, D. (1990). Presleymania: the Elvis factor. *Death Studies*, 14, 277–282.

Ornstein, R. E. (1969). *On the experience of time*. New York: Penguin.

Oyama, T., Hatano, K., Sato, Y., Kudo, M., Spintge, R., and Droh, R. (1983). Endocrine effect of anxiolytic music in dental patients. In R. Droh and R. Spintge (eds.), *Angst, schmerz, musik in der anasthesie* (pp. 143–146). Basel: Editiones Roche.

Ozer, M. (2001). User segmentation of online music services using fuzzy clustering. *Omega*, 29, 193–206.

Paffard, M. K. (1970). Creative activities and 'peak' experiences. *British Journal of Educational Psychology*, 40, 283–290.

Pan, Y. and Schmitt, B. (1996). Language and brand attitudes: impact of script and sound matching in Chinese and English. *Journal of Consumer Psychology*, 5, 263–277.

Panksepp, J. (1995). The emotional sources of "chills" induced by music. *Music Perception*, 133, 171–207.

—— and Bekkedal, M. Y. V. (1997). The affective cerebral consequence of music: happy vs. sad effects on the EEG and clinical implications. *International Journal of Arts Medicine*, 5, 18–27.

—— and Bernatzky, G. (2002). Emotional sounds and the brain: the neuro–affective foundations of musical appreciation. *Behavioural Processes*, 60, 133–155.

Panzarella, R. (1980). The phenomenology of aesthetic peak experiences. *Journal of Humanistic Psychology*, 20, 69–85.

Papadopoulos, T. (2000). Copyright, parallel imports and national welfare: the Australian market for sound recordings. *Australian Economic Review*, 33, 337–348.

—— (2003). Determinants of international sound recording piracy. *Economics Bulletin*, 6, 1–9.

—— (2004). Pricing and pirate product market formation. *Journal of Product and Brand Management*, 13, 56–63.

Papoušek, H. (1996). Musicality in infancy research: biological and cultural origins of early musicality. In I. DeLiège and J.A. Sloboda (eds.), *Musical beginnings: origins and development of musical competence* (pp. 37–55). Oxford: Oxford University Press.

—— and Papoušek, M. (1982). Integration into the social world: survey of research. P. M. Stratton (ed.), *Psychology of the human newborn* (pp. 367–390). London: John Wiley.

Pardun, C. J. and McKee, K. B. (1995). Strange bedfellows: symbols of religion and sexuality on MTV. *Youth and Society*, 26, 438–449.

Park, C. W. and Young, S. M. (1986). Consumer response to television commercials: the impact of involvement and background music on brand attitude formation. *Journal of Marketing Research*, 23, 11–24.

Parncutt, R. (2006). Prenatal development. In G. E. McPherson (ed.), *The child as musician: a handbook of musical development* (pp. 1–31). Oxford: Oxford University Press.

—— and McPherson, G. E. (eds.) (2002). *The science and psychology of music performance*. Oxford: Oxford University Press.

Parris, W. C. V. and Smith, H. S. (2003). Alternative pain medicine. *Pain Practice*, 3, 105–116.

Parsons, M. (1987). *How we understand art*. Cambridge: Cambridge University Press.

Pavlicevic, M. (1997). *Music therapy in context*. London: Jessica Kingsley Publishers.

—— (1999). *Music therapy: intimate notes*. London: Jessica Kingsley Publishers.

—— and Ansdell, G. (eds.) (2004). *Community music therapy*. London: Jessica Kingsley Publishers.

Payne, E. (1967). Musical taste and personality. *British Journal of Psychology*, 58, 133–138.

Payne, H. (1993). *Handbook of inquiry in the arts therapies: one river, many currents*. London: Jessica Kingsley Publishers.

Payne, K. (2000). The progressively changing songs of humpback whales: a window on the creative process in a wild animal. In N. L. Wallin, B. Merker, and S. Brown (eds.), *The origins of music* (pp. 135–150). Cambridge: MIT Press.

Pearsall, P., Schwartz, G. E. R., and Russek, L. G. S. (2002). Changes in heart transplant recipients that parallel the personalities of their donors. *Journal of Near–Death Studies*, 20, 191–206.

Pedersen, W. and Skrondal, A. (1999). Ecstasy and new patterns of drug use: a normal population study. *Addiction*, 94, 1695–1706.

Pegg, C. (1984). Factors affecting the musical choices of audiences in East Suffolk, England. In R. Middleton and D. Horn (eds.) *Popular music 4: performers and audiences* (pp. 51–73). Cambridge: Cambridge University Press.

Pelletier, C. L. (2004). The effect of music on decreasing arousal due to stress: a meta–analysis. *Journal of Music Therapy*, 41, 192–214.

Pepinsky, A. (1944). The growing appreciation of music and its effect upon the choice of music in industry. *Journal of the Acoustical Society of America*, 15, 176–179.

Peretti, P. O. and Kippschull, H. (1990). Influence of five types of music on social behaviors of mice, Mus musculus. *Psychological Studies*, 353, 98–103.

—— and Kippschull, H. (1991). Influence of five types of music on social behaviors of mice, Mus musculus. *Indian Journal of Behaviour*, 15, 51–58.

Perlini, A. H. and Viita, K. A. (1996). Audioanalgesia in the control of experimental pain. *Canadian Journal of Behavioural Science*, 28, 292–301.

Persson, R. S. and Robson, C. (1995). The limits of experimentation: on researching music and musical settings. *Psychology of Music*, 233, 39–47.

Peters, J. (1987). *Music therapy: an introduction.* Springfield: Charles C. Thomas.

Peters, R. J., Kelder, S. H., Markham, C., Peters, L. A., and Ellis, A. (2003). Beliefs and social norms about codeine and promethazine hydrochloride cough syrup (CPHCS) onset and perceived addiction among urban Houstonian adolescents: an addition trend in the city of lean. *Journal of Drug Education*, 33, 415–425.

Peterson, D. L. and Pfost, K. S. (1989). Influence of rock videos on attitudes of violence against women. *Psychological Reports*, 64, 319–322.

Peterson, R. and Berger, D. (1975). Cycles in symbol reproduction: the case of popular music. *American Sociological Review*, 40, 158–173.

Peterson, R. A. and Berger, D. G. (1996). Reply to Alexander: measuring industry concentration, diversity, and innovation in popular music. *American Sociological Review*, 61, 175–178.

Petty, R. E. and Cacioppo, J. T. (1981). *Attitudes and persuasion: classic and contemporary approaches.* Dubuque: William C. Brown.

—— —— and Schumann, D. T. (1983). Central and peripheral routes to advertising effectiveness: the moderating effect of involvement. *Journal of Consumer Research*, 10, 135–146.

Phillips, D. (2001). Celebrity branding aims for the stars. *Brand Strategy*, 154, 10.

Phillips, D. P. (1974). The influence of suggestion on suicide: substantive and theoretical implications of the Werther effect. *American Sociological Review*, 393, 340–354.

Piirto, J. (1991). Why are there so few ? (Creative women: visual arts, mathematicians, musicians). *Roeper Review*, 133, 142–147.

Pincott, G. and Anderson, T. (1999). Lost in music: analysis of music listening in the UK. *Journal of the Market Research Society*, 41, 109–134.

Pincus, B. (2004). Will music and movies muscle in on an overcrowded sporting world? *Marketing Week*, 27, 21 October 2004, 18.

—— (2005). Get in tune with consumers. *Brand Strategy*, 190, 46–47.

Piters, R. A. M. P. and Stokmans, M. J. W. (2000). Genre categorization and its effect on preference for fiction books. *Empirical Studies of the Arts*, 18, 159–166.

Pitt, L. F. and Abratt, R. (1988). Music in advertisements for unmentionable products: a classical conditioning experiment. *International Journal of Advertising*, 7, 130–137.

Plante, T. G., Marcotte, D., Manuel, G., and Willemsen, E. (1996). The influence of brief episodes of aerobic exercise activity, soothing music-nature scenes condition, and suggestion on coping with test-taking anxiety. *International Journal of Stress Management*, 33, 155–166.

Plopper, B. and Ness, M. (1993). Death as portrayed to adolescents through top 40 rock and roll music. *Adolescence*, 28, 793–807.

Plucker, J. A. and Dana, R. Q. (1998). Alcohol, tobacco, and marijuana use: relationships to undergraduate students' creative achievement. *Journal of College Student Development*, 39, 472–483.

Plutchik, R. (1980). *Emotion: a psychoevolutionary synthesis*. New York: Harper and Row.

Podolsky, E. (1954). *Music therapy*. Oxford: Philosophical Library.

Polkosky, M. D. and Lewis, J. R. (2002). Effect of auditory waiting cues on time estimation in speech recognition telephony applications. *International Journal of Human–Computer Interaction*, 14, 423–446.

Pool, M. M., Koolstra, C. M., and van der Voort, T. H. A. (2003). The impact of background radio and television on high school students' homework performance. *Journal of Communication*, 533, 74–87.

Porter, D., Reed, C., and Neuringer, A. (1984). Music discriminations by pigeons. *Journal of Experimental Psychology: Animal Behavior Processes*, 10, 138–148.

Posluszna, J., Burtowy, A., and Palusinski, R. (2004). Music preferences and tobacco smoking. *Psychological Reports*, 94, 240–242.

Posner, M. I. and Keele, S. W. (1968). On the genesis of abstract ideas. *Journal of Experimental Psychology*, 77, 353–363.

Pratt, R. (1993). *Music therapy and music education for the handicapped: developments and limitations in practice and research*. St. Louis: Magna Music Baton.

Pressing, J. (1988). Improvisation: methods and models. In J. A. Sloboda (ed.), *Generative processes in music* (pp. 129–178). Oxford: Oxford University Press.

Preti, A., DeBiasi, F., and Miotto, P. (2001). Musical creativity and suicide. *Psychological Reports*, 89, 719–727.

Price, H. E. and Winter, S. (1991). Effect of strict and expressive conducting on performances and opinions of eighth-grade band students. *Journal of Band Research*, 27, 30–43.

Price, J. J. and Lanyon, S. M. (2004) Patterns of song evolution and sexual selection in the oropendolas and caciques. *Behavioral Ecology*, 15, 485–497.

Priestley, M. (1975). *Music therapy in action*. Oxford: St Martin's.

Prieto-Rodriguez, J. and Fernandez–Blanco, V. (2000). Are popular and classical music listeners the same people? *Journal of Cultural Economics*, 24, 147–164.

Primos, K. (2001). Africa. In D. J. Hargreaves and A. C. North (eds.), *Musical development and learning: the international perspective* (pp. 1–13). London: Continuum.

Pucely, M. J., Mizerski, R., and Perrewe, P. (1988). A comparison of involvement measures for the purchase and consumption of pre-recorded music. *Advances in Consumer Research*, 15, 37–42.

QCA (2002). *Developing new models for music education*. Paper presented to the National Music Education Forum, 17.6.02.

Rabinovich, E., Bailey, J. P., and Carter, C. R. (2003). A transaction–efficiency analysis of an internet retailing supply chain in the music CD industry. *Decision Sciences*, 34, 131–172.

Radocy, R. E. (1975). A naïve minority of one and deliberate majority mismatches of tonal stimuli. *Journal of Research in Music Education*, 23, 120–133.

—— (1976). Effects of authority figure biases on changing judgements of musical events. *Journal of Research in Music Education*, 24, 119–128.

Rajala, A. K. and Hantula, D. A. (2000). Towards a behavioral ecology of consumption: delay–reduction effects on foraging in a simulated internet mall. *Managerial and Decision Economics*, 21, 145–158.

Ramsey, K. L. and Simmons, F. B. (1993). High–powered automobile stereos. *Otolaryngology: Head and Neck Surgery*, 109, 108–110.

Rana, S. A. and North, A. C. (in press). The role of music in everyday life among Pakistanis. *Music Perception*.

Rauscher, F. H. (1999). No title. *Nature*, 400, 827–828.

—— and Hinton, S. C. (2006). The Mozart effect: music listening is not music instruction. *Educational Psychologist*, 41, 233–238.

—— Robinson, K. D., and Jens, J. (1998). Improved maze learning through early music exposure in rats. *Neurological Research*, 20, 427–432.

—— Shaw, G. L., and Ky, K. N. (1993). Music and spatial task performance. *Nature*, 365, 611.

—— —— Levine, L. J., Wright, E. L., Dennis, W. R., and Newcomb, R. L. (1997). Music training causes long-term enhancement of preschool children's spatial-temporal reasoning. *Neurological Research*, 19, 2–8.

—— and Zupan, M. A. (2000). Classroom keyboard instructions improve kindergarten children's spatial-temporal performance: a field experiment. *Early Childhood Research Quarterly*, 15, 215–228.

Raviv, A., Bar-Tal, D., Raviv, A., and Ben-Horin, A. (1996). Adolescent idolization of pop singers: causes, expressions, and reliance. *Journal of Youth and Adolescence*, 25, 631–650.

Rawlings, D., Barrantes, I. V. N., and Furnham, A. (2000). Personality and aesthetic preference in Spain and England: two studies relating sensation seeking and openness to experience to liking for paintings and music. *European Journal of Personality*, 14, 553–576.

—— Twomey, F., Burns, E., and Morris, S. (1998). Personality, creativity and aesthetic preference: comparing psychoticism, sensation seeking, schizotypy, and openness to experience. *Empirical Studies of the Arts*, 16, 153–178.

Reber, R., Schwarz, N., and Winkielman, P. (2004). Processing fluency and aesthetic pleasure: is beauty in the perceiver's processing experience? *Personality and Social Psychology Review*, 8, 364–382.

Reddi, U. (1985). An Indian perspective on youth culture. *Communication Research*, 12, 373–380.

Reddick, B. H. and Beresin, E. V. (2002). Rebellious rhapsody – metal, rap, community, and individuation. *Academic Psychiatry*, 26, 51–59.

Reddy, S. K., Swaminathan, V., and Motley, C. M. (1998). Exploring the determinants of Broadway show success. *Journal of Marketing Research*, 35, 370–383.

Reed, S. K. (1972). On the internal structure of perceptual and semantic categories. In T. E. Moore (ed.), *Cognitive development and the acquisition of language* (pp. 111–144). New York: Academic Press.

Rentfrow, P. J. and Gosling, S. D. (2003). The do re mi's of everyday life: the structure and personality correlates of musical preference. *Journal of Peronality and Social Psychology*, 84, 1236–1256.

Reynolds, W. (1943). Selecting music for the factory. *Personnel*, 20, 95–98.

Rich, M., Woods, E. R., Goodman E., Emans, S. J., and DuRant, R. H. (1998). Aggressors or victims: gender and race in music video violence. *Pediatrics*, 101, 669–674.

Rickard, N. S. (2004). Intense emotional responses to music: a test of the physiological arousal hypothesis. *Psychology of Music*, 32, 371–388.

Rider, M. S. (1985). Entrainment mechanisms are involved in pain reduction, muscle relaxation and music–mediated imagery. *Journal of Music Therapy*, 22, 183–192.

Rider, M. (1990). Imagery, improvisation, and immunity. *Psychotherapy*, 17, 211–216.

Rider, M. S. and Achterberg, J. (1989). Effect of music–assisted imagery on neutrophils and lymphocytes. *Biofeedback and Self Regulation*, 14, 247–257.

—— Achterberg, J., Lawlis, G. F., Goven, A., Toledo, R., and Butler, J. R. (1990). Effect of immune system imagery on secretory IgA. *Biofeedback and Self Regulation*, 15, 317–333.

—— and Weldin, C. (1990). Imagery, improvisation, and immunity. *Arts in Psychotherapy*, 17, 211–216.

Rigg, M. G. (1948). Favorable versus unfavorable propaganda in the enjoyment of music. *Journal of Experimental Psychology*, 383, 78–81.

Rishi, P., Sinha, S. P., Dubey, R. (2000). A correlational study of workplace characteristics and work satisfaction among Indian bank employees. Psychologia, 43, 155–164.

Ritossa, D. A. and Rickard, N. S. (2004). The relative utility of 'pleasantness and liking' dimensions in predicting the emotions expressed by music. *Psychology of Music*, 32, 5–22.

Rob, R. and Waldfogel, J. (2004). Piracy on the high c's: music downloading, sales displacement, and social welfare in a sample of college students. *National Bureau of Economic Research Working Papers: 10874*.

Roballey, T. C., McGreevy, C., Rongo, R. R., Schwantes, M. L., Steger, P. J., Wininger, M. A., and Gardner, E. B. (1985). The effect of music on eating behavior. *Bulletin of the Psychonomic Society*, 23, 221–222.

Robb, S. L. (2000). Music assisted progressive muscle relaxation, progressive muscle relaxation, music listening, and silence: a comparison of relaxation techniques. *Journal of Music Therapy*, 37, 2–21.

Roberts, D. F., Foehr, U. G., and Rideout, V. (2005). *Generation M: media in the lives of 8–18 year olds*. Menlo Park: The Henry J. Kaiser Family Foundation.

—— and Henriksen, L. (1990). *Music listening vs. television viewing among older adolescents*. Paper presented at the annual meeting of the International Communication Association, Dublin, Ireland.

Roberts, K. R., Dimsdale, J., East, P. and Friedman, L. (1998). Adolescent emotional response to music and its relationship to risk–taking behaviours. *Journal of Adolescent Health*, 23, 49–54.

Robinson, J. P. and Hirsch, P. (1969). It's the sound that does it. *Psychology Today*, 3, 42–45.

—— —— (1972). Teenage response to rock and roll protest songs. In R. S. Denisoff and R. A. Peterson (eds.), *The sounds of social change: studies in popular culture* (pp. 222–231). Chicago: Rand McNally.

—— Pilskaln, R., and Hirsch, P. (1976). Protest rock and drugs. *Journal of Communication*, 26, 125–136.

Robinson, T. N., Chen, H. L., and Killen, J. D. (1998). Television and music video exposure and risk of adolescent alcohol use. *Pediatrics*, 102, article no. 54.

Robinson, T. O., Weaver, J. B., and Zillmann, D. (1996). Exploring the relation between personality and the appreciation of rock music. *Psychological Reports*, 78, 259–269.

Rodríguez-González, M. S., Fernández, C. A., and Sabucedo–Cameselle, J. M. (1997). Empirical validation of a model of user satisfaction with buildings and their environments as workplaces. *Journal of Environmental Psychology*, 17, 69–74.

Roe, K. (1985). Swedish youth and music: listening patterns and motivations. *Communication Research*, 12, 353–362.

—— (1995). Adolescents' use of socially disvalued media: towards a theory of media delinquency. *Journal of Youth and Adolescence*, 24, 617–631.

Rogoff, B. (1990). *Apprenticeship in thinking: cognitive development in social context*. New York: Oxford University Press.

—— (2003). *The cultural nature of human development*. New York: Oxford University Press.

Roper, J. M. and Manela, J. (2000). Psychiatric patients' perceptions of waiting time in the psychiatric emergency service. *Journal of Psychosocial Nursing*, 38, 19–27.

Rose, R. F. and Wagner, M. J. (1995). Eminence choices in three musical genres and music media preferences. *Journal of Research in Music Education*, 43, 251–260.

Rosen, S. (1981). The economics of superstars. *American Economic Review*, December, 845–858.

—— (1983). The economics of superstars. *American Scholar*, Autumn, 449–459.

Rosenbaum, J. and Prinsky, L. (1987). Sex, violence, and rock 'n' roll: youth's perception of popular music. *Popular Music and Society*, 11, 79–89.

—— —— (1991). The presumption of influence: recent responses to popular music subcultures. *Crime and Delinquency*, 37, 528–535.

Rosengren, K. E., Wenner, L. A., and Palmgreen, P. (1985). *Media gratifications research*. Beverly Hills: Sage.

Ross, M. (1995). What's wrong with school music? *British Journal of Music Education*, 12, 185–201.

Rossman, G. (2004). Elites, masses, and media blacklists: the Dixie Chicks controversy. *Social Forces*, 83, 61–79.

Rothenbuhler, E. (1985). Programming decision making in popular music radio. *Communication Research*, 12, 209–232.

—— (1987). Commercial radio and popular music: processes of selection and factors of influence. In J. Lull (ed.), *Popular music and communication* (pp. 78–95). London: Sage.

—— and Dimmick, J. (1982). Popular music: concentration and diversity in the industry, 1974–1980. *Journal of Communication*, 32, 143–149.

—— and McCourt, T. (1992). Commercial radio and popular music: processes of selection and factors of influence. In J. Lull (ed.), *Popular music and communication* (2nd edn.) (pp. 101–115). London: Sage.

—— —— (2004). The economics of the recording industry. In A. Alexander, J. Owers, R. Carveth, C. A. Hollifield, and A. N. Greco (eds.), *Media economics: theory and practice* (3rd edn.) (pp. 221–248). Mahwah: Lawrence Erlbaum Associates.

Rouner, D. (1990). Rock music use as a socializing function. *Popular Music and Society*, 14, 97–107.

Royne-Stafford, M. R. and Tripp, C. (2000). Age, income, and gender: demographic determinants of community theater patronage. *Journal of Nonprofit and Public Sector Marketing*, 8, 29–43.

—— —— and Bienstock, C. C. (2004). The influence of advertising logo characteristics on audience perceptions of a nonprofit theatrical organization. *Journal of Current Issues and Research in Advertising*, 26, 37–45.

Rubin, A. M., West, D. V., and Mitchell, W. S. (2001). Differences in aggression, attitudes toward women, and distrust as reflected in popular music preferences. *Media Psychology*, 3, 25–42.

Rubin, D. C., Rahhal, T. A., and Poon, L. W. (1998). Things learned in early adulthood are remembered best. *Memory and Cognition*, 26, 3–19.

Rubin-Rabson, G. (1940). The influence of age, intelligence and training on reactions to classical and modern music. *Journal of General Psychology*, 22, 413–429.

Rudman, L. A. and Lee, M. R. (2002). Implicit and explicit consequences of exposure to violent and misogynous rap music. *Group Processes and Intergroup Relations*, 5, 133–150.

Runfola, M. and Swanwick, K. (2002). Developmental characteristics of learners. In R. Colwell and C. P. Richardson (eds.), *Second handbook of research on music teaching and learning* (pp. 373–397). Oxford: Oxford University Press.

Russell, P. A. (1987). Effects of repetition on the familiarity and likeability of popular music recordings. *Psychology of Music*, 15, 187–197.

Rustad, R. A., Small, J. E., Jobes, D. A., Safer, M.A., and Peterson, R. J. (2003). The impact of rock videos and music with suicidal content on thoughts and attitudes about suicide. *Suicide and Life-Threatening Behavior*, 33, 120–131.

Ruud, E. (1980). *Music therapy and its relationship to current treatment theories*. St. Louis: Magna Music Baton.

Ruud, E. (1998). *Music therapy: improvisation, communication, and culture*. Gilsum: Barcelona.

Ryan, C. and Costa-Giomi, E. (2004). Attractiveness bias in the evaluation of young pianists' performances. *Journal of Research in Music Education*, 52, 141–154.

—— Wapnick, J., Lacaille, N., and Darrow, A. -A. (2006). The effects of various physical characteristics of high–level performers on adjudicators' performance ratings. *Psychology of Music*, 34, 559–572.

Ryan, K., Boulton, M., O'Neill, S. A. and Sloboda, J. A. (2000). Perceived support and children's participation in music. In C. Woods, G. Luck, R. Brochard, F. Seddon, and J. A. Sloboda (eds.), *Proceedings of the 6th International Conference on Music Perception and Cognition* (p. 15). Keele: Keele University Department of Psychology.

Sailer, U. and Hassenzahl, M. (2000). Assessing noise annoyance: an improvement–oriented approach. *Ergonomics*, 43, 1920–1938.

Salmaggi, P., la Torre, R., Nicchia, M., and Pastore, G. (1989). The foetus as psychic entity. *Medicina Psicosomatica*, 34, 249–257.

Salmon, P. (1991). Stress inoculation techniques and musical performance anxiety. In G. D. Wilson (ed.), *Psychology and performing arts* (pp. 219–229). Amsterdam: Swets and Zeitlinger.

Sargent, S. L. and Weaver, J. B. (1996). Exploring the impact of expressed media preferences on perceptions of opposite gender peers. *Paper presented at the annual conference of the International Communication Association, Chicago, May 1996*.

Schachter, S., and Singer, J. E. (1962). Cognitive, social, and physiological determinants of emotional state. *Psychological Review*, 65, 379–399.

Schaller, M. (1997). The psychological consequences of fame: three tests of the self–consciousness hypothesis. *Journal of Personality*, 65, 291–309.

Scheel, K. R. and Westefeld, J. S. (1999). Heavy metal music and adolescent suicidality: an empirical investigation. *Adolescence*, 343, 253–273.

Schellenberg, E. G. (2001). Music and non–musical abilities. *Annals of the New York Academy of Sciences*, 930, 355–371.

—— (2003). Does exposure to music have beneficial side effects? in I. Peretz and R. J. Zattore (eds.), *The cognitive neuroscience of music* (pp. 430–448). Oxford: Oxford University Press.

—— (2004). Music lessons enhance IQ. *Psychological Science*, 15, 511–514.

—— (2006). Exposure to music: the truth about the consequences. In G. E. McPherson (ed.), *The child as musician* (pp. 111–134). Oxford: Oxford University Press.

—— and Hallam, S. (2005). Music listening and cognitive abilities in 10– and 11-year-olds: the Blur effect. In G. Avanzini, L. Lopez, S. Koelsch, and M. Manjno (eds.), *The neurosciences and music II: from perception to performance* (pp. 202–209). New York: New York Academy of Sciences.

Scherer, K. R. and Zentner, M. R. (2001). Emotional effects of music: production rules. In P. N. Juslin and J. A. Sloboda (eds.), *Music and emotion: theory and research* (pp. 361–392). Oxford: Oxford University Press.

Schierman, M. J. and Rowland, G. L. (1985). Sensation-seeking and selection of entertainment. *Personality and Individual Differences*, 6, 599–603.

Schindler, R. M. and Holbrook, M. B. (1993). Critical periods in the development of men's and women's tastes in personal appearance. *Psychology and Marketing*, 10, 549–564.

—— and Holbrook, M. B. (2003). Nostalgia for early experience as a determinant of consumer preferences. *Psychology and Marketing*, 20, 275–302.

Schleimer, J. D. and Freundlich, K. D. (2001). Criminal prosecution of online file sharing. *Journal of Internet Law*, 5, 14–18.

Schlosser, A. E. (1998). Applying the functional theory of attitudes to understanding the influence of store atmosphere on store inferences. *Journal of Consumer Psychology*, 7, 345–369.

Schmidt, L. and Trainor, L. J. (2001). Frontal brain electrical activity (EEG) distinguishes valence and intensity of musical emotions. *Cognition and Emotion*, 15, 487–500.

Schneider, N., Schedlowski, M., Schurmeyer, T. H., and Becker, H. (2001). Stress reduction through music in patients undergoing cerebral angiography. *Neuroradiology*, 43, 472–476.

Schoen, M. (1940). *The psychology of music*. London: Roland.

Schramm, H. (2006). Consumption and effects of music in the media. *Communication Research Trends*, 25, 3–29.

Schubert, D. S. P., Wagner, M. E., and Schubert, H. J. P. (1977). Family constellation and creativity: firstborn predominance among classical music composers. *Journal of Psychology*, 95, 147–149.

Schubert, E. and McPherson, G. E. (2006). The perception of emotion in music. In G. E. McPherson (ed.), *The child as musician* (pp. 193–212). Oxford: Oxford University Press.

Schubert, R. (2004). Modeling perceived emotion with continuous musical features. *Music Perception*, 21, 561–585.

Schulkind, M. D., Hennis, L. K., and Rubin, D. C. (1999). Music, emotion, and autobiographical memory: they're playing your song. *Memory and Cognition*, 27, 948–955.

Schullian, D. M. and Schoen, M. (eds.) (1948). *Music and medicine*. Oxford: Henry Schuman.

Schwadron, A. A. (1967). *Aesthetics: dimensions for music education*. MENC: Washington D. C.

Schwartz, F. J. (1997). Perinatal stress reduction, music and medical cost savings. *Journal of Prenatal and Perinatal Psychology and Health*, 12, 19–29.

Schwartz, K. D. and Fouts, G. T. (2003). Music preferences, personality style, and developmental issues of adolescents. *Journal of Youth and Adolescence*, 323, 205–213.

Scott, A. J. (1999). The US recorded music industry: on the relations between organization, location, and creativity in the cultural economy. *Environment and Planning A*, 31, 1965–1984.

Scott, B. (2002). One tune no longer fits all. *International Journal of Advertising and Marketing to Children*, 3, 49–56.

Seashore, C. E. (1940). Why no great women composers? *Music Educators Journal*, 26, 88.

Seddon, F. (2004). Empathetic creativity: the product of empathetic attunement. In D. E. Miell and K. Littleton (eds.), *Collaborative creativity: contemporary perspectives* (pp. 65–78). London: Free Association Books.

Seelow, D. (1996). Listening to youth: Woodstock, music, America, and Kurt Cobain's suicide. *Child and Youth Care Forum*, 25, 49–60.

Seidman, S. (1992). An investigation of sex–role stereotyping in music videos. *Journal of Broadcasting and Electronic Media*, 36, 209–216.

—— (1999). Revisiting sex–role stereotyping in MTV videos. *International Journal of Instructional Media*, 26, 11–22.

Sellers, P. (1989, 8th May). The ABC's of marketing to kids. *Fortune*, 114–116, 120.

Selm, M. E. (1991). Chronic pain: three issues in treatment and implications for music therapy. *Music Therapy Perspectives*, 9, 91–97.

Selvin, B. (1943). Programming music for industry. *Journal of the Acoustical Society of America*, 15, 131–132.

Serafine, M. L. (1988). *Music as cognition: the development of thought in sound*. New York: Columbia University Press.

Sergeant, D. (1969). Experimental investigation of absolute pitch. *Journal of Research in Music Education*, 17, 135–143.

Shahidullah, S. and Hepper, P. G. (1993a). The developmental origins of fetal responsiveness to an acoustic stimulus. *Journal of Reproductive and Infant Psychology*, 11, 135–142.

—— —— (1993b). Prenatal hearing tests ? *Journal of Reproductive and Infant Psychology*, 11, 143–146.

—— ——(1994). Frequency discrimination by the fetus. *Early Human Development*, 36, 13–26.

Shaver, P. R., Schwartz, J., Kirson, D., and O'Connor, C. (1987). Emotion knowledge: further exploration of a prototype approach. *Journal of Personality and Social Psychology*, 52, 1061–1086.

Shepherd, J. (1982). *Tin Pan Alley*. London: Routledge and Kegan Paul.

—— (2003). Music and social categories. In M. Clayton, T. Herbert, and R. Middleton (eds.), *The cultural study of music: a critical introduction* (pp. 69–79). London: Routledge.

Sherif, M. (1935). An experimental study of stereotypes. *Journal of Abnormal and Social Psychology*, 29, 371–375.

Sherman, B. and Dominick, J, (1986). Violence and sex in music videos: TV and rock 'n' roll. *Journal of Communication*, 36, 79–93.

Sherrer, M. (1971). Kansas City's jazz ambassador Yardbird. *Music Journal*, 23 (May), 53, 55, 58.

Shiraishi, I. M. (1997). A home–based music therapy program for multi-risk mothers. *Music Therapy Perspectives*, 15, 16–23.

Shoup, D. (1995). Survey of performance–related problems among high school and junior high school musicians. *Medical Problems of Performing Artists*, 10, 100–105.

Sicoli, M. L. C. (1995). Life factors common to women who write popular songs. *Creativity Research Journal*, 8, 265–276.

Sidorenko, V. N. (2000). Clinical application of Medical Resonance Therapy Music in high–risk pregnancies. *Integrative Physiological and Behavioral Science*, 35, 199–207.

Siedlecki, S. L. (2005). The effect of music on power, pain, depression, and disability: a clinical trial. *Dissertation Abstracts International: Section B: The Sciences and Engineering*, 65, 3950.

Siegel, S. L. (1983). *The use of music as treatment in pain perception with post surgical patients in a paediatric hospital.* Unpublished MSc thesis, University of Miami.

Signorielli, N., McLeod, D., and Healy, E. (1994). Gender stereotypes in MTV commercials: the beat goes on. *Journal of Broadcasting and Electronic Media*, 38, 91–101.

Silverman, J. and Wilson, D. (2002). *Innocence betrayed: paedophilia, the media and society.* Cambridge: Polity.

Silverman, L. K. (1995). Why are there so few eminent women? *Roeper Review*, 18, 5–13.

Simmons, B. (1992). The effect of censorship on attitudes toward popular music. *Popular Music and Society*, 16, 61–69.

Simon, C. R. and Wohlwill, J. F. (1968). An experimental study of the role of expectation and variation in music. *Journal of Research in Music Education*, 16, 227–238.

Simonton, D. K. (1977a). Creative productivity, age, and stress: a biographical time–series analysis of 10 classical composers. *Journal of Personality and Social Psychology*, 35, 791–804.

—— (1977b). Eminence, creativity, and geographical marginality: a recursive structural equation model. *Journal of Personality and Social Psychology*, 35, 805–816.

——(1980a). Thematic fame and melodic originality: a multivariate computer–content analysis. *Journal of Personality*, 48, 206–219.

—— (1980b). Thematic fame, melodic originality, and musical zeitgeist: a biographical and transhistorical content analysis. *Journal of Personality and Social Psychology*, 38, 972–983.

—— (1984). *Genius, creativity, and leadership: historiometric inquiries.* London: Harvard University Press.

—— (1986). Aesthetic success in classical music: a computer analysis of 1,935 compositions. *Empirical Studies of the Arts*, 4, 1–17.

—— (1987). Musical aesthetics and creativity in Beethoven: a computer analysis of 105 compositions. *Empirical Studies of the Arts*, 5, 87–104.

—— (1988). Creativity, leadership, and chance. In R. J. Sternberg (ed.), *The nature of creativity: contemporary psychological perspectives* (pp. 386–428). Cambridge: Cambridge University Press.

—— (1989). The swan–song phenomenon: last-works effects for 172 classical composers. *Psychology and Aging*, 4, 42–47.

—— (1990). *Psychology, science, and history: an introduction to historiometry*. London: Yale University Press.

—— (1991a). Emergence and realization of genius: the lives and works of 120 classical composers. *Journal of Personality and Social Psychology*, 61, 829–840.

—— (1991b). Latent–variable models of posthumous reputation: a quest for Galton's G. *Journal of Personality and Social Psychology*, 60, 607–619.

—— (1993). Creative genius in music: Mozart and other composers. In P. Ostwald and L. S. Zegans (eds.), *The pleasures and perils of genius: mostly Mozart* (pp. 1–28). Madison: International University Press.

—— (1994). *Greatness: who makes history and why*. London: Guilford Press.

—— (1995). Drawing inferences from symphonic programs: musical attributes versus listener attributions. *Music Perception*, 12, 307–322.

——Simonton, D. K. (1997a). Products, persons, and periods: historiometric analyses of compostional creativity. In D. J. Hargreaves and A. C. North (eds.), *The social psychology of music* (pp. 109–122). Oxford: Oxford University Press.

——Simonton, D. K. (1997b). Creative productivity: a predictive and explanatory model of career trajectories and landmarks. *Psychological Review*, 104, 66–89.

—— (1998a). Fickle fashion versus immortal fame: transhistorical assessments of creative products in the opera house. *Journal of Personality and Social Psychology*, 75, 198–210.

—— (1998b). Achieved eminence in minority and majority cultures: convergence versus divergence in the assessments of 294 African Americans. *Journal of Personality and Social Psychology*, 74, 804–817.

—— (2003). Qualitative and quantitative analyses of historical data. *Annual Review of Psychology*, 54, 617–640.

Simpkins, J. D. and Smith, J. A. (1974). Effects of music on source evaluations. *Journal of Broadcasting*, 18, 361–367.

Singer, S. I., Levine, M., and Jou, S. (1993). Heavy metal music preference, delinquent friends, social control, and delinquency. *Journal of Research in Crime and Delinquency*, 30, 317–329.

Sirgy, M. J., Grewal, D., and Mangleburg, T. (2000). Retail environment, self-congruity, and retail patronage: an integrative model and a research agenda. *Journal of Business Research*, 49, 127–138.

Sivadas, E., Grewal, R., and Kellaris, J. (1998). The Internet as a micro marketing tool: targeting consumers through preferences revealed in music newsgroup usage. *Journal of Business Research*, 41, 179–186.

Skipper, J. K. (1975). Musical tastes of Canadian and American college students: an examination of the massification and Americanization theses. *Canadian Journal of Sociology*, 1, 49–59.

Slater, P. J. B. (2000). Birdsong repertoires: their origins and use. In N. L. Wallin, B. Merker, and S. Brown (eds.), *The origins of music* (pp. 49–63). London: MIT Press.

Sloane, K. D. (1985). Home influences on talent development. In B. S. Bloom (ed.), *Developing talent in young people* (pp. 439–476). New York: Ballantine.

Sloboda, J. A. (1985). *The musical mind: the cognitive psychology of music*. Oxford: Oxford University Press.

—— (1986). Cognition and real music: the psychology of music comes of age. *Psychologica Belgica*, **26**, 199–219.

—— (ed.) (1988). *Generative processes in music: the psychology of performance, improvisation and composition*. Oxford: Oxford University Press.

—— (1991a). Music structure and emotional response: some empirical findings. *Psychology of Music*, **19**, 110–120.

—— (1991b). Musical expertize. In K. A. Ericsson and J. Smith (eds.), *The study of expertize: prospects and limits* (pp. 153–171). Cambridge: Cambridge University Press.

—— (1994). Music performance: expression and the development of excellence. In R. Aiello and J. A. Sloboda (eds.), *Musical perceptions* (pp. 152–172). Oxford: Oxford University Press.

—— (1999a). Musical performance and emotion: issues and developments. In S. W. Yi (ed.), *Music, mind, and science* (pp. 220–238). Western Music Research Institute: Seoul.

—— (1999b). Everyday uses of music listening: a preliminary study. In S. W. Yi (ed.), *Music, mind, and science* (pp. 354–369). Western Music Research Institute: Seoul.

—— (2005). The acquisition of musical performance expertize: deconstructing the 'talent' account of individual differences in musical expressivity. In J. A. Sloboda (ed.), *Exploring the musical mind: cognition, emotion, ability, function* (pp. 275–296). Oxford: Oxford University Press.

—— and Davidson, J. W. (1996). The young performing musician. In I. Deliège and J. A. Sloboda (eds.), *Musical beginnings: origins and development of musical competence* (pp. 171–190). Oxford: Oxford University Press.

—— —— and Howe, M. J. A. (1994). Is everyone musical? *The Psychologist*, **7**, 349–354.

—— —— Howe, M. J. A., and Moore, D. G. (1996). The role of practice in the development of performing musicians. *British Journal of Psychology*, **87**, 287–309.

—— Hermelin, B. and O'Connor, N. (1985). An exceptional musical memory. *Music Perception*, **3**, 155–170.

—— and Juslin, P. N. (2001). Psychological perspectives on music and emotion. In P. N. Juslin and J. A. Sloboda (eds.), *Music and emotion: theory and research* (pp. 71–104). Oxford: Oxford University Press.

—— and O'Neill, S. A. (2001). Emotions in everyday listening to music. In P. N. Juslin and J. A. Sloboda (eds.), *Music and emotion: theory and research* (pp. 415–429). Oxford: Oxford University Press.

—— —— and Ivaldi, A. (2001). Functions of music in everyday life: an exploratory study using the experience sampling method. *Musicae Scientiae*, **5**, 9–32.

Sluckin, W., Hargreaves, D. J., and Colman, A. M. (1983). Novelty and human aesthetic preferences. In J. Archer and L. Birke (eds.), *Exploration in animals and humans* (pp. 245–269). London: Van Nostrand Reinhold.

Sluming, V. A. and Manning, J. T. (2000). Second to fourth digit radio in elite musicians: evidence for musical ability as an honest signal of male fitness. *Evolution and Human Behavior*, **21**, 1–9.

Smith, A. P. (1985). The effects of different types of noise on semantic processing and syntactic reasoning. *Acta Psychologica*, **58**, 263–273.

Smith, C. A. and Morris, L. W. (1977). Differential effects of stimulative and sedative music on anxiety, concentration, and performance. *Psychological Reports*, **41**, 1047–1053.

Smith, H. C. (1947). Music in relation to employee attitudes, piece–work production, and industrial accidents. *International Review of Applied Psychology*, **14**, 59.

Smith, J. D. (1987). Conflicting aesthetic ideals in a musical culture. *Music Perception*, 4, 373–391.

Smith, P. C. and Curnow, R. (1966). 'Arousal hypothesis' and the effects of music on purchasing behavior. *Journal of Applied Psychology*, 50, 255–256.

Smith, R. A. (ed.) (2000). *Readings in discipline–based art education: a literature of educational reform*. Reston: NAEA.

Smith, S. E. (1999). *Dancing in the street: Motown and the cultural politics of Detroit*. London: Harvard University Press.

Smith, S. L. and Boyson, A. R. (2002). Violence in music videos: examining the prevalence and context of physical aggression. *Journal of Communication*, 52, 61–83.

Snyder, M. (1984). When belief creates reality. In L. Berkowitz (ed.), *Advances in Experimental Social Psychology, Vol. 18*. New York: Academic Press.

Soibelman, D. (1948). *Therapeutic and industrial uses of music: a review of the literature*. New York: Columbia University Press.

Sommers-Flanagan, R., Sommers-Flanagan, J. and Davis, B. (1993). What's happening on music television? A gender role content analysis. *Sex Roles*, 28, 745–753.

Soothill, K. and Francis, B. (2002). Moral Panics and the aftermath: a study of incest. *Journal of Social Welfare and Family Law*, 24, 1–17.

Sopchack, A. L. (1955). Individual differences in responses to music. *Psychology Monograph*, 69, No. 11, 1–20.

Sosniak, L. A. (1985). Learning to be a concert pianist. In B. S. Bloom (ed.), *Developing talent in young people* (pp. 19–67). New York: Ballantine.

—— (1990). The tortoise, the hare, and the development of talent. In M. J. A. Howe (ed.), *Encouraging the development of exceptional skills and talents* (pp. 149–164). Leicester: British Psychological Society.

Spangenberg, E. R., Grohmann, B., and Sprott, D. E. (2005). It's beginning to smell (and sound) a lot like Christmas: the interactive effects of ambient scent and music in a retail setting. *Journal of Business Research*, 58, 1583–1589.

Spieth, W. (1956). Annoyance threshold judgments of bands of noise. *Journal of the Acoustical Society of America*, 28, 872–877.

St. John, P. A. (2006). Finding and making meaning: young children as musical collaborators. *Psychology of Music*, 34, 238–261.

St. Lawrence, J. S. and Joyner, D. J. (1991) The effects of sexually violent rock music on males' acceptance of violence against women. *Psychology of Women Quarterly*, 15, 49–63.

Stack, S. (1998). Heavy metal, religiosity, and suicidal acceptability. *Suicidal and Life-Threatening Behavior*, 28, 388–394.

—— (2000). Blues fans and suicide acceptability. *Death Studies*, 24, 223–231.

—— (2002). Opera subculture and suicide for honor. *Death Studies*, 26, 431–437.

—— and Gundlach, J. H. (1992). The effect of country music on suicide. *Social Forces*, 71, 211–218.

—— —— (1994a). Country music and suicide: a reply to Maguire and Snipes. *Social Forces*, 72, 1245–1248.

—— —— (1994b). Psychological versus sociological perspectives on suicide: a reply to Mauk, Taylor, White, and Allen. *Social Forces*, 72, 1257–1261.

—— —— and Reeves, J. L. (1994). The heavy metal subculture and suicide. *Suicide and Life–Threatening Behavior*, 24, 15–23.

Standley, J. M. (1986). Music research in medical / dental treatment: meta–analysis and clinical applications. *Journal of Music Therapy*, **23**, 56–122.

—— (1991a). The role of music in pacification/stimulation of premature infants with low birthweights. *Music Therapy Perspectives*, **9**, 19–25.

—— (1991b). *Music techniques in therapy, counseling and special education*. St. Louis: Magna Music Baton.

—— (1995). Music as a therapeutic intervention in medical and dental treatment: research and clinical applications. In T. Wigram, B. Saperstone, and R. West (eds.), *The art and science of music therapy: a handbook* (pp. 3–22). Langhorne: Harwood.

—— (1996). A meta–analysis on the effects of music as reinforcement for education / therapy objectives. *Journal of Research in Music Education*, **44**, 105–133.

—— (1998). The effect of music and multimodal stimulation on physiological and developmental responses of premature infants in neonatal intensive care. *Pediatric Nursing*, **24**, 532–539.

—— (1999). *The effect of musicreinforced non–nutritive sucking on feeding rate of premature infants*. Paper presented at the Ninth World Congress of Music Therapy, Washington, D.C.

—— (2000). The effect of contingent music to increase non-nutritive sucking of premature infants. *Pediatric Nursing*, **26**, 493–499.

—— (2002). A meta–analysis of the efficacy of music therapy for premature infants. *Journal of Pediatric Nursing*, **17**, 107–113.

—— and Moore, R. S. (1995). Therapeutic effects of music and mother's voice on premature infants. *Pediatric Nursing*, **21**, 509–512, 574.

Stanton, H. E. (1973). The effect of music on test anxiety. *Australian Psychologist*, **8**, 220–228.

—— (1994). Reduction of performance anxiety in music students. *Australian Psychologist*, **29**, 124–127.

Steele, J. and Brown, J. D. (1995). Adolescent room culture: studying media in the context of everyday life. *Journal of Youth and Adolescence*, **24**, 551–576.

Steffenhagen, R. A., McCann, H. G., and McAree, C. P. (1976). Personality and drug use: a study of the usefulness of the Mf Scale of the MMPI in measuring creativity and drug use. Journal of Alcohol and Drug Education, **21**, 8–16.

Stephens, T., Braithwaite, R. L., and Taylor, S. E. (1998). Model for using hip-hop music for small group HIV/AIDS prevention counseling with African American adolescents and young adults. *Patient Education and Counseling*, **35**, 127–137.

Steptoe, A. (1989). Stress, coping, and stage fright in professional musicians. *Psychology of Music*, **17**, 3–11.

—— (2001). Negative emotions in music making: the problem of performance anxiety. In P. N. Juslin and J. A. Sloboda (eds.), *Music and emotion: theory and research* (pp. 291–307). Oxford: Oxford University Press.

—— and Fidler, H. (1987). Stage fright in orchestral musicians: a study of cognitive and behavioural strategies in performance anxiety. *British Journal of Psychology*, **78**, 241–249.

Stermer, E., Levy, N., Beny, A., Meisels, R., and Tamir A. (1998). Ambience in the endoscopy room has little effect on patients. *Journal of Clinical Gastroenterology*, **26**, 256–258.

Sternberg, R. J. (ed.) (1999). *Handbook of creativity*. Cambridge: Cambridge University Press.

—— and Lubart, T. I. (1999). The concept of creativity: prospects and paradigms. In R. J. Sternberg (ed.), *Handbook of creativity* (pp. 3–15). Cambridge: Cambridge University Press.

Stewart, D. W., Farmer, K. M., and Stannard, C. I. (1990). Music as a recognition cue in advertising-tracking studies. *Journal of Advertising Research*, 30, 39–48.

—— and Furse, D. H. (1986). *Effective television advertising: a study of 1000 commercials.* Lexington: Lexington Books.

—— and Koslow, S. (1989). Executional factors and advertising effectiveness: a replication. *Journal of Advertising*, 18, 21–32.

—— and Punj, G. N. (1998). Effects of using a nonverbal (musical) cue on recall and playback of television advertising: implications for advertising tracking. *Journal of Business Research*, 42, 39–51.

Stige, B. (2002). *Culture–centred music therapy.* Gilsum: Barcelona.

Stipek, D. J. (1998). *Motivation to learn: from theory to practice* (3rd edn.). Boston: Allyn and Bacon.

Strasburger, V. C. and Wilson, B. J. (2002). *Youth and media: opportunities for development or lurking dangers? Children, adolescents, and the media.* Thousand Oaks: Sage.

Stratton, V. N. and Zalanowski, A. H. (1994). Affective impact of music vs. lyrics. *Empirical Studies of the Arts*, 12, 173–184.

——Stratton, V. N. and Zalanowski, A. H. (1997). The relationship between characteristic moods and most commonly listened to types of music. *Journal of Music Therapy*, 34, 129–140.

Stratton, V. and Zalanowski, A. (2003). Daily music listening habits in college students: related moods and activities. *Psychology and Education*, 40, 1–11.

Stremikis, B. A. (2002). The personal characteristics and environmental circumstances of successful women musicians. *Creativity Research Journal*, 14, 85–92.

Strobl, E. A. and Tucker, C. (2000). The dynamics of chart success in the U.K.: pre–recorded popular music industry. *Journal of Cultural Economics*, 24, 113–134.

Strouse, J. S. and Buerkel-Rothfuss, N. L. (1987). Media exposure and the sexual attitudes and behaviors of college students. *Journal of Sex Education and Therapy*, 133, 43–51.

—— —— and Long, E. C. J. (1995). Gender and family as moderators of the relationship between music video exposure and adolescent sexual permissiveness. *Adolescence*, 30, 505–521.

—— Goodwin, M. P., and Roscoe, B. (1994). Correlates of attitudes toward sexual harassment among early adolescents. *Sex Roles*, 31, 559–577.

Stryker, S. (1987). Identity theory: developments and extensions. In K. Yardley and T. Honess (eds.), *Self and identity: psychosocial perspectives* (pp. 89–103). New York: Wiley.

Sullivan, M. (2002). The impact of pitch, volume and tempo on the atmospheric effects of music. *International Journal of Retail and Distribution Management*, 30, 323–330.

Sun, S.W. and Lull, J. (1986). The adolescent audience for music videos and why they watch. *Journal of Communication*, 36, 115–125.

Sundstrom, E., Herbert, R. K. and Brown, D. W. (1982). Privacy and communication in an open–plan office: a case study. *Environment and Behavior*, 14, 379–392.

—— Town, J. P., Rice, R. W. and Osborn, D. P. *et al.* (1994). Office noise, satisfaction, and performance. *Environment and Behavior*, 26, 195–222.

Swanwick, K. (1968). *Popular music and the teacher.* Oxford: Pergamon.

—— and Tillman, J. (1986). The sequence of musical development. *British Journal of Music Education*, 3, 305–39.

Sweeney, J. C. and Wyber, F. (2002). The role of cognitions and emotions in the music–approach–avoidance behavior relationship. *Journal of Services Marketing*, 16, 51–69.

Swoboda, B. (1998). Conditions of consumer information seeking: theoretical foundations and empirical results of using interactive multimedia systems. *International Review of Retail, Distribution and Consumer Research*, 8, 361–381.

Szabo, A., Ainsworth, S. E., and Danks, P. K. (2005). Experimental comparison of the psychological benefits of aerobic exercise, humor, and music. *Humor: International Journal of Humor Research*, 18, 235–246.

Tai, S. H. C. and Fung, A. M. C. (1997). Application of an environmental psychology model to in–store buying behaviour. *International Review of Retail, Distribution and Consumer Research*, 7, 311–337.

Tajfel, H. (ed.) (1978). *Differentiation between social groups: studies in the social psychology of intergroup relations*. London: Academic Press.

—— Flament, C., Billig, M. G., and Bundy, R. P. (1971). Social categorization and intergroup behaviour. *European Journal of Social Psychology*, 1, 149–178.

—— and Turner, J. C. (1986). The social identity theory of intergroup behaviour. In S. Worschel and W. G. Austin (eds.), *Psychology of intergroup relations* (2nd edn.) (pp. 7–24). Chicago: Nelson Hall.

Tan, L. P. (2004). The effects of background music on quality of sleep in elementary school children. *Journal of Music Therapy*, 41, 128–150.

Tanabe, P., Ferket, K., Thomas, R., Paice, J., and Marcantonio, R. (2002). The effect of standard care, ibuprofen, and distraction on pain relief and patient satisfaction in children with musculoskeletal trauma. *Journal of Emergency Nursing*, 28, 118–125.

Tanner, J. (1981). Pop music and peer groups: a study of Canadian high school students responses to pop music. *Canadian Review of Sociology and Anthropology*, 18, 1–13.

Tansik, D. A. and Routhieaux, R. (1999). Customer stress-relaxation: the impact of music in a hospital waiting room. *International Journal of Service Industry Management*, 10, 68–81.

Tapper, J., Thorson, E., and Black, D. (1994). Variations in music videos as a function of their musical genre. *Journal of Broadcasting and Electronic Media*, 383, 103–113.

Tarrant, M., Hargreaves, D. J. and North, A. C. (2001). Social categorization, self-esteem, and the estimated musical preferences of male adolescents. *Journal of Social Psychology*, 141, 565–581.

—— and North, A. C. (2004). Explanations for positive and negative behaviour: the intergroup attribution bias in achieved groups. *Current Psychology*, 233, 161–172.

Tarrant, M., North, A. C., Edridge, M. D., Kirk, L. E., Smith, E. A., and Turner, R. E. (2001). Social identity in adolescence. *Journal of Adolescence*, 24, 597–609.

—— —— and Hargreaves, D. J. (2002). Youth identity and music. In R. A. R. MacDonald, D. J. Hargreaves, and D. E. Miell (eds.), *Musical identities* (pp. 134–150). Oxford: Oxford University Press.

Tavassoli, N. T. and Han, J. K. (2002). Auditory and visual brand identifiers in Chinese and English. *Journal of International Marketing*, 10, 13–28.

—— and Lee, Y. H. (2003). The differential interaction of auditory and visual advertising elements with Chinese and English. *Journal of Marketing Research*, 40, 468–480.

Taylor, B. C., Demont-Heinrich, C., Broadfoot, K. J., Dodge, J., and Jian, G. (2002). | New media and the circuit of cyber-culture: conceptualizing Napster. *Journal of Broadcasting and Electronic Media*, 46, 607–629.

Taylor, C. R. and Johnson, C. M. (2002). Standardized vs. specialized international advertising campaigns: what we have learned from academic research in the 1990s. *New Directions in International Advertising Research*, 12, 45–66.

Taylor, S. L. (2004). Music piracy: differences in the ethical perceptions of business majors and music business majors. *Journal of Education for Business*, 79, 306–310.

Tekman, H. G. and Hortacsu, N. (2002). Music and social identity: stylistic identification as a response to a musical style. *International Journal of Psychology*, 37, 277–285.

Tesser, A. and Campbell, J. (1983). Self-definition and self-evaluation maintenance. In J. Suls and A. G. Greenwald (eds.), *Social psychological perspectives on the self* (*Vol. 2*) (pp. 1–31). Hillsdale: Erlbaum.

Teston, G. I. (2002). A developmental perspective of computer and information technology ethics: piracy of software and digital music by young adolescents. *Dissertation Abstracts International: Section B: The Sciences and Engineering*, 62, 5815.

Thompson, K. (1998). *Moral panics*. Oxford: Routledge.

Thompson, S. (2007). Determinants of listeners' enjoyment of a performance. *Psychology of Music*, 35, 20–36.

—— and Williamon, A. (2003). Evaluating evaluation: musical performance assessment as a research tool. *Music Perception*, 21, 21–41.

Thompson, W. F., Schellenburg, E. G., and Husain, G. (2001). Arousal, mood and the Mozart effect. *Psychological Science*, 12, 248–251.

Thorne, S. B. and Himelstein, P. (1984). The role of suggestion in the perception of Satanic messages in rock and roll recordings. *Journal of Psychology*, 116, 245–248.

Thorson, E., Christ, W. G., and Caywood, C. (1991). Effects of issue-image strategies, attack and support appeals, music, and visual content in political commercials. *Journal of Broadcasting and Electronic Media*, 35, 465–486.

Tiggemann, M. and Pickering, A. S. (1996). Role of television in adolescent women's body dissatisfaction and drive for thinness. *International Journal of Eating Disorders*, 20, 199–203.

—— and Slater, A. (2004). Thin ideals in music television: a source of social comparison and body dissatisfaction. *International Journal of Eating Disorders*, 35, 48–58.

Tom, G. (1990). Marketing with music. *Journal of Consumer Marketing*, 7, 49–53.

—— (1995). Classical conditioning of unattended stimuli. *Psychology and Marketing*, 12, 79–87.

Took, K. J. and Weiss, D. S. (1994). The relationship between heavy metal and rap music and adolescent turmoil: real or abstract? *Adolescence*, 29, 613–623.

Top, T. J. (1991). Sex bias in the evaluation of performance in the scientific, artistic, and literary professions: a review. *Sex Roles*, 24, 73–106.

Torrance, E. P. (1974). *Torrance tests of creative thinking*. Lexington: Personnel Press.

Towse, R. (1997). The Monopolies and Mergers Commission's investigation of the U.K. music market. *Journal of Cultural Economics*, 21, 147–151.

Trauger-Querry, B. and Haghighi, K. R. (1999). Balancing the focus: art and music therapy for pain control and symptom management in hospice care. *Hospice Journal*, 14, 25–38.

Trehub, S. E. (2006). Infants as musical connoisseurs. In G. E. McPherson (ed.), *The child as musician: a handbook of musical development* (pp. 33–49). Oxford: Oxford University Press.

Trehub, S., Schellenberg, E. and Hill, D. (1997). The origins of music perception and cognition: a developmental perspective. In I. DeLiège and J. A. Sloboda (eds.), *Perception and cognition of music* (pp. 103–128). Hove: Psychology Press.

—— and Unyk, A. M. (1991). Music prototypes in developmental perspective. *Psychomusicology*, 10, 73–87.

Trevarthen, C. (1999). Musicality and the intrinsic motive pulse: evidence from human psychobiology and infant communication. *Musicae Scientiae, Special Issue (1999–2000)*, 155–215.

—— (2002). Origins of musical identity: evidence from infancy for musical social awareness. In R. A. R. MacDonald, D. J. Hargreaves, and D. E. Miell, D. E. (eds.), *Musical identities* (pp. 21–38). Oxford: Oxford University Press.

Triller, N., Erzen, D., Duh, S., Petrinec-Primozic, M., and Kosnik, M. (2006). Music during bronchoscopic examination: the physiological effects: a randomized trial. *Respiration*, 73, 95–99.

Tse, M. M. Y., Chan, M. F., and Benzie, I. F. F. (2005). The effect of music therapy on postoperative pain, heart rate, systolic blood pressure and analgesic use following nasal surgery. *Journal of Pain and Palliative Care Pharmacotherapy*, 19, 21–29.

Turley, L. W. and Milliman, R. E. (2000). Atmospheric effects on shopping behavior: a review of the experimental evidence. *Journal of Business Research*, 49, 193–211.

Turner, J. C. (1975). Social comparison and social identity: some prospects for intergroup behaviour. *European Journal of Social Psychology*, 5, 149–178.

—— (1987). *Rediscovering the social group: a self-categorization theory*. Oxford: Blackwell.

Turner, M. L., Fernandez, J. E., and Nelson, K. (1996). The effect of music amplitude on the reaction to unexpected visual events. *Journal of General Psychology*, 123, 51–62.

Tusek, D., Church, J. M., Fazio, V. W. (1997). Guided imagery as a coping strategy for perioperative patients. *AORN Journal*, 66, 644–649.

Uetake, K., Hurnik, J. F., and Johnson, L. (1997). Effect of music on voluntary approach of dairy cows to an automatic milking system. *Applied Animal Behaviour Science*, 53, 175–182.

Uhrbrock, R. (1961). Music on the job: its influence on worker morale and production. *Personnel Psychology*, 14, 9–38.

Ungar, S. (2001). Moral Panic versus the risk society: the implications of the changing sites of social anxiety. *British Journal of Sociology*, 52, 271–291.

Unkefer, R. (1990). *Music therapy in the treatment of adults with mental disorders: theoretical bases and clinical interventions*. New York: Schirmer Books.

—— and Thaut, M. (eds.) (2002). *Music therapy in the treatment of adults with mental disorders: theoretical bases and clinical interventions (2nd ed.)*. St. Louis: MMB Music.

Valentine, E. R., Fitzgerald, D. F. P., Gorton, T. L., Hudson, J. A., and Symonds, E. R. C. (1995). The effect of lessons in the Alexander technique on music performance in high and low stress situations. *Psychology of Music*, 23, 129–141.

Van de Goor, L. A., Knibbe, R. A., and Drop, M. J. (1990). Adolescent drinking behavior: an observational study of the influence of situational factors on adolescent drinking rates. *Journal of Studies on Alcohol*, 51, 548–555.

van de Wall, W. (1946). *Music in hospitals*. New York: Russell Sage Foundation.

van de Wijngaart, G. F., Braam, R., de Bruin, D., Fris, M., Maalsté , N. J. M., and Verbraeck, H. T. (1999). Ecstasy use at large-scale dance events in the Netherlands. *Journal of Drug Issues*, 29, 679–702.

van den Bulck, J. and Beullens, K. (2005). Television and music video exposure and adolescent alcohol use while going out. *Alcohol and Alcoholism*, 40, 249–253.

van der Werff, J. J. (1985). Individual problems of self-definition: an overview, and a view. *International Journal of Behavioral Development*, 8, 445–471.

van Eijck, K. (2001). Social differentiation in musical taste patterns. *Social Forces*, 79, 1163–1185.

van Kemenade, J. F. L. M., van Son, M. J. M., and van Heesch, N. C. A. (1995). Performance anxiety among professional musicians in symphonic orchestras: a self–report study. *Psychological Reports*, 77, 555–562.

Vaughn, K. (2000). Music and mathematics: modest support for the oft-claimed relationship. *Journal of Aesthetic Education*, 343, 149–166.

Veitch, J. A. (1990). Office noise and illumination effects on reading comprehension. *Journal of Environmental Psychology*, 10, 209–217.

Verden, P., Dunleavy, K., and Powers, C. H. (1989). Heavy metal mania and adolescent delinquency. *Popular Music and Society*, 133, 73–82.

Vickers, A. (2000). Recent advances: complementary medicine. *British Medical Journal*, 3213, 683–686.

Vietnam studios face the music. (2002). *Far Eastern Economic Review*, 165, 17th January 2002, 8.

Vijayasarathy, L. R. and Jones, J. M. (2000). Intentions to shop using internet catalogues: exploring the effects of product types, shopping orientations, and attitudes towards computers. *Electronic Markets*, 10, 29–38.

Villani, S. (2001). Impact of media on children and adolescents: a 10-year review of research. *Journal of the American Academy of Child and Adolescent Psychiatry*, 40, 392–401.

Vincent, R. C. (1989). Clio's consciousness raised? Portrayal of women in rock videos, re–examined. *Journalism Quarterly*, 66, 155–160.

—— Davis, D. K., and Boruszkowski, L. A. (1987). Sexism on MTV: the portrayal of women in rock videos. *Journalism Quarterly*, 64, 750–755.

Vispoel, W. P. and Austin, J. R. (1993). Constructive response to failure in music: the role of attribution feedback and classroom goal structure. *British Journal of Educational Psychology*, 63, 110–129.

Vitouch, O. (2001). When your ear sets the stage: musical context effects in film perception. *Psychology of Music*, 29, 70–83.

Vitz, P. C. (1966). Affect as a function of stimulus variation. *Journal of Experimental Psychology*, 71, 74–79.

Vogel, H. (1998). *Entertainment industry economics* (4th edn.). Cambridge: Cambridge University Press.

Vokey, J. R. and Read, J. D. (1985). Subliminal messages: between the devil and the media. *American Psychologist*, 40, 1231–1239.

Voss, J. A., Good, M., Yates, B., Baun, M. M., Thompson, A., and Hertzog, M. (2004). Sedative music reduces anxiety and pain during chair rest after open-heart surgery. *Pain*, 112, 197–203.

Vygotsky, L. S. (1966). Genesis of the higher mental functions (abridged translation). In P. H. Light, S., Sheldon, and M. Woodhead (1991). *Learning to think* (pp. 32–41). London: Routledge and Open University Press.

——Vygotsky, L. S. (1978). *Mind and society*. Cambridge: Harvard University Press.

Vygotsky, L. S. (1986). *Thought and language* (revised and edited by A. Kozulin). Cambridge: MIT Press.

Waite, B. M., Hillbrand, M., and Foster, H. G. (1992). Reduction of aggressive behavior after removal of Music Television. *Hospital and Community Psychiatry*, 43, 173–175.

Wakefield, M., Flay, B., Nichter, M., and Giovino, G. (2003). Role of the media in influencing trajectories of youth smoking. *Addiction*, 98, 79–103.

Walberg, H. J., Zhang, G., Cummings, C., and Fillipelli, L. A. *et al*. (1996). Childhood traits and experiences of eminent women. *Creativity Research Journal*, 9, 97–102.

Walker, M. (1985). Backward messages in commercially available recordings. *Popular Music and Society*, 10, 2–13.

Walker, R. (1990). *Musical beliefs: psychoacoustic, mythical, and educational perspectives.* New York: Teachers College Press.

—— (2006). Cultural traditions. In G. E. McPherson (ed.), *The child as musician* (pp. 439–460). Oxford: Oxford University Press.

Wallace, W. T. (1991). Jingles in advertisements: can they improve recall? *Advances in Consumer Research*, 18, 239–242.

Wallach, M. A. and Greenberg, C. (1960). Personality functions of symbolic sexual arousal to music. *Psychological Monographs*, 74, 18.

Wallas, G. (1926). *The art of thought*. London: Watts.

Wallin, N. L. Merker, B., and Brown, S. (eds.) (2000). *The origins of music*. Cambridge: MIT Press.

Walls, K., Taylor, J., and Falzone, J. (1992). The effects of subliminal suggestions and music experience on the perception of tempo in music. *Journal of Music Therapy*, 29, 186–197.

Walsh, G., Mitchell, V. W., Frenzel, T., and Wiedmann, K. P. (2003). Internet–induced changes in consumer music procurement behavior: a German perspective. *Marketing Intelligence and Planning*, 21, 305–317.

Walsh, S. M., Martin, S. C., and Schmidt, L. A. (2004). Testing the efficacy of a creative–arts intervention with family caregivers of patients with cancer. *Journal of Nursing Scholarship*, 36, 214–219.

Walster, E., Aronson, V., Abrahams, D., and Rottmann, L. (1966). Importance of physical attractiveness in dating behaviour. *Journal of Personality and Social Psychology*, 4, 508–516.

Walters, J. and. Gardner, H. (1993). The crystallizing experience: discovering an intellectual gift. In R. J. Sternberg and J. E. Davidson (eds.), *Conceptions of giftedness*. Cambridge: Cambridge University Press.

Wanamaker, C. E. and Reznikoff, M. (1989). Effects of aggressive and nonaggressive rock songs on projective and structured tests. *Journal of Psychology: Interdisciplinary and Applied*, 123, 561–570.

Wang, S. M., Kulkarni, L., Dolev, J., and Kain, Z. N. (2002). Music and preoperative anxiety: a randomized, controlled study. *Anesthesia and Analgesia*, 94, 1489–1494.

Wann, D. L. and Wilson, A. M. (1996). Associations among rock music videos, locus of control, and aggression. *Psychological Reports*, 79, 642.

Wapnick, J., Darrow, A. A., Kovacs, J., and Dalrymple, L. (1997). Effects of physical attractiveness on evaluation of vocal performance. *Journal of Research in Music Education*, 45, 470–479.

—— Mazza, J., and Darrow, A. A. (1998). Effects of performer attractiveness, stage behavior, and dress on violin performance evaluation. *Journal of Research in Music Education*, 46, 510–521.

—— —— and Darrow, A. A. (2000). Effects of performer attractiveness, stage behavior, and dress on evaluation of children's piano performances. *Journal of Research in Music Education*, 48, 323–336.

Ward, B. (1998). *Just my soul responding: rhythm and blues, black consciousness, and race relations*. Los Angeles: University of California Press.

Ward, E., Stokes, G., and Tucker, K. (1986). *Rock of ages: the Rolloing Stone history of rock and roll*. New York: Rolling Stone.

Ward, L. M. (2003). Understanding the role of entertainment media in the sexual socialization of American youth: a review of empirical research. *Developmental Review*, 23, 347–388.

—— Hansbrough, E., and Walker, E. (2005). Contributions of music video exposure to black adolescents' gender and sexual schemas. *Journal of Adolescent Research*, 20, 143–166.

Ward, S., Lampe, H. M., and Slater, P. J. B. (2004). Singing is not energetically demanding for pied flycatchers, Ficedula hypoleuca. *Behavioral Ecology*, 15, 477–484.

Ward, T. B. and Lewis, S. N. (1987). The influence of alcohol and loud music on analytic and holistic processing. *Perception and Psychophysics*, 41, 179–186.

Wartella, E., Heintz, K., Aidman, A., and Mazarella, S. (1990). Television and beyond: children's video media in one community. *Communication Research*, 17, 45–64.

Wass, H., Miller, M. D., and Redditt, C. A. (1991). Adolescents and destructive themes in rock music: a follow-up. *Omega: Journal of Death and Dying*, 23, 199–206.

—— —— and Stevenson, R. G. (1989). Factors affecting adolescents' behavior and attitudes toward destructive rock lyrics. *Death Studies*, 13, 287–303.

—— Raup, J. L., Cerullo, K., Martel, L. G., Mingione, L. A., and Sperring, A. M. (1988–1989). Adolescents' interest in and views of destructive themes in rock music. *Omega: Journal of Death and Dying*, 19, 177–186.

Watson, P. and Valentine, E. (1987). The practice of complementary medicine and anxiety levels in a population of musicians. *Journal of the International Society for the Study of Tensions in Performance*, 4, 26–30.

Webb, S. C. (1995). Role conflicts and coping of African American navy officers. *Dissertation Abstracts International, Section A: Arts and Social Sciences*, 55 *(7-A)*, 2160.

Webster, P. (1992). Research on creative thinking in music: the assessment literature. In R. Colwell (ed.), *Handbook of research on music teaching and learning* (pp. 266–280). New York: Schirmer / Macmillan.

Weick, K. E., Gilfillan, D. P., and Keith, T. A. (1973). The effect of composer credibility on orchestra performance. *Sociometry*, 36, 435–462.

Weiner, B. (1986). *An attributional theory of motivation and emotion*. New York: Springer.

Weinstein, D. (1991). *Heavy metal: a cultural sociology*. New York: Lexington.

Weisberg R. W. (1993). *Creativity: beyond the myth of genius*. New York: W.H. Freeman.

——Weisberg, R. W. (1999). Creativity and knowledge: a challenge to theories. In R. J. Sternberg (ed.), *Handbook of creativity* (pp. 226–250). Cambridge: Cambridge University Press.

Weisskirch, R. S. and Murphy, L. C. (2004). Friends, porn, and punk: sensation seeking in personal relationships, Internet activities and music preference among college students. *Adolescence*, **39**, 189–201.

Wells, A. (1990). Popular music: emotional use and management. *Journal of Popular Culture*, **24**, 105–117.

Wells, D. L., Graham, L., and Hepper, P. G. (2002). The influence of auditory stimulation on the behaviour of dogs housed in a rescue shelter. *Animal Welfare*, **11**, 385–393.

Wenger, E. (1998). *Communities of practice: learning, meaning and identity*. New York: Cambridge University Press.

—— McDermott, R., and Snyder, W. M. (2002). *Cultivating communities of practice*. Boston: Harvard Business School Press.

Werner, C. (1998). *A change is gonna come: music, race, and the soul of America*. Payback Press: Edinburgh.

Wertsch, J. V. (1985). *Vygotsky and the social formation of mind*. Cambridge: Harvard University Press.

Wesner, R. B., Noyes, R., and Davis, T. L. (1990). The occurrence of performance anxiety among musicians. *Journal of Affective Disorders*, **18**, 177–185.

Wester, S. R., Crown C. L., Quatman, G. L., and Heesacker M. (1997). The influence of sexually violent rap music on attitudes of men with little prior exposure. *Psychology of Women Quarterly*, **21**, 497–508.

Westley, F. (1991). Bob Geldof and Live Aid: the affective side of global social innovation. *Human Relations*, **44**, 1011–1036.

Whipple, B. and Glynn, N. J. (1992). Quantification of the effects of listening to music as a noninvasive method of pain control. *Scholarly Inquiry for Nursing Practice*, **6**, 43–58.

Whipple, J. (2003). Surgery buddies: a music therapy program for pediatric surgical patients. *Music Therapy Perspectives*, **21**, 77–83.

Whissell, C. (1996). Traditional and emotional stylometric analysis of the songs of Beatles Paul McCartney and John Lennon. *Computers and the Humanities*, **30**, 257–265.

—— (1999). Phonosymbolism and the emotional nature of sounds: evidence of the preferential use of particular phonemes in texts of differing emotional tone. *Perceptual and Motor Skills*, **89**, 19–48.

—— (2003). The emotional symbolism of two English e–sounds: /i/ as in "cheap" and /I/ as in "chip" active. *Perceptual and Motor Skills*, **96**, 149–165.

Whissell, R. and Whissell, C. (2000). The emotional importance of key: do Beatles songs written in different keys convey different emotional tones? *Perceptual and Motor Skills*, **91**, 973–980.

Whitfield, T. W. A. (1983). Predicting preference for familiar, everyday objects. An experimental confrontation between two theories of aesthetic behaviour. *Journal of Environmental Psychology*, **3**, 221–237.

—— (2000). Beyond prototypicality: toward a categorical–motivation model of aesthetics. *Empirical Studies of the Arts*, **18**, 1–11.

—— and Slatter, P. E. (1979). The effects of categorization and prototypicality on aesthetic choice in a furniture selection task. *British Journal of Psychology*, **70**, 65–75.

Wiebe, G. (1940). The effect of radio plugging on students' opinions of popular songs. *Journal of Applied Psychology*, **24**, 721–727.

Wiesenthal, D. L., Hennessy, D. A., and Lubertacci, F. S. (2003). The effectiveness of music and relaxation training in reducing driver stress. *Proceedings of the Canadian Multidisciplinary Road Safety Conference XIII, 8–11 June 2003, Banff, Canada.*

—— Hennessy, D. A., and Totten, B. (2000). The influence of music on driver stress. *Journal of Applied Social Psychology*, 30, 1709–1719.

—— —— and Totten, B. (2003). The influence of music on mild driver aggression. *Transportation Research Part F: Traffic Psychology and Behaviour*, 6, 125–134.

Wigram, T., Saperston, B., and West, R. (eds.) (1995). *The art and science of music therapy: a handbook.* Langhorne: Harwood Academic Publishers.

Wilkinson, M. (1976). Romantic love: the great equalizer. *The Family Coordinator*, 25, 161–166.

Williamon, A. (ed.) (2004). *Musical excellence: strategies and techniques to enhance performance.* Oxford: Oxford University Press.

—— Thompson, S., Lisboa, T., and Wiffen, C. (2006). Creativity, originality and value in music performance. In I. Deliege and G. Wiggins (eds.), *Musical creativity: current research in theory and practice* (pp. 161–180). Hove: Psychology Press.

Willner, P. and Neiva, J. (1986). Brief exposure to uncontrollable but not to controllable noise biases the retrieval of information from memory. *British Journal of Clinical Psychology*, 25, 93–100.

Wills, G. and Cooper, C. L. (1988). *Pressure sensitive: popular musicians under stress.* London: Sage.

Wills, G. I. (2003). Forty lives in the bebop business: mental health in a group of eminent jazz musicians. *British Journal of Psychiatry*, 183, 255–259.

Wilson, G. D. (1997). Performance anxiety. In D. J. Hargreaves and A. C. North (eds.), *The social psychology of music* (pp. 229–245). Oxford: Oxford University Press.

—— (2002). *Psychology for performing artists (second edition).* London: Whurr.

—— and Roland, D. (2002). Performance anxiety. In R. Parncutt and G. E. McPherson (eds.), *The science and psychology of music performance* (pp. 47–61). Oxford: Oxford University Press.

Wilson, N. C. and Stokes, D. (2004). Laments and serenades: relationship marketing and legitimation strategies for the cultural entrepreneur. *Qualitative Market Research: An International Journal*, 7, 218–227.

Wilson, S. (2003). The effect of music on perceived atmosphere and purchase intentions in a restaurant. *Psychology of Music*, 31, 93–109.

Wingood, G. M., DiClemente, R. J., Bernhardt, J. M., Harrington, K., Davies, S. L., Robillard, A., and Hook, E. W. (2003). A prospective study of exposure to rap music videos and African American female adolescents' health. *American Journal of Public Health*, 93, 437–439.

Winold, C. A. (1963). The effects of changes in harmonic tension upon listener response. *Ph.D. Dissertation, Indiana University.*

Winstock, A. R., Griffiths, P., and Stewart, D. (2001). Drugs and the dance music scene: a survey of current drug use patterns among a sample of dance music enthusiasts in the UK. *Drug and Alcohol Dependence*, 64, 9–17.

—— Wolff, K., and Ramsey, J. (2002). 4–MTA: a new synthetic drug on the dance scene. *Drug and Alcohol Dependence*, 67, 111–115.

Witkin, H. A. (1965). Psychological differentiation. *Journal of Abnormal Psychology*, 70, 317–336.

Wolf, D. P. and Gardner, H. (1981). On the structure of early symbolisation. In R. Schiefelbusch and D. Bricker (eds.), *Early language intervention*. Baltimore: University Park Press.

Wood, D. J. (1998). *How children think and learn* (2nd edn.). Oxford: Blackwell.

—— Bruner, J. and Ross, G. (1976). The role of tutoring in problem solving. *Journal of Child Psychology and Psychiatry*, 17, 89–100.

Wundt, W. M. (1874). *Grundzuge der physiologischen psychologie*. Leipzig: Engelmann.

Yalch, R. F. (1991). Memory in a jingle jungle: music as a mnemonic device in communicating advertising slogans. *Journal of Applied Psychology*, 76, 268–275.

—— and Spangenberg, E. R. (1990). Effects of store music on shopping behavior. *Journal of Services Marketing*, 4, 31–39.

Yalch, R. F. and Spangenberg, E. (1993). Using store music for retail zoning: a field experiment. *Advances in Consumer Research*, 20, 632–636.

—— —— (2000). The effects of music in a retail setting on real and perceived shopping times. *Journal of Business Research*, 49, 139–147.

Yang, F., Li, M., Zhang, M., and Zhang, B. (2003). Effect of music on anxiety of patients receiving eyeground operation. *Chinese Mental Health Journal*, 17, 256–257.

Yarbrough, C. (1975). Effect of magnitude of conductor behaviour on students in mixed choruses. *Journal of Research in Music Education*, 23, 134–146.

Yerkes, R. M. and Dodson, J. D. (1908). The relation of strength of stimulus to rapidity of habit–formation. *Journal of Comparative Neurological Psychology*, 18, 459–482.

Yilmaz, E., Ozcan, S., Basar, M., Basar, H., Batislam, E., and Ferhat, M. (2003). Music decreases anxiety and provides sedation in extracorporeal shock wave lithotripsy. *Urology*, 61, 282–286.

York, N. (2001). *Valuing school music: a report on school music*. London: University of Westminster and Rockschool Ltd.

Young, H. H. and Berry, G. L. (1979). The impact of environment on the productivity attitudes of intellectually challenged office workers. *Human Factors*, 21, 399–407.

Young. S. (2005). Musical communication between adults and young children. In D. E. Miell, R. A. R. MacDonald, and D. J. Hargreaves (eds.), *Musical communication* (pp. 281–299). Oxford: Oxford University Press.

Yung, P. M. B., Kam, S. C., Lau, B. W. K., and Chan, T. M. F. (2003). The effect of music in managing preoperative stress for Chinese surgical patients in the operating room holding area: a controlled trial. *International Journal of Stress Management*, 10, 64–74.

Zachariae, R., Hansen, J. B., Andersen, M., Jinquan, T., Petersen, K. S., Simonsen, C., Zachariae, C. and Thestrup–Pedersen K. (1994). Changes in cellular immune function after immune specific guided imagery and relaxation in high and low hypnotizable healthy subjects. *Psychotherapy and Psychosomatics*, 61, 74–92.

Zajonc, R. B. (1968). Attitudinal effects of mere exposure. *Journal of Personality and Social Psychology*, 9, 1–27.

Zajonc, R. B. (1994). Emotional expression and temperature modulation. In S. H. M. van Goozen, N. E. van de Poll, and J. A. Sergeant (eds.), *Emotions: essays on emotion theory* (pp. 3–27). Hillsdale: Erlbaum.

Zaza, C., Sellick, S. M., Willan, A., Reyno, L., and Browman, G. P. (1999). Health care professionals' familiarity with non–pharmacological strategies for managing cancer pain. *Psycho–Oncology*, 8, 99–111.

Zdzinski, S. F. (1996). Parental involvement, selected student attributes, and learning outcomes in instrumental music. *Journal of Research in Music Education*, 44, 34–48.

Zendel, B.R., Slawinski, E., and Pearson, L. (2003). How music of differing rhythmicities and intensities affects driver performance. *Canadian Acoustics*, 31, 98–99.

Zepeda, L. M. (2002). A and M Records, Inc. Vs. Napster Inc. *Berkeley Technology Law Journal*, 17, 71–90.

Zhang, R., Li, F., Xu, Z., and Feng, Y. (2000). Psychotherapy on negative emotions of coronary heart disease and its clinical implications. *Chinese Journal of Clinical Psychology*, 8, 139–142.

Zhang, X. W., Fan, Y., Manyande, A., Tian, Y. K., and Yin, P. (2005). Effects of music on target–controlled infusion of propofol requirements during combined spinal–epidural anaesthesia. *Anaesthesia*, 60, 990–994.

Zhu, R. and Meyers–Levy, J. (2005). Distinguishing between the meanings of music: when background music affects product perceptions. *Journal of Marketing Research*, 42, 333–345.

Zillman, D., Aust, C. F., Hoffman, K. D., Love, C. C., Ordman, V. L., Pope, J. T, Seigler, P. D., and Gibson, R. J. (1995). Radical rap: does it further ethnic division? *Basic and Applied Social Psychology*, 16, 1–25.

—— and Bhatia, A. (1989). Effects of associating with musical genres on heterosexual attraction. *Communication Research*, 16, 263–288.

—— and Gan, S. (1997). Musical taste in adolescence. In D. J. Hargreaves and A. C. North (eds.), *The social psychology of music* (pp. 161–187). Oxford: Oxford University Press.

—— and Mundorf, N. (1987). Image effects in the appreciation of video rock. *Communication Research*, 14, 316–334.

Zimmerman, L., Nieveen, J., Barnason, S., and Schmaderer, M. (1996). The effects of music interventions on postoperative pain and sleep in coronary artery bypass graft (CABG) patients. *Scholarly Inquiry for Nursing Practice*, 10, 153–170.

Zuckerman, M. (1979). *Sensation seeking: beyond the optimal level of arousal*. Hillsdale: Erlbaum.

Zullow, H. M. (1991). Pessimistic rumination in popular songs and newsmagazines predict economic recession via decreased consumer optimism and spending. *Journal of Economic Psychology*, 12, 501–526.

Name Index

Subject Index